Lecture Notes in Computer Science 16607

Founding Editors

Gerhard Goos
Juris Hartmanis

Samir Chatterjee · Shirley Gregor ·
Gregor Kipping · Gunjan Mansingh

Editors

Design for Better Futures: Beyond the Science of the Artificial

Prototypes and Research-in-Progress

21st International Conference on Design Science Research
in Information Systems and Technology, DESRIST 2026
Münster, Germany, June 8–10, 2026
Proceedings, Part III

Springer

Editors
Samir Chatterjee
Claremont Graduate University
Claremont, CA, USA

Gregor Kipping
University of Liechtenstein
Vaduz, Liechtenstein

Shirley Gregor
Australian National University
Canberra, ACT, Australia

Gunjan Mansingh
University of the West Indies
Kingston, Jamaica

ISSN 0302-9743   ISSN 1611-3349 (electronic)
Lecture Notes in Computer Science
ISBN 978-3-032-28569-0   ISBN 978-3-032-28570-6 (eBook)
https://doi.org/10.1007/978-3-032-28570-6

This Springer imprint is published by the registered company Springer Nature Switzerland AG
The registered company address is: Gewerbestrasse 11, 6330 Cham, Switzerland

If disposing of this product, please recycle the paper.

Preface

Design science research in Information Systems continues to gain strong momentum, and the DESRIST conference series remains at the forefront of this evolution—stimulating intellectual discourse, advancing methodological rigor, and fostering a vibrant global community of scholars and practitioners.

Guided by this year's conference theme, Design for Better Futures: Beyond the Science of the Artificial, this volume constitutes the third of three Springer proceedings volumes for DESRIST 2026. Given the large number of high-quality contributions, Volumes 1 and 2 contain the accepted full research papers, while this volume features a curated collection of research-in-progress and prototype papers that reflect emerging ideas, early-stage innovations, and experimental artifacts that are shaping the future trajectory of design science research. These contributions play a critical role in expanding the design knowledge base by offering novel concepts, preliminary findings, and actionable insights that invite further refinement and validation.

The DESRIST 2026 conference attracted a total of 231 submissions, comprising 108 full research papers, 54 research-in-progress papers, 35 prototype papers, and 34 submissions to the doctoral consortium, student track, and startup and industry forum. Each full research and research-in-progress paper underwent a rigorous double-blind review process by a minimum of two referees, while each prototype paper, as well as the submissions to the doctoral consortium, student track, and startup and industry forum, was evaluated through a single-blind review process by at least two referees. This volume includes 23 research-in-progress papers and 14 prototype papers, resulting in an overall acceptance rate of 42% across these two categories. In addition, 16 prototype submissions were selected as posters and presented interactively to conference attendees, fostering direct engagement and feedback.

The diversity of contributions in this volume underscores the evolving nature of design science research—where iterative development, artifact experimentation, and early validation are essential components of the research lifecycle. These papers highlight innovative applications across domains and demonstrate how design science continues to address complex socio-technical challenges through creative and impactful solutions.

We extend our sincere appreciation to all authors who submitted their work to DESRIST 2026. Their dedication and intellectual contributions were the foundation of this conference. We are equally grateful to the track chairs, program committee members, and reviewers whose expertise and commitment ensured a rigorous and constructive evaluation process.

We also acknowledge the efforts of the organizing committee and volunteers whose hard work made the conference possible. Special thanks go to those who supported the submission and review systems, managed logistics, and coordinated the many aspects required to deliver a successful international conference. We are likewise grateful to our partners at Springer Nature for their valuable support in preparing these proceedings.

We believe that the papers in this volume provide valuable insights into emerging directions in design science research. They not only reflect the current state of innovation but also open new avenues for future inquiry, experimentation, and impact within a vibrant and continuously growing research community.

June 2026

Samir Chatterjee
Shirley Gregor
Gregor Kipping
Gunjan Mansingh
Michael Rosemann
Monica Chiarini Tremblay
Robert Winter

Organization

Conference Co-chairs

Jan vom Brocke   University of Münster, Germany
Leona Chandra Kruse   University of Agder, Norway
Alan Hevner   University of South Florida, USA

Program Co-chairs

Robert Winter   University of St. Gallen, Switzerland
Michael Rosemann   Queensland University of Technology, Australia
Monica Chiarini Tremblay   William & Mary School of Business, USA

General Co-chairs

Samir Chatterjee   Claremont Graduate University, USA
Gunjan Mansingh   University of the West Indies, Jamaica
Shirley Gregor   Australian National University, Australia

Doctoral Consortium Co-chairs

Lisa Seymour   University of Cape Town, South Africa
Alexander Maedche   Karlsruhe Institute of Technology, Germany
Pär Ågerfalk   Uppsala University, Sweden

Prototypes Co-chairs

Oliver Müller   Paderborn University, Germany
Michael Gau   University of Liechtenstein, Liechtenstein
Stephanie Missonier   HEC Lausanne, Switzerland

Impact Forum Co-chairs

Brian Donnellan	Maynooth University, Ireland
Asif Gill	University of Technology Sydney, Australia
Iris Junglas	College of Charleston, USA

Startup and Industry Forum Co-chairs

Timo Strohmann	University of Münster, Germany
Fumi Kurihara	University of Münster, Germany
Thomas Haskamp	University of Münster, Germany

Student Track Co-chairs

Ann-Kristin Cordes	University of Kiel, Germany
Isabel Ramos	Universidade do Minho, Portugal
Stefan Thalmann	University of Graz, Austria

Managing Co-chairs

Fumi Kurihara	University of Münster, Germany
Katrin Bergener	University of Münster, Germany
Timo Strohmann	University of Münster, Germany
Armin Stein	University of Münster, Germany

Proceedings Chair

Gregor Kipping	University of Liechtenstein, Liechtenstein

Website and System Chair

Hans-Henning Näscher	University of Münster, Germany

Communication Chair

Lea Kleinekathöfer   University of Münster, Germany

Track Chairs

Theme Track – Design for Better Futures: Beyond the Science of the Artificial

Jan vom Brocke   University of Münster, Germany
Leona Chandra Kruse   University of Agder, Norway
Alan Hevner   University of South Florida, USA

General Track: From Insight to Impact

Jan Marco Leimeister   University of St. Gallen, Switzerland
Aleksi Aaltonen   Stevens Institute of Technology, USA
Eva Bittner   Hamburg University, Germany
Khushbu Tilvawala   University of Auckland, New Zealand

The Future of Financial Services

Gilbert Fridgen   University of Luxembourg, Luxembourg
Nadine Ostern   Queensland University of Technology, Australia
Roman Beck   Bentley University, USA

Future of Data-Driven and AI-Enabled Design

Hanna Buyssens   ESCP Business School, Germany
Michael Cahalane   University of New South Wales, Australia
Kieran Conboy   University of Galway, Ireland
Amir Haj-Bolouri   University West, Sweden

Future of Healthcare and Wellbeing

Lauri Wessel	European New School of Digital Studies, Germany
Ahmed Abbasi	University of Notre Dame, USA
Kadi Lubi	Tallinn University of Technology, Estonia

Future of Design and Entrepreneurship

Christoph Seckler	ESCP Business School, Germany
Dimo Dimov	University of Bath, UK
Timothy Hor	RMIT University, Australia
Sophie Petzolt	Fraunhofer IAO, Germany

Future of Responsible and Sustainable Design

Thorsten Schoormann	Roskilde University, Denmark
Yenni Tim	University of New South Wales, Australia
Olivia Liu Sheng	Arizona State University, USA
Sarah Hönigsberg	ICN Business School, France

Future of Design Science Education

Matthias Söllner	University of Kassel, Germany
Heikki Topi	Bentley University, USA
Shahper Richter	University of Auckland, New Zealand
Stefano Za	Gabriele d'Annunzio University Chieti-Pescara, Italy

Future of Design Science Methodology

Roman Lukyanenko	University of Virginia, USA
Christine Legner	HEC Lausanne, Switzerland
Dirk Hovorka	University of Sydney, Australia
Kai R. Larsen	University of Colorado Boulder, USA

Future of Ecosystems for Design Science Research

Matthew Mullarkey	University of South Florida, USA
Asif Gill	University of Technology Sydney, Australia
Edona Elshan	Vrije Universiteit Amsterdam, Netherlands

Reviewers

Aleksi Aaltonen	Stevens Institute of Technology, USA
Salar Abaspur	University of Cologne, Germany
Gemza Ademaj	University of Notre Dame, USA
Maike Althaus	Paderborn University, Germany
Yehia Alzoubi	American University of the Middle East, Kuwait
Jana Ammann	LMU Munich, Germany
Katazo Amunkete	Namibia University of Science and Technology, Namibia
Arnold F. Arz von Straussenburg	University of Koblenz, Germany
Tamara Babaian	Bentley University, USA
Dinko Bacic	Loyola University Chicago, USA
Charlotte Bahr	Friedrich-Alexander-Universität Erlangen-Nürnberg, Germany
Madhushi Bandara	University of Technology Sydney, Australia
Christian Bartelheimer	University of Göttingen, Germany
Richard Baskerville	Georgia State University, USA
Ingrid Bauer-Hänsel	University of St. Gallen, Switzerland
Ransome Bawack	Audencia Business School, France
Christian Beecks	FernUniversität in Hagen, Germany
Vincent Beermann	Hasso Plattner Institute, Germany
Daniel Beverungen	Paderborn University, Germany
Manuel Bieri	University of Bern, Switzerland
Grace Billiris	University of Technology Sydney, Australia
Annemarie Bloch	University of Duisburg-Essen, Germany
Mads Bødker	Copenhagen Business School, Denmark
Martin Böhmer	Martin Luther University Halle-Wittenberg, Germany
Marten Borchers	University of Hamburg, Germany
Nina Boulus-Rødje	Roskilde University, Denmark
Tobias Brandt	University of Münster, Germany
Katharina Breiter	University of Hohenheim, Germany
Michael Breitner	Leibniz University Hannover, Germany
Ulrich Bretschneider	University of Kassel, Germany
Constantin Brîncoveanu	Goethe University Frankfurt, Germany
Olivia Bruhin	University of St. Gallen, Switzerland
Lorenzo Matthias Burcheri	University of Luxembourg, Luxembourg
Hanna Buyssens	ESCP Business School, Germany
Michael Cahalane	University of New South Wales, Australia
Marcel Cahenzli	University of St. Gallen, Switzerland

Kevin Carillo	TBS Education, France
Riccardo Cerretani	Gabriele d'Annunzio University Chieti-Pescara, Italy
Samir Chatterjee	Claremont Graduate University, USA
Michele Cipriano	Università Cattolica del Sacro Cuore, Italy
Shannon Colville	Queensland University of Technology, Australia
André Coners	South Westphalia University of Applied Sciences, Germany
Ryan Cook	University of Notre Dame, USA
Marian Cooray	University of New South Wales, Australia
Clinton Daniel	University of South Florida, USA
Danielly de Paula	Hasso Plattner Institute, Germany
Laura Detels	University of Göttingen, Germany
Chedia Dhaoui	University of New South Wales, Australia
Ronja Dobler	University of Münster, Germany
Mateusz Dolata	Zeppelin University, Germany
Ronan Doyle	University of Galway, Ireland
Andreas Drechsler	Victoria University of Wellington, New Zealand
Hanyu Duan	Hong Kong University of Science and Technology, China
Henry Edison	Blekinge Institute of Technology, Sweden
Maarja-Liis Elland	Tallinn University of Technology, Estonia
Edona Elshan	Vrije Universiteit Amsterdam, Netherlands
Jan Enkmann	Hasso Plattner Institute, Germany
Jürgen Fleiß	University of Graz, Austria
Sandro Franzoi	University of Münster, Germany
Natalie Früholz	Fraunhofer IWU, Germany
Michael Gau	University of Liechtenstein, Liechtenstein
Maria George	University of New South Wales, Australia
Matt Germonprez	University of Nebraska Omaha, USA
Heiko Gewald	Neu-Ulm University of Applied Sciences, Germany
Ahmad Ghazawneh	Halmstad University, Sweden
Mona Ghazi	ESCP Business School, Germany
Soham Ghosh	Trinity College Dublin, Ireland
Karoline Glaser	TU Dresden, Germany
Rob Gleasure	Copenhagen Business School, Denmark
Sarah Götz	University of Kassel, Germany
Max Gräser	Leipzig University, Germany
Renate Griessel-Duminy	ESCP Business School, Germany
Nick Große	TU Dortmund University, Germany
Rahel Gubser	Freie Universität Berlin, Germany

Tan Gürpinar	Quinnipiac University, USA
Ram Prasad Gurung	LUT University, Finland
Amir Haj-Bolouri	University West, Sweden
Martin Hänel	University of Kassel, Germany
Thomas Haskamp	University of Münster, Germany
Andreas Hein	University of St. Gallen, Switzerland
Daniel Heinz	Karlsruhe Institute of Technology, Germany
Savindu Herath	ETH Zurich, Switzerland
Malte Högemann	Osnabrück University, Germany
Maike Holtkemper	FernUniversität in Hagen, Germany
Sarah Hönigsberg	ICN Business School, France
Timothy Hor	RMIT University, Australia
Flora Horn	TU Dresden, Germany
Dirk Hovorka	University of Sydney, Australia
Michal Hron	Ghent University, Belgium
Han-Fen Hu	University of Nevada, Las Vegas, USA
Anna Hupe	University of Kassel, Germany
Aida Huskic	Open University of the Netherlands, Netherlands
Jan-Paul Huttner	German Aerospace Center (DLR), Germany
Mirijana Irnich	Osnabrück University, Germany
Christian Janiesch	TU Dortmund University, Germany
Andreas Janson	University of St. Gallen, Switzerland
Alireza Jaribion	University of South Florida, USA
Jonna Järveläinen	University of Jyväskylä, Finland
Florian Johannsen	Schmalkalden University of Applied Sciences, Germany
Frederick K. Johnson	University of California, Berkeley, USA
George Joukhadar	University of New South Wales, Australia
Gustaf Juell-Skielse	University of Borås, Sweden
Jürgen Jung	Frankfurt University of Applied Sciences, Germany
Iris Junglas	College of Charleston, USA
Pieter Kamminga	Open University of the Netherlands, Netherlands
Marlon Kampmann	South Westphalia University of Applied Sciences, Germany
Jesse Katende	University West, Sweden
Matthias Keller	Vlerick Business School, Belgium
Bijan Khosrawi-Rad	Leuphana University Lüneburg, Germany
Theodore Kindong	Linköping University, Sweden
Samuel Kirshner	University of New South Wales, Australia
Hermann Klöckner	Anhalt University of Applied Sciences, Germany
Charlotte Knickrehm	Goethe University Frankfurt, Germany

Christoph Kollwitz   ICN Business School, France
Björn Konopka   TU Dortmund University, Germany
Huda Koulani   University of Kassel, Germany
Diana Kozachek   University of St. Gallen, Switzerland
Julia Maria Kraus   LMU Munich, Germany
Kristin Krebs   University of Wuppertal, Germany
Sylvana Kroop   FHWien der WKW, Austria
Fumi Kurihara   University of Münster, Germany
Jan Laufer   University of Duisburg-Essen, Germany
Seung Jong Lee   Arizona State University, USA
Amelia Li   University of New South Wales, Australia
Mahei Manhai Li   University of Kassel, Germany
Jonas Liebschner   Karlsruhe Institute of Technology, Germany
Eric T. K. Lim   University of New South Wales, Australia
Sebastian Lins   University of Kassel, Germany
Alexander Maedche   Karlsruhe Institute of Technology, Germany
Onkar Malgonde   North Carolina State University, USA
Munir Mandviwalla   University of South Florida, USA
Osama Mansour   Lund University, Sweden
Harry Martin   Open University of the Netherlands, Netherlands
Julian Marx   University of Melbourne, Australia
Secil Matasova   Tallinn University of Technology, Estonia
Martin Matzner   Friedrich-Alexander-Universität
                             Erlangen-Nürnberg, Germany
Valentin Mayer   University of Bayreuth, Germany
Alexander Meier   University of St. Gallen, Switzerland
Christian Meske   Ruhr University Bochum, Germany
Sophia Meywirth   University of Kassel, Germany
Frederik Möller   TU Braunschweig, Germany
Stefan Morana   Saarland University, Germany
Roland M. Mueller   Berlin School of Economics and Law, Germany
Pavankumar Mulgund   University of Memphis, USA
Julian M. Müller   Friedrich-Alexander-Universität
                             Erlangen-Nürnberg, Germany
Sanaz Nabavian   University of Niagara Falls, Canada
Martina Navratilova   South Westphalia University of Applied Sciences,
                             Germany
Maximilian Nebel   TU Dortmund University, Germany
Nicolas Neis   University of Würzburg, Germany
Chloe Nguyen   University of New South Wales, Australia
Giang Tra Nguyen   ESCP Business School, Germany
Anastasija Nikiforova   University of Tartu, Estonia

Kerli Norak	Tallinn University of Technology, Estonia
David Nowak	University of Münster, Germany
Mairead O' Connor	University of New South Wales, Australia
Shawn Ogunseye	Bentley University, USA
Grant Oosterwyk	University of Cape Town, South Africa
Agnieszka Patecka	European University Viadrina, Germany
Asger Balle Pedersen	IT University of Copenhagen, Denmark
Haiat Perozzo	LIUC – Università Cattaneo, Italy
Per Persson	University of Gothenburg, Sweden
Christoph Peters	Bundeswehr University Munich, Germany
Louisa Peters	University of Göttingen, Germany
Dimitri Petrik	University of Stuttgart, Germany
Ralf Plattfaut	University of Duisburg-Essen, Germany
Nadia Pocher	University of Luxembourg, Luxembourg
Jens Pöppelbuß	Ruhr University Bochum, Germany
Matthias Pohl	German Aerospace Center (DLR), Germany
Merle Pohl	European University Viadrina, Germany
Katja Pott	Bern University of Applied Sciences, Switzerland
Nicolas Prat	ESSEC Business School, France
Jan Pries-Heje	Roskilde University, Denmark
Sandeep Purao	Bentley University, USA
Saima Qutab	University of Auckland, New Zealand
Jana-Rebecca Rehse	University of Mannheim, Germany
Alexander Richter	Victoria University of Wellington, New Zealand
Shahper Richter	University of Auckland, New Zealand
Dennis M. Riehle	University of Koblenz, Germany
Roman Rietsche	Bern University of Applied Sciences, Switzerland
Michael Rosemann	Queensland University of Technology, Australia
Kristina Rosenthal	Hochschule Niederrhein, Germany
Matti Rossi	Aalto University, Finland
Linda Sagnier Eckert	Karlsruhe Institute of Technology, Germany
Hannu Salmela	University of Turku, Finland
Alexander Schiller	University of Regensburg, Germany
Hannes Schlieter	TU Dresden, Germany
Tim Schmeckel	University of Agder, Norway
Sofia Schöbel	Osnabrück University, Germany
Dewan Scholtz	University of Galway, Ireland
Thorsten Schoormann	Roskilde University, Denmark
Anika Schröder	Copenhagen Business School, Denmark
Gerhard Schwabe	University of Zurich, Switzerland
Christoph Seckler	ESCP Business School, Germany
Julia Seitz	Karlsruhe Institute of Technology, Germany

Kristina Sen	Vlerick Business School, Belgium
Mike Seymour	University of Sydney, Australia
Shahban Shah	Graz University of Technology, Austria
Forough Shahpasandi	University of Jyväskylä, Finland
Dominik Siemon	LUT University, Finland
Janice Sipior	Villanova University, USA
Lisa Skrzyppek	Ruhr University Bochum, Germany
Marco Smacchia	Gabriele d'Annunzio University Chieti-Pescara, Italy
Balwinder Sodhi	Indian Institute of Technology Ropar, India
Matthias Söllner	University of Kassel, Germany
David Sonnabend	University of Kassel, Germany
Pauline Speckmann	TU Dortmund University, Germany
Fabian Stangl	University of Applied Sciences Upper Austria, Austria
Veda C. Storey	Georgia State University, USA
Gero Strobel	University of Duisburg-Essen, Germany
Timo Strohmann	University of Münster, Germany
Jens Strüker	University of Bayreuth, Germany
Rick Sullivan	HEC Montréal, Canada
Janina Sundermeier	Freie Universität Berlin, Germany
Sampsa Suvivuo	Aalto University, Finland
Sabina Szymoniak	Częstochowa University of Technology, Poland
Masoumeh Tavakoligargari	University of Koblenz, Germany
Katja Thoring	Technical University of Munich, Germany
Antonia Tolzin	University of Kassel, Germany
Evgenia Yvonni Tseloni	University of Luxembourg, Luxembourg
Tuure Tuunanen	University of Jyväskylä, Finland
Umair Ul Hassan	University of Galway, Ireland
Azka Umair	University of Galway, Ireland
Erdi Ünal	Ruhr University Bochum, Germany
Vamsi Vallurupalli	University of Galway, Ireland
Alexander van der Staay	TU Dortmund University, Germany
Christine Van Toorn	University of New South Wales, Australia
John Venable	Curtin University, Australia
Anthony Vigil	University of South Florida, USA
Anna Klara Vohrer	University of St. Gallen, Switzerland
Hendrik Wache	ICN Business School, France
James Wallace	Harvard Business School, USA
David Walter	University of Hildesheim, Germany
Annika Wambsganss	ESCP Business School, Germany
Belinda Wang	University of Sydney, Australia

Blair Wang	Curtin University, Australia
Jingyang Wang	University of Lausanne, Switzerland
Sofie Wass	University of Agder, Norway
Florian Weber	University of Kassel, Germany
Hans Weigand	Tilburg University, Netherlands
Anna Elisabeth Wenzel	TU Dortmund University, Germany
Pauline Weritz	University of Twente, Netherlands
Henning Werminghaus Nusch	South Westphalia University of Applied Sciences, Germany
Oliver Werth	OFFIS - Institute for Information Technology, Germany
Richard Wiebe	University of Würzburg, Germany
Martin Wiener	TU Dresden, Germany
Manuel Wiesche	TU Dortmund University, Germany
Jost Wiethölter	Münster University of Applied Sciences, Germany
Malin Wik	Karlstad University, Sweden
Axel Winkelmann	University of Würzburg, Germany
Anna Wolters	University of Koblenz, Germany
Hetiao Xie	University of Queensland, Australia
Jennifer Xu	Bentley University, USA
Jack Yang	University of New South Wales, Australia
Jongtae Yu	King Fahd University of Petroleum and Minerals, Saudi Arabia
Ryan Yurosko	University of South Florida, USA
Liudmila Zavolokina	University of Lausanne, Switzerland
Anna Zeitsev	University of Tampa, USA
Julian Zerbin	Paderborn University, Germany
Xinyuan Zhang	University of Notre Dame, USA
Xinyue Zhang	University of New South Wales, Australia
Lina Zhou	University of North Carolina at Charlotte, USA
Sandra Zilker	Friedrich-Alexander-Universität Erlangen-Nürnberg, Germany
Markus Zimmer	University of Agder, Norway
Zoe Zoepffel	University of Münster, Germany
Philipp zur Heiden	Paderborn University, Germany

Contents

Future of Data-Driven and AI-Enabled Design

Future of Healthcare and Wellbeing

Future of Design and Entrepreneurship

Future of Responsible and Sustainable Design

Future of Design Science Education

Future of Design Science Methodology

Future of Ecosystems for Design Science Research

Prototypes Track

Theme Track – Design for Better Futures: Beyond the Science of the Artificial

The LLM as Adversary: Designing "Dirty Audit" Assessments to Elicit Evaluative Judgement in Education

Shahper Richter[(⊠)] [ID] and Patrick Dodd

University of Auckland, Auckland, New Zealand
`shahper.richter@auckland.ac.nz`

Abstract. Herbert Simon's foundational definition of the "Science of the Artificial" focuses on the creation of artifacts to satisfy goals. However, Generative AI (GenAI) has fundamentally disrupted this paradigm by automating the creation of complex professional artifacts. In Digital Marketing education, Large Language Models (LLMs) can now produce polished, plausible, and professionally formatted audits on demand, rendering traditional "artifact-creation" assessments insufficient for evidencing human mastery. This presents a critical challenge for Design Science Research (DSR): how do we design for a preferable future where human agency is preserved in a world of automated generation? This Research-in-Progress paper reports on an "LLM-Adversarial" assessment pattern that reimagines the role of the designer. Instead of generating an audit, students are tasked with critiquing a system-generated "Dirty Audit"—a document containing a mix of accurate insights, subtle hallucinations, methodological errors, and strategic omissions. In the initial design cycle ($n = 151$), results indicated strong grade clustering in the A– to B + range, suggesting a "ceiling effect" in the written scaffold. We recommend an evolved artifact design that incorporates an Interactive Oral Assessment (IOA) for the second cycle. We argue that to design for better futures, DSR must pivot from teaching generative competence to teaching evaluative judgement—the ability to govern the artificial.

Keywords: Design Science Research · Beyond the Artificial · Assessment Design

1 Introduction: Beyond the Generation of Artifacts

Digital marketing audits are foundational exercises in undergraduate marketing education, traditionally designed to evaluate students' ability to synthesise data, interpret analytics, and generate actionable strategic recommendations. However, the emergence of large language models (LLMs) and generative AI has dramatically altered the landscape: audit reports can now be generated automatically, often producing coherent outputs that superficially satisfy the requirements of standard assessment tasks. This raises a critical problem: the traditional audit assignment no longer reliably measures the intended constructs of analytical competence, strategic reasoning, and evaluative judgement, as students can achieve high grades without demonstrating deep understanding [3–5].

S. Chatterjee et al. (Eds.): DESRIST 2026, LNCS 16607, pp. 3–14, 2026.
https://doi.org/10.1007/978-3-032-28570-6_1

This problem has significant educational and professional implications. Graduates who rely solely on generative outputs may develop a false sense of competence, reducing employability in data-driven marketing roles where critical analysis of vendor reports, dashboards, and third-party data is essential. From an institutional perspective, assessment validity and academic integrity are at stake, particularly given regulatory guidance emphasising the need to design assessments resilient to foreseeable AI-enabled shortcuts [1, 2, 8]. Existing approaches to mitigating these risks have largely focused on restricting AI use or shifting to supervised, high-stakes testing environments. While effective to some degree, these strategies do not leverage the educational potential of AI nor address the need for scalable, authentic assessment of evaluative judgement [6, 7]. There is therefore a clear gap: how can assessment be redesigned to transform AI from a threat into a tool that strengthens, rather than undermines, the measurement of student competence?

In response, we implemented a Design Science Research (DSR) intervention in a Stage-3 undergraduate digital marketing course. We developed an LLM-adversarial assessment artefact, in which students critique a deliberately flawed, AI-generated "Dirty Audit," identify errors and omissions, and reconstruct the strategic outputs, including a revised SWOT and SMART recommendations. To enhance verification and mitigate the ceiling effect observed in the first cycle, we introduced a seven-minute individual interactive oral assessment (IOA) in Cycle 2, requiring students to defend their critical judgements in real time [10–15]. This paper reports on the design, instantiation, and early implementation of the artefact, and proposes a set of initial design principles for adversarial AI-aware assessment. Our contribution is threefold: (i) a reusable assessment artefact that operationalises LLM-adversarial pedagogy [7, 8], (ii) evidence from the first implementation cycle demonstrating the artefact's potential to elicit evaluative judgement and traceable decision-making, and (iii) initial design principles and recommendations for scaling AI-resilient, integrity-rich assessment [13–17]. We ask: *How can an LLM-adversarial assessment be designed to elicit evaluative judgement, traceable reasoning, and strategic competence in digital marketing education while remaining scalable and verifiable?*

2 Background and Literature Review

The rapid rise of generative AI, particularly LLMs, has significantly disrupted traditional assessment practices in higher education. These models can now generate reports, strategic analyses, and other academic artefacts with high surface coherence while embedding subtle errors or omissions. This risks undermining assessment validity, as grades may reflect AI-assisted outputs rather than independent student competence [3–5]. Regulatory guidance now emphasises assessment redesign over reactive policing, recommending that tasks require authentic student reasoning and verification components [1, 2, 8].

2.1 The Epistemic Threat of GenAI in Assessment

Research shows that LLMs frequently produce outputs that are superficially plausible but contain subtle errors or omissions, a phenomenon referred to as hallucination [6]. These errors can mislead both students and markers, particularly when assignments are designed to measure evaluative judgment rather than mere production of content. Guidance from regulatory and institutional sources emphasizes the importance of designing assessments that require verification, reasoning, and evidence-based decision-making rather than only polished outputs [9].

2.2 Evaluative Judgement as the New Core Competency

Evaluative Judgement (EJ) is defined as "the capability to make decisions about the quality of work of oneself and others." In the pre-AI era, EJ was often implicit. In the AI era, Ma et al. [1] argued it must become the explicit object of assessment. They propose that students must learn to "calibrate" quality against standards, a skill uniquely human in a time of automated production. The "Dirty Audit" design operationalizes this by presenting students with a "near-miss" artifact. By requiring students to identify specific flaws (rather than writing a generic report), the task isolates the faculty of judgment. The student cannot simply prompt an LLM to "fix this audit" without first knowing what is wrong, as the errors are context-specific and subtle [3, 5].

2.3 Interactive Oral Assessment (IOA) as a Verification Mechanism

While written critiques force engagement, they are still susceptible to "prompt-and-paste" if the student uses an LLM to critique the LLM. To secure the assessment, we turn to the Interactive Oral Assessment (IOA). IOAs are unscripted, scenario-based conversations where the assessor plays a role (e.g., a client) and the student defends their work. Unlike traditional viva voce exams, IOAs are designed to be scalable (5–10 min) and authentic. Recent literature positions IOAs as "integrity-rich" verification layers that can validate authorship and probe the depth of understanding that written artifacts conceal [10, 11]. This literature emphasizes that IOAs support a "co-existence of formative and summative purposes," allowing students to demonstrate learning through dialogue in ways that text generators cannot replicate [10].

2.4 Gap in Existing Research

While prior work demonstrates the educational value of erroneous examples and the potential of IOAs, there is limited research integrating these approaches with AI-generated artifacts in a design science framework. Most existing solutions either focus on restricting AI use or on traditional flawed-example pedagogy without explicit scalability or adversarial design. This study addresses this gap by combining LLM-generated controlled errors, scaffolded student critique, and IOAs for verification, providing a structured and reusable approach for AI-resilient assessment [10–17]. In summary, three key insights guide our design: LLMs create epistemic threats because they can produce superficially correct but subtly flawed outputs [6]. Evaluative judgement must be explicitly taught and assessed in the AI era [1, 3, 5]. IOAs provide a scalable, integrity-rich verification mechanism that complements written critique [10, 11].

3   Research Methodology

This research adopts the Design Science Research (DSR) paradigm, which facilitates the creation of innovative artifacts to solve meaningful real-world problems while contributing to the theoretical knowledge base [5]. Given the emergent and disruptive nature of Generative AI in education, DSR is particularly appropriate, as it enables the iterative development of assessment patterns that can adapt to rapidly evolving technological capabilities. We employ the three-cycle view of DSR [6] to structure our inquiry.

3.1   The Relevance Cycle

The relevance of this research is grounded in the immediate "validity crisis" facing higher education. As noted by Swiecki et al. [7], the democratization of GenAI tools has eroded the utility of traditional artifact-creation assessments. In the context of education, this manifests as a disconnect between student grades and actual competency, as students can outsource audit generation to LLMs. This project addresses the practical need for assessment designs that are both scalable and integrity robust. The problem definition is further informed by institutional and sector-wide mandates to redesign assessment for the AI age [8].

3.2   The Rigor Cycle

To ensure the artifact is theoretically grounded, we draw upon two primary knowledge streams. First, we utilize the theory of Evaluative Judgement [1, 3], which posits that in an era of automated production, the critical human competence is the ability to appraise quality. Second, we integrate Constructivist AI Pedagogy [9], which argues for learning designs that position AI not as an oracle, but as a fallible partner requiring active human verification. These theories provide the kernel theories for our Adversarial Assessment design, ensuring that the artifact is not merely a pragmatic fix for cheating but a pedagogically sound instrument for deeper learning.

3.3   The Design Cycle

The core of this research involves the iterative construction and evaluation of the LLM-Adversarial assessment pattern. In Iteration 1 (Pilot), we designed and instantiated the Dirty Audit generator and written critique scaffold in a large undergraduate cohort (n = 151). The evaluation focused on feasibility and initial student engagement. Based on the findings of a "ceiling effect" in Iteration 1, Iteration 2 (Refinement) included the design of an Interactive Oral Assessment (IOA) verification layer. This paper reports on the evaluation of Iteration 1, and the artifact definition for Iteration 2 will be presented in the complete version of this paper.

4 Design of the Artifact

The artefact was designed to address the twin challenges of AI-resilient assessment and authentic evaluative judgement in digital marketing. It operationalises the meta-requirements (MR1–MR4) and consists of three interrelated components: the Dirty Audit generator, the Critique Scaffold, and the Interactive Oral Assessment (IOA). Each component maps directly to the target competences and design requirements.

4.1 Meta-Requirements (MRs)

Based on the integrity threat model and the target learning outcomes (evaluative judgement, evidence-based reasoning, strategic traceability), we defined the following meta-requirements.

MR1 (Adversarial Resistance). The assessment architecture must preclude passive GenAI completion by requiring context-specific forensic analysis and justification, which are unlikely to be achieved through generic LLM prompting alone. Success is indicated when students provide verifiable evidence artefacts (e.g., benchmark tables, tool outputs, documented checks) for high-stakes claims; at least one "error type" requires cross-referencing multiple sections (e.g., analytics vs recommendations), reducing single-shot answers; and students must propose corrections and prioritise impacts rather than merely label "wrong/right." Failure occurs if an LLM can produce a high-scoring submission using only the dirty audit text and generic best-practice advice without external verification [6].

MR2 (Mixed Fidelity / Ecological Validity). The input artefact must simulate realistic third-party output (a vendor report or an AI-assisted audit) by combining valid insights with plausible errors and strategically consequential omissions. Success is indicated when the dirty audit includes a controlled proportion of correct, incorrect, and missing elements across each section; errors are plausible (the kind that would survive a superficial read); and omissions target critical "decision levers" (e.g., measurement governance, competitor benchmarks) rather than trivia. Failure occurs if the audit reads as obviously "fake" or uniformly wrong, prompting blanket scepticism rather than discriminative judgement [7, 8].

MR3 (Traceability). Students must demonstrate a defensible chain of reasoning from detection → correction → SWOT logic → strategic recommendations. Success is indicated when each revised recommendation explicitly cites the corrected audit findings it depends on; SWOT items are grounded in corrected evidence and correctly classified as internal/external; and recommendations are SMART with measurable targets aligned to corrected SWOT priorities. Failure occurs when recommendations remain generic, unmeasured, or disconnected from the corrected analysis [10].

MR4 (Verification). The assessment must include a secure component that verifies authorship and conceptual understanding of the written critique. Implementation in Cycle 2 operationalises verification through a brief, individual, interactive oral assessment (IOA) that requires students to defend their highest-impact corrections and the evidence supporting them. Success is indicated when students can explain (i) why an identified issue matters strategically, (ii) how they validated it, and (iii) how it shaped their revised strategy. Failure occurs when the student cannot reproduce or defend key parts of their submission under questioning [10–12].

4.2   Artifact Component a: The "Dirty Audit" Generator

The Dirty Audit generator produces a controlled, flawed digital marketing audit. Rather than asking an LLM to "make mistakes," a stochastic fault injection process was used, based on a curated Error Catalogue [7, 8]. The catalogue includes error identifiers, section assignments, fault class (data integrity, analytic logic, framework misuse, omission, or strategic incoherence), severity, and detectability. Faults are allocated across audit sections to ensure variability in difficulty and detectability. Analytics and recommendations contain high-severity errors, whereas UX/UI sections include fewer, low-severity faults to maintain plausibility. The output includes both the Dirty Audit and a hidden key mapping all seeded issues to catalogue entries, supporting marking calibration and reproducibility [10, 12] (Table 1).

Table 1. The Error Injection Catalogue

Error Family	Description	Example Injection (The "Dirty" Claim)
E1: Data Integrity	Contradictory or impossible metrics	"According to GA4, the 'Bounce Rate' for the landing page is 12%, indicating high engagement." *(Correction: GA4 uses 'Engagement Rate'; 12% bounce is suspiciously low/legacy metric)*
E2: Methodological	Misinterpretation of valid data	"The Facebook post reached 10,000 users with 50 likes, giving us a 5% engagement rate." *(Math error: 50/10,000 is 0.5%, not 5%)*
E3: Strategic Logic	SWOT misalignment	"A key Opportunity is the company's strong internal video production team." *(Correction: Internal capabilities are Strengths, not Opportunities)*
E4: Omission	Critical silence on risks	The audit recommends aggressive SEO expansion but completely omits technical barriers (e.g., the site is JavaScript-heavy and not indexed)

The LLM (GPT-4) was prompted to generate a 2,500-word audit following a standard professional template, injecting errors from this catalogue at a density of approximately 3 errors per section.

4.3 Artefact Component B: The Critique Scaffold

Students received the Dirty Audit and a structured Critique Matrix designed to operationalise evaluative judgement and enforce traceability (MR3). The scaffold is intentionally tri-phasic—Validate, Diagnose, Repair—to prevent two common failure modes in GenAI-era critique tasks: blanket scepticism ("everything is wrong") and generic improvement lists untethered to evidence.

Validate (Anti-blanket scepticism constraint). Students were required to identify three elements of the audit that were correct and explain why each constitutes good practice in digital marketing analysis, such as appropriate benchmarking logic, correct interpretation of a metric, and valid UX observation with decision relevance. This requirement serves two functions: promoting discriminative judgement, so students distinguish high-quality claims from flawed ones rather than treating "AI-produced" as a cue for rejection, and ensuring ecological realism, because vendor and AI outputs are rarely entirely wrong - competent consultants must extract signals as well as identify noise.

The success criterion for validation required that a "validated" element include the original claim, an explanation of why it is methodologically or strategically sound, and an implication for decision-making.

Diagnose (Critical incident identification + evidence). Students were required to identify five major critical incidents -high-impact errors or omissions - and provide forensic evidence demonstrating why each is incorrect and why it matters strategically. A critical incident is defined as a flaw that would plausibly change business decisions, such as channel allocation, investment priority, targeting, or measurement governance, if left uncorrected.

To avoid superficial critique, each critical incident required students to quote or paraphrase the specific audit statement being challenged, classify the fault type (data integrity, analytic logic, framework misuse, strategic incoherence, or omission), cite a supporting tool output, raw data trace, or credible industry/academic benchmark, explain the decision consequence (what the firm would do wrong if the claim was believed), and provide a corrected statement or analytic interpretation. This structure ensures that the output is not merely error spotting, but a reconstruction of epistemic warrant - students must show how they know something is wrong and what a competent correction looks like.

The quota of five incidents was calibrated to ensure breadth across the audit sections while keeping the workload feasible for a large cohort. It also forces prioritisation: students cannot list minor issues, but must select errors with genuine strategic impact.

Repair (Strategy reconstruction with traceability). Students were required to rewrite the Recommendations section such that the revised strategy directly addresses the diagnosed incidents and aligns with the corrected evidence base. Recommendations were required to be SMART and explicitly reference the corrected SWOT logic.

To operationalise MR3 (Traceability), students were either required or strongly encouraged to include a traceability mapping table showing: Critical Incident $\rightarrow$ Corrected Finding $\rightarrow$ Revised SWOT element $\rightarrow$ Recommendation $\rightarrow$ Metric/Target. The success criterion required that at least one revised recommendation be impossible to justify without resolving a diagnosed error, for example, measurement governance changes following incorrect conversion-rate claims.

4.4 Artefact Component C: Interactive Oral Assessment (Cycle 2 Extension)

Motivation: addressing ceiling effects and outsourcing risk. Cycle 1 results indicated strong performance, with marks clustering at the high end of the distribution (ceiling effects). To increase discriminative power and strengthen MR4 (Verification), Cycle 2 proposes a mandatory seven-minute Interactive Oral Assessment (IOA) as a secure, integrity-rich component [10–12].

IOA design and scenario framing. To ensure reliability and assess authentic understanding, the Interactive Oral Assessment (IOA) employs a standardized consultant-client role-play scenario designed to elicit real-time reasoning. In this dynamic, the evaluator adopts the persona of a defensive client challenging specific audit findings, such as a disputed conversion rate, forcing the student to provide evidential justification, correction logic, and strategic implications.

The assessment follows a consistent three-part prompt structure: an evidence challenge to identify discrepancies and defend corrections; a consequences challenge to articulate the decision-making harms of incorrect data; and a traceability challenge to connect corrections to specific strategic recommendations. Consequently, grading prioritizes evidential competence, reasoning coherence, and strategic traceability over the polish of the written report; responses are deemed insufficient if students rely on vague assertions or cannot reproduce the reasoning behind their own corrections.

This methodology significantly strengthens adversarial resistance against Generative AI by raising the cost of outsourcing, as success requires an authorship-level understanding capable of defending specific claims and tracing evidence to strategy under direct adversarial questioning [10–12].

5 Cycle 1 Implementation and Evaluation

The artefact was implemented with a Stage-3 undergraduate digital marketing cohort (n = 151). Overall performance across the class was strong, with most students achieving grades in the A– to B + range. The most common grade was around B + /A–, indicating strong overall performance. Approximately 39% of students achieved grades in the A– and above range, with another 44% in the B range. Very few students were below the pass threshold, demonstrating strong engagement and understanding of key digital marketing concepts [3, 4].

Exemplar analyses of the submitted critiques indicate that high-performing students were able to identify subtle errors embedded in the Dirty Audit, correctly reclassify SWOT items, and produce traceable recommendations aligned with evidence. The IOA further differentiated student performance, verifying the authenticity of reasoning and the traceability of decision-making. Students who performed well in the written critique generally maintained their performance in the IOA, while some students who appeared proficient on paper revealed gaps when required to justify corrections verbally [10–12].

Limited testing with an LLM red-team confirmed that AI alone could not reliably detect subtle errors or produce traceable strategic reasoning. This validates the adversarial resistance (MR1) of the artefact and supports the value of the tri-phasic Critique Scaffold combined with the IOA in fostering evaluative judgement, evidence-based reasoning, and strategic traceability [6, 7, 10–12].

Observations from student interactions and marker feedback suggest that the artefact successfully operationalises the intended learning outcomes:

Students engage in discriminative judgement rather than blanket rejection.

Students apply strategic reasoning grounded in corrected audit findings.

Students demonstrate traceability, linking errors through corrections to SWOT and revised recommendations.

Overall, the evaluation indicates that the LLM-adversarial assessment is effective at eliciting higher-order evaluative competencies while mitigating risks of AI-assisted superficial completion. The combination of Dirty Audit, Critique Scaffold, and IOA provides a robust, scalable, and integrity-rich assessment model for digital marketing education [10–17].

6 Discussion

6.1 Reflections on Cycle 1: The Validity of Asynchronous Critique

The quantitative "ceiling effect" observed in the pilot cohort presents a significant validity dilemma. While the clustering of high grades could be interpreted as evidence of successful scaffolding (Productive Failure), the lack of failure in the lower tail suggests the task lacked discriminatory power. In an unproctored written environment, distinguishing between a student who has genuinely exercised evaluative judgement and one who has utilized an LLM to perform an "assisted critique" is methodologically fraught. A student can arguably upload the Dirty Audit to a model and request a diagnostic review, thereby bypassing the cognitive struggle intended by the design. This finding empirically underscores the argument by Ma et al. [1] that assessment in the GenAI era must prioritize the process of judgment over the static output. The written critique indicates that an error was identified, but it fails to establish the human agency responsible for that identification. Consequently, we argue that asynchronous adversarial tasks, while necessary for engagement, are insufficient for summative verification without a synchronous defense layer.

6.2 Theoretical Implications: Re-Scoping the Science of the Artificial

This research contributes to the track's call to move "Beyond the Science of the Artificial" by questioning the fundamental object of design in business education. Herbert Simon envisioned a world in which human intelligence designed artifacts to achieve goals. We now inhabit a socio-technical reality where artificial agents generate these artifacts with high fidelity. This shift demands a radical innovation in pedagogical design: a pivot from Generative Design (teaching students to build) to Adversarial Design (teaching students to govern). The "LLM as Adversary" pattern suggests that the "preferable future" is not one in which humans compete with machines on generation speed, but one in which humans retain the epistemic authority to audit machine output. This aligns with Richter et al. [9]'s call for a constructivist reimagining of marketing education, where technology serves as a medium for critical inquiry rather than a production endpoint. By positioning the LLM as a fallible adversary, we preserve human agency in the loop, ensuring that the "Artificial" remains subject to human standards of truth and strategy.

6.3 Nascent Design Principles

Synthesizing the empirical results of Cycle 1 with this theoretical framing, we codify three nascent Design Principles (DPs) to guide the development of future adversarial assessments:

DP1: Plausible Mixed Fidelity. To elicit genuine evaluative judgement, the adversarial stimulus must reside in the "Uncanny Valley" of correctness. If errors are too obvious, the task degrades into trivial copy-editing; if the document is too perfect, the student assumes authority. The design must inject subtle, interpretive errors (e.g., correct data, wrong conclusion) to force deep cognitive engagement.

DP2: Consequentiality. Assessment rubrics must weigh the implications of an error beyond mere detection. In professional practice, a calculation error is less damaging than a strategic misalignment. Therefore, the assessment must require students to trace the "dirty" data to its potential negative impact on business resources, enforcing a logic of corporate responsibility.

DP3: Synchronous Verification. Given the permeability of written texts to AI assistance, adversarial designs must include a synchronous verification loop. The "Dirty Audit" serves as the *stimulus* for learning, but the Interactive Oral Assessment (IOA) serves as the *measure* of learning. This principle asserts that internalized standards can only be reliably tested when the student is required to defend their judgment in real-time, unassisted dialogue.

7 Future Work and Conclusion

This Research-in-Progress paper introduces the "LLM as Adversary" pattern, a DSR artifact designed to reclaim assessment validity in the GenAI era. By inverting the LLM's role from assistant to adversary, we force students to exercise evaluative judgement rather than rely on generative prompting [10]. However, the results from the first design cycle indicate that while this method successfully engages students, a written-only critique format suffers from a "ceiling effect," likely due to the ease with which students can use AI to assist in error detection.

To address this validity gap, the next phase of this research will rigorously test the efficacy of the complete "Dirty Audit + IOA" pattern. We propose a quasi-experimental design for the upcoming 2026 cycle, comparing the treatment cohort against historical control data from the traditional audit assessment. We hypothesize that adding the Interactive Oral Assessment (IOA) will normalize the grade distribution, reduce clustering in the upper bands, and increase the correlation between student confidence and accuracy. The evaluation will use a coding scheme derived from [1] to analyze IOA transcripts for evidence of metacognitive regulation, specifically examining the depth of justification in students' diagnostic reasoning.

Ultimately, this work contributes to a design theory for a future where human experts are defined not by what they generate, but by how they govern the artificial [11, 12]. By shifting the pedagogical focus from artifact creation to adversarial critique, we ensure that human agency remains central to the validation of knowledge in an automated world.

Disclosure of Interests. The authors have no competing interests to declare that are relevant to the content of this article.

References

1. Ma, Y., Zhang, Z., Liu, C.: The double-edged sword effect of GenAI assistance on university students' academic performance: evidence from China. Educ. Info. Technol., 1–26 (2025)
2. Tai, J., Ajjawi, R., Boud, D., Dawson, P., Panadero, E.: Developing evaluative judgement: enabling students to make decisions about the quality of work. High. Educ. **76**(3), 467–481 (2018)
3. Bearman, M., Tai, J., Dawson, P., Boud, D., Ajjawi, R.: Developing evaluative judgement for a time of generative artificial intelligence. Assess. Eval. High. Educ. **49**(6), 893–905 (2024)
4. Stephenson, Z., Johnson-Glauch, N., Cruchley, S.: Interventions and facilitators of oral assessment performance in higher education: A systematic review. Assess. Eval. High. Educ. **50**(7), 1140–1153 (2025)
5. Gregor, S., Hevner, A.R.: Positioning and presenting design science research for maximum impact. MIS Q. **37**(2), 337–355 (2013)
6. Hevner, A.R.: A three cycle view of design science research. Scand. J. Inf. Syst. **19**(2), 4 (2007)
7. Swiecki, Z., et al.: Assessment in the age of artificial intelligence. Comp. Educ. Artif. Intel. **3**, 100075 (2022)
8. TEQSA: Assessment reform for the age of artificial intelligence. Australian Government, Tertiary Education Quality and Standards Agency (2023)
9. Droulers, M., Krautloher, A., Shaeri, S.: Interactive oral assessment: Co-existence of formative and summative purposes. Teach. High. Educ. **31**(1), 67–85 (2026)
10. Perkins, M., Furze, L., Roe, J., Macvaugh, J.: The Artificial Intelligence Assessment Scale (AIAS): a framework for ethical integration of generative AI in educational assessment. J. Univ. Teach. Learn. Prac. **21**(6) (2024)
11. Richter, S., Giroux, M., Piven, I., Sima, H., Dodd, P.: A constructivist approach to integrating AI in marketing education: Bridging theory and practice. J. Mark. Educ. **47**(2), 94–111 (2025)
12. Sotiriadou, P., Logan, D., Daly, A., Guest, R.: The role of authentic assessment to preserve academic integrity and promote skill development and employability. Stud. High. Educ. **45**(11), 2132–2148 (2019)
13. Tan, C.P., Howes, D., Tan, R.K.W., Dancza, K.M.: Developing interactive oral assessments to foster graduate attributes in higher education. Assess. Eval. High. Educ. **47**(8), 1183–1199 (2022)
14. Krautloher, A.: Improving assessment equity using interactive oral assessments. J. Univ. Teach. Learn. Pract. **21**(4), 1–17 (2024)
15. Nallaya, S., Gentili, S., Weeks, S., Baldock, K.: The validity, reliability, academic integrity and integration of oral assessments in higher education: A systematic review. Iss. Educ. Res. **34**(2), 629–646 (2024)

16. Memmert, L., Tavanapour, N., Bittner, E.: Learning by doing: educators' perspective on an illustrative tool for AI-generated scaffolding for students in conceptualizing design science research studies. J. Inf. Syst. Educ. **34**(3), 279–292 (2023)
17. Vlachopoulos, D., Makri, A.: A systematic literature review on authentic assessment in higher education: Best practices for the development of 21st century skills, and policy considerations. Stud. Educ. Eval. **83**, 101425 (2024)

General Track – "From Insight to Impact"

Towards a Theory of Performance Measurement System Design

Charlotte Bahr[(✉)], Willi Tang, Victor Ulherr, and Martin Matzner

Friedrich-Alexander-Universität Erlangen-Nürnberg (FAU), Erlangen, Germany
`{charlotte.bahr,willi.tang,victor.ulherr.bahr,martin.matzner}@fau.de`

Abstract. Deconstructing abstract socio-material systems into action-able design imperatives is essential for translating organizational change requirements into effective IT artifacts. While the design of performance measurement systems (PMS) is often considered a routine design task, the alignment of organizational strategy and requirements with technical constraints remains a complex challenge. This RIP paper suggests using imbrication theory as a lens to conceive a nascent design theory for designing PMS. Using the exploratory case of PMS design at a medium-sized IT service provider, we provide initial insights on how material constraints of existing PMS serve as the primary driver for technological change and the design of a new PMS, translating into two design problems: the design of a technical and conceptual subsystem.

Keywords: Performance Measurement Systems · Imbrication Theory · Decision Support

1 Introduction

Managing organizational performance has become an increasingly complex challenge for contemporary management. In the context of digital transformation, organizations increasingly rely on data-driven approaches to support decision-making based on robust qualitative and quantitative indicators [32]. Intensifying competition further pressures organizations to continuously improve the efficiency of their value creation and operational processes. Organizational and process performance is commonly assessed using *performance measurement systems (PMS)*, which consist of structured sets of indicators designed to measure and represent performance outcomes [21,27]. Within such systems, *key performance indicators (KPIs)* play a central role in supporting both strategic and operational steering [24].

However, while the technical implementation of PMS – often in the form of decision support systems – is often considered a routine design task, PMS projects often turn out to be resource-intensive, costly, and difficult to sustain at a consistently high-quality level due to technical and organizational constraints. This is because PMS design does not only concern the technical realization of collecting, processing, and visualizing data but also involves substantial efforts

S. Chatterjee et al. (Eds.): DESRIST 2026, LNCS 16607, pp. 17–28, 2026.
https://doi.org/10.1007/978-3-032-28570-6_2

in ensuring that the PMS aligns strategic and operational business requirements and covers all dimensions of the business that the decision-makers need to carry out their business. To put it another way, designing DSS requires designing various interdependent subsystems, each of which has unique needs and limitations for the overall DSS design projects.

In this research-in-progress (RIP) paper, we report on our endeavor to conceive a *nascent design theory* [2,9] that describes the complex interplay between changing social and technical requirements in PMS design projects by drawing on *imbrication theory* [15]. Our paper is based on insights from the exploratory case study of a medium-sized IT service provider (ISP) that wanted to implement and configure multi-layered dashboards with varying levels of granularity tailored to different management levels. Our guiding research question (RQ) during the case was as follows:

RQ: *How can performance measurement systems be designed to reconcile the tension between technical constraints and dynamic business requirements?*

In the following sections, we pursue a four-step approach to address this RQ. First, we provide an overview of key concepts such as PMS and their technical implementation. We also introduce our kernel theory, that is, imbrication theory [15], which explicitly addresses mechanisms of change of systems that consist of social and technical subsystems. It is well suited to capture settings where human actors and technology are entangled. Second, we present our exploratory case study that we accompanied, where a mid-sized IT service provider (ISP) sought to introduce a structured control instrument that was developed to replace the existing fragmented and outdated reporting approaches with an integrated, data-driven solution. The company's prototype implementation of such a PMS was the basis for our design theorizing. Third, we provide preliminary results on a firm and design level leading to our final chapter about further steps.

2   Conceptual Background

2.1   Performance Measurement Systems (PMS)

PMS are systematic approaches for capturing, analyzing, and steering organizational performance by translating strategic objectives into measurable indicators [7,21]. Conceptually, PMS define how organizational goals are operationalized through KPIs that make processes transparent and comparable over time [5,18]. Central to PMS design is the alignment between organizational objectives and performance indicators, typically following a top-down logic in which strategic goals determine relevant performance dimensions and guide the selection of KPIs. As such, PMS function primarily as mechanisms of control, coordination, and organizational learning rather than as isolated analytical tools [3,22].

Previous research has acknowledged that organizational performance cannot be captured by a single dimension. Frameworks such as the Balanced Scorecard [12] or the Performance Prism [21] explicitly introduce multiple performance perspectives and can therefore be understood as offering an ensemble view of organizational performance [5]. However, these approaches focus on conceptual perspectives on the firm and its operations, rather than on theorizing how conceptual performance definitions, technical implementations, and organizational arrangements are interrelated. As a result, there is a lack of integrative frameworks that explicitly address the interdependencies across these layers.

Although PMS are often discussed as unified constructs, it is essential to distinguish between their business-level conception and their information-technical realization. At the business level, PMS specify which goals are pursued and which KPIs are required to monitor performance. At the technical level, PMS are instantiated through information systems that collect, process, and aggregate data across organizational processes. Reliable performance measurement depends on standardized process execution and automated data capture. Without these prerequisites, KPIs remain fragmented, delayed, or inconsistent [4].

This distinction is particularly relevant in the context of IT Service Management (ITSM)—a special case of PMS design. In ITSM, standardized process frameworks such as ITIL or COBIT prescribe what activities must be performed and how processes should be structured. These standards are typically linked to organizational objectives that are defined top-down and translated into process-level performance requirements. Consequently, performance measurement in ITSM is tightly coupled to predefined process models, which strongly shape both the selection of KPIs and their technical realization [1,11,19].

The representation of PMS is commonly realized through dashboards, which aggregate and visualize KPIs to provide structured overviews of process performance [29]. Dashboards serve as the interface between conceptual performance definitions and their technical instantiation, making deviations, trends, and distributions observable [33]. Effective dashboards adhere to established design principles such as clarity, consistency, and appropriate granularity, presenting a limited set of relevant KPIs to avoid cognitive overload [4]. Common visualization techniques include traffic-light indicators for rapid status assessment, time-series charts for trend analysis, and bar or pie charts for comparative and proportional insights. The choice of visualization directly influences interpretability and managerial actionability, making dashboard design a critical element of effective PMS implementation [25,33].

2.2 Imbrication Theory

Our research adopts *imbrication theory* as its analytical lens to conceptualize PMS as the outcome of ongoing, intertwined interactions between human action and structural constraints [15]. Imbrication theory is highly influenced by *theories of structuration* [6,8,23], *actor-network theory* [13], and *affordance theory* [17]. It emphasizes that organizational phenomena do not arise from social or technical elements in isolation, but from their repeated entanglement over time. Since a complete discussion of the roots of imbrication theory and its ontological and epistemological assumptions is way out of the scope of this paper, we will focus on a simplified presentation of the key terms and concepts of imbrication theory in the following; for a complete introduction of imbrication theory, we refer to [15] and [16]. Four key terms require a disambiguation for understanding imbrication theory: the distinction between the (1) social and (2) material, the role of (3) agency, and the allegory of (4) imbrication. Similar to the socio-technical systems theory, technology in organizations is viewed as a system of different social and technical subsystems [20,30,31]. Whereas *social* usually refers to elements related to or consequences of *human* behavior and institutions, researchers often use the term *material* (or materiality) to refer to artifacts that may or may not have a structural form, including, for example, physical objects such as computer hardware, buildings, and printed documents or non-physical objects like digital data, frameworks, and so on [16,28]. Imbrication theory proposes that "[organizational] routines and technologies, although distinct empirical phenomena, are ontologically related in the sense that they are both constituted by imbrications of human and material agencies" [15, p. 163]. In this context, *human agency* refers to an individual's ability to influence and realize their goals, whereas *material agency* refers to an artifact's (i.e., a non-human entity) ability to "act" without human control [15]. With *imbrication*, Leonardi [15] refers to how distinct elements (human and material agencies) are arranged in overlapping patterns so that they function interdependently. Depending on whether an existing configuration of human and material agency is perceived as affordances or constraints, this will lead to changes in (human) routines or changes in the material, that is, changes in the technology [15] (see Table 1).

Table 1. Imbrication mechanisms and their impact on routines and technology [15].

Imbrication Mechanism	Consequence
material → *human* "the imbrication of an **existing material agency** with a **new human agency** constitutes a routine" [15, p. 155]	***Perceptions of constraint*** that result in **changes of technology**.
human → *material* "the imbrication of an **existing human agency** with a **new material agency** brings changes to a technology at some level" [15, p. 155]	***Perceptions of affordance*** that result in **changes in routines**.

While previous research has largely viewed imbrication as a mechanism for describing the dynamics of change [15,26], research has recently suggested that it could serve as a lens for design [10,14]. Imbrication theory is particularly suitable for studying PMS design, as performance measurement emerges through continuous interactions between decision-makers, conceptual artifacts such as organizational goals and KPIs, and the technical systems that collect, process, and visualize performance data.

In this study, materiality is understood as the technical PMS, including data sources, analytics components, and dashboards; additionally, the individual KPIs selected also constitute something *material* and exhibit agency as the measures may or may not empower and constrain the cognition and behavior of both the designers of the PMS and the decision-makers using them to assess decisions during daily operations. The *social* aspect of a PMS, the human agency part, includes managers and analysts who define goals, select KPIs, and interpret performance information. By applying an imbrication lens, the study highlights that neither performance definitions, technical implementations, nor organizational roles exist independently but are co-constituted through their mutual interaction in the design and use of PMS. Or, in other words, imbrication can serve as an analogy to describe how different design requirements and principles evolve as a consequence of the continuous sequence of perceived constraints (which lead to changes in technology/design) and perceived affordances (which lead to changes in routines/principles) formed as human goals interact with material capabilities. In this manuscript, we refer to socio-material systems instead of socio-technical systems to stress how performance measures comprising the conceptual, non-technical system can also impose constraints on human agency or facilitate actions.

3 Case: Designing a PMS for a Mid-Sized ISP

This study draws on an exploratory case study conducted at a mid-sized IT service provider. We conducted four semi-structured interviews with C-level executives directly involved in commissioning and using the PMS. The interviews lasted 45 min on average and were conducted in person, audio-recorded, and transcribed (see Table 2). The interview guide comprised open-ended questions focusing on structural requirements, KPI selection, and usability; our goal was to derive the general design requirements for PMS. One researcher had a dual role as both a project participant and an academic, while the others were solely researchers, as acknowledged in Sect. 4.3.

Table 2. Overview of Expert Interviews

ID	Role of the Interviewee	Duration (in Minutes)
Interview 1	Executive Senior Manager (Digital Transformation)	60
Interview 2	Chief Operating Officer (COO)	52
Interview 3	Executive Senior Manager (Operations)	34
Interview 4	Chief Risk Officer (CRO)	62

3.1 Problem Definition

The case is situated in a mid-sized ISP that sought to professionalize its strategic and operational steering through a centralized PMS. Prior to this study, performance measurement practices were characterized by fragmented data sources, partially manual reporting, and heterogeneous KPI definitions across organizational units. As a result, transparency, comparability, and timely interpretation of performance information at the executive level were limited.

3.2   Artifact Design

From a *conceptual perspective*, performance measurement in the organization was primarily driven by top-down defined organizational goals, which were translated into KPIs in an ad hoc and weakly coordinated manner. While management relied on established performance perspectives similar to those popularized by frameworks such as the Balanced Scorecard, these perspectives remained largely disconnected from their technical realization and from concrete organizational roles. As such, performance measurement existed as a set of parallel views rather than as an integrated system spanning conceptual definition, technical implementation, and organizational use.

At the *technical level*, the organization operated multiple operational systems that generated large volumes of process data, particularly in the domains of IT service management and security operations. However, these data were not systematically aggregated or visualized in a unified way. To address this challenge, the organization selected the ServiceNow platform as a common technical foundation, leveraging its shared data model, workflow engine, and analytics capabilities. Within this environment, a prototype was instantiated using the ServiceNow *Control Tower* module, which provides a structured yet configurable framework for layered dashboards.

At the *organizational level*, performance measurement was embedded in a differentiated management structure with distinct information needs across executive roles. The case therefore focused on the design of executive portfolios for the Chief Operating Officer (COO) and the Chief Risk Officer (CRO). These portfolios operationalize role-specific performance concerns through a layered dashboard architecture. At higher levels of abstraction, the dashboards provide aggregated overviews of key performance dimensions, while lower layers enable more detailed, process-oriented perspectives. KPI selection and structuring were informed by literature and qualitative interviews with organizational stakeholders and iteratively refined in collaboration with executive management. Figures 1 and 2 illustrate the preliminary design of the *Control Tower* and its layered structure. Figure 1 presents a high-level view of the *Control Tower*, outlining its overall composition and functional layers. Figure 2 zooms into a role-specific sub-layer, detailing the information required by the CRO.

Rather than treating the artifact as a finalized solution, the case serves as an abstraction of how PMS emerge at the intersection of conceptual performance definitions, technical system affordances, and organizational roles. The case thus provides an empirical setting to study PMS design as an imbricated ensemble of design levels, illustrating how changes at one level shape and constrain the others. In this sense, the case is not presented as a singular instantiation but as a vehicle for developing transferable insights into the design of PMS.

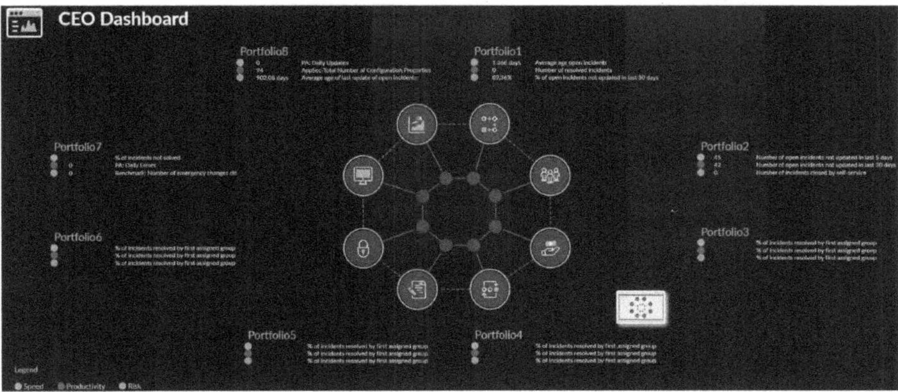

Fig. 1. Control Tower for Chief Executive Officer.

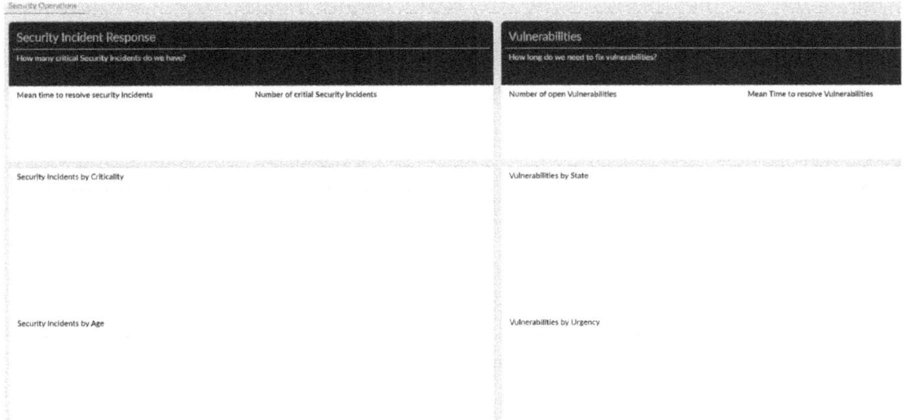

Fig. 2. Sub-layer of Control Tower specified for CRO.

4   Preliminary Results

Our research provides initial insights towards the development of a nascent design theory for PMS. For our theory, we want to disentangle PMS design, that is, the design of a socio-material artifact, into activities at the firm level and activities at the design (or technical artifact) level. The preliminary findings suggest that a PMS should not be conceptualized as a singular, self-contained tool but rather as an imbricated ensemble consisting of interdependent social (human) and material elements—each possessing distinct agency to influence human perception. Using an imbrication theory provides us with the necessary vocabulary and analytical method to distinguish between imbrications of human and material agency, associated perceptions of affordance and constraint, and changes in routines and technology [15].

4.1 Firm Level

In our exploratory case where we analyzed a PMS development project and related design decisions, imbrication theory reveals a path-dependent sequence of socio-material change at the **firm level**. The project begins when C-level management formulated a strategic need to explore a new PMS as existing human agency where organizational decisions are required to be based on a "single-source-of-truth". This intent encountered a significant material constraint, as the existing PMS infrastructure was scattered across disparate data sources and systems, serving as a catalyst for the need to change technology: the design of a new PMS for ITSM. The implementation of the new PMS created new material agency, which provides new affordances. Specifically, the *Control Tower* now offers multi-layered dashboards that provide data representations previously unavailable to executives and that facilitate more informed C-level decision-making. What the imbrication lens highlights is how routines and technologies, while being distinct phenomena, are ontologically related because they both constitute interlocking agencies [15].

4.2 Design Level

However, our current research project indicates that the current framework does not explicitly translate these changes of material agency into actionable imperatives at the **design level**, specifically in the form of *design requirements* and *design principles*. The design of a PMS specifically involves the design of two interlocked sub-systems: the design of the *technical subsystem* comprising the implementation of the technical system and the design of the *conceptual subsystem* comprising the collection of performance measures relevant for C-level.

To bridge this level gap, we have dissected the material agency of the PMS into two design problems: the design of the "technical" and the "conceptual" subsystem. We observed that *design requirements* are primarily derived from the ("to-be") affordances that the stakeholders of an implementation project wish to possess, defining the logic and standards that align with the organizational "spirit" [6] of the system. In contrast, *design principles* constitute the individual design decisions that collectively form the material agency at the system level. With our ongoing study we provide initial insights toward the development of an integrative nascent design theory for PMS that translates changes at the firm level to design decisions and activities at the artifact level. Figure 3 summarizes our current theoretical conceptualization (Fig. 3).

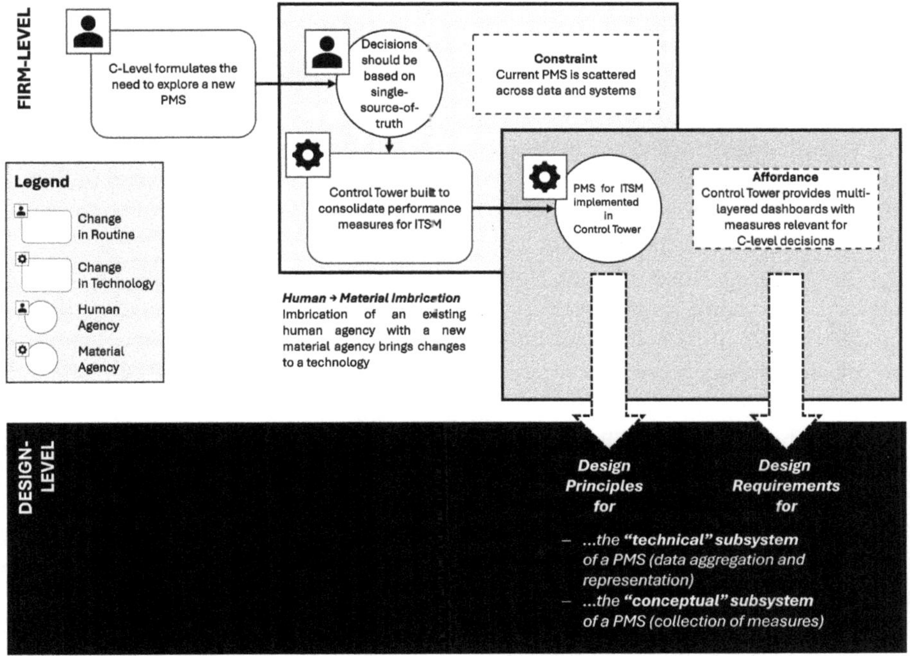

Fig. 3. Preliminary nascent design theory for PMS.

4.3 Limitations

The current study implies several limitations that must be acknowledged when interpreting the preliminary findings.

First, the analysis is based on a single exploratory case situated in one mid-sized IT service provider operating in an ITSM context governed by standardized frameworks such as ITIL. This setting shapes both the nature of the design problems encountered and the imbrication dynamics observed, and may not be representative of PMS design challenges in industries with less formalized process structures or more heterogeneous organizational arrangements. Therefore, it remains an open question which aspects of the emerging design theory are specific to ITSM environments and which reflect more generalizable mechanisms of socio-material change in PMS design.

Second, the paper reports preliminary theoretical insights derived from an ongoing empirical study; the design propositions and principles remain nascent and have not yet been subjected to systematic validation across multiple cases or theoretical triangulation.

Third, one of the researchers was simultaneously involved in the design of the PMS artifact under study, which potentially influenced both the empirical observations and the theoretical interpretations drawn from them.

5 Further Steps

Building on the preliminary results, the next steps of this RIP aim to further substantiate and formalize the emerging theory of PMS design.

First, in response to the single-context limitation of the current study, future research will extend the empirical scope beyond the ITSM context. The initial case is set in a context that tightly couples performance measurement to predefined process models in ways that may not generalize to other settings. Several aspects of our findings appear potentially context-specific: (1) the primacy of material constraints as the primary driver of PMS redesign may be amplified by the high degree of technical standardization inherent to ITSM environments; (2) the relatively clear boundary between conceptual and technical subsystems may be more blurred in industries with less formalized process frameworks; and (3) the role of existing platform affordances in shaping both design requirements and design principles may be less determinative in organizations with more heterogeneous IT landscapes. Comparative case studies in organizations from different industries and with varying organizational structures are therefore planned to empirically distinguish context-specific from generalizable PMS design principles and to assess the broader applicability of the proposed framework.

Second, the preliminary ensemble framework will be refined and operationalized by specifying recurring interaction patterns between organizational goals, KPI definitions, technical system affordances, and organizational roles. This refinement will support the derivation of explicit design propositions and theoretical constructs that explain PMS design as an iterative and recursive process, rather than a linear sequence of design decisions.

Third and finally, subsequent research iterations will place a stronger emphasis on the iterative nature of PMS design by explicitly incorporating feedback loops between empirical observation, theoretical refinement, and artifact redesign. Through these steps, the study aims to advance from preliminary insights toward a robust and empirically grounded theory of PMS design that conceptualizes PMS as evolving design ensembles rather than static, singular systems.

References

1. Axelos (ITIL): ITIL ® Foundation ITIL 4 Edition 2. Technical report (2019)
2. Baskerville, R.L., Kaul, M., Storey, V.C.: Genres of inquiry in design-science research: justification and evaluation of knowledge production. MIS Q. **39**(3), 541–564 (2015)
3. Bititci, U.S., Carrie, A.S., McDevitt, L.: Integrated performance measurement systems: a development guide. Int. J. Oper. Prod. Manag. **17**(5), 522–534 (1997). https://doi.org/10.1108/01443579710167230
4. Bourne, M., Mills, J., Wilcox, M., Neely, A., Platts, K.: Designing, implementing and updating performance measurement systems. Int. J. Oper. Prod. Manag. **20**(7), 754–771 (2000). https://doi.org/10.1108/01443570010330739
5. Brown, D.M., Laverick, S.: Measuring corporate performance. Long Range Plan. **27**(4), 89–98 (1994). https://doi.org/10.1016/0024-6301(94)90059-0

6. DeSanctis, G., Poole, M.S.: Capturing the complexity in advanced technology use: adaptive structuration theory. Organ. Sci. **5**(2), 121–147 (1994). https://doi.org/10.1287/orsc.5.2.121

7. Franco-Santos, M., et al.: Towards a definition of a business performance measurement system. Int. J. Oper. Prod. Manag. **27**(8), 784–801 (2007). https://doi.org/10.1108/01443570710763778

8. Giddens, A.: The Constitution of Society: Outline of the Theory of Structuration. University of California Press, Berkeley, CA (1984)

9. Gregor, S., Hevner, A.R.: Positioning and presenting design science research for maximum impact. MIS Q. 337–355 (2013)

10. Haggerty, N., Compeau, D.: Ruptures during IT-enabled change: a sensemaking and imbrication analysis. MIS Q. **49**(1), 61–90 (2025)

11. Iden, J., Eikebrokk, T.R.: Implementing IT service management: a systematic literature review. Int. J. Inf. Manage. **33**(3), 512–523 (2013). https://doi.org/10.1016/j.ijinfomgt.2013.01.004

12. Kaplan, R.S., Norton, D.P.: The Balanced Scorecard: Measures That Drive Performance, vol. 70. Harvard Business Review Boston, MA, USA (2005)

13. Latour, B.: Reassembling the Social: An Introduction to Actor-Network-Theory. Oxford University Press, Oxford (2005). https://doi.org/10.1093/oso/9780199256044.001.0001

14. Leonardi, P., Rodriguez-Lluesma, C.: Sociomateriality as a lens for design: imbrication and the constitution of technology and organization. Scand. J. Inf. Syst. **24**(2) (2012)

15. Leonardi, P.M.: When flexible routines meet flexible technologies: affordance, constraint, and the imbrication of human and material agencies. MIS Q. **35**(1), 147–167 (2011). https://doi.org/10.2307/23043493

16. Leonardi, P.M.: Theoretical foundations for the study of sociomateriality. Inf. Organ. **23**(2), 59–76 (2013). https://doi.org/10.1016/j.infoandorg.2013.02.002

17. Markus, M.L., Silver, M.: A foundation for the study of IT effects: a new look at DeSanctis and poole's concepts of structural features and spirit. J. Assoc. Inf. Syst. **9**(10) (2008). https://doi.org/10.17705/1jais.00176

18. Marr, B.: Key Performance Indicators (KPI): The 75 Measures Every Manager Needs to Know. Pearson UK (2012)

19. Marrone, M., Kolbe, L.M.: Einfluss von IT-service-management-frameworks auf die IT-organisation. Wirtschaftsinformatik **53**(1), 5–19 (2011). https://doi.org/10.1007/s11576-010-0257-8

20. Mumford, E.: The story of socio-technical design: reflections on its successes, failures and potential. Inf. Syst. J. **16**(4), 317–342 (2006). https://doi.org/10.1111/j.1365-2575.2006.00221.x

21. Neely, A., Gregory, M., Platts, K.: Performance measurement system design. Int. J. Oper. Prod. Manag. **15**(4), 80–116 (1995). https://doi.org/10.1108/01443579510083622

22. Nudurupati, S., Bititci, U., Kumar, V., Chan, F.: State of the art literature review on performance measurement. Comput. Ind. Eng. **60**(2), 279–290 (2011). https://doi.org/10.1016/j.cie.2010.11.010

23. Orlikowski, W.J.: The duality of technology: rethinking the concept of technology in organizations. Organ. Sci. **3**(3), 398–427 (1992). https://doi.org/10.1287/orsc.3.3.398

24. Parmenter, D.: Key Performance Indicators: Developing, Implementing, and Using Winning KPIs. Wiley (2015)

25. Pauwels, K., et al.: Dashboards as a Service. J. Serv. Res. **12**(2), 175–189 (2009). https://doi.org/10.1177/1094670509344213
26. Pentland, B., Vaast, E., Wolf, J.: Theorizing process dynamics with directed graphs: a diachronic analysis of digital trace data. MIS Q. **45**(2), 967–984 (2021)
27. Ravelomanantsoa, M.S., Ducq, Y., Vallespir, B.: A state of the art and comparison of approaches for performance measurement systems definition and design. Int. J. Prod. Res. **57**(15–16), 5026–5046 (2019). https://doi.org/10.1080/00207543.2018.1506178
28. Robey, D., Anderson, C., Raymond, B.: Information technology, materiality, and organizational change: a professional odyssey. J. Assoc. Inf. Syst. **14**(7) (2013). https://doi.org/10.17705/1jais.00337
29. Sarikaya, A., Correll, M., Bartram, L., Tory, M., Fisher, D.: What do we talk about when we talk about dashboards? IEEE Trans. Visual Comput. Graphics **25**(1), 682–692 (2019). https://doi.org/10.1109/TVCG.2018.2864903
30. Sarker, S., Chatterjee, S., Xiao, X., Elbanna, A.: The sociotechnical axis of cohesion for the IS discipline: its historical legacy and its continued relevance. MIS Q. **43**(3), 695–719 (2019). https://doi.org/10.25300/MISQ/2019/13747
31. Sutcliffe, A.G.: Requirements analysis for socio-technical system design. Inf. Syst. **25**(3), 213–233 (2000). https://doi.org/10.1016/S0306-4379(00)00016-8
32. Szukits, Á., Móricz, P.: Towards data-driven decision making: the role of analytical culture and centralization efforts. RMS **18**(10), 2849–2887 (2024)
33. Yigitbasioglu, O.M., Velcu, O.: A review of dashboards in performance management: implications for design and research. Int. J. Account. Inf. Syst. **13**(1), 41–59 (2012). https://doi.org/10.1016/j.accinf.2011.08.002

Customer Contribution-Aware Incident Management: A Problem Space Explication for Digitally Mediated Service Episodes

Peter Hottum[✉] and Daniel Heinz

Karlsruhe Institute of Technology (KIT), Kaiserstr. 12, 76131 Karlsruhe, Germany
{peter.hottum,daniel.heinz}@kit.edu

Abstract. Digitally mediated incident management depends on customer-side input – context, evidence, access enablement, and confirmations – yet these contributions are weakly represented in episode-level operational control. In a remote operations support context, we explicate the problem space of customer contribution-aware incident management and show how contribution dependence produces predictable bottlenecks when customer readiness is unqualified or delayed. Based on seven expert interviews in a large industrial equipment manufacturer and a Gioia-inspired analysis, we identify three recurring challenges: unqualified early contribution signals that leave work readiness ambiguous, ad-hoc intervention in contribution-contingent states that consumes scarce specialist capacity, and contribution-blind routing, scheduling, and pacing that propagates "not-ready" work into expert queues and drives long-tail resolution. Building on these challenges and corresponding deficits, we derive four design objectives for an artifact intended to address these issues and an evaluation logic emphasizing operational benefit, decision defensibility, and acceptability under digital trace constraints.

Keywords: Customer contribution · Incident management · Digitally mediated service episodes · Remote operations support · Design science research

1 Introduction

Incident management in digitally mediated support settings unfolds as an incident episode: a bounded sequence of distributed diagnosis and coordination conducted under workload, skill, and service-level constraints [1, 2]. In ticket-based settings, the initial request message becomes the first coordination artifact that stabilizes shared understanding and shapes subsequent work. Episode progress depends on timely customer-side inputs – situational context, diagnostic evidence, access enablement, and confirmations – while missing, delayed, or inconsistent inputs trigger clarification loops, rework, and extended resolution times even for otherwise routine incidents [1, 2].

Service research frames such episodes as reciprocal resource integration through which actors realize value-in-use in interaction rather than unilateral delivery [3–5]. This co-creation view has been extended to IT service ecosystems, highlighting how value

S. Chatterjee et al. (Eds.): DESRIST 2026, LNCS 16607, pp. 29–41, 2026.
https://doi.org/10.1007/978-3-032-28570-6_3

formation is shaped by multi-actor, multi-level structures beyond dyadic provider–consumer exchange [6]. However, co-creation remains well established only conceptually; existing IT service management guidance is weakly specified at the episode level regarding how readiness is qualified and customer-dependent states are represented and governed during ongoing incidents [7, 8]. As a result, operational control often prioritizes provider-side queue efficiency and throughput, while customer-dependent uncertainty is handled implicitly and inconsistently. A contribution-aware redesign is therefore needed that makes customer-dependent readiness explicit and actionable at the level where incidents are actually coordinated: the episode.

Digitally mediated support amplifies this challenge because episode coordination is enacted primarily through digital artifacts (e.g. tickets, portals, remote-access tools, logs, and automation), so ticket content, timing, and semantics reflect tool affordances and policies that shape what becomes observable and how it is interpreted [9, 10]. The growing role of AI assistance in incident workflows makes this all the more pressing: as AI-drafted content and automated suggestions enter the trace, contribution-aware control becomes even more necessary to keep readiness assessments and decisions regarding routing, escalation, or intervention inspectable and contestable [11–13].

This research-in-progress paper addresses that underspecification within a design science research (DSR) program on customer contribution-aware incident management [14, 15]. The overarching research question is: *How can incident management operations be redesigned to systematically sense, qualify, and leverage customer contribution throughout digitally mediated incident episodes?* The paper provides problem-space grounding from a remote operations support (ROS) context in a large industrial equipment manufacturer. Empirically, it draws on seven semi-structured interviews spanning roles in design, commercialization, and delivery. The interviews reconstruct incident episodes as digitally mediated service interactions and elicit coordination frictions around missing context, delayed confirmations, access enablement, and channel shifts under workload and service-level constraints. Analytically, the study applies a Gioia-inspired coding approach to maintain a transparent link from informant-centric observations to second-order themes and aggregate problem patterns [16, 17].

The analysis yields three recurrent challenges that specify how contribution-blind operational control produces predictable bottlenecks under digital mediation: unqualified early contribution signals that leave work readiness ambiguous, ad-hoc intervention in contribution-contingent states that consumes scarce specialist capacity, and contribution-blind routing, scheduling, and pacing that propagates "not-ready" work into expert queues and drives long-tail resolution. To situate these challenges in a design-oriented framing while remaining agnostic about technical instantiation, the paper adopts a micro-level service platform lens that foregrounds rules of exchange and modular supports shaping evidence requests, confirmations, and decision governance across episodes [18]. The resulting problem-space explication establishes design objectives that a contribution-aware redesign must address, and evaluation criteria to assess the utility and limits of corresponding artifacts.

2 Background and Related Work

2.1 Service Episodes, Customer Contribution, and Service Platforms

Service research conceptualizes service relationships as sequences of episodes in which actors integrate resources through interaction to realize value-in-use [3–5]. Episodes thus provide a micro-level unit of analysis for examining how coordination unfolds over time across roles and organizational boundaries. This perspective fits incident management, where disruptions trigger distributed diagnostic work and progress depends on iterative exchanges of evidence, interpretations, and confirmations anchored in a shared coordination artifact.

We operationalize co-creation at the episode level where incident work is coordinated. In IT service management, the service consumer role is labeled in multiple ways (e.g., user, business representative, site contact); here, customer-side actor denotes the service consumer role involved in the episode [19, 20]. Customer contribution refers to the customer-side provision and enactment of episode-relevant resources – context, evidence, access enablement, and confirmations – required to advance diagnosis and repair. Under ticket-based coordination, these contributions are partially observable through the episode's digital trace, for example in intake completeness, response latency to evidence requests, and confirmation reliability [9, 21].

At the operational level, contribution dependence captures the extent to which episode progress at specific points is contingent on customer-side actions or inputs. It encompasses both operand information artifacts (e.g., logs, screenshots, configuration extracts) and operant resources (e.g., contextual interpretation, diagnostic judgment, and decision rights) that render those artifacts actionable [3, 5]. When contribution dependence is high and contribution is insufficient, episodes enter contribution bottlenecks: provider-side work readiness declines and coordination becomes dominated by evidence chasing, access enablement, and confirmation waiting. In this sense, "waiting on the customer" can be understood as a recurring coordination state with operational consequences that can be represented, anticipated, and governed [1, 2].

Customer contributions shape the conditions under which providers can act, and service research has long emphasized that participation patterns influence service experiences and outcomes [22]. In incident episodes, customer contribution takes an operational form: customer-side actors provide context, enable access, execute checks, deliver confirmations, and coordinate internally across stakeholders with relevant knowledge. When these contributions do not meet the episode's contribution dependence, coordination shifts from diagnosis to securing prerequisites and aligning interpretations, producing bottleneck states characterized by clarification cycles, waiting, and stalled decisions [21, 23].

A service innovation perspective connects these dynamics to a design-oriented framing. Lusch and Nambisan [18] conceptualize service platforms as modular resources and exchange rules that enable interaction among actors and resource bundles. Applied to incident episodes, the platform lens directs attention to exchange rules and modular supports that structure evidence requests, confirmations, escalation decisions, and decision governance across repeated episodes, anchoring the artifact class at the level of interaction structuring while remaining agnostic about specific technical instantiations.

In contemporary IT support, customer contribution is elicited and captured through elements such as portals, standardized forms, workflow states, and routing rules. These elements can reduce ambiguity and increase throughput, but they also shape what becomes visible as "contribution" in the trace. As a result, observable signals such as "a response" or "evidence provided" can differ in operational value depending on completeness, timeliness, and provenance, while system constraints may suppress relevant context [9, 24]. This motivates treating customer contribution as a system-shaped trace that requires qualification – at minimum along completeness, latency, and provenance – to support episode-level operational decision-making under digital mediation.

2.2 Ticket-Based Incident Operations as Trace-Mediated Coordination Work

Ticketing systems make incident episodes empirically tangible because they log coordination as it occurs. Messages, timestamps, status changes, handovers, labels, and resolution markers accumulate into a ticket trace that serves as the canonical digital record of the episode [1]. This trace enables operational learning by making recurring bottlenecks, clarification loops, and escalation dynamics observable, including patterns that contribute to delay variance and long-tail resolution [1, 2].

Ticket-based operations also impose constraints on episode-level mechanisms. Early stages tend to be information-poor because customers report symptoms rather than diagnoses and intake processes often prioritize speed and low friction [25, 26]. Organizations protect specialist capacity, manage risk, and operate under governance constraints that limit aggressive automation [20, 27]; routing and assignment decisions reflect workload distribution, skill structures, and escalation protocols [2]. Accordingly, contribution-aware incident operations must function under sparse early signals, heterogeneous customer contexts, and policies that stabilize work while constraining what can be demanded from customer-side actors and when.

Because the trace captures interaction and control events, coordination breakdowns can leave observable signatures such as repeated clarification cycles, prolonged "waiting" states, reopen and rework after closure, and resolver-group handovers following missing inputs [21, 23]. These signatures provide an empirical entry point for studying contribution dependence and its operational consequences without requiring direct access to underlying intentions or efforts. They also motivate an explicit episode-level representation of readiness and customer-dependent states that can be inferred – within limits – from trace features under digital mediation.

2.3 IT Service Management Guidance and Digital Mediation

IT service management guidance increasingly adopts a co-creation perspective on service relationships. In particular, ITIL 4 positions service management within a broader service value system and frames service provision as a joint provider-consumer activity embedded in end-to-end value creation [7, 28]. Prior work has examined the extent to which this framing aligns with service-dominant logic and co-creation assumptions [8]. However, existing guidance remains largely episode-agnostic with respect to how customer-dependent states are represented and governed during ongoing incidents.

More specifically, current guidance offers only limited episode-level control logic for sensing early contribution signals from the ticket trace, qualifying their sufficiency and reliability for next-step readiness, and linking that assessment to contestable routing and intervention decisions under workload constraints [7, 8]. In practice, this leaves customer-dependent waiting weakly modeled and encourages improvised handling of contribution bottlenecks alongside throughput-oriented control. As a result, incidents may be processed as provider-side workload units even when effective progress depends on unresolved customer-side prerequisites.

Digital mediation intensifies this gap because it shapes how contribution signals are captured and interpreted in the trace [9, 10]. AI assistance sharpens it further: when ticket content and recommendations are partly machine-generated, provenance and interpretability cannot be assumed but must be governed through trace-grounded, contestable rationales [11–13]. Taken together, IT service management guidance provides a useful co-creation vocabulary but still lacks adequate episode-level control logic for qualifying and governing customer-dependent readiness.

3 Study Design for Problem-Space Explication

This research-in-progress paper explicates the problem space, derives design objectives, and specifies goodness-related evaluation criteria for customer contribution-aware incident management within an integrated DSR [14]. It draws on a single in-depth case of a global industrial equipment manufacturer that recently introduced a ROS offering, in which episode progress depends on customer-side inputs such as context, evidence, access enablement, and confirmations exchanged through ticketing and related digital channels. This makes the case suitable for examining contribution dependence as an operational control challenge. Within the broader research program, the purpose of the present study is problem-space explication rather than renewed trace-based analysis of ticket data. Trace-oriented foundations have already been established in prior work [1]. The present paper therefore uses interview-based inquiry to surface coordination frictions, recurring mechanisms, and design-relevant deficits, deliberately foregrounding the practitioner perspective needed for problem-space explication.

The empirical evidence comprises seven semi-structured expert interviews conducted between March 2022 and March 2024 as part of an ongoing research collaboration with the case organization. We purposefully sampled interviewees to cover key vantage points involved in designing, commercializing, and delivering the ROS offering. The sample includes service ownership and development roles as well as customer-facing delivery roles engaged in operational decision-making during standstills. Interviews lasted 50–70 min, were conducted via video, recorded with consent, and transcribed for analysis. Table 1 summarizes interviewees, roles, and interview length. Subsequent work will extend the interview base across additional functions and customer contexts as the broader DSR program progresses.

Interview protocols were designed to reconstruct incident episodes as *digitally mediated service interactions*. Each interview elicited (i) the service offering and its value logic from the interviewee's vantage point, (ii) the operational process by which remote support is initiated and progressed, and (iii) recurring coordination frictions and bottlenecks that shape episode performance under workload and service-level constraints.

Table 1. Overview of interviewees.

ID	Function (years of experience)	Length
I1-ROS	Remote Service Operations Lead (5y)	62 min
I2-BC	Business Center Lead (10y)	57 min
I3-DSA	Digital Services Architect (14y)	50 min
I4-ARCH	Solution Architect (15y)	70 min
I5-BD	Business Development (5y)	65 min
I6-PMDA	Product Manager Data Strategy (4y)	61 min
I7-PM	Product Manager (2y)	65 min

Process elicitation covered recurring scenario variations that influence episode readiness, including situations with an on-site operator available at the customer site and situations in which remote support proceeds with limited on-site assistance. These scenario patterns clarify when provider-side progress becomes contingent on customer-side actions and information, and they help specify which contribution signals and constraints are salient at different points in the episode. Across interviews, particular attention was given to how teams handle missing context, delayed confirmations, access enablement issues, and channel shifts, and how these frictions influence routing, escalation, and intervention choices.

Analytically, we applied a Gioia-inspired approach to maintain a transparent chain from evidence to the problem framing [16, 17]. We captured informant-centric observations as first-order concepts, consolidated them into second-order themes that represent recurring mechanisms and constraints, and aggregated these themes into three recurring challenges (C1-C3) that structure the problem-space explication in Sect. 4. Each challenge concludes with a derived deficit statement that translates the evidence-backed problem framing into design-relevant gaps and directly informs the design objectives in Sect. 5. All claims are anchored through pseudonymized handles (I#–ROLE). Figure 1 in the Appendix provides the data structure that links quote anchors to first-order concepts, second-order themes, and the three challenges.

4 Problem Space Explication

Challenge 1: Unqualified Early Contribution Signals. In digitally mediated incident episodes, progress often stalls when early customer-side contribution cannot be used to qualify work readiness. At intake, tickets may appear triageable, yet critical readiness conditions – context quality, access feasibility, expected responsiveness, and confirmation needs – remain insufficiently qualified.

Interviewees attribute non-qualification to three recurring sources: *semantic ambiguity* of early signals (e.g., "waiting" status without an interpretable reason) (I2-BC), *limited operational usability of evidence* (e.g., data that requires cleaning and interpretation before it supports diagnosis) (I7-PM), and *missing prerequisites for remote progress* (e.g., connectivity and access constraints that restrict feasible remote actions) (I2-BC; I4-ARCH). Contribution further varies with *heterogeneous customer capability and adoption constraints,* shaping whether signals are produced in the expected form and channel (I1-ROS; I7-PM).

From a mechanistic perspective, intake and routing decisions rely on an implicit assumption of timely customer-side readiness. When readiness remains unqualified, provider-side processing proceeds under uncertainty. Once diagnostic work requires concrete evidence, access, or confirmations, gaps become visible and trigger context reconstruction, repeated follow-ups, and coordination overhead under SLA pressure. In the ticket trace, this challenge should surface as *early readiness ambiguity*: intake records with thin context, early on-hold states without a coded reason, artifact uploads arriving only after assignment or first specialist engagement, and early request-reply exchanges focused on making evidence usable before substantive diagnosis begins.

> **Deficit Statement 1:** *Episodes begin without qualified work readiness: early indicators of context quality, responsiveness, access feasibility, and confirmation needs are missing, ambiguous, or operationally unusable, making clarification loops and delayed progress likely.*

Challenge 2: Ad-Hoc Intervention Instead of Systematic Control. When contribution is insufficient relative to contribution dependence, incident teams rely on improvised coordination rather than a staged intervention logic. Episodes enter states in which provider-side progress becomes contingent on customer inputs or actions; when these inputs do not arrive in an actionable form, work readiness drops and coordination shifts toward evidence chasing, access enablement, and confirmation waiting.

Interviewees describe ad-hoc control in two ways. First, they report *channel improvisation and tool workarounds,* shifting to consumer messaging, video calls, photos, or even physical data transfer when formal tools are missing or impractical (I1-ROS; I2-BC; I5-BD). Second, they highlight *breakdowns in tool support and process fit* that fragment episode provenance across channels and agreements, forcing local consolidation work and repeated explanations (I1-ROS; I3-DSA; I4-ARCH). A recurrent constraint is the *resource cost of intervention:* active provider-side guidance binds scarce capacity and becomes difficult to sustain at scale (I6-PMDA; I7-PM).

From a mechanistic perspective, teams face contribution dependence without a decision structure for proportionate interventions (e.g. consolidated requests, explicit deadlines, channel escalation rules, and escalation triggers tied to readiness). As a result, multiple parties request overlapping information, coordination repeats across channels, and episodes accrue delay variance – especially costly when specialist capacity is limited. In ticket traces, this challenge should appear as elevated loop counts, repeated short follow-ups, frequent on-hold toggling, references to off-system channels (e.g., calls, video, messaging), and reopen events following premature closure.

> **Deficit Statement 2:** *When contribution falls short of contribution dependence, teams default to trial-and-error coordination rather than staged, proportionate control, consuming specialist capacity and increasing delay variance.*

Challenge 3: Contribution-Blind Routing, Scheduling, and Pacing. Assignment and scheduling often treat tickets as provider-side workload units rather than episodes with customer-dependent readiness. When routing and pacing ignore contribution-related risk, organizations face misrouting, delayed escalation, specialist overload, and long-tail resolution. Tickets are assigned based on category or skill even when customer-side prerequisites remain unresolved; "not-ready" cases reach scarce experts, who then wait, coordinate, and re-request prerequisites instead of diagnosing.

Interviewees show that customer-dependent feasibility is actively handled in practice, yet largely through local routines rather than explicit design. They report *availability-bounded scheduling* (planning complex actions around customer time windows) (I1-ROS), *readiness-blind routing and escalation* (escalation as a move to secure ownership and expertise; tiering delays shaped by time-of-day constraints) (I1-ROS), and *workload-driven pacing* under queue pressure, including the need to manage ticket 'waves' and scale limits of manual control points (I1-ROS; I6-PMDA). Prioritization and escalation are further shaped by *governance thresholds,* such as downtime economics and service guarantees (I1-ROS; I5-BD; I6-PMDA).

From a mechanistic perspective, contribution dependence makes the effective throughput of provider work conditional on customer responsiveness and feasibility. Without readiness-aware gating, systems propagate "not-ready" work into the wrong queues, delay escalation decisions, and generate long tails under SLA and workload constraints. In ticket traces, this challenge should be observable via resolver-group changes, queue waiting times, escalation markers, time-of-day effects, and SLA breach indicators. Together with late-arriving readiness artifacts, these signatures indicate flow decisions made without qualifying contribution-dependent risk.

Deficit Statement 3: *Routing, scheduling, and pacing operate without readiness-aware gating and therefore ignore customer-dependent coordination risk, yielding misrouting, delayed escalation, and long-tail resolution under SLA and workload constraints.*

5 Design Objectives and Evaluation Logic

Section 4 identifies three recurring deficits that explain why incident episodes stall under digitally mediated conditions: episodes begin without qualified work readiness (D1), contribution bottlenecks are handled through improvised coordination rather than systematic control (D2), and routing and pacing decisions propagate "not-ready" work into scarce expert queues (D3). Taken together, these deficits show that customer contribution is not merely a contextual condition of incident work, but an operational dependency that must be representable and governable at the episode level.

The design objectives derived here therefore do not prescribe a specific technical solution. Instead, they define what contribution-aware incident operations must be able to represent, structure, and justify if they are to handle customer-dependent readiness more effectively under digitally mediated conditions. The accompanying goodness criteria translate this design orientation into a compact evaluation logic for subsequent artifact design and assessment.

Because D1 shows that early ticket signals do not reliably qualify whether provider-side work can meaningfully proceed, contribution-aware operations must treat readiness as an explicit episode property rather than an implicit assumption. D2 further indicates that, once contribution dependence becomes salient, teams need scalable control options that reduce clarification loops without binding scarce capacity. D3 highlights that these mechanisms only translate into performance improvements if flow decisions – routing, scheduling, pacing – are readiness-aware and do not push customer-dependent uncertainty downstream into specialist queues. Across all three deficits, digitally mediated traces are the primary evidence base; therefore, episode states and interventions must remain transparent and contestable across handovers and channels.

Design Objective 1 (Readiness Qualification): *Represent and qualify contribution-dependent work readiness early in the episode – context, usable evidence, access feasibility, and confirmation needs – as an explicit state that prevents uncoded "waiting/on-hold" ambiguity* (addresses D1).

Design Objective 2 (Staged Intervention): *Provide a staged, proportionate intervention logic for contribution-contingent states that specifies requests, follow-ups, interaction-mode changes, and escalation triggers in a way that is feasible under workload and SLA pressure* (addresses D2).

Design Objective 3 (Readiness-aware Flow Control): *Make routing, scheduling, and pacing sensitive to readiness and customer-dependent coordination risk so that "not-ready" work is gated from scarce expert capacity and escalation timing avoids long-tail resolution dynamics* (addresses D3).

Design Objective 4 (Decision Governance): *Anchor readiness states and intervention/flow decisions in trace-grounded rationales that are inspectable and contestable across channels and handovers* (addresses D1-D3).

To avoid treating success as an ex-post interpretation, subsequent solution-space work will evaluate contribution-aware mechanisms against three goodness criteria that directly correspond to the deficits in Sect. 4. The first criterion captures whether the mechanisms actually reduce the bottlenecks identified (D1-D3); the second ensures that the decisions enabled by the artifact remain auditable – particularly important given the trace-mediated governance requirements highlighted across all three deficits; and the third addresses adoption risk: mechanisms that assign blame for contribution failures to either side would undermine the legitimacy needed for operational uptake.

Goodness Criterion 1 (Operational Benefit): *Improved episode performance under realistic workload (e.g., fewer clarification loops and reduced long-tail time-to-resolution patterns).*

Goodness Criterion 2 (Decision Defensibility): *Traceable, auditable rationales for gating, intervention, and escalation decisions across tools and channels.*

Goodness Criterion 3 (Acceptability): *Legitimate and workable mechanisms for both provider and customer roles that avoid punitive attribution while enabling effective control.*

6 Contributions and Outlook

As a research-in-progress paper, this study stops at problem-space explication and design orientation. Its primary contribution is to show how customer contribution dependence becomes an operational control challenge in digitally mediated incident episodes and to specify what customer contribution-aware incident operations must make representable and governable at the episode level.

More specifically, the paper contributes three outcomes to the DSR knowledge base. First, it offers an evidence-based problem framing through three recurring challenges (C1–C3) and their derived deficit statements, including the mechanisms and trace manifestations by which contribution-related frictions surface in day-to-day incident work. Second, it clarifies key implications of digital mediation for inference and accountability by emphasizing observability and provenance limits and motivating trace-grounded, contestable decision governance – particularly where interaction spans multiple channels and handovers. Third, it consolidates these insights into a compact set of design objectives (DO1–DO4) and associated goodness criteria that define the evaluation logic for subsequent solution-space work. Without entering the solution space, the design objectives already indicate the artifact direction: a contribution-aware incident management artifact for making customer-dependent episode states more visible, actionable, and governable under digitally mediated conditions.

The problem-space explication and design objectives established here form a relevance-side foundation for a broader DSR program. Subsequent work translates these findings into a traceable requirements catalog connecting the identified deficits to intervention and flow-control specifications, informed by an extended interview base covering additional roles and customer contexts within the same case organization. Analytically, we will tighten the trace-based evidence logic by establishing which candidate signatures and signals are reliably observable under digital mediation, and how they relate to readiness and contribution-contingent states. A particular concern going forward is AI assistance: as AI-drafted ticket content and automated suggestions enter incident workflows, provenance blurs and unqualified readiness risks being masked rather than surfaced, making contribution-aware control more necessary. These refinements will be integrated into requirements that connect the deficits (D1–D3) to intervention and flow-control needs as well as to governance constraints implied by trace-mediated decision making. This set of requirements will then guide the design and evaluation of an artifact against the design objectives and goodness criteria established in this paper.

Appendix

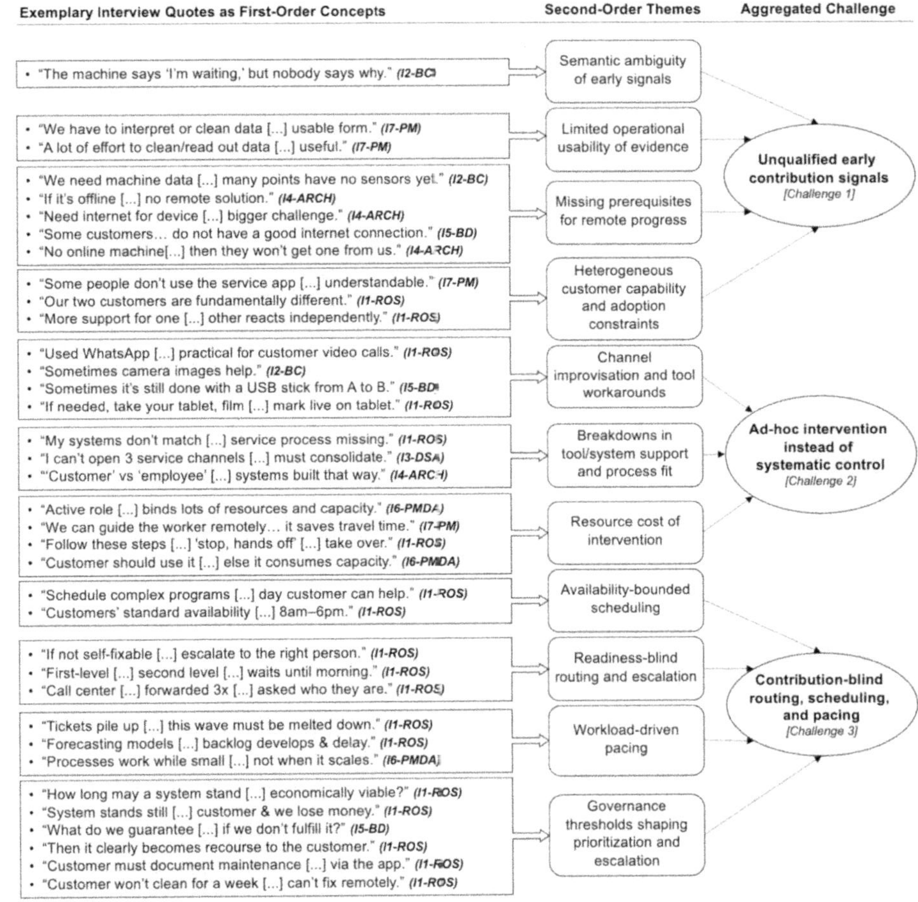

Fig. 1. Overview of Data Structure.

References

1. Satzger, G., Hottum, P.: Management der Interaktionsqualität in industriellen Dienstleistungsnetzwerken. Schmalenbachs Zeitschrift für betriebswirtschaftliche Forschung (zfbf). Sonderheft **69**(15), 150–173 (2015). https://doi.org/10.1007/BF03372939
2. Hottum, P., Reuter-Oppermann, M.: Towards a Customer-Oriented Queuing in Service Incident Management. In: Lübbecke, M.E., et al. (eds.) Operations Research Proceedings 2014, pp. 233–239. Springer, Cham (2016). https://doi.org/10.1007/978-3-319-28697-6_33
3. Vargo, S.L., Lusch, R.F.: Evolving to a new dominant logic for marketing. J. Mark. **68**(1), 1–17 (2004). https://doi.org/10.1509/jmkg.68.1.1.24036

4. Maglio, P.P., Spohrer, J.: Fundamentals of service science. J. Acad. Mark. Sci. **36**(1), 18–20 (2008). https://doi.org/10.1007/s11747-007-0058-9

5. Vargo, S.L., Lusch, R.F.: Service-dominant logic: continuing the evolution. J. Acad. Mark. Sci. **36**(1), 1–10 (2008). https://doi.org/10.1007/s11747-007-0069-6

6. Heidari, M.: Value co-creation in the IT service ecosystem. Griffith University (2023). https://doi.org/10.25904/1912/5147

7. Tuomisto, J.: Value Co-creation in ITIL 4 Framework, Master's Thesis. University of Jyväskylä, Faculty of Information Technology, Jyväskylä, Finland (2022)

8. Cronholm, S., Göbel, H., Åkesson, M.: ITIL Compliance with Service-Dominant Logic. e-Service Journal **11**(2), 74–97 (2020). https://doi.org/10.2979/eservicej.11.2.03

9. Vial, G.: Reflections on quality requirements for digital trace data in IS research. Decis. Support Syst. **126**, 113133 (2019). https://doi.org/10.1016/j.dss.2019.113133

10. Hedman, J., Srinivasan, N., Lindgren, R.: Digital Traces of Information Systems: Sociomateriality Made Researchable. In: ICIS 2013 Proceedings (2013)

11. Bartelheimer, C., Heinz, D., Hönigsberg, S., et al.: Conceptualizing hybrid intelligent service ecosystems. Electron. Mark. **35**, 63 (2025). https://doi.org/10.1007/s12525-025-00798-4

12. Baird, A., Maruping, L.M.: The Next Generation of Research on IS Use: A Theoretical Framework of Delegation to and from Agentic IS Artifacts. MIS Q. **45**(1), 315–341 (2021). https://doi.org/10.25300/MISQ/2021/15882

13. Dellermann, D., Ebel, P., Söllner, M., Leimeister, J.M.: Hybrid Intelligence. Bus. Inf. Syst. Eng. **61**(5), 637–643 (2019). https://doi.org/10.1007/s12599-019-00595-2

14. Johannesson, P., Perjons, E.: An Introduction to Design Science, 2nd edn. Springer Nature Switzerland AG (2021). https://doi.org/10.1007/978-3-030-78132-3

15. Hevner, A.R., March, S.T., Park, J., Ram, S.: Design science in information systems research. MIS Q. **28**(1), 75–105 (2004)

16. Gioia, D.A., Corley, K.G., Hamilton, A.L.: Seeking qualitative rigor in inductive research: notes on the gioia methodology. Organ. Res. Methods **16**(1), 15–31 (2013). https://doi.org/10.1177/1094428112452151

17. Gioia, D.: A systematic methodology for doing qualitative research. J. Appl. Behavioral Sci. **57**(1), 20–29 (2021). https://doi.org/10.1177/0021886320982715

18. Lusch, R.F., Nambisan, S.: Service innovation: a service-dominant logic perspective. MIS Q. **39**(1), 155–175 (2015). https://doi.org/10.25300/MISQ/2015/39.1.07

19. Galup, S.D., Dattero, R., Quan, J.J., Conger, S.: An overview of IT service management. Commun. ACM **52**(5), 124–127 (2009). https://doi.org/10.1145/1506409.1506439

20. Winkler, T.J., Wulf, J.: Effectiveness of IT service management capability: value co-creation and value facilitation mechanisms. J. Manag. Inf. Syst. **36**(2), 639–675 (2019). https://doi.org/10.1080/07421222.2019.1599513

21. Edgington, T.M., Raghu, T.S., Vinze, A.S.: Using process mining to identify coordination patterns in IT service management. Decis. Support Syst. **49**(2), 175–186 (2010). https://doi.org/10.1016/j.dss.2010.02.003

22. Liljander, V., Strandvik, T.: The Nature of Customer Relationships in Services. In: Swartz, T.A., Bowen, D.E., Brown, S.W. (eds.) Advances in Services Marketing and Management, vol. 4, pp. 1–35. JAI Press (1995)

23. Kumar, A., Liu, S.: Analyzing Performance of a Global Help Desk Team Operation – Country Handoffs, Efficiencies and Costs. In: HICSS 2020 Proceedings (2020)

24. Wang, R.Y., Strong, D.M.: Beyond accuracy: what data quality means to data consumers. J. Manag. Inf. Syst. **12**(4), 5–33 (1996)

25. Jäntti, M., Lindström, H.: Exploring quality aspects of customer self-service in IT service provision: A case study. J. Syst. Softw. **234**, 112725 (2026). https://doi.org/10.1016/j.jss.2025.112725

26. Lazarov, A., Shoval, P.: A rule-based system for automatic assignment of technicians to service faults. Decis. Support Syst. **32**(4), 343–360 (2002). https://doi.org/10.1016/S0167-9236(01)00122-1
27. Marabelli, M., Newell, S., Handunge, V.: The lifecycle of algorithmic decision-making systems: organizational choices and ethical challenges. J. Strateg. Inf. Syst. **30**(3), 101683 (2021). https://doi.org/10.1016/j.jsis.2021.101683
28. AXELOS: ITIL® Foundation: ITIL 4 Edition. TSO (The Stationery Office), Norwich (2019). ISBN 978-0-11-331607-6

Nascent Design Principles for Human-Machine Interfaces in Airborne Manned-Unmanned Teaming

Jan-Paul Huttner[1]([⊠])(iD) and Dominik Siemon[2](iD)

[1] German Aerospace Center, Institute of Flight Guidance, Braunschweig, Germany
`jan-paul.huttner@dlr.de`
[2] Department of Software Engineering, LUT University, Lahti, Finland
`dominik.siemon@lut.fi`

Abstract. Manned-unmanned teaming (MUM-T) design remains theoretically fragmented despite growing operational deployment across civilian and military aviation domains. This research-in-progress addresses this gap through a literature-grounded design science study embedded in the echelon design science research framework. Based on a systematic synthesis of 10 fixed-wing MUM-T empirical studies, we derive four theory-grounded, nascent design principles: *Context-Adaptive Automation Intervention, Hierarchical Delegation Granularity, Integrated Temporal-Spatial Plan Visualization,* and *Bidirectional Human-Autonomy Negotiation.* The contribution is positioned as Level 1 nascent design theory, consolidating fragmented findings into actionable prescriptions justified by cognitive engineering and human-automation interaction theories. The principles establish an initial prescriptive knowledge base for subsequent artifact instantiation and evaluation with operational pilots.

Keywords: Manned-Unmanned Teaming · Human-Machine Interface · Design Principles · Design Science Research · Airborne Operations

1 Introduction

The operational landscape of aviation is undergoing fundamental transformation driven by artificial intelligence and autonomous systems. MUM-T reshapes aviation paradigms across domains: search and rescue, maritime surveillance, border protection, agricultural aviation, and sixth-generation fighter programs integrate manned aircraft with autonomous platforms in "system of systems" architectures [1–3]. This dual-use evolution signals a paradigm shift from human-operated aircraft with automated subsystems to *human-autonomy teams* where pilots supervise, coordinate, and collaborate with intelligent autonomous agents possessing decision-making authority. For example, in a civilian search-and-rescue mission, a pilot may need to retask several autonomous assets around changing weather, emerging detections or altered mission objectives while maintaining radio communication and flight control; in a military escort mission, the pilot may need to

S. Chatterjee et al. (Eds.): DESRIST 2026, LNCS 16607, pp. 42–54, 2026.
https://doi.org/10.1007/978-3-032-28570-6_4

approve autonomous task reallocations within seconds under rapidly changing threat conditions.

Despite operational deployment across civilian and military domains, MUM-T human-machine interface (HMI) design remains theoretically fragmented. Empirical studies evaluated specific instantiations addressing interaction modalities [9], adaptive automation [7,17], transparency mechanisms [37], and visualization techniques [23], yet no structured design knowledge guides practitioners developing new MUM-T interfaces. This gap is critical for airborne contexts where pilots supervise multiple autonomous platforms while maintaining concurrent flight control, communication, and tactical decision-making under second-scale time constraints [25,33].

Our research-in-progress addresses this gap by deriving four theory-grounded, nascent design principles from systematic synthesis of 10 fixed-wing MUM-T empirical studies (2019–2024). Note, that "fixed-wing" here relates to the guiding platform, not the Unmanned Aerial Vehicles (UAV). Embedded in the echelon design science research (eDSR) framework [38] and following Möller et al.'s [27] supportive approach, these principles consolidate fragmented findings into actionable, testable prescriptions justified by cognitive and human-automation interaction theories. Each principle specifies a core mechanism, addresses literature-derived requirements, and is supported by convergent evidence from multiple studies. We advance nascent, prescriptive knowledge [13], i.e. Level 1 in Gregor and Hevner's framework, where literature-grounded principles provide testable hypotheses for future artifact instantiation and evaluation.

2   Theoretical Background

Manned-Unmanned Teaming has transitioned from experimental concept to operational doctrine across military and civilian aviation domains, yet the design of human-machine interfaces enabling effective human-autonomy collaboration remains theoretically fragmented [4,31]. While empirical research has evaluated specific MUM-T HMI instantiations such as Bautz et al. [7] who assessed situation awareness (SA) criticality matrices for adaptive automation, Heilemann and Schulte [15,17] validated three-tier delegation in fighter-UCAV (unmanned combat aerial vehicle) scenarios, Tokadli et al. [37] derived information visualization requirements for commercial flight decks or Highland et al. [18] studied trust dynamics in autonomous air combat, these contributions remain *instantiation-specific* rather than *principle-generalized*. Implementers and researchers within the scientific and industrial community lack synthesized, fully-matured and theory-justified principles specifying *what* to design for effective human-autonomy teaming [8].

Existing, normative design guidance still appears too immature for airborne MUM-T contexts. Legacy cockpit standards (MIL-STD-1472 [39]) address single-pilot, single-platform operation, and commercial aviation automation policies (FAA Advisory Circulars [12]) focus on deterministic subsystem automation; and NATO interoperability standards (STANAG 4586 [28]) define technical protocols but do not prescribe HMI design principles for managing cognitive challenges unique to airborne MUM-T: concurrent resource competition (manual flight + communication + autonomous asset supervision), time-critical decision-making (5–30 s tactical windows), and safety-critical coordination where errors risk fratricide or mission failure [9,18]. A NATO educational note explicitly states that STANAG 4586 "does not impose detailed human factors or HMI design requirements" beyond interface protocol standardization [34]. These standards establish compliance baselines but provide no design patterns for workload-adaptive assistance, multi-asset mission visualization, hierarchical task delegation, or bidirectional human-autonomy negotiation in fighter cockpits. Consequently, these standards must be treated as *boundary conditions*, i.e. constraints within which our design principles operate, rather than as sources of prescriptive design knowledge.

The design knowledge gap in airborne MUM-T HMI, which is a fragmented empirical findings without synthesized principles, motivates our research question: **What theory-grounded design principles address the cognitive challenges of supervising multiple autonomous platforms in airborne contexts, and what are their mechanisms, boundary conditions, and empirical support?**

3   Methodology

Our methodological approach follows *literature-grounded Design Science Research* [20,22,27], wherein design principles are derived from systematic synthesis of prior empirical work. Within Gregor and Hevner's [13] DSR knowledge contribution framework, our work constitutes *nascent design theory* (Level 1): we advance from disparate empirical observations to generalized, theory-justified design principles prescribing *how* MUM-T HMIs should be constructed to achieve desired outcomes (reduced workload, maintained situation awareness, calibrated trust). These principles are *hypothetical candidates* requiring validation through artifact instantiation and field evaluation, which is a planned extension of this research-in-progress. Following Möller et al. [27], we employ kernel theories from cognitive engineering (Adaptive Automation Theory [29], Multiple Resource Theory [42], Situation Awareness Theory [10]) and human-automation interaction (Levels of Automation [36], Trust in Automation [24], Mixed-Initiative Interaction [19]) at two stages: (i) deriving meta-requirements from theoretical constructs; and (ii) justifying design principles by explaining mechanisms through which principles achieve intended effects.

Our principles target levels of intervention (LOI) 4–5 contexts [28] where operators control multiple ($\geq$3) autonomous platforms with significant decision-making authority, typical of airforce fighter-UCAV teaming (Next Generation Air Dominance Collaborative Combat Aircraft, Future Combat Air System Remote Carriers, Global Combat Air Programme loyal wingmen) and civilian applications (search and rescue coordination, maritime surveillance, border protection) [2,18]. Airborne MUM-T imposes cognitive demands exceeding ground-based teleoperation and commercial aviation automation: pilots perform concurrent tasks with resource conflicts, face time-critical decision-making (5–30 s tactical windows), and require safety-critical coordination where errors risk fratricide, mission failure, or aircraft loss [9,18,33]. These demands establish boundary conditions for our design principles: they apply to contexts where operators supervise multiple autonomous agents under concurrent task demands, time pressure, and safety constraints. Accordingly, our design principles are intended to cover both civilian and military airborne MUM-T settings, provided these cognitive and operational conditions are present.

This study adopts a DSR approach following the echeloned design science research (eDSR) methodology, which decomposes complex DSR projects into self-contained units delivering validated intermediate artifacts [38]. For design principle development, we follow the supportive approach, deriving principles ex-ante from systematic knowledge bases to guide future artifact design [27]. The eDSR methodology organizes DSR work into five design echelon types: problem analysis, objectives and requirements definition, design and development, demonstration, and evaluation [38]. Our study constitutes the first echelon, focusing on problem analysis and initial objectives and requirements definition. Within eDSR, we treat the resulting design principles as nascent, literature-grounded prescriptive outputs of this echelon that guide later instantiation and evaluation.

A systematic literature review was conducted to establish the knowledge base. At this point in time, the search was executed only in SCOPUS using a query combining MUM-T terminology: TITLE-ABS-KEY (("manned unmanned" OR "manned-unmanned" OR "crewed uncrewed" OR "crewed-uncrewed" OR "manned-unmanned teaming" OR "manned unmanned teaming" OR MUM-T OR MUMT OR "loyal wingman" OR "unmanned wingman" OR CCA OR "collaborative combat aircraft" OR UCAV OR "uncrewed combat aerial vehicle" OR "air-launched effect" OR ALE OR "human machine teaming" OR "human-autonomy teaming") AND ("human machine interface" OR HMI OR "human computer interaction" OR HCI OR cockpit OR avionics OR "pilot-vehicle interface" OR "crew station" OR "workstation" OR "ground control station" OR GCS OR "control station" OR "decision aid*" OR "adaptive interface" OR "adaptive automation" OR transparency OR explainab* OR "situation awareness" OR workload OR trust)) AND PUBYEAR > 2014 AND PUBYEAR < 2027.

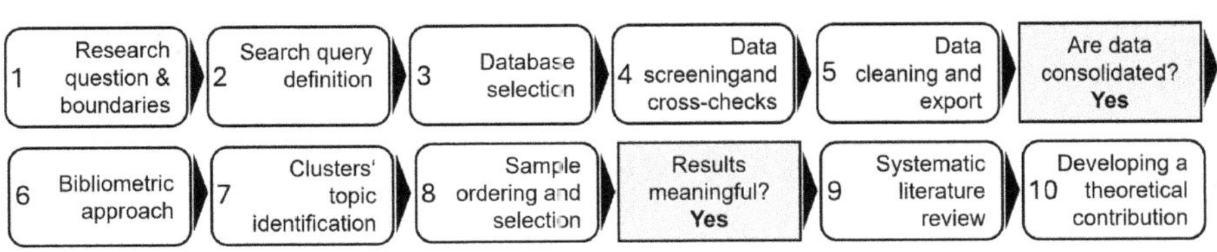

Fig. 1. Simplified B-SLRS Process of Marzi et al. [26]

We adapted the bibliometric-systematic literature review (B-SLRS) approach of Marzi et al. [26], see Fig. 1: we formulated the research question (step 1), defined the query and selected SCOPUS (steps 2–3), refined and cleaned the dataset (steps 4–5), imported the corpus into the bibliometrix tool in RStudio, and conducted thematic map synthesis on abstracts to identify relevant themes (step 6). The "human-autonomy teaming" cluster is one of two clusters, located in the "Motor Themes" quadrant. The other three quadrants in the thematic map are "Basic", "Niche" and "Emerging or Declining" themes. Hence, the "Motor theme" represents the most dense and relevant part of documents [6]. The other motor theme cluster is labeled with "artificial intelligence" but has a lower relevance score. Hence, the human-autonomy cluster, indicating high centrality and density, was selected as our initial source of relevant documents (step 7). Document analysis identified 282 papers strongly associated with this cluster. The papers were ordered according to their associative power to the cluster (step 8), yet none were removed at this point but rather scanned in the next step.

The 282 papers were screened for relevance by two independent coders using ASReview Lab (https://asreview.nl/), a tool for systematic reviews. Inclusion criteria were organized into three tiers. Tier 1 included papers addressing airborne crewed-unmanned teaming with explicit HMI focus: empirical studies, simulations, design frameworks, and systematic reviews examining displays, controls, workload, trust, situation awareness, autonomy transparency, or multi-asset control interfaces. Tier 2 comprised ground or maritime MUM-T domains or adjacent human-autonomy teaming in safety-critical environments, provided HMI challenges were domain-agnostic and transferable to airborne contexts. Tier 3 excluded papers focused purely on autonomy algorithms without human interaction, generic HCI (Human-Computer Interface) without autonomy context, speculative pieces without empirical grounding, and robotics applications lacking operator-interface focus. Screening identified 27 Tier 1 papers. Following full-text examination verifying methodological quality and HMI content depth, 10 papers focusing specifically on fixed-wing MUM-T platforms, which guide the unmanned assets, were selected as the primary knowledge base for this echelon. These papers span from 2019 to 2024 and encompass cockpit interface design, adaptive automation studies, multi-modal interaction research, and human-autonomy teaming transparency investigations. Note, that the downsizing to 10 papers followed an informal author discussion. However, more rigorous methodology and metrics will follow in the ongoing analysis. Steps 9–10 in the B-SLRS process are represented in the following section by deriving and contributing nascent design principles.

4 Design Principle Derivation

From the 10 selected papers, design-relevant findings were extracted following bottom-up clustering. Each paper was analyzed to identify prescriptive statements, empirical findings with design implications, and requirements for effective human-machine interaction in teaming contexts. Extracted elements were coded by underlying mechanisms and grouped into thematic clusters based on addressed human factors challenges.

Clustering yielded four mechanism clusters: adaptive automation intervention (Cluster A), hierarchical task delegation (Cluster B), integrated plan visualization (Cluster C), and bidirectional human-autonomy communication (Cluster D). For each cluster, source-specific findings were synthesized into generalized nascent design principles following the anatomy of a design principle [14]. Table 1 summarizes the design requirements extracted from the literature and serves as the basis for the subsequent principle development.

Table 1. Design Requirements for MUM-T HMI derived from Literature

Source	DR	Description
Bautz et al. 2024 [7]	1	Assistance systems must balance workload and decision-making efficacy without under/overloading pilots
	2	Adaptive assistance must adjust based on operator mental state and environmental assessments
	3	Support situational awareness during multi-UAV delegation under threat
Heilemann & Schulte 2019 [16]	4	Prevent complacency by balancing automation levels and pilot activity in multi-UCAV control
	5	Support task assignment across multiple abstraction levels for varying workload
Heilemann & Schulte 2020 [17]	6	Take-over only tasks human cannot accomplish or are too high risk/cost
	7	Adapt intervention level to mission criticality
Highland et al. 2023 [18]	8	Support cognitive load management for pilots controlling multiple UAVs
	9	Enable real-time measurement and calibration of pilot trust in autonomy
Schulte et al. 2021 [33]	10	Support meaningful human control through adequate workshare/function allocation with controllability and transparency
	11	Manage high work demands from multi-platform mission management
Lindner & Schulte 2020 [25]	12	Keep pilot in decision-making process without overtaxing
	13	Support adaptive transparency to prevent SA loss when autonomy increases
Laudien 2024 [23]	14	Integrate multi-modal interaction (beyond keyboard/mouse) for usability and efficiency
Tokadli et al. 2021 [37]	15	Support bi-directional communication for mission goals, intent, and rationale
	16	Support transparency of behavior, intentions, and goals to build mental model
	17	Support dynamic task allocation based on workload, capabilities, and mission state
	18	Support trust calibration through assessment of skill, experience, and performance

4.1   Cluster A: Adaptive Automation Intervention

The first cluster addresses the challenge of dynamically adjusting automation support based on operator state and mission demands. Source contributions include workload-scaled intervention modes ranging from passive monitoring to automatic execution [15], a situation awareness-criticality matrix determining appropriate levels of automation [7], graduated intervention intensities from hints through simplification to takeover [17], and trust-adaptive interface declutter-ing and augmentation [18]. The common mechanism across these contributions is the real-time assessment of operator cognitive capacity combined with situa-tional demands to determine appropriate automation behavior while preserving human override authority. The resulting nascent design principle is summarized in Table 2.

Table 2. Nascent Design Principle 1: Context-Adaptive Automation Intervention

DP1	Context-Adaptive Automation Intervention
Aim, Implementer, User	HMI designers (implementer) provide appropriate automation support (aim) for pilots controlling multiple autonomous platforms (user).
Context	Airborne MUM-T with variable workload, dynamic situations, and time-critical decisions requiring supervisory control.
Mechanism	Assess operator cognitive state via SA and workload indicators. Evaluate situational criticality. Select graduated intervention intensity from notification to full automation. Preserve override authority.
Rationale	Grounded in adaptive automation theory [29], multiple resource theory [42], and empirical SA-criticality findings [7,17].

4.2   Cluster B: Hierarchical Task Delegation

The second cluster addresses scalable control mechanisms for managing multiple autonomous platforms. Source contributions include three-tier delegation archi-tectures spanning team, task, and parameter levels [15], four-level delegation schemes enabling mission-appropriate control granularity [33], task-based guid-ance paradigms abstracting low-level commands [25], and area-of-responsibility concepts for spatial task abstraction [25].

The unifying mechanism is the provision of multiple abstraction levels that operators can select based on their available cognitive resources and the precision required by current mission demands. Table 3 presents the corresponding nascent design principle.

4.3   Cluster C: Integrated Plan Visualization

The third cluster addresses visualization requirements for complex multi-asset mission planning and monitoring. Source contributions include radial context

Table 3. Nascent Design Principle 2: Hierarchical Delegation Granularity

DP2	Hierarchical Delegation Granularity
Aim, Implementer, User	HMI designers (implementer) provide flexible control precision scaling with cognitive resources (aim) for pilots supervising multiple platforms or swarms (user).
Context	Multi-asset teaming balancing tactical control against mission management with varying cognitive resources.
Mechanism	Provide team-level, agent-level, task-level, and parameter-level delegation enabling goal assignment at appropriate abstraction.
Rationale	Grounded in supervisory control theory [35], hierarchical task analysis [5], and empirical delegation studies [15,33].

menus overlaid on tactical maps for rapid task assignment [15], timeline-based interfaces for temporal task insertion and sequencing [15], real-time feedback mechanisms displaying plan impacts and constraint violations [33], and comparative evaluations of 3D versus augmented 2D representations for mission planning [23]. The common mechanism is the integration of spatial and temporal representations with dynamic feedback on plan consequences. The resulting principle is summarized in Table 4.

Table 4. Nascent Design Principle 3: Integrated Temporal-Spatial Plan Visualization

DP3	Integrated Temporal-Spatial Plan Visualization
Aim, Implementer, User	HMI designers (implementer) provide comprehensive mission awareness and efficient plan modification (aim) for pilots coordinating multiple autonomous assets (user).
Context	Complex teaming requiring spatial, temporal, and resource coordination during pre-flight planning and in-flight replanning.
Mechanism	Provide tactical map displays, timeline interfaces, real-time feedback on plan modifications, and proactive conflict detection.
Rationale	Grounded in cognitive fit theory [40], ecological interface design [41], and empirical evaluations [23,33].

4.4   Cluster D: Bidirectional Human-Autonomy Negotiation

The fourth cluster addresses communication patterns between human operators and autonomous teammates. Source contributions include agent-initiated task allocation suggestions [37], modification notification protocols requiring human approval before execution changes [37], swarm avatar interfaces representing collectives as single entitiy [25,33], and warnings against fully distributed autonomous negotiation due to demonstrated situation awareness degradation [33]. The unifying mechanism is bidirectional communication enabling autonomous initiative while maintaining human approval authority through centralized coordination. Table 5 summarizes the corresponding nascent design principle and Fig. 2 shows the DPs as well as their respective DRs and sources.

Table 5. Nascent Design Principle 4: Bidirectional Human-Autonomy Negotiation

DP4	Bidirectional Human-Autonomy Negotiation
Aim, Implementer, User	HMI designers (implementer) enable human-autonomy collaboration maintaining human authority (aim) for pilots teaming with autonomous agents (user).
Context	Dynamic teaming where autonomous agents can assess situations and propose allocations, but human oversight remains essential.
Mechanism	Provide agent-initiated suggestions, modification notifications, explicit approval interfaces, and centralized coordination displays.
Rationale	Grounded in mixed-initiative interaction [19], team coordination theory [32], and empirical findings [33,37].

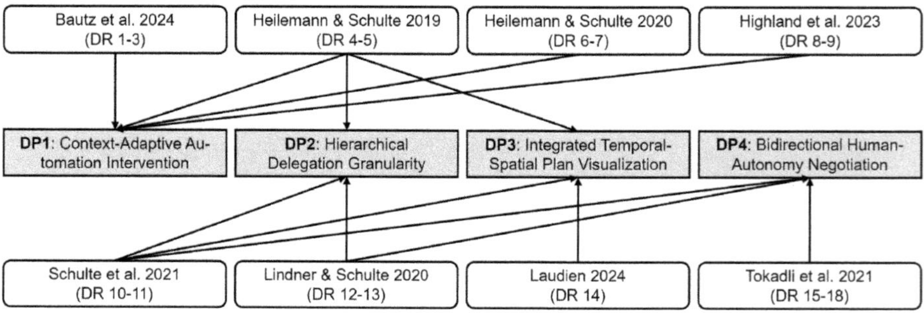

Fig. 2. Mapping of Design Requirements to Design Principles for MUM-T HMI

5 Conclusion and Outlook

Existing guidance for airborne MUM-T leaves room for improvement: legacy standards address single-platform operation [39], commercial policies focus on deterministic subsystem automation [12], and NATO standards define technical protocols without HMI prescriptions [28]. Our nascent principles operationalize kernel theories, hence, adaptive automation [29], supervisory control [35], cognitive fit [40], ecological interface design [41], and mixed-initiative interaction [19], into actionable mechanisms: SA-criticality assessment with graduated intervention, hierarchical delegation, integrated spatial-temporal displays, and agent-initiated suggestions with human approval authority.

The design principles presented in this paper represent the output of echelon 1 in our eDSR research program. Subsequent echelons will expand the knowledge base by incorporating Tier 2 papers and studies from additional domains (rotary-wing, ground, maritime, and space contexts) to validate and refine the principles across operational environments. Echelon 2 will instantiate selected principles in prototype interfaces, while later echelons will conduct demonstration and evaluation activities with domain experts and operational personnel.

For practitioners, our principles provide theory-justified nascent prescriptions complementing standards to address interaction design. For researchers, each mechanism-outcome relationship is testable: failure to produce intended outcomes requires revision. This falsifiability distinguishes our contribution, we make commitments future eDSR echelons can confirm or refute. However, some limitations constrain findings: the 10-study corpus limits grounding and requires maturation across additional contexts [38]; unpublished military research excludes classified knowledge; fixed-wing focus limits transferability. Despite limitations, the study's contribution is an echelon 1 output in the form of nascent, literature-grounded design principles that require later instantiation and evaluation [38].

Research continues through three activities. First, expand the knowledge base with rotary-wing, ground-based, maritime, and space studies to assess generalizability. Second, conduct reusability evaluation [21] assessing accessibility, importance, novelty, actability, and effectiveness. Third, instantiate artifacts in subsequent eDSR echelons [38] through prototype development and human-in-the-loop experimentation. Long-term objective: mid-range design theory integrating principles into coherent frameworks, potentially connecting to abstraction hierarchy frameworks [30,41]. Through this eDSR program, we accumulate validated design knowledge supporting effective HMI for human-autonomy teaming and the youngest research studies [11].

Disclosure of Interests. The authors have no competing interests to declare that are relevant to the content of this article.

References

1. Airbus homepage. https://www.airbus.com/en/products-services/defence/future-combat-air-system-fcas. Accessed 06 Apr 2026
2. Airbus homepage (2024). https://www.airbus.com/en/products-services/defence/uas/crewed-uncrewed-teaming. Accessed 06 Apr 2026

3. U.S. congress hompage (2025). https://www.congress.gov/crs-product/IF12805. Accessed 06 Apr 2026
4. Allworthy, M.: Reimagining Air Superiority: Collaborative Combat Systems for a Contested Battlespace (2025). https://rsdi.ae/en/publications/reimagining-air-superiority-collaborative-combat-systems-for-a-contested-battlespace. Accessed 06 Apr 2026
5. Annett, J., Duncan, K.D.: Task analysis and training design. Technical report 4, Occupational Psychology (1967)
6. Bagdi, T., Ghosh, S., Sarkar, A., Hazra, A.K., Balachandran, S., Chaudhury, S.: Evaluation of research progress and trends on gender and renewable energy: a bibliometric analysis. J. Clean. Prod. **423** (2023)
7. Bautz, J., Schwerd, S., Schulte, A.: Using situational awareness and situative criticality for adaptive planning assistance in MUM-t missions. In: 2024 IEEE International Conference on Systems, Man, and Cybernetics (SMC), pp. 3500–3507. IEEE (2024)
8. Chancey, E.T., et al.: Foundational human-autonomy teaming research and development in scalable remotely operated advanced air mobility operations: research model and initial work. In: AIAA SciTech. National Harbor, MD (2023)
9. Dudek, M., Schulte, A.: Experimental evaluation of UAV task delegation methods. In: 2024 IEEE 4th International Conference on Human-Machine Systems (ICHMS), pp. 1–8. IEEE (2024)
10. Endsley, M.R.: Toward a theory of situation awareness in dynamic systems. Hum. Factors **37**(1), 32–64 (1995)
11. Ernst, J.M., Friedrich, B.T., Friedrich, M.: Mission management in human autonomy teams – an HMI design concept for managing multiple uncrewed aerial systems from a fighter cockpit. In: Intelligent Human Systems Integration, vol. 200 (2026)
12. Federal Aviation Administration: Advisory Circular 25-11B: Electronic Flight Displays. U.S. Department of Transportation (2014)
13. Gregor, S., Hevner, A.R.: Positioning and presenting design science research for maximum impact. MIS Q. **37**(2), 337–355 (2013)
14. Gregor, S., Kruse, L.C., Seidel, S.: The anatomy of a design principle. J. Assoc. Inf. Syst. **21**(6) (2020)
15. Heilemann, F., Schmitt, F., Schulte, A.: Mixed-initiative mission planning of multiple UCAVs from aboard a single seat fighter aircraft. In: Scitech 2019 (2019)
16. Heilemann, F., Schulte, A.: Interaction concept for mixed-initiative mission planning on multiple delegation levels in multi-UCAV fighter missions. In: Karwowski, W., Ahram, T. (eds.) IHSI 2019. AISC, vol. 903, pp. 699–705. Springer, Cham (2019). https://doi.org/10.1007/978-3-030-11051-2_106
17. Heilemann, F., Schulte, A.: Experimental evaluation of an adaptive planning assistance system in manned unmanned teaming missions. In: Schmorrow, D.D., Fidopiastis, C.M. (eds.) HCII 2020. LNCS (LNAI), vol. 12197, pp. 371–382. Springer, Cham (2020). https://doi.org/10.1007/978-3-030-50439-7_25
18. Highland, P., Schnell, T., Woodruff, K., Avdic-McIntire, G.: Towards human objective real-time trust of autonomy measures for combat aviation. Int. J. Aerosp. Psychol. **33**(1), 1–34 (2023)
19. Horvitz, E.: Principles of mixed-initiative user interfaces. In: Proceedings of the SIGCHI Conference on Human Factors in Computing Systems (CHI 1999), pp. 159–166. ACM, New York, NY, USA (1999)
20. Iivari, J.: Distinguishing and contrasting two strategies for design science research. Eur. J. Inf. Syst. **24**(1), 107–115 (2015)

21. Iivari, J., Rotvit Perlt Hansen, M., Haj-Bolouri, A.: A proposal for minimum reusability evaluation of design principles. Eur. J. Inf. Syst. **30**(3) (2021)
22. Kruse, L.C., Purao, S., Seidel, S.: University of liechtenstein: how designers use design principles: design behaviors and application modes. J. Assoc. Inf. Syst. **23**(5), 1235–1270 (2022)
23. Laudien, T.: Assessing state-of-the-art mission planning user interfaces for application to next generation fighter concept of operations. In: 2024 AIAA DATC/IEEE 43rd Digital Avionics Systems Conference (DASC), pp. 1–8. IEEE (2024)
24. Lee, J.D., See, K.A.: Trust in automation: designing for appropriate reliance. Hum. Factors **46**(1), 50–80 (2004)
25. Lindner, S., Schulte, A.: Human-in-the-loop evaluation of a manned-unmanned system approach to derive operational requirements for military air missions. In: Harris, D., Li, W.-C. (eds.) HCII 2020. LNCS (LNAI), vol. 12187, pp. 341–356. Springer, Cham (2020). https://doi.org/10.1007/978-3-030-49183-3_27
26. Marzi, G., Balzano, M., Caputo, A., Pellegrini, M.M.: Guidelines for bibliometric-systematic literature reviews: 10 steps to combine analysis, synthesis and theory development. Int. J. Manag. Rev. **27**(1), 81–103 (2025)
27. Möller, F., Guggenberger, T.M., Otto, B.: Towards a method for design principle development in information systems. In: Hofmann, S., Müller, O., Rossi, M. (eds.) DESRIST 2020. LNCS, vol. 12388, pp. 208–220. Springer, Cham (2020). https://doi.org/10.1007/978-3-030-64823-7_20
28. NATO Standardization Office: Standard interfaces of unmanned aircraft (UA) control system (UCS) for NATO UAV interoperability. Standardization Agreement (STANAG) 4586, Edition 4 (AEP-84 Edition A), NATO (2017)
29. Parasuraman, R., Sheridan, T., Wickens, C.: A model for types and levels of human interaction with automation. IEEE Trans. Syst. Man Cybern. Part A Syst. Hum. **30**(3), 286–297 (2000)
30. Rasmussen, J.: The role of hierarchical knowledge representation in decisionmaking and system management. IEEE Trans. Syst. Man Cybern. **15**(2), 234–243 (1985)
31. Rossetti, L.: Manned-unmanned teaming - joint air power competence centre. J. JAPCC **29**, 42–47 (2020)
32. Salas, E., Sims, D.E., Burke, C.S.: Is there a "big five" in teamwork? Small Group Res. **36**(5), 555–599 (2005)
33. Schulte, A., Heilemann, F., Lindner, S., Donath, D.: Tasking, teaming, swarming: design patterns for human delegation of unmanned vehicles. In: Zallio, M. (ed.) AHFE 2020. AISC, vol. 1210, pp. 3–9. Springer, Cham (2021). https://doi.org/10.1007/978-3-030-51758-8_1
34. Serrano, D.: Key initiatives for interoperability through standardization (2015), systems Concepts and Integration Panel
35. Sheridan, T.B.: Telerobotics, Automation, and Human Supervisory Control. MIT Press, Cambridge (1992). https://mitpress.mit.edu
36. Sheridan, T.B., Verplank, W.L.: Human and computer control of undersea teleoperators. Technical report, Massachusetts Institute of Technology (MIT), Man-Machine Systems Laboratory, Cambridge, MA (1978). https://apps.dtic.mil, technical Report for Office of Naval Research
37. Tokadlı, G., Dorneich, M.C., Matessa, M.: Toward human–autonomy teaming in single-pilot operations: domain analysis and requirements. J. Air Transp. **29**(4), 142–152 (2021). https://arc.aiaa.org/doi/10.2514/1.D0240
38. Tuunanen, T., Winter, R., Vom Brocke, J.: Dealing with complexity in design science research: a methodology using design echelons. MIS Q. **48**(2), 427–458 (2024)

39. U.S. Department of Defense: MIL-STD-1472h: Design criteria standard — human engineering. U.S. Department of Defense Standard (2020)
40. Vessey, I.: Cognitive fit: a theory-based analysis of the graphs versus tables literature. Decis. Sci. **22**(2), 219–240 (1991)
41. Vicente, K.J., Rasmussen, J.: Ecological interface design: theoretical foundations. IEEE Trans. Syst. Man Cybern. **22**(4), 589–606 (1992)
42. Wickens, C.D.: Multiple resources and mental workload. Hum. Factors **50**(3), 449–455 (2008)

Designing a Socio-Technical Support System for Reuse in Low-Code Development: An Echeloned Design Science Research Study

Marlon Kampmann[1]([⊠]) [iD], Peter Alois François[1] [iD], Ralf Plattfaut[2] [iD], and André Coners[1] [iD]

[1] South Westphalia University of Applied Sciences, Haldener Straße 182, 58095 Hagen, Germany
{kampmann.marlon, francois.peter, coners.andre}@fh-swf.de
[2] University Duisburg-Essen, Universitätsstraße 9, 45141 Essen, Germany
ralf.plattfaut@ris.uni-ude.de

Abstract. Low-code development platforms (LCDPs) promise rapid and efficient application development. However, organizations often struggle to scale their low-code initiatives. The lack of professional software engineering techniques, such as reuse, has been identified as a cause of this scaling challenge. The literature offers several (mostly technological) approaches to low-code reuse. In practice, however, reuse typically occurs either through the LCDP's built-in components and marketplaces or through self-developed artifacts in an ad hoc manner, e.g., via copy-pasting, leaving much of the reuse potential untapped. To address this issue, this research-in-progress draws on insights from an ongoing echeloned design science project to develop socio-technical support systems for low-code reuse. We contribute a validated problem statement, as well as design objectives and requirements, to the body of design knowledge.

Keywords: Low-Code Development · Reuse · Design Science Research

1 Introduction

While low-code development platforms (LCDPs) offer organizations a rapid, relatively cost-efficient way to implement software artifacts, many often struggle to scale their low-code initiatives [27]. In recent years, LCDPs have gained significant traction as a means to accelerate application development, reduce reliance on traditional programming skills, better align with business needs, and enable greater agility in software delivery [5, 13, 15, 20]. Through comparatively easy-to-use interfaces and predefined components, LCDPs enable both professional developers and non-IT personnel to configure applications and automations with relatively little effort [2, 5, 20, 30].

One contributing factor to this struggle with scaling is the inconsistent application of established software engineering principles in low-code development activities, particularly reuse [3, 11, 16]. As a result, low-code developers often recreate functionality that already exists rather than reusing previously built solutions, leading to wasted

S. Chatterjee et al. (Eds.): DESRIST 2026, LNCS 16607, pp. 55–67, 2026.
https://doi.org/10.1007/978-3-032-28570-6_5

development capacity and a proliferation of similar components [19]. Over time, the accumulation of such components can complicate maintenance and make the low-code infrastructure rigid [6, 23].

From software engineering research, it is well established that reuse is a key factor for successful and efficient development initiatives [1, 12, 14]. In the context of low-code development, some aspects of reuse appear to be relatively well explored, while others remain insufficiently addressed. On the technical side, the low-code paradigm is based on pre-built, configurable components that users can assemble and reuse via drag-and-drop mechanisms [5]. In addition, many LCDPs offer marketplaces that enable users to share and reuse larger solutions built on the platform [30]. Yet, reuse mechanisms within LCDPs are often underdeveloped, especially for aiding reuse at an organizational level [4, 5, 16]. Similarly, our literature review indicates that the organizational and behavioral dimensions of low-code reuse are considerably less explored. Moreover, we observed in real-world projects that reuse is often carried out in an ad hoc manner, for example, through copy-pasting or drawing on personal knowledge, leaving substantial reuse potential untapped.

Given the apparent underrealized reuse potential in low-code development and the socio-technical complexity of reuse, we embarked on an echeloned Design Science Research (eDSR) project [26] to create design knowledge for socio-technical systems that systematically foster effective and sustainable reuse in low-code settings. This research-in-progress contributes a validated problem statement that summarizes the main problems practitioners face with low-code reuse. We also contribute design knowledge through validated design objectives and requirements for reuse-support systems. Accordingly, this study first investigates which reuse-related concepts in low-code development are documented in the literature and how practitioners perceive them, including the reasons for their limited adoption. To this end, we conducted a structured literature review including 42 papers and complemented it with 20 semi-structured interviews. Future research can build on these results to derive concrete artifacts that support low-code reuse through social, technical, or socio-technical support systems with practical relevance, thereby increasing the long-term success of low-code initiatives.

2 Background

2.1 Low-Code Development

LCDPs facilitate the creation of software applications with minimal reliance on traditional programming. While LCDPs typically require only limited traditional coding to enable users to customize pre-built components, some platforms aim to eliminate coding. Such platforms are commonly referred to as no-code development platforms [29]. LCDPs differ substantially in their scope and capabilities, ranging from lightweight tools for basic data handling to comprehensive, enterprise-grade environments that support workflow automation and cross-platform application development [5]. These different LCDPs typically offer graphical user interfaces that enable users to assemble application logic by manipulating reusable modules, such as those for reading and writing data, accessing databases, or interacting with external services [5, 20]. The comparably low development cost and high deployment speed are key factors driving the adoption of these systems [9]. The ease of configuring predefined artifacts also enables individuals without formal programming skills, often referred to as citizen developers, to create software in LCDPs [2, 20, 22]. Citizen developers are employees with no formal programming experience and typically embedded within the business domain. Due to their deep knowledge of the processes, they are well-positioned to design software closely aligned with operational needs, thereby reducing miscommunication between business units and IT teams [11, 20].

2.2 Low-Code Reuse

LCDPs are built on the principle of reusing technical building blocks, enabling developers to assemble applications from pre-built components provided by platform providers or from external marketplaces [5, 30]. This accelerates development and reduces costs [2, 20]. Viljoen, Hein, and Krcmar [30] conceptualize LCDP from a platform ecosystems perspective, providing an overview of several variables that can influence the reuse of included components. For example, they note that reusable components within an LCDP may be provided by the LCDP vendor or by an external provider. In addition, reuse spans multiple levels, from knowledge to code to entire architectures [7].

However, several issues prevent reuse from reaching its full potential in the low-code setting. For example, many platforms lack structured, user-friendly mechanisms for reusing artifacts created with them [4, 5, 16]. While libraries and marketplaces exist, reusing user-created applications remains challenging, especially in an organizational setting [16]. Therefore, developers frequently find it easier to create new components than to search for, evaluate, and adapt existing ones, especially in citizen developer settings [8]. This re-creation of components rather than reuse leads to redundancy and duplicated logic, which organizations notice as increased maintenance costs and low scalability [19, 23]. Other hurdles to reuse include the availability of reusable artifacts, the high cognitive effort required to locate, access, and understand them, especially those created by others [10], and the low transferability of components across different LCDPs due to proprietary components [5]. As a result, developers often favor short-term speed over the long-term benefits of reuse, contributing to an unmanageable volume of artifacts [6, 23].

3 Research Approach

This study adopts an eDSR approach following the guidelines proposed by Tuunanen, Winter and vom Brocke [26]. The eDSR approach is particularly suited to addressing complex socio-technical problems, as it structures the creation of design knowledge as an iterative, cumulative process organized around self-contained design echelons. Each echelon integrates phase-specific analysis, design, and validation activities. In line with this methodology, each phase of our study is implemented as a self-contained design echelon, as summarized in Table 1.

The objective of the problem analysis echelon was to identify the core problems associated with low-code reuse as a complex socio-technical phenomenon, to assess the extent to which these problems have been addressed in prior research, and to evaluate

Table 1. Design Echelons, Intermediate Artifacts, Validation Criteria, Validation Techniques, and Design Knowledge Contributions (adapted from Tuunanen et al., 2024).

Echelon type	Intermediate artifact	Validation criteria	Validation techniques	Design knowledge
Problem analysis	While low-code reuse is widely perceived as beneficial, practitioners experience substantial difficulties in realizing its potential	- Degree to which the problem has been solved - Solvability	- Structured literature review - Observation of practitioner initiatives - Expert Interviews	*Validated problem statement:* Although LCDPs provide technical mechanisms for reuse, effective reuse extends beyond technical enablement and requires organizational, individual, and procedural support. In practice, low-code reuse remains largely ad hoc, leading to inefficiencies and the underutilization of reusable artifacts Validated objectives: systematic reuse, multi-level reuse, Cognitive relief, Organizational alignment, inclusiveness
Objective and requirements definition	*Overarching design goal:* Enable systematic and effective reuse in low-code development by providing design knowledge that reduces ad hoc reuse practices and improves the purposeful use of reusable artifacts across different reuse levels	- Fit to validate the problem statement - Applicability - Coherence - Completeness - Feasibility - Operatio-nality	- Observation of practitioner initiatives - Expert Interviews	*Validated objectives:* systematic reuse, multi-level reuse, Cognitive relief, Organizational alignment, inclusiveness

Further echelons are part of future research (see Sect. 5)

their solvability. The intermediate artifact in the problem analysis echelon is grounded in real-world observations dating back to 2022. The authors are embedded in a project with six companies that aim to improve their reuse practices in process automation and low-code development. To validate this and to gather design knowledge, we employed a multi-method validation approach comprising a structured literature review and expert interviews. We examined the extent to which the problem has already been solved and whether it is solvable at all [26].

We conducted a structured literature review following the guidelines of Webster and Watson [31]. The review followed a three-step sequential process. As a first step, we used a keyword-based search for "low-code" AND "reuse" across all fields to identify relevant articles, including outlets from both Information Systems and Software Engineering. To this end, we included the AIS Electronic Library (AISeL) (16 hits) and Scopus (113 hits). To further cover the field of software engineering, we included IEEE-Xplore (11 hits) and the ACM Digital Library (222 hits), yielding a total of 362 initial publications. We removed 17 duplicates and filtered the articles, first by title, then by abstracts, excluding those that did not focus on low-code development. This step was shared between two authors. When in doubt, we included the articles for further analysis. Similarly, articles whose titles and/or abstracts did not meet the content criteria, but whose keywords did, were included. This process resulted in 71 included papers. We then conducted a selective forward and backward search [31, 32], identifying 6 new papers as relevant in the backward search. For the forward search, we selected the articles we deemed most relevant and searched for articles citing them in Google Scholar. However, this yielded no additional articles. One publication was excluded because the full text was not available. A total of 77 articles were included in the full-text screening process. Two authors independently coded half of the articles using an inductive coding approach, following the guidelines of Wolfswinkel et al. [32]. We applied a multi-order coding procedure consisting of open, axial, and selective coding [32]. This resulted in distinct categories, including challenges in low-code reuse and technical, managerial, and individual approaches to it.

To complement the literature and validate the problem statement, we conducted 20 semi-structured expert interviews (I) with participants (P) from various companies (C) involved in low-code development, as shown in Table 2. The companies came from a wide range of industries, including manufacturing, consulting, IT services, and construction, with workforces ranging from 50 to over 100,000 employees. The participants were, e.g., professional low-code developers, citizen developers, or consultants using low-code tools. The interviews were conducted through online meetings, recorded, and then automatically transcribed. For the most significant passages, the transcription was manually reviewed and, where necessary, corrected. All interviews were used to validate the problem analysis. We then used the interviews as additional input to formulate and validate the design objectives and requirements. The key validation criteria were consistency with the validated problem statement, applicability, coherence, completeness, feasibility, and operability [26].

Table 2. Summary of Expert Interviews.

#	Participant	Industry	Length
I_1	Manager RPA (P_1)	IT services & consulting (C_1)	58 min
I_2	RPA Developer (P_2), IT Specialist RPA (P_3)	Banking (C_2)	57 min
I_3	RPA Developer (P_2), IT Specialist RPA (P_3)	Banking (C_2)	44 min
I_4	RPA Consultant & Developer (P_4)	Consultancy (C_3)	40 min
I_5	Controller (P_5)	Construction (C_4)	43 min
I_6	Controller (P_6)	Construction (C_4)	43 min
I_7	Lean Manager (P_7)	Construction (C_5)	53 min
I_8	Senior RPA Developer (P_8)	IT consulting (C_6)	18 min
I_9	RPA Developer (P_9)	Insurance (C_7)	19 min
I_{10}	Corporate Strategy Manager (P_{10})	Manufacturing (C_8)	70 min
I_{11}	RPA Developer (P_{11})	IT services (C_9)	56 min
I_{12}	RPA Developer (P_{12})	Manufacturing (C_{10})	63 min
I_{13}	Low-Code App Developer (P_{13})	Energy (C_{11})	53 min
I_{14}	Head of Business Development (P_{14})	Consulting (C_{12})	66 min
I_{15}	Internal IT Consultant (P_{15})	Manufacturing (C_{13})	54 min
I_{16}	Data Control Officer (P_{16})	Energy (C_{14})	53 min
I_{17}	RPA Developer (P_{11})	IT services (C_9)	53 min
I_{18}	Business Process Relationship Manager (P_7)	Manufacturing (C_{15})	52 min
I_{19}	Head of Process Automation (P_{18})	Energy (C_{14})	52 min
I_{20}	Process Manager (P_{19}), Inhouse Consultant (P_{20})	Public Administration (C_{16})	51 min

4 Designing Successful Low-Code Reuse Support

4.1 Problem Analysis

Our initial observations, conducted from 2022 to 2024 across multiple organizational settings, indicate that although low-code reuse is widely perceived as beneficial, practitioners face substantial difficulties in realizing its potential. LCDPs are designed to facilitate reuse through pre-built and configurable components [5, 30]; yet, the availability of technical reuse mechanisms does not automatically translate into systematic reuse behavior. A review of the existing literature shows that research on low-code reuse primarily addresses either technical approaches (e.g., component architectures, platform capabilities [4, 5, 24, 25, 27, 28, 30]) or, to a smaller extent, managerial approaches (e.g., governance structures, citizen development policies, etc. [4, 17, 20]). While these streams provide valuable insights, they remain largely fragmented and focus predominantly on isolated aspects of reuse. As a result, the literature lacks an integrated, stable body of design knowledge that explains how low-code reuse can be effectively and efficiently realized in organizational practice. Prior work primarily focuses on component-level reuse, which is comparatively well understood and technically supported by LCDPs (e.g., [4, 17, 20, 21]). However, broader forms of reuse, such as reuse across abstraction levels, projects, or organizational boundaries, remain insufficiently addressed. As highlighted by François and Plattfaut [7], extending reuse beyond individual components introduces organizational and coordination challenges that are not yet adequately resolved in the literature. One participant stated: *"It's difficult to move code that was used at another customer [...] to other repositories, if such a [fitting] thing even exists. [...] So you tend to just [...] reprogram it."* (I_9).

This gap indicates the absence of organizational and procedural structures for low-code reuse, rather than limitations in the technical capabilities provided by the LCDPs themselves. Consequently, the problem does not lie solely in the absence of reuse mechanisms at the platform level [7] but also in the lack of effective support that enables users to organize, apply, and sustain reuse practices in their organizational contexts. The findings confirm that reuse is regarded as highly relevant and desirable; however, participants consistently reported difficulties in implementing it systematically. Common approaches included copying and pasting existing components, relying on personal recollections of previous solutions, or drawing on individual experience rather than structured reuse strategies. These practices result in inefficiencies, limited scalability, and suboptimal utilization of reusable artifacts. *"When we realize we've had a similar problem before, we look to see where we've done something like that, but not in a structured way."* (P_3 in I_2). Another interviewee (P_7) shared this sentiment: *"And accordingly, I just look at which of the existing flows comes closest to this requirement. And accordingly, I look at what I can copy, so to speak, [...] so that they can import it and then make adjustments"*. Another sub-problem is understanding and adapting artifacts developed internally by another colleague. Documenting artifacts, especially by non-IT personnel, warrants support. *"If you do that [with reuse], then you really have to explain it properly, especially to people who aren't so familiar with it [...] I mean, if you create a more complex flow yourself and then come back a year later and say, hey, wait a minute, how does that work again?"* – (I_7). By combining insights from the literature review with empirical evidence from expert interviews, we arrive at a validated problem statement in line with the eDSR approach [26].

Problem statement: *Although LCDPs provide technical mechanisms for reuse, effective reuse extends beyond technical enablement and requires organizational, individual, and procedural support. In practice, low-code reuse remains largely ad hoc, leading to inefficiencies and the underutilization of reusable artifacts.*

4.2 Objectives and Requirements Definition

Building on the validated problem statement that LCDPs provide technical mechanisms but that effective reuse extends beyond technical enablement and requires organizational, individual, and procedural support, this design echelon specifies the objectives and requirements that guide subsequent design activities for future artifacts. The overarching design goal is to enable systematic and effective reuse in low-code development by providing design knowledge that reduces ad hoc reuse practices and improves the purposeful use of reusable artifacts across different reuse levels. To operationalize this overarching goal, we derive five conceptual design objectives (DO) that articulate the intended target state and serve as a bridge between the problem and solution spaces [18, 26]. From these objectives, we derive six design requirements (DR) that specify the characteristics an artifact should exhibit to achieve the stated objectives. The design requirements are formulated as specific, necessary, and verifiable criteria, thereby providing the basis for evaluating whether a proposed design constitutes a valid realization of the design objectives [26]. The objectives and requirements were derived using a convergent mixed-methods approach, synthesizing insights from prior literature on low-code development and reuse with empirical evidence from the expert interviews, complemented by longitudinal observations of multiple low-code development projects within our research setting with our partner organizations. In line with eDSR guidance, the resulting objectives and requirements were designed and validated against criteria for fit with the validated problem statement, applicability, internal coherence, completeness with respect to stakeholder needs, feasibility, and operationality, thereby ensuring both theoretical soundness and practical viability [26].

The design objectives and requirements address complementary aspects of reuse. Table 3 provides an overview of the results.

Table 3. Design Objectives and Design Requirements.

Design Objective	Design Requirement
DO1: Systematic Reuse: Enable systematic reuse of low-code artifacts beyond informal and ad hoc practices	**DR1** The design must make reusable low-code artifacts explicitly identifiable and weigh up the benefits and efforts of their reuse
DO2: Multi-Level Reuse: Support reuse across multiple levels	**DR2** The design must support the reuse of artifacts across different reuse levels
DO3: Cognitive Relief: Reduce cognitive and coordination efforts	**DR3:** The design must guide practitioners in deciding when and how to reuse artifacts **DR4:** The design must reduce dependency on individual experience and personal memory when reusing low-code artifacts and simplify the understanding of reused artifacts
DO4: Organizational Alignment: Align with organizational structures, roles, and governance practices	**DR5:** The design must support organizational coordination of reuse, including roles, responsibilities, and shared standards

(*continued*)

Table 3. (*continued*)

Design Objective	Design Requirement
DO5: Inclusiveness: Enable both professional developers and citizen developers with varying levels of expertise	**DR6:** The design must be usable by both professional and citizen developers without requiring advanced technical expertise

Together, they capture the core challenges identified in both literature and practice.

DO1: Systematic Reuse. The first design objective aims to enable the systematic reuse of low-code artifacts beyond informal, ad hoc practices. The insight from the first echelon indicates that, despite technical support for reuse, practitioners often rely on personal experience and situational judgment when reusing artifacts, resulting in inconsistent and inefficient reuse practices. Our empirical observations similarly suggest that reusable artifacts are common but underutilized due to a lack of explicit identification and structuring mechanisms. *"If someone says, 'I need this and that,' of course I'll set up the automation, but if I don't document it, etc., it just ends up in a huge, huge mess, and if I reuse it at some point, the whole concept has to be systematic and not a wild jumble."* (*I$_{14}$*).

DO2: Multi-Level Reuse. The second design objective addresses the need to support reuse across multiple levels, including components, reuse knowledge, and process models. Existing studies emphasize that reuse in low-code environments is heterogeneous and spans various abstraction levels, yet most reuse support mechanisms focus on a single level [7, 30]. Interviewees highlighted that effective reuse requires flexibility to transfer artifacts across these levels depending on the development context. P_{13}, i.e., discussed reusing requirements for app development across different projects, which helped him develop the new artifact. P_4 reported that they reused the entire RPA architecture, which saved them substantial time.

DO3: Cognitive Relief. The third design objective focuses on reducing the cognitive and coordination effort required to identify, adapt, check, and apply reusable low-code artifacts. The empirical insights indicate that practitioners struggle not only with finding reusable artifacts but also with deciding when and how to reuse them in a given situation: *"This saves time because you can say, [...] I want to do this and that in our system. What kind of robot is needed for that? And it somehow puts something together or makes a suggestion."* (P_2 in I_3). This effort also extends to testing the reused components in the new context: *"One challenge could be if we have built some kind of error into a prototype that we simply didn't see in the original and that keeps recurring"* (I_5).

DO4: Organizational Alignment. The fourth design objective aims to align low-code reuse with organizational structures, roles, and governance practices. Literature on platform governance and enterprise low-code adoption highlights that reuse is strongly influenced by organizational coordination mechanisms, such as defined responsibilities, shared standards, and reuse policies [30]. Observations from practice indicate that reuse initiatives often fail when they are not embedded adequately within existing organizational structures. *"In principle, they [general reuse guidelines] already exist. But I believe that every department and every company has to adapt and find the best case for itself to reuse."* (I_9).

DO5: Inclusiveness. The fifth design objective addresses inclusiveness by enabling effective reuse for both professional developers and citizen developers with varying levels of expertise. Prior work emphasizes that LDCPs are used by heterogeneous user groups whose technical capabilities differ substantially, which creates tensions between flexibility and usability [5, 10, 28]. Interviewees stressed that reuse mechanisms must remain accessible to non-experts without introducing excessive technical complexity. Another controller from the aforementioned construction company, for example, claimed that a chatbot-based system to explain artifacts he intended to reuse would have been helpful to him, because he did not possess as much technical knowledge as the person who initially developed those components. His status as a citizen developer, therefore, prevented him from participating effectively in reuse.

In the following, we show the design requirements in relation to the design objectives. Each design requirement specifies the characteristics an artifact should exhibit to achieve the stated objective, as derived from the argumentation for that objective. To make the described objectives more concrete and prepare for implementation, design requirements are needed [26]. **DR1** requires that reusable low-code artifacts are explicitly identifiable and distinguishable from non-reusable artifacts, thereby operationalizing systematic reuse (DO1). **DR2** specifies that the design must support reuse across different reuse levels, ensuring that artifacts can be reused at varying levels of abstraction in line with DO2. **DR3** and **DR4** operationalize cognitive relief (DO3) by requiring guidance for reuse decisions and by reducing dependence on individual experience and personal memory. It should simplify the understanding of reused artifacts, e.g., for selecting components. **DR5** translates organizational alignment (DO4) into concrete support for coordination mechanisms, including roles, responsibilities, and shared standards. **DR6** operationalizes inclusiveness (DO5) by requiring usability for both professional and citizen developers without demanding advanced technical expertise.

5 Conclusion and Outlook

From our extensive literature review, we have learned that reusing user-created low-code artifacts in organizational settings can yield significant benefits for low-code development (e.g., scaling low-code initiatives and reducing maintenance effort). However, in our interviews, we noticed that low-code reuse is often pursued only in an ad hoc manner and is hard to realize its full potential. This is consistent with the literature, which describes the mechanisms for low-code reuse in LCDPs as insufficient. Similarly, we could not observe the (primarily technical, but some social) approaches for reuse described in the literature in practice. In response, we proposed that eDSR should be used to address low-code reuse from both social and technical perspectives, ensuring the real-world relevance of the developed approaches. In this work, we therefore proposed validated design knowledge in the form of the problem statement, design objectives, and requirements to guide both lines of inquiry.

In future research, we plan to design two exemplary artifacts: one drawing on our insights to create a technological artifact that aids reuse, and a database for storing and discovering reusable components, including a Large Language Model component. In addition, we plan to develop a selection procedure for low-code components to be reused. By doing so, we aim to contribute to the body of design knowledge and to refine and validate our problem statement and design objectives by pursuing those additional echelons.

Acknowledgments. This work was partially funded by the German Federal Ministry of Research, Technology, and Space (BMFTR, grant number: 13FH034KX0).

Disclosure of Interests. The authors have no competing interests to declare that are relevant to the content of this article.

References

1. Apte, U., Sankar, C.: Reusability-Based Strategy for Development of Information Systems: Implementation Experience of a Bank. MISQ **14**(4) (1990). https://doi.org/10.2307/249791
2. Binzer, B., Winkler, T.J.: Democratizing Software Development: A Systematic Multivocal Literature Review and Research Agenda on Citizen Development. In: Proceedings of the 13th International Conference on Software Business (ICSOB), pp. 244–259 (2022). https://doi.org/10.1007/978-3-031-20706-8_17
3. Binzer, B., Elshan, E., Fürstenau, D. et al.: Establishing a Low-Code/No-Code-Enabled Citizen Development Strategy. MIS Q Exec **23**(3) (2024). https://doi.org/10.17705/2msqe.00097
4. Bock, AC., Frank, U.: In Search of the Essence of Low-Code: An Exploratory Study of Seven Development Platforms. In: 2021 ACM/IEEE International Conference on Model Driven Engineering Languages and Systems Companion (MODELS-C), pp. 57–66 (2021). https://doi.org/10.1109/MODELS-C53483.2021.00016
5. Bock, A.C., Frank, U.: Low-Code Platform. Bus Inf. Syst. Eng. **63**(6), 733–740 (2021). https://doi.org/10.1007/s12599-021-00726-8
6. François, P.A.: Lightweight Shackles Still Bind: Lock-In Effects In Low-Code Development. In: ICIS 2025 Proceedings **14** (2025)
7. François, P.A., Plattfaut, R.: The Reuse of Business Process Automation Artefacts. In: Lecture Notes in Informatics (LNI) - Proceedings **337**, 1923–1942 (2023). https://doi.org/10.18420/inf2023_193
8. François, P.A., Plattfaut, R.: Designing the Organizational Reuse Environment. Enabling Citizen Developers to Reuse Process Automation Artifacts. In: Di Ciccio, C., Fdhila, W., et al. (eds.) Business Process Management Blockchain, Robotic Process Automation, Central and Eastern European, Educators and Industry Forum, pp. 138–153. Springer (2024). https://doi.org/10.1007/978-3-031-70445-1_9
9. François, P.A., Borghoff, V., Plattfaut, R., et al.: Why Companies Use RPA: A Critical Reflection of Goals. In: Di Ciccio, C., Di kman, R. et al. (eds.) Business Process Management, pp. 399–417. Springer International Publishing, Cham (2022). https://doi.org/10.1007/978-3-031-16103-2_26
10. François, P.A., Ciftci, S.A., Janiesch, C., et al.: Large Language Models for Low-Code Process Automation: Lowering the Barriers for Citizen Developers. In: ACIS 2025 Proceedings (2025)
11. Kampmann, M., Femmer, H., Kouadria, D., et al.: Citizen Developers at Work: Roles, Activities, and Interfaces in Low-Code/No-Code Development. In: Proceedings of the 59th Hawaii International Conference on System Sciences (2026)
12. Kim, Y., Stohr, E.A.: Software Reuse: Survey and Research Directions. J. Manag. Inf. Syst. **14**(4), 113–147 (1998). https://doi.org/10.1080/07421222.1998.11518188

13. Krejci, D., Iho, S., Missonier, S.: Innovating with employees: an exploratory study of idea development on low-code development platforms. In: ECIS 2021 Research Papers **118**, 1–16 (2021)
14. Krueger, C.W.: Software reuse. ACM Comput. Surv. **24**(2), 131–183 (1992). https://doi.org/10.1145/130844.130856
15. Lacity, M., Willcocks, L.P.: Innovating in Service: The Role and Management of Automation. In: Willcocks, L., Oshri, I. et al. (eds.) Dynamic innovation in outsourcing. Theories, cases and practices, pp. 269–325. Palgrave Macmillan, Cham (2018). https://doi.org/10.1007/978-3-319-75352-2_9
16. Lethbridge, T.C.: Low-Code Is Often High-Code, So We Must Design Low-Code Platforms to Enable Proper Software Engineering. In: Margaria, T., Steffen, B. (eds.) 10th International Symposium on Leveraging Applications of Formal Methods, pp. 202–212. Springer, Cham (2021). https://doi.org/10.1007/978-3-030-89159-6_14
17. Liu, Y., Zhou, X., Li, D., et al.: A Software Reuse Development Method Based on Base Capability Component Adaptation Model. In: Proceedings of the 2021 5th International Conference on Electronic Information Technology and Computer Engineering, pp. 1480–1485. Association for Computing Machinery, New York (2022). https://doi.org/10.1145/3501409.3501671
18. Maedche, A., Gregor, S., Morana, S., et al.: Conceptualization of the Problem Space in Design Science Research. In: International Conference on Design Science Research in Information Systems and Technology, pp. 18–31. Springer, Cham (2019). https://doi.org/10.1007/978-3-030-19504-5_2
19. Noppen, P., Beerepoot, I., van de Weerd, I., et al.: How to Keep RPA Maintainable? In: International Conference on Business Process Management, pp. 453–470 (2020). https://doi.org/10.1007/978-3-030-58666-9_26
20. Novales, A., Mancha, R.: Fueling Digital Transformation with Citizen Developers and Low-Code Development. MIS Q Exec **22**(3), 221–234 (2023). https://doi.org/10.17705/2msqe.00083
21. Pfeiffer, J., Wortmann, A.: A Low-Code Platform for Systematic Component-Oriented Language Composition. In: SLE 2023: Proceedings of the 16th ACM SIGPLAN International Conference on Software Language Engineering, pp. 208–213. Association for Computing Machinery, New York (2023). https://doi.org/10.1145/3623476.3623516
22. Plattfaut, R., Borghoff, V.: Robotic process automation: a literature-based research agenda. J. Inf. Syst. **36**(2), 173–191 (2022). https://doi.org/10.2308/ISYS-2020-033
23. Průcha, P., Madzík, P.: SiDiTeR: Similarity Discovering Techniques for Robotic Process Automation. In: Business Process Management: Blockchain, Robotic Process Automation and Educators Forum, vol. 491, pp. 106–119 (2023). https://doi.org/10.1007/978-3-031-43433-4_7
24. Sadovnikov, K., Sweijen, R., van der Werf, J.M., et al.: A framework to assess the suitability of low-code for BPM. In ECIS 2023 Research Papers **433** (2023)
25. Seco, J.C., Lourenço, H., Parreira, J., et al.: Nested OSTRICH: hatching compositions of low-code templates. In: Proceedings of the 25th International Conference on Model Driven Engineering Languages and Systems, pp. 210–220. Association for Computing Machinery, New York (2022). https://doi.org/10.1145/3550355.3552442
26. Tuunanen, T., Winter, R., vom Brocke, J.: Dealing with Complexity in Design Science Research: A Methodology Using Design Echelons. MISQ **48**(2), 427–458 (2024). https://doi.org/10.25300/MISQ/2023/16700
27. Viljoen, A., Nguyen, J., Kauschinger, M., et al.: Fostering scalable citizen development in organizations: towards a guiding framework. In: AMCIS 2023 Proceedings, 1–10 (2023)
28. Viljoen, A., Altın, E.N., Hein, A., et al.: Beyond citizen development: exploring low-code platform adoption by professional software developers. In: AMCIS 2024 Proceedings (2024)

29. Viljoen, A., Stelzl, B., Yang, M., et al.: Navigating flexibility and standardisation in low-code/no-code development. Inf. Syst. J. (2025). https://doi.org/10.1111/isj.70001
30. Viljoen, A., Hein, A., Krcmar, H.: Low-code development platform ecosystems. Electron Markets **36**(1), 12 (2026). https://doi.org/10.1007/s12525-025-00848-x
31. Webster, J., Watson, R.: Analyzing the past to prepare for the future: writing a literature review. MISQ **26**(2), xiii–xxiii (2002). https://doi.org/10.2307/4132319
32. Wolfswinkel, J.F., Furtmueller, E., Wilderom, C.P.M.: Using grounded theory as a method for rigorously reviewing literature. Eur. J. Inf. Syst. **22**(1), 45–55 (2013). https://doi.org/10.1057/ejis.2011.51

Towards a Multi-agent LLM-Based Tutoring Tool for Mathematical Argumentation Skills

Huda Koulani[1]([envelope])[ID], Lucia Marchionne[2][ID], Hendrikje Schmidtpott-Schulz[2][ID], Andreas Eichler[2][ID], Andreas Bley[2][ID], and Matthias Söllner[1][ID]

[1] Information Systems and Systems Engineering, University of Kassel, Kassel, Germany
{koulani,soellner}@uni-kassel.de
[2] Institute of Mathematics, University of Kassel, Kassel, Germany
{marchionne,hendrikje.schmidtpott,eichler,
andreas.bley}@mathematik.uni-kassel.de

Abstract. Mathematical argumentation is a core competence that integrates mathematical reasoning with broader critical thinking skills, enabling students to construct coherent and logically structured arguments to evaluate mathematical claims. This skill is essential for undergraduate students across disciplines such as information systems, mathematics, and computer science—yet many struggle to develop it. Recent advances in Large Language Models (LLMs) and multi-agent systems offer a promising opportunity to address these challenges by supporting students in refining their mathematical argumentation within a tutorial setting. In this Research-in-Progress paper, we adopt a Design Science Research approach to generate design knowledge for an LLM-based tutoring tool aimed at fostering students' argumentation skills. Drawing on user requirements and meta-requirements derived from user interviews and theoretical foundations, we derive four design principles and propose a prototype of a multi-agent LLM-based tutoring tool. The system delivers formative feedback on students' proofs and provides tutorial guidance through step-by-step explanations, grounded in theories of formative feedback and tutorial guidance.

Keywords: Mathematical Argumentation · Multi-agent LLM System · Tutorial Guidance

1 Introduction

The ability to construct well-formed arguments is an essential skill for problem-solving and decision-making [4,40]. In mathematics, this ability takes a particularly rigorous form: in contrast to other disciplines, mathematical argumentation is characterized by strict logical validity, where even minor gaps can invalidate an entire argument, and by strong dependencies between reasoning steps that require precise structural coherence. Developing mathematical argumentation skills is essential in undergraduate mathematics, as they support logical reasoning and are needed to construct and verify proofs [12,16]. However, many students struggle with these competencies and supporting their development remains a persistent challenge. Common difficulties include knowing how to begin a proof, constructing logically sound arguments, and expressing ideas in formal mathematical language [33,34,38,43]. Providing structured feedback on mathematical proofs and offering targeted guidance in argument construction are strategies for addressing these challenges and supporting students' learning. However, in large lecture settings, opportunities for individualized guidance are often limited.

Technology-Mediated Learning (TML) tools have emerged as a promising mechanism to address educational challenges [3,11]. Recent research indicates that AI-based TML is effective in enhancing students' argumentation skills [40, 41]. Several systems have been developed to provide learning environments for various mathematical topics [2], evaluate formal proofs [28] or support general mathematical problem-solving [39]. However, none of these systems explicitly focus on delivering informative feedback on students' proof-writing processes. As a result, students often lack guidance on how to build arguments systematically.

Therefore, we investigate how an educational tool should be designed to assist higher education students in improving their mathematical argumentation skills. To ensure practical relevance, we adopt a user-centered design approach that integrates insights from students' perspectives. Following the iterative framework of Design Science Research (DSR) by Peffers et al. [29], we combine user requirements with theoretical foundations to generate design knowledge for viable solutions.

In this Research-in-Progress paper, we propose the design of a multi-agent LLM-based tutoring tool that provides feedback on students' proof attempts and offers guidance on how to improve structure, clarity, and logical coherence. The tool is intended to complement existing teaching practices by offering scalable, individualized support that students can use privately and iteratively.

2 Theoretical Background and Related Work

2.1 Mathematical Argumentation Skills and Student Difficulties

Mathematical argumentation skills involve, among other aspects, constructing and rigorously presenting proofs. This entails deriving necessary conclusions from stated premises using valid logical reasoning [12]. At the same time, argumentation also encompasses informal explanations that support conceptual understanding and promote deeper learning. By encouraging the critical use of reason, such as questioning assumptions, identifying logical gaps, and drawing valid inferences, argumentation plays a central role in both mathematical learning and broader critical thinking [16].

Proof construction is an inherently challenging task and students often encounter a variety of difficulties [30]. Research has documented strategic, logical, and syntactic challenges in students' proof construction. A commonly reported difficulty is not knowing where to begin when faced with a proof task, indicating challenges in initiating a proof and potentially in understanding the logical structure of the given mathematical statements [34]. Beyond this initial obstacle, students often struggle with logical reasoning, including the tendency to treat empirical evidence or specific examples as sufficient proof [38]. These issues frequently manifest in flawed reasoning patterns such as assuming the converse of a statement, beginning proofs by assuming the conclusion, and producing arguments containing logical errors, gaps, or locally incoherent reasoning [33,34,43]. In addition, students face syntactic and technical challenges. These include deficiencies in numerical or algebraic computation, failure to apply relevant knowledge when available, difficulty using definitions effectively, and challenges in interpreting symbolic representations [34,43]. In particular, students may become confused when the same symbol denotes different mathematical objects, when different symbols refer to the same object, or when existence is incorrectly inferred from mere naming [34].

2.2 Tutorial Guidance and Formative Feedback

The difficulties outlined above often persist without guided practice, yet research shows that well-designed feedback can effectively support the development of students' mathematical reasoning [14]. We draw on two complementary theoretical foundations: formative feedback and tutorial guidance.

Following Hattie and Timperley [13], feedback is understood as information provided by a teaching agent about a learner's performance or understanding, intended to reduce the gap between the learner's current state and a desired learning goal. In their framework, effective feedback addresses three core questions: Where am I going? (clarifying learning goals, here the underlying assumptions and statement to be proven), How am I going? (evaluating the validity of a proof attempt), and Where to next? (guiding subsequent improvement). Feedback can operate at multiple levels. This work focuses on task-level feedback (information about the correctness or quality of a proof attempt) and process-level feedback (information about the strategies and reasoning underlying it), while excluding person-focused feedback (e.g., praise), which has been shown to be less effective [36]. Furthermore, effective formative feedback must be designed with attention to both the instructional context and the learner's characteristics [26,36]. From this perspective, feedback must provide actionable information that helps learners understand errors, refine strategies, and progress toward the intended learning goals.

In addition, our work is grounded in the concept of tutorial guidance after Merrill et al. [25], which emphasizes immediate, situation-specific support during problem solving. Rather than simply correcting answers or delivering content, tutorial guidance involves diagnosing learners' reasoning, encouraging promising solution paths, and supporting learners in repairing errors as they occur. In the context of mathematical proof, this means guiding students in how to unpack a statement, select an appropriate proof strategy or justify a step, rather than providing complete solutions.

Together, these theoretical perspectives emphasize a dual approach: directed guidance that helps learners decide how to proceed, and formative feedback that responds to their work with concrete, actionable information for improvement.

While tutorial guidance and formative feedback have been shown to be effective, their provision in practice is often limited by resource constraints, and the quality of support can vary substantially across instructional contexts. As a result, students frequently lack access to consistent, high-quality feedback outside structured instructional settings.

2.3 Multi-agent LLM Systems

LLMs are powerful instruments capable of supporting complex reasoning, planning, and decision-making [7,17,27]. In educational contexts, these capabilities translate into significant potential for enhancing learning through the generation of natural-language feedback [42]. Unlike traditional automated grading systems, which often provide binary or rigid evaluations, LLMs can deliver nuanced feedback that addresses multiple dimensions of student work. These include logical structure, clarity and coherence [18,44]. Because this interaction occurs in natural language, students are more likely to internalize the guidance compared to static output [18]. Furthermore, it enables a form of dialogic, stepwise feedback that was previously only feasible in human tutoring contexts.

Describing all aspects of the desired feedback in a single prompt can overwhelm the model and weaken the quality of the response [23]. To address this challenge, recent studies have proposed using multiple LLMs working collaboratively to manage the complexity of generating high-quality, pedagogically meaningful feedback [6,19,45]. This approach is often formalized as a multi-agent LLM system, in which each agent is assigned a specific role and equipped with a tailored system prompt to perform a distinct part of the task. Communication between agents enables them to exchange intermediate results and coordinate their reasoning [20]. In the context of proof learning, this decomposition aligns naturally with the need to separately assess and guide students on strategy selection, logical validity, and mathematical expression.

2.4 Related Work

TML facilitates the educational process by leveraging educational technologies that alleviate the instructional workload while providing students with the flexibility to engage in learning activities at any time and from any location [3,11]. These technologies have demonstrated effectiveness in diverse educational contexts [15,39,40]. The integration of LLMs into educational applications has enabled natural-language interaction and more adaptive and context-sensitive responses to student input [35]. Furthermore, recent research has explored multi-agent LLM systems in various educational domains, in which multiple specialized agents collaborate, enabling more sophisticated, coordinated support for learners [15,19,45].

On the other hand, the use of LLMs in educational settings introduces well-documented challenges, including the risk of generating hallucinated feedback and a tendency to provide complete solutions rather than supporting students' reasoning processes [37]. Moreover, many recent LLM-based systems focus primarily on general mathematical problem solving or procedural skill acquisition [39], often overlooking the specific demands of mathematical proof construction. These systems rarely address critical aspects of proof writing, such as logical dependency, the coherence of argumentation, and the proper sequencing of reasoning steps.

Beyond LLM-based approaches, formal proof assistants such as Lean [1] have also been employed to support proof learning. While these systems provide precise, logic-based feedback, they require students to express proofs in fully formal languages, which poses a significant barrier to entry for beginner learners. Hybrid approaches that combine natural-language interaction with formal verification, such as LeanTutor [28], aim to mitigate this challenge by enabling more intuitive student engagement. However, despite their promise, such systems typically presuppose the availability of fully formal reference proofs, which limits their applicability in authentic, open-ended learning contexts.

Across these approaches, a common practical constraint is the reliance on typed input for student interaction. In response, recent work has begun exploring the integration of handwritten mathematical input as a complementary interaction modality [2,31]. However, this line of research has largely focused on input recognition and accessibility, with limited attention to the validation of mathematical proofs.

These observations point to the need for systems that complement existing instructional settings by providing accessible, pedagogically grounded support for students' mathematical argumentation.

3   Research Methodology

This Research-in-Progress paper adopts the DSR approach outlined by Peffers et al. [29] to design a multi-agent LLM-based tutoring tool with the goal of supporting university students in developing their mathematical argumentation skills. The adapted research steps are demonstrated in Fig. 1.

First, we define the problem of students' unassisted difficulties in constructing valid mathematical arguments and specify the objectives of a solution in providing individualized feedback on mathematical argumentation that addresses structure, logical rigor, and correctness. Second, we derive design principles from user interviews and theoretical foundations, and instantiate a prototype called *ProofTutor* that directly addresses the identified challenges. As future steps, we plan to conduct ten additional interviews to broaden the user perspective and refine the design knowledge accordingly. Building on this, we will evaluate the tool through a qualitative analysis of student interactions, focusing on its usability and effectiveness in supporting the development of mathematical argumentation skills. Students will solve proof problems using the tool, followed by post-interviews and a survey to capture their experiences.

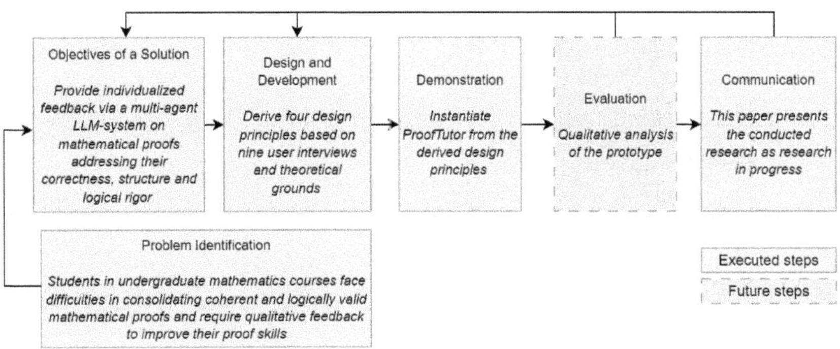

Fig. 1. Research steps following DSR approach by Peffers et al. [29]

3.1 Problem Identification and Objectives of a Solution

Students in undergraduate mathematics courses frequently struggle with constructing mathematical proofs, particularly in knowing how to begin [34], articulating coherent and logically valid arguments [33], and expressing these arguments using appropriate mathematical language [43]. Although essential for developing proof-writing skills [14], instructional feedback from instructors and tutors is often limited in availability, delayed in delivery, and difficult to individualize at scale. As a result, students have few opportunities to engage in iterative revision cycles.

The objective of the proposed solution is to support students' development of mathematical argumentation by providing timely, individualized, and process-oriented feedback on written proofs through an interactive tutoring tool. Specifically, the tool should help students identify appropriate next steps in their reasoning, strengthen the logical structure of their arguments, address gaps in justification, and express their proofs using mathematically precise language. To achieve this, we leverage the ability of LLMs to generate natural-language feedback and adapt recent advances in multi-agent LLM systems, where specialized agents collaborate under the coordination of a central evaluator model that assesses reasoning and synthesizes the final feedback.

3.2 Design and Development

Following the research methodology of Peffers et al. [29], we analyze user perspective and relevant literature and consolidate these insights into user requirements and meta-requirements, from which we derive design principles, as illustrated in Fig. 2.

Deriving User Requirements. To investigate the user perspective, we conducted nine semi-structured interviews with computer science students at a German university, following the guidelines outlined by Rubin [32]. Participants were recruited via an advertisement posted in a first-year mathematics foundation

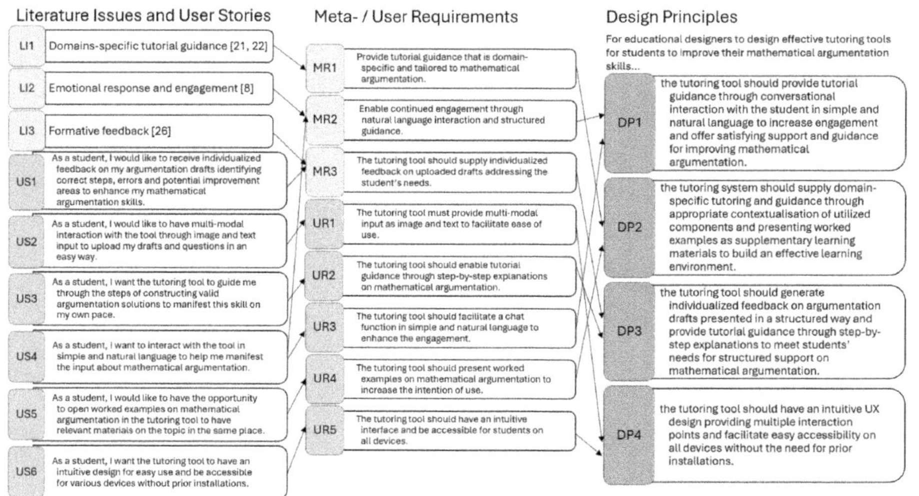

Fig. 2. Overview of derived design principles for LLM-based tutoring tools for mathematical argumentation following the approach of Gregor et al. [10]

course that emphasizes formal mathematics and the development of valid mathematical argumentation. A semi-structured questionnaire was used, comprising five thematic categories and a total of 33 questions. The questions addressed participants' perceived difficulties in constructing mathematical proofs, strategies they have used to overcome these challenges, and their expectations and desires regarding the design, feedback, and usefulness of a tool intended to support the development of mathematical argumentation skills.

The interviews lasted an average of 38 min, with a minimum duration of 18 min and a maximum of 57 min. Participants included five men and four women. With regard to academic standing, eight participants were in their first semester, while one student was in their third semester, having postponed the foundational mathematics course to this term. All interviews were conducted online via Zoom in December 2025 and recorded for subsequent analysis. After transcription, the data were analyzed using Mayring's approach to qualitative content analysis [24]. Three authors independently reviewed the transcripts and performed open coding of the responses. In a second iteration, recurring themes were identified, grouped into coherent categories, and summarized into clusters to derive user stories (**US**) and user requirements (**UR**), following the framework proposed by Cohn [9]. The consolidation of user stories yielded six core user requirements: individualized feedback on mathematical proofs (**UR1**), multi-modal interaction (**UR2**), step-by-step explanations and guidance in proof construction (**UR3**), natural and intuitive dialogue in simple language (**UR4**), provision of worked examples in mathematical argumentation (**UR5**), and an intuitive, device-agnostic design for broad accessibility (**UR6**).

Deriving Requirements from Literature. We analyzed the requirements from the scientific literature on designing tutoring tools to support the development of mathematical argumentation skills. Following the systematic literature review approach outlined by vom Brocke et al. [5], we conducted a review focused on the domains of information systems and technology in education, selecting studies that presented theoretical and practical contributions to the design of tutoring tools in educational settings. A total of 24 studies were selected for in-depth analysis. By summarizing the contributions of these studies and clustering their insights into thematic groups, we consolidated recurring literature issues (**LI**). The analyzed literature emphasized the importance of domain-specific tutoring guidance beyond generic feedback and instruction, highlighting the need for targeted support in mathematical reasoning (**LI1**) [21,22], which was synthesized into **MR1**. Furthermore, emotional response and learner engagement during tutorial interactions (**LI2**) were identified as critical factors [8], and thus incorporated into **MR2**. The integration of formative feedback with tutorial guidance (**LI3**), grounded in formative feedback theory [26], was also reported and consolidated into **MR3**.

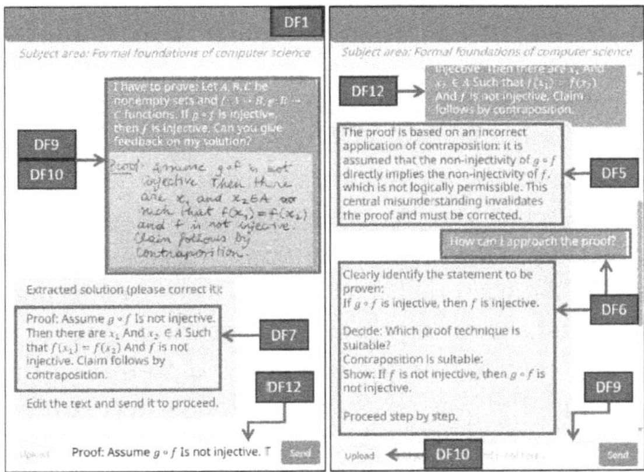

Fig. 3. Screenshots of *ProofTutor* highlighting the instantiated design features (English translation)

3.3 Demonstration

Based on the design requirements previously presented, we derived four design principles (**DP1DP4**) for LLM-based tutoring tools aimed at supporting mathematical argumentation [10]. These principles were instantiated into specific design features (**DF**), which were implemented in our first prototype, *ProofTutor*, as illustrated in Fig. 3. The mapping between design principles and their corresponding design features is detailed in Table 1.

From **DP1**, we derived design feature **DF1**, which implements conversational interaction as a chat between the student and the tool, supplemented by text input (**DF9**) and image input (**DF10**), both of which are derived from **DP4**. The overall design of the prototype follows the conventional structure of conversational interfaces (**DF11**), thereby instantiating **DP4** by promoting an intuitive, user-friendly design. To ensure domain-specific guidance in supporting mathematical argumentation skills (**DP2**), we leveraged LLM-based conversational interaction to enable simple and natural language exchanges (**DF2**). Building on the benefits of multi-agent collaboration discussed in Sect. 2.3, we implemented a multi-agent LLM system where each component acts as a specialized agent, with the overarching flow defined by a pedagogical logic model (**DF3**). To provide tutorial guidance through informative feedback and step-by-step explanations (**DP3**), three specialized LLM agents were designed to divide the workload: one to analyze uploaded drafts, operated by Qwen3 VL 30B A3B Instruct; a second to identify logical errors, structural issues, and correctness gaps (**DF5**), powered by Mistral Large Instruct; and a third to synthesize guidance and deliver step-by-step explanations (**DF6**), operated by Qwen3 30B A3B Instruct 2507. To increase the performance of the agents in the context of mathematical argumentation (**DP2**), each agent was fine-tuned via system prompts and augmented with Retrieval-Augmented Generation (RAG), accessing a curated knowledge base of lecture notes and solved problems on mathematical argumentation (**DF4**). This ensures feedback is grounded in validated pedagogical content. Design feature **DF12** enables students to validate the interpretation of handwritten drafts before submitting them for feedback, ensuring accuracy and reducing the need for manual entry of mathematical symbols, thereby supporting **DP4**. To support the effective presentation of feedback and explanations (**DP3**), we integrated LaTeX-based rendering of mathematical symbols in the frontend, ensuring clarity in notation (**DF7**). Finally, in alignment with **DP4**, the tool was implemented as a web-based application using JavaScript, React, and Python, enabling seamless accessibility across diverse devices and platforms (**DF8**).

Table 1. Instantiation of design principles with design features

	DF1	DF2	DF3	DF4	DF5	DF6	DF7	DF8	DF9	DF10	DF11	DF12
DP1	X											
DP2		X	X	X								
DP3					X	X	X					
DP4								X	X	X	X	X

4   Conclusion and Future Work

This Research-in-Progress paper presents the design and initial development of *ProofTutor*, an LLM-based tutoring tool to support university students in developing mathematical argumentation skills. Following the DSR approach informed the design by a literature analysis of student difficulties, feedback mechanisms, and tutoring strategies, as well as user requirements derived from semi-structured interviews. As next steps, we will conduct ten additional interviews with pre-service mathematics teacher students to further enrich the user perspective and incorporate their requirements into the evolving design knowledge. We will then perform a qualitative evaluation of the prototype with pilot groups to assess its usability and effectiveness in supporting students' learning. Based on these findings, the tool will be refined and iteratively improved. In the longer term, we aim to deploy the system in regular mathematics lectures and conduct a systematic evaluation of its efficacy in authentic learning environments.

Acknowledgments. The authors gratefully acknowledge the computing time granted by the KISSKI project and the access to the SAIA API. This research project is funded by Stiftung Innovation in der Hochschullehre.

References

1. Lean. https://lean-lang.org/. Accessed 29 Jan 2026
2. Mathweb.de. https://mathweb.de/. Accessed 29 Jan 2026
3. Alavi, M., Leidner, D.: Research commentary: technology-mediated learning - a call for greater depth and breadth of research. Inf. Syst. Res. **12**, 1–10 (2001). https://doi.org/10.1287/isre.12.1.1.9720
4. von Aufschnaiter, C., Erduran, S., Osborne, J., Simon, S.: Arguing to learn and learning to argue: case studies of how students' argumentation relates to their scientific knowledge. J. Res. Sci. Teach. **45**(1), 101–131 (2008)
5. Brocke, J.V., Simons, A., Riemer, K., Niehaves, B., Plattfaut, R., Cleven, A.: Standing on the shoulders of giants: challenges and recommendations of literature search in information systems research. Commun. Assoc. Inf. Syst. **37** (2015). https://doi.org/10.17705/1CAIS.03709
6. Cao, J., et al.: From first draft to final insight: a multi-agent approach for feedback generation. In: Cristea, A.I., Walker, E., Lu, Y., Santos, O.C., Isotani, S. (eds.) Artificial Intelligence in Education, pp. 163–176. Springer, Cham (2025)
7. Chen, W., Yu, C., Wang, Y., Chen, M., Xu, Y., Shi, Y.: Echomind: supporting real-time complex problem discussions through human-ai collaborative facilitation. Proc. ACM Hum.-Comput. Interact. **9**(7) (2025). https://doi.org/10.1145/3757587
8. Chinn, S., Heiser, R., Suleiman, J.: Emotional responses to computer-based training materials in education. In: AMCIS 2008 Proceedings, vol. 2, p. 80 (2008)
9. Cohn, M.: User Stories Applied: For Agile Software Development (2004)
10. Gregor, S., Chandra Kruse, L., Seidel, S.: The anatomy of a design principle. J. Assoc. Inf. Syst. **21**(11), 1622–1652 (2020). https://doi.org/10.17705/1jais.00649
11. Gupta, S., Bostrom, R.: Technology-mediated learning: a comprehensive theoretical model. J. AIS **10** (2009). https://doi.org/10.17705/1jais.00207

12. Hanna, G., De Villiers, M.: Proof and Proving in Mathematics Education: the 19th ICMI Study. Springer (2012)
13. Hattie, J., Timperley, H.: The power of feedback. Rev. Educ. Res. **77**(1), 81–112 (2007). https://doi.org/10.3102/003465430298487
14. Hess, K., Smit, R.: Lehrende unterstützen lernende beim mathematischen argumentieren mit feedback-dialogen-eine mixed methods-studie [teachers support learners in mathematical reasoning with feedback dialogues–a mixed methods study]. J. Math.-Didakt. **45**(2), 16 (2024)
15. Hewedy, D.W., Abdelhady, A.S.: Petra: a personalized educational tutoring tool for recursive assistance leveraging multi-model LLMs for dynamic programming learning. In: 2025 15th International Conference on Electrical Engineering (ICEENG), pp. 1–6 (2025). https://doi.org/10.1109/ICEENG64546.2025.11031311
16. Jahnke, H.N., Sommerhoff, D., Ufer, S.: Argumentieren, Begründen und Beweisen [Reasoning, justifying and proving], pp. 369–398. Springer, Heidelberg (2023). https://doi.org/10.1007/978-3-662-66604-3_12
17. Kim, Y.S., Moon, H.S., Lee, S., Lee, T.Y.: 'histochat': leveraging AI-driven historical personas for personalized and engaging middle school history education. Proc. ACM Hum.-Comput. Interact. **9**(7) (2025). https://doi.org/10.1145/3757534
18. Kinder, A., et al.: Effects of adaptive feedback generated by a large language model: a case study in teacher education. Comput. Educ. Artif. Intell. **8** (2025)
19. Le, Q.M., Nguyen, H.D.: Adaptive multi-agent tutoring ai for multimodal mathematics conversational learning. In: Proceedings of the 2nd ACM Workshop in AI-Powered Question & Answering Systems, AIQAM 2025, pp. 36–42. Association for Computing Machinery, New York, NY, USA (2025)
20. Li, X., Wang, S., Zeng, S., Wu, Y., Yang, Y.: A survey on LLM-based multi-agent systems: workflow, infrastructure, and challenges. Vicinagearth **1** (2024). https://doi.org/10.1007/s44336-024-00009-2
21. Ligthart, M.E., et al.: Design specifications for a social robot math tutor. In: Proceedings of the 2023 ACM/IEEE International Conference on Human-Robot Interaction, HRI 2023, pp. 321–330. Association for Computing Machinery, New York, NY, USA (2023). https://doi.org/10.1145/3568162.3576957
22. Liu, B., Zhang, J., Lin, F., Jia, X., Peng, M.: One size doesn't fit all: a personalized conversational tutoring agent for mathematics instruction. In: Companion Proceedings of the ACM on Web Conference 2025, WWW 2025, pp. 2401–2410. Association for Computing Machinery, New York, NY, USA (2025)
23. Liu, N., et al.: Lost in the middle: how language models use long contexts. Trans. Assoc. Comput. Linguist. **12**, 157–173 (2024). https://doi.org/10.1162/tacl_a_00638
24. Mayring, P.: Qualitative Inhaltsanalyse, pp. 601–613. VS Verlag für Sozialwissenschaften, Wiesbaden (2010). https://doi.org/10.1007/978-3-531-92052-8_42
25. Merrill, D.C., Reiser, B.J., Merrill, S.K., Landes, S.: Tutoring: guided learning by doing. Cogn. Instr. **13**(3), 315–372 (1995)
26. Narciss, S., Huth, K.: How to design informative tutoring feedback for multimedia learning. Instr. Des. Multimedia Learn. **181195** (2004)
27. Papachristou, M., Yang, L., Hsu, C.C.: Leveraging large language models for collective decision-making. Proc. ACM Hum.-Comput. Interact **9**(7) (2025)
28. Patel, M., et al.: Leantutor: a formally-verified ai tutor for mathematical proofs. arXiv preprint arXiv:2506.08321 (2025)
29. Peffers, K., Tuunanen, T., Rothenberger, M.A., Chatterjee, S.: A design science research methodology for information systems research. J. Manag. Inf. Syst. **24**(3), 45–77 (2007)

30. Rabin, J.M., Quarfoot, D.: Sources of students' difficulties with proof by contradiction. Int. J. Res. Undergraduate Math. Educ. **8**(3), 521–549 (2022). https://doi.org/10.1007/s40753-021-00152-x
31. Rodrigues, L., et al.: Mathematics intelligent tutoring systems with handwritten input: a scoping review. Educ. Inf. Technol. **29**(9), 11183–11209 (2024)
32. Rubin, J.: Handbook of Usability Testing: How to Plan, Design and Conduct Effective Tests (2008)
33. Selden, A., Selden, J.: Errors and misconceptions in college level theorem proving. In: Proceedings of the Second International Seminar on Misconceptions and Educational Strategies in Science and Mathematics, vol. III, pp. 457–470 (1987)
34. Selden, A., Selden, J.: Overcoming students' difficulties in learning to understand and construct proofs. In: Carlson, M.P., Rasmussen, C. (eds.) Making the Connection, 1 edn, pp. 95–110. The Mathematical Association of America (2008)
35. Sharma, S., Mittal, P., Kumar, M., Bhardwaj, V.: The role of large language models in personalized learning: a systematic review of educational impact. Discov. Sustain. **6**(1), 1–24 (2025)
36. Shute, V.J.: Focus on formative feedback. Rev. Educ. Res. **78**(1), 153–189 (2008). https://doi.org/10.3102/0034654307313795
37. Sonkar, S., Ni, K., Chaudhary, S., Baraniuk, R.G.: Pedagogical alignment of large language models (2024). https://arxiv.org/abs/2402.05000
38. Sowder, L., Harel, G.: Types of students' justifications. Math. Teach. **91**(8), 670–675 (1998)
39. Tonga, J.C., Clement, B., Oudeyer, P.Y.: Automatic generation of question hints for mathematics problems using large language models in educational technology. arXiv preprint arXiv:2411.03495 (2024)
40. Wambsganss, T., Janson, A., Söllner, M., Koedinger, K., Leimeister, J.M.: Improving students' argumentation skills using dynamic machine-learning–based modeling. Info. Sys. Res. **36**(1), 474–507 (2025)
41. Wambsganss, T., Söllner, M., Leimeister, J.M.: Design and evaluation of an adaptive dialog-based tutoring system for argumentation skills. In: International Conference on Information Systems (ICIS) (2020)
42. Wang, T., Wu, T., Liu, H., Brown, C., Chen, Y.: Generative co-learners: enhancing cognitive and social presence of students in asynchronous learning with generative AI. Proc. ACM Hum.-Comput. Interact. **9**(1) (2025)
43. Weber, K.: Student difficulty in constructing proofs: the need for strategic knowledge. Educ. Stud. Math. (2001)
44. Zheng, Q., Mo, T., Wang, X.: Personalized feedback generation using LLMs: enhancing student learning in stem education. J. Adv. Comput. Syst. **3**(10), 8–22 (2023). https://doi.org/10.69987/JACS.2023.31002
45. Zhu, A., Du, Y.: A Role-Aware Multi-Agent Framework for Financial Education QA, pp. 483–491. Association for Computing Machinery, New York, NY, USA (2025). https://doi.org/10.1145/3768292.3770345

A DSR-Informed Intervention to Strengthen Self-Determination in Blended Professional Learning

Pauline Weritz[(✉)] [iD]

University of Twente, Enschede, The Netherlands
`p.weritz@utwente.nl`

Abstract. Blended learning is widely used in professional education, yet many programmes struggle to sustain adult learners' motivation and engagement. Technology-enabled approaches offer a mix of online and offline activities. Limited research has examined how such blended learning environments can be designed to support self-determination, which is central to intrinsic motivation and effective learning. This study addresses this gap by investigating how blended learning can better foster autonomy, competence, and relatedness. Using a Design Science Research approach, both literature and user needs inform the development of initial design principles. Preliminary findings reveal five design principles, namely the importance of a transparent and accessible learning structure, the need for conceptual clarity, going beyond passive consumption to encourage meaningful engagement, relevance, and temporal and cognitive flow of learning. Thereby, this study contributes to the literature on design principles for enhancing self-determination in blended professional learning.

Keywords: Blended Professional Learning · Autonomy · Competence · Relatedness · Design Science Research

1 Introduction

Professional learners often engage in higher education to improve their career prospects, increase their earning potential, and pursue more meaningful personal and professional development in an increasingly dynamic world [1, 2]. Yet these learners, who are typically mid-career practitioners balancing work, study, and personal responsibilities, face distinctive challenges in higher education environments [3]. Their learning needs are shaped by limited time, varying levels of prior knowledge, and a strong demand for practical relevance. In these contexts, blended and digital learning have emerged as a promising approach because they combine face-to-face interaction with self-paced online components and enhance academic and social benefits [4]. However, simply offering information systems (IS) as the key component of blended learning does not guarantee effective learning [5]. From an IS perspective, blended learning environments can be understood as socio-technical systems in which learning outcomes are shaped by the interaction between users, content, processes, and technological artifacts. In particular, learning management systems such as Canvas represent configurable IS artifacts.

© The Author(s), under exclusive license to Springer Nature Switzerland AG 2026
S. Chatterjee et al. (Eds.): DESRIST 2026, LNCS 16607, pp. 80–91, 2026.
https://doi.org/10.1007/978-3-032-28570-6_7

Professional learners frequently report difficulties such as a lack of conceptual clarity, insufficient structure, and limited opportunity to connect theories to their work contexts [6]. These issues often reduce engagement and diminish the perceived value of the learning process, highlighting the need not only for pedagogical adaptation but also for technological redesign [7]. At the core of these challenges lies the question of motivation and satisfaction [8]. Professional learners are not passive recipients of information: their engagement depends heavily on the perceived relevance and usability of learning materials, the transparency of expectations, and the autonomy to navigate learning at their own pace. This makes Self-Determination Theory (SDT) [9, 10] particularly suitable as an explanatory and design-oriented framework. SDT emphasizes three psychological needs (i.e., autonomy, competence, and relatedness) as the basis for sustained intrinsic motivation. Yet many existing blended learning designs fail to intentionally support these needs, leading to challenges in the learning experience, process, and outcomes [11].

First, for the learning experience, students may feel disengaged or overwhelmed due to a one-size-fits-all approach that does not account for their diverse goals, prior knowledge, or preferred learning styles [12]. Second, during the learning process, the absence of a clear structure for self-directed learning can result in confusion about expectations, poor time management, and a lack of ownership over the learning journey [13]. Third, in terms of learning outcomes, when students are not guided to tailor their learning path, the depth and quality of learning may vary widely [14]. Some may fail to meet learning objectives effectively, while others may not be challenged to higher levels of analysis and application. These challenges indicate a need for intervention that not only reorganizes content but redesigns the learning environment to foster motivation through principles grounded in SDT. Hence, the following research question (RQ) is guiding this study: *How can a blended learning environment be designed to enhance the self-determination of professional learners?*

Design Science Research (DSR) is well-suited to address this problem because it focuses on the creation and evaluation of artifacts [15, 16], in this case, a prototype of a blended learning environment, that solves real-world issues while generating theoretical insight. While following a DSR approach, we considered both literature and user views to develop the requirements and design principles (DPs). The goal is to understand the problem and explore how to create a structured, accessible, and practice-oriented online learning space that enhances autonomy, competence, and relatedness, and thereby strengthens learner motivation. With our study, we aim to provide three main contributions: we develop a conceptual design for a blended learning environment, present five DPs for an implementable prototype, and offer lessons learned for educators as a design blueprint for creating blended learning for professionals.

2   Conceptual Background and Related Work

2.1   Professional Learning as the Study Context

Professional learning in adult contexts is shaped by the unique characteristics, needs, and goals of adult learners. Research suggests that adults tend to value learning experiences that support achievement and self-empowerment and are motivated by opportunities to apply knowledge in meaningful ways [17]. Adult learning theory, as summarized by [18], highlights the multidimensional nature of adult learning, integrating cognitive, affective, and contextual dimensions. Despite decades of research, no single comprehensive framework fully captures this complexity [19], which presents challenges for designing effective learning programs. A recurring aim in adult education is to sustain learning motivation, particularly in professional settings where learners must continuously update skills. Context-based learning approaches [20] emphasize the importance of connecting learning activities to real-world environments, making professional learning highly relevance-dependent. Furthermore, lifelong learning has become a defining principle of modern professional development, emphasizing continuous personal and professional growth [21].

As workplaces become more digitally mediated, the importance of developing technological competence, digital literacy, and positive lifelong learning dispositions has increased substantially. [22] highlights that cultivating these competencies helps build a workforce capable of adapting to rapid technological change. Consequently, there is a growing need for learning environments that effectively support adult learners' motivation, autonomy, and sustained engagement.

2.2 Blended Learning Approaches

Blended learning has become a prominent approach in professional learning programs [23], combining face-to-face instruction with technology-supported components, often on digital platforms. While this format is often described as offering the "best of both worlds" [5], enabling flexibility, personalization, and richer learning experiences, current blended learning designs fail to address such benefits and drawbacks (i.e., challenges with workload, digital competences, and learner isolation). A central aspect of blended learning is that it naturally supports self-directed learning. [24] emphasize that self-directed learning involves learners taking control over their learning process, influenced by motivation, self-efficacy, perceived control, and available support. In professional learning, this is particularly relevant, as adult learners often expect a degree of autonomy and seek to align learning with their personal and professional goals. Given the wide variation in blended learning models and the diversity of adult learners, understanding how blended environments can be designed to maximize motivation, engagement, and learning outcomes remains an important area of study (e.g., [25]). This provides a strong foundation for examining blended learning through motivational theories such as SDT.

2.3 Self-Determination in Learning

Self-Determination Theory has a long-established relationship with education, particularly in its ability to explain how learning environments can increase learners' interest and engagement [26, 27]. SDT posits that individuals thrive when their needs for autonomy, competence, and relatedness are supported. When these needs are met, learners experience enhanced intrinsic motivation, greater personal growth, and improved adjustment [27]. Research has shown that self-determination plays a significant role in motivation and learning processes [28]. Studies in blended learning contexts similarly argue for learner-centric designs that foster autonomy and engagement [29]. Online learning environments, in particular, can support or constrain self-determination depending on design choices [30]. Other empirical findings demonstrate that intrinsic motivation, study interest, and self-determined extrinsic motivation correlate positively with perceived autonomy support, competence support, instructional quality, relevance of content, and clarity of requirements [31]. These insights suggest that blended learning environments have the potential to support the psychological needs central to SDT. However, despite the theoretical compatibility between SDT and blended learning, only a limited number of studies have explicitly examined how self-determination influences outcomes within blended learning contexts [32]. This gap highlights the need for further research that links blended learning DPs with adult learners' self-determination.

3 Method

3.1 Rationale for a Design Science Approach

The goal of this study is to understand how blended learning environments can be designed to better support learners' self-determination and to derive actionable DPs for professional learning programs. Because this goal involves both understanding a complex educational problem and shaping a solution that is grounded in user needs, DSR is an appropriate methodological approach. DSR is widely recognized for its ability to generate prescriptive knowledge in the form of DPs, artefacts, and interventions that address real-world problems [33]. In contrast to purely descriptive approaches, DSR combines rigor from the knowledge base with relevance from authentic contexts [34]. This makes DSR particularly suitable for educational innovation, where technological, pedagogical, and motivational factors interact dynamically [35]. Adopting this perspective ensures that the DPs emerging from this study are not only theoretically sound but also directly aligned with the needs, constraints, and expectations found in the professional learning context under investigation. The ethical review board of the researchers' university approved the approach.

3.2 Empirical Foundation and Scientific Knowledge

To develop a rich and evidence-based understanding of the problem space, the study triangulated multiple qualitative and quantitative data sources. This aligns with [36] emphasis on comprehensive problem identification through multi-perspective insights. First, individual interviews with 11 learners working in the public sector captured learners' experiences, perceptions of autonomy and competence support, motivational challenges, and expectations for improvement (total of 143 min). These learners also participated in a short questionnaire about their perceived level of autonomy, competence, relatedness, motivation, and satisfaction with their current learning environment based on established scales by [10]. Second, two expert interviews, conducted with educational support and programme management, contributed institutional and pedagogical perspectives. These conversations clarified operational constraints, programme-level priorities, and interpretations of learner needs. Third, a design workshop with teachers served as a collaborative space to explore design ideas and validate early assumptions about potential improvements. The workshop played an important role in assessing the feasibility and relevance of emerging DPs at an early stage. Together, these data sources formed a robust empirical basis for defining the problem context and identifying user requirements. Their triangulation ensured that the resulting problem understanding was well-grounded, multifaceted, and aligned with DSR expectations for rigorous relevance-cycle activities.

In parallel with the empirical investigation, an extensive literature review informed the rigor cycle. The literature provided established constructs and evidence against which empirical findings were interpreted. Drawing on [33]'s theory-for-design approach, the literature served to frame the theoretical underpinnings of autonomy, competence, and relatedness support, to identify designable elements that could influence motivational processes in blended settings, and highlight research gaps, particularly the limited application of SDT to blended professional learning contexts [32].

3.3 Development and Preliminary Validation

Based on insights from the relevance and rigor cycles, an initial set of DPs was formulated. These principles aim to enhance learners' self-determination by improving autonomy-supportive features, competence scaffolding, and socially connected learning elements in the blended environment. The design cycle remains a work in progress, with further iterations planned to strengthen both the theoretical robustness and practical applicability of the principles. So far, there have been two validation sessions with other teachers and programme management. The next sessions will assess clarity, usefulness, feasibility, and alignment with context-specific constraints.

4 Results

4.1 Problem Identification and Objectives of Solution

The problem space was defined by integrating existing literature, conceptual foundations, and empirical insights from the learner context. The course under investigation serves professional learners (i.e., mid-career public-sector practitioners who combine full-time employment with academic study). These learners bring substantial practice experience, yet also face structural constraints such as limited time, varying levels of prior knowledge, and a strong expectation that learning activities must be immediately relevant to their work. These conditions make their motivational needs central to successful learning design. Through the methods described above, the researchers find that learners in the current blended course experience motivational barriers stemming from unclear structure, insufficient conceptual scaffolding, limited opportunities for applied learning, and weak alignment between online and in-person components. These issues reduce autonomy, competence, and relatedness, which are the core drivers of intrinsic motivation according to SDT. Therefore, the existing blended learning environment is insufficient to support sustained engagement and effective learning for this group.

The objective of this DSR project is to design and evaluate a blended learning environment that enhances the self-determination of professional learners. The solution aims to change the user behavior and support autonomy through clear structure and flexible pathways, competence through scaffolding and applied activities, and relatedness through an authentic public-sector context and alignment with real-world tasks. These objectives are operationalized in the development of a prototype and a set of five DPs guiding its structure and content.

4.2 Design and Development (Artifact)

4.2.1 User Requirements (UR)

To specify the problem and derive design requirements, we combined empirical and theoretical sources. Empirically, we drew on a learner survey, a qualitative needs analysis, and 11 semi-structured interviews with professional learners enrolled in the course. The results highlighted several recurrent issues: difficulty finding materials and navigating the online environment; uncertainty about which content was essential versus optional; insufficient conceptual clarity and limited explanation of theory interactions; desire for more applied, challenging activities to build competence; limited connection between online preparation and public-sector practice; and a need for time to process content before application. Survey responses on motivational factors revealed the lowest evaluation of perceived autonomy, followed by relatedness, competence, and motivation and satisfaction. These findings suggest that the main challenge is not simply content provision, but the design of an IS-supported learning environment that reduces friction, supports self-direction, and strengthens motivational needs.

4.2.2 Literature Requirements (LR)

The motivational challenges in blended learning environments can be understood through complementary theoretical perspectives. SDT [9, 10] provides a central explanatory lens. SDT posits that sustained intrinsic motivation depends on the fulfillment of three psychological needs: autonomy, competence, and relatedness. In blended contexts, autonomy is expressed through flexible access and control over pacing; competence through structured scaffolding and opportunities to apply knowledge; and relatedness through meaningful connections to professional practice and learning communities. Further complementary theories reinforce this perspective. Cognitive Load Theory [37] highlights the importance of reducing extraneous load through clear organization and conceptual clarity. Adult learning theory [38] emphasizes self-directedness, problem-orientation, and relevance to practice, which are the key characteristics of professional learners. Situated learning [39] and transfer of learning frameworks [40] underline the need for authentic tasks connected to real-world contexts. Together, these foundations frame the problem as one of designing a blended environment that intentionally supports motivation, cognitive processing, and professional relevance.

4.2.3 Design Principles

Based on the requirements, we designed five DPs (see Fig. 1). **DP1 emphasizes the importance of a transparent and accessible learning structure in the blended environment.** Professional learners often balance demanding schedules and require immediate clarity regarding where to find materials, how modules are organized, and what is expected in each learning step. Clear navigation, consistent module structures, and flexible access to resources reduce extraneous cognitive load [37], allowing learners to invest their mental resources in meaningful learning rather than searching for information. Such a structure supports autonomy, as learners can navigate at their own pace with fewer procedural barriers [9]. It also prevents frustration and confusion that undermine intrinsic motivation.

DP2 addresses the need for conceptual clarity, particularly when learners have diverse levels of prior knowledge. By distinguishing foundational from optional content and illustrating how theories relate, the learning design provides the scaffolding necessary for building robust mental models. Cognitive Load Theory supports this approach by showing that conceptual structures help manage intrinsic load and facilitate schema construction [41]. From a motivational perspective, such scaffolding enhances competence, one of SDT's core psychological needs. When learners understand what is essential and how ideas connect, they feel more capable of engaging with complex material. Professional learners benefit especially from this structure, as it allows them to efficiently orient themselves regardless of their background, and gradually deepen understanding through optional extensions.

DP3 promotes the design of learning activities that go beyond passive consumption to encourage meaningful engagement. Active learning approaches, such as applied quizzes, problem-based tasks, and scenario-based challenges, are supported by research demonstrating that learners achieve deeper understanding when they actively apply concepts [42]. For professional learners, challenging and applied tasks are central to maintaining engagement because they connect directly to their desire for mastery and practical relevance. Within SDT, these activities strengthen the feeling of competence by offering immediate opportunities to practice and receive feedback. They also increase persistence and intrinsic motivation by turning abstract theory into usable knowledge. DP3 ensures that the learning environment not only informs but also enables learners to perform.

DP4 ensures relevance and is an important driver of motivation for professional learners. Grounding tasks, examples, and cases in the public-sector context provides authenticity and supports transfer of learning [39, 40]. When online tasks mirror real-world decision-making or align directly with assessment tasks, learners can clearly see the value and applicability of the material. In SDT terms, contextual relevance fosters relatedness, as learners feel connected to their professional identity and community. It also supports autonomy, because tasks feel meaningful rather than imposed.

DP5 focuses on the temporal and cognitive flow of learning. Professional learners often struggle with time constraints and benefit from a journey that explicitly guides when to watch, reflect, practice, and prepare. Structuring learning to provide time for conceptual digestion, followed by opportunities for application, aligns with the principles of the Experiential Learning Cycle [42]. A well-sequenced journey, such as moving from micro-lecture to reflection, application, to in-class activities, creates a predictable rhythm. This supports competence by allowing learners to build mastery gradually, and autonomy by making the sequence manageable. This ensures that learners experience learning as a coherent process rather than a fragmented set of tasks.

Overall, the DPs extend beyond generic blended learning recommendations because they are explicitly grounded in SDT and tailored to the context of professional, mid-career learners. Rather than merely aligning with autonomy, competence, and relatedness, they theorize how specific design features within a Canvas-based IS artifact can reduce motivational barriers, support psychological needs, and improve the blended learning experience.

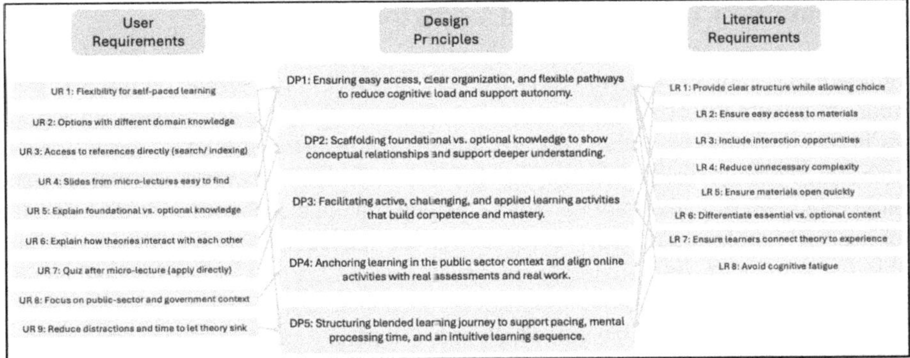

Fig. 1. Developed DPs from user and literature requirements.

4.3 Expected Demonstration and Evaluation

The planned demonstration focuses on translating the five DPs into a functional prototype of a blended learning environment implemented in Canvas. The artifact is conceptualized as a configurable and modular Canvas course prototype rather than a fully developed course. It includes: (1) a transparent module structure with clear navigation, standardized layouts, and flexible access to materials (DP1); (2) conceptual scaffolding through visual theory maps, "core versus optional" content distinctions, and explanatory overviews (DP2); (3) applied quizzes, scenario-based exercises, and reflective tasks that promote active engagement and mastery (DP3); (4) authentic public-sector cases and alignment between online preparation, in-class activities, and assessment tasks (DP4); and (5) a sequenced learning journey that structures preparation, reflection, application, and discussion across time (DP5). In this sense, the prototype represents a proof-of-concept IS artifact that demonstrates how specific Canvas functionalities can be configured to support autonomy, competence, and relatedness in blended learning for professional learners.

Due to the preliminary nature of the research, the evaluation will follow a combined ex-ante and ex-post strategy [33], integrating expert feedback prior to full implementation and user feedback after prototype use. Key evaluation criteria are theoretical validity, completeness, coherence, and feasibility and implementability [43]. A second evaluation phase takes place after learners interact with the prototype in an authentic course context. The evaluation is expected to yield insights into which DPs most strongly support autonomy, competence, and relatedness; whether the conceptual scaffolding (DP2) effectively reduces cognitive load; how well applied activities and public-sector alignment (DP3 and DP4) enhance perceived relevance; whether the structured pacing and flow (DP5) supports learners' time management and mental processing; and areas where navigation, content presentation, or alignment may require refinement. Results from expert interviews may lead to theoretical refinements, while user surveys and interviews will inform practical adjustments to structure, content, and sequencing. The iterative combination of ex-ante and ex-post evaluation will thus support both the rigor and relevance of the developing artifact.

5 Preliminary Discussion and Contribution

Although this study is still in the early stages of the DSR cycle, several preliminary contributions to both theory and practice are emerging. The primary theoretical contribution lies in the development of five DPs that articulate how blended learning environments can be intentionally structured to support the self-determination of professional learners. These principles extend existing design knowledge on blended learning [4, 15] by focusing explicitly on how autonomy, competence, and relatedness can be cultivated within digital learning pathways. Rather than offering isolated features or instructional tactics, the emerging design knowledge proposes a conceptual design that outlines how structure, scaffolding, contextualization, challenge, and pacing can be included in a coherent learner journey.

This conceptual design has the potential to guide future blended learning interventions both within this program and in other professional learning settings. Because professional learners often balance work responsibilities with self-paced study, the principles may generalize to adjacent contexts such as executive education, continuing professional development, and vocational upskilling programs. As the artifact evolves, the DPs may be further refined into testable mechanisms or mid-range theories explaining why and how motivationally supportive blended learning works for professionals.

On the practical level, the study advances understanding of how to meaningfully redesign blended learning environments to address real learner frustrations and motivational challenges. The initial problem analysis surfaced key barriers and problems identified, including unclear structure, overloaded cognitive demands, weak linkage to practice, and limited opportunities for application, which many professional learners frequently encounter but which are rarely addressed holistically. By translating these insights into actionable DPs and, subsequently, into a prototype, the project offers a structured pathway for improving autonomy, competence, and engagement. Educators can apply these early insights to create more motivating, relevant, and manageable online learning experiences that better fit the realities of working professionals.

As a preliminary study, the findings remain limited by the narrow scope of early user input, which currently includes feedback from only two students. Additionally, the DPs have not yet been implemented or empirically tested, and the theorized motivational effects therefore remain hypothetical. The current conceptual design may need to be adapted or extended once expert evaluations and learner data provide clearer insight into feasibility, usability, and motivational impact. As the DSR cycle progresses, these next steps will help transform preliminary insights into robust design knowledge capable of guiding the creation of motivationally supportive blended learning environments across diverse professional settings.

6 Conclusion and Next Steps

This preliminary stage of the DSR project has clarified the core problem facing professional learners in the blended learning course: unclear structure, limited conceptual scaffolding, insufficient opportunities for applied learning, and weak alignment with professional practice. These issues hinder autonomy, competence, and relatedness, underscoring the need for a motivationally supportive blended learning environment grounded in SDT. Based on the theoretical grounding and early feedback from two students, five DPs were formulated to guide the redesign. The initial feedback indicates that the direction is appropriate and that learners value a clearer structure, stronger theoretical framing, and consolidated access to all essential information. The next steps involve building a Canvas prototype that operationalizes these DPs and conducting an ex-ante evaluation through expert interviews. This will be followed by an ex-post evaluation with learners using surveys and qualitative feedback to assess usability, motivation, and perceived relevance. The findings will inform iterative refinement of the artifact and contribute to developing actionable design knowledge for blended learning environments that enhance the self-determination of professional learners.

Acknowledgments. I would like to thank the Professional Learning & Development Centre at the University of Twente and the participants of the post-academic programme. I am also grateful for the support of the Center for Educational Learning and Teaching during my SUTQ trajectory.

Disclosure of Interests. The authors have no competing interests to declare that are relevant to the content of this article.

References

1. Laal, M.: Benefits of lifelong learning. Procedia Soc. Behav. Sci. **46**, 4268–4272 (2012)
2. Freise, L., Ritz, E., Rietsche, R., Beitinger, G., Leimeister, J. M.: How Siemens empowered workforce re- and upskilling through digital learning. MIS Quarterly Executive **24**(3) (2025)
3. Kara, M., Erdogdu, F., Kokoç, M., Cagiltay, K.: Challenges faced by adult learners in online distance education: A literature review. Open Praxis **11**(1), 5–22 (2019)
4. Pei, L., Poortman, C., Schildkamp, K., Benes, N.: Teachers' and students' perceptions of a sense of community in blended education. Educ. Inf. Technol. **29**(2), 2117–2155 (2024)
5. McKenna, K., Gupta, K., Kaiser, L., Lopes, T., Zarestky, J.: Blended learning: Balancing the best of both worlds for adult learners. Adult Learning **31**(4), 139–149 (2020)
6. Gravani, M.N.: Adult learning in a distance education context: Theoretical and methodological challenges. Int. J. Lifelong Educ. **34**(2), 172–193 (2015)
7. Strecker, S., Kundisch, D., Lehner, F., Leimeister, J.M., Schubert, P.: Higher education and the opportunities and challenges of educational technology. Bus. Inf. Syst. Eng. **60**(2), 181–189 (2018)
8. Dang, Y.M., Zhang, Y.G., Ravindran, S., Osmonbekov, T.: Examining student satisfaction and gender differences in technology-supported, blended learning. J. Inf. Syst. Educ. **27**(2), 119–130 (2016)
9. Deci, E.L., Ryan, R.M.: Motivation and lifelong learning. Educ. Psychol. **26**(2), 117–127 (1991)

10. Deci, E.L., Olafsen, A.H., Ryan, R.M.: Self-determination theory in work organizations: The state of a science. Annu. Rev. Organ. Psych. Organ. Behav. **4**, 19–43 (2017)

11. Garrison, D.R., Kanuka, H.: Blended learning: Uncovering its transformative potential in higher education. The Internet and Higher Education **7**(2), 95–105 (2004)

12. Gribbins, M.L., Hadidi, R., Urbaczewski, A., Vician, C.: Technology-enhanced learning in blended learning environments. Comm. AIS **20**(1), 46 (2007)

13. Chai, C.S., Kong, S.C.: Professional learning for 21st century education. J. Comp. Educ. **4**(1), 1–4 (2017)

14. Janson, A., Söllner, M., Leimeister, J.M.: Individual appropriation of learning management systems. AIS Trans. Human-Comp. Interact. **9**(3), 173–201 (2017)

15. Lai, M., Lam, K.M., Lim, C.P.: Design principles for the blend in blended learning. Teach. High. Educ. **21**(6), 716–729 (2016)

16. Bitzer, P., Söllner, M., Leimeister, J.M.: Design principles for high-performance blended learning services delivery. Bus. Inf. Syst. Eng. **58**(2), 135–149 (2016)

17. Diep, A.N., Zhu, C., Cocquyt, C., De Greef, M., Vanwing, T.: Adult learners' needs in online and blended learning. Australian J. Adult Learn. **59**(2), 223–253 (2019)

18. Merriam, S.B.: Adult learning theory for the twenty-first century. New Directions for Adult and Continuing Education (119), 93–98 (2008)

19. Zhang, J., Huang, Y., Wu, F., Kan, W., Zhu, X.: Scaling up online professional development through institution-initiated blended learning programs in higher education. The Internet and Higher Education **65** (2025)

20. Hansman, C.: Context-based adult learning. New Directions for Adult & Continuing Education (2001)

21. Laal, M., Salamati, P.: Lifelong learning; why do we need it? Procedia Soc. Behav. Sci. **31**, 399–403 (2012)

22. McCombs, B.L.: Motivation and lifelong learning. Educ. Psychol. **26**(2), 117–127 (1991)

23. Khoo, E., Berryman, M.: Blended professional learning. Asia Pacific J. Educ., 1–16 (2025)

24. Boyer, S.L., Edmondson, D.R., Artis, A.B., Fleming, D.: Self-directed learning. J. Mark. Educ. **36**(1), 20–32 (2014)

25. Zhang, G., Dang, M., Amer, B., Trainor, K.: Who favor blended learning more: Men or women? (2018)

26. Guay, F., Ratelle, C.F., Chanal, J.: Optimal learning in optimal contexts. Can. Psychol. **49**(3), 233–240 (2008)

27. Ryan, R.M.: The nature of the self in autonomy and relatedness. In: The Self: Interdisciplinary Approaches, pp. 208–238. Springer (1991)

28. Rigby, C.S., Deci, E.L., Patrick, B.C., Ryan, R.M.: Beyond the intrinsic–extrinsic dichotomy. Motiv. Emot. **16**(3), 165–185 (1992)

29. George-Walker, L.D., Keeffe, M.: Self-determined blended learning. High. Educ. Res. Dev. **29**(1), 1–13 (2010)

30. Hsu, H.C.K., Wang, C.V., Levesque-Bristol, C.: Impact of self-determination theory on learning outcomes. Educ. Inf. Technol. **24**(3), 2159–2174 (2019)

31. Müller, F.H., Louw, J.: Learning environment, motivation and interest. South African J. Psychol. **34**(2), 169–190 (2004)

32. Joo, Y.J., Lim, K.Y., Han, S.Y., Ham, Y.K., Kang, A.: Effects of self-determination on learning outcomes in blended learning (2013)

33. Gregor, S., Hevner, A.R.: Positioning and presenting design science research. MIS Q. **37**(2), 337–355 (2013)

34. Peffers, K., Tuunanen, T., Rothenberger, M.A., Chatterjee, S.: A design science research methodology. J. Manag. Inf. Syst. **24**(3), 45–77 (2007)

35. Sein, M.K., Henfridsson, O., Purao, S., Rossi, M., Lindgren, R.: Action design research. MIS Q. **35**(1), 37–56 (2011)

36. Vom Brocke, J., Maedche, A.: The DSR grid. Electron. Mark. **29**, 379–385 (2019)
37. Sweller, J., Ayres, P., Kalyuga, S.: Cognitive Load Theory. Springer (2011)
38. Knowles, M. S.: Andragogy in Action. Jossey-Bass (1984)
39. Lave, J., Wenger, E.: Situated Learning. Cambridge University Press (1991)
40. Bransford, J., Brown, A., Cocking, R.: How People Learn. National Academies Press (2000)
41. Mayer, R.: Multimedia Learning. Cambridge University Press (2009)
42. Kolb, D.A.: Experiential Learning. FT Press (1984)
43. Bichler, M.: Design science in information systems research. Wirtschaftsinformatik **48**(2), 133–135 (2006). https://doi.org/10.1007/s11576-006-0028-8

The Future of Financial Services

AI-Enabled Automation of High-Risk Decision-Making Processes

Pascal Nemecek$^{(\boxtimes)}$, Tobias Zimmermann , Sandro Franzoi , and Jan vom Brocke

University of Münster, Münster, Germany
`{pascal.nemecek,zimmermann.tobias,sandro.franzoi,`
`jan.vom.brocke}@uni-muenster.de`

Abstract. Intelligent Process Automation (IPA) offers strong potential for automating business processes through the application of Artificial Intelligence (AI). However, applying AI to high-risk decision-making processes remains challenging due to regulatory requirements as well as technological and organizational factors. In particular, the EU AI Act imposes strict requirements on human oversight, thereby limiting the potential for automation in high-risk environments. In this research-in-progress paper, we address this gap by conducting an Echeloned Design Science Research (^{e}DSR) project in collaboration with a financial institution to design an AI system for automating the loan approval process. Our problem analysis identifies several challenges, including time-critical and complex decision-making as well as regulatory requirements such as mandatory human oversight, decision justification, accountability, and data privacy. Based on this, we derive validated design objectives and requirements, and we position risk mitigation as a core design challenge. We also provide an outlook for the subsequent echelon types to continue this research project.

Keywords: Intelligent Process Automation · Design Science Research · High-Risk Decision-Making · Artificial Intelligence · EU AI Act

1   Introduction

The rapid advancement of AI enables new decision automation and decision support use cases in the financial sector that impact the banking operating model [9,19]. The implementation of AI systems within IPA initiatives to automate business processes can improve customer experience and operational efficiency, thereby positively impacting financial performance [30]. For example, automating a retail loan approval process can reduce cycle times and improve the quality of loan approval decisions [16].

However, core business processes in the financial sector, such as loan approval, involve high-risk decision-making [26]. This substantially increases the challenges of AI adoption in the banking industry, including organizational, regulatory, and technological factors [19,20]. The EU AI Act reinforces these challenges by imposing requirements on transparency, traceability, human oversight, and the possibility of intervention in high-risk AI systems [31]. Consequently, the design of AI-enabled decision-making processes in such contexts must reconcile automation with human oversight. This reflects the view of Raisch and Krakowski [24], who distinguish between automation, in which machines take over a human task, and augmentation, in which humans collaborate with machines, while arguing that both forms of AI application are not mutually exclusive but interdependent, creating a paradoxical tension. Accordingly, the successful adoption of AI in high-risk decision-making is a sociotechnical design problem, rather than merely a technical or legal challenge, as organizations must define which activities are delegated to AI, which require human judgment, and how both interact within the decision process.

Prior research addresses AI-enabled automation [1,5], the regulatory environment for high-risk AI systems [12,28], and AI applications in financial decision-making [16]. However, the existing research streams remain fragmented with regard to the sociotechnical design knowledge of high-risk decision-making processes in which AI systems automate decision activities while remaining compliant with regulatory constraints such as human oversight [7,28]. We aim to contribute to this research gap by addressing the following research objective: *Design an AI-enabled system to automate high-risk decision-making processes in the financial sector.*

To address this research objective, we collaborated with a large German financial institution to develop an artifact for an automated loan approval process, a high-volume business process with limited time to assess each application. Due to the complex nature of this endeavor, we relied on the ᵉDSR [29] approach for conducting multiple iterations per ᵉDSR echelon type and early validations of the problem statement and the design objectives (DOs) and requirements (DRs).

The paper is structured as follows. Section 2 provides an overview of existing work in the research streams of AI-enabled process automation and the use of AI in high-risk decision-making. Section 3 explains our approach to the ᵉDSR methodology. Next, we present the problem analysis iterations in Sect. 4 and those for the objectives and requirements definition in Sect. 5. Finally, in Sect. 6, we discuss our research progress, contributions, and limitations, and provide an outlook on future research in Sect. 7.

2   Research Background

With the rise of AI, the research stream of IPA has emerged within the fields of workflow automation and robotic process automation [5]. The use of AI models enables the automation of processes that involve complex decision-making or advanced cognitive analysis [5], moving beyond simple, rule-based process activities. Recent advances in AI, particularly through large language models, further extend the scope of automation in business process management by enabling higher-level process understanding tasks, such as detecting inconsistencies across process representations and supporting coherence in process documentation [27], as well as integrating process knowledge from heterogeneous sources [10].

These developments broaden the range of process activities that can be supported or automated by AI. When such AI models are applied to decision-making processes that involve substantial damage potential, such as affecting individuals' fundamental rights, they are classified as high-risk AI systems [28]. Accordingly, this paper builds on the research stream of AI governance, which focuses on the ethically responsible use of AI, including transparency, fairness, non-maleficence, accountability, and privacy [13].

In the EU, the principles of AI governance have been legally formalized in the EU AI Act [23]. For high-risk AI systems, the AI Act specifies technical and organizational measures. Organizational measures include risk management systems, governance mechanisms, and comprehensive documentation of model training, architecture, and instructions for use to ensure transparency [23]. Technical requirements include logging and monitoring capabilities, measures against adversarial attacks and data poisoning, and measures to support robustness and accuracy [15]. Moreover, the AI Act mandates suitable interfaces to enable effective human oversight under Article 14 [28]. Human reviewers need a sufficient understanding of the technology and its decision outcomes [12]. Thus, the design of AI systems must support effective human oversight in practice. Human oversight of AI predictions, therefore, involves a dimension of trust, as human reviewers at least partially rely on the AI system.

IS trust research focuses on human–technology configurations characterized by uncertainty, a lack of total user control, and dependence on technology [21]. Trust in a specific technology is influenced by three beliefs: functionality, helpfulness, and reliability [21]. However, trust in technology needs to be calibrated appropriately to ensure that the user's trust in the AI system aligns with the AI system's actual trustworthiness, meaning its true capabilities [33]. Perceived trustworthiness is shaped not only by the AI system's reliability, but also by design elements such as explanations and confidence cues [33]. Due to the black-box design of many Machine Learning (ML) techniques, the reasoning underlying their decisions is not directly accessible to humans [1]. Explainable AI (XAI) techniques address this challenge by supporting human understanding of how a prediction model arrived at its decision [3], while tailoring such explanations to human overseers requires further investigation, as explanation requirements depend on users' background and relationship to the system [22].

3   Methodology

To address our research objective, we followed the eDSR methodology, which decomposes the Design Science Research (DSR) process into five echelon types, each comprising design/analysis and validation activities. These echelon types are (i) problem analysis, (ii) definition of objectives and requirements, (iii) design and development, (iv) demonstration, and (v) evaluation [29]. We chose this inquiry approach because it reflects the non-linear structure of complex design endeavors and enables us to validate hypotheses early in our DSR project. Consequently, we can articulate truth statements after completing iterative instantiation cycles for each echelon type, even before completing a full DSR cycle.

This research-in-progress paper focuses on the first and second ^eDSR stages, resulting in a validated problem statement and the validated objectives and requirements definition. The individual iterations for the problem analysis, as well as the objectives and requirements definition echelon type and all echelon instances are depicted in Fig. 1 and further described in the subsequent sections.

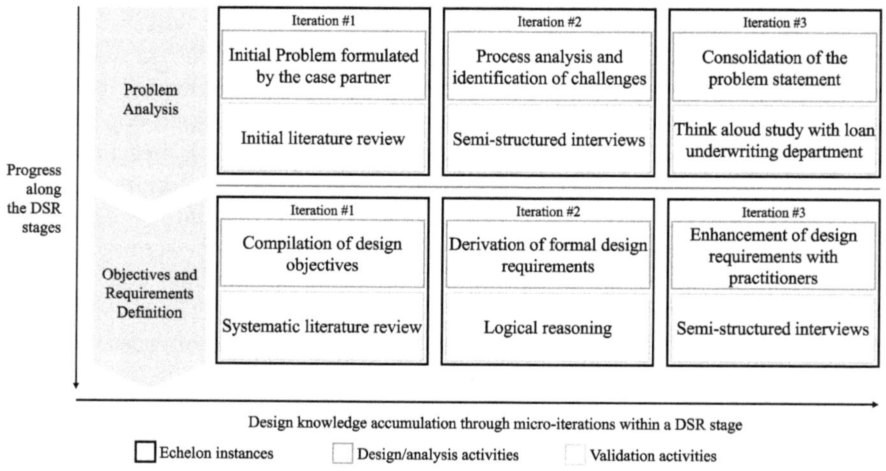

Fig. 1. Hierarchical depiction of instantiated echelons per ^eDSR layer

4   Problem Analysis

Following the ^eDSR methodology, the intermediate artifact of the problem analysis echelon is a validated problem statement [29]. During the first iteration, we developed a preliminary problem statement through an initial literature-based exploration of the challenges associated with AI-enabled automation of high-risk processes, particularly in the financial sector. Previous research has uncovered external challenges, such as regulatory constraints, and internal challenges, including organizational, economic, and technical factors [14,31]. The financial sector is subject to a variety of regulatory requirements, stress tests, and guidelines issued by supervising authorities. AI systems are no exception and are further constrained by the AI Act [12,28]. Organizational factors include the capabilities and governance structures to develop, integrate, and effectively use AI systems [14,20]. The implementation of AI systems is further limited by resource constraints, as training ML models is costly and suitable training data is often scarce. The latter is affected by unstructured data and by data quality issues regarding correctness and completeness [14].

To gain a deeper understanding of the practical challenges involved, we conducted a second iteration of the problem analysis based on eight semi-structured interviews with practitioners from the case organization. The interview participants included two loan underwriters, three process managers, and three legal experts, with varying levels of professional experience (e.g., junior to senior), representing a range of functional perspectives. They were selected because they either contribute operationally to loan approval decisions or shape the organizational, legal, and process-related conditions for these decisions. The interview transcripts were analyzed thematically, using an inductive and semantic approach [4]. This iteration aimed to assess whether the initially identified challenges were perceived as relevant in practice and to uncover additional facets of the problem that emerged in daily decision-making. Across interviews, practitioners discussed both challenges specific to the use of AI in high-risk decision-making contexts and process-related aspects in the loan approval process at the case organization.

The participants mentioned three common themes that challenge the implementation of AI systems to automate high-risk decision-making processes. As the first theme, the interviews revealed a strong awareness of regulatory constraints on the use of high-risk AI systems, particularly with respect to data protection, human oversight, and governance. Participants addressed data privacy laws (in particular, the EU GDPR) that impact model training and decision-making operations. AI training could constitute a restricted form of data use under data protection regulations. Participants also stated that the AI Act's requirement of human oversight limits the potential for automation in high-risk decision-making processes, as such oversight must remain rigorous and effective. Regarding governance, participants referred to risk management, documentation, and control mechanisms to fulfill the accountability and traceability requirements of the AI Act and other sector-specific regulations. The second theme addresses model-related challenges. Interviewees pointed to the black-box nature of AI models, characterized by limited transparency of decision logic and insufficient justification for decisions. Participants also noted that some models are susceptible to manipulative inputs, which may lead to incorrect decisions. The third theme encompassed organizational challenges related to the human-machine interaction. Participants emphasized that too many false-positive decisions would overload human oversight personnel. In relation to this issue, one participant identified the automation bias as a potential source of errors in human oversight. Compared to the initial problem hypothesis, we could validate regulatory, technical, and organizational factors during the second iteration. However, the interviewees did not emphasize economic challenges related to AI adoption. Instead, they viewed AI-enabled process automation as an investment and justified it by the current problem situation, characterized by several process-related aspects.

In the third iteration, we aimed to validate our problem statement through the perspective of the daily activities of the loan underwriters. Therefore, we conducted a think-aloud study to observe how the previously identified challenges manifest during actual decision-making activities under real-life conditions. The study covered a limited set of decision cases reflecting typical decision situations and focused on validating our understanding of the problem situation at the case organization. It was conducted with a loan underwriter who processed credit applications while verbalizing the process activities, decisions, and considerations. Our observations focused on interactions with operational application systems, information use, and decision rationales. The field study corroborated the interview findings by illustrating how process complexity, heterogeneous information sources within a credit application, and time pressure shape everyday decision-making. We also observed that decisions are determined by factual data from the loan application and by fixed rules for credit approval, as set by formal guidelines and legal requirements, but include a risk-benefit assessment based on the loan underwriter's experience, particularly in critical decisions. It is difficult to capture this implicit knowledge comprehensively within a rule-based decision-making system.

Subsequently, we condensed a validated problem statement: *Organizations face the challenge of automating high-risk decision-making processes to improve efficiency and decision quality in complex, time-critical operational decisions that rely partly on implicit human expertise. However, regulatory requirements constitute central design conditions that constrain the scope of automation: first, effective human oversight and control mechanisms are mandatory. Second, decisions must always be justified, even when using black-box AI models. Third, decisions must be fair and unbiased, which may be threatened by limited data quality or imbalances. Fourth, accountability and traceability must be ensured during the prescribed retention period. Fifth, data privacy regulations restrict the use of personally identifiable information.*

5   Objectives and Requirements Definition

The second echelon yields validated design objectives and requirements. According to Tuunanen et al. [29], the validation criteria include fit to the validated problem statement, applicability, completeness, and feasibility. In the first iteration, we conducted a systematic literature review focused on high-risk decision-making or AI systems. We identified relevant articles by conducting a keyword search in Scopus and then snowballing to expand the literature base further. Finally, we included 25 articles and derived seven DOs for high-risk AI systems to automate high-risk decision-making processes.

For reliable decision-making automation and trust in the AI system, the underlying prediction model would need to achieve high predictive performance [6] and reduce misclassification risks, as these would have severe legal and financial consequences [32]. Accordingly, **DO1** is to *automate decision-making with an efficient, fast, and accurate model that incorporates all relevant information from the credit application.* The AI model is trained on historical decisions to

Table 1. Design Objectives and related Design Requirements

DO	Derived Design Requirements
DO1	**DR1.1**: Automated decisions must be made with sufficiently low latency **DR1.2**: Decisions must achieve high prediction accuracy
DO2	**DR2.1**: Use only relevant and permissible data for training and operations **DR2.2**: Training data must not contain systematic biases or missing values
DO3	**DR3.1**: Provide decision-specific explanations identifying the most influential input features **DR3.2**: The decision logic must be comprehensible to human stakeholders **DR3.3**: Provide confidence indicators and known limitations to support appropriate trust calibration by human reviewers
DO4	**DR4.1**: Persist decision outcomes for the required retention period **DR4.2**: Assign a clearly identifiable human overseer to each decision outcome **DR4.3**: Maintain traceability of system versions, model versions, and associated human oversight for each decision during the retention period
DO5	**DR5.1**: Ensure that decisions with legal effects for natural persons are always subject to human review **DR5.2**: Allow human overseers to intervene or halt the decision process **DR5.3**: Provide an overview of pending decisions and their processing status to support oversight prioritization **DR5.4**: Integrate clearly defined handover points between automated processing and human oversight **DR5.5**: Include measures to mitigate automation bias in human oversight
DO6	**DR6.1**: Provide mechanisms to identify model degradation or drift over time **DR6.2**: Ensure robustness against manipulative input data
DO7	**DR7.1**: Minimize the processing of personally identifiable information and support anonymization or pseudonymization

capture past decision patterns, without explicitly formalizing the loan underwriters' expert knowledge. Closely related to decision quality, **DO2** aims to *achieve fairness in decision-making by fulfilling ethical requirements, such as mitigating systematic decision biases* [15,28]. In addition, the system needs to *provide sufficient justification for each decision* (**DO3**). This is important because the stakeholders need to understand why and how a decision was made [2,15]. Besides the individual decision, the overall decision logic of the AI system must also be comprehensible [28]. This justification should also support appropriate trust calibration regarding the AI model's decisions, helping to avoid over-trust or under-trust [33]. Decision understandability must be maintained over the long term to ensure accountability [18,25]. Therefore, **DO4** is intended to *ensure post-decision accountability of the AI system and human reviewers*. Human oversight plays a central role in high-risk decision-making, yet prior research cautions that oversight alone does not guarantee safe and effective outcomes [8,11]. Instead, *the interaction between humans and the AI system must be meaningful and ensure a focused review of the decisions* [2,25], which is expressed as **DO5**. Furthermore, the literature highlights the importance of **DO6**, which addresses the *need for a robust prediction model and continuous monitoring of decision outcomes for drift detection and instability* [11,15]. Finally, **DO7** is to *protect sensitive and personal information* [2,25]. Taken together, these DOs address the problem facets described in the validated problem statement: efficiency and decision quality (**DO1, DO6**), effective human oversight and control mechanisms (**DO5**), decision justification (**DO3**), fair and unbiased decisions (**DO2**), accountability and traceability (**DO4**), and data privacy constraints (**DO7**).

Based on the identified DOs, we derived a set of preliminary DRs that operationalize the objectives into concrete and testable system properties (see Table 1). The DRs were developed through several rounds of logical reasoning, combining insights from the validated problem statement and existing design knowledge in the literature. The DRs primarily concern system-level design while also shaping human-AI interaction, as these dimensions are inherently interdependent. To ensure coherence with the validated problem statement, each DR was mapped to one or more specific problem aspects. While **DR1.1** and **DR1.2** define the fundamental capabilities that the AI system needs to fulfill for high-risk decision-making, other requirements are regulatory-driven. Specifically, **DR2.1** and **DR7.1** address data privacy regulations. Additionally, **DR5.1** builds on Article 22 GDPR, which grants data subjects the right not to be subject to solely automated decisions that produce legal effects or similarly significant effects. **DR4.1–4.3**, **DR5.2–5.5**, and **DR6.1** address the requirements of the AI Act, such as human oversight, accountability, and control mechanisms, as well as other regulations (i.e., DORA for resilient IT operations in the financial sector). Further DRs address technical challenges, such as the black-box nature

Table 2. Design Features and related Design Requirements

Design Feature	Related DRs
DF1: Embed a robust AI prediction model into the operational decision workflow to enable low-latency, high-accuracy decision-making	DR1.1, DR1.2, DR6.2
DF2: Implement a data pipeline that enforces high-quality and reduces imbalances or biases	DR2.1, DR2.2
DF3: Provide a decision-centered justification interface to communicate influencing data features and support meaningful human oversight	DR3.1, DR3.2
DF4: Integrate human oversight and the possibility of intervention in the decision process to preserve human agency	DR4.2, DR5.1–DR5.4
DF5: Implement a logging system that captures decision data and human actions during the retention period to ensure accountability and traceability	DR4.1, DR4.3
DF6: Include deliberate friction and trust calibrations to guide human attention and reduce automation bias	DR3.3, DR5.5
DF7: Implement continuous monitoring and drift-detection mechanisms for data distribution, decision quality, and confidence to sustain reliable decision-making	DR6.1
DF8: Embed privacy-by-design in the data pipeline to limit the exposure of personally identifiable information and comply with data privacy regulations	DR7.1

of AI prediction models (**DR3.1–DR3.3**), data quality issues (**DR2.2**), and susceptibility to manipulated input data (**DR6.2**).

In a third iteration, we validated the DRs through four semi-structured interviews with practitioners, including loan underwriters, executives, and legal experts. The interviewees confirmed the relevance of the DRs by explicitly citing regulatory obligations, particularly regarding data privacy, accountability, and human oversight, and considered the proposed set sufficiently complete with respect to the validated problem statement. In addition, they highlighted a central feasibility challenge: the trade-off between rigorous human oversight and automated decision-making. While extensive human review increases legal defensibility and regulatory compliance, it also limits the achievable benefits of automation. An effective solution design must combine these conflicting goals. This implies that the design of the AI system and human-AI interaction should be considered integral to risk mitigation. Building on this perspective, we derived preliminary design features from the DOs and DRs, as shown in Table 2.

6   Discussion

Despite the early project stage, this research-in-progress report contributes to the design knowledge base on high-risk AI systems in the financial sector by articulating a validated problem statement and validated DOs and DRs. Our contributions are threefold. First, we supplement the normative view of high-risk AI systems driven by the impact severity [28]. While regulatory classifications of high-risk AI systems are necessary, they offer limited guidance for system design. Our study addresses this gap by positioning risk mitigation as a design challenge to reduce the probability of harmful outcomes in AI-enabled decision-making automation. These design decisions are linked to the organization's risk appetite. Second, we underscore the importance of human oversight as a configurable design variable rather than a binary design decision. Meaningful oversight depends on information presentation, attention guidance, and effective process integration to address the trade-off between the degree of automation and the rigor of human control. This finding resonates with the growing emphasis on trustworthy AI [17,33] and automation bias in human-AI interaction [18]. Third, we highlight the role of XAI under the AI Act [23], as our DRs consider explainability as an implicit requirement for meaningful human oversight, particularly where black-box models or complex feature constellations limit the transparency of decision-making. However, explanations must be carefully calibrated to balance sufficient informational support with the risk of information overload.

However, we acknowledge some limitations of our study. First, this research-in-progress report presents preliminary design knowledge, with a focus on the first and second echelon types [29]. Our intermediate results have emerged through formative validations only. The proposed designs have not yet been instantiated or summatively evaluated, which limits the conclusiveness of the findings at this stage. Second, our findings are grounded in a single case within the financial sector and are specific to the regulatory environment in Germany and the EU. While our case provides context-specific insights, its transferability to other sectors or regulatory settings may be limited, offering opportunities for future research. Third, our project focuses on standardized, operational decision-making processes. Therefore, our proposed design knowledge may not be directly applicable to strategic or tactical decision-making contexts, which are typically less structured and require different forms of decision-making capabilities. Finally, ongoing developments in the regulatory environment, including the EU Omnibus initiative and evolving interpretations of indeterminate legal concepts, may affect the applicability of our design knowledge over time.

7   Outlook

This research-in-progress report presents the intermediate results of an ^{e}DSR project focusing on the validated problem statement and objectives and requirements definition for high-risk AI-enabled decision-making processes. Building on the achieved design knowledge, ongoing research in collaboration with the case partner will instantiate the artifact in subsequent ^{e}DSR echelons. During the design and development echelon, we plan to develop an AI-based decision-making system that fulfills our DRs. Together with the case partner, we have already acquired training data from past loan applications to train a prediction model. Furthermore, we plan to validate the proof-of-concept using a mixed-methods approach, including quantitative validation of prediction performance and efficiency, as well as semi-structured interviews to assess the effectiveness of the human-AI interface for oversight. During these echelon instantiations, we will abstract design principles from the evaluation results, thereby generating prescriptive design knowledge. Future research will conduct a summative evaluation by observing the instantiated design in real-world operations to provide proof of value.

Disclosure of Interests. The authors have no competing interests to declare regarding this article.

References

1. Afrin, S., Roksana, S., Akram, R.: AI-enhanced robotic process automation: a review of intelligent automation innovations. IEEE Access **13**, 173–197 (2025). https://doi.org/10.1109/ACCESS.2024.3513279
2. Autili, M., De Sanctis, M., Inverardi, P., Pelliccione, P.: Engineering digital systems for humanity: a research roadmap. ACM Trans. Softw. Eng. Methodol. **34**(5), 1–33 (2025). https://doi.org/10.1145/3712006
3. Barredo Arrieta, A., et al.: Explainable artificial intelligence (XAI): concepts, taxonomies, opportunities and challenges toward responsible AI. Inf. Fusion **58**, 82–115 (2020). https://doi.org/10.1016/j.inffus.2019.12.012
4. Braun, V., Clarke, V.: Using thematic analysis in psychology. Qual. Res. Psychol. **3**(2), 77–101 (2006). https://doi.org/10.1191/1478088706qp063oa

5. Chakraborti, T., et al.: From robotic process automation to intelligent process automation. In: Asatiani, A., et al. (eds.) BPM 2020. LNBIP, vol. 393, pp. 215–228. Springer, Cham (2020). https://doi.org/10.1007/978-3-030-58779-6_15

6. Chen, J., et al.: Designing expert-augmented clinical decision support systems to predict mortality risk in ICUs. KI – Künstliche Intelligenz **37**(2-4), 227–236 (2023). https://doi.org/10.1007/s13218-023-00808-7

7. Dietzmann, C., Heines, R., Alt, R.: The convergence of distributed ledger technology and artificial intelligence: an end-to-end reference lending process for financial services. In: Proceedings of the 28th European Conference on Information Systems (ECIS) (2020). https://aisel.aisnet.org/ecis2020_rp/186/

8. Ehsan, U., Liao, Q.V., Passi, S., Riedl, M.O., Daumé, H., III.: Seamful XAI: operationalizing seamful design in explainable AI. Proc. ACM Hum.-Comput. Interact. **8**(CSCW1), 1–29 (2024). https://doi.org/10.1145/3637396

9. Fares, O.H., Butt, I., Lee, S.H.M.: Utilization of artificial intelligence in the banking sector: a systematic literature review. J. Financ. Serv. Mark. **28**, 835–852 (2023). https://doi.org/10.1057/s41264-022-00176-7

10. Franzoi, S., Delwaulle, M., Dyong, J., Schaffner, J., Burger, M., vom Brocke, J.: Using large language models to generate process knowledge from enterprise content. In: Gdowska, K., Gómez-López, M.T., Rehse, J.R. (eds.) Business Process Management Workshops. BPM 2024. Lecture Notes in Business Information Processing, vol. 534, pp. 247–258. Springer, Cham (2025).https://doi.org/10.1007/978-3-031-78666-2_19

11. Heger, A.K., Passi, S., Dhanorkar, S., Kahn, Z., Wang, R., Vorvoreanu, M.: Towards a responsible AI organizational maturity model. Proc. ACM Hum.-Comput. Interact. **9**(7), 1–33 (2025). https://doi.org/10.1145/3757514

12. Hupont, I., Micheli, M., Delipetrev, B., Gómez, E., Garrido, J.S.: Documenting high-risk AI: a European regulatory perspective. Computer **56**(5), 18–27 (2023). https://doi.org/10.1109/MC.2023.3235712

13. Jobin, A., Ienca, M., Vayena, E.: The global landscape of AI ethics guidelines. Nat. Mach. Intell. **1**, 389–399 (2019). https://doi.org/10.1038/s42256-019-0088-2

14. Jöhnk, J., Weißert, M., Wyrtki, K.: Ready or not, AI comes– an interview study of organizational AI readiness factors. Bus. Inf. Syst. Eng. **63**(1), 5–20 (2021). https://doi.org/10.1007/s12599-020-00676-7

15. Kaur, D., Uslu, S., Rittichier, K.J., Durresi, A.: Trustworthy artificial intelligence: a review. ACM Comput. Surv. **55**(2), 39:1–39:38 (2022). https://doi.org/10.1145/3491209

16. Königstorfer, F., Thalmann, S.: Applications of artificial intelligence in commercial banks - a research agenda for behavioral finance. J. Behav. Exp. Financ. **27**, 100352 (2020). https://doi.org/10.1016/j.jbef.2020.100352

17. Langer, M., Lazar, V., Baum, K.: On the complexities of testing for compliance with human oversight requirements in AI regulation. In: Steffen, B. (ed.) Bridging the Gap Between AI and Reality, pp. 160–169. Springer, Cham (2026). https://doi.org/10.1007/978-3-032-07132-3_11

18. Laux, J., Ruschemeier, H.: Automation bias in the AI act: on the legal implications of attempting to de-bias human oversight of AI. Eur. J. Risk Regul. **16**(4), 1519–1534 (2025). https://doi.org/10.1017/err.2025.10033

19. Lazo, M., Ebardo, R.: Artificial intelligence adoption in the banking industry: current state and future prospect. J. Innov. Manag. **11**(3), 54–74 (2023). https://doi.org/10.24840/2183-0606_011.003_0003

20. Malik, S., Garg, M., Thomas, A., Cillo, V., Del Giudice, M.: Exploration and prioritization of crucial factors of artificial intelligence adoption in credit risk scoring: using the fuzzy analytical hierarchical process. Bus. Process. Manag. J. **31**(5), 1703–1735 (2025). https://doi.org/10.1108/BPMJ-09-2024-0886
21. McKnight, D.H., Carter, M., Thatcher, J.B., Clay, P.F.: Trust in a specific technology: an investigation of its components and measures. ACM Trans. Manag. Inf. Syst. **2**(2), 1–25 (2011). https://doi.org/10.1145/1985347.1985353
22. Meza Martínez, M.A., Mädche, A.: Designing interactive explainable AI systems for lay users. In: ICIS 2023 Proceedings (2023). https://aisel.aisnet.org/icis2023/dab_sc/dab_sc/5/
23. Panigutti, C.: The role of explainable AI in the context of the AI act. In: Proceedings of the 2023 ACM Conference on Fairness, Accountability, and Transparency, pp. 1139–1150 (2023). https://doi.org/10.1145/3593013.3594069
24. Raisch, S., Krakowski, S.: Artificial intelligence and management: the automation-augmentation paradox. Acad. Manag. Rev. **46**(1), 192–210 (2021). https://doi.org/10.5465/amr.2018.0072
25. Sanderson, C., et al.: AI ethics principles in practice: perspectives of designers and developers. IEEE Trans. Technol. Soc. **4**(2), 171–187 (2023). https://doi.org/10.1109/TTS.2023.3257303
26. Santomero, A.M.: Commercial bank risk management: an analysis of the process. J. Financ. Serv. Res. **12**(2), 83–115 (1997). https://doi.org/10.1023/A:1007971801810
27. Schulte, M., Franzoi, S., Köhne, F., vom Brocke, J.: Toward LLM-enabled business process coherence checking based on multi-level process documentation. Process Sci. **2**(1), 22 (2025). https://doi.org/10.1007/s44311-025-00024-6
28. Sunyaev, A., et al.: High-risk artificial intelligence. Bus. Inf. Syst. Eng. **67**(6), 981–994 (2025). https://doi.org/10.1007/s12599-025-00942-6
29. Tuunanen, T., Winter, R., vom Brocke, J.: Dealing with complexity in design science research: a methodology using design echelons. MIS Q. **48**(2), 427–458 (2024). https://doi.org/10.25300/MISQ/2023/16700
30. Villar, A.S., Khan, N.: Robotic process automation in banking industry: a case study on Deutsche Bank. J. Bank. Financ. Technol. **5**(1), 71–86 (2021). https://doi.org/10.1007/s42786-021-00030-9
31. Vuković, D.B., Dekpo-Adza, S., Matović, S.: AI integration in financial services: a systematic review of trends and regulatory challenges. Humanit. Soc. Sci. Commun. **12**(1), 562 (2025). https://doi.org/10.1057/s41599-025-04850-8
32. Weinzierl, S., Zilker, S., Zschech, P., Kraus, M., Leibelt, T., Matzner, M.: How risky is my AI system? A method for transparent classification of AI system descriptions by regulated AI risk categories. In: ICIS 2024 Proceedings (2024). https://aisel.aisnet.org/icis2024/data_soc/data_soc/4/
33. Wischnewski, M., Krämer, N., Müller, E.: Measuring and understanding trust calibrations for automated systems: a survey of the state-of-the-art and future directions. In: Proceedings of the 2023 CHI Conference on Human Factors in Computing Systems, pp. 1–16 (2023). https://doi.org/10.1145/3544548.3581197

Future of Data-Driven and AI-Enabled Design

Making Informal Work Visible: Multimodal AI-Enabled Process Discovery in Public-Sector Meetings

Alina Hafner[(✉)] [iD], Mohamed Aziz Ketata [iD], and Holger Wittges [iD]

Information and Technology, Technical University of Munich, TUM School of Computation, Munich, Germany
{alina.hafner,mohamed.aziz.ketata,holger.wittges}@tum.de

Abstract. This research-in-progress paper presents a design science artifact, the Meeting Process Twin, that extends process discovery to meeting-based decision processes using multimodal data. Unlike prior work that either proposes multimodal process mining conceptually or analyzes meeting corpora without process mining integration, this artifact is fully instantiated and produces conformance diagnostics directly from raw meeting recordings. It transforms public-sector meeting recordings and agenda documents into process-relevant event logs, discovers enacted meeting process models, and compares them with their formal, agenda-based counterparts to identify informal or hidden process variants. The design integrates multimodal event extraction, semantic alignment, and process mining, and is instantiated using data from the LocalView Public Meetings Database. It contributes an instantiated artifact, a governance-oriented walkthrough of detected shadow processes, and transferable design knowledge for multimodal process discovery in domains without structured event logs.

Keywords: Business Process Management · Design Science Research · Multimodal Process Mining · Informal Work

1 Introduction

Business Process Management (BPM) aims to improve organizational transparency, efficiency, and compliance by making work processes explicit, analyzable, and governable. Central to this ambition is the availability of accurate representations of how work is actually performed. BPM research emphasizes that explicit process models are a prerequisite for transparency, analysis, and governance, as they make organizational work observable and comparable across instances and contexts (Dumas et al., 2018; vom Brocke et al., 2014). Classical process mining techniques operationalize this goal by discovering and analyzing process models from structured event logs generated by information systems (van Der Aalst, 2016).

However, many organizational processes unfold largely outside transactional information systems. Meetings are a prominent example. They play a central role in coordination, deliberation, and decision-making in both private and public organizations, yet

S. Chatterjee et al. (Eds.): DESRIST 2026, LNCS 16607, pp. 109–120, 2026.
https://doi.org/10.1007/978-3-032-28570-6_9

they rarely generate machine-readable process traces. Instead, meetings are documented through heterogeneous and weakly structured artifacts such as agendas, minutes, transcripts, and video recordings. As a result, the enactment of meeting procedures remains largely invisible to classical process mining, creating blind spots in BPM analysis. In this work, we focus on the procedural meeting process (agenda progression, motions, voting), not the domain processes discussed within agenda items. While meeting minutes intentionally summarize outcomes and key arguments, they do not preserve the temporal structure, repetitions, or interactional dynamics of the meeting process. The artifact is explicitly not intended to document confidential off-record discussions, but to reconstruct the enacted process structure where documentation is intended but structurally incomplete.

From an organizational perspective, meetings often embody a tension between formal procedures and actual practice. While agendas and procedural rules specify how decisions should be made, the enacted meeting behavior frequently involves informal discussions, deviations from the agenda, and procedural shortcuts. Prior research on organizational routines distinguishes between ostensive routines, understood as the abstract, formalized representation of a process, and performative routines, referring to the situated actions through which work is actually carried out (Feldman and Pentland, 2003). Deviations between the two are common and can be both problematic and productive, yet they remain difficult to observe and analyze systematically.

In governance-sensitive contexts such as public administration, this gap is particularly salient. This challenge aligns with public administration research that treats transparency and accountability (Bovens et al., 2014; Grimmelikhuijsen and Meijer, 2014) as central governance mechanisms, but also highlights their trade-offs and limits: disclosure can enable scrutiny and trust, yet information must be interpretable and actionable to be effective (Fung et al., 2007). Public-sector meetings are subject to formal accountability requirements and are often governed by detailed procedural rules, while at the same time relying heavily on interaction, negotiation, and improvisation. Informal practices that emerge during meetings may facilitate decision-making, but they also raise questions of transparency, legitimacy, and compliance. Without systematic means to surface and analyze these practices, organizations risk either ignoring them entirely or addressing them in an ad hoc and anecdotal manner.

Recent technological developments create new opportunities to address this challenge. Large-scale public datasets now provide access to thousands of hours of aligned meeting videos, transcripts, agendas, and minutes. In parallel, advances in multimodal artificial intelligence have substantially improved the robustness of speech recognition, natural language processing (NLP), and computer vision, enabling the extraction of structured signals from unstructured communication data.

This research-in-progress paper explores this opportunity through a Design Science Research (DSR) approach. We present the Meeting Process Twin: a multimodal, AI-enabled BPM artifact that transforms meeting recordings into process event logs, discovers enacted process models, and compares them with formal agenda-based Business Process Management Notation (BPMN) models. The contribution is threefold: (i) an instantiated artifact demonstrating end-to-end multimodal process discovery, (ii) a detailed governance-oriented walkthrough showing how detected shadow processes support interpretive analysis, and (iii) transferable design principles for AI-enabled process mining in domains without structured event logs. By doing so, the artifact aims to make informal and previously hidden aspects of meeting work visible and amenable to governance-oriented analysis. To structure this design science inquiry, we articulate the following research questions (RQs), which guide the design and instantiation of the proposed artifact:

RQ 1	How can multimodal meeting data (e.g., speech and visual interaction cues) be transformed into task-level events suitable for process discovery?
RQ 2	How can enacted meeting processes be discovered from such events and systematically compared with formal, agenda-based process models?
RQ 3	How can deviations between enacted and prescribed meeting processes be presented in a way that supports governance-oriented interpretation rather than purely technical conformance assessment?

2 Background and Research Objectives

2.1 Public-Sector Meeting Context

The primary application context of this research is formal decision-making meetings in public administration, such as city council, committee, or board meetings. These meetings are characterized by a high degree of procedural formalization alongside inherently interactional and emergent practices.

On the one hand, public-sector meetings are governed by explicit procedural rules, including formally defined agendas, voting procedures, and documentation requirements. These rules are intended to ensure transparency, accountability, and legitimacy of collective decisions (Grimmelikhuijsen and Meijer, 2014). From a BPM perspective, such procedures can be interpreted as ostensive process models that prescribe how the meeting process is expected to unfold. On the other hand, the actual enactment of meetings is shaped by human interaction, negotiation, and situational contingencies. Discussions may extend beyond agenda items, procedural steps may be reordered or skipped, and informal coordination may precede or substitute formal actions. These enacted practices correspond to the performative aspect of routines and are only partially reflected in official records such as minutes. As a result, there is often a systematic gap between formal meeting procedures and how meetings are actually conducted. Importantly, public-sector meetings also differ from many operational business processes in that they are extensively recorded and documented. Video recordings, audio streams, transcripts, agendas, and minutes are frequently made publicly available to fulfill transparency obligations (Meijer, 2009). While these artifacts are primarily intended for human consumption, they constitute a rich but underutilized source of process-relevant data.

From a governance perspective, this context is particularly sensitive. Informal practices and hidden process variants, often discussed as workarounds in IS and BPM research (Alter, 2014; Bartelheimer et al., 2023; Outmazgin and Soffer, 2013), are referred to in this paper as 'shadow processes', i.e., enacted procedural variants that diverge from the prescribed agenda-based process model and are not inherently undesirable (Bartelheimer et al., 2023). They may facilitate consensus-building, address exceptional situations, or compensate for rigid procedures. At the same time, they can raise concerns related to compliance, fairness, and accountability if they systematically diverge from prescribed rules. The challenge, therefore, is not to eliminate informal practices, but to make them visible and interpretable in a way that supports informed governance decisions.

2.2   Research Objectives and Design Orientation

Given the characteristics of the application context, purely observational or descriptive approaches are insufficient to address the research problem. The absence of structured event logs and the heterogeneous nature of meeting data require the construction of a purpose-built artifact that operationalizes theoretical concepts and enables systematic analysis. Accordingly, this work follows a DSR orientation (Hevner et al., 2004). The applied design science process is shown in Fig. 1.

Fig. 1. Design science logic of the study.

We derive design objectives (DOs) that reflect the intended capabilities and contributions of the artifact. These objectives are derived from the problem context and from theoretical considerations regarding process visibility, organizational routines, and governance (Rosemann and Brocke, 2015).

DO1: Enable the extraction of task-level events from multimodal meeting data: The artifact should transform unstructured and weakly structured meeting data, such as speech transcripts and visual interaction cues, into discrete, temporally ordered task events that can serve as input for process analysis.

DO2: Support the discovery and comparison of enacted and formal processes: Based on the extracted events, the artifact should enable the discovery of process models that represent how meetings are enacted in practice and allow systematic comparison with formal, agenda-based BPMN models.

DO3: Facilitate governance-oriented interpretation of deviations: Beyond technical conformance diagnostics, the artifact should present deviations in a way that supports interpretability and informed decision-making by process owners and governance stakeholders (vom Brocke et al., 2014), acknowledging that deviations may be legitimate, recurrent, or even desirable.

3 Artifact Design: Multimodal Process Discovery

The core premise of DSR is that certain organizational problems cannot be adequately studied through observation alone, but require the purposeful design and instantiation of artifacts that operationalize theoretical concepts and enable new forms of analysis (Hevner et al., 2004; Peffers et al., 2007).

In the present case, the phenomenon of interest, i.e., informal and weakly structured meeting processes, does not leave behind structured event logs that could be analyzed using existing BPM techniques (Bartelheimer et al., 2025; Outmazgin and Soffer, 2013). Consequently, it requires an artifact that transforms heterogeneous and unstructured communicative data into process-relevant representations. The contribution of this research therefore lies in the design of such an artifact and in the articulation of the design knowledge embedded within it.

The study follows an iterative DSR logic consisting of problem identification, artifact design, instantiation, and formative evaluation (Hevner et al., 2004). Rather than aiming at theory testing, the goal is to generate design knowledge in the form of a concrete artifact, explicit design decisions, and a structured design space for multimodal process discovery.

3.1 Design Requirements

Based on the problem context outlined in Sects. 1 and 2 and the theoretical grounding in BPM and organizational routines, we derive the following high-level design requirements (DRs) that guide the artifact design:

DR1 (Multimodal Event Extractability): The artifact must be capable of extracting task-level events from heterogeneous multimodal meeting data, including speech transcripts and visual interaction cues. Extracted events should be temporally anchored and interpretable from a BPM perspective.

DR2 (Process Discoverability and Comparability): The extracted events must support the discovery of process models and enable systematic comparison between enacted processes and formal, agenda-based BPMN models.

DR3 (Governance-Oriented Interpretability): The artifact must present deviations between enacted and prescribed processes in a manner that supports interpretation and decision-making by governance stakeholders, rather than limiting output to technical conformance metrics.

These requirements emphasize that the artifact is not merely a technical pipeline, but a socio-technical system intended to support governance-sensitive analysis.

3.2 Key Design Decisions

To address the above requirements, several key design decisions (DDs) were made during artifact design and instantiation. These decisions reflect trade-offs between technical feasibility, interpretability, and deployability, which are particularly relevant in governance contexts.

DD1: Speech Recognition via Whisper: Automatic speech recognition is implemented using OpenAI Whisper (Radford et al., 2022). Whisper provides robust transcription performance on noisy, accented meeting speech and outputs timestamped text segments, which are essential for temporal event alignment (supporting R1). The reliance on an external API and file size constraints are mitigated through audio chunking and timestamp offset correction.

DD2: Visual Event Detection via *MediaPipe Pose*: For the detection of visually observable interaction events (e.g., hand raises during voting), *MediaPipe Pose* (Lugaresi et al., 2019) is used instead of more complex alternatives. This decision prioritizes ease of deployment and sufficient accuracy for the targeted interaction patterns, aligning with R1 while supporting rapid prototyping.

DD3: Rule-Based NLP for Task Event Extraction: Task-level events are extracted from speech transcripts using dependency parsing and domain-specific rules (e.g., actor-verb-object patterns). *Sentence-BERT* (Reimers and Gurevych, 2019) embeddings are used separately for semantic alignment between extracted utterances and agenda items (supporting R3).

DD4: Late Fusion of Multimodal Signals: Audio-based and vision-based event detectors operate independently and are combined through late fusion using temporal proximity and confidence weighting. Late fusion simplifies debugging and allows modality-specific tuning, consistent with established multimodal fusion strategies (Mondal et al., 2024), and supports R1 and R2.

DD5: Semantic Alignment between Informal Speech and Formal Agenda Items: To relate informal meeting utterances to formal agenda items, the artifact employs sentence-level semantic similarity using *Sentence-BERT* embeddings. This enables comparison between enacted and prescribed processes even when terminology differs, supporting R2 without relying on exact keyword matches.

Together, these design decisions instantiate a coherent design strategy that operationalizes multimodal meeting data for BPM analysis while remaining sensitive to governance and interpretability concerns. In the following section, we describe how these design choices are realized in the concrete instantiation of the Meeting Process Twin.

4   Instantiation: The Meeting Process Twin

4.1   Artifact Concept

The Meeting Process Twin is an end-to-end, web-based application that represents the enacted process of a meeting and its relationship to formal procedures. Conceptually, it functions as a digital twin of the meeting process by capturing how the meeting unfolds in practice and aligning this enactment with an agenda-based BPMN representation. The artifact supports the following core capabilities:

- Ingestion of meeting recordings (video and audio) and formal agenda documents,
- Extraction of candidate task events from speech and visual interaction cues,
- Construction of a temporally ordered event log suitable for process mining,
- Discovery of an "as-is" process representing enacted meeting behavior,

- Comparison with a "to-be" process derived from the formal agenda,
- Interactive inspection and governance-oriented interpretation of detected deviations.

By integrating these capabilities into a single artifact, the Meeting Process Twin moves beyond isolated multimodal analysis and enables systematic BPM analysis of meeting-based processes.

4.2 Data Source: *LocalView* Public Meetings Database

The Meeting Process Twin is instantiated and evaluated using data from the LocalView Public Meetings Database (Barari and Simko, 2023), a large, publicly available collection of local government meetings in the U.S. The dataset comprises video recordings, audio tracks, and aligned speech transcripts of formal public meetings collected from publicly accessible sources. The meetings typically follow agenda-driven procedural formats, including discussion, motion, and voting phases, which makes them particularly suitable for process-oriented analysis.

4.3 Architecture and Processing Pipeline

The architecture is organized into four conceptual layers, reflecting the progression from raw multimodal data to governance-relevant process insights.

Multimodal Ingestion Layer: The ingestion layer processes heterogeneous input artifacts, including meeting videos, audio streams, transcripts, and formal agenda documents. Video and audio streams are temporally aligned, while agenda items provide a formal reference structure for subsequent comparison.

Event Extraction Layer: In this layer, candidate task events are extracted independently from different modalities. Speech transcripts are analyzed using NLP to identify task-relevant expressions, while visual streams are analyzed to detect interaction cues such as hand-raise gestures. Each detected event is associated with a timestamp and a confidence score, enabling subsequent fusion and filtering.

Process Mining Layer: Extracted events are transformed into a structured event log that serves as input for process mining techniques. Process discovery is performed to derive a process model representing the enacted meeting process. In parallel, a formal BPMN model is constructed based on the agenda structure, serving as the ostensive reference model.

Governance Interface Layer: The final layer presents discovered processes, formal models, and detected deviations through an interactive user interface. Evidence linking process elements to underlying multimodal data is retained to support interpretation and traceability.

This layered architecture supports modularity and allows individual components to be refined or replaced in future iterations without redesigning the entire system. Figure 2 presents the architecture and processing pipeline. To manage uncertainty in event extraction, the formal-shadow partition is governed by a configurable *Sentence-BERT* cosine similarity threshold (default $t = 0.35$), selected empirically to balance agenda coverage and shadow prevalence. Events whose best agenda match falls below this threshold are classified as shadow rather than silently forced into a formal category.

Visual event detection applies a minimum keypoint confidence of 0.3 per keypoint to suppress false positives from partial or occluded poses. The robustness of findings to threshold choice is assessed through a sensitivity analysis across ten values from t = 0.15 to t = 0.60, confirming that the core findings, i.e., low fitness and high shadow prevalence, hold across the full range tested.

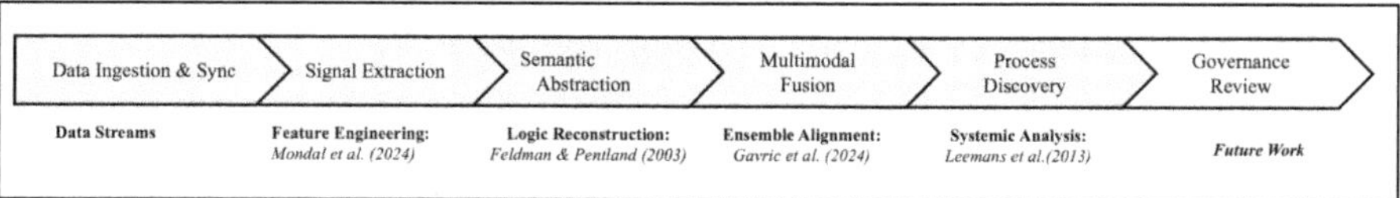

Fig. 2. Data processing pipeline.

4.4 Process Mining, Governance Integration and Implementation

Process mining is implemented using the PM4Py framework (Berti et al., 2023). The extracted event log is analyzed using the Inductive Miner, which produces sound, block-structured process models that can be readily represented in BPMN notation. This choice prioritizes model interpretability and suitability for governance-oriented analysis. To assess the relationship between enacted and prescribed processes, conformance checking is applied using token-based replay and alignment-based diagnostics. These techniques identify deviations such as skipped activities, inserted steps, or unexpected loops in the enacted process relative to the agenda-based model. Crucially, deviations are not treated solely as compliance violations. Instead, they are conceptualized as shadow processes, recurrent or situationally meaningful deviations that may warrant further inspection, formalization, or contextual justification. The artifact surfaces these shadow processes explicitly and links them to supporting evidence from transcripts and video segments. This integration reflects the design objective of supporting governance-oriented interpretation rather than merely producing technical conformance metrics.

The Meeting Process Twin is implemented as an interactive web application using Streamlit, selected for rapid prototyping and ease of deployment. The interface includes a synchronized video player and process visualization, a temporal slider for timeline navigation, a deviation panel listing detected shadow processes, and evidence panels linking process elements to underlying transcript excerpts and video timestamps.

4.5 Preliminary Evaluation

A preliminary technical evaluation demonstrates that the artifact can process real-world meeting recordings end-to-end. To demonstrate how the artifact supports governance-oriented interpretation (DO3), we present a detailed walkthrough of the shadow processes detected in a Seattle city council meeting (January 13, 2026, 118 min, 15 initial agenda items). This walkthrough is not intended as a summative evaluation; it illustrates how the produced artifacts operationalize the conceptual model and enable governance-relevant analysis. Table 1 summarizes the end-to-end run for this meeting. Eight distinct formal activities were detected (*Roll Call, Approval of Consent Calendar, Presentations, Public Comment, Committee Reports, Approval of the Agenda, Ordinance for Floodplain Regulations, Other Business*).

Table 1. Illustrative end-to-end run (one meeting).

Metric	Value
Recording duration	118 min
Agenda items (reference)	15
Total processing time	12 min 34 s
Total events extracted	116
Formal (agenda-aligned)	33 (28%)
Shadow processes detected	83 (72%)
Deduplicated fitness*	0.222
Hardware	Intel i7-11700, 32 GB RAM

*The meeting's lower fitness (0.222 vs. 0.314 mean) reflects its longer duration and higher procedural complexity (15 agenda items, 118 min), which increases opportunities for off-agenda discussion. Cross-meeting variance is expected given that parliamentary rules are interpreted differently across municipalities

Shadow cluster: Opening statements and announcements (minutes 2–7) Immediately after Roll Call, the pipeline detected five shadow events before any agenda item was formally addressed: discussion of a master plan, expressions of inter-city solidarity, announcement of a significant community donation, and standing procedural activities. This represents the common parliamentary practice of opening statements and announcements that occur after *Roll Call* but before the formal agenda begins, a practice so routine that it is rarely formalized in the agenda, yet constitutes meaningful governance activity. From a governance perspective, this cluster illustrates a structural pattern observed across the full dataset: recurring pre-agenda activity that is enacted consistently but never documented in the formal record. The pipeline's evidence links connect each shadow event to the source video and transcript segment, enabling post-hoc review of what was said, by whom, and in what sequence, without requiring a citizen to watch the full 118-min recording. Beyond this cluster, the meeting contained further off-agenda discussions spanning topics such as immigration policy, community access to services, and renters' rights, each surfaced by the pipeline with the same evidence-linking mechanism, and each representing deliberative activity invisible to citizens who consulted only the published agenda.

The artifact's output does not classify these shadow processes as violations or compliance failures. Instead, by surfacing them with evidence links and temporal context, it enables governance stakeholders to ask: should these recurring off-agenda discussions be formalized as standing agenda items? The opening statements cluster, for instance, recurs across multiple meetings in the dataset, suggesting it warrants formal agenda inclusion as a standing item. The artifact thus supports the transition from performative routine (enacted but undocumented) to ostensive routine (formalized and transparent), operationalizing the theoretical framework of Feldman and Pentland (2003) in a concrete governance setting.

The artifact has so far been applied to 54 city council meetings from four U.S. cities (Alameda, Boston, Denver, Seattle), totaling 103.5 h and 26,526 extracted events.

Preliminary results indicate a mean deduplicated fitness of 0.314 and a shadow activity prevalence of 41.9%, with 95.7% of shadow activities classified as innovative. A comprehensive evaluation including ground-truth validation against 9,348 human annotations, sensitivity analysis over key parameters, a multimodal ablation study, and an expert focus group is in preparation for further research.

5 Discussion

This work contributes to BPM and DSR by demonstrating how multimodal AI techniques can be integrated into a governance-oriented process discovery artifact. By extending process mining beyond traditional system event logs, the Meeting Process Twin makes meeting-based decision processes amenable to systematic analysis.

Conceptually, the artifact operationalizes the distinction between ostensive and performative routines in a concrete BPM setting. Rather than treating deviations as noise or failure, it frames informal practices as shadow processes that may warrant interpretation, justification, or formalization. This perspective aligns BPM analysis with organizational research emphasizing flexibility, learning, and situated action.

Beyond the specific artifact, this work yields design knowledge transferable to multimodal process discovery in other domains without structured event logs. First, *late fusion over early fusion*: combining modality-specific detectors independently before merging preserves interpretability and allows modular debugging, which is essential in governance-sensitive deployments where outputs must be explainable. Second, *semantic alignment over keyword matching*: using sentence-level embeddings to relate informal speech to formal process structures enables robust comparison even when enacted behavior diverges substantially in terminology from prescribed models, a pattern likely to recur in any domain where formal specifications and informal practice coexist. Third, *deviation reframing over compliance reporting*: designing the output layer to surface deviations as candidates for interpretation rather than automatically flagging them as violations reflects a broader principle for AI-enabled BPM in human-centered contexts, where the artifact should augment governance judgment rather than replace it. Fourth, evidence linking as a first-class design requirement: retaining provenance links from discovered process elements back to raw multimodal sources is not merely a usability feature but a governance necessity; without it, stakeholders cannot assess, contest, or act on the artifact's outputs. These principles are not specific to public-sector meetings and can inform the design of multimodal process discovery systems in domains such as healthcare rounds, legal proceedings, or collaborative engineering reviews.

From a practical standpoint, the artifact illustrates how publicly available meeting data can be leveraged to support transparency (vom Brocke et al., 2014) and post-hoc governance without enabling real-time monitoring or individual surveillance. By linking deviations to evidence and enabling review, the artifact supports accountability (Bovens et al., 2014) in the sense of an actor-forum relationship where conduct can be questioned, justified, and assessed.

From a theoretical standpoint, the artifact has implications beyond BPM. By making shadow processes systematically visible, it shifts the locus of process ownership (Kohlbacher and Gruenwald, 2011) from those who design formal procedures to those who enact them, raising questions about who is accountable for recurring informal practices and whether they should be formalized. For public organizations, this has direct consequences for transparency mechanisms: if shadow processes are structurally recurrent rather than exceptional, then agenda-based transparency obligations may be systematically incomplete. The artifact thus invites a reconceptualization of procedural transparency not as the publication of intended processes, but as the ongoing reconciliation of intended and enacted ones.

Several limitations must be acknowledged. First, the current implementation assumes a single-camera meeting recording and does not explicitly handle multi-camera setups. Second, the evaluation remains preliminary and focuses on feasibility rather than accuracy or generalizability. These limitations are consistent with the research-in-progress status of the work and provide clear directions for future development.

Further design iterations will explore the integration of Large Language Models (LLMs) for event extraction, alternative process discovery techniques for non-block-structured behavior, and export of BPMN models for use in enterprise BPM tools. For our research, we will next (i) create a manually annotated gold standard for selected meetings to evaluate event extraction accuracy, (ii) conduct expert walkthroughs with public-sector practitioners to assess interpretability and governance utility, and (iii) benchmark alternative extraction approaches, including LLM-based methods, against the current rule-based pipeline. These studies will inform parameter calibration (e.g., similarity thresholds) and extensions such as multi-camera support and BPMN 2.0 export.

6 Conclusion

This paper reported on a DSR project aimed at making informal work visible in meeting-based decision processes. Motivated by the limitations of classical process mining in contexts where structured event logs are absent (Outmazgin and Soffer, 2013), we presented the Meeting Process Twin: a multimodal, AI-enabled artifact that transforms meeting recordings into process-relevant representations and enables comparison between enacted and formal processes. By integrating speech recognition, NLP, visual interaction analysis, semantic agenda alignment, and process mining techniques, the artifact demonstrates the feasibility of multimodal process discovery in governance-sensitive contexts. Rather than treating deviations solely as compliance violations, the Meeting Process Twin surfaces shadow processes as interpretable and evidence-linked phenomena that can support transparency, learning, and informed governance decisions. The results suggest that meeting data, long treated as unstructured and analytically inaccessible, can be systematically incorporated into BPM analysis when approached through an artifact-centered design lens.

References

Alter, S.: Theory of Workarounds. Communications of the Association for Information Systems **34**(1) (2014)

Barari, S., Simko, T.: LocalView, a database of public meetings for the study of local politics and policy-making in the United States. Scientific Data **10**(1), 135 (2023)

Bartelheimer, C., Löhr, B., Reineke, M., Aßbrock, A., Beverungen, D.: Workarounds as a Cause of Mismatches in Business Processes — Insights from a Multiple Case Study. Bus. Inf. Syst. Eng. **67**(3), 339–356 (2025)

Bartelheimer, C., Wolf, V., Beverungen, D.: Workarounds as generative mechanisms for bottom-up process innovation—Insights from a multiple case study. Inf. Syst. J. **33**(5), 1085–1150 (2023)

Berti, A., van Zelst, S., Schuster, D.: PM4Py: A process mining library for Python. Software Impacts **17**, 100556 (2023)

Bovens, M., Schillemans, T., Goodin, R.: Public Accountability. In: Bovens, M., Goodin, R., Schillemans, T. (eds.) The Oxford Handbook of Public Accountability, p. 0. Oxford University Press (2014)

Dumas, M., La Rosa, M., Mendling, J., Reijers, H.A.: Fundamentals of Business Process Management. Springer (2018)

Feldman, M.S., Pentland, B.T.: Reconceptualizing Organizational Routines as a Source of Flexibility and Change. Adm. Sci. Q. **48**(1), 94–118 (2003)

Fung, A., Graham, M., Weil, D.: Full Disclosure: The Perils and Promise of Transparency. Cambridge University Press (2007)

Grimmelikhuijsen, S.G., Meijer, A.J.: Effects of transparency on the perceived trustworthiness of a government organization: evidence from an online experiment. J. Pub. Admin. Res. Theory **24**(1), 137–157 (2014)

Hevner, A., March, S.T., Park, J., Ram, S.: Design science in information systems research. MIS Q **28**(1), 75–105 (2004)

Kohlbacher, M., Gruenwald, S.: Process ownership, process performance measurement and firm performance. Int. J. Product. Perform. Manag. **60**(7), 709–720 (2011)

Lugaresi, C., et al.: MediaPipe: A Framework for Building Perception Pipelines (2019) (arXiv: 1906.08172). arXiv

Meijer, A.: Understanding modern transparency. Int. Rev. Adm. Sci. **75**(2), 255–269 (2009)

Mondal, M., Khayati, M., Sandlin, H.-Â., Cudré-Mauroux, P.: A survey of multimodal event detection based on data fusion. VLDB J. **34**(1), 9 (2024)

Outmazgin, N., Soffer, P.: Business process workarounds: what can and cannot be detected by process mining. In: Nurcan, S., Proper, H.A., Soffer, P., Krogstie, J., Schmidt, R., Halpin, T., Bider, I. (eds.) Enterprise, Business-Process and Information Systems Modeling, pp. 48–62. Springer (2013)

Peffers, K., Tuunanen, T., Rothenberger, M.A., Chatterjee, S.: A Design Science Research Methodology for Information Systems Research. J. Manag. Inf. Syst. **24**(3), 45–77 (2007)

Radford, A., et al.: Robust Speech Recognition via Large-Scale Weak Supervision (2022) (arXiv: 2212.04356). arXiv

Reimers, N., Gurevych, I.: Sentence-BERT: Sentence Embeddings using Siamese BERT-Networks (2019) (arXiv:1908.10084). arXiv

Rosemann, M., Brocke, J.: The Six Core Elements of Business Process Management. Int. Handb. Info. Sys. 105–122 (2015)

van Der Aalst, W.: Process Mining. Springer (2016)

vom Brocke, J., et al.: Ten principles of good business process management. In: Business Process Management Journal, Vol. 20, pp. 530–548. Emerald (2014)

Improving Human Foraging with Hybrid Semantic Graph Retrieval and LLM-Supported Meaning Making

Alexander Meier[(⊠)][iD]

Institute for Information Systems and Digital Business,
University of St. Gallen, St. Gallen, Switzerland
`alexander.meier@unisg.ch`

Abstract. Online search traditionally depends on explicit labels and tags. With the emergence of generative AI and further advancements such as the integration of hybrid graph-vector retrieval, a new kind of information foraging behavior emerges. Humans are now able to engage in richer search-interactions, known as higher-order hermeneutics, that provide the retrieval system with contextual meaning for employing a new type of cue. I study how this new form of foraging behavior impacts cognitive cost and performance in the retrieval of presentation slides, a domain that is inherently multimodal and reliant on contextual narrative meaning. Users externalize narrative meaning to guide foraging. In my online study ($N = 56$), participants constructed a narrative, which guided retrieval via a hybrid graph-vector system. Results show that hybrid graph-vector foraging improves task performance. Building on these preliminary findings, a larger lab-based study is planned. I contribute a perspective: generative-AI-based hermeneutics precedes and enables new information-foraging behavior.

Keywords: Foraging · Hybrid Search · Graph RAG · LLM · Narratives

1 Introduction

Presentation slide creation, an omnipresent medium for knowledge sharing, requires authors to integrate text, numbers, images, and diagrams into a coherent multimodal artifact. Fully AI-generated slides remain inadequate: they oversimplify complex material, yield unreliable results, and dampen critical engagement of the creator [12,32]. Because AI-generated slides often rely on broad but shallow text only data that lack fitting visuals, expert-level knowledge, and corporate design. Consultants, whose work heavily relies on presentation slides for communication, still reuse legacy slides from large repositories to save time and ensure consistency [30]. The core challenge is not merely locating individual slides but integrating them into structured, engaging presentation narratives.

S. Chatterjee et al. (Eds.): DESRIST 2026, LNCS 16607, pp. 121–132, 2026.
https://doi.org/10.1007/978-3-032-28570-6_10

Prior work on organizing information for navigating complex multimodal content is limited. Most studies examine search-engine marketing, product-review search, or social media [11,19,26]. Information Foraging Theory (IFT) frames information seeking as rate-of-gain optimization over information patches [24].

Yet, these models presuppose a static and user-driven search ecology, where information exists a priori and the forager navigates explicit cues. In contrast, contemporary retrieval environments, characterized by knowledge graphs, semantic search, and generative AI, fundamentally alter this ecology [16,20]. Explicit cues can be projected into latent semantic vector space [21], which the system can now follow based on context. This provided narrative context is created beforehand between the user and the system. Meaning and desired outcomes arise through prompting interaction between a human and a Large Language Model (LLM), a so-called hermeneutic loop [14]. Based on the created contextual meaning, information foraging is later partly handed over to the systems. Information comes to the seeker. Thus, I pose the following research question: *How do hybrid semantic graph-vector retrieval systems and LLM-supported narrative meaning creation influence users' information foraging performance, satisfaction, and cognitive cost in multimodal slide retrieval?*

I develop a conceptual model and four testable hypotheses grounded in IFT, and present preliminary empirical results using a prototypical hybrid graph-vector slide retrieval system to instantiate and manipulate the constructs. The study contributes to the literature on human AI systems for interacting with complex multimodal content by demonstrating that a graph-AI slide retrieval system can enhance consultants' foraging task performance, increase satisfaction, and descrease cognitive effort by using a combination of latent and explicit cues and supporting the iterative creation of a meaningful information context.

2   Theoretical Background and Hypothesis Development

IFT borrows the cost-benefit logic of optimal foraging theory, originally used to analyze animal behavior, where animals are understood to navigate their environments in ways that food intake results in energy gain relative to effort and risk [29]. IFT has been introduced to explain why users often take seemingly winding navigation paths yet still gather information near optimally online [24]. The theory positions humans as "informavores", actively seeking and consuming information within environments as a benefit and balancing the cost, such as attention and cognitive effort. Users optimize their information search by following information scent [23]. Pirolli (2007) identified three core constructs of IFT: information scent, information patches, and information diet. The subsequent literature review elaborates on these constructs and situates them within the current discourse in IS, clarifying how each has been instantiated to date.

2.1   Information Foraging in IS

To identify the contextualized discussion in the Information Systems domain of IFT, I conducted a systematic literature review following the established criteria by Webster & Watson (2002) and vom Brocke et al. (2015). This ensured the systematic capture of existing conceptual assumptions and applications of IFT. According to Leidner (2018), the polylithic framework of review and theory development, this systematic literature review itself yields an "assessing review", as the objective is to identify a stream' s patterns and omissions. This also sets the focus for the relevant databases in Information Systems, representing a well-bounded disciplinary stream of socio-technical interplay [3]. I screened the AIS 'basket-of-eight' journals and AIS-affiliated peer-reviewed conferences, including HICSS, PACIS, ECIS, AMCIS, and ICIS. My search string included "INFORMATION" AND "FORAGING". I set no time limit past wards to yield a comprehensive overview.

The search initially yielded 58 results, of which I removed two duplicates. Title and abstract screening reduced the remaining articles to 7. Those seven papers had IFT in their research focus and thus qualified for analyzing the whole paper. I conducted subsequent complementary forward and backward searches, which yielded an additional eight relevant papers.

Early studies embedded the theory in adaptive mobile interfaces, where summaries and color-coded keywords steer handheld users through long pages [1], and in news-aggregator dashboards, where snippet length and thumbnail images represent click-throughs across clustered story groups [6]. In other articles, social-commerce review sites are contrasted with foraging in friends-versus-strangers opinion patches [11] or analyze tag-based social search, where product tags act as cues [31].

Pirolli & Card (1999) defined three core constructs, which I now discuss in the context of the identified literature.

Scent comprises the cues, such as textual, visual, semantic, or structural, that allow humans to estimate the relevance and value of unseen information before committing additional effort. Labels on reviews, textual summaries, risk descriptors, tag keywords, hyperlinks, and text all instantiate scent that is emitted because each lowers the uncertainty of a click or scroll [1,10,11,31].

Moody & Galletta (2015) extend this view by showing that scent can also be computationally and quantitatively inferred from the semantic similarity between a user's task description and the cues on a page. In their approach, latent cues arise when textual elements of the task description and hyperlinks are projected into a latent vector representation of semantic space, and the so-called latent scent is the resulting semantic similarity between the vector of the task and the vectors of the hyperlinks. These latent scent similarity scores closely matched scent evaluations provided by trained human annotators.

Diet represents the cumulative composition and ordering of information items consumed during foraging. Traditionally, diets reflect sequential choices among explicitly presented items, for example, alternating between product reviews [19], when risk-averse users toggle between threat-appraisal and threat-coping pages [27], or accumulating cues across search results [26]. Information that matches the user's evolving diet improves the foraging performance.

Patch is a bounded cluster whose internal links, topology, or social provenance make it worthwhile to exploit locally before considering alternative clusters. Examples include the core-friend review block versus the extended-stranger block [11], the branch of a tree-view mobile page [1], a modular news story grouping [6], or a set of webpages that co-occur in sequences [26].

2.2   From Explicit Navigation to Latent–Hybrid Retrieval

IFT studies still implicitly assume an information environment organized through explicit and human-interpretable structure, such as hierarchical menus, website taxonomies, or manually curated clusters. Hierarchical folder navigation represents the most common retrieval structure identified. Users must manually traverse categories and interpret explicit cues. Also, in knowledge graphs, cues remain explicitly symbolic and human-interpretable. Edge labels, node types, and connectivity patterns convey the relational structure among entities, providing structural cues that make relationships cognitively tractable [17,25].

Generative AI–based retrievers build on latent scent, as already introduced by Moody & Galletta (2015) (see Sect. 2.1), and partially pre-curate the diet. Transformer architectures encode the semantic search meaning provided by the user, along with available information cues, into dense vector embeddings [28]. The resulting semantic similarity between embeddings constitutes latent scent. Thus, the information diet becomes context-responsive. Patches dynamically align with the meaning the user constructs and the latent cue representation of candidate information elements.

Hybrid retrieval systems combine these approaches by using latent semantic scent (via vector similarity) to present only high-scent, explicit, human-interpretable subgraphs. Such systems exploiting both latent scent vector similarity and explicit relational graph structure have recently proven to deliver superior technical document retrieval [2,7] and human AI interaction performance [16,20].

Users may experience lower cognitive cost because less manual navigation is required to locate relevant content. At the same time, the likelihood of encountering high-value items early in the foraging process improves annotated performance. Therefore, I hypothesize (see Fig. 1):

Hypothesis 1a/b: *Hybrid graph-vector-based exploration will lead to higher satisfaction response and lower cognitive effort compared to hierarchical navigation.*

Hypothesis 2: *Hybrid graph-vector-based exploration will positively influence annotated human task performance.*

2.3   Hermeneutics, Meaning-Making, and Interpretive Support

In hermeneutic theories, meaning is not fixed but constructed through an iterative movement between users' prior expectations and the new information they encounter, a circle in which meaning evolves [9]. Henrickson & Meroño-Peñuela

(2025) posit the interaction with an LLM through prompting as part of an iterative process where meaning itself emerges, named as the hermeneutic loop, where "human input informs system output, which informs human input, which informs system output," resulting in a recursive process of meaning-making. The LLM's contribution emerges not from factual accuracy alone but from its ability to provoke, challenge, or expand the user's understanding.

This hermeneutic loop operates upstream of scent-following. Users must articulate a meaningful contextualization of the task, e.g., a narrative, that defines which information items count as valuable. LLM interactions may help users bring their endogenous pre-understandings (Gadamer's Vorverständnis) into explicit externalized form. This provides a meaningful basis on which scent is then followed. Although hermeneutic meaning-making is subjective, interpretations nonetheless vary in quality (coherence, plausibility, and completeness) [18]. I thus hypothesize (see Fig. 1):

Hypothesis 3: *LLM support positively influences the quality of users' contextualized narratives.*

Hypothesis 4: *Narrative quality positively mediates the effect of LLM support on task performance.*

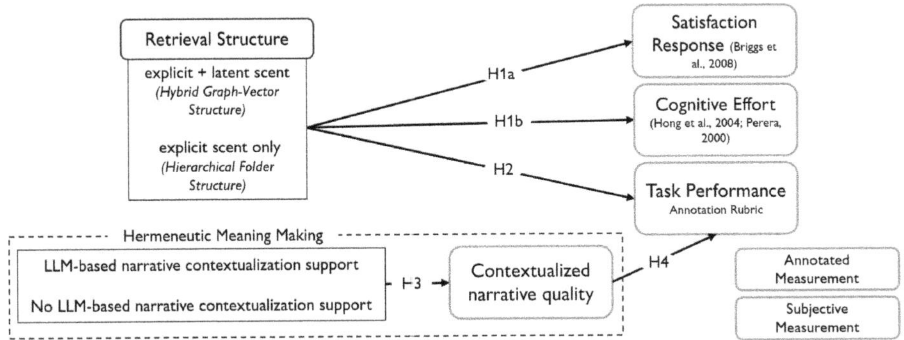

Fig. 1. Research Model.

3 Research Method

3.1 Experimental Design

I tested the model in a 2×2 between-subjects experiment manipulating (1) the retrieval structure (Hybrid graph–vector retriever vs. Hierarchical folder navigation) and (2) LLM-based narrative contextualization support (enabled vs. disabled).

3.2   Tasks and Prototypes

All participants were tasked to create a 10-slide sales proposal pitch on the urgency and business value of cybersecurity and digital resilience by smartly reusing existing firm slides. In consulting, sales proposals are often based on existing services offered, making them suitable for a retrieval task of existing slides. The task was deemed suitable by an employee at the partner level of an actual mid-sized U.S. IT consultancy (USITC). The participants had access to the repository of the USITC. The repository contained around 10,000 slides in total, covering an abundant number of various topics, not limited to cybersecurity.

Hybrid Graph-Vector Retriever. I created a prototype similar to Meier et al. (2025). Similarly, in preparation, all existing slides and the inherent structure in the repository were used to construct a graph database. GPT-4o was used to capture visual and textual content. Based on the textual description, I created a vector representation of each slide using "text-embedding-3-large" of OpenAI. Using a React implementation, the hybrid graph-vector retriever uses the directed narrative represented by a number of user-defined storypoints, depicted as a graph, to suggest candidate slides. Around each storypoint in the narrative, using a shared embedding space, the system retrieves matching slides based on the cosine similarity between the vector representations of each storypoint and slides from the entire repository (Fig. 2).

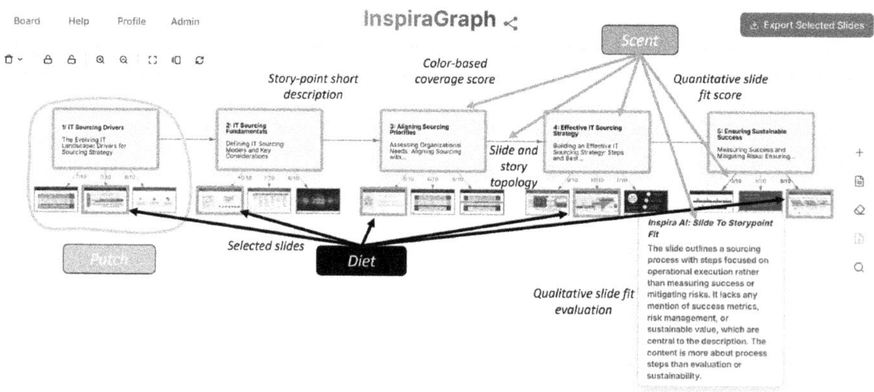

Fig. 2. Instantiated User Interface of a Hybrid Graph-Vector Retriever and Exemplary Information Foraging Theory Concepts.

Employees of USITC, who also provided the slide repository, whose daily work relies on slide production and reuse, provided formative evidence of feasibility. Across five 60–90 min working sessions designed as a task-based co-creation meeting using the partner's live slide repositories, during which at least one employee and a researcher addressed realistic reuse tasks (e.g., assembling a client deck from prior materials) while verbalizing their reasoning as a think-aloud. In total, seven USITC consultants (incl. a design and visualization expert to executives) used the prototype. USITC consultants found the prototype usable for slide-reuse workflows. One USITC consultant remarked it was the "first time I can see how slides from different decks actually fit together into a storyline".

Hierarchical Folder Navigation. The second prototype comprised a traditional folder-based file browser, optimized for previewing presentation slides without the need to open a slide deck in e.g., PowerPoint, but being able to quickly navigate. The prototype's navigation design was inspired by commonly used file-management systems such as Microscft SharePoint, Google Drive, and Dropbox. It accessed the same underlying repository as the *hybrid graph-vector retriever*. However, the content was presented in a thematic, hierarchical folder structure as employed in actual use by the USITC.

To manipulate the second factor of LLM-based narrative contextualization support, the system (when enabled) assisted users, based on GPT 4.1, in creating, formulating, and refining narrative storypoints. In conditions without LLM support, participants created and edited storypoints manually. This aligns with best practice that crafting a narrative before identifying matching content is considered essential [4]. All prototypes captured all clicks, textual input, and navigation patterns for subsequent analysis.

3.3   Participants

56 fluent English participants with self-reported consulting experience were recruited via Prolific. Participants were equally distributed across all four conditions. The average age was 33.91 years, with an average of 6.46 years of consulting experience. Fifteen participants identified as female and 41 as male.

3.4   Measures

Cognitive effort and satisfaction were selected as measures to capture the cost dimension of the foraging task [23]. Following prior work, cognitive effort with five items assesses the mental resources required to interpret and assemble information [15,22], whereas satisfaction with six items captures users' affective evaluation of the system and the foraging experience [5]. Both constructs were measured with items on a 7-point Likert scale in a post survey.

I developed an annotation rubric for task performance with a USITC partner-level employee, who also validated the experimental task (see Sect. 3.2), during a 60-min co-creation session to evaluate annotated foraging performance. The rubric contained nine dimensions, e.g., the existence and quality of "frameworks and methodologies to address cybersecurity and digital resilience gaps", for annotating each participant's final selected slides. One annotator with two years of consulting experience annotated the selected and submitted slides. Additionally, a second annotator will be recruited while ensuring inter-annotator reliability. All participants were asked to define "storypoints", depending on the condition, either without or with the LLM supporting them iteratively. Thus, all participants could externalize and describe their desired meaningful narrative before retrieving and selecting slides, as it is best practice [4]. These storypoints make the contextualized narrative quality. To evaluate this, a second annotation rubric, similar to the overall task performance rubric, with USITC consultants will be developed. The narrative storypoints submitted by the participants will be annotated by at least two experienced consultants while ensuring inter-annotator reliability.

4   Preliminary Results

Table 1. Group comparison: Hybrid Graph-Vector vs Hierarchical Navigation.

Variable	Condition	Mean	SD	p (MWU)	Cliff's δ	Effect Size
Satisfaction	Hybrid graph-vector	5.60	1.26	**.031**	0.34	Medium
	Hierarchical Nav	4.92	1.38			
Cognitive Effort	Hybrid graph-vector	2.89	1.36	**.115**	−0.25	Small
	Hierarchical Nav	3.46	1.08			
Task Performance	Hybrid graph-vector	241.3	86.9	**.021**	0.36	Medium
	Hierarchical Nav	183.9	80.2			

For this work-in-progress online study, I use manifest scale means for the self-reported constructs of satisfaction and cognitive effort. A one-factor exploratory factor analysis (EFA) (polychoric, minres) showed that all satisfaction items loaded strongly on a single factor (λ = .89–.97; uniquenesses $\leq$ .21). Cognitive effort also exhibited a one-factor structure (λ = .78–.97; uniquenesses $\leq$ .39). A two-factor EFA across all items confirmed that satisfaction and effort formed distinct factors, with no cross-loadings $\geq$ .30. The correlation between satisfaction and cognitive effort was moderate and negative (r $\approx$ -.30). Both measures demonstrate acceptable internal consistency, as indicated by their Cronbach's alpha values (α satisfaction = .971; α cognitive effort = .879). Shapiro-Wilk tests indicate non-normal distributions for satisfaction in the Hybrid graph-vector condition (W = 0.785, p < .001) and task performance in both conditions (Hybrid graph-vector: W = 0.910, p = .017; Hierarchical Navigation: W = 0.910, p = .023). Given these violations, I employ Mann-Whitney U (MWU) tests for group comparisons and Cliff's delta for effect size estimation. These methods are robust to non-normality [8]. Supporting Hypothesis 1a, satisfaction was significantly higher in the Hybrid graph-vector condition (M = 5.60) than in the Hierarchical Navigation condition (M = 4.92), U = 523, p = .031 (δ = 0.34). In line with Hypothesis 2, task performance was also significantly better under Hybrid graph-vector (M = 241.3) compared to Hierarchical Navigation (M =

183.9), U = 532, p = .021, δ = 0.36. While Hypothesis 1b posited lower cognitive effort in the Hybrid graph-vector condition, the difference did not reach statistical significance (U = 295, p = .115). Descriptive results show a lower mean effort score (M = 2.89 vs. 3.46, δ = −0.25). To test Hypothesis 3, I will compare contextualized narrative quality using a two-group analysis (e.g., t-test or MWU, depending on distributional assumptions). For Hypothesis 4, I will use PROCESS Model 4 [13] to test whether narrative quality mediates the effect of LLM-based narrative contextualization support on task performance (Table 1).

5   Next Steps, Limitations, and Outlook

Concerning the progress of the online study, the data collection and pre-processing are complete. The next step is annotating the contextualized narrative quality by at least two annotators to test for the mediation effect and add a second annotator for task performance.

The work-in-progress study has several limitations. First, the sample size of this online study restricted statistical power, and online experimental participation limited control over environmental distractions. Self-declared participants' prior consulting, presentation slide creation experience in contrast to actual experience, and prompting skills may have introduced uncontrolled variance. Participants could therefore also differ from real practitioners. To address this, I plan a laboratory experiment with at least 30 participants per condition. Second, task performance and narrative quality are rated by annotators; construct validity remains partly interpretive. Third, although the sales-proposal scenario is realistic for consulting workflows, information foraging in other domains (e.g., research synthesis, software engineering, or e-commerce) involves different retrieval structures and cognitive strategies, which may limit generalizability. Fourth, due to scope constraints and analogous to other IFT studies [19,21], I do not yet examine other IFT mechanisms such as information-diet coherence or patch-switching behavior. Fifth, the hybrid retrieval condition bundles two components, latent semantic vector similarity and explicit graph-structured cues. Because latent cues are not directly interpretable without being surfaced through some form of explicit representation, the two elements necessarily occur together. As a result, the study cannot fully isolate the unique effect of latent scent from the explicit cues through which it is operationalized.

In conclusion, the study aims to provide preliminary evidence that with the introduction of generative AI-based retrievers, information foraging changes. Semantic latent scent, in combination with explicit graph-structured cues, improves foraging task performance and may reduce cognitive cost (lower cognitive effort) while increasing user satisfaction. Further, this study aspires to show that using an LLM in a hermeneutic loop, search is guided by more meaning, leading to even higher task performance.

References

1. Adipat, B., Zhang, D., Zhou, L.: The effects of tree-view based presentation adaptation on mobile web browsing. MIS Q. **35**(1), 99–121 (2011). https://doi.org/10.2307/23043491. https://www.jstor.org/stable/23043491
2. Agrawal, G., Kumarage, T., Alghamdi, Z., Liu, H.: Can knowledge graphs reduce hallucinations in LLMs?: a survey. In: Duh, K., Gomez, H., Bethard, S. (eds.) Proceedings of the 2024 Conference of the North American Chapter of the Association for Computational Linguistics: Human Language Technologies (Volume 1: Long Papers), pp. 3947–3960. Association for Computational Linguistics, Mexico City, Mexico (2024). https://doi.org/10.18653/v1/2024.naacl-long.219. https://aclanthology.org/2024.naacl-long.219/
3. Benbasat, I., Zmud, R.: The identity crisis within the IS discipline: defining and communicating the discipline's core properties. Manag. Inf. Syst. Q. **27**(2) (2003). https://aisel.aisnet.org/misq/vol27/iss2/3
4. Bourgoin, A., Muniesa, F.: Building a rock-solid slide: management consulting, powerpoint, and the craft of signification. Manag. Commun. Q. **30**(3), 390–410 (2016). https://doi.org/10.1177/0893318916629562. http://journals.sagepub.com/doi/10.1177/0893318916629562
5. Briggs, R., Reinig, B., Vreede, G.J.D.: The yield shift theory of satisfaction and its application to the IS/IT domain. J. Assoc. Inf. Syst. **9**(5) (2008). https://doi.org/10.17705/1jais.00160. https://aisel.aisnet.org/jais/vol9/iss5/14
6. Dellarocas, C., Sutanto, J., Calin, M., Palme, E.: Attention allocation in information-rich environments: the case of news aggregators. Manage. Sci. **62**(9), 2543–2562 (2016). https://doi.org/10.1287/mnsc.2015.2237. https://pubsonline.informs.org/doi/10.1287/mnsc.2015.2237
7. Edge, D., et al.: From Local to Global: A Graph RAG Approach to Query-Focused Summarization (2024). https://doi.org/10.48550/arXiv.2404.16130. http://arxiv.org/abs/2404.16130. arXiv:2404.16130
8. Field, A.: Discovering statistics using IBM SPSS statistics. Sage, London Southern Oaks, California New Delhi Singapore, 6th edn (2024)
9. Gadamer, H.G.: Truth and method. Continuum, New York, 2., rev. edn. (2003)
10. Galletta, D.F., Henry, R.M., McCoy, S., Polak, P.: When the wait isn't so bad: the interacting effects of website delay, familiarity, and breadth. Inf. Syst. Res. **17**(1), 20–37 (2006). https://doi.org/10.1287/isre.1050.0073. https://pubsonline.informs.org/doi/10.1287/isre.1050.0073
11. Grange, C., Benbasat, I.: Opinion seeking in a social network-enabled product review website: a study of word-of-mouth in the era of digital social networks. Eur. J. Inf. Syst. **27**(6), 629–653 (2018). https://doi.org/10.1080/0960085X.2018.1472196
12. Guo, Y., Zhang, Z., Liang, Y., Zhao, D., Duan, N.: PPTC Benchmark: Evaluating Large Language Models for PowerPoint Task Completion (2023). http://arxiv.org/abs/2311.01767. arXiv:2311.01767
13. Hayes, A.: Introduction to mediation, moderation, and conditional process analysis: a regression-based approach. Methodology in the social sciences, Guilford Press (2022). https://books.google.ch/books?id=-a3BzgEACAAJ
14. Henrickson, L., Meroño-Peñuela, A.: Prompting meaning: a hermeneutic approach to optimising prompt engineering with ChatGPT. AI Soc. **40**(2), 903–918 (2025). https://doi.org/10.1007/s00146-023-01752-8

15. Hong, W., Thong, J., Tam, K.: The effects of information format and shopping task on consumers' online shopping behavior: a cognitive fit perspective. J. Manag. Inf. Syst. **21**, 149–184 (2004). https://doi.org/10.1080/07421222.2004.11045812
16. Hsuan Yuan, C.W., Yu, T.W., Pan, J.Y., Lin, W.C.: KGScope: interactive visual exploration of knowledge graphs with embedding-based guidance. IEEE Trans. Visual Comput. Graphics **30**(12), 7702–7716 (2024). https://doi.org/10.1109/TVCG.2024.3360690. https://ieeexplore.ieee.org/document/10418108
17. Ji, H., Ke, P., Huang, S., Wei, F., Zhu, X., Huang, M.: Language generation with multi-hop reasoning on commonsense knowledge graph. In: Proceedings of the 2020 Conference on Empirical Methods in Natural Language Processing (EMNLP), pp. 725–736. Association for Computational Linguistics, Online (2020).https://doi.org/10.18653/v1/2020.emnlp-main.54. https://www.aclweb.org/anthology/2020.emnlp-main.54
18. Klein, H.K., Myers, M.D.: A set of principles for conducting and evaluating interpretive field studies in information systems. MIS Q. **23**(1), 67–93 (1999). https://doi.org/10.2307/249410. https://www.jstor.org/stable/249410
19. Li, M., Tan, C.H., Wei, K.K., Wang, K.: Sequentiality of product review information provision: an information foraging perspective. MIS Q. **41**(3), 867-A7 (2017). https://www.jstor.org/stable/26635017
20. Meier, A., Rietsche, R., Li, M.: Developing a hybrid vector-graph retrieval system for entity-preserving and inspiring storyline creation of presentation slides. In: European Conference on Information Systems (ECIS) (2025). https://www.alexandria.unisg.ch/handle/20.500 14171/122503
21. Moody, G.D., Galletta, D.F.: Lost in cyberspace: the impact of information scent and time constraints on stress, performance, and attitudes online. J. Manag. Inf. Syst. **32**(1), 192–224 (2015). https //www.jstor.org/stable/26613982
22. Perera, R.E.: Optimizing human-computer interaction for the electronic commerce environment. J. Electron. Commer. Res. **1**(1), 23–44 (2000). http://www.csulb.edu/web/journals/jecr/issues/20001/paper3.pdf, tex.bibsource: dblp computer science bibliography, https://dblp.org tex.timestamp: Fri, 15 Dec 2023 18:26:00 +0100
23. Pirolli, P.: Information Foraging Theory: Adaptive Interaction with Information. Oxford University Press, New York, NY, US (2007). https://doi.org/10.1093/acprof:oso/9780195173321.001.0001
24. Pirolli, P., Card, S.: Information foraging. Psychol. Rev. **106**(4), 643–675 (1999). https://doi.org/10.1037/0033-295x.106.4.643. https://doi.apa.org/doi/10.1037/0033-295X.106.4.643
25. Reinanda, R., Meij, E., De Rijke, M.: Knowledge graphs: an information retrieval perspective. Found. Trends® Inf. Retrieval **14**(4), 289–444 (2020). https://doi.org/10.1561/1500000063. http://www.nowpublishers.com/article/Details/INR-063
26. Shi, S.W., Trusov, M.: The path to click: are you on it? Mark. Sci. **40**(2), 344–365 (2021). https://doi.org/10.1287/mksc.2020.1253. https://pubsonline.informs.org/doi/10.1287/mksc.2020.1253
27. Wang, J., Xiao, N., Rao, H.R.: Research note–an exploration of risk characteristics of information security threats and related public information search behavior. Inf. Syst. Res. **26**(3), 619–633 (2015). https://doi.org/10.1287/isre.2015.0581. https://pubsonline.informs.org/doi/10.1287/isre.2015.0581
28. Wang, R., Finch, A., Utiyama, M., Sumita, E.: Sentence embedding for neural machine translation domain adaptation. In: Proceedings of the 55th Annual Meeting of the Association for Computational Linguistics (Volume 2: Short Papers), pp.

560–566. Association for Computational Linguistics, Vancouver, Canada (2017). https://doi.org/10.18653/v1/P17-2089. http://aclweb.org/anthology/P17-2089

29. Winterhalder, B., Smith, E.: Hunter-Gatherer Foraging Strategies: Ethnographic and Archeological Analyses. University of Chicago Press, Chicago (1981)

30. Yates, J., Orlikowski, W.: The PowerPoint presentation and its corollaries: how genres shape communicative action in organizations. In: Zachry, M., Thralls, C. (eds.) Communicative Practices in Workplaces and the Professions, pp. 67–92. Baywood Publishing Company, Amityville (2007). https://doi.org/10.2190/CPIC4

31. Yi, C., Jiang, Z.J., Benbasat, I.: Designing for diagnosticity and serendipity: an investigation of social product-search mechanisms. Inf. Syst. Res. **28**(2), 413–429 (2017). https://doi.org/10.1287/isre.2017.0695. https://pubsonline.informs.org/doi/10.1287/isre.2017.0695

32. Zhai, C., Wibowo, S., Li, L.D.: The effects of over-reliance on AI dialogue systems on students' cognitive abilities: a systematic review. Smart Learn. Environ. **11**(1), 28 (2024). https://doi.org/10.1186/s40561-024-00316-7

Design Knowledge Quality in Human-AI Co-Design

Sanaz Nabavian[1]([✉]) [iD] and Jeffrey Parsons[2] [iD]

[1] University of Niagara Falls, Niagara Falls, ON, Canada
sanaz.nabavian@unfc.ca
[2] Memorial University of Newfoundland, Newfoundland, NL, Canada
jeffreyp@mun.ca

Abstract. As Generative Artificial Intelligence (GenAI) is used increasingly to support design activities as a co-designer, assessing design knowledge under the assumption that it will be interpreted and applied by a human designer is becoming insufficient. This dilemma raises two key research questions: (1) What qualities make prescriptive design knowledge applicable and reusable in human–GenAI co-design? and (2) How do different methods for representing and incorporating design knowledge affect these qualities? In this research-in-progress paper, we propose a framework for evaluating prescriptive design knowledge in human–GenAI co-design. Grounded in design science research and informed by recent advances in generative information retrieval, the framework identifies a set of quality criteria (activation, alignment, correctness, consistency, explainability, traceability, efficiency, and final quality) that characterize effective use of design knowledge by GenAI systems. To operationalize the framework, we propose a vignette-based evaluation study comparing different information retrieval techniques and levels of prompt specificity. We further describe how each criterion can be measured. This work establishes a foundation for systematically assessing prescriptive design knowledge in human–GenAI co-design contexts.

Keywords: Human–AI Co-design · Design Knowledge Quality · Design Knowledge Evaluation Framework

1 Motivation and Research Problem

With the growing use of Generative AI (GenAI) as a co-designer (Kadenhe et al., 2025; Yu, 2025; Zhou et al., 2024), the assumption that humans are the sole actors in the development and reuse of design knowledge is becoming obsolete. There are many ways to integrate design knowledge in the process of human–GenAI co-design, such as explicitly providing it to the AI within the prompt, or retrieving it dynamically from external sources (e.g., academic papers, or a design principle repository). The successful reuse of a piece of design knowledge in this context depends on whether the GenAI system can recognize the relevant pieces (e.g., identify appropriate design principles for the context), correctly apply them, and sustain them across iterative interactions. This raises two fundamental research questions:

S. Chatterjee et al. (Eds.): DESRIST 2026, LNCS 16607, pp. 133–141, 2026.
https://doi.org/10.1007/978-3-032-28570-6_11

RQ1: What qualities make a piece of prescriptive design knowledge applicable and reusable in human–GenAI co-design, and
RQ2: How do different methods for incorporating design knowledge (such as information retrieval algorithm or prompt quality) affect this applicability?

Motivated by these questions, we develop a framework for assessing human–GenAI collaboration in design. Specifically, we ask what requirements design knowledge must satisfy for effective use in human–AI co-design, and how such knowledge should be represented and incorporated into GenAI systems. Prior attempts to pose design problems or provide collections of principles to GenAI systems have shown preliminary progress in retrieving appropriate design principles from the repository when users ask for a specific topic; however, it is unclear what else the systems need to reliably identify all the applicable principles or consistently operationalize them across design iterations (Gau & Gnewuch, 2025). Our proposed framework, therefore, serves as an exploratory structure that identifies key aspects of design knowledge and their integration mechanisms that warrant systematic investigation. For each aspect, we draw on existing literature and ongoing research to derive candidate best practices. Rather than claiming definitive solutions, this work-in-progress outlines a research agenda and framework to guide future empirical studies that evaluate these candidate practices across different design settings.

2   Conceptual Foundation

Building on design science research, we first examine the key goals and values expected of prescriptive design knowledge (Iivari et al, 2021; Aier & Fischer, 2011) in human–GenAI co-design. The body of design knowledge must serve not only humans, but also machines and their collaboration.

2.1   Design Knowledge Quality for Humans

Although design science research values evaluation as a main part of the design process (Larsen et al., 2025), in many studies, evaluation is limited to the artifact and how it satisfies specified meta-requirements. Few studies focus on how to evaluate the prescriptive knowledge. The criteria suggested in those studies implicitly assume that the designer is human and capable of interpreting abstraction, resolving ambiguity, and adapting principles to other contexts. A common approach is to first identify the purpose or main goal for which prescriptive knowledge is developed and then assess how well that goal is accomplished using appropriate measurement criteria. For example, Iivari et al. (2021) and Nabavian et al. (2025) considered reusability to be the primary objective of design principles; accordingly, they proposed that the quality and reusability of DPs should be evaluated using criteria such as novelty, actionability, importance, effectiveness, and accessibility. In contrast, Aier and Fischer (2011) define the goal of design theories to be contributing to cumulative progress. Design theories should achieve a more mature and more abstract level of design knowledge that should be comparable to other types of scientific theories. Aier and Fischer use Kuhn's Criteria for scientific progress to develop six criteria to evaluate design theories: accuracy, internal & external consistency, scope, simplicity and fruitfulness of new research findings. Other formats of design knowledge, such as design process, design features, and artifacts, are not the focus of that paper.

2.2 Generative Techniques for Context-Aware Design Knowledge Retrieval

Recent work in generative information retrieval (GenIR) has introduced a range of techniques that move beyond static document lookup toward integrated retrieval–generation systems. These approaches address limitations of traditional retrieval pipe-lines, including weak contextual alignment and poor adaptability to evolving knowledge bases, because they do not rely only on word-level matching (Li et al., 2025). By explicitly structuring knowledge units, controlling retrieval behaviour, and grounding generation through citations, GenIR frameworks enable more reliable and explainable information access, which is particularly important for domain-specific systems (Li et al., 2025).

Retrieval quality depends not only on model capacity but also on what knowledge is represented, how it is structured, how retrieval is triggered (prompt engineering), and how retrieved information is incorporated into generation. As a result, modern systems combine structured identifiers, controlled retrieval strategies, alignment techniques, and citation mechanisms (Gau & Gnewuch, 2025; Li et al., 2025).

Document Identifiers for Design Knowledge. Generative retrieval systems replace traditional indexing with document identifiers (DocIDs) that can be directly generated by language models. Early approaches used numeric identifiers learned through sequence-to-sequence training (e.g., DSI; Metzler et al., 2021), while later methods introduced semantically structured or text-based identifiers to improve interpretability and generalization (Cao et al., 2021; Li et al., 2025). For design principles, DocIDs can encode the principle's intent, scope, or category, allowing the model to retrieve principles directly through generation rather than similarity matching. Multi-view identifiers that combine titles, keywords, or extracted terms have been shown to improve robustness across varied query formulations (Li et al., 2025).

A repository of design principles (DPs) exists and is publicly available with a consistent structure (Gau & Gnewuch, 2025), as well as a large body of scientific papers in which prescriptive design knowledge is embedded in examples, discussions, and methodological narratives that are often difficult for non-expert designers to interpret. Given these heterogeneous input formats, one of the documenting the Multiview Identifiers eNhanceD gEnerative Retrieval (MINDER) emerges as a suitable potential candidate to test, as it supports multiview, text-based identifiers, including titles, substrings, and synthetic pseudo-queries that can jointly represent structured DP artifacts and unstructured explanatory literature. Prior work shows that this multiview generative retrieval mechanism improves robustness and coverage across different query types while preserving interpretability, making it appropriate for exploratory evaluation in design-oriented information systems (Li et al., 2023; Li et al., 2025).

Retrieval with External Knowledge Augmentation. In addition to internalized retrieval, GenIR systems support reliable response generation through external knowledge augmentation. A prominent strategy is retrieval-augmented generation (RAG), in which relevant documents are retrieved from an external corpus and provided as conditioning context during generation (Lewis et al., 2020). This approach allows models to incorporate up-to-date and domain-specific knowledge while maintaining separation between retrieval and generation.

Li et al. (2025) further categorize retrieval augmentation strategies based on retrieval control:1) Sequential retrieval methods retrieve evidence in a fixed pipeline (e.g., ARL2 by Zhang et al. (2024)); 2) Branching retrieval approaches explore multiple retrieval paths in parallel (e.g., REPLUG by Shi et al. (2023)); 3) Conditional retrieval methods dynamically determine whether retrieval is required (e.g., Rowen by Deng et al. (2024)); and 4) Loop-based retrieval approaches interleave retrieval and generation iteratively to support multi-step reasoning (e.g., Search-o1 by Li et al. (2024)). These strategies are particularly relevant for complex design problems requiring iterative clarification or trade-off exploration. Given these characteristics, we identified one method from the Loop-based retrieval approach (i.e., self-RAG) that is suitable for reasoning and fact checking for use in the vignette-based testing approach, which we elaborate below.

Response Generation with Citation. To improve trustworthiness, GenIR systems increasingly emphasize citation-aware response generation, where generated content is explicitly linked to retrieved documents or identifiers. Rather than presenting answers without attribution, citation mechanisms enable users to trace generated claims back to their sources, improving transparency and verifiability. Approaches such as WebGPT (Nakano et al., 2021) and other retrieval-based citation systems demonstrate that explicit citation is essential for professional and high-stakes domains.

In the co-design context, citation-aware generation allows recommendations to be grounded in a design knowledge piece, such as a DP or a design theory. It also enables the human side to review the resources and validate the results. A model like SearChain works well in a knowledge-intensive environment because it improves the explainability and traceability by generating a reasoning chain (Chain-of-Query, CoQ) then interacts with each CoQ separately using retrieval for verification and completion (Asai et al., 2024).

Response Alignment and Personalization. Beyond citation, GenIR research highlights the importance of alignment with user needs and context. Li et al. (2025) describe personal information assistants that adapt responses based on user preferences, prior interactions, or domain-specific requirements. Personalized dialogue systems adjust retrieval and generation strategies across multi-turn interactions, enabling models to refine responses as user intent becomes clearer (Zhang et al., 2023; Wang et al., 2023; Wu et al., 2021).

In addition, domain-specific assistants tailor retrieval and generation mechanisms to specialized domains such as healthcare, education, and academic research (E.g., Zhongjing by Liu et al. (2023), RevGAN by Li and Tuzhilin (2019); EduChat by Dan et al. (2023)). These systems demonstrate that alignment is not limited to surface-level tone or politeness, but extends to domain constraints, boundary conditions, and task-specific evaluation criteria. In the co-design context, such alignment mechanisms are critical for design principle retrieval and adaptation to different design domains, expertise levels, and organizational contexts. In this study, we will not select any model from this approach because our approach does not focus on a specific context.

2.3   Design Knowledge Quality for AI in Co-Design

To assess the quality of design knowledge, we examine the purpose it is intended to serve. In the following, we specify the criteria we propose for this assessment and subsequently suggest corresponding measurements to evaluate each criterion. Unlike reusability or progressiveness criteria, the proposed criteria are not amenable to evaluation based on human judgment or perception, as their assessment primarily requires observing system-level behaviour and outcomes during execution. Only efficiency and effectiveness can be measured qualitatively (Table 1).

Table 1. Prescriptive design knowledge's assessment criteria in the human-AI co-design context

Criterion	Why it matters
Activation (&retrieve)	Can GenAI recognize relevant design knowledge relevant to the problem, context and the personalized query?
Alignment	Can AI align retrieved knowledge to the context, especially for prescriptive knowledge that can be applicable in various contexts/domains?
Explainability	Can humans understand the guidance provided and where it applies? Is it accessible? Can humans verify use?
Traceability	Can humans trace the decisions process, to understand why any relevant piece of design knowledge was not included?
Correctness	Are the design choices valid instantiations of the prescriptive knowledge? Can AI operationalize the knowledge correctly?
Consistency	Does retrieved design knowledge survive iteration?
Efficiency	Is co-design efficient? (time, number of iterations, amount of input data, human effort…)
Final Quality (Effectiveness)	Is the final quality acceptable and better than a sole design by humans? Is it impactful?

2.4   Evaluation of the Criteria

The next step is to define how these criteria should be evaluated across multiple scenarios. We plan to perform a vignette-based study with different IR techniques:

Two implementations for the design knowledge connection to AI will be 1- self-RAG and 2- SearChain and MINDER for document identifier.

We only focus on professional designers and experts using AI as a collaborator, and 3 different iterations from ideation to a more matured design (Kuechler & Vaishnavi, 2008): 1- a very general prompt, which is more suitable for the first round of proto-typing and idea generation (e.g., "Design a website for an online clothing shop") 2- less general by including the meta requirements validated by stakeholders or group of experts (e.g., "Design a website for an online clothing shop with product filtering and an optimized checkout flow") 3- a very specific prompt with meta requirements and deeper explanations of the context, and boundary conditions (e.g., "Design a mobile-first website for an online clothing shop specifying a three-step checkout process, WCAG 2.1 AA accessibility compliance, performance targets under two seconds per page load, and integration of branding guidelines in the attached documents."). We also need a control group that will design for the scenario without an AI-agent collaboration. To evaluate the criteria mentioned in 2.3, we follow the following steps:

Activation. In Human–AI co-design, activation (and retrieval) measures whether the generative AI is able to recognize which knowledge elements, design principles, constraints, or patterns are relevant to a given design problem. This can be evaluated by first defining a reference set of relevant principles established by human experts for the scenario and comparing the AI-activated elements against this ground truth. Quantitatively, this is measured using the proportion of relevant elements successfully retrieved by the AI.

Alignment. After the AI identifies relevant and applicable prescriptive design knowledge for a given design problem, the retrieved knowledge may include mature design theories, design principles that have been validated across multiple domains, or domain-oriented principles that are suitable for more general contexts (e.g., healthcare systems when designing a blood pressure measurement system). While activation concerns whether relevant prescriptive knowledge is retrieved, alignment evaluates whether that knowledge is interpreted and adapted properly in a context-sensitive manner. This criterion assesses whether the AI meaningfully tailors the application of retrieved knowledge to the specific domain, constraints, and design situation rather than applying it uniformly across contexts. Alignment can be evaluated like correctness, through expert assessment of whether AI-supported design decisions are contextually appropriate and justified.

Explainability. This criterion focuses on the extent to which humans can understand and verify the AI's decisions. Evaluations for correctness and alignment require the AI to make explicit which principles or rules were used and how they were applied. Evaluation combines human judgment with task-based verification, using measures such as explanation completeness and alignment between justification and decision. For this study, and to have more control over the whole process, we propose to only include very limited design principles (fewer than 20) that do not have conflicts with each other and have artifacts relevant to the scenario of the study.

Traceability. Traceability addresses whether the decision process can be reconstructed end-to-end, from inputs through intermediate reasoning to final outputs. This is essential for auditability and learning in co-design. It can be measured by analyzing design logs to assess the completeness of decision paths and the rate of omitted rationales. A particularly critical aspect of traceability arises when the prescribed design guidance conflicts with the underlying assumptions or default tendencies of the base model used in the study. For example, if a design principle or meta-requirement calls for reduced transparency, it is important to examine how the model handles this situation and to what extent the resulting decision process remains traceable. This criterion should tell us whether a design decision was made because of patterns learned from training data or because the AI used specific design knowledge it retrieved. For example, suppose we have a relevant design principle suggesting using a more extendable list (such as tag-based designs) rather than a fixed combo box. Therefore, if there is a tag-based list (that complies with the extendable list recommendation) in the final design, traceability shows if the compliance comes from the retrieved design principle or if it is because a vast majority of the training data has this feature. Traceability can complement explainability, which is a more subjective criterion, by clarifying the chain of thought in the process, in a more objective and quantifiable manner.

Correctness. This criterion evaluates whether the AI not only retrieves appropriate knowledge but also operationalizes it properly in concrete design choices. So, if the design principle is to make the user interface simple, does the AI propose a design choice consistent with a simple interface? This criterion is challenging for two reasons: 1) Given the current state of generative AI, it is common for AI systems to claim that they have applied certain guidelines or constraints when, in practice, they have not actually done so; and 2) Even from the human evaluator side, some of the design knowledge presented or formulated abstractly can be interpreted differently because, in many cases, the abstract level of the design principle can manifest in different forms, characteristics or features (Lukyanenko and Parsons, 2020). In our analysis, each AI-supported decision can be reviewed by domain experts to determine validity with respect to requirements and constraints.

Consistency (or stability across iterations). Consistency concerns the robustness of the AI's behaviour when similar inputs are provided over time or when small variations are introduced. This can be tested by running repeated design iterations under controlled changes and comparing the resulting outputs. Metrics such as output similarity or a drift index (change in output relative to change in input) indicate whether the AI maintains coherent reasoning rather than producing erratic or contradictory results.

Efficiency. This criterion evaluates the efficiency of co-design relative to human-only design. It captures both objective and subjective workload. Practical indicators include total time-to-design, number of interaction iterations, volume of human input, intervention rate on AI outputs, and perceived cognitive load. This dimension determines whether the collaboration actually reduces, rather than shifts, design effort.

Final Quality (Effectiveness). This criterion measures whether the outcome of Human–AI co-design is superior to that produced by humans alone. This is best assessed through blind comparative evaluations using expert quality rubrics, cost, requirement compliance, and complemented by end-user acceptance ratings. The difference between AI–Human and Human-only scores (delta-quality) provides a direct measure of the value added by the AI in the co-design process.

3 Conclusion

The goal of this work-in-progress paper is to develop a systematic framework for evaluating prescriptive design knowledge in human–Generative Artificial Intelligence (GenAI) co-design. As GenAI increasingly participates in design activities as a co-designer, evaluating design knowledge solely from the perspective of human interpretation and reuse becomes insufficient. This shift raises two research questions: (1) what qualities make prescriptive design knowledge applicable and reusable when interpreted and applied by GenAI systems? and (2) how can different representation and incorporation techniques be empirically examined to understand their effects on these qualities in human–GenAI co-design contexts?

We address the first question by identifying a set of system-level quality criteria (activation, alignment, correctness, consistency, explainability, traceability, efficiency, and final quality) that characterize whether design knowledge is successfully retrieved, interpreted, and operationalized by GenAI during design activities. In parallel, we incorporate key human-centred evaluation concerns, such as accessibility, impact, and perceived importance, by mapping them to system-level measures: accessibility is reflected through explainability from the human perspective, impact and importance are assessed through the effects of including or excluding design knowledge on resulting designs, and actionability and guidance are captured through correctness of application.

To address the second question, we propose a vignette-based evaluation study that selects 2*3 settings: 2 different genIR models and 3 levels of prompt engineering. Grounded in design science research and informed by recent advances in generative information retrieval, we outline operational measures for each criterion based on observable system behaviour and design outcomes. We further propose evaluating prescriptive design knowledge by embedding it within an AI-supported design system and examining its retrieval, application, and influence on design decisions, rather than relying solely on qualitative methods such as focus groups. One possible option would be to develop a shared, cloud-based evaluation system built directly on the framework proposed in this paper. In such a system, authors could upload their design knowledge and receive a structured score derived from the framework's criteria, based on performance across a set of predefined evaluation scenarios. This approach could support systematic assessment, comparability, and potential reuse. If the community agrees on developing such a system, future research should focus on identifying and defining representative evaluation scenarios, preserving the richness of complex design knowledge, and ensuring fair interpretation across diverse contexts and application domains.

References

Aier, S., Fischer, C.: Criteria of progress for information systems design theories. Inf. Syst. e-Bus. Manage. (2011)

Asai, A., Wu, Z., Wang, Y., Sil, A., Hajishirzi, H.: Self-rag: learning to retrieve, generate, and critique through self-reflection (2024)

Cao, N.D., et al.: *Autoregressive entity retrieval*. Proceedings of the Association for Computational Linguistics (ACL) (2021)

Dan, Y., et al.: Educhat: a large-scale language model-based chatbot system for intelligent education (2023). arXiv preprint arXiv:2308.02773

Gau, M., Gnewuch, U.: Facilitating design knowledge access with a generative AI-based conversational assistant. In: ECIS 2025 Proceedings (2025)

Iivari, J., Hansen, M.R.P., Haj-Bolouri, A.: A framework for light reusability evaluation of design principles in design science research. In: Proceedings of the International Conference on Design Science Research in Information Systems and Technology (DESRIST) (2021)

Kadenhe, N., Al Musleh, M., Lompot, A.: Human-AI co-design and co-creation: a review of emerging approaches, challenges, and future directions. In: Proceedings of the AAAI Symposium Series (Vol. 6, No. 1, pp. 265–270) (2025)

Kuechler, B., Vaishnavi, V.: On theory development in design science research: anatomy of a research project. Eur. J. Inf. Syst. **17**(5), 489–504 (2008). https://doi.org/10.1057/ejis.2008.40

Larsen, K., et al.: Validity in design science. MIS Q. **49**(4), 1267–1294 (2025)

Lewis, P., et al.: Retrieval-augmented generation for knowledge-intensive NLP tasks. Adv. Neural Inf. Process. Syst. (NeurIPS) (2020)

Li, P., Tuzhilin, A.: Towards controllable and personalized review generation (2019). arXiv preprint arXiv:1910.03506

Li, Y., Yang, N., Wang, L., Wei, F., Li, W.: Multiview identifiers enhanced generative retrieval. In: Proceedings of the 61st Annual Meeting of the Association for Computational Linguistics (ACL 2023) (pp. 6636–6648). Association for Computational Linguistics (2023). https://doi.org/10.18653/v1/2023.acl-long.366

Liu, Z., et al.: Pharmacygpt: The ai pharmacist (2023). arXiv preprint arXiv:2307.10432

Lukyanenko, R., Parsons, J.: Design theory indeterminacy: what is it, how can it be reduced, and why did the polar bear drown? J. Assoc. Inf. Syst. **21**(5), 1343–1369 (2020)

Metzler, D., Tay, Y., Bahri, D., Najork, M.: Rethinking search: making domain experts out of dilettantes. In: Acm sigir forum (Vol. 55, No. 1, pp. 1–27). New York, NY, USA, ACM (2021)

Nabavian, S., Parsons, J., Ogunseye, S.: Scale development for measuring design principle Reusability. ICIS 2025 Proceedings. **17** (2025). https://aisel.aisnet.org/icis2025/isdesign/isdesign/17

Nakano, R., et al.: WebGPT: browser-assisted question-answering with human feedback (2021). arXiv. https://arxiv.org/abs/2112.09332 Peffers, K., Tuunanen, T., Rothenberger, M.A., Chatterjee, S.: A design science research methodology for information systems research. J. Manage. Inf. Syst. **24**(3), 45–77 (2007)

Shi, Y., et al.: REPLUG: retrieval-augmented generation with multiple retrieval paths (2023)

Wang, H., et al.: Large language models as source planner for personalized knowledge-grounded dialogue (2023). arXiv preprint arXiv:2310.08840

Wu, Y., Ma, X., Yang, D.: Personalized response generation via generative split memory network. In: Proceedings of the 2021 Conference of the North American Chapter of the Association for Computational Linguistics: Human Language Technologies (pp. 1956–1970) (2021)

Zhang, L., Yu, Y., Wang, K., Zhang, C.: Arl2: aligning retrievers for black-box large language models via self-guided adaptive relevance labeling (2024). arXiv preprint arXiv:2402.13542

Zhang, Y., et al.: Personalized dialogue and adaptive retrieval strategies (2023)

Zhou, J., et al.: Understanding nonlinear collaboration between human and AI agents: a co-design framework for creative design. In: Proceedings of the 2024 CHI Conference on Human Factors in Computing Systems (pp. 1–16) (2024)

Designing Process Mining to Mitigate Electronic Performance Monitoring Risks

Jannis Nacke[1]([⊠]), Ralf Plattfaut[1], and René Riedl[2,3]

[1] University of Duisburg-Essen, Universitätsstraße 2, 45141 Essen, Germany
`jannis.nacke@icb.uni-due.de`
[2] University of Applied Sciences Upper Austria, Wehrgrabengasse 1-3, 4400 Steyr, Austria
[3] Johannes Kepler University Linz, Altenberger Straße 69, 4040 Linz, Austria

Abstract. Process Mining is used to gain transparency into how processes are executed and to support process improvement and operational steering. By transforming digital trace data into performance-relevant insights, Process Mining enables detailed analysis of process behavior. At the same time, such analytics-based transparency can raise concerns related to monitoring and surveillance, as highlighted in research on Electronic Performance Monitoring. This research-in-progress study examines how Process Mining systems can be designed and embedded so that transparency supports positive organizational outcomes rather than being interpreted as surveillance. Drawing on an in-depth qualitative case study at a large utility organization, the study analyzes an organizational context in which Process Mining was predominantly perceived as supportive and enabling despite its strong monitoring capabilities. Using an abductive design science research approach, we identify socio-technical mechanisms that explain how analytics-based transparency is bounded, interpreted, and enacted in practice. Building on these mechanisms, the paper derives a set of design principles that specify how Process Mining systems can be governed, aggregated, framed, introduced, and used to mitigate Electronic Performance Monitoring related risks while fostering trust, learning, and evidence-based process improvement. The study contributes design-oriented insights to Electronic Performance Monitoring and digital surveillance research and provides actionable guidance for the responsible design of analytics-based monitoring systems.

Keywords: Process Mining · Design Principles · Design Science Research

1 Introduction and Research Contribution

In contemporary organizations, digital systems routinely record everyday work activities, producing digital traces through the use of information systems [1, 2]. These traces have become a central resource for how organizations coordinate and improve their work processes [2, 3]. As data collection becomes embedded in everyday operations, process visibility is no longer exceptional but routine. The key question is therefore no longer whether organizations monitor work, but how monitoring systems are designed and embedded so that trace-based visibility enables improvement rather than being perceived as surveillance [4].

S. Chatterjee et al. (Eds.): DESRIST 2026, LNCS 16607, pp. 142–154, 2026.
https://doi.org/10.1007/978-3-032-28570-6_12

Process Mining is an analytics-based technology that uses digital trace data to discover, monitor, and improve organizational processes [5]. By transforming event data into performance-relevant insights, it enables organizations to systematically observe and steer ongoing work processes [6, 7]. As such, Process Mining exemplifies what surveillance research describes as "Surveillance 5.0," where digital traces are translated into actionable insights for decision making [8, 9]. Because it renders work activities visible in performance-relevant ways, it is well suited to be examined through the lens of Electronic Performance Monitoring, even when the primary intent is process improvement rather than employee control.

Prior research on digital surveillance and Electronic Performance Monitoring has documented both risks and opportunities associated with monitoring technologies [8, 10]. Electronic Performance Monitoring has been linked to outcomes such as stress, resistance, and reduced trust [11]. However, these outcomes are not technologically determined but depend on how monitoring systems are designed and enacted in practice [8]. Socio-technical perspectives highlight that perceived surveillance emerges through processes of interpretation and meaning-making beyond technical capabilities alone [4, 10]. In this study, we distinguish between perception, referring to how monitoring is experienced, and interpretation, referring to how monitoring signals are cognitively framed and made meaningful. This distinction provides the conceptual basis for analyzing how monitoring can be enacted differently, which we elaborate in Sect. 2.

Despite extensive research, we still lack design-oriented knowledge on how analytics-based monitoring systems can be configured to realize their benefits without triggering known Electronic Performance Monitoring risks. This gap is particularly pronounced for advanced analytics technologies such as Process Mining, where prior work has focused mainly on technical capabilities rather than organizational and social design choices [7, 8]. Concerns about analytics-driven workplace technologies are also reflected in public and practitioner discussions, where process analytics are frequently framed as intensifying surveillance and control [12, 13]. Against this background, this study examines a positive deviance case: in a qualitative case study at a large German energy provider, Process Mining was predominantly perceived as supportive and enabling, with only limited associations to surveillance and control. This case offers an opportunity to understand how known Electronic Performance Monitoring risks can be mitigated through design and embedding choices. Accordingly, we ask: *How can Process Mining systems be designed and embedded to mitigate known Electronic Performance Monitoring risks and support positive organizational outcomes?*

The objective of this study is to develop preliminary design-oriented knowledge on how Process Mining can be introduced and embedded to mitigate Electronic Performance Monitoring-related risks while enabling outcomes such as trust, learning, and coordination. This study follows a Design Science Research approach to develop preliminary, empirically grounded design principles derived from an in-depth qualitative case study. As a Research in Progress contribution, it explains how negative interpretations can be avoided in a positive deviance setting and motivates subsequent demonstration and evaluation.

2 Conceptual Framing

2.1 Digital Surveillance and Perceived Surveillance

Prior research on digital surveillance in organizations emphasizes that surveillance is not solely defined by the deployment of specific technologies, but by how monitoring practices are socially constructed, interpreted, and experienced by organizational members [14, 15]. Surveillance, in this sense, emerges at the intersection of technical visibility and social meaning-making, rather than being an inherent property of information systems themselves [14, 16]. As a result, identical technologies may be perceived as benign coordination mechanisms in one context and as intrusive surveillance tools in another, depending on organizational norms and power relations [14].

Building on this perspective, scholars increasingly distinguish between objective monitoring capabilities and perceived surveillance [17]. Perceived surveillance refers to employees' subjective interpretations of whether, how, and for what purposes their activities are being observed and evaluated, rather than to the mere presence of data collection technologies [17]. These interpretations are shaped by prior experiences, organizational communication, and the perceived intentions underlying monitoring practices, particularly with respect to performance evaluation and control [17, 18].

Consequently, surveillance can be understood as an interpretative process embedded in socio-technical arrangements, rather than as a direct outcome of technology alone [16]. Digital workplace technologies may substantially increase behavioral visibility without necessarily triggering perceptions of surveillance or control [16]. Whether visibility translates into perceived surveillance depends on whether observed activities are rendered performance-relevant and linked to accountability, evaluation, or sanctioning mechanisms [18, 19].

2.2 Electronic Performance Monitoring

Within the Information Systems and organizational literature, Electronic Performance Monitoring is commonly defined as the use of digital technologies to systematically collect, analyze, and evaluate information about employees' work-related performance [20, 21]. Central to this definition is that monitoring becomes performance monitoring when collected information is perceived as performance relevant, for example in relation to evaluation, comparison, or control of employees' work outcomes [22]. Accordingly, not all forms of digital monitoring qualify as Electronic Performance Monitoring; rather, Electronic Performance Monitoring emerges when monitoring practices are linked to performance assessment and managerial decision-making [8].

Prior research demonstrates that the effects of Electronic Performance Monitoring are highly contingent and context-dependent. While some studies associate Electronic Performance Monitoring with increased productivity, goal clarity, and coordination, others report negative outcomes such as stress, reduced autonomy, and perceptions of unfairness [20, 21]. These mixed findings have led scholars to emphasize the role of moderating factors, including transparency of monitoring practices, employee participation, and perceived procedural fairness [8, 22, 23].

Conceptually, recent work argues that Electronic Performance Monitoring should not be treated as a homogeneous or purely technological phenomenon. Instead, Electronic Performance Monitoring is increasingly conceptualized at the level of its *effects* on employees and organizations, rather than as a fixed system category [8]. From this perspective, technologies may enable performance-related monitoring without necessarily producing Electronic Performance Monitoring related outcomes, depending on how monitoring data are interpreted, communicated, and enacted in organizational practice [8, 16, 22].

This effect-oriented understanding of Electronic Performance Monitoring is particularly relevant in contexts characterized by advanced analytics and data-driven transparency. As monitoring technologies increasingly operate through aggregated and process-oriented analyses, the boundary between performance-relevant monitoring and non-evaluative visibility becomes less clear [6, 8, 22].

2.3 From Analytics to Electronic Performance Monitoring Effects

Recent advances in data analytics have fundamentally expanded organizations' capabilities to generate transparency about work processes and outcomes. In contrast to traditional monitoring systems that focus on individual tasks or behaviors, analytics-based systems increasingly operate on aggregated digital traces to produce insights about patterns, flows, and structural inefficiencies [6]. Within the Information Systems literature, such analytics-based monitoring is typically framed as a means to support process improvement, coordination, and evidence-based decision-making, with limited emphasis on direct performance control [6, 16].

Process mining represents a prominent example of analytics-based monitoring, as it reconstructs end-to-end business processes from event data and enables detailed analyses of process performance, variability, and compliance [6]. Importantly, the primary analytical object of process mining is the process rather than the individual employee. As such, process mining differs conceptually from traditional Electronic Performance Monitoring systems that are explicitly designed to evaluate individual performance or behavior [6, 8].

From an Electronic Performance Monitoring perspective, however, the distinction between process-level analytics and performance monitoring cannot be taken for granted. Prior research emphasizes that monitoring technologies may give rise to Electronic Performance Monitoring effects even when performance evaluation is not an explicit design goal [8, 16, 22]. Analytics-based insights can become performance-relevant when they are interpreted as proxies for individual or group performance, or when they are linked to accountability structures, managerial control, or sanctioning practices [18, 19].

Given the interpretative and context-dependent nature of digital surveillance and electronic performance monitoring, this study adopts a sensitizing rather than deductive use of theory. Concepts from surveillance and electronic performance monitoring research are used to provide analytical orientation without prescribing predefined hypotheses or coding schemes [24]. This approach allows us to remain attentive to how organizational actors themselves interpret analytics-based monitoring practices and their potential performance implications, rather than evaluating these practices against established models a priori [25]. Consistent with the research-in-progress character of this study, theory thus serves as a sensitizing lens to support an empirically grounded exploration of when and how analytics-based monitoring gives rise to electronic performance monitoring effects.

3   Research Design

3.1   Research Setting

The study was conducted in a large, municipally owned utility organization with more than 10,000 employees operating in a highly regulated environment. The organization provides core public services such as energy supply and mobility infrastructure and is characterized by complex, cross-functional, and compliance-intensive business processes. Process mining was introduced as an organization-wide initiative and applied across multiple functional areas, including procurement, logistics, and finance. It was used to analyze end-to-end processes spanning several organizational units, most prominently within procure-to-pay processes. Process mining activities were centrally coordinated through a dedicated Center of Excellence, while being embedded in local operational contexts. This combination of organizational scale, cross-departmental process ownership, and centralized analytical capabilities constitutes a setting in which tensions related to transparency, control, and local discretion naturally emerge, making it particularly suitable for investigating design challenges related to the use of process mining as a form of Electronic Performance Monitoring.

3.2   Data Collection

Data were collected through semi-structured interviews to capture how the use of process mining as an instrument of Electronic Performance Monitoring is designed and experienced in organizational practice. The interviews focused on understanding how specific design decisions shape perceptions of transparency, trust, motivation, and fairness in everyday work contexts. To reflect the socio-technical nature of the design problem, interviews were conducted with two complementary groups: actors involved in the design, implementation, and governance of process mining solutions (system designers), and organizational members who use these systems in their daily work and directly experience their effects (system users). This distinction enabled the integration of intended design rationales and lived usage experiences into the development of design principles. An overview of the interviewees, their organizational responsibilities, and their role as system designer or user is provided in Table 1. All interviews were semi-structured, allowing participants to reflect on concrete experiences while ensuring comparability across cases. Additional details on the interview sample, including its classification and the interview guideline, are provided in the supplementary materials.

Table 1. Overview of interviewees, their organizational responsibilities, and their role

Interviewee	Responsibility	System Designer/User
Interviewee 1	Manager Center of Excellence	Designer
Interviewee 2	Data Engineer COE	Designer
Interviewee 3	Data Engineer COE	Designer
Interviewee 4	Process Excellence Procurement	User
Interviewee 5	Head of Accounts Receivable	User
Interviewee 6	Accounts Receivable Specialist	User
Interviewee 7	Head of Dispatch & Logistics Processes	User

3.3 Research Setting

This study adopts a Design Science Research approach aimed at developing action-able design knowledge for the design and embedding of Process Mining systems. The empirical analysis follows an abductive logic, iteratively moving between empirical observations and conceptual explanations. Interview data were coded and analyzed by the first author [26] to identify recurring patterns, which were subsequently abstracted into mechanisms explaining how specific design choices in Process Mining shape per-ceptions and experiences related to Electronic Performance Monitoring [27, 28]. In a first step, the interview data were coded at a low level of abstraction using first-order concepts that remained close to the informants' language, capturing how process mining was described, interpreted, and enacted by both system designers and system users in everyday work contexts. In a second step, first-order codes were abductively condensed into higher-level mechanisms that explain why certain design choices led to specific outcomes, such as acceptance, perceived fairness, or reduced monitoring concerns [28]. A detailed mapping of first-order codes to higher-level mechanisms is available in the supplementary materials linked in footnote[1]. These mechanisms provide the explana-tory basis for the design principles developed in this study. In a final step, the identi-fied mechanisms informed the derivation of design principles following the anatomy of design principles proposed by Gregor et al. [29], explicitly specifying design objec-tives, prescriptive guidance, and underlying rationales. Extended descriptions of the design principles are also available in the supplementary materials. To structure this derivation, we draw on the design echelons methodology, focusing on the early echelons that connect empirical observations to generalizable design principles [30]. Consistent with prior design science research, the analysis focuses on early echelons and does not cover later stages related to instantiation and implementation, as the goal is the devel-opment of explanatory and prescriptive design knowledge rather than the construction and evaluation of specific artifacts [26, 30].

---

[1] https://github.com/Jannisn12/Designing-Process-Mining.

4 Empirical Findings: Social Outcomes of Process Mining

Interviewees consistently described Process Mining as a tool for operational improvement, with limited references to monitoring individual performance. Across use cases, the primary purpose of analytics was framed in terms of efficiency gains, automation, and quality improvement. As one participant summarized, *"that is actually the main purpose–increasing efficiency and productivity." (Interviewee 7,* Head of Dispatch & Logistics Processes*)*. In everyday practice, Process Mining insights were actively used to identify and discuss process inefficiencies. Analytical results were frequently introduced into workshops and improvement discussions as concrete points of reference. Interviewee 7 who is Head of Dispatch & Logistics Processes, described how process data were used to initiate problem-solving conversations: *"I put the data on the table and said: look, something is going wrong here."* Interviewees further emphasized a high degree of autonomy in exploring and interpreting analytical results. Dashboards were described as spaces for individual sense-making, supported by optional trainings and workshops. As one participant noted, *"I can make many processes significantly more efficient using Celonis, and it also allows me to identify quality issues that we would not detect in SAP" (Interviewee 6,* Accounts Receivable Specialist*)*. This user-led engagement contributed to a perception of Process Mining as an enabling infrastructure for process work rather than a controlling technology. At the same time, participants highlighted practical limitations of Process Mining use. While analytics provided rapid visibility into a large number of potential improvement opportunities, organizations often lacked the resources to implement identified changes. As one interviewee reflected, *"Which processes I focus on is a proactive decision; I regularly review the dashboard to check whether any notable changes have occurred."* (Interviewee 5, Head of Accounts Receivable).

Building on these observed usage patterns, interview data indicate that negative Electronic Performance Monitoring effects did not materialize because Process Mining insights were consistently interpreted as signals of process performance rather than indicators of individual behavior. Interview data indicate that negative Electronic Performance Monitoring effects did not materialize because Process Mining insights were consistently interpreted as signals of process performance rather than indicators of individual behavior. Analytics were introduced to replace vague problem perceptions with shared, data-based views on where processes stalled or looped. As Interviewee 7 noted, *"we wanted to see what actually happens in the process,"* using data to identify structural inefficiencies rather than to evaluate employees. This interpretation was reinforced by how analytical results were communicated and enacted in practice. Rather than demanding higher individual performance, Process Mining applications were framed as tools to simplify work and reduce unnecessary effort. As Interviewee 2 (Data Engineer, CoE) emphasized, *"we don't tell people to work faster–the applications are meant to make their work easier."* Together, these practices limited surveillance-oriented interpretations and positioned Process Mining as an enabling infrastructure for learning and improvement.

5 Why Process Mining Was not Interpreted as Surveillance

Process Mining was not interpreted as surveillance because analytical visibility was bounded in ways that consistently excluded individualized monitoring. Across the case, formal and informal rules defined what could legitimately be analyzed and acted upon, restricting visibility to processes rather than persons. This boundary shaped interpretation in advance by delimiting the object of analysis. As one designer explained, *"there are no names, no personal data, only the process"* (Interviewee 3, Data Engineer, CoE).

A related mechanism operated through the de individualization of analytical outputs via aggregation and abstraction. Dashboards presented results at the level of cases, process steps, suppliers, or organizational units, thereby preventing attribution of outcomes to individual effort. By structurally removing personal identifiers, transparency was experienced as informational rather than evaluative. As the same interviewee noted, *"everything is pooled, you do not see individual people at all"* (Interviewee 3, Data Engineer, CoE). Interpretation was further shaped through consistent process framing of analytical signals. Bottlenecks, loops, and deviations were discussed as properties of workflows and system structures, not as indicators of employee performance. This framing stabilized what kinds of explanations were considered valid and directed attention toward structural causes. As one user described, *"the question is where the process gets stuck, not who did something wrong"* (Interviewee 6, Accounts Receivable Specialist). This interpretive orientation was reinforced through ongoing communicative reframing in everyday use. Designers regularly explained how analytical results should be read and which conclusions should not be drawn from them. Such communication reduced ambiguity and anchored analytics in improvement-oriented narratives. As one designer emphasized, *"we always explain what the numbers mean and what they are not meant for"* (Interviewee 2, Data Engineer, CoE). Transparency was primarily mobilized for learning and steering rather than for control. Analytical insights were used to prioritize issues, coordinate improvement efforts, and identify opportunities for simplification or automation. Dashboards functioned as shared reference points for collective sensemaking instead of instruments for sanctioning. As Interviewee 2 summarized, *"the applications are meant to make work easier, not to push people to work faster"* (Data Engineer, CoE).

Together, these mechanisms enabled a shift of responsibility from individuals to process structures. When deviations occurred, discussions focused on workload drivers, handovers, or system constraints rather than personal accountability. This shift reduced defensiveness and supported collective problem solving. As one user in process excellence noted, *"it is about fixing the process, not blaming the people"* (Interviewee 4, Process Excellence Procurement).

6 Designing Process Mining for Positive Organizational Outcomes

This chapter presents preliminary design principles informed by the empirically identified mechanisms. These principles specify how Process Mining systems can be designed and embedded to mitigate Electronic Performance Monitoring risks and support positive organizational outcomes. Each design principle is grounded in a recurring empirical pattern and the mechanism abstracted from it. The principles are illustrated through empirical observations and examples presented in Sects. 4 and 5. Governance-related observations informed Design Principle 1, aggregation and de-individualization informed Design Principle 2, and process-focused framing informed Design Principle 3. Guided onboarding and communicative clarification informed Design Principle 4, while learning-oriented use of transparency without individual sanction informed Design Principle 5.

Design Principle 1: Governance-Driven Trust and Acceptance: Process Mining systems should be governed by explicit and formal rules that clearly delimit what may and may not be analyzed, thereby fostering trust and acceptance among system users. Such governance defines permissible data scopes, excludes individual-level analysis, and establishes legitimate purposes for analytics use, positioning Process Mining as an improvement instrument rather than a surveillance technology. In organizational contexts with strong co-determination structures, data protection requirements, or heightened sensitivity toward digital monitoring, the involvement of trusted governance actors stabilizes these boundaries and legitimizes analytics use. By clarifying analytical limits upfront and framing monitoring-related signals as informational rather than evaluative, governance reduces uncertainty about managerial intent. As a result, governance substitutes ambiguity with institutional assurance, mitigates defensive reactions, and preserves the legitimacy of Process Mining as a supportive infrastructure for process improvement rather than covert performance monitoring.

Design Principle 2: Design for Aggregated Process-Level Transparency: Process Mining systems should be designed by system designers to provide transparency at an aggregated process level rather than at the level of individual employees. Analytics outputs should be structured around processes, teams, departments, or functional units, thereby excluding individual identifiers and preventing direct performance attribution. Through aggregation and pseudonymization, designers enact a structural boundary that shifts visibility from individual action to process behavior. Bottlenecks, delays, and coordination issues become interpretable as properties of the process rather than as outcomes of individual effort. This enables system users, such as managers and operational staff, to diagnose problems and prioritize improvement without engaging in individual comparison or evaluation. Aggregated transparency reduces perceived surveillance and mitigates typical Electronic Performance Monitoring risks such as fear, mistrust, and defensive behavior. At the same time, it preserves the diagnostic value of analytics for operational and managerial decision making. As a result, Process Mining is stabilized as a process improvement tool rather than being interpreted as a system for monitoring individual performance.

Design Principle 3: Process Focus as a Boundary Against Surveillance: Process Mining systems should be designed and communicated by system designers as instruments for analyzing and improving processes rather than for evaluating individual behavior. Analytical outputs should be consistently framed as process signals such as bottlenecks, loops, handovers, or workload distributions, not as indicators of individual effort or performance. By enforcing this process-focused framing, designers and system users, such as managers and team leads, enact a semantic boundary at the point of interpretation.

Insights are used to identify structural issues and workload drivers instead of attributing responsibility to individual employees. This shifts accountability from persons to processes and stabilizes transparency as a resource for support, relief, and improvement. For system users, a strong process focus clarifies the purpose of transparency and establishes a clear boundary against personal surveillance. Process transparency is perceived as fair and actionable because responsibility is attributed to structures and dependencies rather than to individual effort. This reduces ambiguity and limits defensive or avoidant reactions commonly associated with electronic performance monitoring. In contrast, activity-based or individual-level monitoring blurs interpretive boundaries and invites normative judgments. A stable process focus therefore protects Process Mining's role as an enabling infrastructure for collective problem solving rather than a surveillance tool.

Design Principle 4: Early Immersion Through Guided Onboarding and Transparency: Process Mining systems should be introduced through early, guided onboarding that supports sensemaking by clarifying what is analyzed, how data is generated, and which conclusions are valid. Rather than exposing system users to full analytical complexity upfront, designers should enable stepwise immersion through concrete use cases, example dashboards, and guided walkthroughs. For system designers and internal champions, this principle requires actively structuring early interactions with the system. By explaining data provenance, analytical scope, and limitations, onboarding establishes interpretive boundaries and prevents users from drawing premature or unintended conclusions from transparency. For system users, early immersion reduces uncertainty at a critical moment when analytics are most likely to be misinterpreted as evaluation or control. Guided onboarding creates cognitive grounding and normative clarity, enabling users to appropriate Process Mining as a supportive tool for process understanding rather than a surveillance mechanism. As a result, process-focused interpretations stabilize early and limit the emergence of surveillance-oriented framings.

Design Principle 5: Evidence-Based Steering Without Individual Sanction: Process Mining transparency should be designed to support evidence-based steering and learning rather than individual sanctioning or blame. Analytical insights should inform prioritization, monitoring, and improvement initiatives at a collective level, for example across processes, teams, or organizational units. For system designers, this requires configuring KPIs, dashboards, and drill-down logic in ways that make process performance interpretable and actionable without enabling individual attribution. Transparency should highlight where intervention is needed, not individual actors. For system users, especially managers and team leads, transparency becomes a basis for coordinating actions, allocating resources, and guiding improvement discussions. By anchoring steering decisions in shared metrics rather than personal accountability, this design shifts responsibility from individuals to process structures. As a result, transparency reduces ambiguity and defensiveness, preserves intrinsic motivation, and supports continuous improvement without triggering surveillance-oriented Electronic Performance Monitoring dynamics.

7 Discussion and Implications

This study contributes to Electronic Performance Monitoring and digital surveillance research by showing how negative monitoring effects can be avoided in an analytics-based monitoring setting. Rather than explaining variation across implementations in general, the study examines a positive deviance case in which Process Mining was not predominantly interpreted as surveillance. The findings show that negative Electronic Performance Monitoring effects are not inevitable, but contingent on how analytics are designed, communicated, and governed in practice. The identified mechanisms highlight how design choices shape what analytics make visible, how signals are interpreted, and how responsibility is assigned. In particular, constraining individual level attribution and stabilizing process focused interpretations helped mitigate typical Electronic Performance Monitoring risks such as mistrust, fear, and defensive behavior. At the same time, these insights are bounded: they reflect a setting with clear analytical boundaries, process-oriented use, and supportive communication, and should therefore be understood as explaining how negative interpretations can be mitigated rather than as a general explanation of monitoring outcomes across contexts.

The study also contributes to design science by showing how empirically grounded insights from such a case can inform actionable design principles for socially sensitive analytics contexts. By linking process level transparency, governance, and sensemaking practices to the avoidance of negative Electronic Performance Monitoring effects, the study brings employee perceptions and organizational consequences directly into the design logic. For practitioners, these principles offer guidance on how analytics-based monitoring systems can support learning, coordination, and improvement rather than control. Acceptance and trust do not emerge from user compliance, but from clear analytical boundaries, aggregated transparency, early orientation, and evidence-based steering, underscoring monitoring as a socio technical design problem rather than a user acceptance issue.

8 Conclusion and Next Steps

This research shows that Process Mining, despite its strong monitoring capabilities, does not necessarily trigger negative Electronic Performance Monitoring effects. Instead, its organizational consequences depend on how analytics are designed, communicated, and enacted in practice. By identifying key mechanisms and deriving corresponding design principles, the study offers a structured explanation of how positive organizational outcomes can be enabled through deliberate design choices. As a Research-in-Progress study, this work opens several avenues for future research. Next steps include validating the proposed mechanisms and design principles across additional organizational contexts, examining their long-term stability, and exploring potential boundary conditions. Extending this perspective beyond Process Mining highlights the broader relevance of design-oriented approaches to analytics-based monitoring technologies.

References

1. Freelon, D.: On the interpretation of digital trace data in communication and social computing research. J. Broadcast. Electron. Media 59–75 (2014)

2. Pentland, B.T., Recker, J., Wolf, J., Wyner, G.: Bringing context inside process research with digital trace data. JAIS 1214–1236 (2020)
3. vom Brocke, J., Jans, M., Mendling, J., Reijers, H.A.: A five-level framework for research on process mining. Bus. Inf. Syst. Eng. 483–490 (2021)
4. Grisold, T., Seidel, S., Heck, M., Berente, N.: Digital surveillance in organizations. Bus. Inf. Syst. Eng. 401–410 (2024)
5. van der Aalst, W.: Process mining. Commun. ACM. 76–83 (2012)
6. van der Aalst, W.: Process mining. Springer (2016)
7. Chen, H., Chiang, R.H.L., Storey, V.C.: Business intelligence and analytics: from big data to big impact. MIS Q. 1165–1188 (2012)
8. Kalischko, T., Riedl, R.: Electronic performance monitoring in the digital workplace: conceptualization, review of effects and moderators, and future research opportunities. Front. Psychol. 633031 (2021)
9. Wenzel, R., van Quaquebeke, N.: The double-edged sword of big data in organizational and management research. Organ. Res. Methods 548–591 (2018)
10. Edwards, L., Martin, L., Henderson, T.: Employee surveillance: the road to surveillance is paved with good intentions. SSRN J. (2018)
11. Lund, J.: Electronic performance monitoring: a review of research issues. Appl. Ergonomics 54–58 (1992)
12. Ng, A.: When AI 'optimizes' your workplace (2023)
13. Christl, W.: Digitale Überwachung und Kontrolle am Arbeitsplatz. Von der Ausweitung betrieblicher Datenerfassung zum algorithmischen Management? Cracked Labs (2021)
14. Ball, K.: Workplace surveillance: an overview. Labor Hist. 87–106 (2010)
15. Lyon, D.: Surveillance studies: an overview. Polity Press, Cambridge (2007)
16. Leonardi, P.M., Treem, J.W.: Behavioral visibility: a new paradigm for organization studies in the age of digitization, digitalization and datafication. Organ. Stud. 1601–1625 (2020)
17. Alge, B.J.: Effects of computer surveillance on perceptions of privacy and procedural justice. J. Appl. Psychol. 797–804 (2001)
18. Wells, D.L., Moorman, R.H., Werner, J.M.: The impact of the perceived purpose of electronic performance monitoring on an array of attitudinal variables. Hum. Resour. Dev. Q. 121–138 (2007)
19. Zuboff, S.: In the age of the smart machine. The future of work and power. Basic Books, New York (1988)
20. Bhave, D.P.: The invisible eye? Electronic performance monitoring and employee job performance. Pers. Psychol. 605–635 (2014)
21. Ravid, D.M., White, J., Tomczak, D.L., Miles, A.F., Behrend, T.S.: A meta-analysis of the effects of electronic performance monitoring on work outcomes (2022)
22. Jeske, D., Santuzzi, A.M.: Monitoring what and how: psychological implications of electronic performance monitoring. New. Technol. Work Employ. 62–78 (2015)
23. Alder, G.S.: Examining the relationship between feedback and performance in a monitored environment: a clarification and extension of feedback intervention theory. J. High Technol. Manage. Res. 157–174 (2007)
24. Blumer, H.: What is wrong with social theory? Am. Sociol. Rev. 3–10 (1954)
25. Bowen, G.A.: Grounded theory and sensitizing concepts. Int. J. Qual. Methods 12–23 (2006)
26. Gregor, S., Hevner, A.R.: Positioning and presenting design science research for maximum impact1. MIS Q. 337–355 (2013)
27. Peirce, C.S.: Collected Papers of Charles Sanders Peirce. Harvard University Press (1934)
28. Dubois, A., Gadde, L.-E.: Systematic combining: an abductive approach to case research. J. Bus. Res. 553–560 (2002)
29. Gregor, S., Kruse, L., Seidel, S.: Research perspectives: the anatomy of a design principle. JAIS 1622–1652 (2020)

30. Tuunanen, T., Winter, R., vom Brocke, J.: Dealing with complexity in design science research: a methodology using design echelons. MIS Q 427–458 (2024)

Future of Healthcare and Wellbeing

When Digital Tools Enter the Playground: Designing Information Systems for IT-Distant Care Contexts

Niklas Korte[✉] [iD] and Florian Lüttgenau

University of Münster, 48149 Münster, Germany
`niklas.korte@uni-muenster.de`

Abstract. Information systems increasingly enter care-centered domains with limited digital infrastructure. Design approaches rooted in office-like settings often presume stable users and uninterrupted interaction; in IT-distant contexts, these premises misfit practice. We report a multi-year design science research project in a German all-day school that designed digital support for attendance documentation and coordination of children's whereabouts. Across four iterative design cycles, we built and refined a socio-technical ecosystem. The findings highlight three interrelated challenges shaping design trade-offs: (1) stakeholder heterogeneity across staff, administration, children, and parents with divergent capabilities and accountabilities; (2) temporally fragmented and spatially distributed work that constrains attention for structured digital interaction; and (3) legitimacy- and trust-sensitive dynamics in which privacy and "surveillance" framings weigh as heavily as functional requirements. We develop a sociomaterial explanation of how artifacts become viable through multi-stakeholder alignment and derive implications for design science research in care-oriented environments.

Keywords: IT-distant context · Heterogeneous user · In-situ evaluation · Socio-technical ecosystem

1 Introduction

Information systems (IS) are increasingly expanding into domains that have traditionally been only weakly supported by digital technologies. Beyond administrative and managerial settings, digital systems are now being introduced into social and professional fields such as care, education, crafts, and field-based work [1, 2]. In these domains, digitalization is often associated with promises of modernization, improved coordination, enhanced documentation, and, more recently, data-driven decision-making and AI-supported services [3]. Consequently, organizations are increasingly expected to adopt IS to support everyday work and meet regulatory and accountability requirements. At the same time, these domains follow logics that differ fundamentally from the assumptions underlying much of traditional IS design. Conventional IS approaches have largely evolved in office-like organizational environments and typically assume process-oriented work, rational decision-making, stable roles, and efficiency-driven goals [4].

S. Chatterjee et al. (Eds.): DESRIST 2026, LNCS 16607, pp. 157–168, 2026.
https://doi.org/10.1007/978-3-032-28570-6_13

In contrast, care-oriented and educational settings are characterized by relational work, situational decision-making, emotional engagement, and high variability. Work is organized through interaction, improvisation, and embodied presence rather than through predefined processes. Introducing IS into such environments therefore exposes a fundamental tension between structured system logics and actual everyday practice. This tension has tangible consequences. Users with heterogeneous needs such as educators, children, or cognitively diverse groups are often excluded, underserved, or addressed based on assumptions that do not align with their actual practices and capabilities, leading systems to be resisted, bypassed, or reduced to administrative add-ons. Although IS offer potential for contextual flexibility, for example through adaptive interfaces or accessibility features, this potential remains largely underdeveloped. Accordingly, IT-distant and relational work environments remain underserved and underexplored in IS research and practice.

In this paper, we investigate this design tension through a multi-year Design Science Research (DSR) project conducted in a German open all-day school (Offene Ganztagsschule, OGS) care setting. OGS organizations provide supervision and educational activities for children outside regular school hours and represent a care-oriented, relational work environment that is increasingly subject to digitalization pressures. The project focuses on the design of a digital system for attendance tracking and the coordination of children's whereabouts in daily practice. Beyond the coordination problem, the project reflects mission-driven digital innovation in an under-resourced care-education setting [5]. Over several design phases, we developed and iteratively refined a socio-technical ecosystem consisting of physical terminals, NFC-bracelets, and mobile applications embedded in existing coordination routines. Drawing on longitudinal design documentation and sustained contextual immersion, we analyze how contextual characteristics and user dynamics shaped requirements, design decisions, and socio-technical trade-offs over time. We use the term contextual characteristics to refer to recurring social, temporal, spatial, and organizational features of the setting that shape system use and design decisions. Rather than evaluating a finalized artifact or deriving prescriptive design principles, the study moves beyond a view of IS as separable from their implementation context and aims to deepen our understanding of how digital systems evolve when they are designed for heterogeneous, IT-distant, and care-oriented environments through a sociomaterial lens [6]. The guiding research question is:

What contextual characteristics and user dynamics emerge when digital tools are designed for heterogeneous, IT-distant, and care-oriented environments?

2 Theoretical Background and Related Work

2.1 IS Design and Its Traditional Logic

IS design has historically evolved in close alignment with managerial concerns of efficiency, coordination, and control in organizations [7]. Dominant IS design approaches are typically grounded in a rational-instrumental logic. This traditional logic is based on a set of largely implicit assumptions about work, technology, and users [8]. Work is predominantly framed as a sequence of discrete activities that can be modeled, standardized, and decomposed into clearly assignable tasks [9]. Variability is treated as an exception to be controlled through rules and procedures rather than as a constitutive feature of everyday practice. Technology is typically understood as a relatively stable artifact that can be specified in detail before introduction and then implemented into the organization as a finished solution [10]. The prototypical user of this organization is an adult professional whose primary responsibility includes dealing with documents, data, and formalized communication, and who can reasonably be expected to develop and maintain the competencies needed to handle complex digital tools.

The dominance of this traditional logic has also shaped how IS research conceptualizes the relationship between systems and organizational contexts. Much of the literature [11–13] implicitly assumes office-like or administrative settings in which tasks are temporally and spatially structured, interruptions are manageable, and users can allocate cognitive resources to interacting with the system. For example, workflow research commonly assumes that work can be defined, analyzed, and coordinated as a business process, whereas studies of knowledge work and trace data typically focus on professional, digitally intensive environments in which users can devote sustained attention to informational tasks and system interaction. Under these conditions, the emphasis on efficiency, process control, and standardization is both intelligible and, in many cases, appropriate. However, in cases where these conditions are not met, this traditional logic is inappropriate.

2.2   IS in Non-Traditional and IT-Distant Contexts

Various sectors in which these conditions do not hold are nevertheless, like most areas of contemporary society, subject to ongoing digitalization. These sectors are not primarily organized around knowledge work, but around care work, educational work, or manual and craft work. The core activities in these domains consist either in direct interpersonal engagement or in physically producing and maintaining objects and environments. These environments emphasize empathy, improvisation, and relational work rather than standardization. At the same time, there is also potential for improving and supporting processes through digital means. In addition to the planning and coordination of activities, many of these settings involve documentation, reporting, and communication tasks that can in principle be supported by digital systems. Consequently, there is a growing need for IS research that takes these industries and work contexts as its primary point of reference.

In many of these settings, information technology remains peripheral to the core work and can therefore be described as operating in IT-distant contexts. Here, professional identities and routines are organized around direct interpersonal interaction rather than around technology [14]. In practice, digital devices are often physically and temporally separated from the primary work site, and must be used in short, fragmented intervals rather than in extended sessions. Basic infrastructural and organizational conditions further constrain the integration of IS into everyday practice [15]. From the perspective of practitioners, digital systems may thus appear as external impositions or administrative add-ons, primarily associated with reporting, compliance, or control, rather than as tools that directly support the core relational or manual tasks [16]. This distance between technology and primary work practices shapes how systems are perceived, appropriated, and sometimes resisted or circumvented. Thereby, specific challenges for IS design arise that are not adequately addressed by assumptions derived from digitally saturated office environments.

3 Methodology

3.1 Research Approach

Situated within the field of DSR, this paper adopts a qualitative and interpretive orientation that departs from more normative or principle-driven variants of DSR. Classical DSR approaches often aim at the systematic construction and evaluation of artifacts in order to derive prescriptive design knowledge, such as design principles or methods [7]. While this orientation has proven valuable in relatively stable and well-structured organizational settings [17], it is less suited for contexts characterized by high variability, relational work, and low levels of digital maturity [6]. This research conceptualizes DSR primarily as a contextual and intervention-oriented mode of inquiry that enables the generation of knowledge through sustained engagement with practice. Context is understood as constitutive not only of design requirements and outcomes, but of the design problem itself, which emerges through intervention and use rather than being specified upfront. Design activities therefore serve a dual purpose. On the one hand, they contribute to the development of a functional socio-technical system that supports coordination and documentation needs in the field. On the other hand, they function as an empirical lens through which implicit assumptions, tensions, and contextual logics become visible.

Importantly, this inquiry is coupled with the development of a functional and usable digital system for the research context at hand, without treating the artifact itself as the primary outcome of the research. Consequently, contextual understanding and artifact development are tightly intertwined throughout the project. The goal of this research is not to evaluate the effectiveness or efficiency of a finalized artifact, nor to generalize design rules at this stage. In line with this orientation, the study focuses on contextual characteristics, user dynamics, and design-related turning points that jointly shaped the evolution of the artifact in the OGS setting.

3.2 Research Context: Open All-Day School Care as an IT-Distant Environment

The empirical setting of this study is an OGS in Germany which provides supervision and educational activities for children outside regular school hours and represents a hybrid organizational form situated between formal schooling, childcare, and informal pedagogical work. While they are subject to administrative regulations and accountability requirements, their everyday practices are predominantly shaped by relational, situational, and child-centered logics, emphasizing children's autonomy, self-directed movement, and situational decision-making. From an IS perspective, the OGS constitutes a distinctly IT-distant environment. Digital systems have historically played only a marginal role in daily work, which is instead organized through verbal communication, ad hoc coordination, and embodied presence [18].

At the same time, OGS organizations increasingly face external demands for documentation, transparency, and compliance, particularly with regard to supervision duties, attendance tracking, and data protection. This creates a growing need for digital support systems, despite limited technological infrastructure and heterogeneous digital competencies among user groups [19]. The context involves multiple internal and external stakeholder groups. Internal users include pedagogical staff, children of varying ages and developmental stages, and OGS administrators. External stakeholders comprise parents, umbrella organizations, and public authorities. Notably, children are not only passive subjects of documentation but active users of the system, which introduces additional ethical, developmental, and emotional considerations. These concern, for example, the appropriate handling of children's whereabouts data, age-related differences in attention and interaction capabilities, and the need to avoid experiences of pressure or surveillance in a care setting. In the project, these issues were addressed through simple interaction designs, close alignment with existing routines, and ongoing feedback from staff and parents.

3.3   The Case Study and the Socio-Technical Artifact

The study is embedded in a multi-year Design Science Research project. It aims to support attendance tracking and the coordination of children's whereabouts in the daily routines of the OGS. Rather than replacing existing practices, the system was designed to be embedded into established coordination routines and spatial arrangements within the OGS environment. Its physical presence within the school makes the system visible, tangible, and continuously embedded in everyday social practice. The resulting artifact is a hybrid socio-technical ecosystem combining NFC-enabled terminals, children's wristbands, and a staff-facing mobile application.

3.4   Design Cycles

Our DSR project unfolded through four iterative cycles that combined artifact building with formative evaluation in the field (Fig. 1). Across cycles, the socio-technical artifact evolved into an integrated system. The first cycle consolidated the design problem and initial requirements based on practitioner input, specifying central use cases (e.g., attendance and supervision documentation), key stakeholder groups, and boundary conditions such as data protection and accountability. Building on this framing, the second cycle translated requirements into conceptual designs and early prototypes of the hardware and software components. In the third cycle, the emerging system was iteratively tested and refined in-situ; live trainings and interviews served as evaluation to identify breakdowns in interaction routines and integration into practice, which were translated into concrete revisions of the artifacts (terminal, wristbands, and mobile app). The fourth cycle focused on pilot implementation and stabilization: a two-week live pilot validated feasibility in production use and supported targeted adjustments prompted by issues observed during sustained operation. Figure 1 summarizes the four cycles and the corresponding artifact versions.

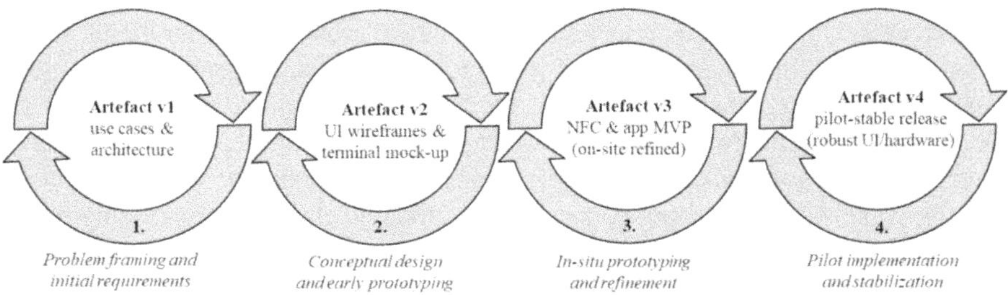

Fig. 1. Overview of the four DSR cycles and the evolving socio-technical artifact (v1–v4)

3.5 Data Collection and Analysis

Data collection followed a qualitative, longitudinal strategy aligned with the study's interpretive DSR orientation. Given the focus on understanding contextual characteristics and user dynamics, data were collected across conceptualization, prototyping, design, implementation, and use phases in production. The primary data sources include ethnographic field notes from repeated site visits to the OGS, documenting daily routines, coordination practices, breakdowns, and informal interactions among educators and children. These observations were complemented by detailed notes taken during training workshops, stakeholder meetings, and feedback sessions involving administrative actors, pedagogical staff, and parents. In addition, transcripts and summaries of design discussions, informal conversations, and reflective debriefings among the research team were collected to capture evolving interpretations and design rationales. As part of the data collection strategy, MyDesignProcess, a web-based tool for documenting DSR processes introduced by vom Brocke et al. [20], was used to structure and document design phases, activities, and key decisions throughout the project. The tool supported longitudinal documentation and maintained a transparent design trace linking contextual observations, design choices, and artifact evolution.

Data collection spanned 26 months and included 8 site visits to the OGS, 42 stakeholder meetings and feedback sessions, and 3 workshops and training sessions involving pedagogical staff, administrative actors, and, where relevant, parents and children. This longitudinal corpus enabled us to trace how contextual observations, interaction breakdowns, and stakeholder concerns accumulated and informed subsequent design decisions.

Data analysis followed a qualitative and interpretive approach aimed at identifying recurring contextual characteristics, tensions and user dynamics that shaped the design and evolution of the digital system. While contextual insights informed ongoing design work throughout the project, the formal analysis reported in this paper was conducted retrospectively in the later project phase, drawing on material collected across all four design cycles. In this retrospective analysis, we reviewed field notes, meeting notes, and design documentation comparatively across the project in order to identify recurring episodes, breakdowns, and tensions related to system use, coordination, and stakeholder interaction. This comparative reading enabled us to consolidate higher-level patterns and reconstruct those moments in which initial design assumptions were revised, which we conceptualize as turning points in the design process.

4 Findings

4.1 Contextual Characteristics

Our observations and interviews show that everyday work is organized around the care, safety, and participation of children rather than around the execution of predefined procedures. Staff are responsible for supervising groups, responding to individual needs, coordinating activities, and maintaining a sense of order and well-being in the group. These responsibilities extend beyond task execution to the ongoing management of social dynamics, emotions, and transitions between activities and spaces. The rhythms of work in this environment are dynamic and often unpredictable. Children arrive and leave at different times, groups reconfigure throughout the afternoon, and small incidents regularly disrupt planned activities. On-site engagements and trial interactions further indicated that the setting affords little uninterrupted time for explanation or concentrated system use: ambient noise, continuous movement, and frequent interruptions constrain sustained attention and complicate the establishment of stable interaction routines.

Practitioners constantly shift attention between multiple parallel demands: monitoring the group, engaging in one-on-one interactions, coordinating with colleagues, and handling practical issues such as snacks, materials, or room changes. As a result, work is frequently organized through ad hoc reactions and local judgements rather than through stable, formally modelled processes. Across field visits, coordination was predominantly achieved through informal, verbal communication and embodied cues. Staff relied on brief conversations, shared routines, and mutual observation to distribute responsibilities and react to emerging situations. Documentation and digital systems played a subordinate role in moment-to-moment coordination; they were typically used before or after direct interaction with children, or in short intermissions when the situation allowed. This organization of work leaves limited uninterrupted time and cognitive bandwidth for structured digital interaction.

4.2 Observed Design Challenges

Across the design cycles, our empirical material revealed a set of recurring challenges that shaped how the system could be meaningfully introduced and used in the OGS setting. These challenges mainly arose from the limited contextual understanding with which the design work initially started. Coming from more office-like environments, the team was unable to anticipate many of the practical constraints and contingencies that structure everyday work in the OGS.

First, the user landscape proved to be more heterogeneous than initially anticipated. The setting brought together pedagogical staff, administrative personnel, children from different age groups, and parents, with considerable variation in digital literacy not only between these groups but also within them. Some children were already familiar with tablets or wearable devices, others had little or no prior experience. Among pedagogical staff, some used digital devices extensively in their private lives, whereas others reported that they rarely interacted with such technologies at all. Because digital tools are not central to the professional role in this context, most digital literacy stemmed from unevenly distributed private experience rather than from organizational training. This made it difficult to assume a "typical user" and to define a single interaction logic that would be equally appropriate for all.

A second cluster of challenges concerned the relationship between system use and relational work. In everyday practice, interactions with children consistently took precedence over digital interaction. Staff routinely interrupted or postponed system use when children approached them with questions, conflicts, or requests for attention, and several practitioners expressed discomfort with spending time "at the device" while the group was active. An early evaluation session in which developers, pedagogical staff, and children jointly tried out the app and hardware made this very tangible: the noise level in the room made focused explanation difficult, children spontaneously engaged with the terminals and wristbands, and one developer was even accidentally knocked to the ground by a running child. This moment became a first turning point in the project, as it highlighted how little uninterrupted time and physical stability were available for concentrated system use.

A third set of challenges concerned project communication and stakeholder interfacing between two markedly different worlds. In the OGS, work was fast-paced and interruption-rich, and staff had to respond immediately to children's needs and transitions. By contrast, the development team worked with planned cycles, meetings, and technical abstractions that presupposed time for explanation and reflection. In the early stages, mediated communication through the project manager was indispensable. It enabled translation between vocabularies, helped align expectations, and reduced coordination overhead for staff whose attention was continuously absorbed by situational demands. Over time, however, this bridging arrangement became less conducive to design work because it inevitably filtered situated concerns and limited the developers' direct exposure to the material, spatial, and temporal conditions of use. As a result, feedback cycles risked becoming detached from practice, and design decisions were more likely to reflect second-hand interpretations than lived interaction dynamics. As routines stabilized and relationships matured, the project manager could gradually step back, which enabled several turning points in the project. The development team engaged more directly with staff and, when relevant, with parents and the data protection officer. It also coordinated directly with the school administration to secure Wi-Fi provisioning. These direct encounters improved mutual understanding, made implicit assumptions visible in situ, and supported adaptations that were more tightly aligned with local routines and constraints.

4.3 How Turning Points Reoriented the Design Work

For the design team, several moments in the project acted as turning points that changed their understanding of the design problem. The first in-situ evaluation in the after-school care setting made it clear that staff had far less time and attentional capacity for focused interaction than initially assumed. Rather than designing for sustained, screen-centered use, the team began to treat very brief, interruptible interactions as the primary use case. This shift pushed simplification of interaction flows, reduction of steps, and immediate legibility of system states from secondary usability goals to central design requirements. A concrete instance of this reorientation concerned the NFC terminals used by children. In an early iteration, both an NFC logo and the project logo were printed side by side on the device. Because the two logos were visually similar, children could not identify the functional interaction point. Unlike adult users, they lacked familiarity with the NFC symbol as a culturally established signifier for contactless interaction. In a subsequent iteration, the project logo was removed, leaving only the NFC symbol as the sole visual cue. This simplification resolved the ambiguity and enabled self-explanatory use without verbal instruction.

A second turning point related to the organization of project communication. Working largely through a central coordinating person had initially seemed efficient, but over time it became apparent that this gateway structure filtered and delayed how practices in the OGS and the system design informed each other. As the team recognized this, communication and participation arrangements themselves became part of the design problem. This led to a stronger emphasis on direct encounters with pedagogical staff and, where feasible, children, for example through joint workshops and on-site feedback sessions alongside the existing coordination role.

Further turning points emerged around data protection and infrastructure. Concerns voiced by parents highlighted that the system would be evaluated not only in terms of functionality. Questions of data protection rights and supervision of children moved into the foreground of design work. At the same time, the discovery of uneven Wi-Fi coverage during initial tests showed that connectivity and device placement could not be treated as neutral background conditions, but had to be checked and negotiated as part of the design. Taken together, these turning points shifted the focus from adapting a preconceived solution to a new setting towards articulating what it means to design a digital system that responds to the specific relational, emotional, and material conditions of the after-school care context.

5   Discussion

Our theoretical contribution is not that context matters, but how emotional, stakeholder-intensive contexts shape design work. We distinguish designing systems to elicit emotions from designing for emotional contexts. In our case, the artifact had to fit a care-and-trust-sensitive environment in which legitimacy concerns (e.g., parental "surveillance" framings) became as decisive as functional requirements (e.g., attendance tracking and a staff-facing overview of children's whereabouts across spaces). This shows that emotional alignment is a multi-stakeholder achievement: viability emerges only when workability, comprehensibility, and acceptability converge across the involved actor groups. The turning points we report capture moments in which initial design assumptions broke down, and the team had to reframe the problem and simplify interaction concepts. In this way, they make visible how design knowledge in IT-distant care-education settings emerges through iterative renegotiation of what is feasible and appropriate in the local practice.

Methodologically, our study suggests that interpretive DSR in IT-distant settings benefits from deliberate context entry and sustained on-site engagement. Several key constraints and evaluation criteria only became visible in situ, for instance during live training and trials embedded in everyday routines. This implies that data collection should be organized around moments of actual use (not only interviews) and supported by systematic, lightweight documentation of design decisions and breakdowns (e.g., via myDesignProcess.com) to maintain traceability across cycles. Finally, our cycles show that iteration helped to uncover breakdowns in everyday routines, in which taken-for-granted practices became problematic and, as a result, provided concrete guidance for subsequent design decisions.

In practical terms, our findings specify how designers can reduce friction when deploying digital artifacts in care-and education settings characterized by multi-user use and high legitimacy demands. In the OGS, viable solutions had to work for pedagogical staff under time pressure, be understandable for children, and remain acceptable to parents, including in terms of trust and data protection perceptions. Systems should therefore prioritize adaptability and accessibility through simple, interruptible interactions and clear system states, rather than relying on sustained attention or extensive training. Finally, designers should check socio-material preconditions early (e.g., connectivity, device placement, spatial routines) and use early in-situ prototyping and live trials to identify constraints that are unlikely to surface in workshop-only settings.

This study is grounded in one specific care-education setting, a German OGS, and in a particular socio-technical configuration, namely a hybrid hardware/software solution consisting of terminals, NFC-wristbands, and a mobile web application. While this focus enables deep contextual insight, it limits how far the findings can be transferred to other IT-distant domains or to settings in which coordination technologies are purely software-based. Moreover, our analysis emphasizes contextual characteristics and design-related turning points rather than long-term effectiveness outcomes of a finalized artifact. As a research-in-progress study, we will continue in-situ validation to further consolidate the artifact and refine interaction routines, accessibility, and socio-material fit, in order to derive empirically grounded design principles.

6 Conclusion

Introducing digital systems into IT-distant and relational care contexts reveals tensions that are not primarily about "resistance", but about mismatches between structured system logics and everyday experiential logics of care, supervision, and participation. In this research-in-progress study, we reported insights from the longitudinal design science project in a German OGS, where a hybrid solution (terminals, NFC wristbands, and a staff-facing app) is being developed and validated in situ. Our findings show how heterogeneous users, relational work, and legitimacy concerns (e.g., parental trust and data protection perceptions) shaped requirements and socio-technical trade-offs over time. Read through a social entrepreneurship lens, the project can be understood as mission-driven digital innovation that seeks to create social value in an under-resourced care-education setting, while continuously negotiating legitimacy with diverse stakeholders. At this stage, we therefore contribute contextual understanding and analytically grounded turning points as a foundation for later, more transferable design knowledge for such environments. Next, we will deepen in-situ validation and use the upcoming transfer and scaling activities to test how the solution remains workable across sites.

Next, we will deepen in-situ validation by accompanying the continued development and use of the prototype in additional OGS settings. Through further observation and documentation of artifact evolution, use routines, and stakeholder interactions across sites, we aim to deepen the present findings and derive more transferable design implications for developing information systems in IT-distant care contexts.

References

1. Chen, Y., Lehmann, C.U., Malin, B.: Digital information ecosystems in modern care coordination and patient care pathways and the challenges and opportunities for AI solutions. J. Med. Internet Res. **26** (2024)
2. Herterich, M., Peters, C., Neff, A., Uebernickel, F., Brenner, W.: Mobile work support for field service: a literature review and directions for future research
3. Vial, G.: Understanding digital transformation: a review and a research agenda. Managing Digital Transformation **28**, 118–144 (2019)
4. van der Aalst, W.M.P., Jablonski, S.: Dealing with workflow change: identification of issues and solutions. Comput. Syst. Sci. Eng. **15**, 267–276 (2000)
5. Qureshi, I., Pan, S.L., Zheng, Y.: Digital social innovation: an overview and research framework. Inf. Syst. J. **31** (2021)
6. Orlikowski, W.J.: Sociomaterial practices: exploring technology at work. Organ. Stud. **28**, 1435–1448 (2007)
7. Bichler, M.: Design science in information systems research. Wirtschaftsinformatik **48**(2), 133–135 (2006). https://doi.org/10.1007/s11576-006-0028-8
8. Orlikowski, W.J., Iacono, C.S.: Desperately seeking the 'IT' in IT research: a call to theorizing the IT artifact. Inf. Syst. Res. **12**, 121–134 (2001)
9. van der Aalst, W., van Hee, K.M.: Workflow management: models, methods, and systems. MIT press (2004)
10. Boudreau, M.-C., Robey, D.: Enacting integrated information technology: a human agency perspective. Organ. Sci. **16**, 3–18 (2005)
11. Aaltonen, A., Stelmaszak, M.: The performative production of trace data in knowledge work. Inf. Syst. Res. **35**, 1448–1462 (2024)
12. Schultze, U.: A confessional account of an ethnography about knowledge work. MIS Q. **24**, 3–41 (2000)
13. Tarafdar, M., Cooper, C.L., Stich, J.-F.: The technostress trifecta-techno eustress, techno distress and design: theoretical directions and an agenda for research. Inf. Syst. J. **29**, 6–42 (2019)
14. Coiera, E.: When conversation is better than computation. J. Am. Med. Inform. Assoc. **7**, 277–286 (2000)
15. Lindeman, S., Svensson, M., Enochsson, A.-B.: Digitalisation in early childhood education: a domestication theoretical perspective on teachers' experiences. Educ. Inf. Technol. **26**, 4879–4903 (2021)
16. Sosa-Alonso, J.J., Rivero, V.M.H., Mesa, A.L.S., Aguilar, A.B.: Adoption of digital educational resources by early childhood education teachers: a fad or a conviction? Comput. Educ. **238**, 105396 (2025)
17. Peffers, K., Tuunanen, T., Rothenberger, M.A., Chatterjee, S.: A design science research methodology for information systems research. J. Manag. Inf. Syst. **24**, 45–77 (2007)
18. Nielsen, J.A., Mathiassen, L., Newell, S.: Theorization and translation in information technology institutionalization: evidence from Danish home care. MIS Q. **38**, 165–186 (2014)

19. Afzal, M., Panagiotopoulos, P.: Coping with digital transformation in frontline public services: a study of user adaptation in policing. Gov. Inf. Q. **41**, 101977 (2024)
20. vom Brocke, J., et al.: Tool-support for design science research: design principles and instantiation (2017). Available at SSRN 2972803

A Theory-Driven LLM Agent Design for Generating Synthetic Data in Tele-Triage

Hetiao Slim Xie[1(✉)] [iD], Morteza Namvar[1] [iD], Saeed Akhlaghpour[1] [iD],
and Andrew Staib[2,3] [iD]

[1] Business School, The University of Queensland, Brisbane, Australia
hetiao.xie@uq.edu.au, {m.namvar,
s.akhlaghpour}@business.uq.edu.au
[2] Princess Alexandra Hospital, Brisbane, Australia
ndrew.Staib@health.qld.gov.au
[3] Centre for Health Services Research, The University of Queensland, Brisbane, Australia

Abstract. Data scarcity in sensitive domains, such as healthcare, poses a profound challenge for the design of computational artifacts. Tele-triage, a promising frontier in digital health, remains hindered by the lack of patient self-report data essential for developing artificial intelligence (AI) solutions. To address this challenge, this research-in-progress study proposes a theory-driven large language model (LLM) agent design for generating synthetic data in tele-triage. We translate complex patient self-report phenomenon into analyzable and structured theoretical synthesis, which informs the design process. The proposed artifact comprises a theory-driven workflow and agent architecture designed to transform clinical notes from leading Australian hospitals into synthetic patient self-reports that authentically reflect subjective behavior. We will demonstrate validity of the artifact through comparative and ablation experiments in downstream applications, as well as on-site expert evaluations conducted by clinicians. We expect to make methodological contributions to this promising domain.

Keywords: Tele-triage · synthetic data · design science · LLM agents

1 Introduction

The widespread adoption of digital health solutions has accelerated patients' willingness to access telemedicine [1], which lays a foundation for the feasibility of tele-triage. Tele-triage, also referred to as virtual triage or online triage, is the use of online technology to supplement or replace elements of the traditional triage process [2]. It remotely determines the patient's condition and level of care needed based on patient self-reported information [3]. Under the dual challenges of emergency department (ED) overcrowding and rising healthcare demand [4], the rise of tele-triage paves a bright and vital path. However, this process currently mainly relies on efforts from online registered nurses who review patients' self-reported symptoms then use structured guidance of triage protocols and their professional expertise to make tele-triage decisions [1]. The shortage of healthcare professionals makes it highly difficult to scale this service to meet the needs of a large patient population [5].

S. Chatterjee et al. (Eds.): DESRIST 2026, LNCS 16607, pp. 169–180, 2026.
https://doi.org/10.1007/978-3-032-28570-6_14

Recent advancements in artificial intelligence (AI) technologies are revolutionizing the field of healthcare, while simultaneously creating opportunities for scalable tele-triage solutions. Machine learning (ML), natural language processing, and large language model (LLM) technologies have been widely adopted across the healthcare domain to assist in enhancing decision-makings of both clinicians and patients [6]. Regardless of other developments, the success of these models relies on a core foundation: high-quality data [7]. Data is the fuel to AI, while data scarcity serves as a key barrier hindering technological innovation and the development of AI artifacts. Especially in the healthcare domain, due to strict privacy regulations and high personnel costs, dataset collection and processing are extremely time-consuming and labor-intensive [7]. The model unreliability or the inability to initiate training caused by data scarcity, in turn, makes it impractical to collect data through the actual use of AI models [8]. The consequence of this paradox is the lack of patient self-report data to train AI models and support subsequent AI adoption [9], which severely weakens the potential contributions this field could offer to healthcare systems and patients [2, 3].

Synthetic data has emerged as a widely recognized solution to this problem, involving the creation of artificial data that resembles real-world data to support model development [10]. This approach has evolved from early statistical methods that generated structured data to the current use of LLMs to produce contextually diverse textual data [11]. In particular, recent LLM agents have shown great potential in generating human-like synthetic data by simulating human behaviors or decision-making processes [12]. A key problem that can be formulated is how to effectively and systematically build characteristics of human behavior to guide LLM agents in simulating complex human actions. Extant research predominantly relies on exhaustive prompt engineering to describe phenomena [13], rather than rigorously conceptualizing the domain to develop systematic methodologies for capturing its essential mechanisms. Especially in tele-triage, we currently lack a comprehensive understanding of patient self-report behavior. This research gap leaves this promising area largely unexplored. Therefore, we propose the following research question: *"How can we design a systematic approach to simulate patient self-report in tele-triage for generating synthetic data using LLM agents?"*.

Information Systems (IS) scholars have a long-standing tradition of theory-driven design, which involves conceptualizing or theorizing a phenomenon to inform the development of an artifact [14, 15]. Building on this, we propose a theory-driven LLM agent design for generating synthetic data in tele-triage. This LLM agent framework enables the generative transformation of clinician-recorded medical notes into synthetic patient self-reports. We integrate three theories from interdisciplinary literature to conceptualize patient self-reporting behavior in tele-triage, thereby establishing theoretical synthesis. Guided by the computational design science (CDS) paradigm [16, 17], we operationalize these synthesis to inform the LLM agent's workflow, prompt engineering, and underlying computational modules. Finally, through preliminary analysis and a comprehensive roadmap for future computational and field evaluations, we expect to demonstrate that the synthetic data generated via our approach offers superior utility for downstream tele-triage applications.

2 Background

2.1 Tele-Triage: Current Landscape and Challenges

Tele-triage, as a component of telemedicine and broader digital health technologies, leverages telecommunication tools to evaluate patients' reported symptoms and clinical acuity, thereby determining the urgency of their healthcare needs [2]. For example, patients can use tele-triage services to understand the severity of their symptoms and potential treatments, helping them decide whether to visit an ED or another healthcare institution. Effective tele-triage systems improve healthcare delivery by redirecting low-acuity patients to appropriate non-ED settings [4], ensuring timely and suitable care for patients [18], and reducing delays in emergency presentation [2].

At present, tele-triage is most commonly delivered by registered nurses who conduct patient assessments through telephone calls or online messaging platforms [3]. An Australian telephone triage toolkit implemented across several states specifies that triage nurses evaluate patients by systematically eliciting information about symptom severity and applying predefined clinical protocols to guide decision-making [19]. However, this approach has limited scalability due to its heavy reliance on a large workforce of trained medical professionals [4]. Moreover, because clinicians must assess patients sequentially, it creates systemic delays and operational bottlenecks.

Given the potential of AI solutions to deliver rapid clinical assessment and decision support in digital health without incurring additional labor costs, a growing body of research has investigated the application of AI techniques in tele-triage [5]. However, training such AI-enabled tele-triage models requires patient self-report data, which is currently lacking. As a result, existing studies have largely relied on data drawn from closely related application scenarios. These data sources include telephone recordings [9] and symptom keywords generated by patients using online self-symptom checker systems [20]. Consequently, the mismatch between training data and real-world data causes the trained AI models to struggle to achieve satisfactory performance [18].

2.2 Data Scarcity Paradox in Healthcare

Data scarcity typically encompasses deficiencies across three dimensions: sample volume, expert annotation, and data representation [7]. Within the healthcare sector, data scarcity remains a persistent challenge driven by factors such as stringent privacy regulations, fragmented digital infrastructure, and high cost of clinical experts [8]. Such scarcity significantly undermines both the design and the evaluation of AI artifacts. A lack of high-quality data often leads to model overfitting, where performance on limited datasets fails to be generalized to the complexities of real-world scenarios. Furthermore, restricted datasets can introduce algorithmic bias and impede the ability to rigorously demonstrate the effectiveness of an AI artifact during evaluation [6, 16].

In emerging fields such as tele-triage, data scarcity further evolves into a "chicken-and-egg" paradox—a vicious cycle. Since large-scale, commercially deployed tele-triage AI models are currently nearly non-existent, the opportunity to collect patient self-report data during real-time use is unavailable [2]. This lack of data makes the training of such AI models fundamentally unreliable from the outset. Due to strict ethical requirements, underperforming models cannot be authorized for clinical deployment, thereby trapping the field in the stagnant loop of the data scarcity paradox [7].

2.3 Synthetic Data and LLM Agent Approaches

Synthetic data has paved a promising path for the development of AI models in sensitive domains. It refers to artificial data created through various technical means that resembles real-world data [10, 11]. Early synthetic data primarily utilized statistical methods to capture the statistical characteristics of existing datasets. While simple and practical, these methods were limited to generating structured data [7]. Later, the introduction of ML and deep learning enabled researchers to capture the complex distributions of high-dimensional data through advanced methods such as generative adversarial networks [8]. In the LLM era, data synthesis has shifted toward semantic-level simulation. Research requiring synthetic text data has begun to turn toward using LLMs to generate human-like natural language [12].

Table 1. Current LLM agent designs for behavioral simulation and data synthesis

References	Scenario	Simulation / synthetic results	Theory use	Theory-driven design
[21]	Economic experiments	Economic behaviors	Yes	No
[22]	Medical education	Patient conversations	No	No
[24]	Urban planning	Citizen opinions	Yes	No
[25]	Illness diagnosis	Patient conversations	No	No
[26]	Political discussions	Public opinions	No	No

As the frontier of LLMs, LLM agents leverage LLMs as foundation models, integrating structured design components to establish intelligent system frameworks capable of autonomous planning and task execution [12]. Extant research has begun exploring the assignment of specific personas to these agents, enabling them to conduct behavioral simulations within specialized contextual environments. For instance, by employing extensive textual prompts, researchers can prompt LLMs to simulate rational agents within economic models, thereby facilitating the collection of synthetic behavioral data for experimental economics [21]. Similarly, researchers can also utilize techniques such as retrieval-augmented generation techniques to incorporate external health-related data, allowing LLMs to stimulate patients for the purpose of medical education [22]. Beyond prompt engineering, LLM agents can integrate diverse architectural workflows. For example, the ReAct framework deconstructs the working process into iterative stages—reasoning, acting, and observing—thereby enhancing logical coherence [23]. Furthermore, complex multi-agent systems leverage the collaborative dynamics between multiple agents to generate higher-quality outputs [24].

However, the majority of current behavioral simulations prioritize describing phenomena over explaining mechanisms. They rely on extensive prompt engineering or other techniques to make AI appear human, rather than architecting these behaviors based on underlying behavioral mechanisms [25, 26]. This approach lacks a robust foundation, as model outputs are highly sensitive to minor prompt variations and lack both interpretability and replicability [27]. Even where research adopts theory, there is a lack of deep engagement in integrating these theories into the actual design of the LLM agents; instead, theory is often relegated to a post-hoc tool for explaining outputs. Table 1 presents key insights derived from our analysis. From a design science perspective, without a systematic methodology, the validity and utility of the resulting artifact remain unverified [16]. This necessitates a move toward a more rigorous, systematic, and theory-driven approach to data synthesis.

3   Research Method

3.1   Grounding Patient Self-Report Behaviors in Tele-Triage in Theories

Transforming a vague and complex phenomenon into a concept or construct that can be systematically examined and utilized is a crucial prerequisite for empirical design [28]. Conceptualizing patient self-report in tele-triage allows this multifaceted phenomenon to be translated into a structured, analyzable construct, thereby revealing the underlying behavioral mechanisms. Accordingly, we conceptualize patient behavior in tele-triage by drawing on the theories in extant literature. Then we develop theoretical synthesis that can guide the subsequent design of artifact by capturing the essential explanatory behavior mechanisms and providing conceptual principles. To examine how patients perceive and interpret their symptoms, and react to the tele-triage AI model, it is essential to adopt a theoretical foundation that captures both individual-level cognitive factors and the influence of the broader environment.

Common-Sense Model Is particularly well-suited to be our foundational framework, as it synthesizes the diverse cognitive and psychological perspectives required to explain how patients manage their health conditions. As a theoretical framework, it explains how individuals perceive, interpret, and manage health threats and illness [29]. In the context of tele-triage, the Common-Sense Model can help understand how the individual forms a common-sense or lay belief about their illness, such as perceived type, cause, and consequences of the illness. The key theoretical constructs of Common-Sense Model include socio-cultural context, cognitive illness representation, and emotional illness representation [29]. The broader social and cultural environment fundamentally impacts and shapes how patients perceive and interpret illness. Existing research has examined the moderating role of various socio-structural variables, including social factors, socio-ecological factors, and cultural factors [30]. Cognitive illness representation refers to the set of organized beliefs and perceptions that individuals hold across five dimensions of illness: identity, cause, timeline, consequences, and controllability [29]. In the context of tele-triage, where medical intervention is limited, these perceptions emerge as timely rational interpretations triggered by self-perceived symptoms. The illness perception also encompasses the emotional responses elicited by the condition, often manifested as anxiety or fear.

Affordance Actualization Theory Is another theoretical perspective to further explain how patients adapt behaviors to the perception of the affordance of tele-triage AI. The assumption of Common-Sense Model does not fully capture the unique characteristics of AI-enabled tele-triage. In this context, the health action involves patients reporting their symptoms to an AI system rather than interacting directly with healthcare professionals. This human-AI interaction and technology adoption underscores the rationale and necessity of incorporating Affordance Actualization Theory [31]. Accordingly, patients' use of AI-enabled tele-triage systems (i.e., their self-report behavior) depends not only on the system's technical features but also on how these features are cognitively interpreted and perceived by patients. When patients engage with the AI system, their behavioral decisions are shaped by their perception of these affordances, such as perceived system functionalities, patients' digital and health literacy, and external information and social cues available in the environment [32]. This implies that factors such as patients' trust in AI systems, their psychological expectations of system capabilities, institutional trust, and social norms collectively shape perceived affordances [33]. Ultimately, affordance perception subtly influences actualization, reflected in how patients articulate their self-report content in natural language to the system.

Heuristics Allows us to theorize a critical yet understudied dimension of the patient self-report behavior: situational factors. Rather than assuming patients act as perfectly rational information processors, a heuristic perspective acknowledges that self-report in tele-triage is deeply embedded in the immediate environment [34]. Specifically, situational constraints such as time pressure fundamentally alter the reporting process. Under such pressure, patients often experience acute cognitive overload and emotional tension, which significantly diminish their capacity for systematic and exhaustive symptom description. Consequently, patients do not articulate their health conditions through a purely rational or comprehensive lens. Instead, faced with the trifecta of time constraints, heightened anxiety, and limited medical literacy, they rely on cognitive shortcuts (heuristics) to interpret and express their perceived illness.

3.2 The Design of LLM Agent for Generating Synthetic Data

Grounded in theoretical synthesis, we propose an LLM-based multi-agent framework designed to generate synthetic patient self-report data within the tele-triage context (Fig. 1). This framework incorporates six meticulously designed agents, each endowed with specialized functional roles to simulate the behavioral mechanisms underlying patient self-reports. Furthermore, we introduce a novel algorithmic module engineered to capture the manifestation of heuristics in patient self-report behavior. Through this framework, we can convert clinical notes into synthetic patient-report data. The following sections provide an in-depth elaboration of these architectural specifications.

Workflow. The overall workflow of this framework is grounded in the conceptualization of patient self-report as articulated in its core theoretical foundation, the Common-Sense Model. First, the socio-cultural Agent simulates the theoretical synthesis of socio-cultural context and is responsible for initializing the simulation environment. Based on the demographic data of each representation, it constructs persona profiles that simulate factors such as the patient's age, education level, and cultural background [21]. By propagating environment memory to every agent within the framework, it establishes the baseline linguistic style, health literacy level, and communication norms for all subsequent operations.

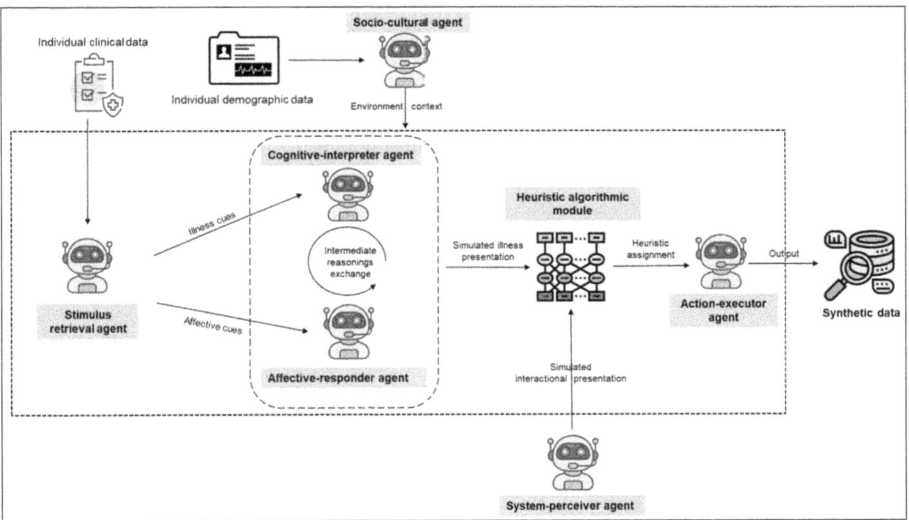

Fig. 1. The framework of the proposed LLM agent

Then, the stimulus retrieval agent automatically retrieves information from the external dataset of clinician notes provided. Functioning as a filter, it autonomously determines which symptoms are significant and stores the identified symptoms for subsequent information distribution. Following this, the cognitive-interpreter agent receives an objective description of the clinical information to generate a structured understanding of the condition, simulating the process of a patient identifying their own symptoms. In parallel, the affective-responder agent generates emotional states (e.g., anxiety, panic, or composure) based on the received information of conditions. During this process, the cognitive-interpreter agent and affective-responder agent will exchange memory to simulate perceptual biases triggered by emotional states [30].

In addition, the system-perceiver agent operates independently of the illness itself to evaluate the current AI-enabled tele-triage environment. This agent integrates external social cues to simulate the patient's trust in AI, their digital literacy, and their psychological expectations regarding system accuracy. These factors determine the patient's mindset and communicating strategies when interacting with the AI solutions [34]. Finally, the system-perceiver agent, along with the two aforementioned agents, passes downstream the structured semantic parameters which are encodings that store their reasoning memory and configurations.

The structured semantic parameters will be transmitted to the heuristic algorithmic module for centralized internal processing. Unlike the anthropomorphic agents, this module is a mathematical modeling component designed to simulate the bounded rationality of a patient assessing their illness. Through computational operations, it simulates how factors such as time pressure and limited medical knowledge compel patients to utilize cognitive shortcuts [34]. It results in final expressions that are often fragmented and not entirely rational.

As the terminal point of the process, the action-executor agent integrates all memories processed by the heuristic module, transforming abstract cognitive, emotional, and environmental perceptions into final natural language text. These synthetic patient self-report texts correspond one-to-one with the representation in the clinical dataset.

Prompt Engineering Strategy. To ensure that the generated synthetic data strictly adheres to the theoretical synthesis defined within our multi-agent framework, we have designed a structured and parameterized prompt engineering strategy. Unlike general zero-shot prompting, which relies on the model's inherent training distribution, our approach utilizes a parameterized system prompt specifically tailored for the final action-executor agent [35]. Under this strategy, the other six agents operate with independent prompts designed not to output natural language, but to generate specific states and intermediate parameters. The action-executor agent then dynamically assembles these generated states and parameters to produce the final natural language output.

For each agent, the prompt architecture consists of three modular components populated dynamically at runtime: (1) Role configuration. This component ingests individual demographic data to establish the agent's socio-cultural background and automatically constructs the patient's persona. (2) State configuration. This component builds psychological states based on the specific theoretical synthesis followed by each agent. We translate these theoretical synthesis into clear language with unbiased examples within the prompt. (3) Operation configuration. This component restricts the agent's potential out-of-bounds behaviors. We strictly define the scope of each agent's responsibilities to ensure they only execute their designated duties. Due to space limitations, we are unable to provide full prompt examples as they are extensively detailed.

Heuristic Algorithmic Module. To simulate the irrationality and uncertainty inherent in human perception with greater accuracy, we construct this heuristic module to computationally manipulate the information transmitted between agents. Specifically, when the upstream cognitive-interpreter agent identifies objective symptoms, it is tasked with generating an intensity score $I_{obj}^{(i)}$ (ranging from 0 to 1) based on the objective physical attributes of the medical condition. However, the final symptoms self-reported by patients are rarely objective or exhaustive. Instead, driven by heuristic mechanisms, patients tend to prioritize reporting symptoms that possess higher perceived saliency. This perception is heavily influenced by psychological factors, specifically the psychological coefficients $P_{affective}^{(i)}$ and $P_{system}^{(i)}$ simulated by the affective-responder agent and the system-perceiver agent.

To model this, we construct an exponential modulation function. In this calculation, for patients with higher anxiety levels $Heur_i$,, objective signals are exponentially amplified, which causes even smaller discomforts to occupy more attention during the patient's self-report. Conversely, for more tolerated patients (lower $Heur_i$), attention remains focused solely on the most physically significant symptoms. Additionally, we introduced a stochastic error term ε (ranging from 0 to 1) to simulate the error in perceiving the actual condition caused by differences in individual medical knowledge.

$$Heur_i = I_{obj}^{(i)} \cdot \exp\left(P_{affective}^{(i)} + P_{system}^{(i)}\right) + \varepsilon$$

Ultimately, the module ranks the $Heur_i$ scores and passes the highest value as a logit term within the structured semantic parameters to the downstream agent, action-executor agent, to produce a stochastic self-report influenced by heuristic decisions.

4 Preliminary Evaluation and Future Work

4.1 Data Collection and Preliminary Evaluation

In this research, we collaborated with a major public tertiary teaching hospital in Australia. After obtaining research ethics and governance clearance, we accessed their dataset from the electronic medical record system comprising 161,455 non-identifiable records of adult patient presentations, spanning the period from July 2023 to July 2025. The dataset includes over 40 distinct data features across the triage, treatment, and disposition phases. For the preliminary evaluation, we randomly sample 1,000 records, which include diagnosis information, clinical notes, and demographic data. We further implement the Qwen-Agent framework using Qwen-3 (8B) as the backbone LLM to execute our design. We provide an shorten example of data pair below:

Original: *"Left sided CP worse on insp rad to jaw w social stressors-relationship Son work has plan and means-intoxicatedHx Anxiety-Lexapro Kresta: sees cardiologist for sameHR126 reg teary 97%RA T36.0 help seeking good insight/eye contact...".*

Synthetic: *"My chest hurts. Left side. It's sharp when I breathe and I can feel it in my jaw. It's moving up. I already see a cardiologist for this, but it's bad right now. My heart is pounding fast. I'm on Lexapro for anxiety but it's not working. I've had some drinks tonight because of stress, and it's all too much...".*

Furthermore, we evaluate the utility of our synthetic data by using it to fine-tune a ClinicalBERT model. The fine-tuned model will execute the downstream predictive tasks in tele-triage and compare the results with other data sources. To establish a baseline for comparison, we also fine-tune the same model using the 1,000 original clinical notes. Due to the absence of existing specialized tele-triage datasets, we utilize a telephone triage dataset for performance testing. The fine-tuned ClinicalBERT models aims to predict whether a patient should be referred to the ED based on the telephone triage transcripts. The results (Table 2) indicate that the synthetic data generated by our theory-driven framework provide superior performance enhancements to models.

Table 2. Comparative Evaluation of Our Method and Its Variants

	Accuracy	Precision	Recall	F1
No data	0.548	0.535	0.592	0.562
Original data	0.632	0.627	0.671	0.648
Our synthetic data	0.715	0.704	0.756	0.729

4.2 Future Work

In future research, our primary focus will be to comprehensively evaluate the utility of our proposed LLM agent. First, we intend to establish a robust baseline by collecting primary data from human participants. We plan to conduct surveys and simulations with individuals who have prior healthcare experience, prompting them to simulate interactions with a tele-triage model to report their symptoms. By acquiring this authentic human data, we aim to further validate and refine our multi-agent framework.

Secondly, we will conduct a more in-depth computational investigation into the validity of our generated synthetic data. Regarding our comparative studies, we plan to incorporate a broader range of data resources to fine-tune downstream tele-triage models. Furthermore, we will perform ablation studies by systematically removing individual components of our design, including both the underlying theoretical synthesis and the computational modules. This approach will allow for assessing whether the superior performance of our framework is indeed derived from our innovative design elements.

Additionally, we plan to conduct a field evaluation to assess the quality of the generated synthetic data. We are collaborating with leading Australian health services and hospitals. In this evaluation, experienced clinicians will review the synthetic data to ensure that the generated data adhere to real-world patient norms and characteristics.

5 Conclusion

The challenge of data scarcity significantly hinders digital innovation and AI deployment within the tele-triage domain, thereby obstructing its vast potential to enhance patient care and healthcare efficiency. Drawing upon the promise of LLM agents in synthetic data generation and addressing the current gap in systematic, theory-driven methodologies, we propose an LLM agent artifact designed to generate synthetic patient self-report data.

Building on existing efforts and outlining future research directions, this research-in-progress study offers three potential contributions to the knowledge bases of IS and digital health. For IS, first, our study provides a novel and valid computational artifact for generating synthetic data, aimed at tackling grand societal challenges. Second, we expect to contribute new knowledge on theory-driven LLM agent design to make methodological contributions, thereby developing design principles for LLM agent design. Finally, for digital health, we will offer insights into overcoming data scarcity in tele-triage and provide a foundation for future research on developing effective AI-based tele-triage models.

Acknowledgments. This study was partially funded by The PA Research Foundation, Australia.

Disclosure of Interests. The authors have no competing interests to declare that are relevant to the content of this article.

References

1. Nguyen, L., Ngwenyama, O., Bandyopadhyay, A., Nallaperuma, K.: Realising the potential of digital health communities: a study of the role of social factors in community engagement. Eur. J. Inf. Syst. **33**(6), 1033–1068 (2024)
2. Farzandipour, M., Nabovati, E., Sharif, R.: The effectiveness of tele-triage during the COVID-19 pandemic: a systematic review and narrative synthesis. J. Telemed. Telecare **30**(9), 1367–1375 (2024)
3. Ziebart, C., Kfrerer, M.L., Stanley, M., Austin, L.C.: A digital-first health care approach to managing pandemics: scoping review of pandemic self-triage tools. J. Med. Internet Res. **25**(1), e40983 (2023)
4. Sun, S., Lu, S.F., Rui, H.: Does telemedicine reduce emergency room congestion? Evidence from New York State. Inf. Syst. Res. **31**(3), 972–986 (2020)
5. Naved, B.A., Luo, Y.: Contrasting rule and machine learning based digital self triage systems in the USA. Npj Digital Med. **7**(1), 1–10 (2024)
6. Thirunavukarasu, A.J., Ting, D.S.J., Elangovan, K., Gutierrez, L., Tan, T.F., Ting, D.S.W.: Large language models in medicine. Nat. Med. **29**(8), 1930–1940 (2023)
7. Bansal, M.A., Sharma, D.R., Kathuria, D.M.: A systematic review on data scarcity problem in deep learning: solution and applications. ACM Comput. Surv. **54**(10s), 1–29 (2022)
8. Alzubaidi, L., et al.: A survey on deep learning tools dealing with data scarcity: definitions, challenges, solutions, tips, and applications. J. Big Data **10**(1), 46 (2023)
9. Inokuchi, R., Iwagami, M., Sun, Y., Sakamoto, A., Tamiya, N.: Machine learning models predicting undertriage in telephone triage. Ann. Med. **54**(1), 2989–2996 (2022)
10. Joshi, I., Grimmer, M., Rathgeb, C., Busch, C., Bremond, F., Dantcheva, A.: Synthetic data in human analysis: a survey. IEEE Trans. Pattern Anal. Mach. Intell. **46**(7), 4957–4976 (2024)
11. Wei, L., Chen, S., Lin, J., Shi, L.: Enhancing return forecasting using LSTM with agent-based synthetic data. Decis. Support Syst. **193**, 114452 (2025)
12. Park, J.S., O'Brien, J., Cai, C.J., Morris, M. R., Liang, P., Bernstein, M.S.: Generative agents: Interactive simulacra of human behavior. Proceedings of the 36th Annual ACM Symposium on User Interface Software and Technology, (pp. 1–22) (2023)
13. Zhu, L., Huang, X., Sang, J.: How reliable is your simulator? analysis on the limitations of current llm-based user simulators for conversational recommendation. Companion Proceedings of the ACM Web Conference 2024 (pp. 1726–1732) (2024)
14. Liu, X., Wang, G.A., Fan, W., Zhang, Z.: Finding useful solutions in online knowledge communities: a theory-driven design and multilevel analysis. Inf. Syst. Res. **31**(3), 731–752 (2020)
15. Yang, Y., Qin, Y., Fan, Y., Zhang, Z.: Unlocking the power of voice for financial risk prediction: a theory-driven deep learning design approach. MIS Q. **47**(1), 63–96 (2023)
16. Fang, X., Hu, P. J., Chau, M., Chen, H.: Computational Design Science: A Critical Information Systems Research Area Contributing to Artificial Intelligence and Data Science (2025). *Available at SSRN 5455094*
17. Rai, A., et al.: Editor's comments: Diversity of design science research. MIS Q. **41**(1), iii-xviii (2017)

18. Hall, J.N., Galaev, R., Gavrilov, M., Mondoux, S.: Development of a machine learning-based acuity score prediction model for virtual care settings. BMC Med. Inform. Decis. Mak. **23**(1), 200 (2023)

19. Hawkins, J., Jones, P., McShane, B., Morris, H., Ollett, L., Sanderson, L.: Telephone triage toolkit for children's cancer services: a quality initiative. Eur. J. Oncol. Nurs. **56**, 102036 (2022)

20. Riboli-Sasco, E., et al.: Triage and diagnostic accuracy of online symptom checkers: systematic review. J. Med. Internet Res. **25**(1), e43803 (2023)

21. Horton, J.J.: Large language models as simulated economic agents: what can we learn from homo silicus?. Natl. Bureau Econ. Res. (2023)

22. Yu, H., et al.: Simulated patient systems powered by large language model-based AI agents offer potential for transforming medical education. Commun. Med. **6**(27) (2025)

23. Yao, S., et al.: React: Synergizing reasoning and acting in language models. The 18th International Conference on Learning Representations (2022)

24. Guo, N., Cong, W., Su, Y., Zhang, S., Man, Q.: The influence of social interaction and emotional states on residents' decision-making on energy-efficiency retrofit: an improved multi-agent simulation approach. Eng. Constr. Architectural Manage. 1–19 (2025)

25. Zolnour, A., et al.: LLMCARE: early detection of cognitive impairment via transformer models enhanced by LLM-generated synthetic data. Front. Artif. Intell. **8**, 1669896 (2025)

26. Wagner, S.S., Behrendt, M., Ziegele, M., Harmeling, S.: The power of llm-generated synthetic data for stance detection in online political discussions. The 13th International Conference on Learning Representations (ICLR) (2025)

27. Mohammadi, M., Li, Y., Lo, J., Yip, W.: Evaluation and benchmarking of llm agents: a survey. Proceedings of the 31st ACM SIGKDD Conference on Knowledge Discovery and Data Mining V. **2** (pp. 6129–6139) (2025)

28. Bringmann, L.F., Elmer, T., Eronen, M.I.: Back to basics: the importance of conceptual clarification in psychological science. Curr. Dir. Psychol. Sci. **31**(4), 340–346 (2022)

29. Leventhal, H., Diefenbach, M., Leventhal, E.A.: Illness cognition: using common sense to understand treatment adherence and affect cognition interactions. Cogn. Ther. Res. **16**(2), 143–163 (1992)

30. Hagger, M.S., Orbell, S.: The common sense model of illness selfregulation: a conceptual review and proposed extended model. Health Psychol. Rev. **16**(3), 347–377 (2022)

31. Strong, D., et al.: A theory of organization-ehr affordance actualization. J. Assoc. Inf. Syst. **15**(2) (2014)

32. Shao, Z., Zhang, J., Zhang, L., Benitez, J.: Uncovering post-adoption usage of AI-based voice assistants: a technology affordance lens using a mixed-methods approach. Eur. J. Inf. Syst. **34**(3), 475–501 (2025)

33. Huang, D.-H., Chueh, H.-E.: Chatbot usage intention analysis: veterinary consultation. J. Innov. Knowl. **6**(3), 135–144 (2021)

34. Ly, D.P.: The influence of the availability heuristic on physicians in the emergency department. Ann. Emerg. Med. **78**(5), 650–657 (2021)

35. Li, L., Zhang, Y., Chen, L.: Personalized prompt learning for explainable recommendation. ACM Trans. Inf. Syst. **41**(4), 1–26 (2023)

An Agentic Workflow for Patient Medical History Summarization and Visualization

Jennifer Xu[(⊠)] [iD] and Tamara Babaian [iD]

Bentley University, Waltham, MA, USA
`{jxu,tbabaian}@bentley.edu`

Abstract. Agentic AI provides opportunities to transform healthcare. This research-in-progress paper reports our pilot study exploring the design of an agentic workflow for summarizing and visualizing patient medical history based on both structured EHR (Electronic Health Records) data and unstructured clinical notes. Our research is different from prior medical text summarization work by its scope, integrating both structured and unstructured data spanning a patient's lifetime, and by a hybrid system architecture that clearly delineates responsibilities between agentic AI components and traditional programming modules based on their respective strengths. We derive a set of preliminary design principles for developing agentic systems that support life-long patient medical history summarization and visualization. An implemented proof-of-concept prototype demonstrates the feasibility of the proposed approach and will be used to assess its potential utility and usability for medical professionals.

Keywords: Summarization · Large Language Models · Agentic Workflow · Electronic Health Records · Visualization

1 Introduction

Electronic Health Records (EHRs) play an important role in supporting clinical decisions, such as diagnosis, medication prescription, and care plan development [14]. However, since a patient's medical history may extend over a long period of time [20] and the information about encounters, labs, immunizations, and surgeries may be scattered in multiple structured databases and unstructured text, it remains a challenge for doctors to quickly build an accurate, complete overview of the medical history, especially if the patient's conditions are complex and involve many encounters with multiple hospitals, clinics, and rehabilitation centers. In situations where immediate clinical decisions must be made, it is critical for doctors to be able to access the holistic summary of patient history promptly and easily. Unfortunately, at present, most EHR systems are not intelligent enough to automatically consolidate and summarize both structured and unstructured patient medical data [12].

Traditional machine learning and natural language processing (NLP) techniques have been used to summarize unstructured medical data [12]. The recent advancements in generative AI show promising directions in using large language models (LLMs) to process

© The Author(s), under exclusive license to Springer Nature Switzerland AG 2026
S. Chatterjee et al. (Eds.): DESRIST 2026, LNCS 16607, pp. 181–193, 2026.
https://doi.org/10.1007/978-3-032-28570-6_15

medical text data, such as clinical notes, lab reports, and discharge summaries [18, 25]. LLMs have been employed in a range of medical applications, including clinical decision support, clinical documentation and narrative generalization, patient interaction, drug discovery, and biomedical research [21]. Moreover, LLM-based agentic systems orchestrating multiple agents have emerged to support more complex medical and clinical tasks [8, 11, 21]. In these multi-agent systems, different agents perform different subtasks (e.g., planning, diagnosing, and monitoring) and collaborate to achieve high level of autonomy and adaptability [11].

This research-in-progress paper presents our exploratory study of using an agentic workflow for patient medical history summarization and visualization in the EHRs context. What distinguishes our approach from prior research is (a) the scope of the summarized information, which is a variety of structured and unstructured data from a life-long patient history, and (b) the system architecture that properly divides the responsibility between LLM-based agents and traditional programming components according to the strengths of each.

We propose a set of preliminary design principles for developing agentic workflows for summarizing and visualizing patient life-long medical histories based on EHR data. A proof-of-concept prototype system that embodies these principles is implemented to validate the feasibility of our approach. Our future work will evaluate the practical utility of the workflow and the prototype for medical professionals.

2 Literature Review

2.1 Agentic AI in Healthcare

Electronic Health Records (EHRs) are digital repositories of patient medical information and serve a critical role in the medical and healthcare domain [14]. An EHR database usually consists of a large number of structured tables related to different aspects of patient health, including demographics, encounters, labs, tests, vital signs, medications, procedures and treatments, social history, and billing information [16]. Some EHR systems may also store unstructured data, such as clinical and progress notes, radiology images, and reports.

Researchers have strived to leverage the wealth of EHR data for improving patient care. The advancements of LLMs and agentic AI have shown their potential in transforming the healthcare and medical industry in various applications areas [11]. LLMs have been used in to automatically transcribe doctor-patient conversations and generate summary reports [15]. GPT-4 was used to generate comprehensive clinical notes based on transcribed doctor-patient communication to streamline and automate the clinical documentation process, thereby helping doctors focus on patient care, reducing documentation workload and risk of burnout [25].

Although LLMs can achieve impressive performance in narrowly defined knowledge-intensive tasks (e.g., medical Q&A), they lack the ability to work autonomously [4]. One of the most important recent trends in AI is the transition from LLMs to agentic systems that consist of autonomous computational agents that can perceive, plan, reason, act, and adapt [21]. In the healthcare domain, this shift brings new opportunities to integrate LLM-based agents into clinical workflows to help address more complex problems, such as clinical decision support, triage, diagnosis, patient interaction and engagement, and scientific discovery [4, 8, 11, 21]. For example, TriageAgent is an agentic system that can analyze patient information and make more accurate triage recommendations based on clinical guidelines [17].

In the area of clinical decision support, several agentic systems have been proposed. For example, MedAgent Pro consists of a planner agent that generates a diagnostic plan based on medical knowledge integrated using the RAG (Retrieval-Augmented Generation) technology, and several other agents that are responsible for retrieving multi-modal patient data, performing analysis, making diagnostic recommendations, and verifying the diagnoses. LLMs serve as the cognitive core throughout the entire pipeline [28]. Similarly, MAGDA is a diagnostic agent based on a large vision-language model for screening radiology images, detecting diseases, and providing diagnostic assistance [5]. To assist doctors in identifying rare and newly emerging diseases, LLM-based agents in MedAssist retrieve medical knowledge from the Web, extract records of patients in similar conditions, and present the results in user-friendly interfaces [30]. MDAgents assigns different roles to a team of agents (e.g., Moderator, Recruiter, General Doctor, Specialist) to emulate the collaborative decision-making process among human medical professionals [13]. RareAgents [7] and ColaCare [29] adopt similar role-based structure to simulate multidisciplinary medical collaboration, in which doctor-agents with diverse clinical expertise provide diagnostic recommendations, and coordinator agents moderate discussions and debates among doctor-agents.

2.2 Medical Information Summarization

Research on medical information summarization mostly focuses on automatically generating summaries or notes to reduce the documentation burden of doctors [12, 16]. A review of summarization approaches [12] identifies *temporality*, *uncertainty*, and *medical pertinence* as the key dimensions of quality of medical summaries. It is found that the majority of research is focused on summarizing structured EHR data or unstructured text, and only a small percentage of studies (~10%) integrate both structured and unstructured data. Another literature survey [16] shows that most reviewed research focuses on summarizing single encounters of patients instead of the patient's entire medical history involving multiple encounters over a long period of time and across different clinical facilities.

A number of NLP techniques and LLMs have been employed in patient information summarization. In a recent study, several NLP techniques (e.g., Recurrent Neural Network, BART, and Reinforcement Learning) are tested and compared in terms of their performance in summarizing clinical encounters for discharge note generation [24]. The Flan-T5 model was fine-tuned to generate EHR information summaries based on clinician specified topics [18]. A fine-tuned GPT model (e.g., GPT-4) was used to summarize various clinical documents (e.g., radiology reports, patient questions, and doctor-patient dialogs) [25].

Researchers have cautioned against the use of traditional NLP metrics, such as ROUGE and BLEU, when evaluating the summarization performance, because these metrics are not sufficient to gauge the quality of generated summaries due to their failure to capture clinical contexts and knowledge [2]. In addition, because LLMs are often prone to hallucinations, additional measures and analyses, such as faithfulness and factuality [24], omission rate and error analysis [2], and safety analysis [25] are needed to ensure the quality of medical information summary in clinical contexts.

2.3 Medical History Visualization

The need for improving presentation of patient medical history within EHRs has been acknowledged in prior studies (e.g., [1, 12]). In addition to presenting textual summaries, researchers have explored a variety of graphical approaches that encompass the use of different types of plots and interaction techniques (see [27, 31] for recent reviews).

Reflecting the *temporality* aspect of medical information [12], timelines have long been used for visualizing patient history [9, 22]. A recent study [9] evaluated three different timeline-based visual summarization tools by deploying them in a hospital for a month. The study showed that the design presenting primary events (treatments, exams, prescriptions, etc.) side-by-side on a timeline, abstracted for overview and with details available on request, was most preferred by the hospital medical and administrative personnel. The features most valued by practitioners were the ease of obtaining an overview and the accessibility of more detailed information.

Beyond the inherent *uncertainty* stemming from the inconsistent use of medical terms, incompleteness or inaccuracies in the health data records, summarization can introduce further errors of omission and loss of information due to data aggregation [19]. Counteracting these effects requires careful crafting of summaries and providing access to the original information for verification and detailed review.

Medical pertinence requires that information be selected, summarized, and presented in the way that is targeted for a specific type of problem or decision. For example, a sepsis-risk monitoring system, SepsisLab [32] illustrates this principle: the system not only visualizes the likelihood of the onset of sepsis, but also combines this with illustrated actionable recommendations for reducing the uncertainty. Another approach [33] visualizes the trace of medical diagnosis and treatment by explicitly connecting the pertinent items of history, such as symptoms, tests, conditions, and treatments.

3   Methodology and Artifact Design

We adopt the design science research methodology [10] in this study. To establish the relevance of the problem to the current practice, we have conducted a preliminary study and interviewed a group of medical professionals about the use of AI in their work, and, specifically, about the way they review patient history within EHRs. Our findings from this study are reported in (citation removed for double-blinded review). The interviews have shown: (1) Reviewing patient history within existing EHR interfaces is a time-consuming process involving extensive search and filtering of information relevant to the patient condition. (2) Medical practitioners in different roles welcome AI-based help in identifying and presenting relevant information to avoid spending time in search and aggregation of pertinent data. (3) Different medical tasks and specialties vary in the scope and nature of the information that must be reviewed by the practitioner.

Our design artifacts include the agentic workflow, the prototype system that implements the workflow, and a set of preliminary design principles for developing effective patient history summarization using LLM-based agents and information visualization.

3.1 Requirements

Based on our literature review and findings from the interviews, we identified several requirements for the workflow and the prototype system. From the perspective of functional requirements, the system must be able to (1) summarize the medical history of a patient including all encounters, (2) handle diverse aspects of medical information (e.g., lab results, vital signs, prescriptions, care plans, etc.), (3) integrate both structured EHR data and unstructured clinical notes, (4) identify significant conditions and diseases from the clinician's perspective, and (5) visualize the history summary by addressing the *temporality*, *uncertainty*, and *medical pertinence*.

From the perspective of performance requirements, the system should also achieve *factuality* (i.e., no hallucinations), *completeness* (i.e., no omission of significant conditions), *consistency* (i.e., summaries across patients are similar in format), and *user friendliness* (i.e., summaries are presented in an intuitive, easy-to-understand manner).

3.2 System Architecture

To fulfill the functional and performance requirements, our agentic workflow consists of both LLM-based agents and traditional programming components. The workflow begins with a user query, which can be a clinician's request for a specific patient's medical history. The system retrieves relevant structured EHR data and unstructured clinical notes, generates a holistic overview of the patient's medical history, identifies critical or significant medical conditions, and presents intuitive visualization of the results. Figure 1 presents this agentic workflow, in which EHR Data Retrieval, Note Retrieval, Consolidation, and History Visualization are programming components involving no LLMs, and Note Summarizer, Note Summary Critic, History Summarizer, and History Summary Critic are LLM-based agentic components.

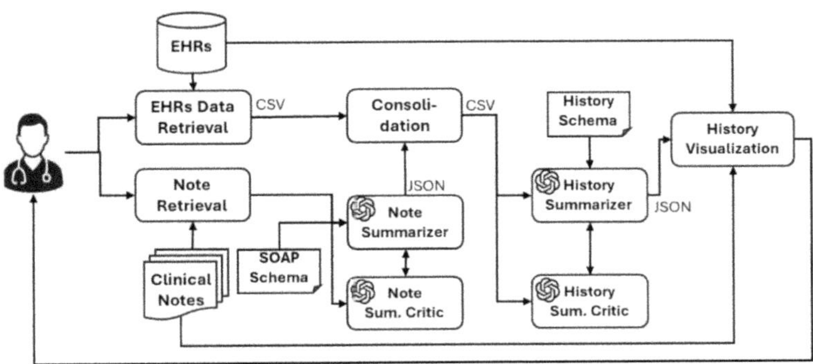

Fig. 1. System architecture

EHR Data Retrieval. Based on the user query, this component retrieves and extracts the patient's past encounters from the EHR databases. The size of the returned results may vary greatly across patients due to their ages and the complexity of their medical conditions. For example, a senior with multiple serious complications and chronic diseases may have hundreds of encounters, each of which is associated with multiple examinations, labs, and procedures.

Note Retrieval. In clinical settings, doctors or physicians may sometimes write additional notes to document observations, findings, and concerns that are not captured in standard EHR entries [24]. This component is used to retrieve unstructured clinical notes associated with some encounters of the patient.

Note Summarizer. This component is an LLM-based agent responsible for summarizing individual clinical notes, which may vary greatly in content, length, format, and personal style, and producing a summary in a standard format for each note.

Note Summary Critic. To ensure the quality of the note summaries generated by LLMs, which often suffer from hallucinations and omission errors [2], this agent serves as an evaluator to assess the output of Note Summarizer. This agent evaluates the factuality and completeness of the generated summaries, identifies the issues (e.g., hallucination), and makes recommendations for revising the prompt. The original prompt is then updated by integrating the recommendations made by the critic.

Consolidation Is used to produce input to the History Summarizer by combining the retrieved EHR entries and note summaries.

History Summarizer. This agent takes consolidated input and generates a holistic, concise summary of the patient's medical history. It also identifies any significant conditions or diseases (e.g., hypertension) based on the LLM's general medical knowledge.

History Critic. Similar to the Note Summary Critic, this agent's role is to assess the quality of the generated history summary and identify possible hallucinations, errors, and omissions.

History Visualization. This component provides interactive visualization of the patient's medical history. It presents the history summary and allows access to the full details of the history based on which the summary is created.

3.3 Implementation

Data. Since patient medical data are confidential and protected under the HIPPA regulation, it is impossible for us to access EHR data of real patients. In this research, we employed synthetic EHR data generated by Synthea, an open-source patient population simulation service [26]. For the pilot study, we generated a small sample of 14 patients with varying demographics and medical conditions. In this sample, the average age of the patients is 36.8 years (max = 61, min = 8); 57.1% (n = 8) of the patients are male; the average number of encounters per patient is 33.5 (max = 102; min = 12).

The EHR data generated by Synthea are organized in a standard FHIR (Fast Healthcare Interoperability Resources) relational schema [3], which includes several tables:

patients, encounters, observations, medications, conditions, procedures, allergies, immunizations, and care-plans. A patient may have many encounters, each of which may be associated with multiple observations (e.g., labs and vital signs), medications, etc.

The Synthea service cannot generate unstructured clinical notes. For each patient, we randomly selected 10% of the encounters and prompted OpenAI's GPT-4o to generate a clinical note for each of the encounters.

In the workflow, the data retrieval components are implemented using regular SQL queries with returned structured data are in CSV files and clinical notes in MS Words.

Summarization. We use OpenAI's Responses API[1], which enables the development of agents with persistent memory, specialized knowledge, and tool use (e.g., Code Interpreter, Function Calling) to implement agentic components.

For Note Summarizer, we employ a zero-shot learning strategy to prompt GPT-5 and assign the LLM a clinical note summarization expert role. To ensure the consistency of format in the returned summaries, we explicitly request the LLM to generate the result using the SOAP method for clinical documentation [6]. The SOAP includes (a) Subjective narrative about patient's perspectives, feelings, and symptoms; (2) Objective findings by the clinician or based on test results; (3) Assessment or diagnosis; (4) Plan regarding treatment, follow-up, and next steps [6]. SOAP notes are formulated based on a JSON output schema and inserted into the prompt as part of the instruction.

The prompt for the Note Summary Critic requests the LLM to compare the note summaries against the original clinical notes, score the summary's *factuality*, *completeness*, and *consistency*, identify issues, and suggest prompt revisions, using the Critic Output Schema.

Like in the Note Summarizer, the prompt for History Summarizer provides detailed instructions on how to summarize each CSV table (e.g., encounters, lab results) and format the result using the predefined History Summary Output Schema. The output schema has specific sections for the identified major conditions, risk factors, abnormal labs/vital signs, and a timeline narrative. For each identified condition or disease, we request the LLM to cite the original source (encounter entry or clinical note file name). Table 1 presents a snippet of the prompt for the History Summarizer and the output schema, showing the instructions for the *major conditions* section. Instructions for other sections are omitted for brevity. To enable LLM's processing of patients with long, complicated medical histories, we use vector stores for long text and DuckDB[2] to manage a bulk of CSV entries.

Similar to Note Summary Critic, History Critic is prompted to compare the generated summary against the original data and assess the quality of the history summary.

We have tested individual components of the prototype extensively for quality, but have not yet formally evaluated its overall performance. Section 5 discusses plans for full-scale evaluation and user studies with medical professionals.

Visualization. To present patient history summary in a form that reflects both temporal and medical relationships of the history items, we developed an interactive visualization using Python Dash framework. Figures 2 and 3 show the major components of the visualization interface based on a sample patient record.

---

[1] https://platform.openai.com/docs/api-reference/responses.

[2] https://duckdb.org/.

Table 1. Prompt snippet for History Summarizer and the output schema

Prompt:
You are a clinical history summarization expert. You will receive structured entries from a patient's EHRs (e.g., encounters, medications, labs, procedures). Your job is to produce an accurate, clinically useful, and consistently structured summary in JSON that follows the provided JSON output schema exactly.

General rules:
  - Follow the JSON schema strictly: use exactly the specified fields and structure.
  - For every patient, maintain a similar level of detail and structure so that summaries are comparable.
  - If a section has no relevant information, return an empty array (never omit the field).
  - Do NOT invent facts that are not supported by the input.
  - Be concise but clinically meaningful: prioritize information that materially affects care decisions.

Section-specific instructions:
  1. Patient ...
  2. Major conditions
        a.   Array of arrays. Each inner array MUST be: [condition_name, timeframe_or_onset, current_status_or_severity, ids_of_source_encounters]
        b.   Include all clinically significant chronic conditions when possible. If there are more than 10, include the 10 most important and capture the rest at a high level in the timeline_narrative.
        c.   If no chronic conditions are documented, return an empty array.
  3. Risk factors ...
  4. Medications ...
  5. Abnormal labs/vitals ...
  6. Procedures ...
  7. Care plans ...
  8. Timeline narrative ...

History Summary Output Schema:
```
{...
    "Medications": {
      "type": "array",
      "description": (
         "Current medications and the most clinically relevant past medications. "
         "Each inner array is: [medication_name, indication, dose_or_regimen_if_known, "
         "timeframe_or_status (e.g., current, stopped 2022), ids_of_source_encounters]. "
         "Include all current medications, and up to 5–10 of the most important past medications. "
         "If no medications are documented, return an empty array."),
      "minItems": 0,
      "maxItems": 15,
      "items": {
        "type": "array",
        "minItems": 3,
        "maxItems": 4,
        "items": {"type": "string"}
      }, },}
```

On this interface, the top of the screen displays the Patient Summary narrative. Underneath it, a timeline displays key items identified by the History Summarizer agent. Those items (*Themes* in the visualization) include *major conditions, abnormal lab results,* and *medications.* Continuous themes, such as lasting medical conditions, are displayed using a colored bar extending from the date of diagnosis to the current date or date they resolved. Themes are displayed side-by-side, so that their *temporal* relationship with each other can be easily identified, helping assess their co-occurrence and causal relationships. Filtering components appear above the timeline and allow focusing it on a designated time period and/or specific themes of interest, facilitating *medical pertinence*. Hovering over an event reveals some details, as shown in Fig. 2 for a Lab Systolic Blood Pressure event. Clicking on an event displays details (Fig. 3, left panel, Selected Event Details) and the history of all Systolic Blood Pressure measurements from the *full* patient history (Fig. 3, right panel, Theme Details Over Time) to put this event in perspective.

4 Preliminary Design Principles

Through agentic workflow design and prototype implementation, we developed a set of preliminary design principles for medical history summarization and visualization.

Properly divide the responsibility between agentic and traditional software components. Agentic systems may have different levels of autonomy ranging from a low degree of "agenticness" to complete autonomous design [23]. Traditional programming components follow static rules and procedures to produce deterministic output. LLM-based agents can function autonomously and adapt to dynamic environments [11]. Based on their different strengths, properly dividing the labor between the two types of components in a workflow allows them to complement each other and maximize the benefits. In our study, knowledge-intensive and context-dependent tasks (e.g., summarization and critic) are assigned to agentic components. For example, History Summarizer can identify major conditions and complications of a patient based on the LLM's extensive medical knowledge. Several other tasks (e.g., data extraction and consolidation, visualization), instead, are accomplished through predefined programming components. Thus, in the context of our study, such a division of responsibility is more beneficial than a completely autonomous end-to-end agentic workflow.

Leverage the tool use capability of LLM-based agents. One of the important features of agents is their ability to use tools [4, 11, 23]. Since both structured EHR data and unstructured clinical notes must be considered in this study, different tools are used in the agentic components in the workflow. Specifically, to identify the SOAP information from clinical notes, the Note Summarizer utilizes the File Search tool provided by the Responses API; to force History Summarizer to examine the entire medical history of a patient (i.e., all encounters) instead of the default behavior of the model that only considers the "most relevant" information, we use the Code Interpreter tool to process structured CSV data.

Control the uncertainty of LLM-generated output. LLMs often generate nondeterministic output that may vary between executions even given the same prompt. This may be problematic from the clinical perspective due to this uncertainty and lack of predictability. To address this problem, we set the model temperature, a parameter for LLM randomness, to be close to 0. More importantly, in addition to detailed instructions in the prompt, we provide clearly defined output schemas (see Table 1) for the LLM to follow. These approaches help minimize variations between executions.

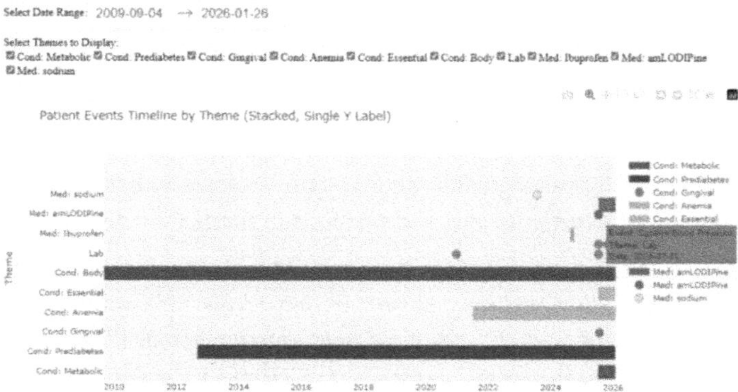

Fig. 2. Patient summary and timeline

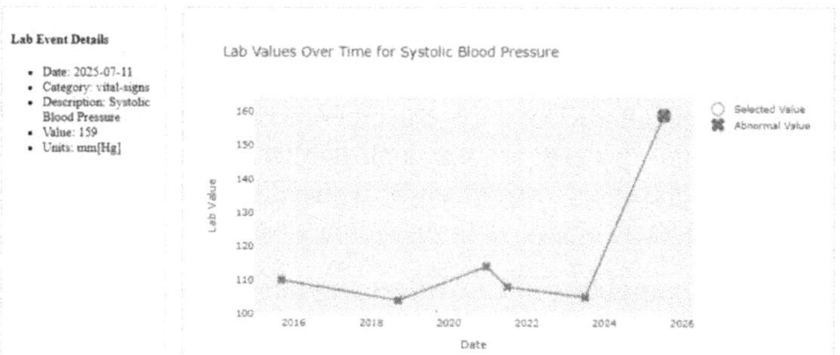

Fig. 3. Theme Details view (left) shows details of the selected abnormal lab result; Theme Over Time view (right) displays all lab values from the patient history, including the selected one

Minimize hallucinations and omission errors. LLM hallucinations and omission errors are serious problems, especially in the context of clinical decision-making [2]. We employ multiple methods to minimize such errors. First, explicit rules in the prompts and output schemas prohibit the LLM from making up facts not found in the data. For example, if no major condition is found for a patient, the corresponding section in the summary can be empty (see Table 1). Second, LLM is requested to cite the sources (i.e., the encounter ID or clinical note file) for any identified conditions, risk factors, medications, abnormal vital signs, etc. Third, for both Note Summarizer and History Summarizer, the associated Critic agents assess the quality of the generated output and identify errors.

Use a timeline to display the essential patient history and provide quick access to detailed information. Conditions, treatments, labs, and prescription medications displayed side by side on an interactive timeline provide a comprehensive view of all essential components of the patient's medical history. This requires the summarization workflow to preserve the timing information and references to the original encounters from the full patient history for all items. Access to the detailed information on which the summary is based is necessary to reduce uncertainty when making medical decisions, verify completeness and validity of the AI generated summary.

Dynamically adjust details of interest. While the summary already focuses on a subset of all patient events, namely the significant current conditions and risk factors, the visualization must enable hiding the themes and details irrelevant to a specific medical decision, leaving only the themes that are medically pertinent. Our current prototype implements this via filtering based on selection of dates and specific themes.

Provide a way to link items of the history that are medically related. In our current version, this task is implicitly accomplished by History Summarizer, which uses its medical knowledge to identify medications and lab tests related to specific conditions. In the future, we plan to create explicit linking of the tests and procedures used to diagnose conditions, care plans and treatments and to make these connections explicit in the visualization.

5 Concluding Remarks and Future Work

LLMs and agentic AI provide opportunities to transform healthcare. This research-in-progress reports our pilot study exploring the design of an agentic workflow for summarizing and visualizing patient medical history. Our design artifacts include not only the specific workflow and prototype but also a set of preliminary design principles for agentic workflows in the context of EHR summarization and visualization. This workflow is extensible as new components can be added to it. For example, multi-modal agents can be inserted to process and summarize imagery data (e.g., X-ray images). The workflow can also be customized to medical specialties by focusing only on patient medical history that is relevant to specific diseases or conditions.

Our future work will include several important directions. First, we will extend this pilot to a full-scale study with a large set of patient data. Second, we will evaluate the performance of the Summarizers (independent from the scores produced by Critics) using both traditional metrics (e.g., precision and recall) and LLM-oriented summarization metrics (e.g., factuality and completeness). The performance of the prototype will be evaluated by involving healthcare professionals in assessing its usability and clinical utility.

References

1. Amir, O., et al.: From care plans to care coordination: opportunities for computer support of teamwork in complex healthcare. In: Proceedings of the 33rd Annual ACM Conference on Hu-man Factors in Computing Systems, pp. 1419–1428 (2015)

2. Asgari, E., et al.: A framework to assess clinical safety and hallucination rates of LLMs for medical text summarisation. npj Digital Med. **8**, 274 (2025)

3. Ayaz, M., et al.: The Fast Health Interoperability Resources (FHIR) standard: systematic literature review of implementations, applications, challenges and opportunities. JMIR Med. Inform. **9**(7), e21929 (2021)

4. Banerjie, S., et al.: Agentic AI in healthcare: a comprehensive survey of foundations, taxonomy, and applications. TechRxiv (2024). https://doi.org/10.36227/techrxiv.176238073.312 62603/v1

5. Bani-Harouni, D., et al.: MAGDA: multi-agent guideline-driven diagnostic assistance. In: Proceedings of the Foundation Models for General Medical AI. Springer, Cham (2025)

6. Cameron, S., Turtle-Song, I.: Learning to write case notes using the SOAP format. J. Couns. Dev. **80**(3), 286–292 (2002)

7. Chen, X., et al.: RareAgents: advancing rare disease care through LLM-empowered multi-disciplinary team (2024). arXiv, https://doi.org/10.48550/arXiv.2412.12475

8. Choi, J., et al.: MALADE: orchestration of LLM-powered agents with retrieval augmented generation for pharmacovigilance (2024). https://doi.org/10.48550/arXiv.2408.01869

9. Fujita, K., et al.: The improvement of the electronic health record user experience by screen design principles. J. Med. Syst. **44**(1), 1–6 (2020)

10. Bichler, M.: Design science in information systems research. Wirtschaftsinformatik **48**(2), 133–135 (2006). https://doi.org/10.1007/s11576-006-0028-8

11. Karunanayake, N.: Next-generation agentic AI for transforming healthcare. Inform. Health **2**(2), 73–83 (2025)

12. Keszthelyi, D., et al.: Patient information summarization in clinical settings: scoping review. JMIR Med. Inform. **11**(1), e44639 (2023)

13. Kim, Y., et al.: MDAgents: an adaptive collaboration of LLMs for medical decision-making. In: Proceedings of the Advances in Neural Information Processing Systems, pp. 79410–79452 (2024)

14. Kruse, C. S., et al.: Adoption factors of the electronic health record: a systematic review. JMIR Med. Inform. **4**(2), Article e5525 (2016)

15. Lee, C., et al.: Improving clinical documentation with AI: a comparative study of Sporo AI Scribe and GPT-4o mini (2024). arXiv, https://doi.org/10.48550/arXiv.2410.15528

16. Li, L., et al.: A scoping review of using large language models (LLMs) to investigate electronic health records (EHRs) (2024). arXiv, https://doi.org/10.48550/arXiv.2405.03066

17. Lu, M., et al.: TriageAgent: towards better multi-agents collaborations for large language model-based clinical triage. Findings of the Association for Computational Linguistics: EMNLP (2024)

18. Madzime R., Nyirenda, C.: Enhanced electronic health records text summarization using large language models (2024). arXiv. https://doi.org/10.48550/arXiv.2410.09628

19. Pivovarov, R., Elhadad, N.: Automated methods for the summarization of electronic health records. J. Am. Med. Inform. Assoc. **22**(5), 938–947 (2015)

20. Porter, R., et al.: LLMD: a large language model for interpreting longitudinal medical records (2024). arXiv. https://doi.org/10.48550/arXiv.2410.12860

21. Radi, A.M.A., et al.: Agentic large-language-model systems in medicine: a systematic review and taxonomy (2025). TechRxiv. https://doi.org/10.36227/techrxiv.175736231.12300949/v1

22. Sepehri, K., et al.: Beyond the bulging binder: family-centered design of a digital health information management sys-tem for caregivers of children living with health complexity. In: The 2023 CHI Conference on Human Factors in Computing Systems, pp. 1–19 (2023)

23. Shavit, Y., et al.: Practices for governing agentic AI systems. OpenAI (2023)

24. Shing, H.C., et al.: Towards clinical encounter summarization: learning to compose discharge summaries from prior notes (2021). arXiv. https://doi.org/10.48550/arXiv.2104.13498

25. Van Veen, D., et al.: Adapted large language models can outperform medical experts in clinical text summarization. Nat. Med. **30**(4), 1134–1142 (2024)
26. Walonoski, J., et al.: The "Coherent Data Set": combining patient data and imaging in a comprehensive, synthetic health record. Electronics **11**(8), 1199 (2022)
27. Wang, Q., Laramee, R.S.: EHR STAR: the state-of-the-art in interactive EHR visualization. Comput. Graph. Forum **41**(1), 69–105 (2022)
28. Wang, Z., et al.: MedAgent-Pro: Towards evidence-based multi-modal medical diagnosis via reasoning agentic workflow (2025). arXiv. https://doi.org/10.48550/arXiv.2503.18968
29. Wang, Z., et al.: ColaCare: enhancing electronic health record modeling through large language model-driven multi-agent collaboration. In: Proceedings of the ACM on Web Conference 2025. ACM, 2250–2261 (2025)
30. Xu, R., et al.: MedAssist: LLM-empowered medical assistant for assisting the scrutinization and comprehension of electronic health records. In: Proceedings of the Companion Proceedings of the ACM on Web Conference 2025, pp. 2931-2934 (2025)
31. Zerlik, M., et al.: Visualization techniques for summarizing single patient health data to support physicians' clinical decisions–A scoping review. Studies in Health Technology and Informatics, IOS Press (2024)
32. Zhang, S., et al.: Rethinking human-AI collaboration in complex medical decision making: A case study in sepsis diagnosis. In: Proceedings of the CHI Conference on Human Factors in Computing Systems, pp. 1–18 (2024)
33. Zhang, Z., et al.: AnamneVis: a framework for the visualization of patient history and medical diagnostics chains. In: Proceedings of the IEEE VAHC Workshop, pp. 1–4 (2011)

Future of Design and Entrepreneurship

Leading Through Change: Designing an AI Companion for Decision Support from Continuous Conversation with Strategic Decision Makers

Jan vom Brocke[1,2(✉)], Bianca van Dellen[2], Zoë Zoepffel[1], Tobias Zimmermann[1], and Timo Strohmann[1]

[1] University of Münster, 48149 Münster, Germany
`jan.vom.brocke@uni-muenster.de`
[2] University of Liechtenstein, 9490 Vaduz, Liechtenstein

Abstract. Design Science Research (DSR) has extensively studied how organizations cope with constant change; however, existing contributions have largely focused on the design and management of processes at an operational level. Strategic decision making has received comparatively little attention, even though such decisions set the essential framework for organizational adaptability. In this research in progress paper, we extend DSR to provide support for strategic decision making in contexts of change. We present and evaluate the solution design of an AI Strategy Companion for strategic decision making, which is built on data derived from continuous conversations with senior decision makers about their experiences in dealing with change. We identify four design features for AI Strategy Companions and, based on an evaluation with strategic managers, derive five design requirements critical to their design. The results have implications for both research and practice and open up promising avenues for future research.

Keywords: Change · Transformation · Strategic Change · Entrepreneurship · Strategic Decision Making · AI Companion · AI Strategy Companion · Design Science Research · DSR

1 Introduction

Contemporary organizations operate in an environment characterized by persistent volatility, increasing complexity, and accelerating change [1, 2]. Technological innovation, geopolitical uncertainty, demographic shifts, and societal transformation continuously reshape the conditions under which firms compete and evolve [2]. Within this context, an organization's ability to adapt to change is considered a fundamental capability [3]. While adaptability is often discussed as an organizational attribute, a growing body of research emphasizes that change is ultimately enacted through human agency, most notably through the decisions and interpretations of senior executives [4]. Strategic decision makers play a pivotal role in framing transformation initiatives, allocating resources, and legitimizing change trajectories within their organizations [5].

S. Chatterjee et al. (Eds.): DESRIST 2026, LNCS 16607, pp. 197–208, 2026.
https://doi.org/10.1007/978-3-032-28570-6_16

Entrepreneurship therefore extends beyond the mere founding of new ventures and encompasses the critical examination of existing structures as well as the proactive shaping of a firm's future development. Consequently, understanding how strategic decision makers conceptualize and navigate change has become an important research priority. Senior executives are increasingly required to make high-stakes decisions under conditions of uncertainty, ambiguity, and incomplete information [6]. These decisions often involve competing objectives, long time horizons, and consequences that extend beyond organizational boundaries [7]. Executives tend to face decisions for the first time, and they rarely have systematic access to the experiential knowledge of peers who face similar challenges in different organizational or institutional contexts [8, 9]. Although many strategic challenges recur across firms, industries, and countries, the associated experiential knowledge typically remains tacit and fragmented [2]. Opportunities for structured peer-level learning are limited, and it is often unclear whether comparable situations have been encountered elsewhere, how they were interpreted, and which courses of action proved effective [1]. As a result, strategic decision making frequently relies on individual experience and intuition, while increasingly facing first-time decisions of a particular kind, increasing the risk of avoidable errors during periods of transformation. We conclude by identifying the specific problem statement: *Strategic decision makers lack decision support on how to deal with continuous change.* Our objective is to contribute to solving this problem, and so we ask: *How can we support strategic decision makers to deal with change, specifically providing access to experiential knowledge to inform decision making?*

In this research in progress paper, we present an evaluation of the solution design for an AI companion aimed at assisting entrepreneurial decision making in strategic renewal, referred to as the AI Strategy Companion. The focus is on the design and initial evaluation rather than an exhaustive problem statement. The intent is to showcase the potential of an AI companion to inspire strategic decision makers. This study identifies four design features and derives five critical design requirements from evaluations with strategic managers. A notable aspect is its longitudinal design, capturing strategic reasoning through ongoing interactions with senior decision makers.

The remainder of this paper is structured as follows. First, we present the relevant research background, introducing strategic decision making, intelligent decision support for executives, and AI companions. We then describe the research design, outlining how we applied a design science research approach to develop and evaluate the solution design of an AI Strategy Companion. We then introduce the solution design and subsequently present the results of our initial evaluation. We discuss implications for both practice and research and outline future research directions.

2   Background

2.1   Strategic Decision Making

For this research it is essential to recognize the nature of strategic decision making, including leadership and executive reasoning. The relevance of researching decision making processes is particularly evident in the number and breadth of existing research in this field. Previous research has addressed strategic decision making in a broad and general manner [10, 11]. With an increasingly volatile economic environment, a wealth of literature has emerged on decision making in a dynamic world [1, 10]. However, the examination of decision making by entrepreneurs and top managers has been of special interest in the existing literature [1, 9, 12].

In the digital age and a volatile environment, decision making is anything but easy. Therefore, decision makers are often supported by predictive models that are supposed to make an accurate forecast about the consequences [2]. The decision making process of corporate leaders covers numerous areas and has a tremendous impact on stakeholders such as employees [12]. Nevertheless, it should not be forgotten that decisions are often made not by one person but by a management team, which is why companies can benefit from understanding the dynamics of team decision making [13]. In the early stages of team development, individual decision making styles shape the approach, while in later stages, past performance primarily serves as a feedback mechanism that guides further decision making strategies [13].

Nauhaus [14] addresses the issue of rationality in decision making in his study about strategic decision making in the digital age. Strategic decision makers use a variety of expert signals as rationalizing heuristics that go beyond pure financial indicators and help them make more informed investment decisions in uncertain situations [14]. Despite limited rationality, digitalization enables more rational and comprehensive decisions—but only if sufficient high-quality and reliable information is available [14].

Despite a lot of research on strategic decision making the optimal methods for assisting decision makers in dynamic, unpredictable scenarios with numerous interdependencies remain ambiguous [1, 9, 12]. Contemporary decision support methodologies primarily emphasize the accuracy of forecasts and the efficacy of data processing [14]. Nevertheless, they often fail to effectively facilitate strategic decision making that is iterative, collaborative, and contextually aware, particularly in dynamic situations [13]. This study therefore addresses the question of how decision support can be designed to better assist strategic decision makers in such contexts.

2.2 Information Systems for Strategic Decision Making

In an increasingly digitized world, systems that can intelligently support companies in strategic decision making are coming to the fore in science [15–17]. But digital support for decision making processes has been a topic of discussion for quite some time, long before the emergence of artificial intelligence (AI) in recent years [18]. It can therefore be said that three stages of research have been completed: (1) The foundation [18], (2) differentiation and maturity [19] until it then transitioned to (3) AI transformation [16]. Gorry and Scott Morton [18] laid the foundation for decision support systems with their research. According to this study, management decision making should be supported by a new type of digital tool [18].

The current era of decision support (from around 2024 onwards) is characterized by the transition from passive tools to active partners in the decision making process, which is summarized under the terms decision intelligence and algorithmic leadership. AI systems are increasingly being viewed as Machines as Teammates (MaT) that actively participate in the problem-solving process [15]. MaT systems participate in cognitive steps such as identifying causes, designing solutions, and evaluating consequences [15].

An essential aspect of modern intelligent agents is their ability to learn from explicit feedback from humans in order to provide more accurate information later on. Strategic decision makers want systems that they can actively coach [20]. This iterative process continuously improves the quality and relevance of the information provided, making the system a reliable source for future decisions [20].

In modern frameworks for intelligent decision support systems, the storage of human knowledge plays a central role [17]. The system has a dedicated knowledge layer that receives information from three sources: internal memory, other integrated systems, and human experts who feed their knowledge directly into the system [17]. Descriptive knowledge (facts), procedural knowledge (processes), and inferential knowledge (logic) are stored. Knowledge-management-based systems support individual and organizational memory by enabling access to knowledge across groups, for example through electronic forums or expert systems [17].

Consequently, there is a need for decision support approaches that go beyond predictive analytics and instead function as interactive partners in complex decision processes, particularly in environments characterized by continuous change.

2.3 AI Companions

Recent advances in AI and natural language processing have enabled conversational systems that move beyond short-term, task-oriented interaction toward sustained, relational engagement with users [21, 22]. These systems are commonly referred to as AI companions and are distinguished from traditional chatbots and virtual assistants by their emphasis on longitudinal interaction, social responsiveness, and adaptive dialogue across repeated encounters [23, 24].

AI companions are designed to establish continuity and familiarity over time rather than to optimize isolated task execution [22, 23]. This design orientation builds on the Computers Are Social Actors (CASA) paradigm, which shows that users apply social norms and relational expectations to interactive technologies that display social cues such as natural language, responsiveness, and apparent intentionality [25, 26]. As a result, conversational agents capable of sustained interaction are frequently engaged as social interaction partners rather than purely instrumental tools [27].

Design-oriented research has identified persistence, adaptivity, and socio-emotional responsiveness as core characteristics distinguishing AI companions from reactive assistants [23, 27, 28]. Unlike transactional agents that reset interactional context, AI companions accumulate interaction histories and adapt their conversational behavior based on prior exchanges, enabling open-ended and evolving dialogue [21, 22]. These properties support interaction patterns that more closely resemble ongoing interpersonal exchange than episodic information retrieval.

From a design science perspective, AI companions represent a distinct class of digital artifacts characterized by longitudinal engagement and relational continuity [23]. Prior literature conceptualizes such systems as emphasizing continuity, shared interaction history, and adaptive dialogue, rather than discrete, task-bounded exchanges [22, 27, 28]. These characteristics align AI companions conceptually with theoretical accounts that treat reflection and interpretation as ongoing processes, thereby motivating their consideration in contexts where decision making unfolds over time.

3 Research Design

In this research paper, the authors highlight the importance of presenting current AI capabilities to senior management for informed strategic decision making before engaging in system design discussions. They adopt an effectuation logic, focusing on available resources and potential solutions amidst uncertainty and rapid technological changes. The feedback from executives and the demonstration of the AI Strategy Companion prototype are deemed crucial for uncovering latent assumptions and expectations that might remain obscured through traditional problem analysis.

Our study follows a DSR approach with the objective of generating prescriptive design knowledge for AI Strategy Companions in contexts of continuous organizational change [29]. Given the complexity of the problem domain, the evolving understanding of both problem and solution spaces, and the longitudinal nature of the empirical setting, we adopt the echeloned design science research (eDSR) methodology as the overarching research design [30]. As argued, we focus on presenting and evaluating the *solution design* of the AI Strategy Companion for strategic decision making. We consider it important to first demonstrate and explore what can be achieved with an AI Strategy Companion in this application context, in order to stimulate the imagination of our target group—strategic decision makers. Validation occurs through participant feedback and illustrative scenarios, aligning with eDSR's focus on early error detection [31, 32]. Based on the results of this research in progress, we intend to go back to the problem, objective echelon, conduct more thorough design and validation of each echelon.

We present a socio-technical design with the AI Strategy Companion at the center, essentially enlarged regarding an appropriate data collection strategy from strategic decision makers as well as a dissemination strategy of the AI towards strategic decision makers. The study targets strategic decision makers from large firms in the DAX, ATX, and SMI, as well as family-owned enterprises in Germany, Austria, Switzerland, and Liechtenstein, involving 75–100 executives across various industries. Regarding the data collection strategy, the study employs a longitudinal interview design to capture ongoing strategic reasoning, treating continuous conversational data as digital traces supported by a dedicated architecture for analysis. The study aims to provide insights into executive reasoning as a process, contributing to research on strategic decision making and DSR by establishing design objectives for AI Strategy Companions.

4 Solution Design of a Strategic Decision Making Companion

The core challenge in designing an AI Strategy Companion is that much of the data required to inform such a system is not publicly available: While general knowledge about strategic decision making can be accessed through existing publications, our research aims to capture the lived experiences of strategic decision makers themselves.

In order to get to strategic decision makers' experience, we have created *Leaders Unplugged*, a research initiative designed to capture strategic decision making through continuous, structured conversations with senior executives. With *Leaders Unplugged*, strategic decision makers agree to participate in interviews over an extended period of time, during which they report on personal change projects and share their experiences in pursuing and achieving their goals. We have developed an information systems architecture that uses an LLM at the center of the AI Strategy Companion to capture, analyze, and provide data for strategic decision support, which we illustrate in Fig. 1.

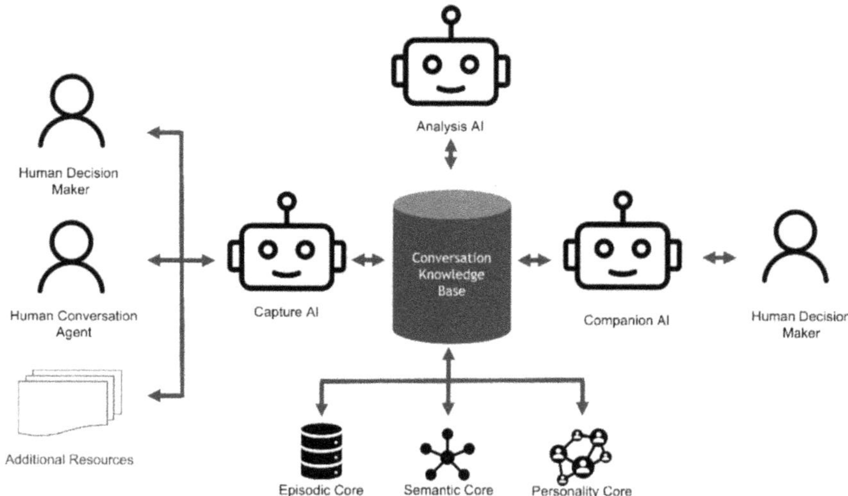

Fig. 1. Design of the AI Strategy Companion Architecture for Decision Support

Leaders Unplugged is a longitudinal research initiative capturing executive reasoning through continuous, structured conversations with senior decision makers. Rather than relying on one-off, retrospective interviews, the initiative invites strategic decision makers to engage in repeated sessions with a human conversational agent over approximately three months, focusing on real-time change challenges. These conversations are recorded and transcribed to create a corpus of "strategic episodes" documenting how leaders interpret signals, weigh trade-offs, and revise judgments. Building on this, an LLM-based AI Strategy Companion structures peer-derived experience, identifies recurring patterns in strategic reasoning, and supports decision makers through reflective prompts and contextualized retrieval.

Technically, a capture AI orchestrates the ingestion of raw discourse from human decision makers into a conversation knowledge base. This repository is an integrated memory system supported by three structural cores, the episodic, semantic, and personality cores, storing narrative context, structural industry patterns, and behavioral traits. An analysis AI continuously monitors this knowledge base to identify recurring themes, while the companion AI acts as the primary interface, providing real-time decision support through a facilitated dialogue that emphasizes reflection over simple automation.

The solution distinguishes itself from standard retrieval-augmented generation systems through four specific Design Features (DFs) on instantiation-level grounded in advancements in neuro-symbolic AI and personality-adaptive design:

DF1 - Dual-Memory Ingestion Architecture: The system incorporates both generalized structural knowledge and specific context-driven experiences. It distinguishes between semantic and episodic memory, organizing data into two parallel streams: the semantic core creates a structured "world model" of industry patterns, while the episodic core saves detailed narratives in a vector database. This architecture supports theories suggesting that separating memory systems improves an agent's ability to conduct complex reasoning, surpassing mere pattern matching [33].

DF2 - Hybrid Neuro-Symbolic Retrieval: To synthesize these distinct memory types, the solution implements a concurrent retrieval strategy that addresses the limitations of standard vector-only retrieval in multi-hop reasoning. Symbolic retrieval identifies high-level structural clusters and causal chains, while neural retrieval performs similarity searches to retrieve the specific anecdotes that ground these patterns in reality. This approach integrates knowledge graphs with vector retrieval to significantly reduce hallucinations and improve complex information extraction [34].

DF3 - Agentic Facilitation Protocol: A strategic companion must facilitate reflection rather than providing passive outputs. To mitigate automation bias, the system employs an agentic workflow based on the ReAct paradigm. During the observe & reason phase, the agent analyzes intent to detect operational offloading. Crucially, the system instantiates a refusal rule: if a binary decision is requested, the system is programmed to refuse and instead offer a "reflective challenge" comparing peer trade-offs, enabling the system to act as an active cognitive partner [35].

DF4 - Personality-Adaptive Reasoning: To ensure the AI is perceived as an authentic social actor, the system adapts to its user based on the Five Factor Model. Building on the CASA paradigm, the system automatically infers personality traits from conversational language use. Linguistic cues are processed to allow the agent to dynamically adapt its communication style, social role, and degree of anthropomorphism to match preferences. Personalizing the interaction style in this manner is shown to improve communication and rapport, enabling sustained relational engagement [36].

5 Initial Evaluation of the Solution Design

In this chapter, we report on our initial evaluation of the design solution with strategic decision makers. We implemented the software and recruited an initial group of senior decision makers who agreed to contribute to the *Leaders Unplugged* initiative. As this is a research in progress paper, we intentionally adopted a more lightweight approach for the first evaluation. At this point, we analyzed 92 min of interviews and think-aloud protocols with two senior decision makers from the investment goods sector as data input, which is appropriate for a research in progress paper. For the purposes of this research in progress paper, we keep the description concise and do not detail the implementation. Instead, we focus on reporting first evaluation results from key executives working with the solution. The prototype used in the evaluation by the decision makers is publicly available[1].

We employed an exploratory, formative evaluation methodology typical of early-stage Design Science Research (DSR) to assess the feasibility and conceptual validity of an AI Strategy Companion for strategic decision making, focusing on gathering initial

---

[1] https://leaders-unplugged.uni-muenster.de.

design feedback rather than evaluating effectiveness [37, 38]. Through sessions with two strategic decision makers—qualified as senior executives and owners with decision authority over an organization's strategic direction - we collected first insights into the perceived usefulness of the solution design. Each participant used the AI Strategy Companion prototype for approximately 30 min. We assessed feedback using a think-aloud protocol and subsequently conducted open interviews with each participant to explore how they experienced their interaction with the AI companion.

The interviewees (B1 and B2) engaged with the prototype and shared their thoughts through a think-aloud procedure, and subsequent open interviews.

Our first concern was whether senior decision makers would be willing to engage in the planned continuous conversations and support the capture of data for the LLM:

"Leaders Unplugged addresses a real gap in strategic decision making. Access to the thinking of accountable peers — not theory, not consultants — significantly strengthens decision quality. That's why I'm fully willing to participate and contribute to my own experience. (Int. B1)"

Then, we were eager to learn to what extent the senior executives would find the solution design useful:

"Observing how different leaders behave in challenging situations is a great learning opportunity for me. I could see how peers act under pressure, which approaches they choose, and what consequences these behaviors have [...]. Experiencing this across different companies worldwide creates a powerful source of learning. (Int. B2)"

From the evaluation, it also emerged that the permanent and spontaneous availability of AI, as well as the informality and anonymity of the query, are viewed positively.

"What would be truly valuable, is the ability to query what I want to know exactly when I need it [...] that I can reach this or that peer at a given moment. Being able to access such insights precisely provided by AI when needed, without having to worry about how perfectly I formulate or articulate my question, [...]. This kind of temporal and spatial independence would be more than ideal. (Int. B1)"

The findings endorse the notion that executive reasoning can be captured and structured through continuous conversational data. The concept of an AI Strategy Companion is pertinent to the actual experiences of senior decision makers.

"I would love to work with AI in this context. [...] What would be truly valuable, however, is the ability to access and reflect on the knowledge and decisions of real, accountable decision makers through AI. Being able to query and consider how responsible executives have approached comparable situations would create immense value. Otherwise, the perspectives available to us are largely those of consultants or theoretical frameworks from books—often written by individuals who do not themselves bear ultimate decision responsibility. (Int. B2)"

Both interviews revealed a clear consensus against viewing AI as an autonomous decision maker. Strategic decision makers described the system as a cognitive partner that aids individuals while ensuring managers retain full control and accountability. The AI should identify patterns, suggest alternatives, and question assumptions, which highlights the importance of AI-driven decision support systems.

"Being able to query an AI that is grounded in the knowledge and experiences of real peers would address a very real and currently unmet need. It would allow us to learn from one another much faster [...]. (Int. B1)"

The participants also valued the underlying data basis, which they perceived as particularly trustworthy and insightful, because it reflects the experiences of other senior decision makers. They noted that counseling peers facing similar strategic issues is valuable in uncertain situations where decisions are complex and difficult to reverse.

"It is certainly more credible for me, because while consultants may have broader exposure and see many cases, only other entrepreneurs truly understand what it means to sit in my chair as a family business owner. (Int. B1)"

Trust is crucial for the acceptance of AI Strategy Companions, influenced by organizational context and decision making roles. Preliminary evaluation suggests the solution's feasibility and value, with ongoing research to assess the companion's capabilities among strategic decision makers. The data collection method is being refined, and future steps involve extensive interviews with larger groups and a longer timeline to solidify the study's empirical basis. A list of potential interviewees has been prepared, leveraging access to high-level executives.

6 Implications

In this research in progress paper, we have presented and evaluated the solution design of an AI Strategy Companion for strategic decision makers. The AI system we propose is inherently socio-technical as it is based on data we gain from conversation with decision makers, and it aims to serve decision makers to strategically deal with change. Our initial evaluation confirms that strategic decision makers value the system, which suggests that we continue our more detailed work on the solution.

Based on our research, we see first design requirements emerging, which we intend to further investigate in future research:

DR1 - Sensemaking over Optimization: specifies that AI Strategy Companions for strategic leadership must support sensemaking and reflection rather than optimize or recommend singular "best" decisions.

DR2 - Human-in-the-Loop by Design: requires that the system stimulates strategic reasoning while preserving executive judgment and accountability.

DR3 - Trust through Transparency: requires traceable reasoning paths, explainable patterns, and clear references to peer-derived insights.

DR4 - Contextual Anchoring: captures the need to ground AI support in the executive's organizational, temporal, and strategic context rather than decision models.

DR5 - Seamless Process Integration: requires that AI Strategy Companions align with existing leadership routines and strategic workflows instead of behavioral change.

Beyond contributions to knowledge on the design of AI companions for strategic decision making, our research provides two methodological points of reflection.

First, our research follows a non-linear approach that emphasizes early solution presentation prior to detailed problem analysis, reflecting the dynamic nature of technology-driven design science research, particularly with AI artifacts. Early design representations help surface latent needs and foster stakeholder engagement, which is especially valuable in strategic decision making contexts where stakeholders often struggle to articulate requirements for non-existent artifacts. We therefore consider this approach beneficial for DSR projects more generally, as it supports envisioning digital futures and articulating requirements through early solution design.

Second, our engagement with strategic decision makers resulted in a continuous dialogical inquiry approach that goes beyond isolated interviews. We see this as a promising methodological direction for DSR more broadly, as ongoing conversations with practitioners can serve as a sustained strategy of inquiry. Such an approach opens access to a novel data base grounded in continuous, real-world experience.

While this study offers early insights into the eDSR approach, it has limitations, including a lack of systematic problem analysis due to early solution design involvement and a small evaluation sample of two senior decision makers. Building on the overall positive feedback, future research will further advance problem understanding, requirements definition, and the iterative refinement of the solution, proof of concept, and proof of value. At its current stage, this study is exploratory rather than evaluative, providing a basis for early-stage insights and particularly enabling early error detection within the eDSR approach.

References

1. Chirico, F., et al.: Entrepreneurial decision-making under uncertainty and competing goals. Strat. Entrep. J. 1–17 (2026)
2. Cohee, G.L., Barnhart, C.M.: Often wrong, never in doubt: Mitigating leadership overconfidence in decision-making. Organ. Dyn. **53**, 1–7 (2024)
3. Yang, E., DiBenigno, J.: Opportunistic change during a punctuation: how and when the front lines can drive bursts of incremental change. Organ. Sci. **36**, 40–64 (2025)
4. Cannella, A.A., Jr., Monroe, M.J.: Contrasting perspectives on strategic leaders: toward a more realistic view of top managers. JOM **23**, 213–237 (1997)
5. Snihur, Y., Zott, C., Kiss, A.N.: Incumbent response to business model innovation: The role of CEO opportunity framing. Strat. Entrep. J. **19**, 225–255 (2025)
6. Srikanth, K., Ungureanu, T.: Organizational adaptation in dynamic environments: Disentangling the effects of how much to explore vs. where to explore. SMJ. **46**, 19–48 (2025)
7. Smith, W.K.: Dynamic decision making: A model of senior leaders managing strategic paradoxes. Acad. Manage. J. **57**, 1592–1623 (2014)
8. Olson, B.J., Parayitam, S., Bao, Y.: Strategic decision making: the effects of cognitive diversity, conflict, and trust on decision outcomes. JOM **33**, 196–222 (2007)
9. Arendt, L.A., Priem, R.L., Ndofor, H.A.: A CEO-adviser model of strategic decision making. JOM **31**, 680–699 (2005)

10. Schwenk, C.R.: Strategic decision making. JOM **21**, 471–493 (1995)
11. Hendry, J.: Strategic decision making, discourse, and strategy as social practice. JMS. **37**, 955–977 (2000)
12. Westaby, J.D., Probst, T.M., Lee, B.C.: Leadership decision-making: a behavioral reasoning theory analysis. Leadersh. Q. **21**, 481–495 (2010)
13. Zhu, X.S., Wolfson, M.A., Dalal, D.K., Mathieu, J.E.: Team decision making: the dynamic effects of team decision style composition and performance via decision strategy. JOM **47**, 1281–1304 (2021)
14. Nauhaus, S., Luger, J., Raisch, S.: Strategic decision making in the digital age: expert sentiment and corporate capital allocation. JMS. **58**, 1933–1961 (2021)
15. Seeber, I., et al.: Machines as teammates: a research agenda on AI in team collaboration. Inf. Manag. **57**, 103–174 (2020)
16. Juenke, A.S.M., Khosrawi-Rad, B., Strohmann, T., Robra-Bissantz, S.: Leading by Algorithm: Investigating User Requirements for Automated Leadership Agents. In: AMCIS 2025 Proceedings, pp. 1–10 (2025)
17. Onwujekwe, G., Weistrofer, H.R.: Intelligent decision support systems: an analysis of the literature and a framework for development. Inf. Syst. Front. **27**, 2027–2058 (2025)
18. Gorry, G.A., Scott Morton, M.S.: A Framework for management information systems. Sloan Manage. Rev. **13**, 55–70 (1971)
19. Arnott, D., Pervan, G.: A critical analysis of decision support systems research. J. Inf. Technol. **20**, 67–87 (2005)
20. Duan, Y., Ong, V.K., Xu, M., Mathews. B.: Supporting decision making process with "ideal" software agents – What do business executives want? Expert Syst. Appl. **39**, 5534–5547 (2012)
21. Diederich, S., Brendel, A.B., Morana, S., Kolbe, L.: On the design of and interaction with conversational agents: an organizing and assessing review of human-computer interaction research. J. Assoc. Inf. Syst. **23**, 96–138 (2022)
22. Nißen, M., et al.: See you soon again, chatbot? A design taxonomy to characterize user-chatbot relationships with different time horizons. Comput. Human Behav. **127**, 1–15 (2022)
23. Strohmann, T., Siemon, D., Khosrawi-Rad, B., Robra-Bissantz, S.: Toward a design theory for virtual companionship. Hum.-Comput. Interact. **38**, 194–234 (2022)
24. Skjuve, M., Følstad, A., Fostervold, K.I., Brandtzaeg, P.B.: My chatbot companion - a study of human-chatbot relationships. Int. J. Hum. Comput. Stud. **149**, 1–14 (2021)
25. Nass, C., Moon, Y.: Machines and mindlessness: Social responses to computers. J. Soc. Issues **56**, 81–103 (2000)
26. Nass, C., Steuer, J., Tauber, E.R.: Computers are social actors. In: Proceedings of the SIGCHI conference on Human factors in computing systems celebrating interdependence - CHI '94. ACM Press, New York, New York, USA (1994)
27. Krämer, N.C., Eimler, S., Rosenthal-von der Pütten, A.M., Payr, S.M.: Theory of companions: what can theoretical models contribute to applications and understanding of human-robot interaction? Appl. Artif. Intell. **25**, 474–502 (2011)
28. Bickmore, T.W., Picard, R.W.: Establishing and maintaining long-term human-computer relationships. ACM Trans. Comput. Hum. Interact. **12**, 293–327 (2005)
29. Hevner, A.R., March, S.T., Park, J., Ram, S.: Design Science in Information Systems Research. Manag. Inf. Syst. Q. **28**, 75–105 (2004)
30. Tuunanen, T., Winter, R., vom Brocke, J.: Dealing with complexity in design science research: A methodology using design echelons. Manag. Inf. Syst. Q. **48**, 427–458 (2024)
31. Sonnenberg, C., vom Brocke, J.: Evaluations in the Science of the Artificial – Reconsidering the Build-Evaluate Pattern in Design Science Research. In: Peffers, K., Rothenberger, M., and Kuechler, B. (eds.) Design Science Research in Information Systems. Advances in Theory and Practice, pp. 381–397. Springer, Berlin, Heidelberg (2012)

32. Venable, J., Pries-Heje, J., Baskerville, R.: FEDS: A framework for evaluation in design science research. Eur. J. Inf. Syst. **25**, 77–89 (2016)
33. Kim, T., Cochez, M., Francois-Lavet, V., Neerincx, M., Vossen, P.: A machine with short-term, episodic, and semantic memory systems. In: Proc. 37th Conf. AAAI Artif. Intell, pp. 48–56. Association for the Advancement of Artificial Intelligence (AAAI) (2023)
34. Sarmah, B., et al.: HybridRAG: Integrating Knowledge Graphs and vector Retrieval Augmented Generation for efficient information extraction. In: Proceedings of the 5th ACM International Conference on AI in Finance. Association for Computing Machinery, New York, NY, USA (2024)
35. Yao, S., et al.: ReAct: Synergizing Reasoning and Acting in Language Models. In: Proceedings of the Eleventh Intern. Conference on Learning Representations (ICLR '23). OpenReview.net, Kigali, Rwanda (2023)
36. Ahmad, R., Siemon, D., Gnewuch, U., Robra-Bissantz, S.: Designing Personality-Adaptive Conversational Agents for Mental Health Care. Inf. Syst. Front. **24**, 923–943 (2022)
37. Hambrick, D.C., Mason, P.A.: Upper echelons: The organization as a reflection of its top managers. Acad. Manage. Rev. **9**, 193–206 (1984)
38. Finkelstein, S., Hambrick, D.C., Cannella, B.: Strategic Leadership: Theory and Research on Executives, Top Management Teams, and Boards. Oxford Univ. Press, Oxford (2009)

Future of Responsible and Sustainable Design

Balancing Openness and Security in Digital Energy Ecosystems

Theodore Kindong[✉] ⓘ, Gianluigi Viscusi ⓘ, and Björn Johansson ⓘ

Linköping University, Campus Valla, 58183 Linköping, Sweden
`{theodore.kindong,gianluigi.viscusi,Bjorn.se.johansson}@liu.se`

Abstract. This paper presents a design framework for energy management systems (EMS) that positions openness and information security as interdependent dimensions, jointly shaping innovation in digital energy ecosystems. Rather than considering them as opposing forces, the framework frames them as characterized by a dynamic interplay that requires continuous recalibration in response to evolving technological and organizational contexts. Accordingly, we conceptualize openness as a facilitator of innovation, interoperability, and data-driven collaboration among diverse actors, including utilities, regulators, technology providers, and end-users. Yet, we also acknowledge that openness amplifies vulnerability by increasing the number of interfaces, data exchanges, and system dependencies, thereby exposing EMS to potential external exploitation.

Keywords: Digital energy ecosystems · Energy Management Systems · Openness · Security

1 Introduction

The digitalization of power grids has fundamentally changed how energy systems are designed, operated, and secured [1, 2]. Smart grids, which form the backbone of an emerging "Energy Internet," [3] rely on real-time collection, transmission, and analysis of user consumption patterns and grid conditions to enhance reliability, flexibility, and sustainability [4, 5]. However, this extensive data interconnection creates a new layer of vulnerability, making power grid infrastructures susceptible to threats such as unauthorized data access, manipulation, inaccurate forecasting, operational disruptions, and even large-scale blackouts [6, 7]. Accordingly, cybersecurity emerges as a central determinant of how power grids are designed, developed, and governed, requiring an integrated understanding of technical architectures, organizational complexity, and policy environments [8, 9]. As Fan and Gong [7] highlight, the interconnected nature of smart grid metering and control systems introduces complex vulnerabilities that demand continuous innovation in encryption and intrusion detection. This is because smart meters enable real-time optimization but remain exposed to data manipulation and unauthorized access [10, 11]. Similarly, cloud-based data handling techniques such as deduplication can lead to breaches if not properly secured, underscoring the need for adaptive cybersecurity frameworks [4]. Nevertheless, Herath et al. [12] further show that organizational

© The Author(s), under exclusive license to Springer Nature Switzerland AG 2026
S. Chatterjee et al. (Eds.): DESRIST 2026, LNCS 16607, pp. 211–223, 2026.
https://doi.org/10.1007/978-3-032-28570-6_17

adoption of security solutions is tied to the innovation process and is influenced by technological and environmental factors that shape resilience. Consequently, cybersecurity serves not only as a protective mechanism but also as a driver of innovation, especially for advanced energy management systems (EMS) in smart grids, which transform traditional consumers into active prosumers [3]. Furthermore, while openness has been widely studied as a driver of digital innovation [13], there is a need for further research investigating how openness *and* information security jointly influence the design of EMS. This study addresses this gap as the overarching problem for EMS, and we propose a design framework that views openness and security as interdependent design dimensions for resilient and innovative EMS, guided by the following research question: *Are security concerns pivotal to EMS innovation? How can security concerns be addressed in EMS development?*

To address these questions, we present a design framework instantiated in a case study in Sweden. By bridging insights from information systems security theory [6, 14, 15] with empirical perspectives from smart grid research [5, 7, 16], this ongoing study contributes to the development of a design framework to understand mechanisms that make security a driver of innovation in EMS. This article is structured as follows. First, we present the theoretical background, followed by an outline of the research method. Next, we introduce the design framework, its constructs, and guiding principles, which are then applied to the Swedish Data Hub Project as an illustrative case. Finally, the paper concludes with a summary and an outline of future work.

2 Theoretical Background

2.1 Information Security in Energy Management Systems

The transition from a centralized power grid to smart grids transforms traditional consumers into active prosumers [7] and increases reliance on interconnected digital control and data infrastructures, making cybersecurity a foundational requirement for EMS. Effective security in this context asks for not only technical mechanisms such as encryption, authentication, anomaly detection, and access control, but also socio-technical governance arrangements, as cybersecurity capabilities depend on institutional readiness and organizational culture [12, 15]. This becomes increasingly critical as EMS complexity grows, as they connect and govern what can be seen as a *digital energy ecosystem* [17], where heterogeneous, time-critical energy data must be exchanged securely under low-latency, energy-constrained conditions [8, 18]. At the same time, emerging cryptographic and data-management technologies, including blockchain-based access control, and cryptographic frameworks such as homomorphic encryption, offer strong potential for maintaining confidentiality and functionality in smart grid environments, but only if aligned with organizational capacity and governance structures [19–21].

Moreover, involvement of multiple stakeholders, including utilities, regulators, technology providers, and prosumers, further expands system openness and interoperability, increasing both innovation opportunities and exposure to cyber risk. Empirical studies on smart meters show that despite existing safeguards measures, smart meters remain vulnerable to data manipulation, false data injection, and privacy breaches [10, 11, 16, 22], and local breaches caused by weak authentication or insecure communication channels can rapidly propagate across interconnected grids [5, 22]. These conditions create trade-offs between openness and security, as organizations struggle to balance innovation, compliance, and efficiency when adopting new security measures [12, 14]. Schneier and Vance [9] note that growing system complexity amplifies security challenges, and each new digital interface enlarges the attack surface of national power grids [12, 14], enabling cyber vulnerabilities to trigger cascading physical disruptions [11]. Regarding this issue, state-of-the-art research has proposed resilient and adaptive security architectures for EMS, including fuzzy-based optimization and anomaly-detection frameworks [23] as well as integrated smart-home cybersecurity architectures that combine encryption, intrusion detection, and authentication [24]. However, smart grid vulnerabilities, as discussed in this paper, highlight the need for multi-layered, security-by-design approaches spanning device authentication, secure communication, anomaly detection, and incident response. Hence, EMS security must be understood as an evolving socio-technical challenge [25] rather than a static compliance task, requiring information systems engineering frameworks that integrate security as an adaptive and innovation-enabling foundation for resilient and trustworthy digital energy ecosystems.

2.2 Openness in Energy Management Systems

Openness, referring to accessible resources, participatory processes, or democratizing effects [26], has been an important topic in technology and innovation management for both research and practice over the last twenty years, particularly in questioning the role of information technology as an enabler for leveraging it as a source of innovation [26, 27]. As to this issue, open innovation is defined as "a distributed innovation process based on purposively managed knowledge flows across organizational boundaries, using pecuniary and non-pecuniary mechanisms in line with each organization's business framework"(p.17 [28]). Then, considering now the domain of interest of this paper, openness in EMS refers to the degree of transparency, interoperability, and accessibility embedded in the system's architecture as well as in the system's data flows through *interoperability standards* [29]. As energy infrastructures evolve toward decentralized and intelligent networks, openness has become a key driver of innovation, user participation, and *stakeholder collaboration*, like in *peer-to-peer energy market* [30]. El-Hawary [2] underscores that smart grids depend on open standards, interoperable communication protocols, and *shared data platforms* to coordinate utilities, distributed energy resources, and consumers. This is further strengthened by advances in technology, as Kim et al. [31] demonstrate how blockchain-based EMS architectures can foster decentralized and transparent energy markets through peer-to-peer trading and traceable transactions, reducing reliance on central authorities [31]. This is expected to promote trust and accountability, while empowering prosumers to play an active role in energy generation and distribution. However, achieving openness in EMS requires navigating complex trade-offs between accessibility, innovation, and security. Herath et al. [12] argue that organizational adoption of open technologies depends on readiness, regulation, and the balance between opportunity and risk. Thus, while openness enables collaboration and interoperability in EMS, it also introduces new risks to data privacy and integrity. Regarding this issue, Goel et al. [4] note that cloud-based openness in large-scale EMS data sharing can expose sensitive data if not properly secured. Similarly, Fan and Gong [7] warn that open communication protocols broaden the smart grid attack surface, increasing vulnerability to cyber intrusions. Therefore, openness should be understood not as unrestricted access but as controlled transparency, supported by governance and cybersecurity mechanisms across all system layers. We argue that when openness and security are co-engineered, open EMS architectures can drive innovation, support multi-stakeholder collaboration, and enhance sustainability. Thus, we propose a framework that rethinks EMS innovation security in a changing digital world and in the context of the green transition.

3 Research Method

This paper adopts a design science research (DSR) method [32–34], following the guidelines and activities outlined by [34] and their elaboration by [35] based on the concept of "echelons" to address complex projects in the domain of energy transition, the subject of this paper. The aim is to produce an artifact in the form of a framework [33]. Regarding those activities, in the previous sections, we have summarized the results of the *problem analysis* and the *objectives and requirements definition* echelons [35]. In what follows, we first present the design framework in Fig. 1 as the artifact resulting from the *design and development* echelon. Then, we apply the artifact to the Swedish National Data Hub case (part of the *demonstration* echelon [35]). It is worth noting that this paper aims to *communicate* [34] the intermediate artifacts from the current iterations for each of the above-mentioned echelons. Future work will be dedicated to further iterations to further theorize on the artifact [36] and include the instantiations of the *evaluation* echelon [35]. This is also in accordance with the cycles identified for the two layers of DSR (design and theory-oriented) by [37]. Thus, the paper presents the results of two of the three sub-practices (theorize, build, and evaluate) making up design research [37]. Regarding the paper's contribution, we position it as an exaptation [32], extending known cybersecurity and open innovation frameworks from information systems [38] into the new domain of digital energy ecosystems. Moving beyond socio-technical framing, we offer prescriptive knowledge in the form of a design framework that defines the means-end relationships between openness and security. Accordingly, we formalize the problem space by specifying stakeholder needs and requirements [39] and provide a compelling problematization [40] of the digital energy transition rather than a simple gap-spotting exercise.

3.1 The Artifact

This section introduces the Digital Energy Ecosystem (DEE) design framework as the artifact resulting from activities 1–3 of the DSR. Figure 1 aims to support understanding of how DEE evolve as digitalization increases, with new technologies making up the Energy Internet.

The DEE focuses on the joint role of *openness* through elements like shared data platform, interoperability standards, stakeholder collaboration, and peer-to-peer energy market (*Open Innovation Layer* in Fig. 1) and *information security* (*Secure Architecture*

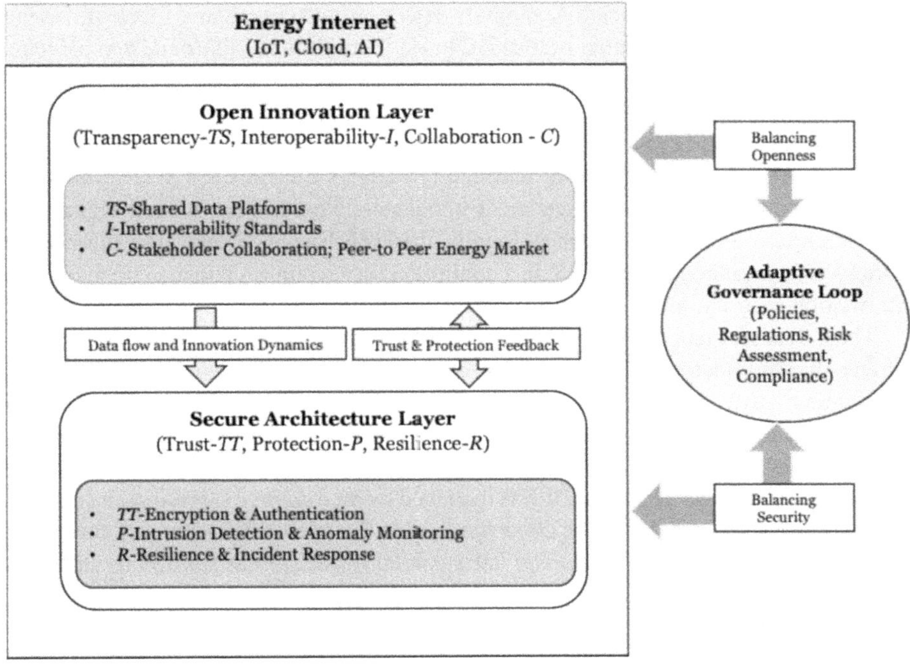

Fig. 1. DEE Design framework

Layer in Fig. 1) in shaping innovation in smart grid infrastructures. Rather than treating openness and security as opposing objectives, the DEE framework conceptualizes them as interdependent design dimensions that must be continuously aligned as technologies, organizational practices, and regulatory conditions evolve. Moreover, in our proposed DEE framework, openness refers to interoperable architectures, shared data infrastructures, and participatory system design that enable collaboration among utilities, regulators, technology providers, and end users [2, 23, 31]. Thus, openness supports innovation by facilitating data-driven coordination and prosumer participation, increasing connectivity, data exchange, and interface exposure, which introduces additional security and privacy risks [3, 6]. On the other hand, information security in this framework is treated as a foundational design requirement that ensures confidentiality, integrity, and availability of EMS data and services [5, 20]. This is achieved through i) security mechanisms such as *encryption, authentication, anomaly monitoring,* and *resilience and incident response* (see the *Secure Architecture Layer* in Fig. 1), and ii) governance controls to preserve trust and operational resilience within open ecosystems (see the *Adaptive Governance Loop* in Fig. 1) [6, 24, 27]. However, excessively rigid security controls may slow innovation, illustrating the need for balance rather than unilateral optimization. Then, overly rigid approaches can constrain experimentation and slow innovation. Accordingly, our proposed framework, shown in Fig. 1, conceptualizes EMS development as a balancing loop between two co-evolving design principles. The *first design principle* is 1) an Open Innovation Layer emphasizes interoperability, shared data infrastructures, and participatory system design [31]. The *second design principle* is 2) a Secure Architecture Layer embeds encryption, authentication, anomaly detection, and governance mechanisms that preserve trust within open ecosystems [7, 24, 41]. Furthermore, a *third design principle* (3) is that these layers (design principles 1 and 2) interact through adaptive governance, where organizational, regulatory, and technological mechanisms dynamically adjust the level of openness and security according to context-specific risks and innovation goals [8, 12]. The cited case of Svenska Kraftnät (Sweden's transmission system operator) incident exemplifies the consequences of imbalance, where openness and digital integration outpace security governance. Finally, the DEE framework rethinks information systems (IS) engineering for EMS as a continuous co-evolution between openness and information security, innovation, and control.

Thus, Transformative Performance (TP_{DEE}) denotes the system's overall ability to achieve digital transformation objectives, enabling innovation through openness while maintaining trustworthy, resilient operations under cyber risk. TP_{DEE} must be treated as a composite measure of innovation benefits moderated by security risks and governance effectiveness. In TP_{DEE}, innovation and security are not trade-offs, but mutually reinforcing principles. Then, the DEE is managed by an *Adaptive Governance Loop* that seeks to balance the benefits of the *Open Innovation Layer* with the necessary constraints of the *Secure Architecture Layer*. The latter can be formalized as follows to model the overall system performance and quantify the inherent trade-off.

$$TP_{DEE} = F_{G}c \cdot \frac{V_I}{R_S^a}$$

Table 1. The framework components, variables, and their role in the formalization.

Components	Variables	Elements in Design framework	Role in Formula
Open Innovation layer	V_I (Innovation Value)	Transparency (*TS*), Interoperability (*I*), Collaboration (*C*)	Benefits derived from openness
Secure Architecture layer	R_S (Security Risk)	Trust (*TT*), Protection (P), Resilience (R)	Cost/constraint (risk) associated with security robustness
Adaptive Governance Loop	F_G (Governance Factor)	Policies, Regulations, Risk Assessment, Compliance	Balancing mechanism that moderates the trade-off

Moreover, this formalization of the framework enables us to test the overall DEE Transformative Performance (TP_{DEE}) and to capture the trade-off between the benefits derived from openness (Innovation) and the costs/constraints associated with security. This is because the DEE Transformative Performance (T) is a function of the Innovation Value (cap R sub s) and is balanced by the Governance Loop Factor ($F_{G}c$), which varies depending on the organization's capacity to manage it. Here we consider capacity as related to i) the capabilities required for, e.g., understanding and applying regulations, doing risk assessments, acting on the Secure Architecture Layer (TT, P, R), as well as ii) the overall information capacity of the organization defined as "the current stock of understandings informed by a given installed base" (p. 81 [42]).

Moreover, inspired by the G-expectation model [43], we introduce a nonlinear risk-sensitivity exponent α, since real-world digital energy ecosystems exhibit cascading dependencies in which small security failures can propagate rapidly across interconnected components. The exponent a therefore models the empirically observed nonlinear escalation of impact under increasing cyber risk. And we set $\alpha > 1$ to reflect that this amplification effect moves the framework beyond a linear cost-benefit relation. Thus, the framework is analytically interpretable through its main constructs and design principles (see also Table 1), which emphasize the interaction between the Open Innovation and Secure Architecture layers, moderated by an Adaptive Governance Loop.

3.2 A DEE Vignette: The Swedish Datahub Project

The Swedish national Data Hub was a key initiative under the Nordic Energy Regulators (NordREG) framework to harmonize the Nordic electricity retail market. It was launched in 2018 [44] but was put on hold in September 2020 [44–46]. The project was expected to be implemented by Svenska Kraftnät (SVK), Sweden's transmission system operator, with oversight from the Swedish Energy Markets Inspectorate (*Energimarknadsinspektionen*, Ei), which had been tasked by the Swedish government to establish a comprehensive data hub encompassing all metering data for the country's electricity market. The introduction of the Data Hub was expected to bring significant changes to the Swedish electricity market by enabling a supplier-centric market framework, allowing consumers to rely on a single electricity trading company for both distribution and consumption invoicing. Additionally, the hub aimed to promote new energy-efficiency services by enhancing market transparency and competition through improved access to and exchange of metering data. Moreover, the Data Hub was envisioned as a transformative digital energy ecosystem infrastructure, intended to consolidate all metering information, streamline market operations, and facilitate innovative energy services [29, 30]. However, on 22 September 2020, Svenska Kraftnät's board formally decided to place the project on hold, citing "delays in the legislation and other uncertain circumstances." Despite earlier planning and procurement efforts, the legislative package necessary for enabling the hub had been repeatedly postponed.

By the time the hold was enacted, only about 20% of development had been completed [45, 46]. The absence of legal clarity prevented key market participants from committing to processes such as data migration or certification, effectively stalling the project. Thus, using our proposed formalization and normalizing the units across variables, we map how the delay in legislation affected key variables and why the project could not proceed safely in Table 2. This allows us to show how the framework supports EMS providers' understanding and the elicitation of requirements for balancing open innovation and security in digital energy ecosystem development initiatives.

Table 2. Mapping of the Data Hub vignette to our formula

Dimension	Variable	Meaning in formula	Target (before delay)	Observed during delay	Interpretations for managers
Innovation & data hub Value	V_I	Expected data hub innovation value (services, interoperability, market efficiency)	3.5	3.5 (unchanged)	High innovation potential remains but cannot compensate for governance and risk deficiencies
Governance & Regulatory Alignment	F_G	Governance effectiveness multiplier (clarity of roles, data stewardship, regulatory mandates)	1.2	0.7	Regulatory delays weaken governance alignment; unclear mandates significantly reduce system performance
Operational & Residual Risk	R_S	Residual risk after controls (legal uncertainty, unclear processes, cyber obligations)	1.6	2.2	Risk increases due to incomplete compliance frameworks and unclear responsibilities across DSOs/retailers
System Fragility & Interdependence	α	Sensitivity exponent (non-linearity of risk propagation in a grid-coupled digital ecosystem)	1.8	2.0	Higher fragility emerges as delays create inconsistent implementations and misaligned processes

(continued)

Table 2. (continued)

Dimension	Variable	Meaning in formula	Target (before delay)	Observed during delay	Interpretations for managers
Computed digital energy ecosystems Transformative Performance	TP_{DEE}	Calculated system performance readiness	≥ 1.0 (launch threshold)	≈ 0.50	The system cannot be safely launched; postponement is justified due to low governance and high risk
Managerial Decision Outcome		Based on performance function outcome	Proceed with deployment	Project on hold	Formula shows the system became unbalanced: high innovation but insufficient governance and too much risk

4 Discussion

The mapping of the vignette to our formula, as shown in Table 2, presents a scenario where the data hub, positioned as a potentially transformative DEE initiative capable of offering standardized data access to multiple stakeholders, including retailers, aggregators, and distribution system operators in Sweden, failed to materialize. While promising advanced functionalities, such as enabling flexible markets and providing real-time metering services, which could drive innovation and efficiency in energy management and market operations, the Swedish data hub project was put on hold because regulatory and compliance requirements were not addressed on time. The vignette highlights the significant role the adaptive governance loop in our design framework plays in open innovation, particularly in a DEE. Reinforce the importance of addressing non-negotiable requirements, including regulations, early to facilitate early compliance [47]. This is because governance factors provide oversight structures, and in the vignette, these structures were not yet finalized, leaving critical elements, such as roles, data-sharing obligations, and liability allocations, ambiguous. This ambiguity diminishes governance effectiveness, as stakeholders may have unclear expectations or responsibilities, thereby reducing the multiplier effect of the governance factor. Consequently, residual risk within the system increases. In the case of the Swedish data hub, an increase in residual risk led to incomplete onboarding procedures, unclear access rights, and unresolved legal responsibilities, creating vulnerabilities. This vulnerability meant market actors could inadvertently overstep boundaries or fail to comply with their obligations, increasing the likelihood of operational or legal failures and putting the project on hold.

Moreover, the vignette emphasizes the ecosystem's fragility due to high interdependence between the market and grid systems. Any disruption or inconsistency, such as fragmented oversight or uneven implementation, can propagate across the system, exacerbating systemic sensitivity. This suggests that while the data hub promises innovation, its success depends on factors such as effective governance, clear regulatory frameworks, and robust risk management. These factors are made visible in a structured way to EMS providers through the DEE design framework and guide their design.

5   Conclusion and Future Work

This paper proposes a design framework to help EMS providers understand the interactions between open innovation and security in a digital energy ecosystem. Then, the Swedish Data Hub vignette illustrates this point from a real case perspective: despite strong innovation potential, delays in regulatory decision-making reduced the governance factor and heightened residual risk. Thus, the design framework provides a structured approach to rethinking EMS innovation. Also, the framework clarifies why projects can stall even when technologies are mature and illustrates that systemic viability depends as much on institutional readiness, regulatory clarity, and coordinated risk control as on technical innovation. Finally, our design framework's main contribution lies in making these interdependencies explicit, measurable, and integrable within digital energy ecosystem design by EMS providers.

Despite the potential contribution, future research would examine whether the risk sensitivity exponent α captures nonlinearity at the conceptual level but does not currently distinguish among different classes of cascading failures (technical, organizational, regulatory), potentially oversimplifying complex interdependencies. Also, the framework assumes a single aggregated governance factor, with each operational entity evolving at a different speed. Hence, future research, as anticipated in the method, will focus on further theorizing the artifact [36] and on completing the evaluation of the proposed artifact. As to the issue, instances of that echelon will include comparative studies across the Nordic Data Hub initiatives to further validate and refine the framework, thereby supporting the development of a generalizable theory of socio-technical performance in digital energy ecosystems.

Acknowledgments. This work has been conducted within the program "Resistance and Effect – on the smart grid for the many people" funded by the Kamprad Family Foundation, Sweden.

Disclosure of Interests. The authors declare no conflict of interest related to the research presented in this paper.

References

1. Dhara, S., Shrivastav, A.K., Sadhu, P.K.: Smart grid modernization: Opportunities and challenges. Electric Grid Mod. (2022)
2. El-Hawary, M.: The Smart Grid—State-of-the-art and future trends. Eighteenth International Middle East Power Systems Conference (MEPCON). IEEE, Cairo, Egypt (2016)

3. Joseph, A., Balachandra, P.: Smart grid to energy internet: a systematic review of transitioning electricity systems. Ieee Access **8**, 215737–215805 (2020)
4. Goel, A., Prabha, C., Malik, M., Sharma, P.: Security concerns and data breaches for data deduplication techniques in cloud storage: a brief meta-analysis. Int. J. Safe. Secur. Eng. 14, (2024)
5. Jimeno, J., Anduaga, J., Oyarzabal, J., De Muro, A.G.: Architecture of a microgrid energy management system. European Trans. Electr. Power **21**, 1142–1158 (2011)
6. D'Arcy, J.P.: The misuse of information systems: The impact of security countermeasures. Lfb Scholarly Pub. Llc (2007)
7. Fan, X., Gong, G.: Security challenges in smart-grid metering and control systems. Technology Innovation Management Review 3 (2013)
8. Plachkinova, M.: A taxonomy for risk assessment of cyberattacks on critical infrastructure (TRACI). Commun. Assoc. Inf. Syst. **52**, 1 (2023)
9. Schneier, B., Vance, A.: Guest Editorial: "Complexity is the Worst Enemy of Security": Studying Cybersecurity Through the Lens of Organizational Complexity1. Manag. Inf. Syst. Q. **49**, 205–210 (2025)
10. Díaz Redondo, R.P., Fernández-Vilas, A., Fernández dos Reis, G.: Security aspects in smart meters: Analysis and prevention. Sensors **20**, 3977 (2020)
11. Gui, Y., Siddiqui, A.S., Tamore, S.M., Saqib, F.: Security vulnerabilities of smart meters in smart grid. In: IECON 2019-45th Annual Conference of the IEEE Industrial Electronics Society, pp. 3018–3023. IEEE (Year)
12. Herath, T.C., Herath, H.S., D'Arcy, J.: Organizational adoption of information security solutions: An integrative lens based on innovation adoption and the technology-organization-environment framework. ACM SIGMIS Database: the DATABASE for Adv. Info. Sys. **51**, 12–35 (2020)
13. Nambisan, S., Lyytinen, K., Majchrzak, A., Song, M.: Digital Innovation Management: Reinventing Innovation Management Research in a Digital World. Mis Quart **41**, 223–238 (2017)
14. Balozian, P., Leidner, D.: Review of IS security policy compliance: Toward the building blocks of an IS security theory. ACM SIGMIS Database: The DATABASE for Adv. Info. Sys. **48**, 11–43 (2017)
15. Cram, W.A., D'arcy, J., Proudfoot, J.G.: Seeing the forest and the trees. MIS Q. **43**, 525-A524 (2019)
16. Bendiab, G., Grammatikakis, K.-P., Koufos, I., Kolokotronis, N., Shiaeles, S.: Advanced metering infrastructures: Security risks and mitigation. In: Proceedings of the 15th international conference on availability, reliability and security, pp. 1–8. (Year)
17. Idries, A., Krogstie, J., Rajasekharan, J.: Challenges in platforming and digitizing decentralized energy services. Energy Informatics **5**, 8 (2022)
18. Zeng, M., Cheng, Z., Huang, X., Xu, H.: A low-power consumption security data fusion model for Industrial Internet of Things. Int. J. Comput. Appl. **47**, 312–322 (2025)
19. Kukreja, B., Malik, S.K., Sharma, A.: A Novel Citadel Security Framework for Cyber Data using CryptSteg Techniques. Int. J. Performab. Eng. 20 (2024)
20. Thenmozhi, R., et al.: Attribute-based adaptive homomorphic encryption for big data security. Big data **12**, 343–356 (2024)
21. Yusoff, Z.Y.M., Ishak, M.K., Rahim, L.A., Asaari, M.S.M.: Improving Smart Home Security via MQTT: Maximizing Data Privacy and Device Authentication Using Elliptic Curve Cryptography. Comp. Sys. Sci. Eng. 48 (2024)
22. Khattak, A.M., Khanji, S.I., Khan, W.A.: Smart meter security: Vulnerabilities, threat impacts, and countermeasures. In: International Conference on Ubiquitous Information Management and Communication, pp. 554–562. Springer (Year)

23. Ramya, K., Teekaraman, Y., Kumar, K.R.: Fuzzy-based energy management system with decision tree algorithm for power security system. Int. J. Computat. Intel. Sys. **12**, 1173–1178 (2019)
24. Alkatheiri, M.S., Alqarni, M.A., Chauhdary, S.H.: Cyber security framework for smart home energy management systems. Sustain. Ener. Technol. Assess. **46**, 101232 (2021)
25. Bolton, R., Foxon, T.J.: Infrastructure transformation as a socio-technical process—Implications for the governance of energy distribution networks in the UK. Technol. Forecast. Soc. Chang. **90**, 538–550 (2015)
26. Schlagwein, D., Conboy, K., Feller, J., Leimeister, J.M., Morgan, L.: "Openness" with and without Information Technology: a framework and a brief history. vol. 32, pp. 297–305. SAGE Publications Sage UK: London, England (2017)
27. Whelan, E., Conboy, K., Crowston, K., Morgan, L., Rossi, M.: The role of information systems in enabling open innovation. J. Assoc. Inf. Syst. **15**, 4 (2014)
28. Chesbrough, H., Bogers, M.: Explicating Open Innovation: Clarifying an Emerging Paradigm for Understanding Innovation. In: Chesbrough, H., Vanhaverbeke, W., West, J. (eds.) New Frontiers in Open Innovation. Oxford University Press (2014)
29. Lee, E.-K.: Advancing building energy management system to enable smart grid interoperation. Int. J. Distrib. Sens. Netw. **12**, 3295346 (2016)
30. Wörner, A., et al.: Bidding on a Peer-to-Peer Energy Market: An Exploratory Field Study. Inf. Syst. Res. **33**, 794–808 (2022)
31. Kim, S.M., Lee, T., Kim, S., Park, L.W., Park, S.: Security issues on smart grid and blockchain-based secure smart energy management system. In: MATEC Web of conferences, p. 01001. EDP Sciences (Year)
32. Gregor, S., Hevner, A.R.: Positioning and presenting design science research for maximum impact. MIS Q. **37**, 37–56 (2013)
33. Hevner, A.R., March, S.T., Park, J., Ram, S.: Design Science in Information Systems Research. MIS Q. **28**, 75–105 (2004)
34. Peffers, K., Tuunanen, T., Rothenberger, M., Chatterjee, S.: A Design Science Research Methodology for Information Systems Research. J. Manag. Inf. Syst. **24**, 45–77 (2007)
35. Tuunanen, T., Winter, R., Brocke, J.v.: Dealing with complexity in design science research: A methodology using design echelons. Mis. Quart **48**, 427–458 (2024)
36. Kuechler, W., Vaishnavi, V.: A Framework for Theory Development in Design Science Research: Multiple Perspectives. J. Assoc. Inf. Syst. **13**, 395–423 (2012)
37. Goldkuhl, G.: Activity Cycles in Design Research: A Pragmatic Conceptualisation of Inter-related Practices. In: Helfert, M., Donnellan, B. (eds.) Design Science: Perspectives from Europe, vol. 388, pp. 49–60. Springer International Publishing, Cham (2013)
38. Whelan, E., Conboy, K., Crowston, K., Morgan, L., Rossi, M.: Editorial: The Role of Information Systems in Enabling Open Innovation. J. Assoc. Inf. Syst. **15**, XX-XXX (2014)
39. Maedche, A., Gregor, S., Morana, S., Feine, J.: Conceptualization of the problem space in design science research. International conference on design science research in information systems and technology, pp. 18–31. Springer (2019)
40. Chatterjee, S., Davison, R.M.: The need for compelling problematisation in research: The prevalence of the gap-spotting approach and its limitations. Info. Sys. J. 31 (2021)
41. Muzzammel, R., Arshad, R., Mehmood, S., Khan, D.: Advanced energy management system with the incorporation of novel security features. Int. J. Electr. Comp. Eng. **10**, 3978 (2020)
42. Viscusi, G., Batini, C.: Digital information asset evaluation: Characteristics and dimensions. Smart Organizations and Smart Artifacts: Fostering Interaction Between People. Technologies and Processes, pp. 77–86. Springer (2014)
43. Peng, S.: Multi-dimensional G-Brownian motion and related stochastic calculus under G-expectation. Stochastic Processes and Their Applications **118**, 2223–2253 (2008)

44. NordREG: Implementation of data hubs in the Nordic countries: Status Report (2019)
45. NordREG: Implementation of data hubs in the Nordic countries (2021)
46. Svenska Kraftnät, https://www.svk.se/en/stakeholders-portal/electricity-market/data-hub/
47. Kosenkov, O., et al.: Systematic mapping study on requirements engineering for regulatory compliance of software systems. Inf. Softw. Technol. **178**, 107622 (2025)

Future of Design Science Education

Integration is Key: Designing AI-Based Teaching Assistants for ERP Education

Christopher Gillespie[1]([⊠]) [iD] and Hannah Sperling[2,3] [iD]

[1] Grand Valley State University, 1 Campus Drive, Allendale, MI 49401-9403, USA
gillesch@gvsu.edu
[2] SAP SE, Dietmar-Hopp-Allee 16, 69190 Walldorf, Germany
hannah.sperling@sap.com
[3] University of Mannheim, 68161 Mannheim, Germany

Abstract. The rapidly evolving enterprise resource planning (ERP) market demands innovative educational approaches that leverage artificial intelligence (AI) capabilities. Current ERP education faces significant challenges: educators struggle with complex system functionality while students require personalized, hands-on education that many higher education institutions cannot efficiently provide. This research in progress explores how AI can enhance current practice-based ERP education curricula to best benefit both student learning and alleviate pressure on instructors. Following a design science research approach, we leverage discriminative AI capabilities to design and implement a conversational ERP teaching assistant (TA). Our solution integrates with SAP S/4HANA to allow for real-time, personalized support based on students' input data. Preliminary evaluation based on user tests and expert feedback confirms that our ERP TA fosters learning by helping to troubleshoot students' work, which saves instructors significant time and mental resources. Conversational rigidity and remaining gaps in theoretical business process content remain limiting factors. As our research continues, we plan to expand the curriculum base and incorporate generative AI capabilities to enhance conversational abilities.

Keywords: SAP S/4HANA · education · learning

1 Introduction

Advances in artificial intelligence (AI) present significant potential for the traditionally challenging field of enterprise resource planning (ERP) education. To realize this potential while ensuring effective quality education, educators require teaching designs that carefully calibrate the application of AI in the classroom. Working toward effective, modern, and scalable ERP teaching, this paper focuses on the development of a conversational agent as teaching assistant (TA) for ERP education integrated with SAP S/4HANA. The ERP market is expected to grow to an estimated $40.6 billion in 2033 [9], fueling the need for innovative educational formats that combine different modes of teaching and technology in ERP education. However, many educators already struggle with the demands of effectively conveying the complex workings of ERP functionality [31]. Although equipping future professionals with ERP skills remains of utmost importance, educational institutions face financial and organizational constraints in offering scalable, innovative ERP education formats [27].

The scant research that exists on AI-facilitated ERP education has so far remained limited to commercial large language models (LLMs) fine-tuned to ERP curricula [7]. In these studies, students' abilities to design the right prompts to their problems limits the utility of their generative AI TA. Moreover, these models remain prone to 'hallucinations' and can only theoretically explain general ERP principles. Instructors are regularly caught up spending most of their time checking students' hands-on ERP exercises, which proves challenging in the classroom. Without access to real ERP student input data through system integration, AI-assisted ERP education falls short of its potential impact on both instructor experience as well as student learning.

While advances in AI technologies provide opportunities for effective learning, their proliferation has also produced problems in the educational sphere. Research shows that the unauthorized use of LLMs by students, e.g., for the completion of writing assignments, can undermine teaching efforts [8]. Even authorized use of AI in the classroom has drawbacks, as it can lead to students feeling disconnected to their teachers [4]. Moreover, erroneous instructions, i.e., 'hallucinations', can subvert learning benefits and erode trust in AI recommendations [16]. Nonetheless, carefully planned applications of educational AI tools harbor benefits, as they can improve student learning by providing cost-efficient individualized assistance at scale [36]. This is especially valuable for resource-intense subjects like ERP education, in which educators usually administer communal face-to-face instructions as well as hands-on practice sessions where students complete assignments individually [33]. Hence, our ongoing study addresses the following research question: *How should an AI-based TA be designed to most effectively benefit student learning as well as instructor teaching experience in ERP education?*

Beyond modernizing teaching formats, answering this question promises significant insight to solving longstanding challenges in ERP education. Moreover, focusing on the integration of ERP training systems with AI capabilities for individualized, hands-on learning in real-time offers design recommendations for future educational technologies beyond the use of fine-tuned LLMs. Focusing on SAP S/4HANA, a globally leading ERP system [30], we explore how AI should be integrated in ERP education to most effectively assist both instructors and students. Using a design science approach, we build on a constructivist conception of learning for the design and preliminary evaluation of an integrated, conversational ERP teaching assistant (TA) for both theoretical and hands-on ERP education. Building on the presented preliminary findings, we aim to further align our solution to the established success factors of ERP education as well as educational use of AI.

For this research-in-progress paper, we use insights from a user test with higher education ERP students as well as qualitative feedback from ERP instructors for a first evaluation of our design. Our preliminary results are twofold: First, our study shows how AI can help establish a real-time integration of conversational ERP TAs with learners' ERP systems. Second, our research illustrates how discriminative AI helps realize the potential of such real-time integration by allowing learners to engage with the ERP

TA in natural language for error detection and troubleshooting. Currently, our design remains limited by conversational rigidity and gaps in ERP training data, which we aim to develop further. As our research progresses, we plan to (1) refine and extend existing design constructs from theory to the specific context of AI-assisted ERP education, (2) extend constructivism learning theory by showing how teaching designs should integrate AI in ERP education, and (3) support practitioners and instructors with guidelines for implementing AI-based functionality to effectively teach ERP.

2 Related Work

2.1 AI as a Tool to Improve Education

Statistical learning theory distinguishes between discriminative and generative AI models [21]. Discriminative models are used for classification, regression, and clustering tasks to directly map input to output without generating new data [19]. A classification task could for example involve distinguishing between different transactions involved in an ERP exercise to decide if specific transactional data should direct to pre-defined learning help. In comparison to discriminative methods, generative models produce new data by learning the joint probability distribution of the training data, producing less accurate classification results [19]. When designing AI-based TAs for ERP education, model selection must carefully weigh these tradeoffs to maximize pedagogical value while minimizing potential drawbacks.

Educators increasingly use AI models to improve and facilitate teaching, e.g., by automating feedback and assessment through computerized adaptive tests or automated essay scoring [11]. Automated learning assessments can improve grading accuracy and offer personalized feedback to students [23], reducing instructors' time and cognitive load [11]. Moreover, the customization of curricula and personalization of teaching content to individual learners' needs can improve uptake and retention, increasing overall learning quality [5]. At the same time, the use of AI in the classroom can estrange students from their instructors [4]. Thus, AI tools should complement rather than replace face-to-face education to preserve human interaction.

In the context of interactive teaching, conversational agents (CAs) have become a fixture in educational research. Pedagogical CAs simulate human dialogue through interaction with voice or text, providing interactive learning scenarios [37]. Researchers have categorized CAs into rule-, retrieval-, or generative-based, as well as hybrid models [14]. Rule-based CAs provide answers based on manually specified rules, which ensure response accuracy but limit dialogue complexity [25]. While retrieval-based CAs also query predefined data, the use of similarity measures allows more coherent replies that remain constrained only by the quality of the knowledge base [15]. Generative-based CAs dynamically produce output from large amounts of training data, using sequence-to-sequence frameworks [32]. Based on statistical inference, their output can include 'hallucinations' and requires filtering to prevent inappropriate responses [22]. Hybrid models combine design choices of different categories of CAs [14]. Ensuring response accuracy is crucial to foster the use of pedagogical CAs, as response inconsistencies undermine user trust [16]. Moreover, availability and perceived usefulness of CAs impacts user satisfaction and fosters autonomous learning [36]. Research shows that digital literacy, e.g., the ability to use conversational technology, moderates individuals' motivation to use CAs, in turn impacting learning engagement [7]. For ERP TA's, these findings suggest that hybrid CA architectures offer the necessary combination of precision for system-based error detection with conversational fluidity.

2.2 Challenges in ERP Education

Due to their breadth, complexity, and interdependence, ERP functionalities are generally difficult to master, especially as ERP systems become increasingly enriched with AI capabilities [26]. Students with little to no experience with IT and business processes often struggle to understand the integration benefits that ERP systems offer [17]. As a result, researchers and practitioners have introduced numerous teaching formats to effectively convey ERP skills. Most importantly, ERP curricula are commonly taught as a combination of lectures and exercise sessions, in which students engage in hands-on ERP system work [33]. Facing regular academic staff turnover, upskilling instructors for these exercise sessions remains a challenge for higher education institutions [31]. Gamification approaches use ERP simulations and often foster interaction between students that work together in groups [17]. To help students understand ERP concepts and business process integration, Chiang et al. [7] proposed course schedules including generative AI-based CAs. After a lecture followed by a hands-on session operating an ERP system, students in the study engaged in short interactive learning sessions with commercial generative AI-based CAs that were trained on ERP curriculum data and subsequently tested by instructors. The authors find support for the idea that the use of AI-based CAs in ERP teaching contributes to students' learning engagement [7]. However, standalone without system integration, the study's generative AI-based CAs used in separate teaching blocks could not provide feedback on students' hands-on work.

In addition to being difficult to learn, ERP skills also prove challenging to teach. ERP software is very complex and requires a high degree of familiarity with the system, which is why educators may shy away from offering hands-on training [31]. ERP exercises require practical tasks and often simultaneous feedback and assistance [33]. As a time and labor-intensive offering, many universities do not have the financial resources to support ERP education [27]. Taken together, existing work suggests untapped potential regarding integrated AI functionalities into ERP education, potentially alleviating challenges in both ERP learning and teaching.

3 Research Design

This study follows the design science research (DSR) methodology to design and evaluate an integrated, AI-based conversational ERP TA. DSR emphasizes the development of innovative artifacts that address real-world problems and contribute to both practical application and the academic knowledge base [13]. We employ Peffers et al.'s approach [24] to structure our research into six steps as illustrated in Fig. 1.

The starting point of our DSR project was the observation of working but improvable ERP teaching in higher education. Thus, our research can be seen as both client/context

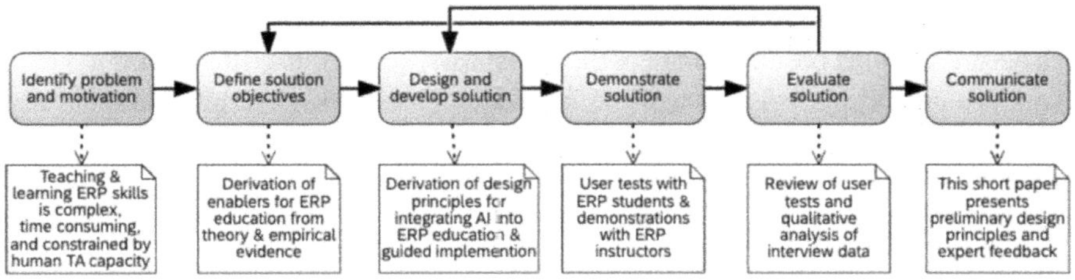

Fig. 1. Structure of this research according to Peffers et al. [24].

initiated as well as problem-centered [24]. Sharing extant researchers' motivation to effectively convey ERP skills, we worked backward to retroactively identify problems and improvement potentials with the currently dominant approach of combining theoretical and hands-on ERP education. This motivation and resulting research problem were defined in the introduction. Our related work section reviews AI capabilities as potential solutions to the limitations of the current gold standard in ERP education. Triangulating insights from constructivism learning theory and classroom practice, the next section derives objectives and design principles that guide artifact design and development. This research-in-progress paper lays out the current state of the artifact as well as preliminary evaluation results. Our research effort is iterative in nature, as is often the case in DSR projects [24]. Here, we focus on the initial design cycle, which informs subsequent artifact improvement and serves as a starting point for future evaluation and communication efforts.

4   Objectives

We derive enablers of effective ERP education from our analysis of extant literature as well as insights from empirical observation in the classroom. Since skills and abilities cannot merely be transferred from one individual to another, hands-on ERP exercises that challenge students to think for themselves are common [33]. This is in line with a constructivist conception of learning, which centers around the idea that in order to learn, "students need to actively construct knowledge in their own minds" [2]. Interactive learning formats foster learning by deepening students' constructive and interactive engagement [6]. However, increased cognitive load due to complex course demands can lead to faltering motivation and engagement in learning [10]. Thus, to enable effective ERP education, instructors should combine interactive, multi-modal teaching formats while offering enough assistance to safeguard student engagement. Hands-on ERP exercises place the learner at the center, as constructivism learning theory recommends [2]. However, in hands-on system work, learners often get stuck at a certain point in the business process they are working on. To help students overcome these difficulties and form ERP and business process knowledge, they require assistance. As opposed to directly providing answers and fixing student errors, effective ERP education secures student learning outcomes by helping them to solve their problems themselves.

To ensure applicability and realize benefits for instructors, which ultimately improve educational outcomes, enablers of effective ERP education include the perspective of

ERP educators as well. In many cases, erroneous ERP data input occurs many exercise steps before students become aware of their mistakes, which makes them hard to identify and fix. To enable students to continue, instructors must spend significant amounts of time troubleshooting their work [31]. Thus, time as a resource to engage with students interpersonally as opposed to troubleshooting data input in students' practice systems becomes a critical enabler of effective ERP education.

5 Design and Development

5.1 Design Principles and Context

Based on our literature review and practical insights on the enablers of effective ERP education, we derived four design principles (DPs) for the first design cycle of developing AI-enhanced teaching assistance for ERP education. Table 1 lists these DPs in a format as proposed by Gregor et al. [12] to facilitate adaptability in similar contexts. All DPs apply to the context of AI-assisted ERP education as laid out in the previous section.

Table 1. Design Principles.

Title	Aim & Mechanism	Rationale	Source
Learner-centricity	Personalization through integration and relevant, accurate support	Free up instructor resources, erroneous AI output diminishes user trust and use	[16, 31]
Guided discovery	"Explain, don't solve" ensures learning success	Learning occurs through individuals' active construction of knowledge	[2]
Effortlessness	Simple, easy-to-use design reduces cognitive load	Digital efficacy moderates willingness for self-learning	[36]
Resourcefulness	Making effective use of limited time and financial resources	Scant resources in ERP higher education	[31]

Enhancing ERP education with integrated AI functionality remains a challenge with numerous pitfalls. First, teaching the complexities of ERP systems demands hands-on exercise work, where success hinges on personalized and relevant support. Although commercial generative AI-based models have made it comparatively easy to imitate human dialogue, they cannot trouble-shoot highly relevant ERP system work. Moreover, AI tools must be accurate for students to use them [16]. Therefore, our development prioritizes integrating AI functionality with ERP practice systems and remains limited to discriminative AI capabilities that ensure accuracy. Second, effective learning requires students to actively construct knowledge [2]. Thus, our design follows the paradigm of "explain, don't solve" in prioritizing guided discovery. By positively impacting user satisfaction, ease of use increases the use of conversational AI [7]. Thus, we prioritize simplicity in our design choices. Lastly, our aim is to develop a resourceful solution, since time and financial resources in higher education institutions remain limited [31].

To fulfill the outlined design principles, the on-premises ERP system SAP S/4HANA 2021 SPS01 (02/2022) hosted at Grand Valley State University (GVSU) under administration by the first author serves as a starting point. While most higher education institutions obtain their SAP ERP systems from external hosting centers [33], GVSU host their own SAP S/4HANA systems. Although this allows for more system access, proprietary software cannot be modified or requires extensive coding to make changes. As a result, we ruled out automated AI assessment or feedback directly through the ERP practice system, e.g., as visible recommendations in the ERP interface. Even if the code base could be tweaked, frequent system updates would not be able to handle custom code extensions, and the use of multiple ERP systems for different courses would require time-consuming upgrades (GVSU has approximately four ERP servers running at any given time).

5.2 Developing an AI-Based ERP Teaching Assistant

Based on our reasoning in the previous section, we decided to focus on the integration of AI by means of a hybrid CA running in parallel to the ERP practice system. For the initial design of such an ERP teaching assistant (TA), we tracked ideas and requirements over the course of multiple ERP classes at GVSU in a thought protocol encompassing 107 notes by January 2026. Our development was organized in five architectural layers, namely (1) the ERP application layer, (2) the configuration layer (non-ERP data), (3) the API integration layer (ERP-facing services), (4) the Natural Language Processing (NLP) and routing layer, and (5) the User Interface (UI) layer. These layers remain logically separated to strengthen security controls, simplify maintenance, and support scalable deployment.

(1) ERP application layer. An SAP S/4HANA system and undergraduate course on enterprise information systems forms the basis of our development as described in the previous section. As an example, the course and system configuration includes a student hands-on exercise to create new materials according to their assigned company code.

(2) Configuration layer. To manage information not kept in the ERP system, such as ERP learning documents as well as instructional configuration and environment routing, we implemented a MySQL Community Edition database [20]. The database serves two main purposes. First, based on the students' input and identified problems (e.g., wrongful creation of two materials instead of one), it stores ERP learning documents, e.g., describing how to change material data in the system. Second, it maintains mapping tables that associate exercises to business processes (e.g., procurement) and associations with ERP server/client environments. This enables high flexibility in instructional use, allowing for different sections of the same course to run distinct configurations and models based on an instructor's requirements. Separate API calls specify where student's transactional data resides for each transaction in the different exercises and business processes. Since there are many potential input fields in an ERP system, our configuration queries only the minimum necessary data to validate or guide the user to ensure efficiency and timely responses. If numerous users encounter a similar issue when querying the system for help, targeted validation checks with extended data coverage remain possible.

(3) API integration layer. Individualized assistance for hands-on ERP exercises by a CA requires ERP system integration. We employed remote function calls (RFCs) [28] to integrate our ERP TA with the ERP practice systems. For RFC connections, the ERP connector stack supports development in C + +,.NET, or Java, of which we chose Java to ensure compatibility with Apache web server as described in (4). From an architecture standpoint, we modularized the REST APIs into multiple libraries and host them on a separate Apache port from the *Bot Libre* application. This allows a separation of the front-facing layer (see Fig. 2, bottom right) and a backend integration layer (ERP-facing APIs, top left). This design helps support future scalability, including load balancing across multiple ERP application servers if required. Moreover, *Bot Libre* in this configuration protects access to the REST API's that access the ERP servers by serving as a router through the chat sessions.

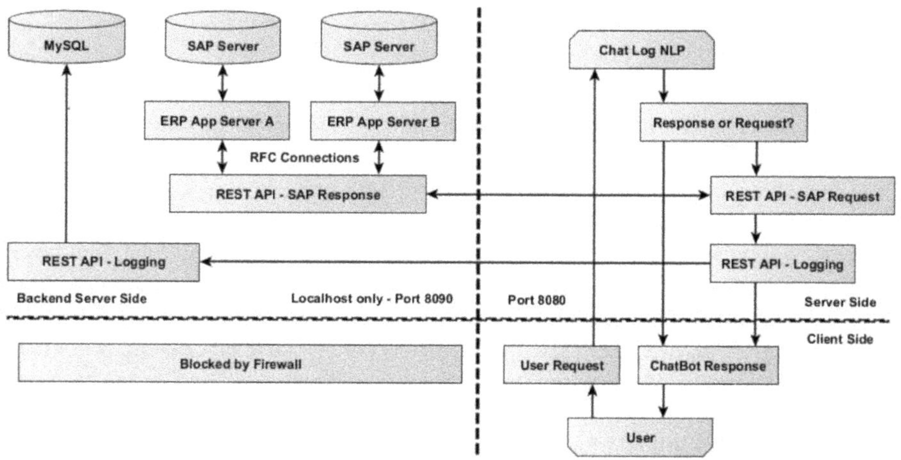

Fig. 2. System interface of ERP TA's APIs to ERP system. Students interact with ERP TA (bottom right). The browser-based ERP TA (top right) communicates with the ERP backend (top left) via REST API. A firewall (bottom left) ensures communication to the ERP backend only through the authorized ERP TA.

(4) NLP layer. To standardize development and to enhance delivery, our solution leverages *Bot Libre*, an open-source platform for building, hosting, and deploying hybrid CAs [35]. *Bot Libre* is installed on Apache web server [1] that allows for reliable, maintainable architecture. Utilizing *Bot Libre*'s discriminative AI capabilities minimizes computational and hardware requirements in comparison to fully generative AI approaches. Moreover, its intent- and pattern-driven design prevents AI 'hallucinations' by ensuring that all responses and actions remain explicitly bound to predefined keywords, intents, and REST API calls [3, 29]. Language input patterns were implemented in so-called self-script files for *Bot Libre*'s NLP functionality. The self-scripts are depicted as Chat Log NLP in Fig. 2. Using rule- and pattern-driven NLP as opposed to generative AI is necessary, as this is the crucial step that connects the learner prompt to the transaction, the associated exercise, and their associated system input.

(5) UI layer. Students interact with the ERP TA through their web browser, which queries them for their course and SAP credentials to support their inquiry (Fig. 3).

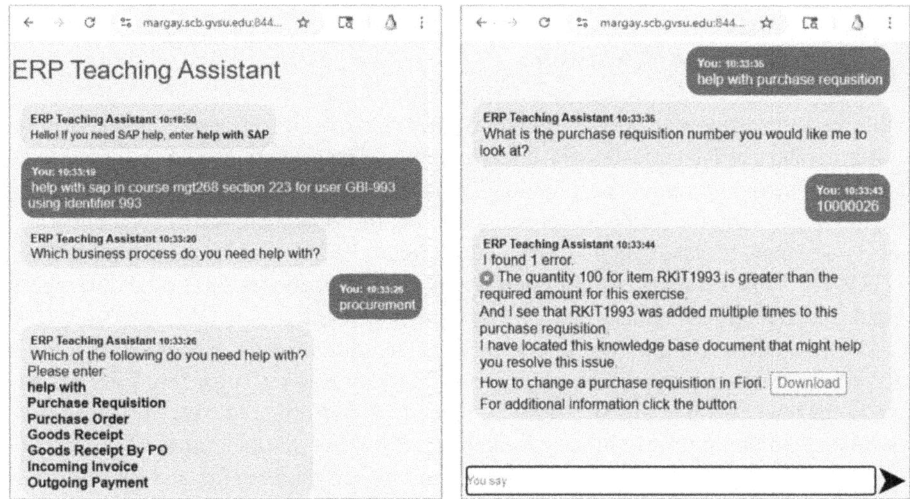

Fig. 3. ERP TA interface with exemplary chat protocols.

6 Demonstration and Evaluation

At this stage of this ongoing research project, we conducted a pilot user test through application in two ERP courses at GVSU with participation of 33 (32) students using the ERP TA in 3,542 (1,735) total calls. Moreover, we demonstrated our design in a focus group discussion with four ERP higher education specialists and professors from different universities and interviewed two ERP learning experts from SAP SE based on a demonstration of our ERP TA. At this stage, we started qualitative content analysis [18] of existing data, but plan to collect more feedback through semi-structured interviews with higher education ERP instructors and students.

We evaluate our solution based on our observations and the feedback collected so far. Both academic and professional ERP instructors confirmed that troubleshooting assistance by our ERP TA would save them significant amounts of time they could then use to cater to learners directly. They appreciated the ERP TAs read-only functionality, which offers only system details and resource suggestions to safeguard student learning. At the same time, suggestions included expanding the curriculum knowledge stored in the system to incorporate general business process knowledge. In combination with generative AI capabilities, this could allow for more comprehensive context of theoretical concepts in addition to suggestions based on ERP transactional data.

In line with this, some students criticized the ERP TAs relative conversational rigidity compared to commercial CAs. Evidence from the classroom confirms that students' digital literacy and experience with technology impact the extent of their ERP TA use. Surprisingly many students had very limited experience interacting with AI-generated responses in general. The students that readily explored ERP TA's functionalities to assist them in hands-on class- and homework sometimes struggled to convey their intent in cases of misunderstandings. At the same time, there were no complaints around response times or wrong output.

7 Discussion and Next Steps

In this research article, we provide initial insight into the design principles of an AI-based TA that enhances ERP education for both students and instructors. Based on the feedback of this first design iteration, we plan to expand our ERP TA's capabilities by including generative AI elements for better human dialogue. Informed by constructivism learning theory, we plan to systematically evaluate students' ERP learning success attributable to ERP TA. This promises insights into how ERP TA responses should be designed to nudge students into thinking about ERP systems holistically.

Our research highlights the importance of integration when including AI tools in ERP education in two important ways. First, integration is key regarding ERP practice system data access, as it unlocks teaching benefits by offering custom troubleshooting assistance. Second, our preliminary findings confirm that an integration of discriminative and generative AI capabilities is crucial to balance the benefits and drawbacks of AI use in education. It might be tempting for higher education professionals to revert to commercial generative AI offerings due to their accessibility and ease of use. However, as out research shows, generative AI capabilities alone fall short of the complex ERP teaching needs. Rather than adapt generic commercial systems, AI-based teaching solutions must be purpose-built to ensure pedagogical success and balance precision with flexibility.

Acknowledgments. We thank the SAP Product & Solution Learning & Enablement team for their expertise and support throughout this work.

Disclosure of Interests. Christopher Gillespie is an SAP system administrator and adjunct ERP instructor at Grand Valley State University in MI, USA. Dr. Hannah Sperling is research expert at SAP SE and adjunct lecturer at the University of Mannheim in Germany.

References

1. Apache HTTP Server Project: https://www.apache.org/. Last accessed 12 January 2026
2. Bada, S.O.: Constructivism learning theory: a paradigm for teaching and learning. IOSR J. Res. Method Educ. **5**(6), 66–70 (2015)
3. Bloch, J.: Effective Java, 3rd edn. Addison-Wesley, Boston, MA (2018)
4. Center for Democracy & Technology: https://cdt.org/press/cdt-survey-research-finds-use-of-ai-in-k-12-schools-connected-to-negative-effects-on-students-including-their-real-life-relationships/. Last accessed 07 January 2026
5. Chen, L., Chen, P., Lin, Z.: Artificial intelligence in education: a review. IEEE Access **8**, 75264–75278 (2020)
6. Chi, M.T.H., Wylie, R.: The ICAP framework: linking cognitive engagement to active learning outcomes. Educational Psychologist **49**(4), 219–243 (2014)

7. Chiang, Y.-H., Huang, C.-S., Hung, L.-S., et al.: Enhancing enterprise resource planning learning through generative AI teaching assistants: A motivation – opportunity – ability perspective. Innov. Educ. Teach. Int. **62**(5), 1447–1466 (2025)

8. Cotton, D.R.E., Cotton, P.A., Shipway, J.R.: Chatting and cheating: Ensuring academic integrity in the era of ChatGPT. Innov. Educ. Teach. Int. **61**(2), 228–239 (2024)

9. Allied Market Research: https://www.alliedmarketresearch.com/erp-market. Last accessed 07 Jauary 2026

10. Evans, P., Vansteenkiste, M., Parker, P., et al.: Cognitive load theory and its relationships with motivation: a self-determination theory perspective. Educ. Psychol. Rev. **36**(7), 6–31 (2024)

11. Gardner, J., O'Leary, M., Yuan, L.: Artificial intelligence in educational assessment: 'Breakthrough? Or buncombe and ballyhoo?' J. Comput. Assist. Learn. **37**(5), 1207–1216 (2021)

12. Gregor, S., Jones, D.: The anatomy of a design theory. J. Assoc. Inf. Syst. **8**(5), 312–335 (2007)

13. Hevner, A.R., March, S.T., Park, J., et al.: Design science in information systems research. MIS Q. **28**(1), 75–105 (2004)

14. Hussain, S., Ameri Sianaki, O., Ababneh, N.: A survey on conversational agents/chatbots classification and design techniques. In: Barolli, L., Takizawa, M., Xhafa, F., et al. (eds.) WAINA-2019, vol 927, pp. 946–956. Springer International Publishing, Cham (2019)

15. Ji, Z., Lu, Z., Li, H.: An Information Retrieval Approach to Short Text Conversation, arxiv.org/pdf/1408.6988 (2014)

16. Kahr, P., Rooks, G., Snijders, C., et al.: Good Performance Isn't Enough to Trust AI: Lessons from Logistics Experts on their Long-Term Collaboration with an AI Planning System. Proceedings of the 2025 CHI Conference on Human Factors in Computing Systems, pp. 1–16 (2025)

17. Léger, P.-M.: Using a simulation game approach to teach ERP concepts. J. Inf. Syst. Educ. **17**(4), 441–447 (2006)

18. Mayring, P.: Qualitative content analysis: theoretical foundation, basic procedures and software solution, 1st edn. SSOAR, Klagenfurt (2014)

19. McTear, M.: Conversational AI: dialogue systems, conversational agents, and chatbots. Springer Nature Switzerland AG, Cham (2022)

20. MySQL Community Edition: https://www.mysql.com/products/community/. Last accessed 12 January 2026

21. Ng, A., Jordan, M. I.: On Discriminative vs. Generative classifers: A comparison of logistic regression and naive Bayes. In: Advances in Neural Information Processing, p. 15 (2002)

22. Ouyang, L., Wu, J., Jiang, X., et al.: Training language models to follow instructions with human feedback. In: Advances in Neural Information Processing 36, pp. 1–15 (2022)

23. Owan, V.J., Abang, K.B., Idika, D.O., et al.: Exploring the potential of artificial intelligence tools in educational measurement and assessment. Eurasia J. Math. Sci. Technol. Educ. **19**(8), 1–15 (2023)

24. Peffers, K., Tuunanen, T., Rothenberger, M., et al.: A design science research methodology for information systems research. J. Manag. Inf. Syst. **24**(3), 45–77 (2008)

25. Peng, Z., Ma, X.: A survey on construction and enhancement methods in service chatbots design. CCF Trans. Pervas. Comp. Interact. **1**(3), 204–223 (2019)

26. Ranasinghe, H., Gide, E., Eikhodr, M.: The Significance of GenAI Empowered ERP Systems Course Teaching in Quality Education. In: 2024 21st International Conference on Information Technology Based Higher Education and Training (ITHET), pp. 1–7. IEEE (2024)

27. Ravi, S.: Enterprise Systems (ES) Software in Business School Curriculum - Evaluation of Design and Delivery. J. Inf. Syst. Educ. **18**(1), 69–83 (2007)

28. Remote Function Call (RFC): https://help.sap.com/docs/SUPPORT_CONTENT/cpp/336187 6526.html?locale=en-US. Last accessed 12 January 2026

29. Richardson, L., Ruby, S.: RESTful web services, 1st edn. O'Reilly, Sebastopol, CA (2007)
30. SAP SE: https://news.sap.com/2025/10/sap-a-leader-gartner-magic-quadrant-cloud-erp-pro duct-centric-enterprises/. Last accessed 07 January 2026
31. Schwade, F., Schubert, P.: The ERP Challenge: An Integrated E-learning Platform for the Teaching of Practical ERP Skills in Universities. Procedia Comp. Sci. **100**, 147–155 (2016)
32. Sutskever, I., Vinyals, O., Le, Q.V.: Sequence to Sequence Learning with Neural Networks https://arxiv.org/pdf/1409.3215 (2014)
33. Soellner, S.: Digital Elements for SAP ERP education and training: results from a systematic literature review. Int. J. Eng. Pedag. (iJEP) **11**(4), 115–130 (2021)
34. Deloitte: https://image.marketing.deloitte.de/lib/fe31117075640474771d75/m/1/147c324b-c7f5-4884-b3f7-06cf12247406.pdf. Last accessed 07 January 2026
35. Bot Libre: https://www.botlibre.org. Last accessed 16 January 2026
36. Wang, L., Li, W.: The Impact of AI Usage on University Students' Willingness for Autonomous Learning. Behav. Sci. **14**(10), 956–972 (2024)
37. Weber, F., Wambsganss, T., Rüttimann, D., et al.: Pedagogical Agents for Interactive Learning: A Taxonomy of Conversational Agents in Education. In: Valacich, J., Barua, A., Wright, R., et al. (eds.) Proceedings of the 42nd Conference on Information Systems (2021)

Redesigning the Master's Thesis for Epistemic Adequacy Using Design Science Research in a Generative AI (LLM)–Supported Context

Sylvana Kroop[✉]

University of Applied Sciences, Department of Digital Economy, FHWien der WKW, Vienna, Austria
sylvana.kroop@fh-wien.ac.at

Abstract. Traditional master's thesis formats rely heavily on extensive written text as primary evidence of scholarly competence. Under widespread use of generative AI and large language model (LLM)–based tools, this evidentiary logic becomes epistemically fragile, as fluent academic writing can no longer be assumed to reflect independent cognitive effort. As a result, established thesis assessment practices risk losing epistemic adequacy. In response, this Research in Progress paper reports on an ongoing Design Science Research (DSR) redesign of the master's thesis to reestablish epistemic adequacy. This paper proposes a four-stage thesis format with substantially reduced textual scope (~30 pages), grounded in and mapped to Hevner et al.'s DSR framework. The paper contributes (1) an analysis of broken epistemic assumptions in traditional thesis formats, (2) corresponding design decisions, and (3) early insights from the first three stages completed at a university of applied sciences. The results inform iterative refinement and invite community discussion.

Keywords: Design Science Research · master's thesis redesign · generative AI · epistemic adequacy · assessment design

1 Introduction

The long-written master's thesis has long served as the prevailing capstone format in higher education. In its classic form, it relies heavily on extended written text as evidence of scholarly competence. Yet this format was designed for a world in which writing was a scarce cognitive achievement. In generative AI environments with widespread access to LLM-based tools, polished academic prose is no longer a scarce output and can no longer be treated as a reliable proxy for understanding, independence, and research competence. Recent literature on academic integrity and AI highlights both opportunities and risks, but offers only limited actionable solutions for preserving the evidentiary function of assessment under these conditions [1]. At the same time, information systems education research has repeatedly shown that curricula and pedagogical structures must evolve with changing practice and technologies. Topi and Spurrier [12], for example, advocate a generalized process framework for systems analysis and design education that bridges traditional and agile approaches. In parallel, technology-mediated learning research suggests that competence signals can be strengthened by focusing on observable reasoning and skill development rather than textual output alone [13]. Building on these developments, this paper argues that traditional master's thesis formats are epistemically broken, that LLMs make this visible, and that Design Science Research (DSR) enables a principled redesign. Drawing on Hevner's DSR framework and guidelines [2,3], we propose a four-stage, reduced-scope (~30 pages) master's thesis format and report early insights from its first implementation cycle.

How can a master's thesis format be redesigned, using Design Science Research principles, to reestablish epistemic adequacy in a generative AI (LLM)-supported educational context?

The remainder of this paper reviews related work, outlines the problem diagnosis, presents the proposed four-stage thesis format and its design rationale, and concludes with early insights, limitations, and next steps.

2   Related Work

Our work draws on two intersecting bodies of literature: epistemic adequacy in assessment and Design Science Research (DSR) as an educational and methodological framework. Epistemic adequacy can be understood as adequacy-for-purpose, i.e., whether assessment practices provide appropriate epistemic warrant for the claims they support [8]. Under LLM-supported conditions, this raises the question of whether written text still functions as valid evidence of competence. DSR, by contrast, provides a well-established paradigm for producing and evaluating artifacts as knowledge contributions, supported by process models and guideline-based framings that connect relevance, rigor, and evaluation [2,3,9]. Although DSR has matured into a broad research program, its use in master's thesis contexts remains comparatively underrepresented and has traditionally been more common at doctoral level [4]. Recent work nonetheless shows growing interest in DSR education and supervision at the master's level [6,10,11,14]. More broadly, the present redesign resonates with competency-based and portfolio-oriented assessment approaches in emphasizing observable performance across multiple artifacts rather than a single final text. However, the present work is specifically DSR-driven in that it ties assessment to the staged production, justification, and evaluation of an artifact within a relevance–rigor framework. Despite this emerging literature, existing work rarely questions the traditional monolithic, long-form master's thesis artifact itself; generative AI therefore creates both urgency and opportunity to redesign the thesis as an assessment artifact that remains epistemically adequate.

3   Problem Diagnosis

Generative AI and LLM-based tools do not merely introduce a new integrity challenge; they expose a deeper epistemic vulnerability in traditional master's thesis assessment: fluent academic writing can be produced with limited independent cognitive effort, weakening the inferential link between the submitted document and the student's competence. Systematic reviews on AI and academic integrity emphasize that higher education institutions face a rapidly evolving landscape in which both benefits and risks coexist, while robust assessment responses remain underdeveloped [1]. This aligns with technology-mediated learning research showing that competence-relevant evidence increasingly needs to be grounded in observable reasoning processes and skill development rather than textual fluency alone [13]. In design-oriented and practice-oriented degree programs, this fragility is amplified because the expected contribution is often tied to solution development and evaluation, whereas traditional master's thesis formats remain predominantly text-centred. Consequently, the key breakdowns include: (i) writing quality and stylistic sophistication no longer functioning as reliable competence signals, (ii) authorship and independence becoming difficult to infer from the final document, (iii) problem understanding and methodological accountability remaining insufficiently observable in monolithic submissions, and (iv) evaluation often being superficial or retrofitted. These epistemic problems are summarized in Table 1 and serve as the basis for the design rationale in the subsequent section, which maps each problem to specific design decisions in the proposed four-stage DSR-based master's thesis format and to the corresponding DSR guideline(s) [2,3].

4   Proposed Artifact: Four-Stage DSR-Based Master's Thesis Format

This section presents the proposed artifact of our ongoing Design Science Research (DSR) project: a redesigned master's thesis format explicitly anchored in Hevner et al.'s [3] DSR framework and operationalized as a four-stage, milestone-based assessment process. The artifact responds to the epistemic challenge that, in LLM-supported educational contexts, written output alone is no longer a sufficiently reliable proxy for independent understanding, decision-making, and methodological competence. Accordingly, the redesigned format shifts assessment emphasis from text volume to traceable research decisions, theory-grounded requirements, and evaluation evidence.

4.1   Anchoring the Four-Stage Thesis in Hevner et al.'s DSR Framework

The theoretical foundation of the redesigned thesis format is the widely adopted DSR framework by Hevner et al. [3]. To strengthen conceptual consistency, we deliberately adopt DSR terminology (e.g., problem space, knowledge base, develop/build, justify/evaluate). In our applied university context, this is particularly suitable because master's candidates are expected to address real-world innovation challenges situated in their professional practice.

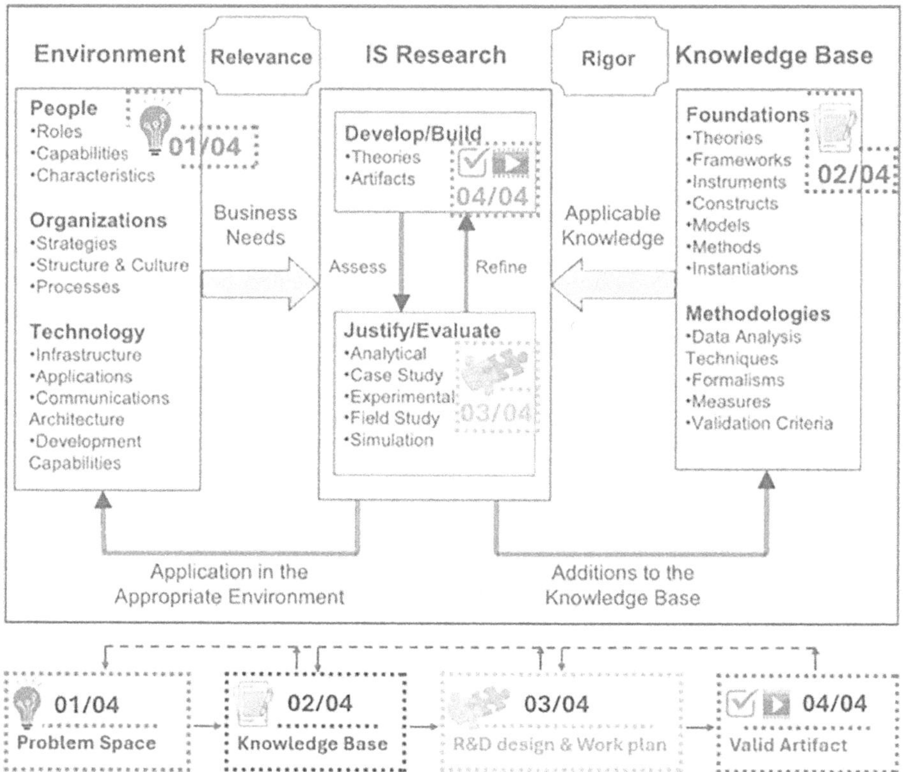

Fig. 1. Mapping of the four-stage master's thesis format onto Hevner et al.'s Design Science Research (DSR) framework. [3]

Figure 1 maps the proposed four-stage master's thesis format onto Hevner et al.'s DSR framework. It shows the staged progression from problem identification (Problem Space, 01/04) and knowledge grounding (Knowledge Base, 02/04) to design specification and success criteria (R&D Design & Work Plan, 03/04) and the development and evaluation of a validated artifact (Valid Artifact, 04/04). Part 03/04 bridges design and evaluation by specifying the artifact and its evaluation plan prior to implementation. Building on this mapping, each stage operationalizes a specific aspect of the framework: Part 01/04 addresses relevance, Part 02/04 establishes rigor, Part 03/04 specifies how develop/build and justify/evaluate will be carried out, and Part 04/04 integrates the full DSR cycle through implementation, demonstration, and iterative evaluation.

4.2   Overall Structure and Governance of the Four-Stage Master's Thesis Process

The redesigned master's thesis is structured as four consecutive parts that together form one coherent thesis artifact. Each part constitutes a self-contained, assessable deliverable with an explicit scope limit, defined submission requirements, and a dedicated review and feedback cycle. Importantly, each part is considered final once submitted and reviewed; it is not revised retroactively. Improvements are carried forward into subsequent parts. This forward-only principle increases transparency and comparability in assessment and makes student learning progress visible across stages. Each part follows a three-step interaction pattern:

1. an optional draft submission,
2. an on-campus meeting including a short presentation and structured feedback discussion with supervisors, and
3. the final submission of the revised version for formal review.

The staged structure supports both process visibility and timely completion by providing fixed milestones and reducing the risk that students postpone the thesis indefinitely after completing coursework. The design is complemented by cohort-based coordination through shared deadlines and peer exchange.

4.3   Assessment Logic and Weighting Across Stages

The four stages are weighted to reflect their epistemic role within the DSR process and to align assessment incentives with demonstrable competence rather than textual production.

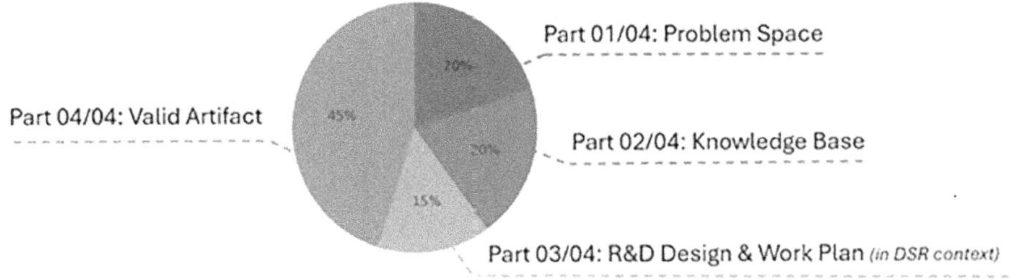

Fig. 2. Assessment weighting across the four stages of the redesigned master's thesis format

As shown in Fig. 2, the weighting is deliberately asymmetric. The highest weight is assigned to the Valid Artifact (45%) because, in DSR, the strongest evidence of competence lies in developing and validating a meaningful artifact in context, including transparent justification of design decisions and evaluation outcomes. The Problem Space (20%) and Knowledge Base (20%) ensure early relevance and rigor, while the R&D Design & Work Plan (15%) provides methodological accountability without outweighing implementation and evaluation outcomes. In addition, the assessment criteria are explicitly aligned with Hevner et al.'s [3] DSR guidelines. While specific guidelines are foregrounded in the early stages, the final stage requires coherence across the full guideline set, including artifact quality, evaluation, contribution, rigor, and communication.

4.4   Stage 01/04: Problem Space (20%)

Purpose. Part 01/04 establishes relevance by defining and empirically exploring a user-centered innovation challenge rooted in the student's professional environment.

Core Activities and Evidence. Students conduct at least three semi-structured interviews with relevant stakeholders from their work or business context. The aim is less theoretical saturation than a quick, practice-grounded start to the thesis process. Students then perform an initial qualitative content analysis to extract key themes and insights. Interview guides and transcripts are provided as appendices to enable transparency and traceability.

Theoretical Grounding. In addition to empirical exploration, students identify at least two high-quality scientific publications addressing their problem area, complemented by two current practitioner-oriented articles. This initiates the knowledge base early while ensuring that the problem framing is informed by both research and practice.

Deliverable. The written submission is limited to 5 pages of continuous text (excluding appendices) and includes (a) the problem description grounded in interviews and supported by an initial literature review, (b) the initial research question, and (c) a preliminary artifact idea that plausibly addresses a potential solution to the problem.

Primary DSR Focus. Part 01/04 primarily emphasizes DSR guideline 2 (Problem Relevance), supported by guideline 1 (Design as an Artifact) and guideline 7 (Communication of Research).

4.5   Stage 02/04: Knowledge Base (20%)

Purpose. Part 02/04 establishes rigor by grounding the planned artifact and research trajectory in existing scientific knowledge.

Core Activities and Evidence. Students conduct a systematic literature review following PRISMA 2020 reporting principles. The knowledge base explicitly builds on Part 01/04: students may refine the problem statement, research question, and artifact description based on literature insights, and they are expected to narrow the problem space to ensure feasibility. A central output is a theory-informed requirements specification for the artifact. Students derive and document concrete requirements, ideally prioritized (e.g., via MoSCoW), and traceably link them to both literature and interview evidence from Part 01/04. The resulting requirements list becomes a bridge to Part 03/04, where evaluation methods and test scenarios must be aligned with these requirements.

Deliverable. The written submission is limited to 10 pages of continuous text (excluding appendices, figures, and tables) and includes (a) a refined problem framing, (b) the systematic literature review and synthesis, and (c) the derived artifact requirements.

Primary DSR Focus. Part 02/04 primarily supports guideline 5 (Research Rigor) and prepares guideline 3 (Design Evaluation) by making evaluation criteria explicit through the requirements specification, and guideline 7 (Communication of Research).

4.6   Stage 03/04: R&D Design and Work Plan (15%)

Purpose. Part 03/04 translates relevance and rigor into a methodologically traceable plan for design, development, and evaluation.

Core Activities and Evidence. Students specify (a) a detailed research and development design and (b) a concrete work plan. The R&D design includes selected methods and test scenarios to iteratively evaluate the artifact requirements derived in Part 02/04. Students are expected to justify method choices and provide operational details (e.g., participant characteristics, technical setup, tools for data collection and analysis, and data handling procedures). A work plan, ideally presented as an iterative Gantt chart, lists concrete work steps and time allocations.

Deliverable. The written submission is limited to 5 pages of continuous text (excluding figures such as process diagrams, test scenario visualizations, and the Gantt chart). The work is self-contained and explicitly connects to Parts 01/04 and 02/04.

Primary DSR Focus. Part 03/04 operationalizes guideline 1 (Design as an Artifact) by planning iterative development cycles, strengthens guideline 3 (Design Evaluation) through explicit evaluation design, and reinforces guideline 5 (Research Rigor) through methodological transparency.

4.7   Stage 04/04: Valid Artifact (45%)

Purpose. Part 04/04 constitutes the culmination of the thesis process. Students implement, demonstrate, and validate an artifact that addresses the defined problem space and satisfies the theory-grounded requirements.

Core Activities and Evidence. Students develop the artifact iteratively and conduct evaluation activities aligned with the R&D design. Evaluation must demonstrate the artifact's utility, efficacy, and limitations in context using appropriate empirical and/or analytical methods. The final deliverable includes the artifact itself, a concise written documentation of the research process and results, and a video-based demonstration that includes a live test scenario.

Deliverable. The written documentation is limited to 10 pages of continuous text (excluding appendices and supporting material). Together with the artifact and video, it forms the final master's thesis submission and supports the final examination.

Primary DSR Focus. Part 04/04 requires coherence across the full set of Hevner et al.'s [3] DSR guidelines: artifact quality, problem relevance, design evaluation, research contribution, rigor, search process, and communication.

4.8   Implementation Roadmap and Milestone Design

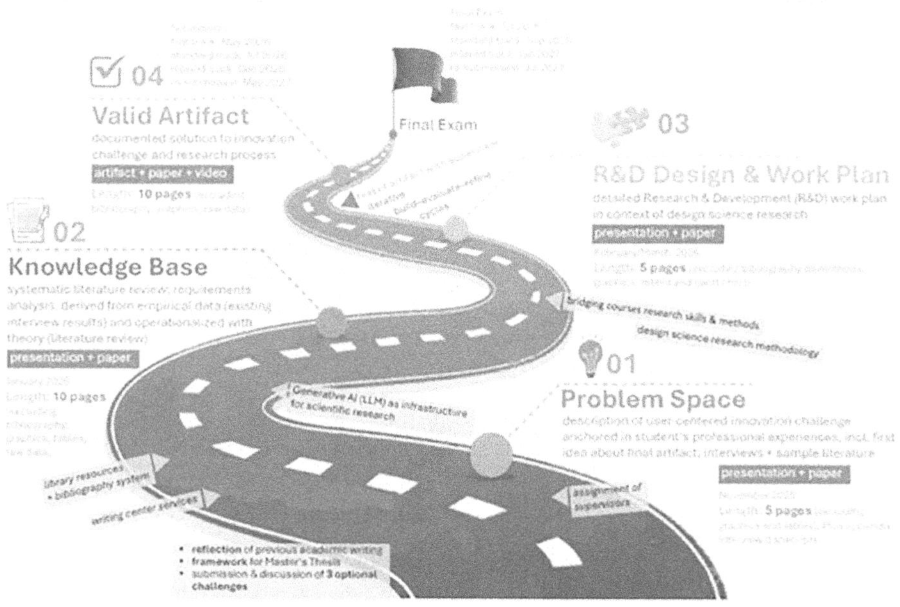

Fig. 3. First test run: Redesigning the master's thesis as a four-stage Design Science Research process with a reduced scope (~30 pages)

Figure 3 illustrates the first test run of the redesigned thesis format, including the sequencing of stages, expected deliverables, and page limits. The roadmap operationalizes the four-stage structure as a shared trajectory with explicit milestones, enabling cohort-level coordination while still supporting individualized problem contexts and artifacts. Two submission tracks ("fast track" and "standard track") provide flexibility without sacrificing structure. Both are designed to allow students to complete the thesis in a predictable timeframe and graduate as a cohort, addressing delayed completion after coursework.

5   Design Rationale: Mapping Epistemic Problems to Design Decisions and DSR Guidelines

This section makes the design rationale of the proposed four-stage master's thesis format explicit by mapping key epistemic problems of traditional thesis assessment under generative AI (LLM) conditions to corresponding design decisions in our redesigned thesis concept. Following the logic of DSR, the mapping documents (1) the epistemic problem diagnosis, (2) the design decisions embodied in the artifact, and (3) their theoretical grounding in Hevner et al.'s DSR guidelines. Table 1 summarizes this mapping and provides a transparent rationale for why specific structural and assessment-related choices were made and how they are intended to reestablish epistemic adequacy in an LLM-supported educational context.

Table 1. Design rationale mapping: epistemic problems under generative AI (LLM) conditions, corresponding design decisions, and alignment with Hevner et al.'s DSR guidelines (G1–G7).

Epistemic problem (LLM context)	Design decision (4-stage format)	Hevner et al.	Intended epistemic effect
Writing quality and stylistic sophistication no longer indicate competence	Reduced scope (~30 pages) + stage-specific page limits; assess decisions and evaluation evidence, not writing volume	G5, G7	Competence evidenced via justification, methodological traceability, and evaluation outcomes
Authorship and independence cannot be inferred from the final text	Staged deliverables + milestone-based reviews; explicit accountability for claims and decisions	G1, G7	Responsibility becomes assessable through traceable decisions and defensible claims
Problem understanding is insufficiently observable in monolithic theses	Dedicated Part 01/04 (Problem Space) with interviews and empirically grounded problem articulation	G2, G1	Relevance and problem framing evidenced through stakeholder needs and contextual constraints
Premature building or literature-only work without solution trajectory	Part 02/04 (Knowledge Base): systematic review + theory-informed requirements derived from literature and interviews	G5, G4	Requirements create traceability from knowledge base to design choices and evaluation criteria
Evaluation is often superficial or retrofitted	Part 03/04 (R&D Design & Work Plan): explicit evaluation strategy, test scenarios, and methods before implementation	G3, G6, G5	Evaluation becomes planned, justified, and inspectable; success criteria defined ex ante
Thesis overload causes delays and prolonged time-to-degree	Four sequential stages with fixed milestones, draft options, and structured feedback cycles	G6, G7	Progress becomes manageable and visible; iterative refinement supported through checkpoints
Assessment drifts toward formal compliance or text quality	Stage-specific assessment criteria aligned with DSR + asymmetric weighting (Part 04/04 = 45%)	G3, G4, G5	Judgment focuses on epistemically meaningful evidence: artifact quality, rationale, and validation
Traditional master's thesis formats misfit DSR, where contributions stem from design decisions, artifacts, and evaluation—not writing volume	Part 04/04 (Valid Artifact): implement, demonstrate, and validate the artifact; concise documentation + video demo	G1, G3, G4, G7	DSR contribution logic becomes central: validated artifact and evaluation evidence in context

Across the mapping, two design principles recur. First, the redesigned thesis format deliberately shifts assessment from text-centric evidence toward decision- and evaluation-centric evidence, addressing the epistemic fragility of written output under LLM conditions. Second, the staged structure operationalizes DSR's iterative logic by separating **Problem Space, Knowledge Base, R&D Design & Work Plan**, and **Valid Artifact** into assessable milestones. Together, these decisions aim to reestablish epistemic adequacy by making students' reasoning, methodological rigor, and evaluative competence inspectable while maintaining feasibility through reduced scope and structured supervision. The following section examines how these intended effects appeared in practice during the first implementation cycle and what early design knowledge can be derived from Stages 01/04 to 03/04.

6   Early Insights, Emerging Design Knowledge, and Limitations

The redesigned four-stage master's thesis format is currently being implemented in two newly introduced master's programs at FH Wien der WKW: *Digital Technology & Innovation* (MSc, $n = 20$) and *Digital Innovation* (MA, $n = 19$), resulting in a first cohort of $n = 39$ students. At the time of writing, all 39 had submitted Stages 01/04 to 03/04. The findings reported here are based on an interpretive, practice-based evaluation of this first implementation cycle. Before implementation, I discussed the redesign with the head of our Digital Economy department. We agreed on three core decisions: a four-stage process, a substantially reduced thesis length (~30 pages), and explicit embedding in Design Science Research (DSR). Based on this, I designed and coordinated the rollout and collected observations from on-campus discussions, meetings, emails, chats, student evaluations, submission artifacts, and supervisor feedback reports. The resulting insights are therefore early, context-bound, and not statistically generalizable.

6.1   What Became Visible in Practice

Three early findings stand out. First, written text alone proved insufficient as evidence of competence. What mattered in practice was less whether students produced polished prose than whether they could make, explain, and defend decisions in relation to a bounded problem, a knowledge base, and an evolving artifact. This aligns with work suggesting that competence signals must increasingly be grounded in observable reasoning rather than textual fluency alone [13]. A particularly revealing outlier was *Case 1*: one student submitted formally strong documents, openly listed *"OpenAI – ChatGPT"* and *"Google AI Pro – Gemini"* as tools used, and stated that *"The final synthesis and analysis remain the original work of the author."* At the same time, the student contributed meaningfully only in the first required on-campus session, remained nearly silent in the second, and was absent from the third. The supervisor therefore could not determine whether feedback had been understood, critically processed, or merely passed on to an AI assistant. The case shows that transparent AI disclosure does not by itself make reasoning inspectable. However, in most cases, the staged process made engagement substantially more visible than a traditional one-shot thesis format would have done. One implication is therefore not to reduce supervision overall, but to reallocate effort away from repeatedly reading long, text-heavy documents and toward focused discussion.

Second, traceability emerged as the strongest practical mechanism for epistemic transparency. Across the first three stages, the most convincing submissions were not the longest, but the ones that made their logic visible: how problem insights led to requirements, how requirements informed design choices, and how these choices were to be evaluated. This became especially clear in *Case 2*, where a compact traceability matrix in Part 03/04 dramatically improved readability and discussability. More broadly, once students were encouraged to make stage-specific traceability chains visible, their work tended to become both more concise and more assessable. Traceability thus functioned not merely as documentation, but as a pedagogical mechanism that shifted attention from writing volume to reasoning.

Third, the staged structure generated productive pressure and improved progress. Despite the fact that most students study part-time while working full-time, all 39 students remained in the process through Stages 01/04 to 03/04. In my prior experience, such cohort-wide continuity is exceptional. One supervisor summarized the effect in an email: *"nirgendwo gibt es einen Prozess für Abschlussarbeiten, der besser strukturiert und sorgfältiger ausgearbeitet ist als in diesen beiden Studiengängen der FH Wien. Das macht das Betreuen sehr angenehm."* At the same time, the process also exposed tensions. In *Case 3*, one student submitted 88 pages for Part 01/04, formally meeting the task requirements but clearly failing to delimit the problem. Only after lower evaluations in subsequent stages did a coherent focus emerge. This suggests that staged constraints can expose conceptual diffusion early enough for intervention, but also confirms that the model is demanding for both students and supervisors.

6.2   Emerging Design Knowledge

Taken together, the first three stages suggest five provisional design principles. First, assessment in AI-supported thesis environments should focus less on textual output and more on the visibility of decisions, explanations, and responsibility. Second, traceability should be treated as a central design mechanism rather than as a secondary documentation concern. Third, strong milestone structure appears to be a powerful anti-procrastination mechanism in part-time master's contexts. Fourth, scaffolding should be expertise-sensitive rather than uniformly standardized, consistent with the expertise reversal effect [5]. Finally, the redesign seems pedagogically strongest when it makes the thesis readable as a sequence of visible decisions under constraint rather than as a single polished text artifact.

These insights also clarify key tensions for the next iteration. The *forward-only* logic increases transparency and comparability, but it requires students to demonstrate learning through visible improvement in subsequent stages rather than by rewriting earlier parts. Likewise, the "three interviews" rule in Part 01/04, originally introduced as a pragmatic simplification, risks being misunderstood as a scientific standard; the next test run should therefore move toward theoretical saturation instead of a fixed number. Ultimately, the success of the model hinges on both student compliance and supervisor sensemaking. Some participants demanded and valued detailed guidance, while others preferred to forgo it, trusting in the potential of academic freedom.

6.3   Limitations and Next Steps

The present paper remains limited in several respects. Most importantly, the evidence is still restricted to the first three stages of one implementation cycle in two newly introduced programs at a single university of applied sciences. The most heavily weighted stage, Part 04/04 (Valid Artifact), is not yet complete, and no final judgments can therefore be made about artifact quality, evaluation quality, or final examination performance. In addition, the findings are based on interpretive analysis of heterogeneous qualitative material collected in the course of program coordination and implementation. This yields rich process insight, but also entails the limitations of situated practitioner research, including role proximity, selective visibility, and limited external validity. From a DSR perspective, this matters not only for the final artifact, but also for the frameworks through which artifact quality and evidentiary adequacy are interpreted [7]. Finally, the current cohort benefited from unusually intensive coordination during a first pilot cycle; it therefore remains unclear how robust the model would be under less favorable supervisory ratios, fully online conditions, or weaker institutional support structures.

Next steps include completing the final stage, consolidating lessons learned across the full four-part cycle, and translating the most stable insights into improved design instruments for the second test run. These include stronger traceability scaffolds, clearer communication of the forward-only logic, more expertise-sensitive support for students and supervisors, and refined reviewer templates with stage-specific and optionally expandable criteria. Future work should also position the redesign more explicitly in relation to broader assessment design literature in order to clarify what is specifically DSR-driven in the present model and what draws on more general principles of inspectable assessment. Even at this interim stage, however, the first implementation cycle suggests that redesigning the master's thesis as a staged DSR process is a promising response to the erosion of text-based competence evidence in AI-supported higher education.

References

1. Balalle, H., Pannilage, S.: Reassessing academic integrity in the age of AI: a systematic literature review on AI and academic integrity. Soc. Sci. Humanit. Open **11**, 101299 (2025)
2. Hevner, A., Chatterjee, S.: Design science research in information systems. In: Hevner, A., Chatterjee, S. (eds.) Design Research in Information Systems: Theory and Practice, pp. 9–22. Springer, Boston (2010)
3. Hevner, A.R., March, S.T., Park, J., Ram, S.: Design science in information systems research. MIS Q. **28**(1), 75–105 (2004)
4. Hevner, A.R., vom Brocke, J.: A proficiency model for design science research education. J. Inf. Syst. Educ. (JISE) **34**(3), 264–278 (2023)
5. Kalyuga, S., Ayres, P., Chandler, P., Sweller, J.: The expertise reversal effect. Educ. Psychol. **38**(1), 23–31 (2003). https://doi.org/10.1207/S15326985EP3801_4

6. Knauss, E.: Constructive master's thesis work in industry: guidelines for applying design science research. In: Proceedings of the 43rd International Conference on Software Engineering: Joint Track on Software Engineering Education and Training, ICSE-JSEET 2021, Virtual Event, Spain, pp. 110–121. IEEE Press (2021)
7. Kroop, S.: Artifact validity in design science research (DSR): a comparative analysis of three influential frameworks. In: Chatterjee, S., vom Brocke, J., Anderson, R. (eds.) Local Solutions for Global Challenges, pp. 199–215. Springer, Cham (2025)
8. Lusk, G., Elliott, K.C.: Non-epistemic values and scientific assessment: an adequacy-for-purpose view. Eur. J. Philos. Sci. **12**(2), 35 (2022)
9. Peffers, K., Tuunanen, T., Rothenberger, M.A., Chatterjee, S.: A design science research methodology for information systems research. J. Manag. Inf. Syst. **24**, 45–77 (2007)
10. Pekkola, S.: Reflections on supervising the postgraduate students' design science research thesis. J. Inf. Syst. Educ. **34**(3), 326–332 (2023)
11. Schlimbach, R., et al.: A teaching framework for the methodically versatile DSR education of master's students. J. Inf. Syst. Educ. **34**(3), 333–346 (2023)
12. Topi, H., Spurrier, G.: Invited paper: a generalized, enterprise-level systems development process framework for systems analysis and design education. J. Inf. Syst. Educ. **30**(4), 253–265 (2019)
13. Wambsganss, T., Janson, A., Söllner, M., Koedinger, K., Leimeister, J.M.: Improving students' argumentation skills using dynamic machine-learning-based modeling. Inf. Syst. Res. **36**(1), 474–507 (2025)
14. Weber, I.: Design Science Research als wissenschaftliche Herangehensweise für Abschlussarbeiten mit Gestaltungsauftrag in anwendungsorientierten Studiengängen. In: 35. Jahrestagung des Arbeitskreises Wirtschaftsinformatik an Hochschulen für Angewandte Wissenschaften im deutschsprachigen Raum (AKWI), Berlin, pp. 101–116. GITO (2022)

Future of Design Science Methodology

Reuse in Design Science Research: The Example of a Distributed Ledger Technology Design Knowledge Library

Max Gräser[(✉)] [iD] and Rainer Alt [iD]

Information Systems Institute, Leipzig University, 04109 Leipzig, Germany
{max.graeser,rainer.alt}@uni-leipzig.de

Abstract. Design science research (DSR) knowledge reuse remains a neglected aspect, with limited systematic collection and reuse of design knowledge across projects. This research-in-progress paper proposes the development of a design knowledge library for distributed ledger technology (DLT) to enable systematic reuse of DLT knowledge in future DSR projects. The research design follows established design science processes and draws on literature, interviews, and workshops. Initial findings from analyzing selected literature identify five requirement categories, nine design principles, and twelve features for DLT instantiation. The research contributes theoretically by advancing DSR knowledge reuse and practically by bridging the gap between DLT adoption decisions and implementation. Two e-commerce prototypes will demonstrate the library's applicability, with one utilizing directed acyclic graphs to extend beyond blockchain-specific applications.

Keywords: Design knowledge reuse · design knowledge library · blockchain · DLT

1 Motivation

Design science research (DSR) knowledge reuse appears to be a neglected aspect of DSR [1, 2]. Reuse is often limited and does not follow direct paths, resulting in knowledge that is neither synthesized nor reused across DSR projects [3–6]. Recent research points to ways to reuse knowledge more systematically [3, 7] as a possible path to accumulate knowledge in the era of "DSR Knowledge contributions" [4, 8]. However, reuse options are available in other fields (e.g., software engineering), but no single standardized method for reuse exists [3], and the challenge of gathering design knowledge within the DSR community remains unresolved [9]. One potential solution could be to develop libraries that collect artifacts [10]. Related proposals also exist for a repository for DSR processes (the steps followed in a DSR project) [11]. A similar approach is feasible for other DSR knowledge [12], and it could be inspired by existing libraries, such as those in the software (e.g., GitHub) or in the document domain (e.g., academic publication libraries). Design knowledge itself is not a fixed term and includes different concepts [4,

S. Chatterjee et al. (Eds.): DESRIST 2026, LNCS 16607, pp. 255–264, 2026.
https://doi.org/10.1007/978-3-032-28570-6_20

13]. For this study, design knowledge comprises requirements, principles, and features, which are often derived as prerequisites for DSR instantiations [14]. These three types of design knowledge represent a suitable form for knowledge reuse and can be classified as "Solution Design Knowledge for Entity Realization" [13]. Although the exact form of such a design knowledge library has not yet been determined, the concept is appealing because a systematic collection of design knowledge would support conducting DSR projects and knowledge transfer to practice. A library's fundamental purpose is to store, organize, and provide access to knowledge. In the area of DSR, a library may collect and structure design knowledge to make it reusable across projects. This might also positively impact the setup of DSR projects, as researchers can access existing knowledge more easily and arrive at prototypical instantiations more quickly. Beyond what such a library might look like, the scope of these libraries remains unclear; they could cover a variety of topics, including specific technologies, methods, or phenomena. Starting with a specific technology is a pragmatic first step because it offers a clearly bound yet widely studied problem space, enabling systematic structuring and comparison of design knowledge across multiple projects before extending to broader topics such as methods or phenomena. In the future, libraries could expand to include varying topics to facilitate cross-domain use of design knowledge, following more advanced knowledge reuse journeys [3]. As a technology domain for such a design knowledge library, distributed ledger technology (DLT) appears to be a suitable choice for the following reasons.

DLT enables participants to securely share and maintain data across a distributed network, creating an immutable, tamper-proof record of transactions [15–17]. The most common forms of DLT are based on blockchain technology and alternatives like directed acyclic graphs [18] have receive less attention within the information systems (IS) community. Despite high interest in IS research [19], DLT still encounters challenges in practical adoption, and many projects have failed, for example, in the supply chain industry [20]. Among others, successful implementation requires meeting specific requirements first, often identified using decision trees [21, 22] or by defining its characteristics to determine suitable application areas [23]. While this initial step helps identify the right environment for DLT, it does not specify how to implement it. Building on this, researchers increasingly use DSR to systematically instantiate DLT in suitable environments [24–30]. Although each DSR project varies due to different problem and solution spaces, commonalities emerge in its application, leading to overlapping design knowledge such as requirements, principles, and features. Collecting this knowledge, despite the uniqueness of each project, could benefit the academic community and decision-makers by creating a design knowledge library to support future DSR efforts and improve the application of DLT in suitable environments. The reuse journey can be best described as "Maintaining" [3] since its goal is to collect, expand, and organize DSR knowledge on DLT for future DSR projects.

This research-in-progress paper aims to conceptualize the research approach and outline the development and potential form of a DLT design knowledge library. This is a first step toward the overall research goal of developing a DLT design knowledge library and toward answering the research question: *Which DLT design knowledge can be reused for future design science projects?* The research also serves as an initial step toward developing a general approach to design knowledge libraries, with DLT as the first test object.

To prepare for answering the research question, this paper begins by outlining the research design. After that, the initial results present findings from a first literature review (on DSR knowledge of DLT) in the Senior Scholars' List of Premier Journals of the AIS. The research-in-progress paper closes with an expected contribution and a research agenda for publication in an IS journal.

2 Research Design

To develop and evaluate a DLT design knowledge library, the DSR research paradigm is adopted. The approach is based on BAUSTEIN [31] and follows the DSR process outlined by Peffers et al. (2007) [32]. The research design involves four phases: first, identifying the problem and defining solution objectives; second, designing and developing the DLT design knowledge library in iteration 1; third, demonstrating and evaluating the library in iteration 2; and finally, communicating the results of the DSR project. This process aligns with the problem-solving design configuration proposed by BAUSTEIN [31]. Figure 1 shows the four-phased DSR process following the six steps outlined by Peffers et al. (2007) [32] and using BAUSTEIN notation [31].

From a DSR perspective, the main motivation is to demonstrate the reuse of design knowledge. The project employs a specific technology, DLT, as an example of how a design knowledge library can be built to facilitate reuse in future DSR efforts. From a technological perspective, DLT still struggles to gain widespread adoption despite its potential. Creating a DLT design knowledge library helps practitioners and researchers better understand DLT's capabilities and how they can be instantiated. This chapter details the planning and strategy for the research approach.

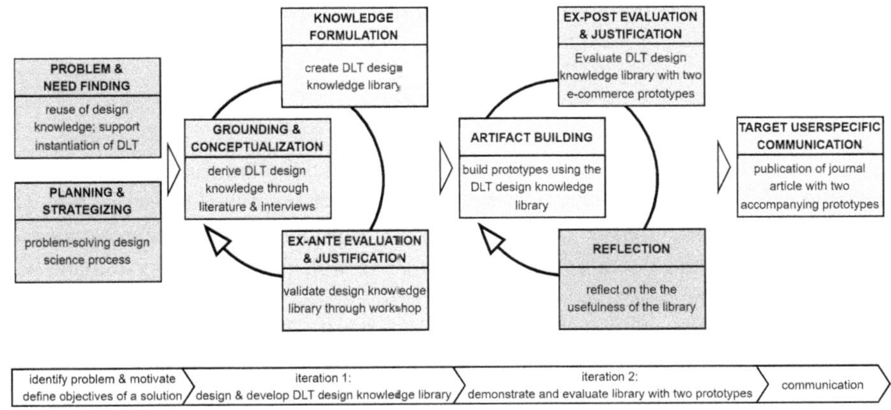

Fig. 1. The research design presented in BAUSTEIN notation

In iteration 1, the goal is to create a design knowledge library. The first step is systematically reviewing existing literature to extract relevant knowledge, focusing on studies that use DSR processes to develop DLT artifacts in the form of prototypical instantiations and are published in leading IS journals and conferences. Additionally, interview data is employed to validate and refine this knowledge. Next, the information is organized and structured into the design knowledge library through qualitative content analysis. It is planned to develop an interactive web application that presents design knowledge in a structured, intuitive way, making it easier to reuse. The web application will help researchers find the right design knowledge for their DSR projects by providing matching services [33], which are planned to be implemented with large language models. This approach could be useful in other domains as well and is being tested in this research with DLT. The final step involves evaluating the library through a workshop and making necessary adjustments to prepare for iteration 2. The outcome of iteration 1 is thus the design and development of the DLT design knowledge library.

In iteration 2, the library is tested in prototypical environments. Two prototypes (software instantiations) are developed that utilize the library as input, both situated in the e-commerce sector. One is an electronic product catalog that employs DLT, while the second use case will be determined in collaboration with e-commerce practitioners. Because e-commerce is not yet a primary application area for DLT, unlike, for example, supply chain management, testing in this domain aims to demonstrate the library's applicability across DLT use cases. Additionally, e-commerce's suitability for DLT has been the subject of research interest [34, 35]. One of the prototypes will utilize directed acyclic graphs to demonstrate the library's applicability to DLT broadly, not just blockchain. Insights gained from developing these prototypes serve as an evaluation of the library. The second iteration concludes with a reflection on the library's performance and an assessment of its validity [36]. Iteration 2 will be completed twice, once for each prototype. The results of iteration 2 include the two prototypes and the evaluated design knowledge library. Regarding communication, the DSR project will result in two publications, including this research-in-progress paper and two prototypes. This is further detailed in the last chapter of this paper.

3   Initial Results

To gain initial insights, a literature review in the Senior Scholars' List of Premier Journals of the AIS is conducted, focusing on publications that combine DLT with DSR. This review is intended to demonstrate the feasibility and aims of the future research endeavor; the full paper will present a more comprehensive and well-documented systematic literature review covering additional journals and conferences relevant to the DSR domain [37]. The journals were queried using *("blockchain" OR "DLT" OR "distributed ledger technology") AND "design"*, then the results were refined by title, abstract, and full text. Searching the eleven journals, an initial set of seven publications was identified [24–30]. The inclusion criteria were that the publications develop design knowledge for using DLT in software instantiations (usually in the form of prototypical instantiations). This includes, first and foremost, publications that provide a software prototype, as well as those that offer design knowledge for the instantiation of IS with DLT, such as the principle of "storing only public data on-chain" [30]. Additionally, the publication should include at least one of the three design knowledge types, namely requirements, principles, or features. Publications that create frameworks for other DLT aspects, such as regulation [38] or the development process [39] were excluded.

The data analysis led to five requirement categories, nine design principles, and twelve features for the instantiation. It is visible that some requirements are often addressed with DLT, particularly the need to prevent data manipulation. This is directly related to the immutable nature of DLT [23], but it also involves other features, such as cross-validating inputs with off-chain data or ensuring that system changes are made by a majority. Another common requirement is ensuring data privacy, typically achieved by storing only selected data on-chain (since it cannot be erased) or using smart contracts to validate privately stored data anonymously. Less frequently mentioned requirements include handling large data volumes by storing minimal data on-chain; incentivizing participation through token rewards; and promoting inclusiveness by ensuring all participants benefit from royalties when tokens are minted. This analysis of a relatively small number of publications already shows that there are various potential applications of DLT in the field of DSR.

Additionally, the analysis identified recurring requirements, principles, and features. For example, the requirement to prevent data manipulation is formulated as "prevent manipulation" [24], "identity management and verification", as well as "transparency and completeness of collected data relevant to transaction" [29], and "enable tamper-resistant data generation, processing, and exchange" [25]. The requirement to prevent data manipulation can, among others, be fulfilled by the principle cross-validation ("Sensor data is certified on the basis of cross validation" [25]) or joint approval of changes ("Require joint approval for changes to computation mechanisms" [24]). To implement the principle cross-validation, the feature plausibility check with off-chain data ("Certification Service: Sensor Data Certification" [25]) and for the principle joint approval, the feature configure policy so changes can only be made by a majority ("Governance policies enforce that any changes to the private data collection or the smart contract require the joint approval of both the information provider and the information recipient" [24]) can be used. Table 1 maps these relationships, starting with typical requirements, showing how they are addressed by design principles and ultimately instantiated as features. The table also presents an initial concept for the DLT design knowledge library, but the future version will be an interactive web application.

4 Expected Contribution and Research Agenda

This research offers several theoretical and practical contributions to DSR and DLT. From a theoretical standpoint, the reuse of design knowledge within the DSR community could transform how DSR is conducted. Exploring knowledge reuse journeys [3] is a logical initial step toward synthesizing knowledge across DSR projects. This research proposes a design knowledge library for knowledge reuse, which would contain design knowledge in the form of requirements, principles, and features. Furthermore, it addresses the variability in DSR knowledge formulation, aiming to establish a common understanding of DLT knowledge while respecting guidelines for knowledge formulation [6, 40]. In this way, the library can also serve as a blueprint for capturing design knowledge in other

Table 1. Initial concept for the DLT design knowledge library

Requirement	Principle	Feature
Prevent data manipulation [24, 25, 29]	Manipulation-resistant storage and auditability [24–27, 29]	Save hash of private data in public DLT [24, 25]
		Distributed immutable data storage of DLT [26, 27, 29]
	Cross-validation [25]	Plausibility check with off-chain data [25]
	Joint approval of changes [24]	Configure policy so changes can only be made by a majority [24]
Ensure data privacy [24–27]	Publicly verifiable private data [24, 27, 30]	Smart contract with a non-reversible function to validate private data [24]
		Store only non-private data on chain [25, 27, 30]
	Data sovereignty principle [25, 26]	Provide data access management [25, 26]
Handle large data volumes [25]	Linear scalability [25]	Hybrid architecture with on- and off-chain transactions [25]
Motivate participation [27, 28]	Incentives for participation [27, 28]	Monetary reward (e.g., token) [27, 28]
		Reputational reward (e.g., soulbound token) [27]
Inclusiveness [28]	Royalties for random issuance [28]	Randomized token minting [28]

DSR domains. To support this goal, the design knowledge library for DLT contributes to DLT research by enabling better assessment of DLT applications and providing a foundation for developing software instantiations with DLT. Additionally, the study offers a comprehensive overview of existing DLT DSR research. The two planned prototypes are designed to emphasize the DLT aspect using directed acyclic graphs, which have been overlooked in the IS community so far. Additionally, the potential of e-commerce as an application area for DLT remains to be evaluated, but it offers promising avenues [34, 35].

From a practitioner's perspective, the DLT design knowledge library bridges the gap between the decision to use DLT, which may be assessed with decision trees, and its implementation. Despite existing research on DLT development processes [39], a synthesized DSR perspective can support practitioners in designing and developing DLT-based systems. The prototypes will demonstrate the library's usefulness and applicability, with a focus on practical relevance, by developing two prototypes in the e-commerce sector.

Building on the initial research design, this paper will be further developed with the goal of publication in a journal by the end of 2026. The upcoming steps include conducting a systematic literature review, performing interviews, and using qualitative content analysis to build the DLT design knowledge library. The library will be evaluated through a workshop as part of completing iteration 1. Subsequently, the two prototypes will be developed and evaluated to finish iteration 2. Early results from the literature review indicate the project's feasibility but also highlight several challenges to be addressed in future development. A key challenge is the variation in knowledge formulation, which will be tackled by creating categories and subcategories for requirements, principles, and features. At the most detailed level, citations from the literature and interviews will be included to ensure transparency [41] and a clear understanding of the design knowledge and its context. This also pertains to the second challenge, which is the existence of n:m relationships between requirements, principles, and features; for example, one requirement might be satisfied by several principles and vice versa [29]. For actual library use, this could result in too many options to choose from, which is why we plan to implement matching services [33] using large language models to provide researchers with recommendations for their DSR projects. The third challenge is how to represent the library, since a simple table or mapping diagram becomes impractical as the library grows and the relationships between knowledge types become more complex (e.g., features used across principles, as shown in Table 1). Therefore, it is planned to develop an interactive web application to display the knowledge, thereby enabling more intuitive reuse and improving the library's practical usability. This blueprint could then be used for other DSR knowledge domains as well.

Disclosure of Interests.   The authors have no competing interests to declare that are relevant to the content of this article.

References

1. Legner, C., Pentek, T., Otto, B.: Accumulating Design Knowledge with Reference Models: Insights from 12 Years' Research into Data Management. J. Ass. Info. Sys. **21**, 735–770 (2020). https://doi.org/10.17705/1jais.00618
2. Schoormann, T., Möller, F., Hansen, M.R.P.: How Do Researchers (Re-)Use Design Principles: An Inductive Analysis of Cumulative Research. In: Chandra Kruse, L., Seidel, S., Hausvik, G.I. (eds.) The Next Wave of Sociotechnical Design: 16th International Conference on Design Science Research in Information Systems and Technology, DESRIST 2021, Kristiansand, Norway, August 4–6, 2021, proceedings, vol. 12807, pp. 188–194. Springer, Cham (2021)
3. Schoormann, T., Hansen, M., Möller, F.: Advancing design knowledge reuse: a framework for circular design principles. Comm. Ass. Info. Sys. **56**, 430–460 (2025). https://doi.org/10.17705/1CAIS.05618
4. vom Brocke, J., Winter, R., Hevner, A., et al.: Special issue editorial – accumulation and evolution of design knowledge in design science research: a journey through time and space. J. Ass. Info. Sys. **21**, 520–544 (2020). https://doi.org/10.17705/1jais.00611

5. Reining, S., Ahlemann, F., Mueller, B., et al.: Knowledge accumulation in design science research: ways to foster scientific progress. ACM SIGMIS Database: the DATABASE for Advances in Information Systems **53**, 10–24 (2022). https://doi.org/10.1145/3514097.351 4100

6. Iivari, J., Hansen, M.R.P., Haj-Bolouri, A.: A Framework for Light Reusability Evaluation of Design Principles in Design Science Research. In: DESRIST 2018 Proceedings (2018)

7. Khosrawi-Rad, B., Grogorick, L., Strohmann, T., et al.: Toward a Method for Design Science Research Meta-Studies to Improve the Reusability of Design Principles. In: Mandviwalla, M., Söllner, M., Tuunanen, T. (eds.) Design science research for a resilient future: 19th international conference on design science research in information systems and technology, DESRIST 2024, Trollhättan, Sweden, June 3–5, 2024: proceedings, pp. 182–196. Springer, Cham (2024)

8. Akoka, J., Comyn-Wattiau, I., Prat, N., et al.: Knowledge contributions in design science research: Paths of knowledge types. Decis. Support Syst. **166**, 113898 (2023). https://doi.org/ 10.1016/j.dss.2022.113898

9. Folha, R., Carvalho, A.: Towards Managing Design Science Knowledge with Large Language Models. In: AMCIS 2024 Proceedings (2024)

10. Lukyanenko, R., Parsons, J.: Research perspectives: design theory indeterminacy: What is it, how can it be reduced, and why did the polar bear drown? J. Ass. Info. Sys. **21**, 1343–1369 (2020). https://doi.org/10.17705/1jais.00639

11. Gau, M., Maedche, A., vom Brocke, J.: Towards an open repository for design science research: a meta-model and its instantiation for the representation of design science research processes. Enterprise Modelling and Information Systems Architectures (EMISAJ) **18**, 1–22 (2023). https://doi.org/10.18417/emisa.18.4

12. Hilts, A., Yu, E.: Design and evaluation of the goal-oriented design knowledge library framework. In: Mai, J.-E. (ed.) Proceedings of the 2012 iConference, pp. 384–391. ACM, New York, NY, USA (2012)

13. Drechsler, A., Hevner, A.R.: Utilizing, Producing, and Contributing Design Knowledge in DSR Projects. In: Chatterjee, S., Dutta, K., Sundarraj, R.P. (eds.) Designing for a Digital and Globalized World, pp. 82–97. Springer International Publishing, Cham (2018)

14. Möller, F., Guggenberger, T.M., Otto, B.: Towards a method for design principle development in information systems. In: Hofmann, S., Müller, O., Rossi, M. (eds.) Designing for Digital Transformation. Co-Creating Services with Citizens and Industry: 15th International Conference on Design Science Research in Information Systems and Technology, DESRIST 2020, Kristiansand, Norway, December 2–4, 2020, Proceedings, 1st ed. 2020, vol 12388, pp. 208–220. Springer International Publishing; Imprint Springer, Cham (2020)

15. Ballandies, M.C., Dapp, M.M., Pournaras, E.: Decrypting distributed ledger design-taxonomy, classification and blockchain community evaluation. Cluster Comput. **25**, 1817–1838 (2022). https://doi.org/10.1007/s10586-021-03256-w

16. Sunyaev, A.: Internet Computing. Springer Nature Switzerland, Cham (2024)

17. Alt, R., Gräser, M.: Distributed ledger technology. Electronic Markets 35 (2025). https://doi. org/10.1007/s12525-025-00784-w

18. Kannengießer, N., Lins, S., Dehling, T., et al.: Trade-offs between Distributed Ledger Technology Characteristics. ACM Comput. Surv. **53**, 1–37 (2020). https://doi.org/10.1145/337 9463

19. Lei, C.F., Ngai, E.W.: Blockchain from the information systems perspective: Literature review, synthesis, and directions for future research. Info. Manage. **60**, 103856 (2023). https://doi. org/10.1016/j.im.2023.103856

20. Lacity, M., O'Leary, D.E., Conway, D.: Developing Capabilities for B2B Commerce on Public Decentralized Networks. MIS Q. Exec. **23**, 467–481 (2024)

21. Wüst, K., Gervais, A.: Do you Need a Blockchain? In: 2018 Crypto Valley Conference on Blockchain Technology Proceedings, pp. 45–54 (2018)
22. Pedersen, A.B., Risius, M., Beck, R.: A ten-step decision path to determine when to use blockchain technologies. MIS Q. Exec. **18**, 99–115 (2019)
23. Treiblmaier, H.: Toward More Rigorous Blockchain Research: Recommendations for Writing Blockchain Case Studies. Frontiers in Blockchain 2 (2019). https://doi.org/10.3389/fbloc.2019.00003
24. Bossler, L.F., Buchwald, A., Spohrer, K.: And No One Gets the Short End of the Stick: A Blockchain-Based Approach to Solving the Two-Sided Opportunism Problem in Interorganizational Information Sharing. Inf. Syst. Res. **36**, 1565–1586 (2025). https://doi.org/10.1287/isre.2022.0065
25. Chanson, M., Bogner, A., Bilgeri, D. et al.: Blockchain for the IoT: Privacy-Preserving Protection of Sensor Data. J. Ass. Info. Sys. **20**, 1274–1309 (2019). https://doi.org/10.17705/1jais.00567
26. Anderson, C., Carvalho, A., Kaul, M., et al.: Blockchain innovation for consent self-management in health information exchanges. Decis. Support Syst. **174**, 114021 (2023). https://doi.org/10.1016/j.dss.2023.114021
27. Anderson, C., Shrestha, P., Bhunia, S., et al.: Blockchain-based token system for incentivizing peer review: A design science approach. Decis. Support Syst. **197**, 114514 (2025). https://doi.org/10.1016/j.dss.2025.114514
28. Carvalho, A., Zavolokina, L., Bhunia, S., et al.: Designing a fair and inclusive digital asset-based name-image-likeness marketplace. Decis. Support Syst. **201**, 114580 (2026). https://doi.org/10.1016/j.dss.2025.114580
29. Große, N., Möller, F., Schoormann, T., et al.: Designing trust-enabling blockchain systems for the inter-organizational exchange of capacity. Decis. Support Syst. **179**, 114182 (2024). https://doi.org/10.1016/j.dss.2024.114182
30. Schlatt, V., Sedlmeir, J., Feulner, S., et al.: Designing a Framework for Digital KYC Processes Built on Blockchain-Based Self-Sovereign Identity. Info. Manage. **59**, 103553 (2022). https://doi.org/10.1016/j.im.2021.103553
31. Schoormann, T., Möller, F., Chandra Kruse, L., et al.: BAUSTEIN —A design tool for configuring and representing design research. Inf. Syst. J. **34**, 1871–1901 (2024). https://doi.org/10.1111/isj.12516
32. Peffers, K., Tuunanen, T., Rothenberger, M.A., et al.: A Design Science Research Methodology for Information Systems Research. J. Manag. Inf. Syst. **24**, 45–77 (2007). https://doi.org/10.2753/MIS0742-1222240302
33. Alt, R., Ehmke, J.F., Haux, R., et al.: Towards customer-induced service orchestration - requirements for the next step of customer orientation. Electron. Mark. **29**, 79–91 (2019). https://doi.org/10.1007/s12525-019-00340-3
34. Treiblmaier, H., Sillaber, C.: The impact of blockchain on e-commerce: A framework for salient research topics. Electron. Commer. Res. Appl. **48**, 101054 (2021). https://doi.org/10.1016/j.elerap.2021.101054
35. Madlberger, M., Niu, R., Fan, Y.: Blockchain and electronic commerce: Transforming networks, platforms, and value creation. Electron. Mark. **35** (2025). https://doi.org/10.1007/s12525-025-00851-2
36. Larsen, K.R., Lukyanenko, R., Mueller, R.M., et al.: Validity in Design Science. MIS Quarterly **49**, 1267–1294 (2025). https://doi.org/10.25300/MISQ/2024/18064
37. vom Brocke, J., Simons, A., Niehaves, B., et al.: Reconstructing the Giant: On the Importance of Rigour in Documenting the Literature Search Process. In: ECIS 2009 Proceedings (2009)
38. Benedict, G., Gill, A.Q.: A regulatory control framework for decentrally governed DLT systems: Action design research. Info. Manage. **59**, 103555 (2022). https://doi.org/10.1016/j.im.2021.103555

39. Fahmideh, M., Abedin, B., Shen, J.: Towards an integrated framework for developing blockchain systems. Decis. Support Syst. **180**, 114181 (2024). https://doi.org/10.1016/j.dss.2024.114181
40. Gregor, S., Kruse, L., Seidel, S.: Research perspectives: the anatomy of a design principle. J. Ass. Info. Sys. **21**, 1622–1652 (2020). https://doi.org/10.17705/1jais.00649
41. Hevner, A.R., Parsons, J., Brendel, A.B., et al.: Transparency in design science research. Decis. Support Syst. **182**, 114236 (2024). https://doi.org/10.1016/j.dss.2024.114236

Dynamic Design Thinking, Building Innovation into the DSR Process

Frederick K. Johnson[(⊠)] [iD]

Berkeley Haas School of Business, University of California, Berkeley, CA 94720, USA
frederick.johnson@berkeley.edu

Abstract. Design Science Research has given the field a rigorous foundation for building and evaluating artifacts, but it has never fully solved the method-selection problem. Researchers know the stages. They know the evaluation criteria. What they often lack is structured guidance on which generative design methods to apply at each point in the process, and that gap quietly undermines both the creativity and the transparency of the work. This paper addresses that gap directly. The hybrid DSR framework introduced here embeds Kumar's seven modes of innovation within each stage of Peffers et al.'s six-step process model, anchored by Hevner et al.'s DSR guidelines and Gregor and Hevner's contribution types and artifact levels. The central question driving the work is straightforward: can a structured integration of Peffers' process with Kumar's innovation modes reduce method-selection friction and support more balanced, creative rigor in complex research environments? The answer, grounded in four completed DSR cycles and structured expert interviews, is yes; however, the mechanism matters. The problem is not the tension between rigor and creativity. It is the absence of curated, stage-aligned method options that leaves researchers defaulting to implicit choices at precisely the moments when deliberate ones would produce better outcomes. The framework operationalizes innovation not as a departure from process; rather, as the deliberate selection of human-centered, generative methods at each DSR stage. The DSR. Navigator, a prototype AI-driven tool, instantiates the revised framework in practice. This research-in-progress contributes a mid-level method artifact to the DSR community and sets the stage for rigorous validation and broader platform development.

Keywords: Design science research · innovation integration · method selection · hybrid DSR framework · DSR process enhancement · design methodology

1 Introduction

1.1 Dynamic Design Thinking: A Working Definition

Throughout the evolution of Design Science Research (DSR), the field has made an undeniable and lasting mark on how we understand the relationship between knowledge and the built world. From Herbert Simon's foundational framing of design as the science of the artificial [11], to March and Smith's distinction between design and natural science research, and through to the modern IS contributions of Walls, Widmeyer, and El Sawy, the trajectory of DSR has been one of increasing rigor and disciplinary clarity.

© The Author(s), under exclusive license to Springer Nature Switzerland AG 2026
S. Chatterjee et al. (Eds.): DESRIST 2026, LNCS 16607, pp. 265–277, 2026.
https://doi.org/10.1007/978-3-032-28570-6_21

Within information systems, Hevner et al. established the guidelines, principles, and relevance cycles that formalized DSR as a legitimate and productive research paradigm [3]. Peffers et al. added structural clarity through a widely adopted six-step process model [9]. Gregor and Hevner further defined how contributions should be classified and communicated [1, 2]. And Sein et al. extended the paradigm through Action Design Research, connecting organizational intervention to design iteration [10].

What these contributions share is a common orientation toward process structure and evaluative rigor, and a relative silence on how researchers should generate creative, context-sensitive options at each stage of that process. This is the gap that the concept of Dynamic Design Thinking addresses. As used in this paper, Dynamic Design Thinking refers to a mode of conducting DSR in which the researcher moves fluidly between structured process steps and curated, stage-aligned innovation methods, drawing from a deliberate palette of generative techniques rather than relying on ad hoc or implicit method choices. It is not a departure from DSR rigor; it is an enrichment of it.

1.2 Research Question and Motivation

The central question motivating this paper is: How can a structured integration of Peffers' DSR process with Kumar's seven modes of innovation reduce method-selection friction and support balanced, creative rigor for researchers and practitioners operating in complex environments?

This question emerged from repeated practical friction encountered across four completed DSR cycles [4–7], during which the challenge of selecting appropriate methods at each process stage. The DSR process is consistently slowed down by unnecessary cognitive load that leaves the internal design logic of as study implicit rather than transparent. The hybrid framework proposed here is a direct response to that experience.

1.3 Defining Innovation in the DSR Context

Before proceeding, it is important to define what this paper means by innovation. The framework does not claim that DSR lacks novelty, it clearly does not. What it lacks is structured access to human-centered, generative design methods that expand a researcher's option space at each stage of the process.

In this paper, innovation refers specifically to the deliberate application of design methods that support discovery, reframing, and concept generation within a structured research process. This definition draws from Kumar's characterization of design innovation as a planned, mode-based approach to moving from intent to realized offering [8]. The approach aligns well with Hatchuel's critique of bounded rationality in design, which calls for expandable rationality, the capacity to expand both the problem space and the artifact space simultaneously. DSR identifies what to build; the hybrid framework provides curated method options for how to build it from a creative perspective while maintaining rigor, with greater levels of transparency.

2 Related Work

2.1 Method Guidance Gaps in DSR

The foundational DSR literature provides robust structural guidance. Peffers et al.'s six-step model offers a clear process sequence [9]; Hevner et al.'s guidelines provide evaluative standards and design principles [3]; and Gregor and Hevner's contribution taxonomy clarifies how artifacts should be positioned and communicated within the scholarly community [1, 2]. Figure 1 illustrates the Peffers et al. (2007) process model that serves as the structural backbone of the hybrid framework proposed in this paper.

However, despite its strength and long history of success, DSR often lacks clear pathways for method selection, especially regarding innovation. Guideline, structure, and rigor are certainly required, yet that comes at the cost of creativity. Within applied research, these limitations are problematic where practitioners struggle with how to balance design, context, and contribution. There is much to consider when practitioners are challenged when turning a new idea into a complete DSR roadmap. This repeated rigor slows early progress and adds unnecessary cognitive load.

Yet, if we consider a different perspective, we can see we are in the golden age of innovation. Building on that perspective and prior design cycles that applied Peffers' framework [9] to the development of a digital transformation (Dx) adoption models [4–7], this paper proposes a hybrid approach based on Peffers er al. 2007 model in Fig. 1.

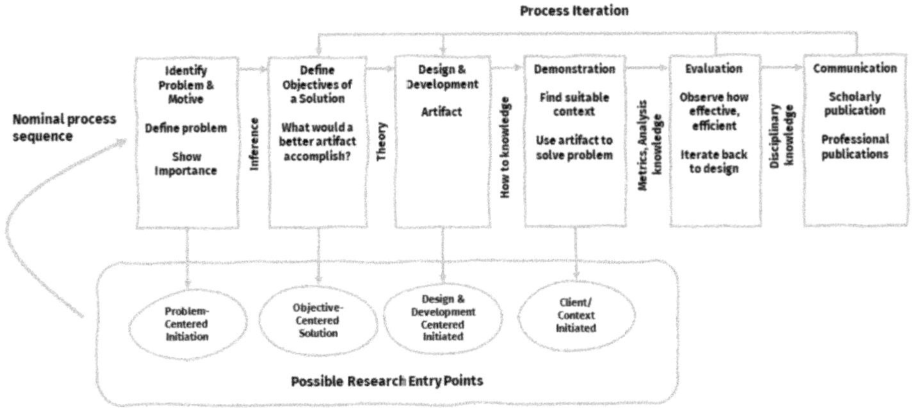

Fig. 1. Peffers et al. (2007) DSR Method Process Model [9]

However, what this body of work does not provide is grounded guidance on which specific design methods a researcher should select at each DSR stage. Less experienced practitioners and those operating in complex, regulated environments face a genuine challenge in determining which methods best support their work at any given point in the process. The DSR grid proposed by vcm Brocke and Maedche offers one useful lens for planning and communicating DSR projects across six core dimensions [13], and Venable et al.'s framework for DSR methodology selection provides complementary guidance at the level of research strategy [12]. More recently, Schoormann et al.'s BAUSTEIN tool has taken a design-tool approach to configuring and representing design research [14]. Each of these contributions advances the field, yet none addresses the within-stage method selection problem from the perspective of integrating innovation modes into the process itself.

2.2 Bridging Innovation and Rigor

The case that DSR can and should embrace more generative design orientations has been made from multiple directions. Hevner, vom Brocke, and Maedche have addressed the role of digital innovation within DSR, arguing that the field must engage more directly with innovation-driven design processes [15]. From design theory, Hatchuel's concept of expandable rationality challenges the assumption that design problems are fixed and known in advance, suggesting instead that both the problem and the artifact evolve together through the design process. This perspective is particularly relevant for DSR practitioners working in fast-moving technological environments where problem spaces are not stable.

Kumar's 101 Design Methods provides a structured, mode-based catalog of innovation techniques [8], illustrated in Fig. 2, that spans from early intent-sensing through to realized offerings. These methods are widely used in innovation practice but have rarely been embedded as explicit options within formal DSR frameworks. Prior work [4–7] demonstrates the practical value of drawing on these techniques across multiple DSR cycles, and the friction experienced during that work, particularly around method selection and design logic transparency, motivates the integration proposed here.

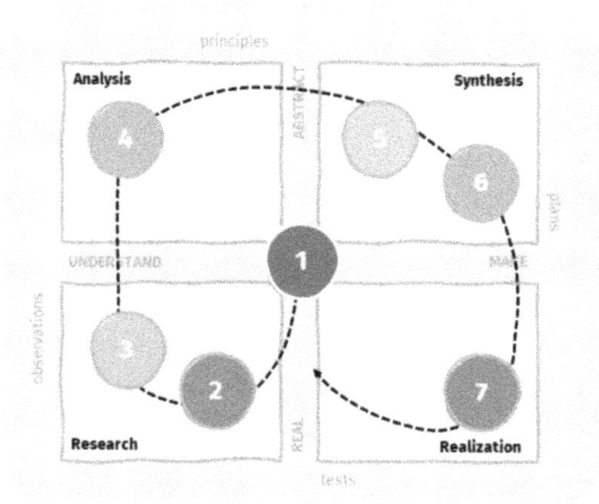

Fig. 2. Kumar, (2013) Seven Modes of Innovation [8]

3   Hybrid Framework: Design and Rationale

3.1   The Logic of Integration

The hybrid artifact in Fig. 3 combines Peffers et al.'s six-step DSR process model [9] with Kumar's seven modes of innovation [8], layered with Hevner et al.'s DSR guidelines 3 (evaluation) and 7 (communication) [3], and anchored by Gregor and Hevner's contribution types and artifact levels [1, 2]. The resulting structure is not a replacement of Peffers' model but an extension of it, one that makes method selection explicit, stage-aligned, and traceable.

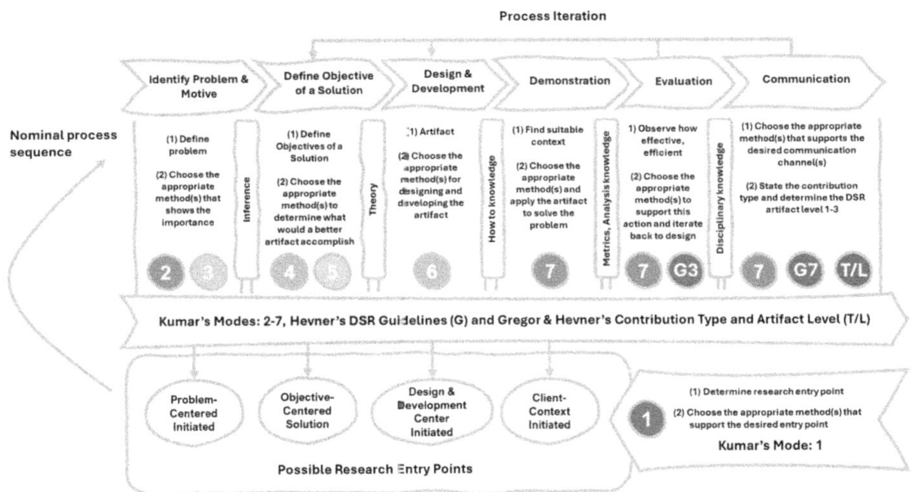

Fig. 3. The Design Science Hybrid Innovation Framework

The integration logic follows a straightforward principle: each stage of Peffers' process represents a distinct epistemic task, and each of Kumar's seven modes offers a cluster of methods calibrated to support a corresponding type of cognitive and design work. Mode 1 (Sense Intent) supports the pre-research framing work that precedes formal problem identification. Modes 2 and 3 (Know Context; Know People) are well-suited to the problem identification and motivation stage, where understanding the stakeholder landscape is critical. Modes 4 and 5 (Frame Insights; Explore Concepts) align naturally with the objective's definition stage, where the researcher must move from observed problems to design goals. Mode 6 (Frame Solutions) supports the design and development stage. Mode 7 (Realize Offerings) spans demonstration, evaluation, and communication, supporting prototyping, testing, and the translation of findings into publishable contributions.

This alignment reflects the epistemic logic of each stage: early stages demand contextual understanding and problem reframing (analysis-oriented modes); middle stages demand creative synthesis and concept generation (synthesis-oriented modes); and later stages demand realization and communication (implementation-oriented modes). This structure mirrors the observation-to-realization arc described in Kumar's original framework [8] and maps coherently onto Peffers' process sequence [9]. Critically, this integration does not prescribe a single method for each step; it provides a curated palette from which researchers make contextually appropriate, deliberate selections, this is the mechanism through which the framework reduces cognitive load.

3.2 The Revised Framework Design

Table 1 presents the complete mapping of the revised hybrid framework design from Fig. 3, specifying for each Peffers stage the corresponding Kumar mode cluster, the alignment rationale, and the DSR elements engaged. Figure 4 shows the revised artifact, and how it operationalizes this mapping as an iterative, card-driven research process.

Table 1. The New Hybrid Framework Design: Stage-Mode Alignment with Rationale

Step	Peffers Stage	Kumar Mode(s)	Alignment Rationale	SR Element
Step 1	Research Entry Point	Mode 1: Sense Intent (1.1–1.14)	Entry sensing requires intent clarification before formal problem definition. Mode 1 methods support this orientation work	Kumar Mode 1
Step 2	Identify Problem & Motivate	Mode 2: Know Context (2.1–2.8); Mode 3: Know People (3.1–3.15)	Problem identification demands contextual and stakeholder understanding. Modes 2–3 provide structured methods for observation, interviews, and context mapping	Kumar Modes 2–3
Step 3	Define Objectives	Mode 4: Frame Insights (4.1–4.18); Mode 5: Explore Concepts (5.1–5.17)	Moving from problem to solution objectives requires insight synthesis and concept exploration. Modes 4–5 support analytical reframing and generative ideation	Kumar Modes 4–5

(continued)

Table 1. (*continued*)

Step	Peffers Stage	Kumar Mode(s)	Alignment Rationale	SR Element
Step 4	Design & Development	Mode 6: Frame Solutions (6.1–6.10)	Artifact design requires structured solution framing. Mode 6 provides prototyping, solution evaluation, and vision-building methods	Kumar Mode 6
Step 5	Demonstration	Mode 7: Realize Offerings (7.1–7.9)	Demonstration involves finding a suitable context and applying the artifact. Mode 7 includes pilot and prototype testing methods calibrated for this purpose	Kumar Mode 7
Step 6	Evaluation	Mode 7: Realize Offerings; Hevner Guideline 3	Evaluation demands observational, analytical, and experimental rigor. Mode 7 methods support structured testing; Hevner's Guideline 3 anchors evaluative standards	Guideline 3; Mode 7
Step 7	Communication	Mode 7; Hevner Guideline 7; Contribution Types 1–5; Artifact Levels 1–3	Communication requires audience calibration, contribution framing, and artifact classification. Guideline 7 and Gregor & Hevner's taxonomy provide the necessary tools	Guideline 7; Gregor & Hevner [1, 2]

A key feature of this framework is that method selection is no longer an ad hoc or implicit process. It becomes a formal, traceable element of the research design, one that the DSR.Navigator tool (described in Sect. 5) operationalizes in real time. The round-based structure shown in Fig. 4 supports iteration, method swapping, and replay; the researcher can refine, backtrack, or skip stages based on contextual judgment.

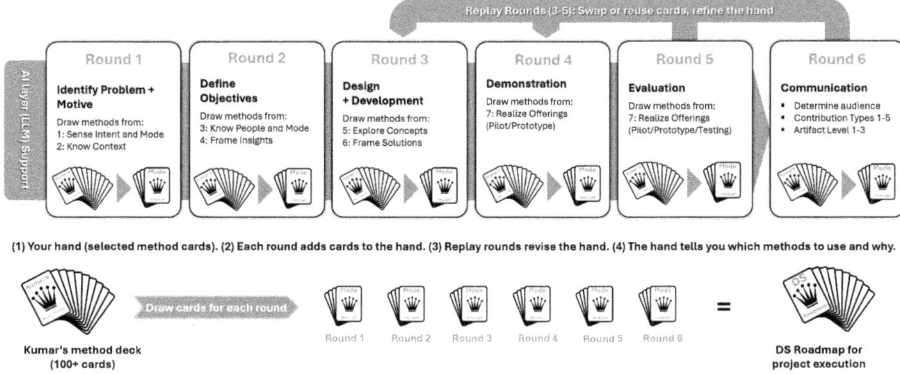

Fig. 4. The Revised Design Science Hybrid Innovation Framework

3.3   A Worked Example: Problem Identification to Objectives

To make this concrete, take a researcher looking into why AI-driven tools stall in regulated manufacturing environments. Before anything else, Round 1 asks them to slow down and become clear on the intent. Mode 1 supports that because this is orientation work, and skipping this phase is exactly how researchers end up solving the wrong problem with the right methods.

Round 2 is where problem identification begins. Modes 2 and 3 cover this stage, and the researcher picks whatever fits their context. Maybe that is a User Research Plan. Maybe it is Expert Interviews or direct observation in the field. The framework does not prescribe a single path. It lays out a set of stage-appropriate options and asks the researcher to choose deliberately and write that choice down. That documentation is not administrative. It is what keeps the design logic visible as the work evolves.

Round 3 moves into defining objectives. Modes 4 and 5 carry that work. A researcher might use a Summary Framework to organize what the problem identification stage surfaced, or Opportunity Mapping to push from findings into a defined solution space. Again, the specific method is less important than the fact that the choice was made on purpose and connects clearly to what came before.

Round 4 is design and development, Mode 6. Round 5 covers demonstration and evaluation, both drawing from Mode 7. These three rounds in the middle can be replayed. The researcher swaps methods, refines the artifact, runs another cycle if the design needs it. That flexibility is built in, not bolted on.

Round 6 is communication. Mode 7 again, but the focus shifts to what Gregor and Hevner's describe as contribution types and artifact levels. These elements provide the researcher with a framework for positioning the work and making the contribution legible to the community it is meant to reach. This last step is often skipped or rushed. The fundamental idea supports a framework that treats the entire DSR process as one full iterating stage that allows for change, growth and innovation without sacrificing rigor.

4   Lessons from Prior DSR Cycles

To ground the revised framework in applied practice, this section draws on three completed DSR cycles conducted between 2021 and 2025 within the context of biopharma digital transformation [4, 6, 7]. These cycles are not background; they are the evidence. Each one used the author's dissertation as its structural and theoretical origination point, and each one moved the artifact forward in a way that directly informed both the hybrid framework and the DSR.Navigator, discussed in Sect. 5. The progression was not linear by accident. It was the result of making more deliberate design decisions at each stage of the process, which is exactly what the framework is built to support.

The first cycle started where most hard problems start, with a gap that existing tools could not close [6]. Biopharma IT leaders had no structured way to evaluate and select digital transformation frameworks, and the generic models available were not built for regulated, operationally complex environments. The artifact developed in this cycle established the baseline: a PLS-SEM adoption model grounded in TAM, TAM2, and Pharma 4.0 hallmark elements, validated against 210 industry professionals. The model explained a strong share of the variance in both Intention to Use and Perceived Usefulness, with adjusted R^2 values of 0.784 and 0.797 respectively. Predictive relevance was confirmed through blindfolding, and PLSpredict showed the model consistently outperforming the naïve linear benchmark on every indicator. Ease of Use turned out to matter more than Perceived Usefulness in driving adoption, a finding that contradicted the conventional TAM narrative and immediately raised the next question. The model was intentionally compact, and that constraint was deliberate. It created a clean foundation with enough room left to build on.

The second cycle took that finding seriously and pushed further [7]. By incorporating TAM3 and UTAUT constructs, Perceived Enjoyment and Perception of External Control, and introducing Perceived Ease of Use as a formal endogenous variable, the model became structurally richer and empirically sharper. The extended model outperformed the initial one on every benchmark that mattered. BIC dropped meaningfully for both Intention to Use and Perceived Usefulness, signaling a genuine improvement in fit, not just added complexity. R^2 values held strong across all three endogenous constructs, and Q^2 predictive relevance climbed across the board. PLSpredict CVPAT confirmed the advantage was real, statistically significant negative average loss differences across all constructs, with PLS RMSE lower than the linear model on every single indicator. The headline result was hard to ignore: Perceived Ease of Use was nearly eight times more influential on Intention to Use than Perceived Usefulness. That is not a refinement. That is a reframing of the adoption logic entirely, and it set the trajectory for everything that followed.

The third cycle was where the model became unified [4]. Three domain-specific constructs were introduced, Business Domain Application, Framework Interoperability, and Digital Maturity Model Relevance, and the model was validated against 273 biopharma professionals across manufacturing, clinical, and commercial functions. R^2 values remained strong across all four endogenous constructs, with Intention to Use at 0.609, Perceived Usefulness at 0.642, Perceived Ease of Use at 0.605, and Job Relevance at 0.489. Q^2 predictive relevance was large across the majority of indicators, and PLSpredict confirmed the model's superiority over the linear benchmark on RMSE across every indicator. Framework Interoperability emerged as a medium-effect driver of Job Relevance, and multi-group analysis surfaced something no prior cycle had the architecture to find adoption logic varies significantly by functional role. Non-IT leaders leaned on structural elements to assess usefulness. IT leaders weighted ease and strategic alignment. Executives operated from a different logic altogether. That kind of role-based differentiation is not visible in a compact baseline model. It took three cycles of deliberate construct expansion to get there.

What the progression shows was meaningful with merit. The artifact demonstrated a high predictive level because the design decisions become much more intentional at each stage. The framework did not just organize the process, it created the conditions for asking better questions, selecting more context-appropriate methods, and building constructs that reflected how the problem actually worked in the field. That is the argument for the initial hybrid model. Not that this model guarantees improved fit, but that it replaces implicit, undocumented choices with deliberate, stage-aligned ones, and the difference shows up in the results.

5   The DSR.Navigator: Prototype and Future Work

5.1   Artifact Description

The DSR.Navigator is an AI-assisted decision-support tool that operationalizes the revised hybrid framework in practice, as seen in Fig. 4. Its purpose is not to automate DSR decision-making but to reduce the friction associated with method selection, roadmap construction, and contribution framing. The tool walks researchers through each of the six DSR stages, presents curated method options from the Kumar palette appropriate to that stage, and generates a customized Strategic DSR Roadmap based on the researcher's problem type, artifact goal, and desired contribution level. Figure 5 illustrates the launch page user interface.

Fig. 5. The DSR.Navigator, Prototype Interface

A functioning prototype has been developed and is being evaluated with a subset of the expert interview participants. The prototype accepts researcher inputs regarding problem context, artifact type, and research entry point, and produces stage-level method recommendations, artifact classification guidance, and communication pathway suggestions aligned with Gregor and Hevner's contribution framework [1, 2]. An integrated functionality that includes a DSR.CopyEditor, providing structured peer-review-level feedback on draft DSR papers, checking for logical argument flow, DSR alignment, academic tone, and contribution clarity.

5.2 Design Validity Considerations

A critical next step for this research is addressing design validity across the three dimensions proposed by Larsen et al. [16]: Is the artifact better? Is it known why it is better? And for whom and in what contexts is it effective? The current research-in-progress has produced preliminary evidence on the first dimension through structured expert evaluation, with participants consistently rating the revised round-based prototype as clearer and more usable than the original framework. Addressing the second and third dimensions, causal explanation and boundary conditions, requires a more formal evaluation study, which is planned as the primary next step.

Regarding the technical architecture of the DSR.Navigator, the question of whether a Retrieval-Augmented Generation (RAG) approach would offer greater traceability and domain-specificity than the current prototype architecture is under active consideration. A RAG-based approach could provide more controlled, source-grounded method recommendations, a feature that would strengthen the tool's credibility in academic research contexts and improve its auditability.

5.3 Scope Considerations

One concern raised in the expert interviews is worth addressing directly: does a tool that generates structured roadmaps risk reinforcing the procedural rigidity that the framework seeks to overcome? The DSR.Navigator is designed as a decision-support tool, not a prescriptive engine. It presents options and rationale, not mandates. The round-based structure of the prototype explicitly supports iteration, method swapping, and replay, the researcher can refine, backtrack, or skip stages based on their own judgment. Whether this design intent is realized in practice is a question the validation study will address directly.

6 Conclusion

This paper introduces a hybrid DSR framework that embeds Kumar's seven modes of innovation within Peffers et al.'s six-step process model, anchored by Hevner et al.'s guidelines and Gregor and Hevner's contribution framework. The framework addresses a specific and documented gap: the absence of structured, stage-aligned method guidance within established DSR processes. The contribution is a mid-level method artifact, not a replacement of existing DSR theory, but a coherent extension of it.

The framework's core claim is that innovation integration in DSR is not about departing from rigor. It is about providing researchers with a deliberate, curated palette of generative design methods at each process stage, making method selection transparent, traceable, and contextual appropriate. Across four DSR cycles and a structured expert evaluation study, this integration has shown practical value in reducing method-selection friction and improving the communicability of design logic.

The DSR.Navigator operationalizes this framework as an AI-assisted tool for researchers and practitioners. Both the framework and the tool represent works in progress, with formal design validity evaluation as the immediate next step. The longer-term vision is a research support platform that extends the hybrid framework's reach into doctoral education, interdisciplinary research design, and innovation-driven professional practice.

References

1. Gregor, S., Hevner, A.R.: Positioning and presenting design science research for maximum impact. MIS Q. **37**(2), 337–355 (2013)
2. Gregor, S., Jones, D.: The anatomy of a design theory. J. Assoc. Inf. Syst. **7**(5), 312–335 (2006)
3. Bichler, M.: Design science in information systems research. Wirtschaftsinformatik **48**(2), 133–135 (2006). https://doi.org/10.1007/s11576-006-0028-8
4. Johnson, F.K.: A digital transformation framework for biopharma manufacturing, Doctoral dissertation. Claremont Graduate University, Claremont, CA (2023)
5. Johnson, F.K.: A unified digital transformation adoption model for the biopharmaceutical industry. Preprint, ResearchGate (2026). https://doi.org/10.13140/RG.2.2.27953.03683
6. Johnson, F.K., Uwaoma, C.: A digital transformation adoption model for biopharma manufacturing. SSRN Electron. J. (2023). https://doi.org/10.2139/ssrn.4355793

7. Johnson, F.K., Uwaoma, C.: PLS-based evaluation of a digital transformation adoption model. In: Sarstedt, M., Ringle, C.M., Hair, J.F. (eds.) State of the Art in Partial Least Squares Structural Equation Modeling (PLS-SEM). Springer, Cham (2023)

8. Kumar, V.: 101 Design Methods: A Structured Approach for Driving Innovation in Your Organization. Wiley, Hoboken (2013)

9. Peffers, K., Tuunanen, T., Rothenberger, M.A., Chatterjee, S.: A design science research methodology for information systems research. J. Manag. Inf. Syst. **24**(3), 45–77 (2007)

10. Sein, M.K., Henfridsson, O., Purao, S., Rossi, M., Lindgren, R.: Action design research. MIS Q. **35**(1), 37–56 (2011)

11. Simon, H.A.: The Sciences of the Artificial, 3rd edn. MIT Press, Cambridge (1996)

12. Venable, J., Pries-Heje, J., Baskerville, R.: Choosing a design science research methodology. In: ACIS 2017 Proceedings (2017)

13. vom Brocke, J., Maedche, A.: The DSR grid: six core dimensions for effectively planning and communicating design science research projects. Electron. Mark. **29**, 379–385 (2019)

14. Schoormann, T., Möller, F., Chandra Kruse, L., Otto, B.: BAUSTEIN—a design tool for configuring and representing design research. Inf. Syst. J. **34**(6), 1871–1901 (2024)

15. Hevner, A., vom Brocke, J., Maedche, A.: Roles of digital innovation in design science research. Bus. Inf. Syst. Eng. **61**(1), 3–8 (2019)

16. Larsen, K.R., et al.: Validity in design science. MIS Q. **49**(4), 1267–1294 (2025)

Future of Ecosystems for Design Science Research

Designing Open Access Platforms for Multilingual Language Awareness in Early Childhood Education

Mara Burger[1]([✉]) [iD], Niklas Kloth[1] [iD], and Christina vom Brocke[2] [iD]

[1] University of Münster, 48149 Münster, Germany
{mara.burger,niklas.kloth}@uni-muenster.de
[2] University of Teacher Education of the Grisons, 7000 Chur, Switzerland
christina.vombrocke@phgr.ch

Abstract. Linguistic diversity is important in Early Childhood Education and Care (ECEC), yet pedagogically appropriate and adaptable materials to foster multilingual language awareness remain scarce. Practices often stay implicitly monolingual, leaving educators with limited support for systematically managing linguistic diversity in everyday settings. This paper addresses this gap by proposing an open access web platform at the center of a platform that supports multilingual early childhood language awareness through multimodal storytelling and complementary resources. Drawing on Cognitive Load Theory, the platform provides an individually paced multilingual story environment and serves as repository for educational material, enabling educators to reduce cognitive load for children and foster early language awareness. Following an echeloned Design Science Research (eDSR) approach, we iteratively derived design requirements, implemented a functional prototype, and conducted a preliminary evaluation with parents, educators, multilingual ECEC researchers, and software experts. The evaluation suggests that the platform is perceived as useful and usable, while highlighting improvement needs around role-specific entry points and interface refinements. This study is interdisciplinary in nature, integrating contributions from information systems, computer science and language education, and it contributes initial design principles for multilingual ECEC platforms and highlights directions for future implementation in real-world educational settings.

Keywords: Early Childhood Education and Care · ECEC · Educational Technology · Design Science Research · DSR

1 Introduction

Early childhood is a critical period for the development of cognitive and social foundations of language learning [1]. Currently, linguistic diversity is increasingly the norm rather than the exception, especially in multilingual countries like Luxembourg, Switzerland, or border regions like Tyrol, where both German and Italian are spoken simultaneously [2]. Many children grow up navigating multiple languages across home, educational, and community settings—latest, when they join kindergarten or preschool [3].

S. Chatterjee et al. (Eds.): DESRIST 2026, LNCS 16607, pp. 281–293, 2026.
https://doi.org/10.1007/978-3-032-28570-6_22

Whereas the need for children to develop their "own cultural identity, language and values," [4] is acknowledged in literature and the United Nations (UN) Charta [4, 5]. Simultaneously multilingualism is anchored in Article 3 the Treaty of the European Union and thereby is a core of the European Union (EU) values. Despite this reality, Early Childhood Education and Care (ECEC) practices and learning materials often remain predominantly monolingual, limiting opportunities to systematically support early multilingual development and value children's linguistic diversity. Although current research consistently demonstrates benefits of early multilingual exposure, educators frequently lack pedagogically appropriate materials and tools for that cause [6]. Current research underscores the necessity to provide multilingual pedagogical support in ECEC, as educational practitioners struggle offering adequate support for children with a multilingual background, leading to children feeling left out [5].

Available resources are often limited to single-language or bilingual formats or are insufficiently adaptable to the linguistic diversity present in ECEC settings, resulting in fragmented and uneven implementation of multilingual pedagogical approaches needed for teaching children language awareness.

Despite the growing linguistic diversity in ECEC settings, existing resources remain largely restricted to single-language formats, hindering the effective implementation of multilingual pedagogical approaches. This creates a critical lack of adaptable digital tools in the education sector, leaving educators without the innovative means necessary to support children in increasingly diverse environments. This gap underscores the need for research and design efforts that examine how digital materials and tools can meaningfully support multilingual learning from the earliest stages of education. Therefore we ask: *How can an open access multilingual ECEC platform be designed for children, educators, and parents to effectively foster early language awareness?*

The developed artifact is encompassed in a multidisciplinary project, aiming to find an adequate solution by designing a platform and multilingual resources. In an emerging setting where needs and users were not yet defined, we followed an echeloned Design Science Research (eDSR) approach to (1) derive preliminary design principles (DPs), (2) create a viable platform, dynamically evolving as an artifact to the emergent needs, and (3) evaluate the artifact with different experts.

In the following, we give an overview of multilingual education and its importance in the EU. Next, we present our eDSR approach. Followed by that, we present our results grounded in insights from literature analysis and ten in-depth interviews with ECEC experts, which inform the derivation of initial design knowledge on how digital platforms can support multilingual language awareness in ECEC contexts under real-world constraints. Finally, we discuss our findings, highlight our limitations, and give an outlook for our future steps.

2 Research Background

2.1 Multilingual Early Childhood Education

Multilingualism is an increasingly common characteristic of ECEC contexts. Children grow up with diverse linguistic repertoires shaped by family languages, migration, regional and minority languages, and transnational practices [2]. Research has consistently identified early childhood as a particularly sensitive phase for language acquisition, cognitive development, and identity formation [5]. Consequently, multilingual education in early childhood is not a marginal concern, but a central issue closely linked to educational equity, inclusion, and long-term learning trajectories.

Despite growing awareness of the benefits of early multilingual exposure, multilingual pedagogical approaches remain unevenly implemented in ECEC settings. Empirical research indicates that while educators often express positive attitudes towards linguistic diversity, multilingual practices are frequently implemented implicitly and situationally rather than as systematically embedded pedagogical approaches. Studies conducted in early childhood education contexts show that multilingual practices often depend on individual educator initiative rather than being structurally anchored within institutional frameworks [9, 10]. Learning materials and pedagogical resources in particular continue to reflect predominantly monolingual orientations [11, 12]. Early childhood educators are therefore confronted with considerable challenges. They are expected to support children's language development, respond to diverse linguistic backgrounds, collaborate with families, and create inclusive learning environments—often without sufficient professional preparation or access to appropriate resources [5, 13]. Research highlights that existing educational materials frequently privilege a dominant societal language and rarely reflect children's full linguistic repertoires [10].Hence, educators rely heavily on personal expertise, informal strategies, and improvisation, leading to variations in the quality and sustainability of multilingual support across settings.

Addressing these challenges is essential in light of the broader aims of early childhood education, including social participation, equal educational opportunities, and the recognition of diversity as a resource rather than a deficit. Research on multilingual pedagogies and translanguaging demonstrates that valuing and integrating children's home languages can support language development, strengthen identity formation, and foster positive attitudes towards linguistic and cultural diversity among all children [6, 7, 9]. Conversely, the marginalization of home languages in early educational contexts may negatively affect children's sense of belonging and participation.

In this context, digital platforms and resources are gaining increasing relevance to design innovative platforms. Digital technologies are already part of many children's everyday lives and are gradually becoming more visible in early childhood education settings [14]. When grounded in early childhood pedagogy, digital resources offer opportunities to support multilingual education by enabling flexible language integration, multimodal input e.g. audio, visual, and interactive elements, and adaptation to diverse linguistic contexts [15, 16]. Digital formats also facilitate the inclusion of multiple languages and can support collaboration with families by enabling the integration of home languages and culturally relevant content [17–19].

Importantly, the pedagogical value of digital platforms does not lie in replacing established early childhood practices, but in complementing and extending them within a new platforms [18]. Digital resources can function as mediating tools that support educators in implementing multilingual pedagogies more consistently and sustainably, thereby addressing some of the structural challenges identified in current practice [18, 19]. However, research also indicates the lack of high-quality, evidence-based digital resources specifically designed to foster multilingual development in early childhood education. Many existing digital tools are either insufficiently aligned with early childhood pedagogy or do not adequately address multilingual learning needs [11, 12].

Against this background, multilingual early childhood education emerges as a field in which digital platforms hold significant but still underexplored potential to design innovative multilingual learning platforms. Investigating how digital platforms can support multilingual pedagogical goals is therefore both timely and necessary to promote inclusive and developmentally appropriate learning opportunities from the earliest stages of education.

2.2 Digital Platforms for Early Childhood Education

Multiple commercial platforms exist in early childhood education for learning foreign or secondary languages. DuolingoABC [20] is a dedicated children program to teach children a language in a gamified approach, promoting their literacy and phonetic awareness. Similarly, Abblino Kids [21] aims for an AI-based voice and text chat to individually teach various languages. Mondly Kids [19] is situated in between the previous ones, offering a similar gamified approach and chatbot interactions to learn languages. Little Pim [22] is a video-based platform presenting individual lessons and offers offline resources for parents to study different languages together. DinoLingo [23] offers a gamified approach for young children as well as a language-platform for schools for homework assignment directly on the platform.

While the identified platforms focus on educating vocabulary use of young children of a specific language and language awareness in a specific language, there exists no platform assisting early childhood education professionals by enabling them to foster language awareness and literacy competencies as well as helps them to break down language barriers, when children with different mother tongues join a group of children. Most of the identified platforms are focused on a direct child interaction with an individual device, which most of the elementary schools or kindergartens in Europe do not offer for their children and for educational purposes, do not want children early to interact with digital devices for educational purposes. Therefore there is.

3 Method

To investigate the problem of no open access digital platform to create digital platforms to foster multilingual early childhood language awareness, we apply an eDSR approach by [24]. Generally, DSR is defined as a methodology aimed at designing and evaluating innovative artifacts that are created to solve pressing real world problems [25]. The eDSR approach uses echelons, small self-reliant parts to organize the entire DSR project.

The echelons are problem analysis, objectives and requirements definition, design and development, demonstration, and evaluation and iterations can be done within each echelon [24]. The echelons for our iterations colored in white are shown in Fig. 1.

3.1 Problem Analysis

A1 Problem Scoping: Through a literature analysis of multilingual language awareness, a market analysis of digital platforms currently available, and a close collaboration with 10 multilingual ECEC researchers from different countries in the EU we understood the need to create an open access platform for multilingual ECEC. We see that many digital platforms for children lack the facet of multilingual language awareness.

3.2 Objectives and Requirements

A2 Defining Objectives: Through insightful iterative discussions with 10 ECEC researchers, each session lasting between 30 min and 1 h, and through literature analysis we gathered the requirements for the platform. The requirements are explained in detail in the next chapter. The ECEC researchers provided different viewpoints from different stakeholders, such as children, parents and kindergarten teachers which they have been in contact with beforehand and they therefore understood the different needs of the various user groups and provided us with the requirements.

3.3 Design and Development

A3 Prototype Development: With these requirements at hand, we used Figma [26] to create the first clickable mockup as first design of the platform.

A5 Functional Prototype: With the information at hand from A4 we used internal feedback loops and iterations to design a functional prototype. This prototype is a functional platform that holds the open-access materials, created by our pedagogical ECEC research partners to foster open-access early childhood language awareness.

3.4 Demonstration

A4 Mockup Demonstration: We presented our mockup in a small informal meeting with 10 of our ECEC research partners and the experts gave insights into the first design. Through the insights of the researchers, we created a proof-of-concept (PoC), validated the core concept and aligned the next steps for building the next step of our artifact.

A6 Prototype Demonstration: For this demonstration, we showed eight ECEC experts, parents, and ECEC teachers the prototype in an online and in-person meeting.

3.5 Evaluation

A7 Qualitative Evaluation: We used four interviews with ECEC experts and a focus group with four frontend and software developers to gather insights into the usefulness and design of the platform. The insights show the PoC as the qualitative feedback highlights the importance of the platform and the important features. Additionally, the insights also show where improvements can be implemented.

To evaluate our approach and prototype, we conducted four semi-structured interviews with ECEC experts and a focus group with four experts from different software backgrounds, shown in Table 1. We followed information systems guidelines for stakeholders qualitative research to evaluate the first prototype [27, 28]. We interviewed parents, ECEC experts and software developers in Germany to gather insights into different perspectives of the platform, user perspectives and expert designer perspectives. Our interview partners stem from various backgrounds to address the multitude of perspectives and the multilingual researchers contribute their academic experience in multilingual ECEC as well as their insights into the work with children and kindergarten, while parents had children in the age for kindergarten and contributed their experience with digital platforms. The software and frontend developers contributed their perspective on the design of the platform and if design features could be implemented differently.

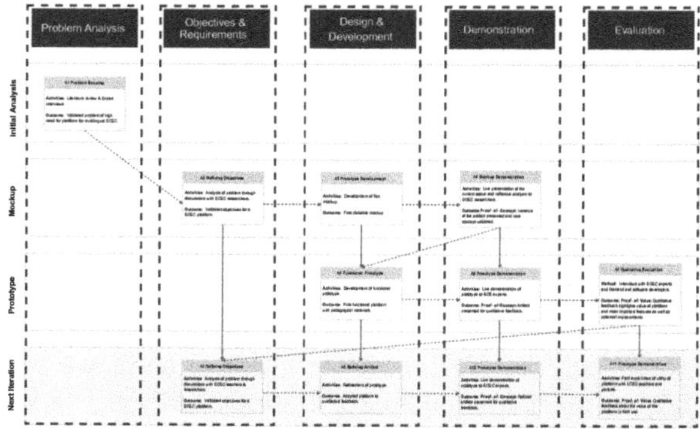

Fig. 1. eDSR approach and future steps

All feedback partners were asked about their impression of the platform regarding design and utility of multilingual language awareness for the target groups. Questions for pedagogical experts focused on pedagogical usage and interaction with children, while questions for software developers focused on platform design and structure. Thereby, we aimed for meaningful feedback and a first PoV of our prototype.

The interviews were automatically transcribed by noScribe [29], manually reviewed and analyzed through a deductive analysis afterwards in *MAXQDA*.

In the next iteration, shown in grey in Fig. 1, we will adapt the design based on the feedback and create a proof-of-value (PoV).

Table 1. Overview of Evaluation Participants

Denotation	Role	Method	Duration
MR-1	Multilingual ECEC Researcher	Interview	33

(continued)

Table 1. (*continued*)

Denotation	Role	Method	Duration
P	Parent	Interview	36
EP	Education Professional / Parent	Interview	47
MR-2	Multilingual ECEC Researcher	Interview	43
FD-1	Frontend Developer	Focus Group	36
FD-2	Frontend Developer	Focus Group	36
SD-1	Software Developer	Focus Group	36
SD-2	Software Developer	Focus Group	36

4 Preliminary Result

4.1 Design Requirements and Design Features

The open-access, web-based digital platform is specifically designed for multilingual ECEC. This platform serves as a central hub for educational resources to foster language awareness. The design and functionality of the platform were informed by the distinct requirements of its primary user groups: kindergarten children, ECEC teachers, and parents and were communicated with the design team through our cooperating partner, the ECEC researchers. The platform design is depicted in Fig. 2. In the following, the design requirements (DRs) and our design features (DFs) are explained.

DR 1 Platform should minimize Cognitive Load for Children: The interface of the platform should prioritize visual simplicity to prevent overstimulation and distractions for young children. This requirement is derived from the teachers and experts and connects to literature, that reducing cognitive load [30] ensures that children remain focused on educational content.

DF 1.1 Design for Primary User Accessibility: The interface was engineered to minimize cognitive load for young children who may not yet possess digital literacy or reading skills. To achieve this, the platform employs a minimalist layout with a clear visual hierarchy. During story playback, the platform removes all peripheral navigation elements, such as menus or sidebars, to center the child's attention on the content itself.

DR 2 The platform should provide different modes of navigation: To respect the multitude of user, the platform needs to be accessible from computers, tablets, mobile phones or similar [31]. Also, the platform interface should provide possibilities to address multiple navigation options to allow a non-disruptive experience due to different preferences and due to different devices being available for teachers and parents.

DF 2.1 Navigation mechanisms: Moving through a story is implemented via multiple interaction modalities; dedicated large-scale buttons for ease of use for children, swiping gestures for touchscreens, and a click-and-drag modality for traditional mouse users. These redundant controls ensure that physical or developmental differences in fine motor skills do not affect the navigation through the content.

DR 2.2 Easily interact with multiple languages: A core requirement is to switch between languages for each story. Thereby, children should be able to gain a sense of language awareness and are able to curiously interact with different languages.

DF 2.3 Multilingual switching mechanisms: A critical feature of the "Storytime" artifact is the ability to switch languages dynamically. The platform supports an interface available in various languages and content narrated or written in over 15 languages, including English, German, French, as well as minority languages like Romansh.

DF 2.4 Synchronous state: The platform is designed so that a user can switch the language while remaining on the same page or "picture" of a story. This ensures that children can compare the phonetics or scripts of different languages for the exact same narrative moment, facilitating immediate linguistic comparison.

DR 3 Facilitate Content Presentation for Auditory and Literacy Development: As the children may have different prior knowledge and cognitive abilities, it is important for educators to address them individually and customize their multilingual experience based on their multilingual background and literacy level [32]. Therefore children need to be able to either listen to the stories or also read together with educators.

DF 3.1 Dual-Mode Presentation: The system allows users to choose between two functional modes for each story: "Listen & Watch", where the priority is on hearing the stories and watching the respective pictures. In the "Read" mode, the text is displayed in a dedicated text-container below the image.

DR 4 Individually paced Interaction: The platform should prioritize relationships with teachers and parents over the interaction and relationship with the platform. The platform should not function like a TV show or like an audiobook where information is pushed towards the child, which hinders their sense of agency and curiosity [33, 34].

DF 4.1 Individually paced Interaction: The platform is engineered to function similarly to a traditional picture book as the progression to the next narrative segment is controlled manually through clicking or swiping on user readiness. This feature prioritizes interpersonal interaction through discussing with children between pages instead of passive consumption of content.

DR 5 The Platform should enable Offline Adult-Child Interaction: In many kindergarten, there is no sufficient digital equipment available. Many kindergarten only have one computer for administration, resulting in kindergarteners to use their own phones or tablets with their mobile plan [35]. As this is not sufficient for many educational settings, it is necessary to provide sufficient models for offline and analog use.

DF 5.1 Hybrid Media Decoupling: To foster integration in the physical classroom, the platform allows for the independent use of its digital components, such as playing the optionally downloadable audio while utilizing physical, downloaded printouts of the story illustrations. This decoupling of audio and visual streams empowers teachers to lead offline storytelling sessions. This also allows that children can play with the story pictures while listening to native speaker multilingual narration, which can be downloaded depending on their selected language.

DF 5.2 Granular Selection Interface: Within the activity categories, the platform employs a grid-based selection interface, offering a broad overview for educators or parents. Apart from individual downloads, they can use radio buttons to select individual activities across multiple stories for bulk-downloading. This eases the preparation phase of educators.

DF 5.3 Accessibility: The platform's architecture emphasizes open accessibility. By hosting resources in standardized formats, the artifact ensures easy offline usage. Furthermore, the inclusion of dedicated guides for "Dialogic Reading" and "Story Reading" provide educational instructions on how the digital artifact should be used to achieve desired educational outcomes.

The platform aims at solving the problem of providing high-quality, multilingual, and child-accessible multilingual content through a design that balances extreme simplicity for the child with high-utility resource management for teachers and parents.

Fig. 2. Overview of Platform Design

4.2 Preliminary Design Principles

We propose an initial set of DPs that are relevant for other designers and researchers and derive the DPs according to [36].

DP 1 Mediated Agency and Offline Synergy: For designers and developers, enabling self-paced learning and interpersonal interaction for children and adults in digital educational settings requires mechanisms such as (a) manual progression that pauses the narrative until children are ready, (b) interaction anchors like audio stopping, and (c) hybrid delivery modes with downloadable or printable analog companions that mirror digital content. Actively involving teachers and parents supports user agency and offline interpersonal engagement, helping prevent passive consumption and thereby contributing to educational success.

DP 2 Context-Preserved Multilingual Synchronicity: For designers and developers to support context-preserved multilingual exploration for children, teachers, and parents in multilingual ECEC settings, mechanisms should include (a) dynamic language switching with instant access across languages and (b) synchronous state maintenance that keeps the toggle anchored to the current narrative element. Involving teachers and parents is essential, as maintaining narrative continuity during language switches enables immediate phonetic and script comparison, fostering linguistic curiosity and pedagogical inclusion across diverse digital environments.

4.3 Preliminary Evaluation

We report preliminary qualitative results from semi-structured interviews with educational professionals, parents, multilingualism researchers and software designers, as denoted in Table 1. Across education-focused partners, the prototype was evaluated as a relevant response to the need for more systematic support of early multilingual development. Interviewees acknowledged the underlying problem and assessed the platform's concept and structure as a suitable approach for the designated user base (EP, MR-1, MR-2, P). One multilingual researcher highlighted the stepwise structure and clear navigation, stating that the platform is self-explanatory (MR-1).

Ease of use was reported as a consistent theme. Parents, educators, and multilingual researchers described the interface as simple, "uncluttered" and non-distracting, which they considered beneficial for children (MR-1, EP, FD-2, SD-1, SD-2). Parents and educators compared the story experience to picture-book interaction; the stepwise pacing was viewed as supporting active engagement rather than passive listening. The option to display text when needed was highlighted as an advantage over audio-only stories, enabling children and educators to interact.

The participants explained their different viewpoints on the independent use of the platform by children (MR, P, EP). Perspectives differed by role: Researchers tended to be more cautious and promoted parental or educational support, while the interviewed parents were more optimistic, arguing that children quickly learn common app interaction patterns e.g., play/pause, swiping and can navigate it independently. Parents and educational researchers also reported that the individual pacing of the stories can foster creative, discussion-based interaction with images and spoken content, potentially supporting language awareness (P).

Educators and educational researchers emphasized limited digital infrastructure in some kindergartens e.g., only one computer for administration or reliance of the educators on private devices (MR-2, EP). Consequently, download and print options were repeatedly described as essential. Interviewees also noted that they had not used a comparable platform before, contrasting the prototype's segmented story progression with typical audio stories children listen to independently. An educator emphasized the benefit of language switching for listening comprehension, pointing to native-speaker audio and the value of noticing phonological similarities across languages as "very beneficial for listening comprehension [similarities] encourage the children to think about what a word might mean" (EP).

Several usability issues emerged. A frequent point of confusion was the distinction between "listening" and "reading," suggesting a need for clearer labeling or mode cues (FD-1, FD-2, SD-1, SD-2, EP). One practitioner requested language selection within the full-screen story view to enable rapid switching during spontaneous child interaction

(EP). While this was discussed, it was originally rejected as visual overhead. Finally, the hybrid "one-size-fits-all" concept was criticized as blurring child-and adult-facing components; parents, software designers, and some educators suggested role-specific entry points e.g., separate areas for children, educators, parents. Further requests included additional audio controls, e.g., rewind/repeat.

5 Discussion

This study sets out to address a persistent gap in multilingual ECEC. While linguistic diversity is increasingly the norm, educators and families still face a shortage of developmentally appropriate and open-access resources that support multilingual language awareness in everyday practice. The current problem centers around multilingual pedagogical approaches that are often implemented unevenly, largely because materials and institutional structures remain predominantly monolingual [9, 10]. Building on established research that highlights early childhood as a sensitive period for language development, identity formation, and inclusion [7, 8], the platform prototype is a modern response. In this context, our artifact contributes a child-centered story-focused platform combining multimodal story presentation with minimal cognitive load evaluated by interviewees and supported by literature, flexible multilingual switching, and downloadable material to bridge the varying extent of digitalization in kindergartens.

Methodologically, the work demonstrates how eDSR can be applied in an emerging setting where requirements are developed collaboratively with researchers from multiple disciplines. An agile work setting helped to agree on a set of design requirements and early design principles grounded in stakeholder input.

Multilingual language awareness in early childhood is best supported when digital resources (1) keep interaction simple and paced, (2) treat language switching as a pedagogical feature rather than a settings option, and (3) remain resilient to infrastructural limitations through offline portability and adult-facing preparation tools. The preliminary findings suggest that this stance resonates with educators, researchers, and parents, while also pointing to specific interface refinements needed to clarify roles, reduce ambiguity, and better support spontaneous, dialogic use.

Although our artifact shows its benefit in our evaluation, the current evidence remains preliminary. Our interviews provide a PoC and a first PoV through interviews and a focus group, however a PoV demonstrated through a field analysis remains to be done. For future work, we propose adapting the requirements based on the insights of the qualitative feedback. Through reiteration and adaptation of the current prototype to the adapted requirements and the development of an improved artifact, a PoC can be demonstrated to ECEC teachers and parents and evaluated in a naturalistic setting trough field experiments to create a PoV.

6 Conclusion

This paper addressed the lack of high-quality, evidence-based, open-access digital platforms and resources that can support multilingual learning and language awareness in early childhood education. Building on multilingual pedagogy and translanguaging research, we designed and implemented a web-based platform that complements established early childhood practices by enabling flexible language integration and multimodal storytelling. As our main contribution, we developed a platform as a central hub for multilingual stories and accompanying educational activities, designed around the needs of three primary stakeholders: Children, educators, and parents. The platform combines child-centered, low-distraction interaction and offers a hybrid media decoupling with adult-oriented preparation and offline portability through downloadable story components and guides. Key platform capabilities include dynamic multilingual switching, with synchronous state retention, dual-mode story presentation, child-paced navigation, and a deliberate bridge to offline adult-child interaction through printable and reusable materials. Future research could investigate the use of such platforms in a naturalistic setting, for example, in kindergarten or with parents to assess learning outcomes and long-term pedagogical value.

Acknowledgments. This research was funded by the European Union (EU Funding Erasmus+ 2024-1-LU01-KA220-HED-000245349: "Digital, multilingual and cross-sectoral early childhood education through school-university-business synergies (AGENTIVE)").

References

1. Bialystok, E.: Bilingual education for young children: review of the effects and consequences. Int. J. Biling. Educ. Biling. **21**(6), 666–679 (2018)
2. Bergeron-Morin, L., Peleman, B., Hulpia, H.: Working with multilingual children and families in early childhood education and care (ECEC): guidelines for continuous professional development of ECEC professionals. Publications Office of the European Union (2023)
3. Kirsch, C., Duarte, J.: Multilingual Education in Europe. In: Chapelle, C.A. (ed.) The Encyclopedia of Applied Linguistics, pp. 1–9. John Wiley & Sons, Ltd (2025)
4. European Parliament: The Treaty on European Union (2012). https://eur-lex.europa.eu/res ource.html?uri=cellar:2bf140bf-a3f8-4ab2-b506-fd71826e6da6.0023.02
5. Kirsch, C., Aleksic, G.: The effect of professional development on multilingual education in early childhood in Luxembourg. Rev. Eur. Stud. **10**(4), 148–163 (2018)
6. Carim, A., Nkomo, S.A.: A systematic literature review of the feasibility of a translanguaging pedagogy in the foundation phase. J. Lang. Lang. Teach. **11**(2), 195–210 (2023)
7. García, O., Wei, L.: Translanguaging. Language, Bilingualism and Education. Palgrave Pivot London, Basingstoke, UK (2014)
8. Cummins, J.: Language, power and pedagogy: bilingual children in the crossfire. Bilingual Education and Bilingualism 23. Multilingual Matters (2000)
9. Kirsch, C., Aleksic, G., Mortini, S., Andersen, K.: Developing multilingual practices in early childhood education through professional development in Luxembourg. Int. Multilingual Res. J. **14**(4), 319–337 (2020)
10. Kirsch, C., Seele, C.: Translanguaging in early childhood education in luxembourg: from practice to Pedagogy. In: Panagiotopoulou, J.A., Rosen, L., Strzykala, J. (eds.) Inclusion, Education and Translanguaging, pp. 63–81. Springer VS Wiesbaden (2020)
11. Repo, E., Aerila, J.-A., Tyrer, M., Harju-Luukkainen, H.: Multilingual learning environments in early childhood education in Finland. J. Early Child. Educ. Res. **13**(1), 221–248 (2024)
12. Kirsch, C.: Monolingual and translingual dialogic reading practices in early childhood education. Creat. Educ. **15**, 2259–2278 (2024)
13. Kirsch, C., Aleksic, G.: Multilingual education in early years in Luxembourg: a paradigm shift? Int. J. Multiling. **18**(4), 534–550 (2021)

14. Konca, A.S.: Digital technology usage of younge children: screen time and families. Early Child. Educ. J. **50**, 1097–1108 (2022)
15. Flewitt, R., Messer, D., Kucirkova, N.: New directions for early literacy in a digital age: the iPad. J. Early Child. Lit. **15**(3), 289–310 (2015)
16. Neumann, M.M.: Using tablets and apps to enhance emergent literacy skills in young children. Early Child. Res. Q. **42**, 239–246 (2018)
17. Palviainen, A.: This Is the normal for us: managing the mobile, multilingual, digital family. In: Wright, L., Higgins, C. (eds.) Diversifying Family Language Policy. Bloomsbury Publishing (2021)
18. Liu, S., Reynold, B.L., Thomas, N., Soyoof, A.: The use of digital technologies to develop young children's language and literacy skills: a systematic review. SAGE Open **14**(1), 1–18 (2024)
19. Chen, J.J., Rivera-Vernazza, D.: Communicating digitally: building preschool teacher-parent partnerships via digital technologies during COVID-19. Early Child. Educ. J. **51**, 1189–1203 (2023)
20. Duolingo: duolingoABC (2026). https://abc.duolingo.com/
21. abblino: Language Learning for Kids (2026)
22. Little Pim: Little Pim (2026). https://www.littlepim.com
23. Dinolingo: dinolingo (2026). https://dinolingo.com
24. Tuunanen, T., Winter, R., vom Brocke, J.: Dealing with complexity in design science research: a methodology using design echelons. MIS Q. **48**(2), 427–458 (2024)
25. Hevner, A., March, S.T., Park, J., Ram, S.: Design science in information systems research. MIS Q. **28**(1), 75–105 (2004)
26. Figma: Figma (2026). https://www.figma.com
27. Myers, M.: Qualitative Research in Business Management. Sage Publications (2019)
28. Myers, M., Newman, M.: The qualitative interview in IS research: examining the craft. Inf. Organ. **17**, 2–26 (2007)
29. Dröge, K.: Datenaufbereitung durch Transkription. In: Gras, J., Schieferdecker, R. (eds.) Einführung in Qualitative Sozialforschung. Grundlagen für Studierende pädagogischer Studiengänge, pp. 224–234. Julius Klinkhardt, Bad Heilbrunn (2025)
30. Sweller, J.: Cognitive load theory. Psychol. Learn. Motiv. **55**, 37–76 (2011)
31. van der Vlies, R.: Digital strategies in education across OECD countries: Exploring education policies on digital technologies. OECD Education Working Papers (2020)
32. Oshechepkova, E., Kartushina, N., Razmakhnina, K.: Bilingualism and development of literacy in children: a systematic review. Psychol. Russ. **16**(1), 3–25 (2023)
33. Clemente-Suárez, V.J., et al.: Digital device usage and childhood cognitive development: exploring effects on cognitive abilities. Children **11** (2024)
34. Radesky, J., Hiniker, A.: From moral panic to systemic change: making child-centered design the default. Int. J. Child-Comput. Interact. **31** (2021)
35. Knauf, H.: Digitalisierung in Kindertageseinrichtungen. Frühe Bildung **9**(2), 99–101 (2020)
36. Gregor, S., Kruse, Chandra Kruse, Leona, Seidel, S.: Research perspectives: the anatomy of a design principle. J. Assoc. Inf. Syst. **21**(6), 1622–1652 (2020)

From Collaboration to Toolkit: Applying eDSR in a Generative AI Knowledge Management Project

Dmitry Kudryavtsev[(⊠)] [iD], Umair Ali Khan [iD], Jukka Remes [iD], and Janne Kauttonen [iD]

Haaga-Helia University of Applied Sciences, Ratapihantie 13, Helsinki, Finland
dmitry.kudryavtsev@haaga-helia.com

Abstract. The creation of complex research-based artefacts for innovation increasingly relies on industry–university collaboration, yet such projects are difficult to organize due to evolving problem spaces, multiple stakeholders, and high technological uncertainty. This paper argues that these conditions require correspondingly complex research methodologies and demonstrates the application of echeloned Design Science Research (eDSR) for planning and coordinating industry-focused research projects. The paper presents the Generative AI-enhanced Knowledge Management (GAIK) project as a use case. GAIK is an ERDF (European Regional Development Fund.) co-research initiative that aims to develop a business-oriented Generative AI toolkit supporting three key knowledge processes: how companies create, synthesize, and access critical business knowledge. The methodological contribution lies in the integration of eDSR with the University–Industry Linkages (UIL) framework. By aligning eDSR iterations and echelons with UIL phases—pre-linkage, establishment, engagement, advancement, and potential latent phases—the paper shows how design knowledge creation and university–industry collaboration can be jointly structured. This integration supports both systematic artefact development and effective collaboration in complex, industry-embedded research projects.

Keywords: design science research · university-industry linkages · generative AI · knowledge management

1 Introduction

The creation of complex research-based artefacts, such as digital toolkits, platforms, and socio-technical systems, has become an important mechanism for fostering innovation in modern economies. Increasingly, such artefacts are developed through industry–university collaboration, as industry seeks access to advanced research expertise and universities aim to translate research outcomes into practical and economic impact. These collaborations are further reinforced by public innovation policies, such as ERDF co-research funding, which explicitly promote joint research and measurable industry uptake.

S. Chatterjee et al. (Eds.): DESRIST 2026, LNCS 16607, pp. 294–305, 2026.
https://doi.org/10.1007/978-3-032-28570-6_23

Despite their importance, industry-focused research projects remain difficult to organize and execute. They operate in open-ended, evolving, and multi-stakeholder settings where problem definitions, objectives, and solutions emerge iteratively. Companies often expect tangible, near-term outcomes, while universities pursue generalized and reusable research results. Managing this tension, while simultaneously addressing technical uncertainty and public funding requirements, poses significant challenges for both research design and collaboration.

This paper argues that the creation of complex research-based artefacts via industry–university collaboration requires correspondingly complex research approaches. In particular, it highlights the value of echeloned Design Science Research (eDSR) as a means of organizing and planning such projects. eDSR enables large, applied research efforts to be decomposed into manageable units while supporting iterative learning, early validation, and cumulative knowledge creation. The paper further demonstrates that aligning eDSR with established University–Industry Linkages (UIL) perspectives helps structure collaboration across different phases of relationship development.

The argument is illustrated through the Generative AI-enhanced Knowledge Management (GAIK) project, an ERDF co-research initiative involving three universities and multiple companies. The project aims to develop a business-oriented Generative AI toolkit that improves how companies create, synthesize, and access critical business knowledge, with a particular focus on supporting small and medium-sized enterprises. Companies participate in the co-development of the toolkit through iterative experimentation, proofs-of-concept, and feedback.

By presenting GAIK as a use case, the paper shows how eDSR, combined with a phased view of UIL, can support both the creation of reusable design knowledge and the practical organization of industry collaboration. In doing so, the paper contributes insights into how complex research-based artefacts can be systematically developed and transferred into practice under real-world constraints.

2 Background

2.1 Economic and Institutional Drivers

Creating complex research-based artefacts requires sustained university–industry cooperation due to both economic imperatives (companies' limited internal R&D capacity and competitive pressures) and institutional policy drivers. European innovation policy explicitly supports this cooperation under ERDF 2021–2027. The cooperation is monitored through various indicators, including enterprises cooperating with research organizations, and SMEs introducing product or process innovation. These indicators are linked to Policy Objective 1 of Regulation (EU) 2021/1060, signalling that universities should contribute research-based knowledge and companies adopt innovations through collaboration.

2.2 Challenges of the Applied Industry-Focused Research Projects

Creating complex artefacts through university–industry collaboration is challenging because the work is undertaken in open-ended, evolving, multi-stakeholder settings.

Ambiguous and evolving problem spaces. Collaborative innovation projects rarely begin with fully specified problems. Partners bring distinct perspectives, leading to shifting definitions of needs and objectives. Coordination requires continuous reframing of problem–solution boundaries rather than reliance on fixed early specifications (Tuunanen et al, 2024).

Limits of linear development models. Sequential approaches are insufficient for complex DSR projects, as they cannot adequately address evolving problem and solution spaces (Tuunanen et al, 2024). Managing complexity benefits from decomposing the overall effort into discrete, manageable "research chunks" or intervention cycles (Mullarkey, Hevner, 2019).

Managing complexity across artefacts, iterations, and abstraction levels. Complex industry-embedded projects produce many intermediate artefacts (e.g., requirements, design principles, prototypes, demonstrations) before a mature solution emerges. Organizing, validating, and communicating these contributions requires decomposing the overall effort into smaller, self-contained units of design knowledge rather than treating the artefact as a single monolithic outcome (Mullarkey, Hevner, 2019; Tuunanen et al, 2024).

Hard to find balance between industry needs and research goals. Many companies expect a ready-made or quick solution, while universities are interested in research results that are available to the public, generalized, reusable, and innovative, addressing typical business problems (Kudryavtsev et al., 2025).

Value proposition articulation and early engagement. An additional challenge concerns articulating a clear value proposition for industry partners. The return on cooperation with universities is not always evident to companies (except for recruiting students), as such cooperation costs time and other resources, and the value is not always clear. (Kudryavtsev et al., 2025).

2.3   Methodological Foundations (DSR, eDSR, UIC Phases)

Design Science Research (DSR) Provides the foundational paradigm for creating research-based artefacts addressing real-world organizational and societal problems. Peffers et al. (2007) conceptualize DSR as six core activities – problem identification, objectives definition, design and development, demonstration, evaluation, and communication – emphasizing that the process is inherently iterative with multiple possible entry points.

Echeloned DSR (eDSR) Extends DSR for large-scale, industry-embedded research programs involving evolving problem and solution spaces, multiple stakeholders, and continuous change (Tuunanen et al, 2024). eDSR introduces a hierarchical organizing logic through three dimensions: *layers* (macro-level design logic, corresponding to five echelon types: problem analysis, objectives/requirements definition, design and development, demonstration, evaluation); *strata* (levels of abstraction over time, corresponding to project iterations—not linear phases); and *echelons* (self-contained, logically coherent units of design knowledge combining specific activities with validation and intermediate artefacts). This enables nonlinear iteration, early and continuous validation, parallel work, and cumulative knowledge accumulation (Fig. 1).

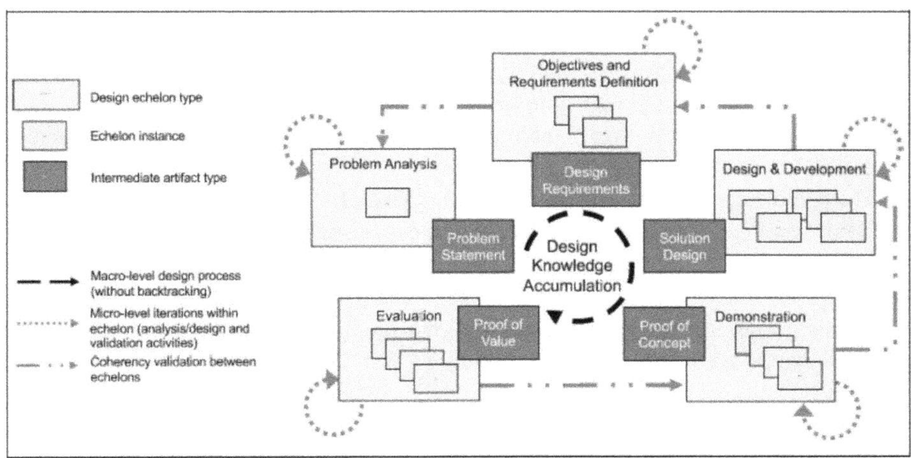

Fig. 1. The eDSR Metamodel (Tuunanen et al, 2024)

University–Industry Linkages.
The collaboration context for creating complex artefacts is addressed by the University–Industry Linkages (UIL) framework proposed by Plewa et al. (2013), which conceptualizes UIL as a dynamic, relational process rather than a transactional exchange. UILs evolve through phases such as pre-linkage, establishment, engagement, advancement, and potential latent phases, with each phase characterized by different success drivers, including trust, communication, mutual understanding, and individual actor commitment.

3 GAIK Use Case

3.1 Generative AI-Enhanced Knowledge Management (GAIK) Project

Generative AI has significant potential to increase the productivity of knowledge work. However, tangible business value from Generative AI implementation projects is still limited. According to BCG's report (de Bellefonds et al, 2024), "Only 26% of companies have advanced beyond the proof-of-concept stage to generate value." Similarly, an MIT report (Challapally et al, 2025) states, "Despite \$30–40 billion in enterprise investment into GenAI, 95% of organizations are getting zero return." Adopting Generative AI and creating value from it is especially challenging for small and medium-sized enterprises (SMEs), which lack the technical expertise and capabilities to implement GenAI solutions effectively. Our AI consultancy in the Finnish AI Region (FAIR)[1] project and

---

[1] https://www.fairedih.fi/.

analysis of consultancy data show that most companies lack the technical expertise to implement AI ideas (Khan et al., 2025).

To address this issue, we initiated Generative AI-enhanced Knowledge Management (GAIK) project[2] (Feb 2025-Jan 2027), which is aimed at developing a business-oriented GenAI toolkit that will improve three knowledge processes: how companies create, synthesize, and access critical business knowledge. It will enable companies and technology providers to develop and implement Generative AI solutions using business data, using reusable and tested toolkit components: software modules & components, no-code assets, management frameworks and templates, process models, guidelines, templates, and reusable knowledge models.

The project consortium includes 3 universities and 4 companies. Haaga-Helia University of Applied Sciences (HHUAS) coordinates the project and is mainly involved in the toolkit design and interaction with companies. The University of Helsinki (UH) and Tampere University (TAU) primarily provide expertise in specific areas, more specifically, in large language models and computational linguistics (UH) and the business value of generative AI for knowledge management (TAU). Our consortium is also extending cooperation with solution user companies, tech providers and international partners.

3.2 GenAI Toolkit as an iS Artefact

To enable reuse and guide the development and implementation of GenAI, we are creating a knowledge-focused toolkit for SMEs within the GAIK project. This toolkit applies a knowledge management perspective for GenAI solution development and implementation by helping to leverage the company's own knowledge assets and improve knowledge processes (capture, synthesis, and access).

The key requirements of the toolkit include: 1. Combination of business- and technical-level support; 2. Support for the whole life-cycle: requirements analysis, development, implementation & operation; 3. Suitability for SMEs with low AI maturity and limited tech expertise.

The GenAI toolkit design principles are presented in (Kudryavtsev et al., 2025b). Review and limitations of existing frameworks, methods and tools for supporting GenAI solution development and implementation are also presented in this paper.

The GAIK Toolkit is structured into six layers: Strategy, Requirements, Business, Implementation, Security & Compliance, and Guidance. Together, these layers cover the full lifecycle from planning to deployment and governance.

For example, the Business layer includes tools such as the GenAI product canvas for describing and structuring use cases and workflows, while the Implementation layer provides both code-based modules and no-code assets (e.g., prompt templates) to support solution development, integration, and evaluation.

For a more detailed toolkit description, see the toolkit website: https://gaik-project. github.io/gaik-toolkit/

---

[2] https://gaik.ai/.

3.3 ERDF Co-Research Funding Requirements

We selected the Innovation and Competence Networks National Theme Research Project Call 1/2024 as the most suitable funding instrument for our project. The call supported strengthening research and innovation capabilities, promoting the adoption of advanced technologies, and is part of the Innovation and Skills in Finland 2021–2027 programme funded by the European Regional Development Fund (ERDF).

It aims to promote new knowledge-intensive innovation and business ecosystems, renew business-driven expertise, and improve the faster use of research results in companies' operations and competence development.

The call particularly values projects that support the development, piloting, and commercialization of SME products, services, materials, or production methods; respond to business-driven RDI needs; and strengthen collaboration between research organizations and industry.

Call's Output indicators include companies cooperating with research institutes, co-development platforms and networks, and companies participating in co-development. Result indicators include SMEs innovating in products or processes, innovations and services developed through networks and ecosystems, and companies making use of RDI infrastructure.

3.4 Co-Development with Companies

Companies are involved in the co-development of the toolkit with universities.

We have two categories of cooperating companies: 1. Technology users (companies from various industries using AI and other IT to develop their products, services and processes), 2. Technology providers (including technology developers, vendors, IT consultants).

Technology user companies will primarily use the toolkit to create generative AI solutions for their knowledge processes. Technology providers will help us (universities) to develop some toolkit components. Technology user companies are in the focus of our cooperation. We have two cohorts of technology user companies:

Cohort 1. 4 companies are involved in co-development with us (universities). Analysis of their requirements for GenAI solutions for knowledge tasks helped us formulate the requirements for the toolkit. Design and development of the solutions for these companies helped us identify the required building blocks and create them. Evaluation and testing of the solutions helped us to prepare evaluation methods that can be adapted and included in the toolkit. During the first iteration, we attracted the interest of such companies. During the second iteration, we established cooperation with interested companies and signed agreements with them. During the third iteration, we organised joint work with these companies - planned the projects, defined the deliverables, timeline, responsibilities, and data management practices. During the 4th iteration, we started to produce tangible results for companies (Proofs-of-Concept) and evaluate these results together with them.

Cohort 2. These technology user companies will join our project at a later stage. They will use the first versions of our toolkit, which are also involved in co-development, but mainly through their feedback on how it can be improved. We aim to attract these companies during iteration 4 through the toolkit launch event.

Technology providers (including technology developers, vendors, and IT consultants) will help our consortium to develop the toolkit by producing or contributing to several toolkit components. This contribution will be implemented in 2026 (Q3) as an outsourcing activity.

We aim to establish a sustainable community of users and developers of the GAIK open-source toolkit. The core of the community will consist of project consortium members (3 universities and 4 companies from the first cohort), cohort 2 technology-user companies, and partner technology provider companies. The "second circle" of the community will include interested companies and universities. The project's outcomes will be shared with industry stakeholders through the community (network of professionals) established around GenAI-enhanced knowledge management. This community will further promote practical applications of the toolkit and provide a platform for knowledge exchange and networking.

3.5   University-Industry Collaboration Challenges in the GAIK Project

The GAIK project amplifies general collaboration challenges through its specific context. Problem spaces are especially ambiguous: companies differ widely in AI maturity, data readiness, and understanding of GenAI, requiring continuous refinement of use cases and requirements. Linear development is ill-suited, as rapid GenAI advances require frequent reassessment of technical feasibility and design choices. Managing complexity across artefacts, iterations, and abstraction levels is challenging–aligning the toolkit components (software modules, guidelines, templates, process models, evaluation methods etc.) across iterations while ensuring coherence and reusability demands sustained coordination. Balancing company needs, research goals, and funding demands is challenging. Companies want quick, practical results, while universities focus on broader, reusable knowledge. Meanwhile, ERDF funding requires clear industry collaboration and measurable innovation.

3.6   GAIK Project Iterations and Echelons

The echeloned design science research (eDSR) methodology was applied to organize and plan the GAIK project. The Fig. 2 depicts a four-iteration (eDSR) program in which each iteration (I1–I4) is initiated by explicit objectives and operationalized through design echelons, research activities, and progressively evolving university–industry linkages. The objectives are primarily aligned with the UIL success drivers for the corresponding UIL phase. The appendix provides details on the milestones and dissemination materials for each iteration.

Companies collaborate with universities to co-develop a generative AI (GenAI) toolkit for knowledge processes. Consistent with Plewa et al.'s UIL framework (2013), cooperation primarily evolved through the pre-linkage, establishment, and engagement phases, whereas later phases remain prospective at the current stage of the project.

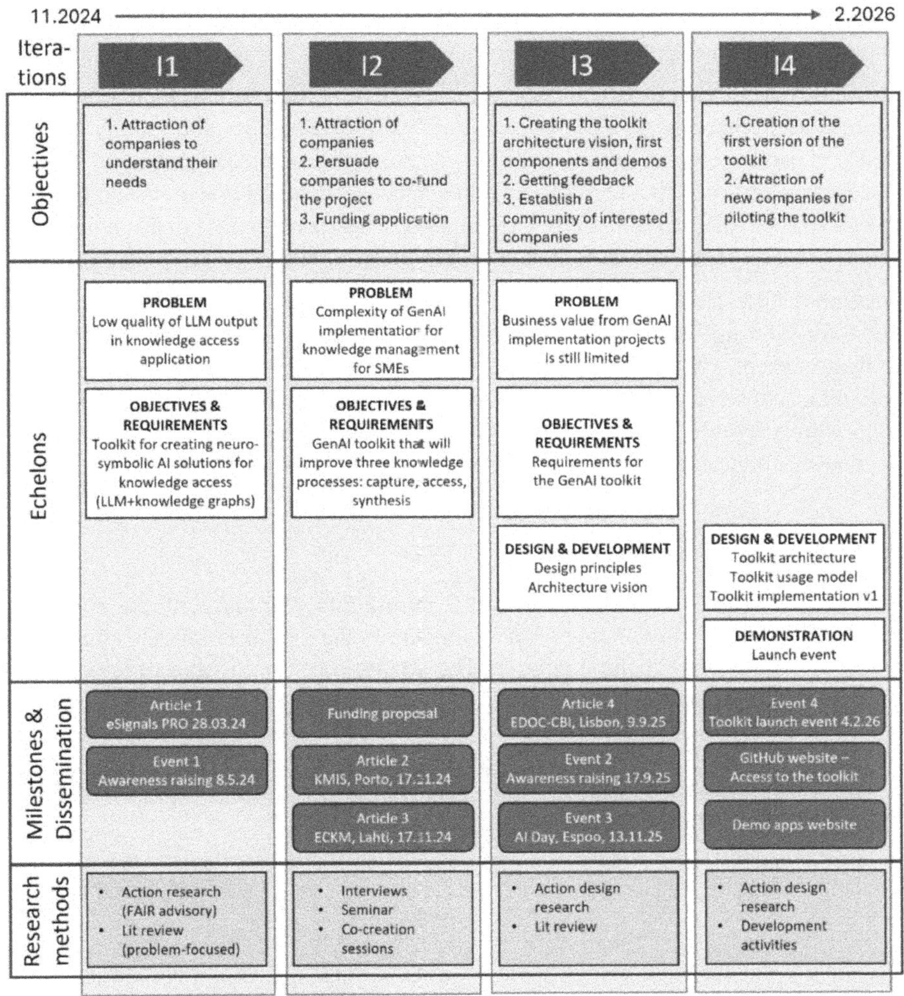

Fig. 2. GAIK project iterations and echelons (till 4.2.2026)

Iteration 1 (I1): Pre-linkage and problem framing focused on attracting companies and understanding their needs in GenAI-supported knowledge work. The main activities included problem analysis, initial requirements definition, literature review, advisory work, and informal discussions with companies. Cooperation at this stage was exploratory and informal. UIL phase–pre-linkage. The main milestones and dissemination results are presented in the appendix (see Article 1 and Event 1).

Iteration 2 (I2): Project establishment focused on formalizing collaboration, securing company commitment and co-funding, and obtaining external funding. Industry needs were translated into structured toolkit requirements through interviews, seminars, and co-creation sessions. With Cohort 1 companies, cooperation moved into the establishment phase of the UIL framework through formal agreements, defined roles, and shared project planning.

Iteration 3 (I3): Joint design and early engagement focused on developing the toolkit vision, initial components, early demonstrations, and a broader community of interested companies. Universities and Cohort 1 companies worked together on concrete projects, and these collaborations directly informed the identification of the toolkit building blocks. UIL phase with cohort 1 companies: Engagement. This phase emphasized design, development, demonstration, and early dissemination.

Iteration 4 (I4): Delivering the first full version of the toolkit and attracting new companies for piloting. With Cohort 1 companies, the universities develop and evaluate proof-of-concept solutions, while the results help define and produce components for the toolkit. At the same time, Cohort 2 companies are engaged through the toolkit launch event, mainly by testing early versions and providing feedback for further refinement. UIL phases: Engagement for Cohort 1 companies, and Pre-linkage with Cohort 2.

3.7 Future Plans and Roadmap

We plan to have 3 extra iterations of eDSR during this year and until the end of the project. These iterations will produce new versions of the toolkit and should attract more companies to the GAIK community (see Fig. 3). Moving from toolkit development to its application is essential.

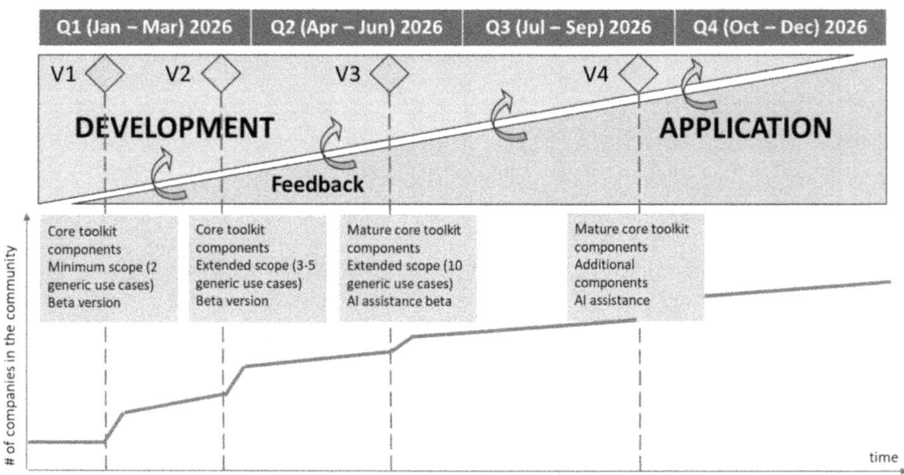

Fig. 3. Roadmap for the GAIK toolkit development and adoption

4 Theoretical and Practical Implications

This study contributes to design science research by showing that artefact development and collaboration processes can be co-structured through the alignment of eDSR and UIL. While eDSR organizes the creation and validation of design knowledge, UIL explains the evolution of collaboration relationships. Their integration introduces a synchronization mechanism in which design iterations are aligned with collaboration phases, enabling more effective coordination of stakeholder engagement, expectation management, and knowledge production in complex projects.

We can suggest the following steps for successful university-industry cooperation during the eDSR project based on the GAIK project experience:

Step 1. Identification of the UIL phase/-s for each iteration (stratas in eDSR).
Step 2. Definition of UIL success and success drivers based on the corresponding framework (Plewa et al., 2013) for the identified UIL phase and project iteration.
Step 3. Alignment of R&D project objectives and plan with UIL success definition and its drivers.

In case of a problem-centered DSR project, step 1 can be assisted by the following reference iterations and mappings (Table 1).

Table 1. Links between DSR project iterations, eDSR echelon types and UIL phases

Iteration and project stages	Main layers or echelon types in eDSR	UIL phase/-s
Iteration 1: Project initiation and consortium building	Problem statement v1 & Design requirements v1 (preliminary)	Pre-linkage phase
Iteration 2: Project proposal preparation (funding application)	Problem statement v2 & Design requirements v2 (more mature and detailed)	Establishment phase
Iteration 3: Project delivery, artifact development	Solution design, Proof of Concept, Proof of value	Engagement phase
Iteration 4: Project delivery, artifact usage and adoption (with more users)	Solution design (improvement), Proof of Concept, Proof of value	Pre-linkage phase, Establishment phase, Engagement phase
Iteration 5: Follow-up project/-s initiation	New Problem statement & corresponding Design requirements	Advancement phase

Each iteration may include sub-iterations, if needed. Sub-iterations will help to deepen knowledge (e.g. move from high-level vision to a detailed implementation).

5 Conclusions

This paper examined the creation of complex research-based artefacts through industry–university collaboration and argued that such efforts require correspondingly complex research methodologies. Using the Generative AI-enhanced Knowledge Management (GAIK) project as a use case, the paper demonstrated how echeloned Design Science Research (eDSR) can be applied to plan, organize, and coordinate a multi-year, industry-embedded research program under public co-research funding conditions.

The main contribution of the paper lies in the integration of eDSR with the University–Industry Linkages (UIL) framework, showing how design echelons and iterations can be aligned with evolving phases of collaboration. This integration supports both systematic design knowledge creation and the effective organization of university–industry collaboration, addressing challenges related to ambiguity, complexity, and stakeholder alignment.

The GAIK project illustrates how this combined approach enables the development of a reusable, business-oriented Generative AI toolkit while maintaining research rigor and industry relevance. Future work will focus on advancing the toolkit, expanding the user community, and further evaluating the proposed methodological integration across additional industry contexts.

Acknowledgments. The present work is part of the Generative AI-Enhanced Knowledge Management in Business (GAIK) project, which is co-funded by the European Union (European Regional Development Fund).

Appendix. GAIK Project Main Dissemination Materials

Iteration 1:
Article 1: Khan, U. A., Kudryavtsev, D. & Kauttonen, J. (28.3.2024) Enhancing generative AI for accessing enterprise knowledge. eSignals PRO. Haaga-Helia University of Applied Science. Helsinki. Accessed 28.3.2024. http://urn.fi/URN:NBN:fi-fe2 024032813633
Event 1: Awareness-raising seminar "generative AI-enhanced knowledge management in business" was organized at the 25+ onsite participants and 30+ online participants attended the seminar. 25+ onsite participants and 30+ online participants attended the seminar.
Iteration 2:
Article 2: Kudryavtsev D., Khan U. and Kauttonen J. (2024). Transforming Knowledge Management Using Generative AI: From Theory to Practice. In Proceedings of the 16th International Joint Conference on Knowledge Discovery, Knowledge Engineering and Knowledge Management - Volume 3: KMIS; ISBN 978-989-758-716-0, SciTePress, pages 362-370. https://doi.org/10.5220/0013071400003838
Article 3: Kudryavtsev, D., Khan, U. A., Kauttonen, J., Kaski, T., Remes, J., Wuokko, A., Yangarber, R., Pivovarova, L., Wu, Y., Seppänen, M., Myllärniemi, J., & Sorri, K. (2025). Building a Generative AI toolkit for leveraging knowledge processes: The GAIK project report. 26th European Conference on Knowledge Management (ECKM 2025), Lahti, Finland. pp. 1317-1321.
Iteration 3:
Article 4: Kudryavtsev, D., Khan, U. A., Remes J., Kauttonen J. (2025). Reuse and guidance for generative AI solution development and implementation: Knowledge management perspective. EDOC-CBI Forum 2025. 29th International Conference on Enterprise Design, Operations, and Computing & 27th International Conference on Business Informatics, Lisbon, Portugal. In press.

Event 2: GAIK Event 17th of September 2025 https://gaik.ai/events/gaik-event-2025/

Iteration 4:

Event 3: GenAI Toolkit Launch – Feb 4, 2026 https://gaik.ai/events/gaik-toolkit-off icially-launched-presentations-demos-and-materials-available/

GitHub website: https://gaik-project.github.io/gaik-toolkit/ for the GAIK toolkit access.

Demo apps website: https://gaik-demo.2.rahtiapp.fi/, which shows the results of the GAIK toolkit usage.

References

Annex I of Regulation (EU) 2021/1060, of 24 June 2021 Common output and result indicators (2021–2027 period) URL: https://eur-lex.europa.eu/legal-content/EN/TXT/HTML/?uri=CELEX:32021R1058&from=EN#d1e32-83-1

Challapally A., Pease C., Raskar R., Chari P.: The GenAI Divide-State of AI in Business 2025. MIT Nanda (2025)

de Bellefonds, et al.: Where's the Value in AI? BCG report (2024). https://www.bcg.com/publications/2024/wheres-value-in-ai

Khan U.A., Kauttonen J., Kudryavtsev, D.: AI adoption in finnish SMEs: key findings from AI consultancy at a European digital innovation hub. Proceedings of the IEEE 23rd World Symposium on Applied Machine Intelligence and Informatics (SAMI 2025), January 23–25 2025, Stará Lesná, Slovakia. P. pp. 465–470 (2025). https://doi.org/10.1109/sami63904.2025.10883271

Kudryavtsev, D., Khan U. A., Kauttonen J., Kaski T.: Bridging the academia-industry gap by a co-design and co-research approach for generative AI adoption. UAS J.–J. Finnish Univ. Appl. Sci. 1 (2025a). https://urn.fi/URN:NBN:fi-fe2025031819161

Kudryavtsev, D., Khan, U. A., Remes J., Kauttonen J.: Reuse and guidance for generative AI solution development and implementation: knowledge management perspective. EDOC-CBI Forum 2025. 29th International Conference on Enterprise Design, Operations, and Computing & 27th International Conference on Business Informatics, Lisbon, Portugal. In press (2025b)

Mullarkey, M.T., Hevner, A.R.: An elaborated action design research process model. Eur. J. Inf. Syst. **28**(1), 6–20 (2019)

Peffers, K., Tuunanen, T., Rothenberger, M.A., Chatterjee, S.: A design science research methodology for information systems research. J. Manag. Inf. Syst. **24**(3), 45–77 (2007)

Plewa, C., Korff, N., Johnson, C., Macpherson, G., Baaken, T., Rampersad, G.C.: The evolution of university–industry linkages: a framework. J. Eng. Technol. Manage. **30**, 21–44 (2013)

Tuunanen, T., Winter, R., Brocke, J.V.: Dealing with complexity in design science research: a methodology using design echelons. MIS Q. **48**(2), 427–458 (2024)

Prototypes Track

Navigating Complexities at Home: A Residential Decision Support System for Flexible Electricity Consumption

Lorenzo Matthias Burcheri[✉][ID], Hicham Rahali[ID], Mehdi Testouri[ID], Raphael Frank[ID], and Gilbert Fridgen[ID]

Interdisciplinary Centre of Security, Reliability and Trust, University of Luxembourg, Kirchberg-Luxembourg, Luxembourg
`lorenzo.burcheri@uni.lu`

Abstract. Households are increasingly expected to adjust electricity use in response to dynamic system conditions, yet most lack the information needed to interpret fluctuating prices, carbon intensities, and generation patterns. Addressing this gap, we designed a smartphone application that simplifies, contextualizes, and personalizes key system signals to support intuitive household decision-making. Following a multi-year design science research process, we developed a customizable master indicator, complementary single indicators, and alert-based cues. We evaluated these features in a staggered field experiment with high-frequency smart-meter data from 23 households in Luxembourg. The results provide exploratory evidence that environmental cues can activate selective pro-environmental behavior, price responsiveness remains limited in high-income contexts, and urgent, risk-framed signals trigger stronger behavioral responses than encouragement-based cues. The study advances understanding of transparency-based digital interventions in demand response settings and offers actionable guidance for practitioners and policymakers seeking to make dynamic consumption more accessible.

Keywords: Energy Transition · Demand Response · Residential Decision Support System

1 Introduction

Europes decarbonization efforts increasingly depend on households adjusting electricity use in response to dynamic system signals such as hourly prices and carbon intensities. This marks a shift away from long-standing flat-rate consumption and requires consumers to assume a more active role in managing demand [12]. Prior research highlights information as a central enabler of such behavior: households need transparent, comprehensible, and actionable system information to identify opportunities for efficient and sustainable consumption [4,9]. However, despite growing policy interest in demand response, most consumers still receive limited guidance in interpreting fluctuating prices, carbon intensities,

S. Chatterjee et al. (Eds.): DESRIST 2026, LNCS 16607, pp. 309–315, 2026.
https://doi.org/10.1007/978-3-032-28570-6_24

or generation patterns. Energy-management assets—such as rooftop PV, home batteries, or automated control systems—are often positioned as technological solutions to support this transition. Yet adoption remains limited, amongst others, due to high up-front investment costs [11]. As a result, many households lack accessible tools to navigate the complexity of dynamic electricity systems, regardless of whether they possess such technologies. To address this practical gap, we developed a smartphone app that simplifies and personalizes key system signals, such as hourly CO2 intensity and retail prices, to support routine consumption decisions. By contextualizing system dynamics, the app helps users align routines with environmental and economic objectives. We evaluated the app in an eight-week field experiment in Luxembourg in 2025.

2   Problem Awareness and Suggestion Phase

We source the problem statements, resulting design requirements and guidance from an earlier work by [1][1] following a five-step DSR model according to [7] and a design principle development approach based on [5] (Table 1).

Table 1. Problem Statements (P) and Resulting Design Requirements (DR).

Problem Statement	Design Requirement
P1. High perceived tariff complexity in dynamic electricity tariffs overwhelms consumers, reduces their ability to process information and make economically beneficial decisions, increases perceived risks and lowers self-confidence [8].	**DR1.** Simplification as means to reduce complexity of decision-relevant information signals.
P2. Households struggle to adjust their energy use to dynamic system conditions because information is often untimely, insufficiently contextualized, and not delivered in a format that supports immediate decision-making [13].	**DR2.** Timely availability of contextualised data in an understandable format.
P3. Households often fail to translate information into actual behavioral change because, despite understanding dynamic pricing signals, they lack the practical guidance, knowledge, and means to act on them effectively [6].	**DR3.** Framing information actionable so that households can infer adequate demand response.
P4. Individuals often struggle to engage with dynamic electricity tariffs because complex or poorly designed visualizations exceed many users graphical literacy, and thus increase the cognitive burden of interpreting dynamic information [10].	**DR4.** Creating infographics or visual cues that are intuitive and interpretable.
P5. Households differ widely in their price sensitivity, environmental values, and motivational drivers, meaning that persuasive energy interfaces must accommodate heterogeneous preferences or should allow personalisation [2].	**DR5.** Building features that are customisable and thus tailor information to the respective user.

---

[1] In [1], concrete design cues were derived from a large-scale consumer survey and discrete choice experiments. We iteratively refined the prototype through a series of workshops with business practitioners.

3   Development Phase

The research team opted for an Android/iOS application that provides real-time information, particularly for contexts in which users can remotely operate appliances via control apps (e.g., initiating a preset washing cycle). The prototype is illustrated in Fig. 1. A prototype video is provided through the open research repository Zenodo[2].

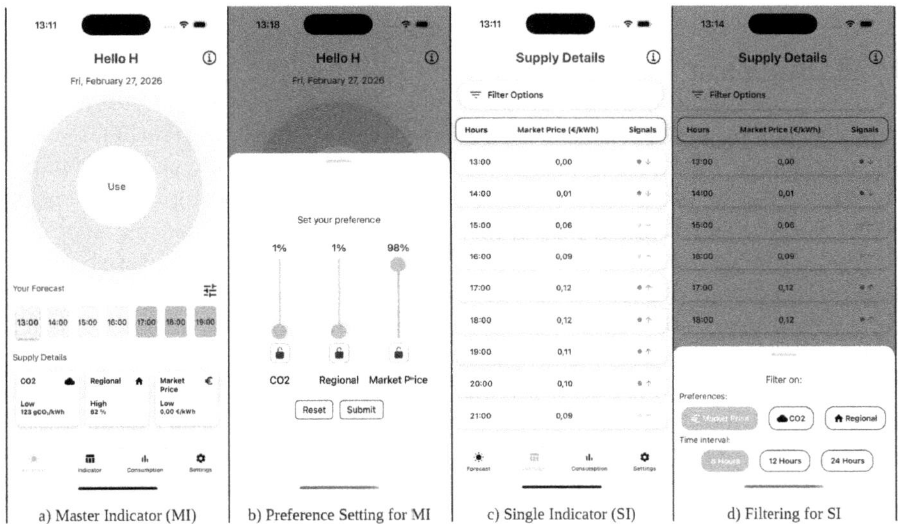

Fig. 1. Application User Interface: Master Indicator, Preference Setting, Single Indicator and Filtering.

To reduce the cognitive burden associated with interpreting volatile energy data[3], we designed an intuitive master indicator that aggregates key energy information into a single hourly signal (Fig. 1a). Using a traffic-light scheme (green, yellow, red), complemented by textual labels (Use, Moderate, Avoid) and a pulsing animation as a non-color cue, the indicator enables immediate and intuitive decision-making while supporting users with color-vision limitations. The indicator is fully customizable: households can weight the electricity price, CO2 impact, and regional energy production according to their preferences (Fig. 1b)[4]. The system recalculates the hourly values accordingly and provides short-term forecasts to support anticipatory planning. The system also issues actionable

---

[2] Accessible via https://doi.org/10.5281/zenodo.19129091

[3] Data is sourced from ENTSO-E, with Energy-Charts, serving as a fallback. For variables not publicly available, such as hourly CO2 intensity of the electricity mix, we developed machine learning models to generate accurate predictions.

[4] If users assign too little preference towards the price, the system will present a warning that the preference setting could lead to economically disadvantageous outcomes.

notifications based on the personalized master indicator, alerting users to favorable or unfavorable consumption windows within the upcoming six hours.

Real-time consumption feedback from a smart-meter-enabled data pipeline further contextualizes these signals for a household, improving interpretability and user engagement. Beyond the master indicator, the interface offers optional detailed views of the underlying single indicators (prices, CO_2 impact, and regional generation shares), presented in color-coded tables that are configurable according to users' preferred time resolutions (Fig. 1c and d). Arrow-based cues highlight hourly changes for users with color-vision or numeracy constraints.

4 Evaluation Phase

To assess the impact of the application, we used a staggered treatment-control group rollout of features over two months in Luxembourg, allowing us to compare the same users before and after receiving each feature, isolating feature-specific effects while controlling for user-specific factors and common time shocks. A two-week pre-treatment period ensured baseline comparability, satisfying the parallel trend assumption for a treatment-control group analysis. After excluding inactive users and a few data-quality outliers, the final analytical sample comprised 23 households. Participating households were reimbursed based on their price-responsive behavior through vouchers at the end of the experiment, mirroring a realistic dynamic pricing scenario. Although the sample was small, high-frequency, real-time household-level data (15 min consumption data gathered through the Smarty+ IoT Device) support the exploratory analysis. We evaluated three feature types: (1) Single Indicators (SIs), (2) the Master Indicator (MI), and (3) alert notifications. First, we applied a Difference-in-Differences analysis to estimate overall treatment effects [3].

Second, we used a high-dimensional fixed-effects regression model to capture the behavioral responses according to the type of information that was provided through the single and master indicators (favorable-green signal vs. unfavorable-red signal). The SIs produced a significant cumulative increase of 44.33 kWh per user over the course of the experiment. The MI showed an average cummulative, but non-significant, 8.5 kWh reduction and should be treated as qualitative trend conditional on the rather small sample size (Table 2).

Table 2. Overall Treatment Effects in kWh of the Single and Master Indicator.

Treatment	Coefficient	Robust Std. Error
Single Indicator	+44.33***	15.01
Master Indicator	−8.50	23.17

Significance Levels: *** p < 0.01 ** p < 0.05 * p < 0.1.

Detailed hourly regression models found qualitative, immediate reductions after alert notifications: on average −1 kWh in the first hour and −0.5 kWh in the second, fading out thereafter (Fig. 2). This suggests time-discounting behavior, with users prioritizing immediate alerts over those concerning later hours.

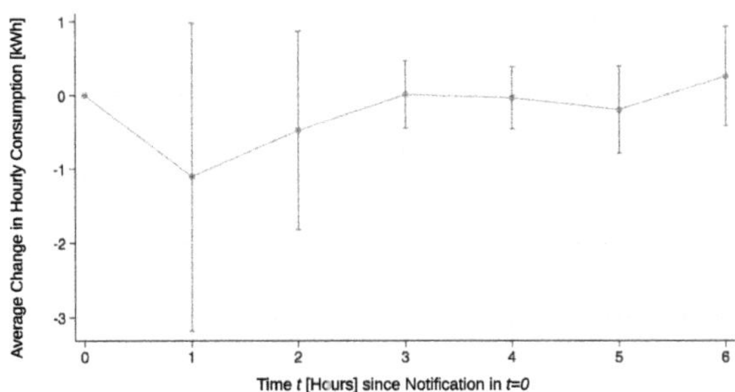

Fig. 2. Average Change in Hourly Consumption in kWh after Receiving an Alert.

Most individual SIs were not statistically significant (Table 3), except for the green CO2 signal, which indicated a highly significant hourly increase in consumption by 0.072 kWh—being the driver of the overall consumption increase observed in Table 2. Users increased consumption during low-carbon periods, while high-carbon periods showed only weak, non-significant conservation tendencies. This suggests that pro-environmental motivations were selective and may exhibit moral licensing effects. Price and Regional Share SIs had no significant effects, consistent with low price salience in high-income settings and Luxembourgs long-standing import dependence. Disaggregating the MI revealed that red phases produced a significant hourly reduction of 61 Wh, while green phases showed no significant effect. The asymmetry indicates that urgent, risk-framed cues trigger stronger responses than encouragement-based cues.

Table 3. Hourly Effects in kWh of the Single and Master Indicator Signals.

Treatment	Coefficient	Robsut Std. Error
Red Price (SI)	−0.003	0.046
Green Price (SI)	−0.011	0.049
Red CO2 Impact (SI)	−0.280	0.022
Green CO2 Impact (SI)	+0.072***	0.023
Red Regional Share (SI)	−0.010	0.049
Green Regional Share (SI)	+0.035	0.041
Red Signal (MI)	−0.061*	0.035
Green Signal (MI)	−0.015	0.033

Significance Levels: *** $p < 0.01$ ** $p < 0.05$ * $p < 0.1$.

5   Conclusion

5.1   Relevance for Research and Limitations

This DSR study advances energy-informatics research by showing how CO2 signals, visualizations, and salient alerts influence household behavior in dynamic consumption settings. Using a staggered field experiment with high-frequency smart-meter data, the study uncovers selective pro-environmental action, limited price responsiveness in high-income contexts, and the impact of urgency-based cues. These findings refine current understandings of digital nudging in demand-response environments. Given the small sample, additional evaluations are needed to strengthen statistical power and generalizability.

5.2   Relevance for Practice

For practitioners, this study illustrates that transparent user-centric information systems can make dynamic electricity environments actionable for households. Environmental signals, intuitive visualizations, and timely alert notifications could effectively prompt flexible consumption, indicating economic viability for emerging dynamic tariff models such as those of Octopus Energy or Tibber. In addition, policymakers could enhance consumer engagement by promoting user-centric information services and by implementing alert-based congestion-management signals that enable rapid and targeted interventions during grid outages.

Acknowledgments. This research was funded in part by the Luxembourg National Research Fund (FNR) and PayPal, PEARL grant reference 13342933/Gilbert Fridgen. The authors gratefully acknowledge the Fondation Enovos under the aegis of the Fondation de Luxembourg in the frame of the philanthropic funding for the research project LetzPower!.

References

1. Burcheri, L.M., Fridgen, G., Marxen, H., Kumari, J.: Towards a persuasive decision support interface for the sustainable use of dynamic electricity tariffs. In: Chatterjee, S., Vom Brocke, J., Anderson, R. (eds.) Local Solutions for Global Challenges, vol. 15704, pp. 282–297. Springer (2025)
2. Buryk, S., Mead, D., Mourato, S., Torriti, J.: Investigating preferences for dynamic electricity tariffs: the effect of environmental and system benefit disclosure. Energy Policy **80**, 190–195 (2015)
3. de Chaisemartin, C., et al.: Using did_multiplegt_dyn to estimate event-study effects in complex designs: overview, and four examples based on real datasets. arXiv (2025). https://doi.org/10.48550/arXiv.2510.19426
4. Dalén, A., Krämer, J.: Towards a user-centered feedback design for smart meter interfaces to support efficient energy-use choices: a design science approach. Bus. Inf. Syst. Eng. **59**(5), 361–373 (2017)

5. Gregor, S., Kruse, L., Seidel, S.: Research perspectives: the anatomy of a design principle. J. Assoc. Inf. Syst. **21**(6) (2020)
6. Jessoe, K., Rapson, D.: Knowledge is (less) power: experimental evidence from residential energy use. Am. Econ. Rev. **104**(4), 1417–1438 (2014)
7. Kuechler, B., Vaishnavi, V.: On theory development in design science research: anatomy of a research project. Eur J. Inf. Syst. **17**(5) (2008)
8. Layer, P., Feurer, S., Jochem, P.: Perceived price complexity of dynamic energy tariffs: an investigation of antecedents and consequences. Energy Policy **106** (2017)
9. Lossin, F., Kozlovskiy, I., Sodenkamp, M., Staake, T.: Incentives to go green: an empicircal investigation of monetary and symbolic rewards to motivate energy savings. In: Proceedings of the Twenty-Fourth European Conference on Information Systems (ECIS), İstanbul, Turkey (2016)
10. Reis, I.F.G., Lopes, M.A.R., Antunes, C.H.: Energy literacy: an overlooked concept to end users' adoption of time-differentiated tariffs. Energ. Effi. **14**(4) (2021)
11. Rezvani, Z., Jansson, J., Bodin, J.: Advances in consumer electric vehicle adoption research: a review and research agenda. Transp. Res. Part D: Transp. Environ. **34**, 122–136 (2015)
12. Schlereth, C., Skiera, B., Schulz, F.: Why do consumers prefer static instead of dynamic pricing plans? An empirical study for a better understanding of the low preferences for time-variant pricing plans. Eur. J. Oper. Res. **269**(3), 1165–1179 (2018)
13. Tiefenbeck, V., Wörner, A., Schöb, S., Fleisch, E., Staake, T.: Real-time feedback reduces energy consumption among the broader public without financial incentives. Nat. Energy **4**(10), 831–832 (2019)

Selbstlernen.app 2.0 – A Feedback-Oriented Mobile Application for Supporting Self-regulated Learning in Higher Education

Madeleine Dormeyer[1] and Alexander Herwix[2,3]([✉])

[1] Faculty of Mathematics and Natural Sciences, University of Cologne, Cologne, Germany
`mdormeye@smail.uni-koeln.de`
[2] Faculty of Management, Economics and Social Sciences, University of Cologne, Cologne, Germany
[3] Department of Applied Information Technology, University of Gothenburg, Gothenburg, Sweden
`herwix@wiso.uni-koeln.de`

Abstract. Self-regulated learning (SRL) is a key prerequisite for academic success in higher education, yet many students struggle to plan, monitor, and adapt their learning processes effectively. While digital learning environments generate rich behavioural data, existing mobile and learning analytics-based solutions often address only isolated phases of SRL or provide descriptive feedback that is difficult for learners to interpret and act upon. This paper presents a mobile application designed to support SRL through feedback-oriented learning analytics. The prototype is grounded in the SRL model of Winne and Hadwin and in feedback concepts that distinguish between feed-up, feed-back, and feed-forward. The application scaffolds the creation and conduct of learning sessions, captures learner-generated data such as goals, tasks, focus time, mood, and perceived strategy effectiveness, and translates these data into visualisations and reflection prompts intended to support metacognitive adaptation. The prototype follows an offline-first architecture and is designed for flexible use in everyday learning contexts. Its evaluation combined expert feedback, a one-week field test with six students, a survey, and follow-up interviews. The results indicate that the application is perceived as useful, intuitive, and particularly valuable for structuring learning sessions and supporting reflection on learning behaviour. It thus demonstrates the potential of feedback-oriented mobile analytics to strengthen SRL in higher education.

Keywords: Self-regulated Learning · Learning Analytics · Feedback

1 Design of the Artefact

Self-regulated learning (SRL) is closely linked to academic success, yet many students in higher education find it difficult to plan, monitor, and adapt their learning effectively [2,15]. When learners struggle to identify discrepancies between intended and actual performance, feedback becomes an important source of guidance [4,7]. This is particularly relevant in higher education, where large class sizes and limited instructional resources make it difficult to provide timely and individualised feedback at scale. At the same time, digital learning environments generate behavioural data that can be used to provide learning analytics (LA)-based support [1,8,9]. Existing applications, however, often focus only on isolated aspects of the SRL cycle or rely mainly on descriptive visualisations that require learners to possess sufficient feedback literacy to interpret them productively [8,9,13].

Against this backdrop, the objective of this study was to completely redesign the existing mobile application *Selbstlernen.app*, which has been shown to support students with learning difficulties in self-monitoring and attention [10], into a more comprehensive application that supports SRL in higher education through feedback-oriented learning analytics. The application was developed as part of a master's thesis using the Design Science Research (DSR) process proposed by Peffers et al. [12]. Its conceptual foundation is the four-phase SRL model by Winne and Hadwin [14], which conceptualises learning as a cyclical process of task definition, goal setting and planning, enactment, and metacognitive adaptation (see Fig. 1). The feedback logic further draws on the distinction between feed-up, feed-back, and feed-forward [7], and on the importance of combining external feedback with learner reflection [4,11].

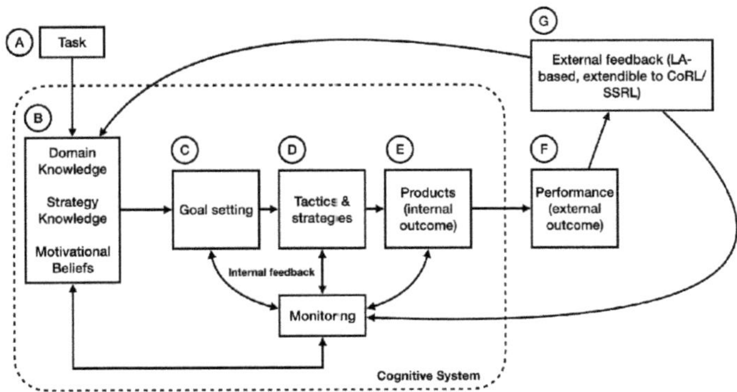

Fig. 1. The conceptual framework for the development of the mobile application.

The primary user group consists of students in higher education. The design particularly considers learners with different levels of prior SRL competence, ranging from students who require stronger scaffolding for planning and reflection to students who benefit from reviewing patterns in their own learning behaviour. The main use cases are: preparing a structured learning session, conducting the session with lightweight monitoring support, comparing intended and actual learning behaviour after completion, reflecting on the effectiveness of selected learning strategies, and establishing a sustainable learning routine over time.

To address these use cases, the prototype implements four central feature areas. First, the artefact scaffolds learning sessions by requiring users to define at least one goal or task, select at least one learning strategy, configure duration and timing, and optionally activate notifications and in-session focus prompts (see Fig. 2). Sessions can be one-time or recurring, and learners may choose between a simple focus timer and a Pomodoro-based timer. During enactment, the timer-centred interface displays goals and tasks as a checklist, thereby keeping intended objectives visible throughout the session (see Fig. 3, red border).

Second, the artefact provides LA-based feedback through locally generated visualisations and progress tracking (see Fig. 4). It collects selected learner-generated data, including completed goals and tasks, focus and break time, responses to in-session focus prompts, mood, and perceived strategy effectiveness. These data are aggregated after session completion and displayed in a statistical overview. The main purpose of the visualisations is to make discrepancies between planned and actual performance visible, for example with regard to goal completion or expected versus actual focus time. When recurring sessions are available, the visualisations also support the identification of patterns over time, such as temporal study habits or recurring relationships between mood, strategy use, and performance.

Third, the prototype scaffolds self-reflection immediately after each learning session (see Fig. 3, red border). Before accessing the statistical overview, learners are asked to review their session, rate their mood, assess the perceived effectiveness of their selected learning strategies, and optionally document further observations in a free-text field. This feature complements behavioural data with subjective self-assessments to support metacognitive adaptation.

Fourth, the artefact supports long-term engagement through recurring sessions, reminders, cumulative statistics, and continuity-oriented progress views (see Fig. 3, yellow border). These features are intended to strengthen routine formation and make learning activity visible over time. The application follows an offline-first architecture and operates without external backend infrastructure. As a result, it is accessible independent of network availability and can be used ubiquitously in mobile learning settings. Although social and cooperative learning modes were considered conceptually, they were not implemented within the project scope because real-time synchronisation and user-to-user interaction were incompatible with the chosen standalone architecture.

More information about the mobile application, including download options, access to the source code, and ways to contribute to its development, is available at: https://selbstlernen.app.

Fig. 2. Screenshots of the session creation workflow

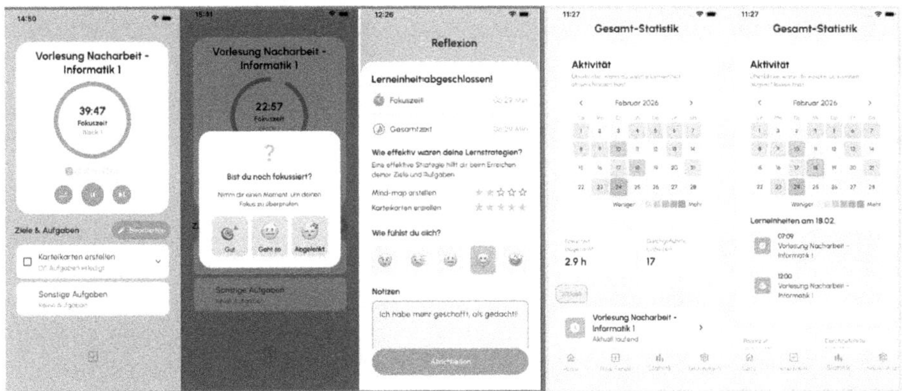

Fig. 3. Screenshots of the session enactment workflow (red border) and general activity statistics (yellow border). (Color figure online)

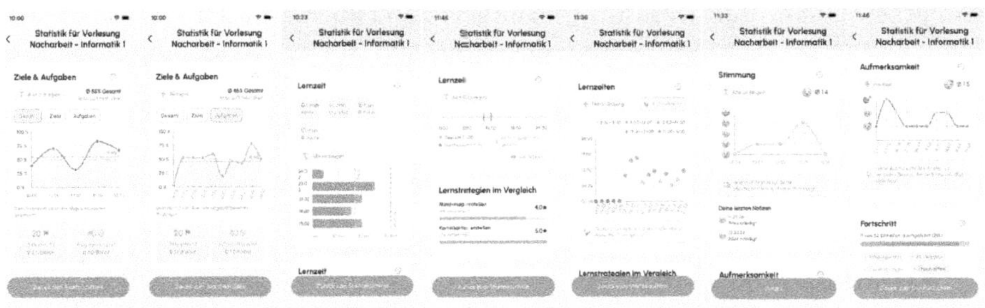

Fig. 4. Screenshots of available session statistics.

2   Significance to Research

The prototype is significant to research because it demonstrates how SRL theory, feedback theory, and mobile learning analytics can be translated into a coherent software instantiation. In contrast to many LA-based interventions which outsource analytics in the form of dashboards or visualisations, the artefact presented here embeds data capture within a structured learning workflow, linking planning, enactment, feedback and reflection in a single application [1,8,9]. This is important because prior research has repeatedly shown that LA-based feedback is often limited by missing feed-forward guidance and by the assumption that learners can interpret analytics without additional scaffolding [8,9,13].

The artefact further represents an improvement-oriented DSR contribution [6]. It builds on an already established problem space and on insights from earlier work on the Selbstlernen.app, yet differs in its conceptualisation by foregrounding feedback-oriented LA, strategy reflection, and longitudinal support for individual learners. The prototype therefore contributes knowledge about how a theory-grounded mobile artefact can operationalise the four phases of SRL while simultaneously making learner-generated data usable for metacognitive adaptation.

3 Significance to Practice

The artefact is also significant to practice because it addresses a persistent challenge in higher education: supporting students' self-regulation in everyday learning situations without relying exclusively on scarce instructor feedback. For learners, the application offers a lightweight but structured way to transform vague study intentions into concrete learning sessions, maintain attention during enactment, and reflect on whether selected strategies and routines are effective.

For educational practice, the prototype shows how SRL support can be implemented outside institutional learning management systems. Since the artefact is designed as a standalone, offline-first mobile application, it can be adopted with comparatively low infrastructural requirements. This makes it particularly suitable for contexts in which flexible, personal, and device-based support is more realistic than institutionally integrated analytics systems. At the same time, the evaluation suggests that the artefact may have transfer potential beyond university study, for example in other contexts in which planning, persistence, and reflection are important.

4 Evaluation

The prototype was evaluated using a mixed-methods design that combined qualitative and quantitative methods in three phases. In the first phase, an exploratory expert interview was conducted after the fifth development sprint in order to assess the usefulness of the initial visualisations and identify missing feedback elements. In the second phase, a revised test version of the application was used by six students from different academic backgrounds over a period of one week. After the field test, participants completed a survey based on the Technology Acceptance Model (TAM) [5]. The survey addressed perceived usefulness, perceived ease of use, support for the SRL phases, motivational features, and the usefulness of the implemented visualisations in relation to feed-up, feed-back, and feed-forward. In the third phase, two expert interviews and two follow-up user interviews were conducted and analysed using thematic analysis [3].

Across the field setting, participants generally perceived the application as easy and intuitive to use and reported a positive overall impression of its usefulness for structuring their learning. The LA-based feedback was generally regarded as helpful, but differences emerged between the visualisations. In particular, visualisations relating to goals and tasks as well as the focus-time chart were perceived as more useful for informing subsequent learning behaviour, whereas the mood chart and the focus-prompt visualisation were considered less helpful because meaningful conclusions were more difficult to derive from them. With regard to motivation, notifications appeared to support regular use for some participants, but they were not clearly perceived as increasing motivation to learn on their own.

The qualitative interviews added further depth to these findings. Experts emphasised the relevance of actionable feedback and considered the integration of learning-strategy evaluation particularly valuable, as many students have only limited awareness of effective strategies. At the same time, they suggested stronger trend indicators, additional pre-session reflection elements, and mechanisms to better address distraction during active learning sessions. Overall, the evaluation indicates that the prototype is a promising and usable artefact for supporting SRL through feedback-oriented mobile design. At the same time, it confirms that the interpretability and actionability of analytics-based feedback remain critical design challenges.

Acknowledgments. During the preparation of this work the authors used ChatGPT EDU in order to help distill the content of the master's thesis for this prototype paper. After using this service, the authors reviewed and edited the content as needed and take full responsibility for the content of the published article. The authors would also like to thank all students and academic colleagues who contributed to the development and evaluation of the mobile application, in particular those who participated in the field test, survey, and follow-up interviews.

References

1. Baars, M., Viberg, O.: Mobile learning to support self-regulated learning: a theoretical review. Int. J. Mob. Blended Learn. **14**(4), 1–12 (2022)
2. Bjork, R.A., Dunlosky, J., Kornell, N.: Self-regulated learning: beliefs, techniques, and illusions. Annu. Rev. Psychol. **64**(1), 417–444 (2013)
3. Braun, V., Clarke, V.: Using thematic analysis in psychology. Qual. Res. Psychol. **3**(2), 77–101 (2006)
4. Butler, D.L., Winne, P.H.: Feedback and self-regulated learning: a theoretical synthesis. Rev. Educ. Res. **65**(3), 245–281 (1995)
5. Davis, F.D.: Perceived usefulness, perceived ease of use, and user acceptance of information technology. MIS Q. **13**(3), 319–340 (1989)

6. Gregor, S., Hevner, A.R.: Positioning and presenting design science research for maximum impact. MIS Q. **37**(2), 337–355 (2013)
7. Hattie, J., Timperley, H.: The power of feedback. Rev. Educ. Res. **77**(1), 81–112 (2007)
8. Heikkinen, S., Saqr, M., Malmberg, J., Tedre, M.: Supporting self-regulated learning with learning analytics interventions: a systematic literature review. Educ. Inf. Technol. **28**(3), 3059–3088 (2023)
9. Matcha, W., Uzir, N.A., Gasevic, D., Pardo, A.: A systematic review of empirical studies on learning analytics dashboards: a self-regulated learning perspective. IEEE Trans. Learn. Technol. **13**(2), 226–245 (2019)
10. Melzer, C., Herwix, A.: App-based self-monitoring as an intervention to support attention in students with learning difficulties. Front. Educ. **9** (2024). https://doi.org/10.3389/feduc.2024.1270484
11. Nicol, D.J., Macfarlane-Dick, D.: Formative assessment and self-regulated learning: a model and seven principles of good feedback practice. Stud. High. Educ. **31**(2), 199–218 (2006)
12. Peffers, K., Tuunanen, T., Rothenberger, M.A., Chatterjee, S.: A design science research methodology for information systems research. J. Manag. Inf. Syst. **24**(3), 45–77 (2007)
13. Tsai, Y.S.: Why feedback literacy matters for learning analytics (2022). https://doi.org/10.48550/arXiv.2209.00879, version 3
14. Winne, P.H., Hadwin, A.F.: Studying as self-regulated learning. In: Hacker, D.J., Dunlosky, J., Graesser, A.C. (eds.) Metacognition in Educational Theory and Practice, pp. 277–304. Lawrence Erlbaum Associates, Mahwah, NJ (1998)
15. Zimmerman, B.J.: Becoming a self-regulated learner: an overview. Theory Into Pract. **41**, 64–70 (2002)

Contextualized Interpretability for AI Model Quality Assessment: Designing an LLM-Based Decision Companion for Domain Experts in LCNC Environments

Benjamin Gigerl[1]([✉]) [iD], Claris Chung[2] [iD], and Stefan Thalmann[1] [iD]

[1] University of Graz, Universitätsstraße 15, 8010 Graz, Austria
{benjamin.gigerl,stefan.thalmann}@uni-graz.at
[2] University of Canterbury, Private Bag 4800, 8140 Christchurch, New Zealand
claris.chung@canterbury.ac.nz

Abstract. Low-Code/No-Code (LCNC) platforms increasingly enable domain (non-technical) experts to develop AI models. However, assessing AI model quality remains challenging for domain experts, as evaluation metrics such as precision, recall, and confusion matrices are often presented as decontextualized technical outputs. This limits transparency, understanding, and trust, and reinforces reliance on data scientists. Grounded in Sensemaking Theory, this work introduces an LLM-based conversational assistant designed to support contextualized interpretability in AI model quality assessment. Embedded within LCNC environments, the assistant facilitates a structured "what" and "why" dialogue that explains evaluation metrics and elucidates the underlying causes of specific model behaviors. Particular emphasis is placed on the confusion matrix as a central sensemaking task, linking quantitative metrics to concrete classification outcomes. By translating technical evaluation results into domain-specific, contextual explanations, the artifact strengthens sensemaking, supports informed decision-making, and enables domain experts to assess and iterate on AI models.

Keywords: Contextualized Interpretability · AI Model Quality Assessment (AIMQA) · Low-Code/No-Code (LCNC)

1 Design of the Artifact

Problem Statement. The continuous advancement of Artificial Intelligence (AI) increasingly influences strategic decision-making, business models, and managerial cognition, as organizations must interpret and navigate the new opportunities and constraints introduced by AI-enabled systems (Jorzik et al., 2024). Facilitating this shift, Low-Code/No-Code (LCNC) platforms have popularized a development approach driven by domain experts rather than traditional technical specialists (Polzer & Thalmann, 2022). While LCNC platforms democratize access to AI development, the persistent "black-box" nature of many AI models, combined with insufficient technical guidance, introduces a significant evaluation gap (Buchmann et al., 2024; Kumar & Sharma, 2022).

S. Chatterjee et al. (Eds.): DESRIST 2026, LNCS 16607, pp. 323–328, 2026.
https://doi.org/10.1007/978-3-032-28570-6_26

As a result, domain experts often struggle to establish trust and reliability, particularly when model assessments are presented through decontextualized metrics that are neither interpretable nor aligned with their domain-specific expertise (Netten et al., 2021). One potential response to this challenge is to enhance the AI literacy of domain experts. However, such efforts are typically resource-intensive and difficult to scale across organizations (Eilers et al., 2017). An alternative and still underexplored approach lies in providing targeted tool-based guidance that supports domain experts during AI model quality assessment. Such guidance holds promise for improving sensemaking by embedding interpretability directly into the evaluation process of the created AI model (Aselmaa et al., 2017; Elshawi et al., 2019; Kumar & Sharma, 2022). Accordingly, this study addresses the following research question (RQ):

RQ: How can a contextualized interpretability artifact be designed to support domain experts in evaluating AI model quality in LCNC environments?

This research question underscores the need for a design artifact that not only presents model performance metrics but also fosters shared understanding among heterogeneous actors involved in LCNC AI development (Särner et al., 2024). Following the Design Science Research (DSR) paradigm (Hevner, 2007), this study focuses on the development of an interactive design artifact named **AIMQA** (AI Model Quality Assessment).

Use Case and Features. The proposed artifact was specifically designed to support the evaluation of AI models generated within LCNC environments, exemplified by a customer churn prediction use case. To ground the artifact design in empirical insights, a Think-Aloud study was conducted with 14 participants who developed a variety of AI use cases using LCNC platforms, covering the full pipeline from data input to model deployment. The study was carried out using KNIME[1], an open-source LCNC platform that is widely adopted in both academia and industry. In the study, a recurring pattern emerged: participants consistently emphasized that *"The model should be as readable and simple as possible."* For contextualized interpretability, three core design requirements emerged that guide the development of the three core features of the proposed artifact. The first feature is an accessible explanation of a confusion matrix. Participants sought an overview of overall model quality, an explicit visualization of error types, and transparent visibility of critical misclassifications, particularly false negatives (e.g., missed churn cases). Consequently, the artifact must provide clear, accessible explanations of AI model quality metrics that link quantitative metrics to concrete classification outcomes. The second feature is an interactive dialogue for business-oriented interpretation. Domain experts are accustomed to asking use case-specific, business-oriented questions without engaging deeply with technical details. The third feature is the explicit explanation of model behavior, avoiding speculative outputs or hallucinations. Rather than generic explanations, participants requested explanations that are grounded in the concrete modeling context, such as the underlying LCNC workflow and feature configurations. The AIMQA operationalizes these three design features by embedding a context-aware, LLM-based decision companion into the LCNC environment. In doing so, it aims to enhance contextualized interpretability and support domain experts in making informed, confident judgments about AI model quality. **SCREENCAST**: https://business-analytics.uni-graz.at/en/research/aimqa.

---

[1] KNIME Analytics Platform (https://www.knime.com/knime-analytics-platform).

2 Significance to Research

The core innovation of AIMQA lies in its ability to provide hypothesis-driven and data-driven insights that extend domain experts understanding of AI model quality. Through explicit "what" and "why" explanations, AIMQA triggers an additional reasoning process within the sensemaking activities of domain experts, enabling them to explore advanced workflow settings, data characteristics, and model outputs in a structured and interpretable manner. By fostering this additional reasoning, AIMQA empowers domain experts to regain agency in a landscape where automation often unintentionally reinforces the "black-box" nature of AI models, feature engineering, and hyperparameter optimization. This shift is critical, as traditional automated processes often limit transparency and stifle the critical reflection necessary for high-stakes decision-making (Bachinger et al., 2024). To visualize this shift, Fig. 1 illustrates this contrast by comparing an automized LCNC-driven process without sensemaking iteration to the revised AI development process enabled by the proposed artifact AIMQA.

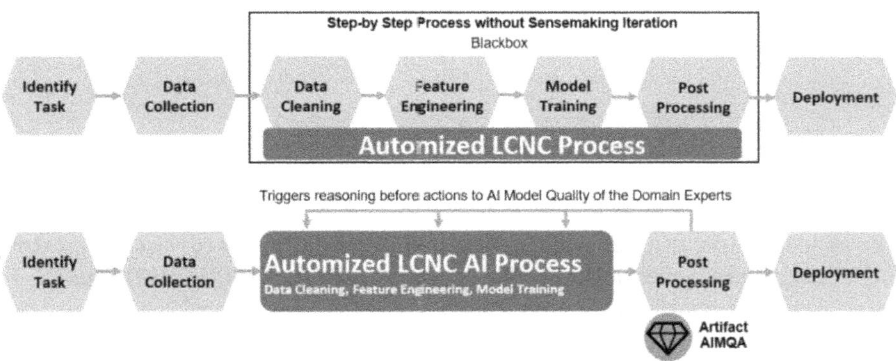

Fig. 1. Automized LCNC Process versus AIMQA augmented LCNC process.

3 Significance to Practice

The system is implemented as a two-phase cycle consisting of five core AIMQA functional components that facilitate sensemaking for domain experts. The process begins in the domain experts standard LCNC development environment, where they independently build task-specific pipelines regardless of the artifact (see *Fig. 2*). The specific interventions of AIMQA begin with (1) **automated data extraction**, where a custom KNIME macro (Metanode) captures node configurations and performance metrics from the created workflow. The evaluation then shifts to the AIMQA sensemaking environment after these extracted files are imported. This phase involves (2) **secure deployment and validation** on the Snowflake AI Data Cloud and (3) **LLM-powered integration** using Claude 3.5 Sonnet to ground explanations in the specific modeling context. Domain experts then engage in (4) **contextual dialogue and guidance** through a chatbot interface to interpret AI model quality in domain-specific language. Finally, (5) **iterative model improvement** empowers the domain expert to return to their standard KNIME environment to proactively refine the model for better reliability based on the insights gained from AIMQA.

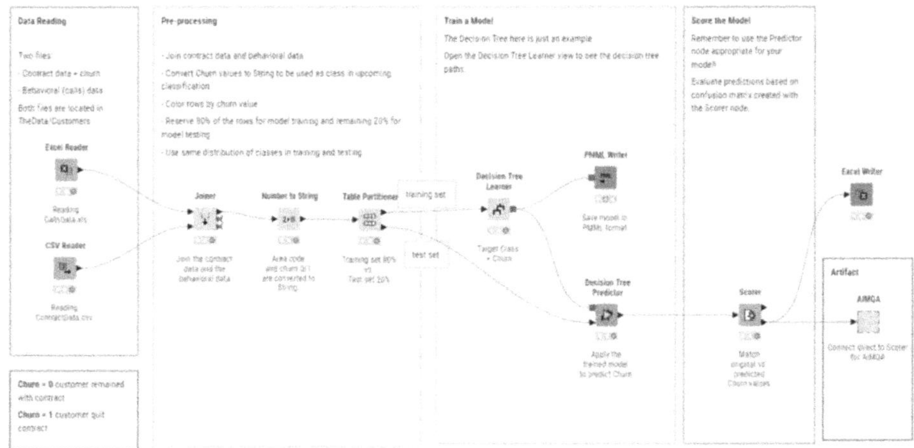

Fig. 2. KNIME churn prediction workflow with AIMQA.

The AIMQA evaluation cycle involves the three features to facilitate the sense-making of domain experts. **First**, the accessible explanation of the confusion matrix is realized through the transition from automated data extraction to secure deployment and validation, which converts quantitative scoring into a structured, visual representation of error types and critical misclassifications. **Second**, the interactive dialogue for business-oriented interpretation is powered by LLM integration and contextual dialogue and guidance functionalities. By assigning the LLM a domain-specific role, the system enables experts to interrogate model quality using domain language rather than technical jargon (according to *Fig. 3*). **Finally**, the explicit explanation of model behavior is ensured by grounding the contextual dialogue in the layers of information provided by automated data extraction, which prevents hallucinations and ensures that all responses are rooted in the concrete modeling context and workflow configurations. This integrated approach culminates in iterative model improvement, as the clarity provided by these features empowers experts to proactively refine their models.

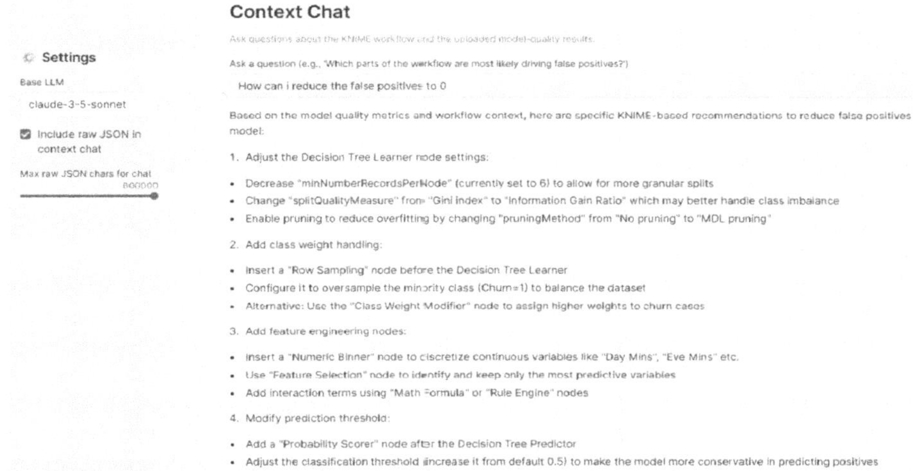

Fig. 3. Context-aware AIMQA decision companion interface.

4 Initial Evaluation and Conclusion

The AIMQA was presented twice in a qualitative field setting to assess its potential in supporting sensemaking and interpretability of AI model quality within an LCNC environment (KNIME + Snowflake). A total of 20 domain experts and Information Systems scholars participated in these sessions, where they were shown a demonstration of the artifact and completed a seven-question survey. The evaluation results indicated that the majority of participants found the presentation of evaluation metrics and the linkage to concrete classification outcomes clear and understandable, confirming the confusion matrix as a valuable sensemaking anchor. Furthermore, the LLM-based dialogue was perceived as highly useful for uncovering the causes of specific model behaviors through interactive, "why-oriented" explanations. While the structured data upload effectively reduced technical complexity for domain experts, feedback suggested that the integration of technical node configurations could be made even more explicit to further enhance explanatory credibility. Although the assistant supported users in deriving actionable improvement steps, participants identified a strong demand for more explicit guidance on how to act upon evaluation results, comparative views across multiple model versions, and scenario-based explanations to illustrate the impact of metric changes on domain outcomes. Particularly, no participant rated any aspect of the artifact's interpretability support as difficult to understand or not understandable.

The development of AIMQA addresses a critical evaluation gap in the democratization of AI by providing a structured, contextualized interpretability layer for domain experts in LCNC environments. By integrating automated data extraction from KNIME with an LLM-assisted dialogue interface, the artifact effectively triggers the additional reasoning processes necessary for domain experts. Initial evaluations with PhD-level experts confirm that while quantitative metrics are well understood, the true value of the system lies in its ability to translate technical "black-box" outputs into plausible, domain-specific explanations that empower users to take the "driver's seat" in model refinement.

Future iterations will focus on strengthening prescriptive guidance and comparative model analysis to further support sustained improvements in AI model quality.

Disclosure of Interests. The authors have no competing interests to declare that are relevant to the content of this article.

References

Aselmaa, A., et al.: Using a contextualized sensemaking model for interaction design: a case study of tumor contouring. J. Biomed. Inform. **65**, 145–158 (2017)

Bachinger, F., Zenisek, J., Affenzeller, M.: Automated machine learning for industrial applications–challenges and opportunities. Procedia Comput. Sci. **232**, 1701–1710 (2024)

Buchmann, T., Peinl, R., Schwägerl, F.: White-box LLM-supported low-code engineering: a vision and first insights. In: ACM/IEEE 27th International Conference on Model Driven Engineering Languages and Systems (MODELS Companion '24), Linz, Austria, pp. 1–5 (2024)

Eilers, D., Köpp, C., Gleue, C., Breitner, M. H.: It's not a bug, it's a feature: how visual model evaluation can help to incorporate human domain knowledge in data science. In: Thirty-Eighth International Conference on Information Systems (ICIS), South Korea, pp. 1–17 (2017)

Elshawi, R., Al-Mallah, M.H., Sakr, S.: On the interpretability of machine learning-based model for predicting hypertension. BMC Med. Inform. Decis. Mak. **19**, 1–32 (2019)

Hevner, A.: A three cycle view of design science research. Scand. J. Inf. Syst. **19**(2), 87–92 (2007)

Jorzik, P., Klein, S.P., Kanbach, D.K., Kraus, S.: AI-driven business model innovation: a systematic review and research agenda. J. Bus. Rese. **182**, 114764 (2024)

Kumar, P., Sharma, M.: Data, machine learning, and human domain experts: none is better than their collaboration. Int. J. Hum.-Comput. Interact. **38**(14), 1307–1320 (2022)

Netten, N., Suijker, A., Bargh, M.S., Choenni, S.: Operationalization of a glass box through visualization: applied to a data-driven profiling approach. In: 20th Conference on e-Business, e-Services and e-Society (I3E), Galway, Ireland, pp. 292–304 (2021)

Polzer, A.K., Thalmann, S.: The impact of AutoML on the AI development process. In: Proceedings of the 2022 Pre-ICIS SIGDSA Symposium, pp. 1–16 (2022)

Särner, E., Yström, A., Lakemond, N., Holmberg, G.: Prospective sensemaking in the front end of innovation of AI projects. Res. Technol. Manag. **67**(4), 72–83 (2024)

Automated Documentation for Reproducible Research: The Reproducible AI Documentation (RepAID) Tool

Armin Haberl[(⊠)] and Stefan Thalmann

University of Graz, Graz, Austria
`{armin.haberl,stefan.thalmann}@uni-graz.at`

Abstract. Artificial Intelligence (AI) and Machine Learning (ML) are increasingly transforming how researchers outside of computer and data science analyze and extract meaningful insights from data. The introduction of low-code tools, such as the KNIME Analytics Platform, empowers researchers without extensive coding expertise to leverage complex ML methods. However, the highly automated internal processes of these tools often lack transparency and complicate thorough research documentation. This is ever more problematic as scientific journals and conferences demand comprehensive documentation of ML workflows to ensure research reproducibility. To address this gap, we introduce the Reproducible AI Documentation (RepAID) tool, designed to support researchers in documenting ML workflows and meeting reproducibility standards. RepAID consists of two KNIME components that extract workflow metadata and utilize Large Language Models (LLMs) to generate custom reproducibility reports. Initial evaluation results demonstrate that RepAID can generate accurate workflow documentation and is adaptable to varying reporting guidelines and requirements. These findings contribute to the ongoing discussion on how to support reproducible research with low-code ML tools. Furthermore, feedback from researchers familiar with low-code ML highlights the utility of the prototype and encourages further development to strengthen human oversight and ensure responsible use of automated research documentation.

Keywords: Low-Code · Machine Learning · Reproducibility · Documentation · Automation

1 Design of the Artifact

This paper introduces the **Reproducible AI Documentation (RepAID)** tool designed to enhance the reproducibility of ML research. RepAID extends the low-code data science platform KNIME[1] with custom components to extract ML workflow information and generate comprehensive research documentation based on specified guidelines or requirements. The RepAID components are available on the KNIME Hub to facilitate reuse within the research community, and a screencast demonstrating the prototype can be accessed online (see Sect. 6).

---

[1] https://www.knime.com/.

S. Chatterjee et al. (Eds.): DESRIST 2026, LNCS 16607, pp. 329–336, 2026.
https://doi.org/10.1007/978-3-032-28570-6_27

1.1 Problem Statement

AI and ML methods are increasingly used in research to extract meaningful insights from data outside computer and data science [1]. While ML can support scientific discovery, there is a growing debate around the transparency and reproducibility of these methods [2]. Especially, the insufficient documentation of utilized datasets, code and implementation details threaten the reproducibility of ML research findings [3, 4]. The development of low-code ML tools has empowered researchers without coding expertise to use ML methods in various scientific domains outside computer or data science [5]. However, their lack of shareable code, limited transparency of automated ML processes, and often limited ML expertise of these researchers can further threaten the documentation quality of ML research [5, 6]. Various journals and conferences have implemented documentation guidelines and checklists to tackle these reproducibility concerns, see e.g., [7]. While these measures can help to improve documentation practices [4, 7], they also impose additional documentation effort on researchers. The core problem faced by researchers with limited computer and data science expertise knowledge utilizing low-code ML tools is therefore the mismatch between increasingly high documentation requirements in ML research and the limited transparency and documentation support provided by established low-code tools. To address this problem, we designed and developed RepAID within the KNIME Analytics Platform to support the reproducibility of low-code ML research.

1.2 User Groups and Use Cases

The main user group for RepAID are researchers outside computer and data science that need to provide detailed documentation of their low-code ML workflows for scientific publications. With the increasing use of low-code ML tools in research, especially in life sciences [8], the user group of RepAID is expanding as well. The need for documentation support within low-code ML tools was also identified in a pre-study of this paper, where six researchers from various scientific disciplines implemented and documented low-code ML projects and tried to reproduce each other's findings. This led to the development of design requirements that also recommended automated research documentation.

To support the reproducibility of ML research, the documentation should typically include a textual description of the ML workflow and detailed information about the used datasets, code, and the experimental setup [9]. For low-code ML the documentation can further include visual descriptions of the workflow and other forms of executable instructions instead of code. The main use case of RepAID is therefore the automated generation of customized reproducibility reports for low-code ML workflows. This should allow researchers to comply with reporting requirements of journals and conferences while lowering the barriers and reducing manual effort.

We differentiate two main ways of using RepAID for research documentation. Firstly, researchers can let the system generate default documentation that aligns with requirements mentioned in the ML reproducibility literature [2, 9] covering information such as data preparation steps, hyperparameters, and model evaluation methods. This is useful, when conferences and journals do not provide reproducibility guidelines. Secondly, researchers can provide specific documentation requirements (e.g. journal guidelines) to RepAID and generate custom reports based on these requirements.

1.3 Features

The RepAID tool consists of two KNIME components that are responsible for extracting workflow information, filtering this information, and generating a reproducibility report based on specified documentation requirements. Figure 1 shows how the two components *Result to Report* and *Generate Report* are used within a KNIME workflow.

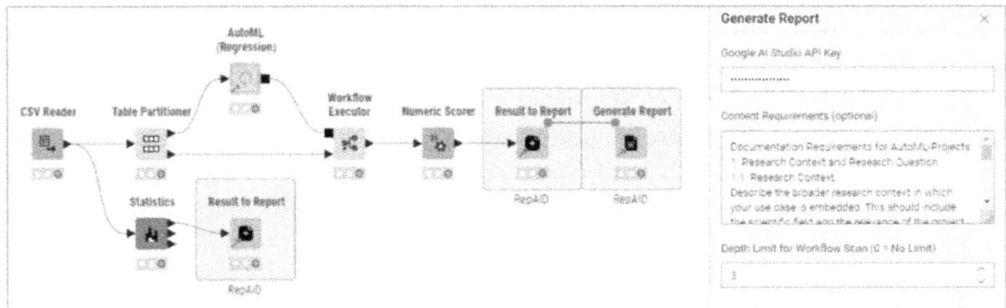

Fig. 1. KNIME Workflow with highlighted RepAID Components

The component *Result to Report* is used to append certain outcomes of the ML workflow such as model performance or data statistics to the reproducibility report. This manual selection of output data is necessary to avoid the inclusion of irrelevant data or entire datasets in the final report. The component *Generate Report* performs the main documentation steps such as data extraction, filtering and report generation. It requires researchers to provide an API Key for Google AI Studio to enable the use of LLMs for report generation. Researchers can also specify optional content requirements in the input dialog as well as a depth limit for the inclusion of deeply nested workflow components. The internal processes of RepAID begin when a researcher configures the *Generate Report* component and executes it within a given KNIME workflow.

Data Extraction: Once the component is started it gathers all available information saved in the KNIME workflow such as settings, connections between nodes, as well as software and hardware configurations. This data is then transformed from the initial XML format into a more compact YAML format using a custom Python script. In this step, information from nodes that surpass the workflow depth limit is removed to ensure a reasonable report size for large and deeply nested workflows. Information stored in instances of the *Result to Report* component is also added during this step.

Requirements Refinement: To ensure that the specified report requirements are suitable for filtering workflow data and guiding report generation, they are refined by an LLM. After initializing Google AI Studio using the supplied API key, the Gemini 2.5 Flash model is used to adapt the report requirements to explicitly state all workflow information that needs to be included in the final documentation. Gemini 2.5 Flash was chosen for its large context window, low latency and cost-efficiency[2]. The prompts within RepAID utilize a zero-shot prompting strategy with role, task and constraint descriptions. All prompts used in RepAID components can be accessed through the KNIME Hub repository[3].

Data Filtering: The information extracted from the ML workflow is subsequently filtered based on the refined report requirements. This filtering is necessary, since the extracted workflow data can be extremely large for complex ML workflows and can surpass the context window of the LLM. Thus, the information for each component in the KNIME workflow is filtered separately using Gemini 2.5 Flash. During this filtering step repetitive settings and configurations that do not affect ML outcomes are either summarized or removed from the workflow data.

Report Generation: After the individual parts of the workflow data are filtered, they are aggregated into a single YAML string and added to the report generation prompt. This prompt utilizes the same prompting strategy as before, incorporates the refined report requirements, defines how to format the final report, and is also executed by the Gemini 2.5 Flash model. Once the report is generated in markdown format, a custom Python script is used to add an image of the visual KNIME workflow, convert the report to the Microsoft Word format and save it to the user's download directory.

2 Significance to Research

There is an ongoing academic discussion on the reproducibility of ML research that highlights several critical barriers, including poor documentation practices, limited access to code and data, and the inherent randomness of ML algorithms [4]. To overcome these barriers, several solutions have been proposed, such as dedicated hosting services for code and data, the use of random seeds to ensure deterministic training, and the introduction of documentation guidelines and checklists by journals [4]. While these solutions are promising for traditional ML research where computer scientists implement ML algorithms using code, it is unclear whether they also apply to low-code ML tools. By developing RepAID we aim to broaden the scope of the academic discussion on ML reproducibility and highlight both barriers and possible solutions to reproducible research with low-code ML tools. While these tools provide highly automated ML pipelines that do not require manual programming, they often lack the transparency of internal processes required by academic research [5, 10]. Furthermore, the lack of shareable code and limited interoperability between different tool vendors complicates the reuse of low-code ML workflows [11]. These difficulties can be exacerbated when researchers using low-code tools have limited technical expertise and fail to recognize which specific implementation details must be documented to aid reproducibility [5, 6]. Consequently, it can be more difficult for research utilizing low-code ML tools to comply with documentation requirements. RepAID is designed to address these challenges and expand both the understanding and the solution space for reproducible research with low-code ML tools.

---

[2] https://ai.google.dev/gemini-api/docs/models/gemini-2.5-flash.

[3] https://hub.knime.com/arminhaberl/spaces/Public/RepAID/Prompts.

3 Significance to Practice

The RepAID tool has the potential to greatly reduce the effort required to document workflows developed within low-code ML environments. By allowing researchers to provide specific reporting requirements as input for automated report generation, RepAID enables them to easily adapt their documentation to various standards. This is particularly valuable when submitting research to different journals or adapting to evolving reproducibility guidelines. By integrating documentation directly into the ML environment, the process becomes an integral part of the workflow rather than an afterthought. While the current prototype of RepAID is a first step, it also serves as a blueprint for developers of established low-code ML platforms. By demonstrating the potential of using LLMs to automate the generation of adaptable ML documentation, tool vendors can adopt this principle to develop future low-code ML tools that provide comprehensive documentation out-of-the-box. This can lead to tools that are better suited for scientific use, especially since research reproducibility is often not the focus of established ML platforms [12]. While RepAID was developed to support the documentation of low-code ML research, it can also be useful for industry researchers. By streamlining the documentation of ML applications, RepAID can facilitate knowledge transfer within organizations, support regulatory compliance, and help foster ML adoption.

4 Initial Evaluation

To evaluate whether the documentation generated by RepAID can meet academic standards, we conducted lab tests using existing KNIME workflows and collected feedback from researchers familiar with low-code ML tools.

4.1 Lab Testing

The KNIME workflows used for lab testing were originally developed in a pre-study for this paper, in which researchers created ML workflows using KNIME and manually documented their steps to ensure reproducibility. To evaluate RepAID, we used the prototype to automatically generate documentation for these same workflows and compared the output against the researchers' original manual records.

We found that the documentation generated using RepAID closely followed the provided reporting requirements and contained correct information about datasets, ML training settings, and outcomes. The reports generated by RepAID were also remarkably consistent in their structure, content, and style. This was a main difference from the manually created reports, which varied greatly in their comprehensiveness depending on the data science expertise of the researchers creating them. While both the researchers and RepAID thoroughly documented the high-level processes of the ML workflows, the automated reports provided more insight into the internal processes of various KNIME components, such as automated data cleaning. Additionally, the explanation and interpretation of performance metrics were often more comprehensive in the automated reports compared to the manual reports.

Despite these promising results, certain aspects of the automated reports warrant further improvement of RepAID. Since RepAID can only access data stored within the ML workflows, it lacks the contextual information needed to document aspects such as dataset sources or specific hardware configurations. Thus, future versions of the tool should allow researchers to provide this context information through a separate configuration option. Finally, the reports created by RepAID include only a single image of the visual ML workflow, while many researcher-created reports included screenshots of all relevant configuration views within KNIME. This lack of visualization can make reports more difficult to understand and should be addressed in future versions of RepAID.

4.2 User Feedback

To further evaluate RepAID, we demonstrated the prototype to six researchers familiar with the documentation of low-code ML workflows and collected their feedback through semi-structured interviews (average duration: 35 min). Each researcher also received both the automated and original reports used in lab testing for comparison.

Overall, the researchers highlighted the potential time savings that RepAID can enable, since research documentation is often associated with considerable effort. One interviewee explained: "I think that [the tool] can take a lot of work off your hands. Because when I now say how much effort it was to create this 15-page report, that was a lot of effort [...] [but now] it is only two clicks, and it is generated in a minute." The researchers also considered the RepAID prototype easy to use and stated they would use it in their research. One interviewee explained: "Whenever it makes things easier for me as user, I would want to use it [in future projects]". After comparing the reports, the researchers also noted the standardization potential and high degree of technical detail of the automated reports. One researcher explained, "The report is very detailed and [...] in some areas even more detailed than my own report. [...] My impression is that it would work very well to reproduce the workflow like that."

The most frequently mentioned concern was the risk of automation bias, where researchers might trust the results of RepAID without manually checking the outcome. One researcher explained, "As soon as there is something written down [...] then it is less likely that it is changed again. [...] it must be clear that this is just a first draft and the person is still responsible." To address these concerns, several researchers suggested incorporating human oversight into the prototype. This could include interactive report generation, where parts of the report must be confirmed for correctness, or the inclusion of placeholders that researchers can fill with contextual information not available to RepAID. Overall, the interviewees stressed the importance of sufficient data science expertise to use low-code ML in research and to allow for the critical examination of automated reports. One researcher explained: "It is the question, if it makes sense to use these statistical methods at all, if I cannot understand them [...] because if I cannot understand what happens, I also cannot check if the report is 100% correct." The researchers also suggested that any use of automated research documentation must always be made transparent and comply with the guidelines of the journals to which it is submitted. One interviewee explained: "It likely depends on the journal, whether they allow the use of generative AI [...] and also if it were only in the appendix, I would have to specify that anyway."

5   Conclusion

This paper introduces the RepAID tool, which allows researchers to automatically generate documentation for low-code ML workflows according to specified guidelines or requirements. RepAID fills an important gap to overcome the reproducibility issues of AI/ML research and primarily supports researchers outside computer and data science using low-code ML tools. The RepAID prototype consists of two custom components within the KNIME Analytics Platform and utilizes LLMs to generate adaptable reproducibility reports. While initial evaluation results demonstrate the utility of the prototype, further development is warranted to strengthen human oversight and ensure responsible use of low-code ML platforms in general and automated research documentation specifically. Future research should focus on providing an in-depth evaluation of RepAID and experimentally testing its effects on documentation quality, research reproducibility, and research practices.

6   Links to External Resources

- **Screencast:** https://business-analytics.uni-graz.at/en/research/repaid/
- **KNIME Hub:** https://hub.knime.com/arminhaberl/spaces/Public/RepAID

Disclosure of Interests.   The authors have no competing interests to declare that are relevant to the content of this article.

References

1. Wang, H., et al.: Scientific discovery in the age of artificial intelligence. Nature **620**, 47–60 (2023). https://doi.org/10.1038/s41586-023-06221-2
2. Gundersen, O.E., Kjensmo, S.: State of the Art: Reproducibility in Artificial Intelligence Proceedings of the AAAI Conference on Artificial Intelligence, vol. 32 (2018). https://doi.org/10.1609/aaai.v32i1.11503
3. Koenigstorfer, F., Haberl, A., Kowald, D., Ross-Hellauer, T., Thalmann, S.: Black box or open science? assessing reproducibility-related documentation in AI research. Proceedings of the 57th Hawaii International Conference on System Sciences, vol. 57 (2024)
4. Semmelrock, H., et al.: Reproducibility in machine-learning-based research: overview, barriers, and drivers. AI Mag. **46** (2025). https://doi.org/10.1002/aaai.70002
5. Haberl, A., Thalmann, S.: Automated machine learning in research–a literature review. Proceedings of the 58th HICCS (2025). https://doi.org/10.24251/HICSS.2025.899
6. Pletzl, S., Haberl, A., Ross-Hellauer, T., Thalmann, S.: Reproducible AutoML: an assessment of research reproducibility of Nc-Code AutoML tools. Wirtschaftsinformatik 2024 Proceedings (2024)
7. Pineau, J., et al.: Improving reproducibility in machine learning research (A Report from the NeurIPS 2019 Reproducibility Program). J. Mach. Learn. Res. **22**, 1–20 (2021)
8. Castro, G.A., et al.: Automated Machine Learning in medical research: a systematic literature mapping study. Artif. Intell. Med. **171**, 103302 (2026). https://doi.org/10.1016/j.artmed.2025.103302

9. Gundersen, O.E.: The fundamental principles of reproducibility. Philosophical transactions. Series A, Mathematical, Physical, and Engineering Sciences, vol. 379, 20200210 (2021). https://doi.org/10.1098/rsta.2020.0210

10. Sun, Y., Song, Q., Gui, X., Ma, F., Wang, T.: AutoML in the wild: obstacles, workarounds, and expectations. Proceedings of the 2023 CHI Conference on Human Factors in Computing Systems (2023). https://doi.org/10.1145/3544548.3581082

11. Quaranta, L., Azevedo, K., Calefato, F., Kalinowski, M.: A multivocal literature review on the benefits and limitations of industry-leading AutoML tools. Inf. Softw. Technol. **178**, 107608 (2025). https://doi.org/10.1016/j.infsof.2024.107608

12. Gundersen, O.E., Shamsaliei, S., Isdahl, R.J.: Do machine learning platforms provide out-of-the-box reproducibility? Futur. Gener. Comput. Syst. **126**, 34–47 (2022). https://doi.org/10.1016/j.future.2021.06.014

PaperMate: A Prototype for Supporting Comprehension of Scientific Texts for Non Native Academic Readers

Martin Hänel[1] , Kevin Fred Mwaita[2] , Thiemo Wambsganss[3](✉) , and Matthias Söllner[1]

[1] University of Kassel, Kassel, Germany
haenel@uni-kassel.de
[2] Free University of Bozen-Bolzano, Bozen, Italy
kmwaita@unibz.it
[3] Bern University of Applied Sciences, Bern, Switzerland
thiemo.wambsganss@bfh.ch

Abstract. Reading comprehension is essential for accessing scientific knowledge, yet many students, especially non native readers, struggle to understand complex academic texts. Comprehension theory shows that understanding requires the coordinated interaction of multiple subskills and the construction of a coherent situation model. Existing reading support systems typically address only isolated aspects such as summarization or simplification, resulting in superficial understanding. We present PaperMate, a canvas based reading support system designed to support situation model construction. Grounded in the Active Reader View, the artifact integrates simplification, structural guidance, essentialization, and contextual clarification within a unified and user controlled interface. This enables readers to flexibly combine support based on individual needs. The artifact was developed through multiple iterative design cycles including proof of concept, proof of value, laboratory studies, and field tests, and is continuously refined. The work demonstrates how holistic reading support can be operationalized in a concrete artifact and contributes to theory grounded design of reading support systems.

Keywords: Design Science Research · Reading Comprehension · Reading Support System · Non Native Readers · Active Reader View

1 Design of the Artifact

Reading scientific literature is a core requirement in higher education, yet many students struggle to construct meaningful understanding from complex texts [1, 2]. These challenges are particularly pronounced for non native readers, who face systematic linguistic, structural, and conceptual barriers when engaging with English language publications [3, 4]. As scientific knowledge is predominantly communicated in English [5, 6], non native readers are placed at a structural disadvantage when accessing and processing academic content [1, 3]. This creates an issue of equity in science, as access to knowledge

S. Chatterjee et al. (Eds.): DESRIST 2026, LNCS 16607, pp. 337–344, 2026.
https://doi.org/10.1007/978-3-032-28570-6_28

and participation in academic discourse becomes unevenly distributed across language backgrounds[4, 7].

Non native readers require significantly more time to process academic texts [1], recall less information and make more comprehension errors [3], and report negative impacts on academic performance which directly undermines subject learning and academic success [8].

At the same time, effective reading for scientific texts is rarely explicitly taught, leaving students without adequate support [9, 10]. Educational settings further exacerbate this problem. Providing individualized reading support is time intensive [11], personalized feedback is often lacking [12] and many reading situations occur without teacher guidance [13]. Consequently, students are frequently left alone with texts that exceed their current comprehension abilities.

Despite substantial progress in reading support technologies, existing systems fail to address these challenges. Prior approaches typically focus on isolated interventions such as summarization [14], simplification [15, 16], explanations [17], or structural visualization [18]. The Accessible Text Framework conceptualizes these approaches as distinct categories, including compressing, simplifying, experiencing, and reviewing systems [19]. However, these functions are usually implemented separately, requiring users to switch between tools [20]. As a result, existing systems fail to align with comprehension theory and do not adequately support situation model construction [14–17, 21]. Readers process the explicit content of a text, referred to as the textbase, without constructing a deeper situation model that integrates meaning, context, and prior knowledge [21].

However, meaningful understanding requires precisely situation model construction [21]. This process depends on the coordination of multiple interacting subskills such as lexical access, syntactic parsing, inference generation, coherence building, and metacognitive regulation [22]. When these processes are not sufficiently supported, readers remain at a superficial level of understanding.

To address this gap, we present PaperMate, a canvas based reading support system designed to support comprehension of scientific texts through integrated, comprehension theory grounded functionality. The artifact targets non native novice readers in self directed learning contexts, such as students who must independently read English language scientific literature as part of their studies. A typical use case involves a student working through a research paper and encountering multiple comprehension challenges, including unfamiliar terminology, unclear structure, and dense argumentation. Instead of relying on fragmented tools, the student interacts directly with the text and selectively applies different forms of support within a unified interface.

The design of PaperMate is grounded in the Active Reader View [22], which conceptualizes reading as an active and goal directed process. This implies that effective reading support must support multiple comprehension processes simultaneously. Different readers struggle with different aspects of a text, and even within a single reading session, the type of support required may change. Consequently, the system adopts a user controlled approach, allowing readers to decide when, where, and how support is applied.

The artifact is structured around five design principles [23, 24]. The first principle, Simplify, reduces linguistic complexity through paraphrasing, translation, and contextual explanations, thereby supporting lexical and syntactic processing. The second principle, Structure, makes discourse organization explicit by highlighting relationships between parts of the text, supporting understanding of the author's argumentation. The third principle, Essentials, condenses content into key propositions, reducing cognitive load and helping readers focus on the most relevant information. The fourth principle, Conversational Support, enables contextual clarification through user driven interaction, allowing readers to ask questions about specific text segments and receive targeted explanations. The interaction design enables users to flexibly combine multiple forms of support within a single workflow displayed in Fig. 1. For example, a student may first simplify a sentence to understand its basic meaning, then analyze its structure to understand its role within the argument, and finally extract key ideas to summarize the content. This integrated interaction supports the construction of a coherent understanding.

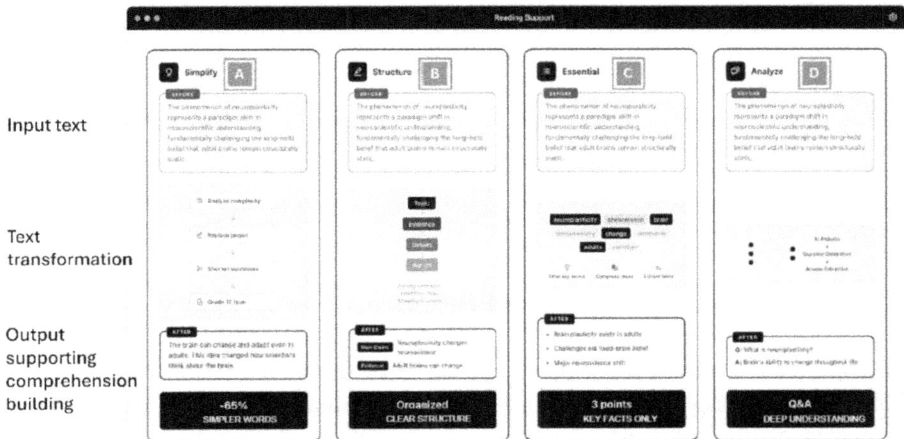

Fig. 1. Conceptual foundation DP1-DP4 instantiated in the artifact. Each principle addresses a distinct dimension of comprehension while contributing to a coordinated support system.

Canvas interaction workflow is displayed in Fig. 2. Users begin by uploading a scientific text, which is displayed within the system. While reading, users can select specific passages that they find difficult to understand. For each selected passage, users can choose one of the four support functions. The system then transforms the selected content and presents the result as a sticky note anchored directly to the original text. This ensures that all support remains localized, traceable, and in accordance with the fifth design principle.

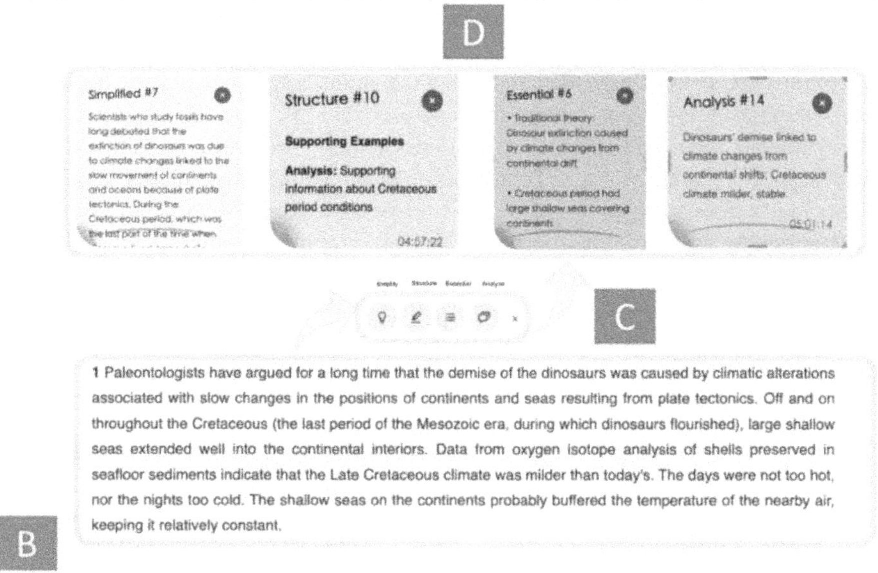

Fig. 2. Canvas interaction workflow: Users select text passages and apply support functions, which generate anchored sticky notes that provide localized, traceable, and context grounded reading support (DP5).

2   Significance to Research and Practice

PaperMate contributes to design science research by translating established theories of reading comprehension into a concrete and implementable artifact. While prior work has acknowledged the importance of multi level comprehension support [19, 22], systems have largely failed to embed these theoretical insights into user calibrated reading systems [25, 26]. PaperMate addresses this gap by aligning different system functionality [19] and linguistic comprehension theory [21, 22].

Furthermore, the artifact contributes to the design knowledge on reading support systems by demonstrating how multiple support functions can be combined within a unified interface [19, 27]. Prior systems typically implement isolated functions. In contrast, PaperMate integrates these functions within a single canvas based environment [28], thereby addressing the fragmentation highlighted in the Accessible Text Framework. This integration provides a design pathway for future systems that aim to support comprehension holistically rather than isolated.

In addition, the artifact contributes to research on human computer interaction in learning contexts by emphasizing user controlled and context sensitive support [29]. Instead of applying uniform transformations, the system enables readers to dynamically select and combine support functions based on their individual needs. This aligns with the Active Reader View, which conceptualizes reading as an active and adaptive process shaped by reader resources and goals [22].

From a practical perspective, PaperMate addresses a critical challenge in higher education, namely the ability of students to independently engage with and understand scientific literature. Many students, especially non native readers, face significant barriers when working with academic texts [1]. At the same time, institutions often lack the resources to provide individualized support, particularly in self-directed learning contexts [30]. The system provides a scalable solution to this problem by enabling students to access adaptive, on demand support directly within the reading process. At the same time, the artifact encourages active engagement with the text rather than passive consumption. While it initially lowers barriers to accessibility, it also supports the development of deeper comprehension over time by guiding users toward constructing a situation model of the text [31]. Overall, PaperMate demonstrates how theory grounded design can be translated into practical solutions that improve both accessibility and quality of learning [31].

3 Evaluation of the Artifact and Design Science Research Process

The development of PaperMate followed the three-cycle view of design science research as proposed by Hevner [32] with multiple evaluations displayed in Fig. 3. The artifact was developed through multiple iterative design cycles, including problem analysis, requirements derivation, design principle development, proof of concept, proof-of-value evaluations in the form of laboratory studies, and field tests [33]. These cycles informed the refinement of the system and ensured alignment with both theoretical foundations and user needs. The process began with problem analysis grounded in both literature [34] and observed challenges in academic reading contexts, particularly among non native readers. Based on these insights, requirements for a reading support system were derived and translated into initial design principles that reflect key dimensions of comprehension theory.

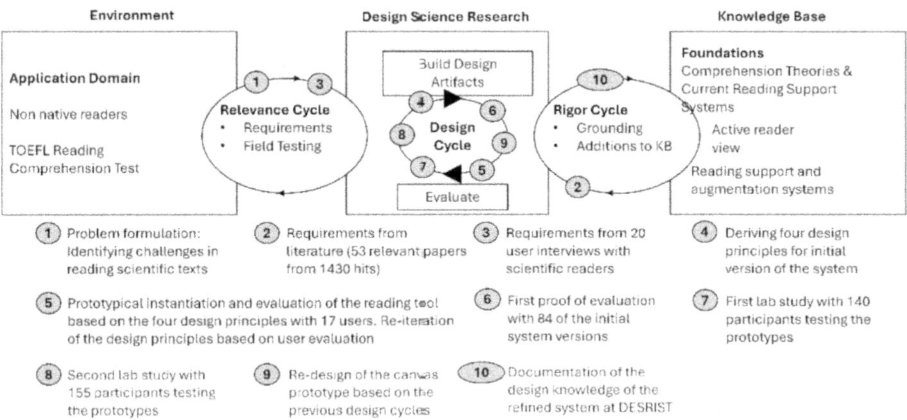

Fig. 3. Design science research journey of PaperMate, illustrating multiple iterative cycles of prototype refinement and evaluation across successive design stages [32].

These principles were instantiated in an initial proof of concept prototype, which enabled basic interaction with different forms of reading support. Early proof of value evaluations focused on feasibility and perceived usefulness.

Subsequent design cycles focused on refining the artifact through more advanced system implementations and controlled laboratory studies. These studies allowed for systematic observation of user interaction with the system and provided insights into how different support functions are used in practice. In particular, they informed the redesign of the interface toward a more integrated and user controlled canvas based approach, addressing limitations of earlier versions. In addition, the artifact is currently being evaluated in field-based settings through upcoming field based tests in realistic usage contexts. These evaluations contribute to validating the prototypes applicability in real world scenarios [33].

The current version of PaperMate represents the outcome of this iterative process and continues to be further developed based on ongoing evaluation and feedback. This approach reflects the core logic of design science research [32], where knowledge is generated through the design, implementation, and continuous evaluation of artifacts to address real-world challenges [35, 36].

Screencast of the prototype.

https://youtu.be/xQPcIFSJhqQ.

Disclosure of Interests. The authors have no competing interests to declare that are relevant to the content of this article.

References

1. Hellekjær, G.O.: Academic English reading proficiency at the university level: a Norwegian case study. Read. Foreign Lang. **21**, 198–222 (2009)
2. PISA 2022 Results (Volume I). https://www.oecd.org/en/publications/pisa-2022-results-vol ume-i_53f23881-en.html. Last accessed 09 Sep 2025
3. Trenkic, D., Warmington, M.: Language and literacy skills of home and international university students: how different are they, and does it matter? Bilingualism: Lang. Cogn. **22**, 349–365 (2019)
4. Amano, T., et al.: The manifold costs of being a non-native English speaker in science. PLoS Biol. **21**, 1–27 (2023). https://doi.org/10.1371/journal.pbio.3002184
5. Elnathan, R.: English is the language of science — but precision is tough as a non-native speaker. Nature (2021). https://doi.org/10.1038/d41586-021-00899-y
6. Behaviour, E.N.H.: Scientific publishing has a language problem. Nat. Hum. Behav. **7**, 1019–1020 (2023). https://doi.org/10.1038/s41562-023-01679-6
7. Uccelli, P., Galloway, E.P., Barr, C.D., Meneses, A., Dobbs, C.L.: Beyond vocabulary: exploring cross-disciplinary academic-language proficiency and its association with reading comprehension. Read. Res. Q. **50**, 337–356 (2015). https://doi.org/10.1002/rrq.104
8. Cruz Neri, N., Guill, K., Retelsdorf, J.: Language in science performance: do good readers perform better? Eur. J. Psychol. Educ. **36**, 45–61 (2021). https://doi.org/10.1007/s10212-019-00453-5
9. Barr, R.B., Tagg, J.: From teaching to learning—A new paradigm for undergraduate education. Change: Mag. High. Learn. **27**, 12–26 (1995). https://doi.org/10.1080/00091383.1995.105 44672
10. Howard, P.J., Gorzycki, M., Desa, G., Allen, D.D.: Academic reading: comparing students' and faculty perceptions of its value, practice, and pedagogy. J. Coll. Read. Learn. **48**, 189–209 (2018). https://doi.org/10.1080/10790195.2018.1472942

11. Pressley, M., Johnson, C.J., Symons, S., McGoldrick, J.A., Kurita, J.A.: Strategies that improve children's memory and comprehension of text. Elem. Sch. J. **90**, 3–32 (1989). https://doi.org/10.1086/461599

12. Swart, E.K., Nielen, T.M.J., Sikkema-de Jong, M.T.: Supporting learning from text: a meta-analysis on the timing and content of effective feedback. Educ. Res. Rev. **28**, 100296 (2019). https://doi.org/10.1016/j.edurev.2019.100296

13. Michaelis, J.E., Mutlu, B.: Reading socially: transforming the in-home reading experience with a learning-companion robot. Sci. Robot. **3**, 1–11 (2018). https://doi.org/10.1126/scirobotics.aat5999

14. Xu, S., Jiang, H., Lau, F.C.M.: User-oriented document summarization through vision-based eye-tracking. In: Proceedings of the 14th international conference on Intelligent user interfaces. pp. 7–16. Association for Computing Machinery, New York, NY, USA (2009). https://doi.org/10.1145/1502650.1502656

15. Alonzo, O.: The use of automatic text simplification to provide reading assistance to deaf and hard-of-hearing individuals in computing fields. SIGACCESS Access. Comput. **3**, 1 (2022). https://doi.org/10.1145/3523265.3523268

16. Agrawal, S., Carpuat, M.: Do text simplification systems preserve meaning? A human evaluation via reading comprehension. http://arxiv.org/abs/2312.10126 (2024). https://doi.org/10.48550/arXiv.2312.10126

17. Chung, S., Jeon, H., Shin, S., Hoque, M.N.: Reading.help: supporting EFL readers with proactive and on-demand explanation of english grammar and semantics, http://arxiv.org/abs/2505.14031, (2025). https://doi.org/10.48550/arXiv.2505.14031

18. Ariasi, N., Mason, L.: Uncovering the effect of text structure in learning from a science text: an eye-tracking study. Instr. Sci. **39**, 581–601 (2011). https://doi.org/10.1007/s11251-010-9142-5

19. Heuer, H., Glassman, E.L.: Accessible text tools: where they are needed & what they should look like. In: Extended Abstracts of the 2023 CHI Conference on Human Factors in Computing Systems. pp. 1–7. ACM, Hamburg Germany (2023). https://doi.org/10.1145/3544549.3585749

20. Liu, W., Huang, H., Saleem, A., Zhao, Z.: The effects of university students' fragmented reading on cognitive development in the new media age: evidence from Chinese higher education. PeerJ **10**, 1–18 (2022). https://doi.org/10.7717/peerj.13861

21. Kintsch, W.: The role of knowledge in discourse comprehension: a construction-integration model. Psychol. Rev. **95**, 163–182 (1988). https://doi.org/10.1037/0033-295X.95.2.163

22. Duke, N.K., Cartwright, K.B.: The science of reading progresses: communicating advances beyond the simple view of reading. Read. Res. Q. **56**, S25–S44 (2021). https://doi.org/10.1002/rrq.411

23. Gregor, S., Kruse, L.C., Seidel, S.: Research perspectives: the anatomy of a design principle. J. Assoc. Inf. Syst. **21**, 2 (2020). https://doi.org/10.17705/1jais.00649

24. Hänel, M., Wambsganss, T., Söllner, M.: Towards effective AI-Driven reading assistants: a design science exploration. In: Thirty-Second European Conference on Information Systems (ECIS 2024). pp. 1–16., Paphos, Cyprus (2024)

25. Kosch, T., Schmidt, A., Thanheiser, S., Chuang, L.L.: One does not Simply RSVP: mental workload to select speed reading parameters using electroencephalography. In: Proceedings of the 2020 CHI Conference on Human Factors in Computing Systems. pp. 1–13. Association for Computing Machinery, New York, NY, USA (2020). https://doi.org/10.1145/3313831.3376766

26. Higasa, T., Tanaka, K., Feng, Q., Morishima, S.: Keep eyes on the sentence: an interactive sentence simplification system for english learners based on eye tracking and large language models. In: Extended Abstracts of the CHI Conference on Human Factors in Computing

Systems. pp. 1–7. Association for Computing Machinery, New York, NY, USA (2024). https://doi.org/10.1145/3613905.3650792

27. Alonzo, O., Hassan, S.: A review of 25 years of human-computer interaction research on reading support technologies for people with disabilities published in the ACM digital library. In: Proceedings of the 27th International ACM SIGACCESS Conference on Computers and Accessibility. pp. 1–21. ACM, Denver Colorado USA (2025). https://doi.org/10.1145/3663547.3746355

28. Amin, R.M., Kühle, O.H., Buschek, D., Butz, A.: Composable prompting workspaces for creative writing: exploration and iteration using dynamic widgets. In: Proceedings of the Extended Abstracts of the CHI Conference on Human Factors in Computing Systems. pp. 1–11. Association for Computing Machinery, New York, NY, USA (2025). https://doi.org/10.1145/3706599.3720243

29. Schreiber, G.: Reconsidering agency in the age of AI. Filozofia **79**, 529–537 (2024). https://doi.org/10.31577/filozofia.2024.79.5.5

30. Winkler, R., Söllner, M., Leimeister, J.M.: Enhancing problem-solving skills with smart personal assistant technology. Comput. Educ. 1–15 (2021). https://doi.org/10.1016/j.compedu.2021.104148

31. Bittner, E., Oeste-Reiß, S., Kirmse, R., Poser, M., Wiethof, C.: Cognitive load theory approach to hybrid intelligence: tackling the dual aim of task performance and learning. ICIS 2024 Proceedings (2024)

32. Hevner, A.: A three cycle view of design science research. Scand. J. Inf. Syst. **19**, 87–92 (2007)

33. Venable, J., Pries-Heje, J., Baskerville, R.: FEDS: a framework for evaluation in design science research. Eur. J. Inf. Syst. **25**, 77–89 (2016). https://doi.org/10.1057/ejis.2014.36

34. vom Brocke, J., Simons, A., Riemer, K., Niehaves, B., Plattfaut, R., Cleven, A.: Standing on the shoulders of giants: challenges and recommendations of literature search in information systems research. Commun. Assoc. Inf. Syst. **37** (2015). https://doi.org/10.17705/1CAIS.03709

35. Tuunanen, T., Winter, R., vom Brocke, J.: Dealing with complexity in design science research: a methodology using design echelons. MISQ **48**, 427–458 (2024). https://doi.org/10.25300/MISQ/2023/16700

36. Schoormann, T., Möller, F., Chandra Kruse, L., Otto, B.: BAUSTEIN—A design tool for configuring and representing design research. Inf. Syst. J. **34**, 1871–1901 (2024). https://doi.org/10.1111/isj.12516

Designing and Building Personalized Agentic AI for Job Seekers

Matt Mullarkey$^{(\boxtimes)}$ ⓘ and Denis Edwards ⓘ

University of South Florida, Tampa, FL, USA
{mmullarkey,denisedwards}@usf.edu

Abstract. This paper presents the design, implementation, and simulation-based evaluation of a multi-agent agentic AI system that supports job seekers across the full lifecycle of a job search. Applying the elaborated Action Design Research (eADR) method, we diagnose the challenges candidates face within AI-driven recruitment systems and design a governed, hybrid multi-agent architecture integrating ten specialized LLM-powered agents, a coordinator agent, multi-tier memory, and human-in-the-loop (HITL) oversight. We implement the system as a ~17,000-line prototype using Python, LangGraph, Claude Sonnet, PostgreSQL, and a React dashboard, then evaluate it through simulation using actual candidate profiles with live LLM calls. Results confirm the architecture correctly orchestrates agents, enforces governance, and produces actionable outputs across career alignment, job discovery, application orchestration, and interview preparation. The source code is publicly available on GitHub.

Keywords: Agentic AI · Multi-Agent Systems · Job Search · eADR · LLM

1 Design of the Artifact

1.1 Problem Statement

The job search process is complex, multistage, and cognitively demanding. While employers have rapidly adopted AI throughout recruitment—résumé parsers, predictive analytics, screening tools, and automated interviews [5]—candidates lack equivalent AI-powered tools that operate across the full job search lifecycle. Up to 79% of U.S. employers use AI in hiring, yet candidates report increasing exhaustion, with 35% abandoning lengthy applications and 43% citing the application process as the primary driver of employer perception [3]. This asymmetry motivates our central question: *can an agentic AI system effectively support job seekers across the full lifecycle of a job search?* This problem is particularly acute because the job search lifecycle spans weeks to months, requires coordination across ten or more distinct activity domains, and demands both creative output (résumé tailoring, cover letter writing) and analytical reasoning (offer comparison, salary negotiation)—a combination that neither traditional automation nor single-step generative AI adequately addresses.

In collaboration with a startup developing a job seeker platform, we applied the elaborated Action Design Research (eADR) method [6] to diagnose this problem, design a

S. Chatterjee et al. (Eds.): DESRIST 2026, LNCS 16607, pp. 345–351, 2026.
https://doi.org/10.1007/978-3-032-28570-6_29

multi-agent solution, implement a working prototype, and evaluate it through simulation. eADR extends ADR [8] by distinguishing Diagnosis, Design, Implementation, and Evolution stages, each producing identifiable artifacts through iterative researcher–practitioner intervention cycles. Our diagnosis decomposed the job search into ten distinct activity domains (career alignment through onboarding), each elaborated as a task with inputs, outputs, context, constraints, and subgoals. This decomposition revealed that existing candidate-facing tools (job board search, résumé builders) address isolated tasks but fail to provide the sustained, multi-step orchestration that a comprehensive job search demands. The cognitive load of managing ten parallel workflows—each with its own tools, timelines, and decision points—is a primary source of the frustration documented in candidate surveys [1].

1.2 User Groups and Use Cases

The primary user group is active job seekers—professionals seeking new employment across career levels. The system addresses ten core use cases corresponding to the decomposed job search lifecycle: (1) career self-assessment and goal setting, (2) résumé and profile optimization, (3) job discovery and opportunity matching and scoring, (4) application preparation and submission, (5) assessment and skills testing preparation, (6) interview preparation and coaching, (7) offer evaluation and negotiation, (8) communication and follow-up management, (9) relationship and network tracking, and (10) onboarding coordination. A secondary user group is career coaches and advisors who can leverage the system's outputs to augment their guidance. Each use case was validated with practitioners who confirmed the decomposition reflects real-world job search workflows.

1.3 Features and Architecture

Through feasibility analysis, we determined that generative AI alone is insufficient for long-horizon, multi-step job search workflows. Agentic AI—where agents use LLMs for reasoning, orchestration, planning, memory, and tool interaction [2]—proved more suitable. Unlike single-prompt generative AI, agentic systems maintain state across interactions, pursue goals over multiple steps, and coordinate specialized sub-tasks through structured delegation—capabilities essential for a process that unfolds over weeks or months and requires different expertise at each stage. Three validated design principles guide the architecture:

DP1: Multi-agent design is warranted for domain-spanning, role-diverse, governed solutions. **DP2:** A hybrid approach is needed for tasks requiring human nuance; governance ensures HITL checkpoints. **DP3:** A coordinating agent is essential for managing multiple agents, domains, and governance.

The resulting artifact (Fig. 1) integrates: **Ten specialized agents** for each use case, coordinated by a supervisor agent that sequences tasks, enforces guardrails, prevents duplicates, and triggers HITL approval for high-risk actions. The ten agents are: Career Alignment (validates target roles, identifies skill gaps), Profile Optimization (ATS keyword analysis, résumé formatting), Job Discovery (multi-dimensional fit scoring across skills, salary, location, experience, and culture), Application Orchestration (tailored cover letters, submission tracking), Assessment Preparation (company-specific practice questions), Interview Coach (STAR story generation, company research), Negotiation (counter-offer strategies, market benchmarking), Communication (recruiter message classification, response drafting), Relationship Tracking (contact strength scoring, networking recommendations), and Onboarding (30/60/90 day plans, pre-start checklists). **Multi-tier memory** provides Redis for session cache, PostgreSQL for long-term persistence and audit, and Pinecone for semantic vector search. A **governance engine** implements risk assessment, rate limiting (max ten applications/day), content filtering (PII redaction), and HITL approval queuing. A **HITL portal** surfaces all human-required decisions as structured approval requests. The reference architecture draws on the agentic AI framework class model defined by Derouiche et al. [2] (Fig. 2).

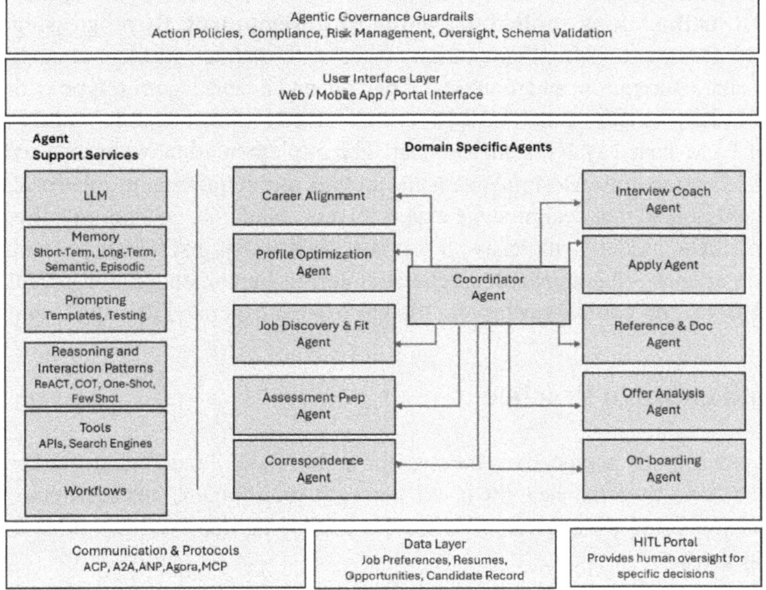

Fig. 1. Job Seeker Agentic AI System Architecture

2 Significance to Research

This work contributes to three research areas. First, it advances **agentic AI systems design** by providing a validated architecture for governed, hybrid multi-agent systems in a complex, human-sensitive domain. While multi-agent systems have been studied extensively in simulation and game environments, applications to real-world, multi-step professional workflows remain scarce. The recruitment domain is particularly instructive because it combines long-horizon goal pursuit (weeks to months), multi-stakeholder interaction (candidates, recruiters, hiring managers), heterogeneous data sources (job boards, company sites, salary databases), and high-stakes decisions requiring human oversight—a combination of characteristics shared by many professional domains that stand to benefit from agentic AI. Our ten-agent architecture with supervisor coordination demonstrates how MAS principles apply to domains requiring sustained goal pursuit, adaptive personalization, and human oversight—characteristics absent from typical MAS benchmarks.

Second, the research contributes **design principles for HITL governance in agentic systems**. The three design principles (DP1–DP3) provide transferable guidance for other domains where autonomous AI must coexist with human judgment—healthcare decision support, legal document review, and financial advisory, among others. The principles were validated through expert peer review and confirmed through implementation.

Third, the system provides an empirical demonstration of how LLM-powered agents can be composed into a coherent multi-agent workflow with shared state, where each agent's output becomes input to downstream agents—creating a pipeline of increasingly refined career intelligence from a single candidate profile. Fourth, the work demonstrates the **eADR methodology applied to agentic AI development**. By progressing through Diagnosis, Design, and Implementation stages with distinct artifacts at each stage, a problem characterization, an architectural design, and a working prototype with simulation evaluation, we show that eADR [6] is well suited to the emergent, rapidly evolving nature of LLM-based systems engineering. The implementation cycle surfaced knowledge (LLM output non-determinism, async architecture requirements, platform-specific deployment issues) that design-stage expert review could not. This finding directly supports the eADR model's emphasis on progressing through distinct stages with artifact evaluation at each—the knowledge generated during Implementation was qualitatively different from, and complementary to, the knowledge generated during Design.

3   Significance to Practice

From a practitioner perspective, the system addresses a documented market failure: employers have invested heavily in AI-powered recruitment, but candidates remain largely unsupported by equivalent tools. The prototype demonstrates practical utility in several ways:

Cognitive load reduction. By decomposing the job search into ten automated agent workflows, the system eliminates the most repetitive and time-consuming tasks—job board monitoring, résumé tailoring per posting, cover letter generation, and follow-up scheduling—while preserving human agency over consequential decisions (which jobs to apply to, whether to accept an offer). In our simulation, the system produced differentiated outputs for five distinct job postings in a single 60-s run—each with a uniquely tailored résumé summary, customized cover letter, and role-specific interview preparation materials.

Personalization at scale. Each agent operates on the candidate's full profile, career goals, and interaction history. The ATS keyword analyzer tailors résumés to specific postings; the fit scorer weights skills, salary, location, experience, and culture; the interview coach generates company-specific STAR stories. This level of personalization would require hours of manual effort per application.

Governed automation. The HITL governance model ensures that high-risk actions (submitting applications, accepting offers, sending communications) require explicit human approval, addressing practitioner concerns about autonomous AI taking irreversible actions in professional contexts. Rate limiting and PII redaction provide additional safety guardrails.

The startup collaborating on this research has incorporated the design principles and architecture into their product roadmap, providing early evidence of practitioner adoption. The simulation demonstrated that a single workflow execution produces outputs that would require several hours of manual effort: a tailored résumé, five scored job matches, cover letters, interview preparation materials, and a negotiation strategy. This cost-benefit ratio suggests significant practical value at scale.

4 Evaluation

In traditional ADR, evaluation occurs through formative and summative assessments embedded within each design cycle (Sein et al., 2011). Both Sein et al. (2011) and Mullarkey and Hevner (2019) explicitly permit surrogate evaluation mechanisms when real-world deployment is impractical within the research timeline. Because this research represents a prototype solution not yet ready for field deployment, simulation was selected as the primary evaluation strategy. This choice is methodologically consistent with the eADR framework, which recognizes that ensemble-level artifacts whose value properties emerge from the interaction of multiple components can be rigorously evaluated through controlled execution rather than longitudinal field observation.

The simulation employed in this study is grounded in real artifacts rather than hypothetical constructs. It uses actual candidate profiles and resumes, market-relevant executive job postings, and LLM-generated outputs that are functionally identical to those the system would produce in live deployment. The only synthetic element is employer-response logic, which cannot be ethically or practically instantiated within a research context. In this respect, the approach is analogous to usability testing in HCI research, where a real system is evaluated under controlled laboratory conditions rather than in unconstrained field use. Following Mullarkey and Hevner (2019), the simulation functions as a controlled laboratory instantiation for artifact evaluation, explicitly scoped to functional behavior rather than ecological outcomes—a defensible and epistemologically precise boundary for a prototype-stage contribution.

4.1 Simulation-Based Implementation Evaluation

The implemented prototype was evaluated by creating and executing a simulation engine against real candidate profiles— with actual résumé, skills inventory, and career goals loaded from PostgreSQL. Each simulation randomly samples 5 of 20 curated job postings to ensure variability across executions. Results:

Agent orchestration. The supervisor correctly sequenced all ten agents. Career Alignment identified target roles and skill gaps. Profile Optimization achieved ATS scores of 80–92/100. Job Discovery scored five postings with fit scores of 0.65–0.93, correctly distinguishing strong from poor matches. Application Orchestration generated tailored cover letters and triggered HITL approval for submissions. Interview Coach produced company-specific STAR stories mapped to target company culture. Negotiation generated counter-offer strategies with market salary benchmarking. Communication classified simulated recruiter messages by type (interview invite, rejection, inquiry) and generated context-appropriate responses. Relationship Tracking scored contact strength across recency, frequency, depth, and relevance dimensions.

Governance enforcement. Rate limits enforced (max ten applications/24 h). PII content filtering active (SSN and credit card pattern redaction in all outbound text). HITL approval correctly triggered for high-risk actions—specifically, the system paused before submitting any application and surfaced a structured approval request containing the job title, company, fit score, and generated cover letter for human review. These behaviors could not have been validated through design review alone.

End-to-end data flow. All results persisted to PostgreSQL and streamed via Server-Sent Events to the React dashboard in real time, confirming full-stack integration from LLM reasoning through database persistence to frontend visualization. The React dashboard provides a live simulation view with agent status panels showing active/done/error states, a scrolling log of agent outputs, scored job cards with fit percentages, and an application lifecycle tracker. Simulation runs are persisted and can be compared across executions through the simulation history viewer, enabling longitudinal evaluation of system behavior across different job pool samples.

Implementation also revealed practical considerations invisible to design evaluation: LLM output non-determinism requires defensive JSON parsing; async-first architecture is essential for concurrent execution; platform-specific issues (Windows event loop policies) affect deployment. These findings confirm the eADR principle that authentic evaluation through instantiation generates knowledge beyond design-stage review. The implementation validated all three design principles: DP1 was confirmed as the ten-agent decomposition enabled effective specialization, with inter-agent data flow (e.g., career alignment output informing profile optimization keywords) producing emergent system-level intelligence. DP2 was confirmed as HITL checkpoints correctly paused workflows for human approval on consequential actions. DP3 was confirmed as the coordinator successfully sequenced all agents and enforced governance policies.

4.2 Limitations and Future Work

The simulation operates against curated job postings rather than live job board APIs; real-world deployment will introduce additional integration challenges. Evaluation involved limited candidate profiles; broader testing across diverse demographics, career levels, and markets is needed. HITL oversight thresholds remain untested with diverse user populations. LLM reasoning brittleness and incomplete memory coherence across long sessions introduce technical constraints. Future research will address these limitations through field testing with diverse candidate populations, integration with live employer systems (LinkedIn, Indeed), and investigation of continuous learning mechanisms that enable agents to adapt to evolving labor-market trends. This would advance the research into the Evolution stage of the eADR process model, where the artifact is iteratively refined based on longitudinal field observations.

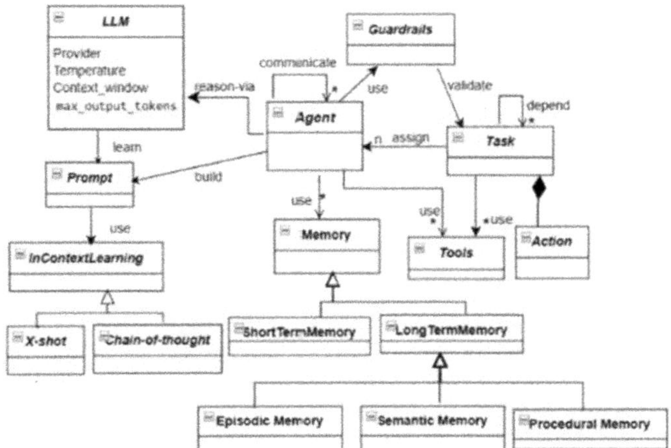

Fig. 2. Agentic AI Solution Class Model (after Derouiche et al. [2])

Acknowledgments. The authors thank the practitioner collaborators who contributed to the design evaluation and the anonymous reviewers for their constructive feedback.

Disclosure of Interests. The authors have no competing interests to declare that are relevant to the content of this article.

References

1. Dadaboyev, S.M.U., Abdullayeva, J., Abbosova, N., Suleymenova, A., Mamadjanova, K.: Role of artificial intelligence in employee recruitment: systematic review. Discover Glob. Soc. **3**(1), 1–16 (2025). https://doi.org/10.1007/s44282-025-00246-w
2. Derouiche, H., Brahmi, Z., Mazeni, H.: Agentic AI frameworks: architectures, protocols, and design challenges. arXiv (2025). https://doi.org/10.48550/arXiv.2508.10146
3. Employ Inc.: 2025 Job Seeker Nation Report: Job market truths—What's driving candidates in 2025 (2025). https://www.employinc.com/resources/2025-job-seeker-nation-report/
4. LangChain, Inc.: LangGraph: Build resilient language agents as graphs (2025). https://langchain-ai.github.io/langgraph/
5. Mori, M., Sassetti, S., Cavaliere, V., Bonti, M.: A systematic literature review on AI in recruiting and selection. Pers. Rev. **54**(3), 854–878 (2025). https://doi.org/10.1108/PR-03-2023-0257
6. Mullarkey, M.T., Hevner, A.R.: An elaborated action design research process model. Eur. J. Inf. Syst. **28**(1), 6–20 (2019). https://doi.org/10.1080/0960085X.2018.1451811
7. Raza, H.: AI-powered hiring: Balancing efficiency and potential. LinkedIn (2025)
8. Sein, M., Henfridsson, O., Purao, S., Rossi, M., Lindgren, R.: Action design research. MIS Q. **35**(1), 37–56 (2011)

LitFlow: An Integrated, AI-Augmented Systematic Literature Review Platform

Hans-Henning Näscher[✉] ⓘ, Timo Strohmann ⓘ, and Jan vom Brocke ⓘ

University of Münster, Münster, Germany
`{hans.naescher,timo.strohmann,jan.vom-brocke}@uni-muenster.de`

Abstract. Systematic literature reviews (SLRs) are central to rigorous research but remain resource-intensive and dependent on fragmented toolchains. At the same time, artificial intelligence (AI)-based support for review tasks often lacks transparency and limits researcher control. This paper presents LitFlow, a web-based platform for AI-augmented SLRs developed following the echeloned design science research (eDSR) methodology. LitFlow integrates multi-database search, criteria-based screening, structured data extraction, and audit-trail generation within a single workspace. Its augmentation approach provides AI recommendations with confidence scores, justifications, and source references, while final decisions remain with the researcher. The platform is built on a community-extensible architecture. A formative evaluation with five researchers confirmed the perceived value of the integrated workflow and the augmentation-oriented design. Participants also raised socio-technical concerns, including potential anchoring effects from AI recommendations, which inform directions for future iterations. LitFlow contributes a working demonstration of transparent, researcher-controlled AI support across the full SLR workflow.

Keywords: Systematic Literature Review · AI Augmentation · Design Science Research

1 Introduction

Systematic literature reviews (SLRs) are well-established for ensuring research rigor but demand substantial resources. Reviews often require months of work, involve large volumes of papers, and depend on fragmented toolchains that lack native interoperability [1–3]. At the same time, large language models (LLMs) offer new opportunities to support review tasks like screening and data extraction [4]. However, these advancements raise concerns about transparency, auditability, and the preservation of researcher judgment [5, 6]. SLRs thus represent a promising domain for AI-based tool development in information systems (IS) [7].

This paper presents LitFlow, a web-based platform for artificial intelligence (AI)-augmented SLRs. The artifact is developed following the echeloned design science research (eDSR) approach [8]. LitFlow has progressed through three eDSR iterations: (1) an initial prototype focused on problem scoping through literature review and the derivation of meta-requirements, (2) an empirically grounded tool usage study based on a survey of 178 researchers, and (3) the design and implementation of the current web-based platform. This paper reports on the third iteration and serves as a demonstration echelon. LitFlow follows an augmentation paradigm in which AI provides recommendations, explanations, and confidence estimates across the review workflow, while final decisions remain with the researcher. Beyond its immediate function, LitFlow is designed as a community-extensible artifact that supports independent verification, local adaptation, and community-driven refinement of AI-supported review practices.

2 Design of the Artifact

2.1 Problem Statement and Target Users

Current SLR practice faces two related challenges. It is both time-consuming and fragmented across tools for search, screening, extraction, and reporting [1, 2], and emerging AI-based support often favors automation over methodological transparency and researcher agency [5, 6]. In response, LitFlow supports individual researchers and small teams conducting SLRs by integrating key tasks such as multi-database searching, criteria-based screening, structured data extraction, and audit-trail generation for methods reporting. To clarify the specific gap that LitFlow addresses, the following section positions the artifact relative to the most widely used SLR support tools before presenting the design requirements (DRs) and features (DFs).

2.2 Positioning Relative to Existing Tools

Existing tools such as Rayyan[1], Covidence[2], ASReview [9], and EPPI-Reviewer[3] cover multiple review stages and have increasingly incorporated AI, from screening prioritization and relevance sorting to LLM-assisted data extraction. However, AI-generated outputs typically lack per-decision transparency: researchers receive rankings or suggestions without interpretable justifications, confidence scores, or provenance linking recommendations to specific textual evidence. Furthermore, configurability and workflow coverage remain inversely related: ASReview and EPPI-Reviewer are open source or source-available but concentrate their AI on screening, while the tools with broader workflow coverage (Covidence and Rayyan) remain proprietary. As of early 2026, no existing tool integrates transparent, configurable AI augmentation across the full SLR workflow from search through reporting while preserving researcher decision authority and auditability at every stage.

2.3 Design Process and Design Requirements

The artifact was developed using the eDSR methodology [8], which structures DSR projects into five recurring echelons: problem analysis, objectives and requirements,

---

[1] https://www.rayyan.ai/.

[2] https://www.covidence.org/.

[3] https://eppi.ioe.ac.uk/cms/Default.aspx?tabid=2914.

design and development, demonstration, and evaluation. These echelons are repeated across successive iterations.

The following DRs emerged within the problem definition echelons of the three iterations. They draw on four distinct sources of design knowledge: (1) literature on structured analysis of SLR support tools and their limitations [1, 10–13]; (2) literature-derived DRs for AI use in research workflows such as transparency, auditability, explainability, interoperability, and researcher control [5, 7, 14–16]; (3) an online survey with 178 researchers on tool usage and unmet needs; and (4) iterative development cycles with formative feedback from members of the research group, which served as a continuous validation mechanism throughout the design process. Across these sources, five consolidated DRs guide the artifact design (Table 1).

Table 1. DRs and their knowledge sources.

DR	Description	Sources
DR 1 – End-to-end workflow integration	The system must provide a seamless pipeline across search, screening, extraction, and reporting, eliminating manual data transfers between isolated tools	Survey; [7, 17]
DR 2 – Transparent AI augmentation	All AI-generated outputs must be inspectable, accompanied by confidence scores, justifications, and source references	[6, 14]
DR 3 – Researcher-in-the-loop	Final decisions on inclusion, exclusion, and interpretation remain with the researcher; the system recommends, the human confirms	[5–7, 15]
DR 4 – Auditable provenance	The system must log all decisions with timestamps, actor attribution, and rationale to support reproducibility and compliance with emerging AI disclosure requirements	Survey; [10, 12, 14]
DR 5 – Open, community-extensible architecture	Core functionality must be freely accessible. The system's development must be guided by its research community, with structured mechanisms for collaborative contribution to the platform's evolution	Survey; [1, 14]

These five DRs are operationalized through a set of concrete design features (DFs), each traceable to one or more requirements.

2.4 Design Features

The following design features operationalize the DRs identified in Sect. 2.3. Each DF is described below together with its requirement traceability.

DF 1 Search and import (addressing DR 1): The platform supports parallel search across academic databases (e.g., Scopus, Web of Science, PubMed, IEEE Xplore) via application programming interfaces (APIs) and manual import of standard bibliographic formats. Duplicates within the search results are automatically removed. An AI-supported query refinement function proposes synonyms, related terms, and Boolean logic improvements. The researcher reviews and approves all changes.

DF 2 AI-augmented screening with researcher control (addressing DR 1, DR 2, DR 3): Reviewers define inclusion and exclusion criteria. Screening proceeds in two stages: title/abstract screening and full-text screening, both supported by the same criteria-based AI assistant. The screening workspace presents the record and the assistant side by side (see Fig. 1). The system shows the AI recommendation, confidence, and justification per criterion. The researcher remains the final decision-maker and can accept, reject, or override suggestions. Exclusion reasons are documented at the criterion level.

DF 3 PDF retrieval and viewer (addressing DR 1): LitFlow provides integrated full-text retrieval via API-based access to open-access repositories and manual upload. A built-in PDF viewer with highlighting, annotation, and in-text search is available throughout the platform—during screening, data extraction, and synthesis. This allows researchers to consult source documents without switching tools.

DF 4 Structured data extraction (addressing DR 1, DR 2, DR 3): Reviewers define custom extraction schemas (e.g., method, sample, findings, theory). The AI pre-fills fields using LLM-based extraction and returns structured outputs with confidence scores and links to source passages. Reviewers validate or correct entries in a dedicated interface.

DF 5 Audit trail and reporting (addressing DR 4): LitFlow logs all AI-assisted and human decisions with timestamps and user attribution. The system computes agreement metrics between AI recommendations and human decisions (e.g., Cohen's κ [18], precision, recall, and F1). It supports the export of decision histories and generates AI transparency documentation for methods reporting.

DF 6 Community-driven extensibility (addressing DR 5): LitFlow is freely accessible and follows a community-driven development model in which the research community actively shapes the platform's evolution. Structured contribution mechanisms allow researchers to propose and collaboratively develop new features, review workflows, and integrations. This positions LitFlow not as a static tool but as a shared infrastructure that evolves with the practices and needs of its user community.

The following section describes the technical realization of these design features in the current prototype.

2.5 Prototype Demonstration

LitFlow[4] is implemented as a modular web application with a backend built on FastAPI[5](Python) and PostgreSQL. The backend is organized into feature-based modules (e.g., search, screening, extraction, reporting). LLM integration is abstracted through a provider-agnostic layer that supports multiple commercial and open-source model backends, allowing review teams to select or replace AI providers without modifying application code. The frontend is a React single-page application with a component-based user interface. The entire stack is containerized for reproducible deployment. This architecture supports the extensibility goal of DF 6. New database connectors, extraction templates, LLM backends, and reporting modules can be added as isolated components without cross-cutting changes.

A screenshot of the user interface is included in Fig. 1.

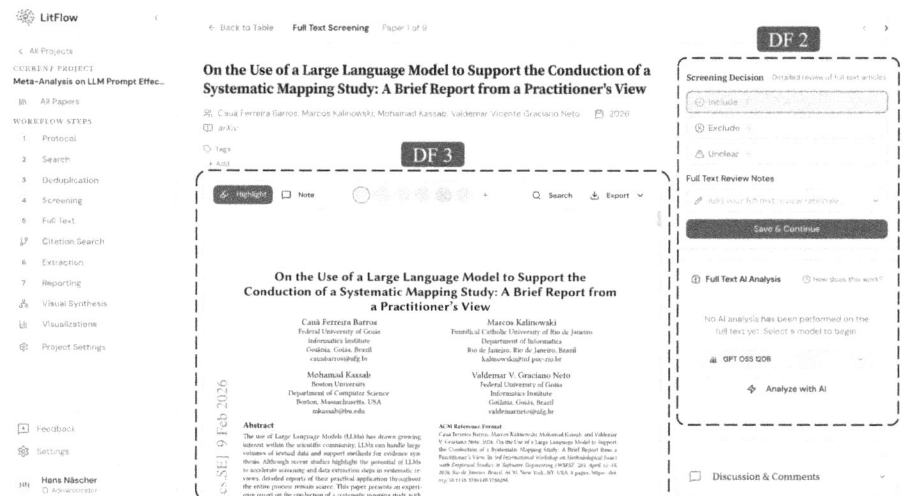

Fig. 1. Full-text screening workspace showing the integrated PDF viewer (left) and the AI-augmented screening panel (right)

3 Significance to Research

LitFlow offers three research contributions. First, it demonstrates an augmentation-first approach to AI-supported literature reviews. While prior work has emphasized the importance of transparency, auditability, and researcher agency, these principles have rarely been operationalized within a single artifact [7, 19]. LitFlow makes these design goals concrete and observable in a working platform.

---

[4] The screencast can be accessed at https://youtu.be/4mIKnQdIl3E.

[5] https://fastapi.tiangolo.com/.

Second, the artifact illustrates methodological integration by treating AI as a second reviewer rather than an opaque assistant. By quantifying agreement between AI recommendations and human decisions through established metrics, LitFlow connects review-method quality assurance with AI evaluation practice in a form that is interpretable for researchers and editors.

Third, LitFlow is designed to provide a foundation for community-driven, AI-augmented review systems. Its transparent development practices are intended to enable independent verification, comparative evaluation across contexts, and collaborative refinement of the artifact. To support this, we are establishing a community platform[6] where researchers can share adaptations, report experiences, and contribute to the ongoing development of the tool. This positions LitFlow as a shared experimental platform for accumulating design knowledge on human–AI collaboration in evidence synthesis.

4 Significance to Practice

LitFlow addresses the practical challenges researchers face when conducting SLRs. The platform improves efficiency by integrating search, screening, extraction, and reporting within a single workspace, and by using AI to assist with selected tasks. This reduces manual overhead and makes larger review projects more feasible for small teams.

Regarding review quality and consistency, criteria-based AI recommendations, explicit justifications, and agreement metrics help reviewers apply inclusion and exclusion criteria more consistently and make decision quality visible during the process, not only after publication.

The platform also supports methodological onboarding. The structured workflow, explicit criteria handling, and traceable AI suggestions provide guidance for less experienced researchers while still supporting advanced users.

Finally, the community-driven and interoperable design reduces adoption barriers for institutions that cannot rely on commercial review platforms. It is planned that research groups can inspect, adapt, and extend the system for their own domains, and community-shared templates or modules can reduce duplicated effort across projects.

5 Evaluation

We conducted a formative evaluation to assess workflow completeness, perceived researcher control, and the transparency of AI-generated outputs. Given the prototype maturity of the artifact, we adopted a qualitative, exploratory design rather than a summative performance comparison. We selected think-aloud interviews because they capture reasoning processes and usability issues in real time. Five researchers (four PhD students, one postdoctoral researcher) in IS, all with prior SLR experience, participated in individual one-hour sessions. Each session covered the full workflow from project creation through reporting, including multi-database search, deduplication, AI-augmented screening, structured data extraction, and audit report generation. This allowed us to verify that LitFlow executes the core SLR process end-to-end. Sessions

---

[6] https://litflow.org/community/.

were screen-recorded and transcribed. We note a technical limitation: one session was partially affected by API outages, which restricted the demonstration of AI-assisted features for that participant. Findings from this session are included for workflow-related observations but excluded from AI-specific themes.

Across sessions, participants' feedback clustered around three recurring observations. First, participants consistently identified the integrated workflow as the platform's primary value, particularly multi-database search with database-specific query previews. AI support in query refinement was perceived as less useful than assistance during screening and extraction. Second, all participants indicated they felt in full control of their review decisions, describing the AI as a restrained assistant rather than an autonomous agent. Confidence indicators and justifications were regarded as comprehensible, though some questioned the interpretability of the scoring logic. Third, three participants independently raised socio-technical concerns beyond usability. They noted that viewing AI recommendations before forming an independent judgment may introduce anchoring effects that weaken the researcher agency the tool seeks to preserve. One proposed a delayed-reveal mode in which the researcher screens first and compares with AI assessments afterward. Two cautioned that early reliance on AI support may impede the development of foundational literature appraisal skills, a risk they framed as skill non-acquisition rather than deskilling. A related concern was that reporting AI use may invite peer-reviewer skepticism regardless of actual process rigor.

These findings provide initial formative evidence supporting the usefulness of the integrated workflow and the augmentation-oriented design. At the same time, the socio-technical tensions around anchoring, skill development, and community acceptance point to design directions for future iterations, such as configurable AI-reveal timing, that go beyond interface refinement. As a next step, we plan a comparative evaluation with three conditions: (A) traditional tools, (B) LitFlow with AI augmentation enabled, and (C) LitFlow with AI features disabled. This design will allow us to separate the effects of workflow integration from the effects of AI support. Planned measures include time to completion, review quality (inter-rater reliability against a reference set), and cognitive load.

References

1. Marshall, C., Brereton, P., Kitchenham, B.: Tools to support systematic reviews in software engineering: a cross-domain survey using semi-structured interviews. In: Proceedings of the 19th International Conference on Evaluation and Assessment in Software Engineering, pp. 1–6. ACM, Nanjing China (2015). https://doi.org/10.1145/2745802.2745827
2. Tell, P., Cholewa, J.B., Nellemann, P., Kuhrmann, M.: Beyond the spreadsheet: reflections on tool support for literature studies. In: Proceedings of the 20th International Conference on Evaluation and Assessment in Software Engineering, pp. 1–5. ACM, Limerick Ireland (2016). https://doi.org/10.1145/2915970.2916011
3. Vom Brocke, J., et al.: Standing on the Shoulders of Giants: Challenges and Recommendations of Literature Search in Information Systems Research. CAIS 37, 205–224 (2015). https://doi.org/10.17705/1cais.03709
4. Felizardo, K.R., Lima, M.S., Deizepe, A., Conte, T.U., Steinmacher, I.: ChatGPT application in Systematic Literature Reviews in Software Engineering: an evaluation of its accuracy to

support the selection activity. In: Proceedings of the 18th ACM/IEEE International Symposium on Empirical Software Engineering and Measurement, pp. 25–36. ACM, Barcelona Spain (2024). https://doi.org/10.1145/3574805.3686666

5. Ngwenyama, O., Rowe, F.: Should We Collaborate with AI to Conduct Literature Reviews? Changing Epistemic Values in a Flattening World. JAIS **25**, 122–136 (2024). https://doi.org/10.17705/1jais.00869

6. Schryen, G., Marrone, M., Yang, J.: Exploring the scope of generative AI in literature review development. Electron Markets. **35**, 13 (2025). https://doi.org/10.1007/s12525-025-00754-2

7. Wagner, G., Lukyanenko, R., Paré, G.: Artificial intelligence and the conduct of literature reviews. J. Inf. Technol. **37**, 209–226 (2022). https://doi.org/10.1177/02683962211048201

8. Tuunanen, T., Winter, R., Vom Brocke, J.: Dealing with Complexity in Design Science Research: A Methodology Using Design Echelons. MISQ **48**, 427–458 (2024). https://doi.org/10.25300/MISQ/2023/16700

9. De Bruin, J., et al.: ASReview LAB v.2: Open-source text screening with multiple agents and a crowd of experts. Patterns **6** (2025). https://doi.org/10.1016/j.patter.2025.101318

10. Al-Zubidy, A., Carver, J.C., Hale, D.P., Hassler, E.E.: Vision for SLR tooling infrastructure: Prioritizing value-added requirements. Inf. Softw. Technol. **91**, 72–81 (2017). https://doi.org/10.1016/j.infsof.2017.06.007

11. Harrison, H., Griffin, S.J., Kuhn, I., Usher-Smith, J.A.: Software tools to support title and abstract screening for systematic reviews in healthcare: an evaluation. BMC Med. Res. Methodol. **20**, 7 (2020). https://doi.org/10.1186/s12874-020-0897-3

12. Hassler, E., Carver, J.C., Hale, D., Al-Zubidy, A.: Identification of SLR tool needs – results of a community workshop. Inf. Softw. Technol. **70**, 122–129 (2016). https://doi.org/10.1016/j.infsof.2015.10.011

13. Van Der Mierden, S.: Software tools for literature screening in systematic reviews in biomedical research. ALTEX **36**, 508–517 (2019). https://doi.org/10.14573/altex.1902131

14. Bolaños, F., Salatino, A., Osborne, F., Motta, E.: Artificial intelligence for literature reviews: opportunities and challenges. Artif. Intell. Rev. **57**, 259 (2024). https://doi.org/10.1007/s10462-024-10902-3

15. Tingelhoff, F., Brugger, M., Leimeister, J.M.: A guide for structured literature reviews in business research: The state-of-the-art and how to integrate generative artificial intelligence. J. Inf. Technol. **40**, 77–99 (2025). https://doi.org/10.1177/02683962241304105

16. Wagner, G., Prester, J., Mousavi, R., Lukyanenko, R., Paré, G.: Generative artificial intelligence for literature reviews. J. Inf. Technol. (2026). https://doi.org/10.1177/02683962261425675

17. Messeri, L., Crockett, M.J.: Artificial intelligence and illusions of understanding in scientific research. Nature **627**, 49–58 (2024). https://doi.org/10.1038/s41586-024-07146-0

18. Cohen, J.: A Coefficient of Agreement for Nominal Scales. Educ. Psychol. Measur. **20**, 37–46 (1960). https://doi.org/10.1177/001316446002000104

19. Tomczyk, P., Brüggemann, P., Vrontis, D.: AI meets academia: transforming systematic literature reviews. EuroMed J. Bus. **21**, 345–369 (2026). https://doi.org/10.1108/EMJB-03-2024-0055

Prototyping VR Training Using Design Thinking and ADR

Stefan Nilsson[(✉)] [iD], Daniel Sjölie, Ulf Andersson, Zakarias Mortensen, Darmin Poturovic, Jesse Katende, and Amir Haj-Bolouri

School of Business, Economics and IT, University West, Trollhättan, Sweden
`stefan.nilsson@hv.se`

Abstract. Train managers face a challenging work environment, characterized by a heightened risk of passenger aggression within spatially confined environments. Further, the rarity of threatening incidents makes skill development difficult. This paper presents the design and development of a Virtual Reality (VR) training artifact aimed at equipping train managers with de-escalation skills through immersive VR simulation of threatening onboard scenarios. Developed in collaboration between SJ (Sweden's largest train operator), University West, and VR developer Tenstar, the project operationalizes Design Thinking (DT) as the micro-level method within an Action Design Research (ADR) framework. Two Minimum Viable Products (MVPs) were developed as boundary objects to surface tacit practitioner knowledge and validate scenarios before committing to costly VR development. A modular JSON-based architecture decouples scenario content from the VR implementation, enabling rapid iterations without modifying the underlying VR environment. Evaluation indicates strong perceived utility and confirms that the design process successfully captured the complexity of real onboard work practices. The paper contributes a methodological approach for developing VR training artifacts in complex, practice-embedded contexts.

Keywords: Design thinking · VR training · de-escalation · ADR

1 Introduction

This research project concerns the design and development of a Virtual Reality (VR) training application aimed at equipping onboard train managers with skills for handling threatening and potentially violent situations in their working environment. Train managers face a uniquely challenging work environment characterized by a threefold problem. First, public transportation represents an environment in which frontline staff face a disproportionately high rate of passenger aggression. Second, this aggression occurs within a highly specific physical context: the train carriage is a confined, moving space that severely restricts escape routes, forcing train managers to handle threats within intimate spatial proximities for an indeterminate period until the train can stop. Third, while potentially violent events are fortunately rare, their infrequency creates a pedagogical paradox: it is exceedingly difficult for train managers to build skills in handling authentic threats.

© The Author(s), under exclusive license to Springer Nature Switzerland AG 2026
S. Chatterjee et al. (Eds.): DESRIST 2026, LNCS 16607, pp. 360–366, 2026.
https://doi.org/10.1007/978-3-032-28570-6_31

This paper sits at the intersection of two distinct complexities: the situated and partly tacit work practices of onboard train staff, and the demands of developing for virtual reality. VR remains a rapidly evolving technology in which both hardware and software capabilities are advancing faster than the design and development processes used to govern them. This is a gap that researchers have documented as a persistent absence of refined best practices [1, 2]. Navigating this fragmented landscape requires developers to maintain simultaneous competence across a broad range of disciplines, including programming, 3D modeling, animation, and audio engineering, each of which imposes its own demands on the development process. Critically, when requirements change late in development, as they frequently do in domains where user needs are complex, the associated cost in time and skilled effort is substantial [3]. This combination of domain complexity and technical fragility provides the practical motivation for this paper.

1.1 Background

The necessity for effective de-escalation has become a critical occupational requirement within public transportation. Currently, organizations in need of de-escalation training predominantly rely on theoretical and didactic training models to address these issues, occasionally supplemented by basic practical exercises [4]. However, these theoretically oriented courses included in the basic training for train managers systematically fail to capture the in-situ affective and environmental challenges of handling real-world aggression. Because authentic, threatening encounters are difficult to safely replicate in a traditional classroom setting, there is a distinct lack of high-fidelity, work-integrated training that adequately prepares staff for the psychological stress of the train carriage.

To address this gap, this paper outlines the design and development process of a VR safety training artifact. This project is a collaborative effort between Sweden's largest train operator, SJ, University West, and the VR developer Tenstar. The objective is to supplement the operator's current training regimen by providing a high-fidelity VR environment where train managers can experience threatening situations and practice skills in de-escalation. VR presents a unique opportunity to safely and repeatedly simulate these rare, high-stakes events, offering trainees an array of escalating challenges while deeply immersing them in the authentic spatial conditions of a train carriage.

The paper is structured as follows: it will first outline the design process and the rationale for how we proceeded to address the above-mentioned challenges, present the significance to research and for practice, outline the evaluation of the artifact and the results, and finally discuss the next steps in the design process.

2 Design of the Artifact

Developing this class of application challenges the design process from several perspectives. It requires a deep understanding of actual work practices of train managers and the complexity of de-escalation practices onboard trains, and the time-consuming effort to design both the virtual train carriage, the scenario within it as well as the VR interface to suit a non-technical target audience. In an effort to navigate this complexity, the day-to-day design activities were guided by a user-centric Design Thinking (DT) approach

[5], which was operationalized within an overarching Action Design Research (ADR) framework [6]. More specifically, we utilized the five steps of DT (empathize, define, ideate, prototype, and test) as the operational steps of the first two stages of the ADR model: Problem Formulation, and Building, Intervention and Evaluation (BIE), and as such constituted micro-iterations that progressively refined the outcome artifact within the overarching ADR process. In a sense, in this project DT disciplines the practice, and ADR disciplines the research.

Motivated by the complexity of the work practices of train managers, and the risk of developing a detailed, high-fidelity prototype at high cost without having verified the effectiveness and correctness of the proposed design, we utilized rapid iterations through the five DT steps. Particular emphasis was placed on the empathize and define stages of the process by engaging in close collaboration with all stakeholders in the project. Collaboration has been identified as one of the four core mechanisms for DT to provide impact in organizations [7], and as such had a great influence in how the project was conducted.

The project started with open discussions with instructors and experienced train managers on the topic of work practices, familiarizing ourselves with the challenges train managers face onboard trains. Subsequently, analysis of secondary data such as detailed incident reports was combined with primary empirical data collection such as onboard observations, roleplaying, group interviews, and focus group sessions with train staff. These activities helped us create an initial idea of who the end users are, their work practices, and the challenges they face onboard trains, outlining an early version of the problem definition. These sessions cemented the initial assumptions regarding complex work practices and informed the subsequent ideation stage. The ideation also had a collaborative focus and was conducted both in sessions within the design team at University West, and together with SJ and Tenstar. The understanding of the problem and ideation sessions led to the development of early prototypes in the form of two Minimum Viable Products (MVPs).

The two MVPs developed during this project served a dual purpose within the design process. Understood broadly as a form of boundary objects [8], they facilitated communication and collaboration both within the design team and between the design team and the train managers, making tacit practitioner knowledge accessible in ways that, for example, interviews alone could not achieve. Each MVP was oriented toward a separate design challenge. The first, called "NarVis" (short for Narrative Visualization; see Fig. 1) focused on de-escalation as a practice, probing the complexity of how train managers read, interpret, and respond to threatening situations, and surfacing the nuanced judgements that underpin their professional expertise. The second MVP, implemented in the VR prototyping tool ShapesXR, shifted attention to the physical environment itself, exploring the spatial constraints of the train carriage and how these shaped both user behavior and the experiential quality of the VR simulation. Together, the two MVPs functioned as both evaluation instruments and empathy tools, generating relevant knowledge while deepening the team's understanding of the users' lived work context.

In order to enable non-technical designers to make rapid design changes in the scenario as new knowledge of work practices was generated from the design process iterations, a modular architecture was developed in which scenario content was defined

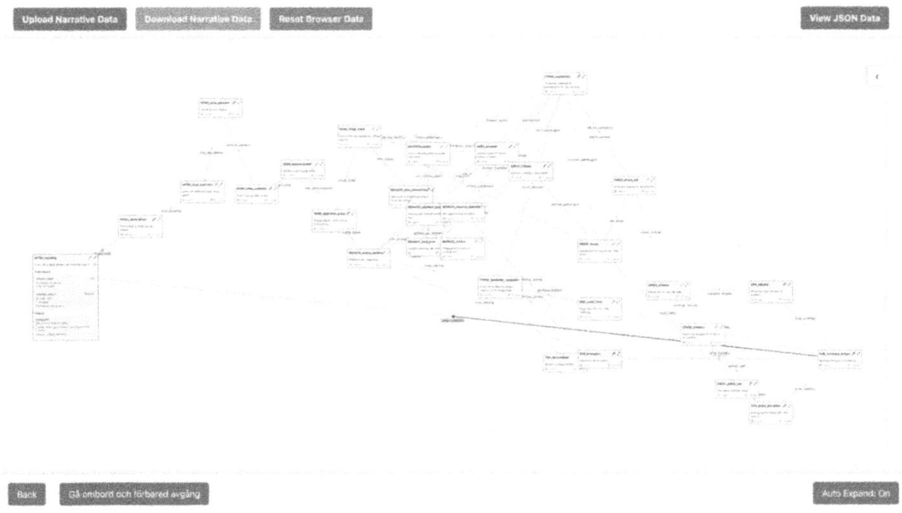

Fig. 1. The NarVis scenario visualization MVP.

through structured JSON data files, specifying each scene, the actors present, their behavior, dialogue, and the interaction options available to the user. This separation of content from implementation meant that narrative decisions could be revised without triggering costly changes to a VR environment. The NarVis MVP allowed both the design team and project stakeholders to step through the scenario scene by scene, evaluating the internal logic and coherence of the narrative before committing development resources to its realization. In this way, NarVis acted as a low-cost pre-validation layer.

As the scenario was evolving through JSON development, the VR prototype (see Fig. 2) was beginning to take shape in Unreal Engine. While effort was devoted to developing 3D train models and creating passenger models and animations, the scenario narrative continued to be based on the same JSON structure as the NarVis MVP. The JSON data is read by Unreal Engine at runtime, so alterations to the JSON file directly influence key parts of the simulation. The JSON also specifies dialogue, i.e., what each person on the train says, including the player. A value in the JSON corresponds to a filename with the recorded speech, and as such, what is said and what the player hears within the train can be dynamically altered without modifying anything in Unreal Engine.

Fig. 2. The VR prototype with a proximity warning, highlighting that the user is too close to the passenger.

3 Significance to Research

This paper makes a methodological contribution through the combination of ADR and DT. The general approach of using DT methodology in day-to-day activities is an instantiation of the overarching ADR BIE cycles. More specifically, the use of MVPs rapidly produces artifacts that both facilitate the understanding of a complex problem area, by mediating between stakeholders, and reduce the risk of costly, time-consuming development when working with complex work practices. In a sense, the empathy-focused orientation of DT directly addresses ADR's stated premise that artifacts are shaped by organizational contexts [6].

4 Significance to Practice

This VR training offers train managers the opportunity to develop de-escalation skills in a safe and repeatable environment, without risk to themselves or passengers. Exposure to realistic threatening scenarios before encountering them in practice may reduce the cognitive and emotional burden on staff in the moment, supporting more considered and effective responses. For train operators, this represents a scalable and cost-effective supplement to existing training, offering experiential learning that is difficult to achieve through conventional role-play or classroom-based instruction alone.

5 Evaluation

While evaluation of the MVPs has been an ongoing effort throughout the project, evaluation of the current VR prototype has been conducted with 21 experienced train managers, ticket inspectors and instructors. Participants were divided into two groups, each spending a day testing the prototype in VR, answering interview questions and participating in focus group sessions. In total, we conducted two 2-h demo sessions (with 10 and 11 participants, respectively), six group interviews of 60–80 min and four focus group sessions of 60–80 min. To assess how well the design process with the MVPs facilitated the understanding of the real-world practices of the train managers, the evaluation dimensions for this paper consisted of two components: 1) Overall impression and 2) Narrative accuracy.

Overall, the participants showed a positive attitude towards the use of the VR prototype as a training tool. They mentioned both the usefulness for newly hired train managers, and the opportunity for more experienced train managers to update and re-align their knowledge and skills. The prototype was also perceived as a form of safe experimental space; several participants, independent of one another, described the prototype as a rare chance to 'do wrong', deliberately testing suboptimal responses (e.g., standing too close to a passenger or being overly provocative) in ways that would be impossible in real work settings. This turned the prototype into both an outlet for frustration and a 'what happens if…' playground.

Regarding the narrative accuracy, the design process managed to capture many of the complexities involved in their work practices. The way the virtual passengers acted and the dialogue in the VR simulation were highly rated as realistic by the participants. This highlights that the knowledge of the work practices gained through testing with various MVPs during the design process iterations has been transferred well to the VR prototype. The more generic layout of the train carriage and its passengers, all controlled with an external JSON file, has worked well in enabling a lean prototyping process. One thing the participants noted as lacking was a more varied repertoire of choices in the VR environment, highlighting the complex work practices in which a wide variety of actions are possible to de-escalate a situation.

A low-cost MVP like NarVis, acting as a boundary object between designers and practitioners, allowed us to rapidly try out ideas and validate the scenario's accuracy, thus supporting vital collaboration [7]. Using JSON as a portable data format for both the NarVis MVP and the functional VR prototype supported a development cycle in which scenario validity could be tested in the VR environment, and alterations could be made 'on the fly' by updating the JSON data, addressing the issue of costly VR development in uncertain, complex contexts. With this approach, we can continue refining the VR environment, for example, by adding more choices to the user interface, reducing the need for costly and time-consuming adjustments to the VR environment when updating the scenario.

Challenges ahead include fine-tuning the scenario and further testing its validity with end-users. In later stages of the project, finalizing the environment with higher-fidelity models of the train and passengers, refining the user interface, and developing interaction modalities will become central.

Disclosure of Interests.   The authors have no competing interests to declare that are relevant to the content of this article.

References

1. Krauß, V., Boden, A., Oppermann, L., Reiners, R.: Current Practices, Challenges, and Design Implications for Collaborative AR/VR Application Development. In: Proceedings of the 2021 CHI Conference on Human Factors in Computing Systems, pp. 1–15. ACM, New York, NY, USA (2021). https://doi.org/10.1145/3411764.3445335
2. Ashtari, N., Bunt, A., McGrenere, J., Nebeling, M., Chilana, P.K.: Creating Augmented and Virtual Reality Applications: Current Practices, Challenges, and Opportunities. In: Proceedings of the 2020 CHI Conference on Human Factors in Computing Systems, pp. 1–13. ACM, New York, NY, USA (2020). https://doi.org/10.1145/3313831.3376722
3. Karre, S.A., Reddy, Y.R.: Model-based approach for specifying requirements of virtual reality software products. Front. Virtual Real. 5 (2024). https://doi.org/10.3389/frvir.2024.1471579
4. Engel, R.S., McManus, H.D., Herold, T.D.: Does de-escalation training work?: A systematic review and call for evidence in police use-of-force reform. Criminol. Public Policy **19**(3), 721–759 (2020). https://doi.org/10.1111/1745-9133.12467
5. Brown, T.: Design thinking. Harv. Bus. Rev. **86**(6), 84–92 (2008)
6. Sein, M.K., Henfridsson, O., Purao, S., Rossi, M., Lindgren, R.: Action Design Research. MIS Q. **35**(1), 37–56 (2011). https://doi.org/10.2307/23043488
7. Mayer, S., Schwemmle, M.: The impact of design thinking and its underlying theoretical mechanisms: A review of the literature. Creat. Innov. Manag. **34**(1), 78–110 (2025). https://doi.org/10.1111/caim.12626
8. Lortie, J., Cox, K., DeRosset, S., Thompson, R., Kelly, S.: Unpacking the minimum viable product (MVP): a framework for use, goals and essential elements. J. Small Bus. Enterp. Dev. **32**(1), 212–235 (2025). https://doi.org/10.1108/JSBED-02-2024-0075

Developing AI Literacy of Novice Adult Learners Outside of Formal Education Settings – a Prototype

Alexander Rinkowski[(✉)] [iD] and Dennis Kundisch [iD]

Paderborn University, Paderborn, Germany
`{alexander.rinkowski,dennis.kundisch}@upb.de`

Abstract. The diffusion of generative AI has made AI Literacy a critical societal issue, yet a large proportion of novice adult learners remains underserved by existing educational approaches. Existing approaches either lack theoretical grounding, fail to reach novices with low digital literacy, or do not address adults outside formal learning contexts. To address this gap, we design and evaluate a theory-grounded, practice-oriented AI Literacy course for novice adult learners outside formal learning settings using Action Design Research. The prototype implements a multi-session course artifact including guided instruction and hands-on interaction with LLMs to transition learners without prior experience toward AI-assisted, self-directed learning. Grounded in a digital literacy framework and Dynamic Skills Theory, the artifact aims to iteratively develop AI Literacy as critical knowledge and functional skills. Distinctive design features, such as low-tech metaphors, are implemented to create an end-user-oriented course structure and novice-friendly communication of content. The prototype was evaluated in multiple field iterations with novice adult learners. Longitudinal data was collected using a mixed-methods design, combining self-reported and behavioral data. Results consistently indicate substantial improvements in interaction strategies and conceptual understanding of AI across heterogeneous learners. We provide a reusable course design and synthesize five design principles to support the design and refinement of courses, especially those for novice adult learners outside formal learning settings.

Keywords: AI literacy · AI competence · AI skills · GenAI · Generative AI · Action Design Research

1 Design of the Artifact

1.1 Problem Statement

Since late 2022, the widespread public availability of a new class of powerful AI systems has fundamentally redefined how society engages with AI. This has made AI Literacy (AIL) to become a central issue in the digital divide. Among others, AIL is essential for fostering informed, democratic debates on AI regulation and is increasingly demanded

S. Chatterjee et al. (Eds.): DESRIST 2026, LNCS 16607, pp. 367–374, 2026.
https://doi.org/10.1007/978-3-032-28570-6_32

in the labor market. This shift implies that AIL is now about developing basic AI competencies across the general public rather than upskilling selected AI specialists. However, the widespread demand for AI education conflicts with the reality of low digital literacy rates. For instance, the EU Commission currently reports that nearly half of all adults in the EU still lack basic digital literacy – this issue is particularly pressing for adults aged 55 and older, among whom the rate is 63% [1]. The proposed artifact addresses this issue with a design that breaks with existing designs.

Designing AI education artifacts entails both practical and theoretical challenges. First, there is the practical issue of developing AIL of millions of novice learners without the support of a formal education setting. While many practice-oriented resources (e.g., blog posts with prompting tips) exist that partially address this issue, they lack the necessary conceptual grounding to communicate why their suggestions work. This is problematic for end-users because it fails to support the development of an accurate conceptual mental model of AI systems, which is a core part of AIL and, therefore, a design requirement of any AIL course. Further, these tips are at risk to translate poorly across models or into newer versions. This creates a need for research artifacts that integrate actionable guidance with conceptual grounding. A few such artifacts have been proposed by other researchers. However, they overwhelmingly address learners in formal education settings (e.g., K-12, undergraduates, or teachers) or in specialized fields (e.g., medicine). In contrast, the proposed artifact addresses the design problem of developing a theoretically grounded AIL course that is accessible to novice adult learners outside of formal education settings.

Designing such an artifact entails several key design challenges. First, the artifact must be accessible to a heterogeneous group of learners, including those with low levels of digital literacy. For instance, massive online courses were disregarded as a potential design choice in favor of in-person learning due to this practical constraint. Second, establishing a sound theoretical basis is challenging because AIL literature is still emerging and AI systems are evolving rapidly. This complicates the measurement of AIL and the identification of relevant content elements, such as the properties and mechanics of current AI systems, which are resistant to the rapid changes in the AI field. The presented artifact addresses these design challenges in novel ways and presents a set of general design principles that are drawn from the initial evaluation of the prototype.

1.2 Use Cases and User Groups

A Design for Novice Adult Learners and Course Designers. The presented artifact addresses two main groups of users. The first group is the end-user, or learner. The artifact, particularly the prototyped version, focuses on the under-researched group of novice adult learners who are not part of the formal education system. The main use case for this user group is overcoming the practical challenge of developing AIL without prior AI knowledge to a point that enables them to use and learn with AI systems sustainably. The main goal is to achieve a level of AIL where users can self-learn with the help of large language models (LLMs), triggering a cycle of self-empowerment. To support this use case, the design focuses on the dyadic human-AI relationship and each learner's personal learning journey. The second user group consists of course designers and practitioners. This group's main use case is searching for theoretical and practical insights to improve existing AIL courses or create new ones. To address this use case, a set of general design principles is drawn from the theoretical foundations of the course design and from the practical insights that were gained from end-user testing of the prototype. These principles can be adopted by other course designers and practitioners. Adopting the prototype version of the artifact or the derived principles is subject to this study's understanding of AIL.

A Generative AI View of AIL. The definition of AI used in this study establishes a boundary condition for both use cases, as the artifact is designed to develop AIL only within the adopted view of AI. Conceptualizing AIL is a complex endeavor that cannot be adequately described in this section. The keyword 'AI Literacy' first appeared in scientific articles around 2016; however, scientific research on the education of AI systems has a much richer history. The meaning of AI itself has shifted many times since late John McCarthy coined the term in 1955 [2]. Typically, at least three properties can be associated with AI: (1) AI algorithms often combine properties of cognition (reasoning) and action; (2) They either imitate human behavior or showcase other intelligent behavior (for instance, consider how early versions of AlphaGO learned from analyzing human games and later versions increased performance by learning entirely through self-play); (3) Only state-of-the-art algorithms are labeled as AI (outdated technologies tend to lose the AI label). Since the term AIL was popularized during the ongoing AI boom, it is typically associated with generative AI algorithms, often foundational LLMs, that descend from the transformer architecture, such as ChatGPT. The use cases of the presented course are limited to this view.

1.3 Features

Theory-Ingrained Design. The artifact follows Action Design Research to integrate theoretical grounding and practical design considerations. The design process followed the iterative development in stages and principles of the IT-dominant Build-Intervention-Evaluation schema described by Sein et al. [3]. The artifact draws on several ideas from literature. Its kernel theory consists of a conceptual framework from digital literacy literature and a skill development theory from educational psychology.

First, the conceptualization of the focal multidimensional construct of AIL draws on the Digital Literacy Framework (DLF) by Smahel et al. [4], which partitions literacy into Critical Knowledge (CK) and Functional Skills (FS). This view is adopted as it represents a more mature conceptualization of literacy compared to the still-emerging AIL literature. Furthermore, it mirrors common AI definitions by incorporating both cognitive and action-related components. This aligns well with the end-user use case of developing a productive dyadic human-AI interaction.

Second, the artifact draws on the Neo-Piagetian, constructivist Dynamic Skills Theory (DST) [5]. DST would describe literacy as a set of independently evolving skills beginning with basic capabilities [5]. This aligns with the need to accurately represent heterogeneous novice learners. Further, DST emphasizes the context dependence of performance [6], aligning with AI-assisted learning and informing design decisions regarding the level of support (scaffolding) provided throughout the course. DST would describe literacy development as an iterative construction in which subskills combine to form more complex skills [5]. This progression is described at both micro and macro levels [5], informing design considerations at the session (micro) and course (macro) levels.

Design at Macro and Micro Level. Figure 1 provides an overview of the artifact at the macro level. It illustrates how insights from DLF and DST are instantiated in the prototyped artifact. The course develops CK and FS in parallel, integrating the conceptualization of DLF with the progression mechanism described in DST. At the macro level, the course is structured in three phases: it begins with a broad introduction to foundational concepts, then develops key mechanisms and properties in focused sessions, and finally returns to a broader view, integrating these aspects at a higher level. This reflects the progression described by DST at the macro level. The resulting hourglass pattern exemplifies the integration of complementary ideas from educational psychology, such as the spiraled curriculum [7] and elaboration theory [8]. At the micro level, each session first develops CK and FS as separate building blocks and then integrates them. Furthermore, the level of scaffolding is continuously adjusted based on learners' needs, drawing on the core ideas of DST. These insights are translated and extended into a set of design considerations.

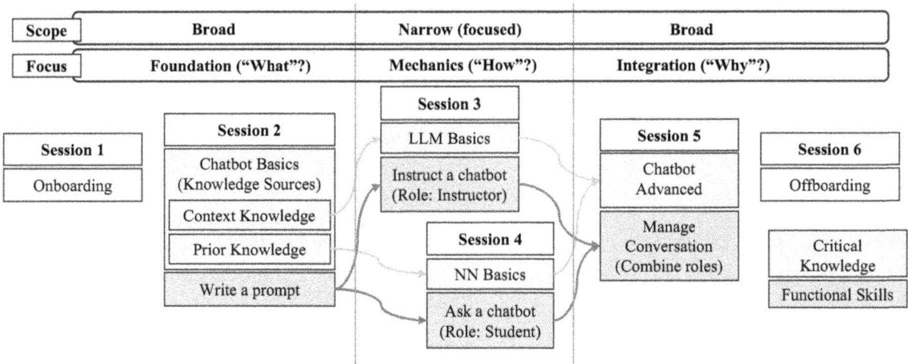

Fig. 1. Overview of the artifact prototype at a macro level

Theoretical and Practical Considerations. Table 1 summarizes the set of technical (T), pedagogical (P), and content (C) design considerations based on the kernel theory and practical requirements. While presented as separate categories, the interplay of these considerations is aligned with the TPACK framework [9]. The considerations address six main goals (G): presenting AI in a usable way while acknowledging its rapid changes (G1), meeting learners at their individual level (G2), accounting for learner heterogeneity (G3), managing cognitive load continuously (G4), ensuring a safe learning environment (G5), and enabling sustained use and self-directed learning (G6).

AI learning content was identified through a review of literature, existing courses, and expert feedback, resulting in a broad view of AI. As the development of FS requires concrete technologies, LLMs were selected as the primary focus (C1 → G1). In the baseline session LLMs are introduced and contextualized within the broader field of AI

Table 1. Pedagogy (P), content (C), and technology (T) considerations in the artifacts' design

ID	Description
P1	**Hourglass instructional design:** Start with broad overview, narrow into focused deep dives, then widen again to integrate insights by building on established knowledge
P2	**Establishing a baseline:** Introduce core CK and FS elements early to establish a common baseline and reduce prior variance across participants' AIL
P3	**Supporting sustained use:** Include dedicated offboarding to enable chatbot access on participants' personal devices and promote continued independent learning
P4	**Strategic scaffolding reduction:** Start with strong initial guidance, then gradually reduce to foster independent exploration as learners' AIL develops
C1	**Aim for a holistic AI view:** Span from general AI concepts to concrete technologies (e.g., LLMs), including technical, ethical, and societal perspectives
C2	**Cover generic and specific content:** Include both generic and AI-specific conversation strategies to reduce misguided use of AI (e.g., treating AI as all-knowing)
C3	**Top-down ordering:** Start with familiar applications and progress toward details of underlying concepts. Start with broad "what?" and work towards "how?" and "why?"
C4	**Translation into low-tech version:** Translate properties and mechanics of technical concepts into familiar and intuitive everyday metaphors that convey their main ideas
T1	**Chatbot selection:** Choose widely accessible, high-performing, and familiar chatbots, prioritizing practical relevance and ease of use over custom API-based solutions
T2	**Privacy considerations:** Protect novice learners' data and privacy through anonymous accounts, credentials, privacy settings, explicit guidance, and devices

(P2 → G1), and learners interact with ChatGPT to establish a common baseline (T1, P2 → G2, G3). Like a driver's license, the course content is structured top-down, starting from concrete applications and only adding technical detail of underlying concepts if needed for safe use or basic understanding (C3 → G2, G4). Further, these details are translated into novice-friendly, low-tech metaphors and discussed in dedicated focus sessions (P1, C4 → G4). In contrast, many existing artifacts follow bottom-up structures derived from traditional AI courses designed for AI engineers. In this artifact, each session begins with guided instruction (scaffolding) and gradually transitions to self-directed exploration (P4 → G4, G6). To facilitate self-exploration, learners are reminded of generic interaction strategies (e.g., formulating tasks unambiguously) in addition to prompting guidance based on LLM properties (C2 → G2, G4). Finally, to enable sustained self-directed learning, the course concludes with guidance on using LLMs on personal devices (P3 → G6). Until then, learners work with anonymized accounts on provided devices to ensure a safe learning environment (T2 → G5).

2 Evaluation

Evaluation Design. To inform the Build-Intervention-Evaluation cycles [3], feedback was collected from experts and end-users. End-user feedback was gathered during the prototype execution using a mixed-methods design – specifically a concurrent triangulation equal-status design [10]. Measurement of real AIL development is challenging due to many potential sources of biases. To ensure validity, quantitative and qualitative data were collected indirectly (self-reported) and directly (performance tests). Primary data sources included session observations, anonymized chatbot interaction history, and an anonymized learning journey booklet. The latter was specifically designed for the course and included exercises, perception tests, notes, and self-reflections of learners, including the MAILs questionnaire [11].

Evaluation Setting. The artifact was first tested in mid-2025 in cooperation with the Volkshochschule (VHS) Paderborn, which provided facilities, advertising, and feedback. While the learning environment and scheduling were taken into consideration for the prototype's design, the VHS did not influence the artifact's content or design. The setting provided workstations for twelve participants and standard digital presentation materials. The first evaluation was conducted with twelve heterogeneous participants (most aged 55 +) over three weeks with two 2:15 h sessions per week. The prototype has since been executed three additional times under similar conditions. Participants self-selected into the course based on a description emphasizing a practice-oriented, novice-friendly AI course at a minimal fee intended to prevent no-show registrations.

Results. Across all iterations, the prototype consistently improved AIL among heterogeneous learners. For example, in self-reported MAILs data, learners typically started at ≤ 2 points (0–10 scale), improved consistently after each session, and ended at ≥ 8 points on average (excluding two advanced MAILs items outside the course scope). These improvements were also evident in chatbot interactions, performance tests, and observations. Many participants lacked prior experience with chatbots or a basic understanding of AI. They typically progressed from using the chatbot like a search engine to engaging in full conversations including elements of prompt engineering and conversation management strategies. They also demonstrated improved conceptual understanding of LLMs and broader AI during discussions in later sessions. Almost all participants showed sufficient signs of self-directed learning capabilities and a willingness for sustained use, suggesting that the positive follow-up feedback from selected participants was representative of the group. Subsequent iterations also included participants who self-selected into the course based on word-of-mouth recommendations.

3 Significance to Research and Practice

Usefulness for End-users. While the evaluation indicates that the prototype can address the underlying problem of AIL among novice adult learners, it is still limited in its scalability. Field tests demonstrated a meaningful impact on end-users by enabling AI-assisted, self-directed learning. Many end-users reported improved access to information that was previously unobtainable for them due to issues with internet search.

Usefulness for Course Designers. Insights from the artifact design and the field evaluations were synthesized into five design principles. In addition to the design features, these provide actionable guidance for designing and refining AIL courses. Table 2 summarizes these five principles. The principles also reflect potential innovations for current courses, as the AI course landscape keeps evolving.

Table 2. Five design principles for AIL educational artifacts for novice adult learners

Principle	Description
1 Low-tech elements	Translate AI properties and mechanics into low-technical elements
2 Actionable theory	Streamline all theory elements into practical and actionable insights
3 Generic strategies	Include generic (not just AI-specific) interaction strategies
4 Reflected user	Highlight the importance of a reflected use to learners
5 Engineer interactions	Focus on engineered interactions over prompt engineering

Innovativeness. The evaluation revealed five novel design insights. (1) Translating technical AI concepts into metaphors proved highly effective for participants. For example, they developed an understanding of how information provided earlier in an interaction influences subsequent LLM behavior, without requiring knowledge of underlying mechanisms such as autoregression or context windows. (2) The results further show that theoretical elements must be carefully streamlined into actionable guidance. When CK and FS elements were not sufficiently connected, learners struggled to translate knowledge into action. For example, framing a chatbot interaction as a conversation with a stranger rather than a friend (CK) can be streamlined by advising users to provide all relevant information a stranger would need. This can be streamlined more gradually by subsequently showing learners the effect of two prompts with different levels of detail and explicitly deriving actionable advice (FS). (3) This example also highlights how generic interaction strategies can guide users to communicate effectively with LLMs. Despite their promising impact and little added cognitive load, these strategies are often overlooked in AI courses, which tend to emphasize LLM-specific advice.

(4) This example additionally highlights the importance of making users aware of the relevance of their own behavior and role in the interaction. While many AI courses focus on AI systems and their properties, they often neglect to make users understand the importance of their behavior in the interaction. (5) Finally, the results suggest a shift from prompt engineering toward managing interactions at the conversation level (context engineering). This includes strategies such as structuring conversations, resetting context, or using separate, disconnected interactions for ideation and verification.

Disclosure of Interests. The authors have no competing interests to declare that are relevant to the content of this article.

References

1. EU Commission: https://digital-decade-desi.digital-strategy.ec.europa.eu/datasets/desi/charts/desi-indicators. Last accessed 21 March 2026
2. McCarthy, J., Minsky, M. L., Rochester, N., Shannon, C. E.: http://jmc.stanford.edu/articles/dartmouth/dartmouth.pdf. Last accessed 21 March 2026
3. Sein, M.K., Henfridsson, O., Purao, S., Rossi, M., Lindgren, R.: Action design research. MIS Q. **35**(1), 37–56 (2011). https://doi.org/10.2307/23043488
4. Smahel, D., et al.: Theoretical Integration of ySKILLS: Towards a New Model of Digital Literacy. KU Leuven, Leuven (2023). https://doi.org/10.5281/zenodo.11242207
5. Fischer, K.W.: A theory of cognitive development: The control and construction of hierarchies of skills. Psychol. Rev. **87**(6), 477–531 (1980). https://doi.org/10.1037/0033-295X.87.6.477
6. Lerner, R.M., Damon, W.: Handbook of child psychology: Vol. 1. Theoretical models of human development, 6th edn. John Wiley & Sons, Hoboken (2006)
7. Bruner, J.S.: The process of education. Harvard University Press, Cambridge (1960)
8. Reigeluth, C.M.: In search of a better way to organize instruction: The elaboration theory. J. Instr. Dev. **2**(1), 8–15 (1979). https://doi.org/10.1007/BF02984374
9. Koehler, M., Mishra, P.: What is technological pedagogical content knowledge (TPACK)? Contemp. Iss. Technol. Teacher Educ. **9**(1), 60–70 (2009)
10. Venkatesh, V., Brown, S., Sullivan, Y.: Conducting mixed-methods research: From classical social sciences to the age of big data and analytics. Virginia Tech Publishing, Blacksburg (2023)
11. Koch, M.J., Carolus, A., Wienrich, C., Latoschik, M.E.: Meta AI literacy scale: Further validation and development of a short version. Heliyon. **10**(21), e39686 (2024). https://doi.org/10.1016/j.heliyon.2024.e39686

TerrainGrade: An Artifact for Flood Susceptibility Mapping

Thomas Roderick[1,2]($\boxtimes$) iD, Monica Chiarini Tremblay[2] iD, Rajiv Kohli[2] iD, and Arturo Castellanos[2] iD

[1] AI for Natural Disasters, LLC, Canton, GA, USA
`tom@aifornaturaldisasters.com`
[2] Raymond A. Mason School of Business, William & Mary, Williamsburg, VA, USA
`{monica.tremblay,rajiv.kohli,arturo.castellanosbueso}@mason.wm.edu`

Abstract. Flood hazard information in the United States is conveyed primarily through regulatory floodplain maps that are costly to update and difficult to integrate with modern geospatial analytics. This paper presents TerrainGrade, a design science artifact that generates cell-level flood susceptibility estimates using open national hydrologic data within a machine learning pipeline implemented on an H3 hexagonal grid (approximately 85 m cells).

TerrainGrade estimates inundation likelihood across multiple flood scenarios and aggregates the results into a Flood Susceptibility Index (FSI). Training labels are derived by converting modeled river flows to water levels and comparing them with local terrain elevation using the Height Above Nearest Drainage (HAND) metric. In a pilot covering 2.2 million cells in the US state of Maryland, spatial cross-validation demonstrated out-of-fold AUC values of 0.984, 0.978, and 0.969 for increasing flood severity thresholds. Defined FEMA flood zones receive substantially higher susceptibility scores despite not being used for training.

TerrainGrade provides a scalable method for generating continuous flood susceptibility surfaces from open federal datasets, enabling flood risk screening and resilience analysis across large geographic domains.

Keywords: Flood susceptibility · Design science research · H3 spatial index · Machine learning · National Water Model · CFIM · HAND

1 Design of the Artifact

1.1 Problem Statement

Flood risk in the United States is documented primarily through FEMA's National Flood Hazard Layer (NFHL), which provides binary flood-zone designations derived from engineering studies of varying vintage. Those maps are indispensable for regulation and insurance, but they are not designed as a uniform analytical substrate for machine learning. They do not provide a continuous susceptibility gradient, do not differentiate among multiple return periods in a

S. Chatterjee et al. (Eds.): DESRIST 2026, LNCS 16607, pp. 375–381, 2026.
https://doi.org/10.1007/978-3-032-28570-6_33

uniform geospatial cell-based representation, and remain incomplete in many locations. Previous work on digital vulnerability frameworks has similarly highlighted the inadequacy of binary regulatory classifications for capturing the continuous, spatially heterogeneous nature of community flood exposure [9].

There is a similar complementary gap in hydrologic modeling. The NOAA National Water Model (NWM) provides continental streamflow estimates over a large NHDPlus river network, but it does not directly yield a cell-based inundation layer. The Catchment Flood Inundation Mapping (CFIM) framework addresses part of this gap by combining HAND-derived terrain with hydraulic property tables and synthetic rating curves that convert discharge to stage and inundation depth at fine spatial resolution [6,7].

Consistent with the Design Science Research paradigm, which emphasizes the construction and rigorous evaluation of artifacts to address relevant organizational and societal problems [4], we propose TerrainGrade as an information technology artifact that bridges this gap. It combines a *model artifact*, the Flood Susceptibility Index, with a *method artifact*, the reproducible pipeline that converts hydrologic simulations, terrain data, and network attributes into cell-level flood probabilities. The artifact is designed to operate on a uniform H3 grid, to learn from hydrologically grounded labels rather than regulatory polygons, and to produce continuous susceptibility estimates suitable for downstream analytical systems.

1.2 Design Requirements

The design requirements for TerrainGrade are based on three structural limitations in the existing flood information infrastructure. First, regulatory flood maps assign binary zone designations at irregular polygon boundaries, preventing the construction of continuous susceptibility gradients suitable for machine learning pipelines or downstream resilience analysis. Second, hydrologic simulation outputs operate at the reach level and are not directly translated into spatially uniform cell-level predictions. Third, existing systems create dependencies on proprietary data or regulatory products that limit reproducibility and broad deployment.

Drawing on an established DSR methodology [3,4], we derive four design requirements for this class of artifacts:

DR1 (Uniform Spatial Representation): A flood susceptibility artifact must represent analysis units as uniform discrete spatial cells that support consistent prediction, storage, and downstream aggregation across administrative and hydrological boundaries.

DR2 (Physically Grounded Supervision): Training labels must be derived from physically interpretable hydrologic simulations rather than regulatory classifications, producing susceptibility estimates that are decoupled from policy artifacts and capable of expressing continuous hazard gradients.

DR3 (Open-Data Instantiability): The artifact must be fully instantiable from publicly available federal data infrastructure, without proprietary data dependencies, to support reproducibility and scalable deployment.

DR4 (Structure-Preserving Validation): Predictive validity must be assessed using holdouts that respect the natural spatial dependency structure of the domain, preventing inflated generalizability estimates from geographic leakage across watershed boundaries.

1.3 Artifact Architecture

TerrainGrade is instantiated through a reproducible data-engineering and modeling workflow rather than a single monolithic model. Terrain predictors are derived from NASADEM elevation data and aggregated to H3 resolution 10 cells ($\sim$85 m) using zonal summaries and neighborhood statistics. Each cell is linked to NHDPlus HR catchments and reach attributes such as stream order, drainage area, and reach slope [8]. The hierarchical hexagonal grid provides uniform spatial units and stable neighborhood structure for machine learning and downstream spatial aggregation [2], satisfying DR1.

Hydrologic labels are then constructed from NWM retrospective hourly streamflow, satisfying DR2. Annual maxima for 1979–2023 are extracted by reach and fitted with generalized extreme value distributions to estimate return-period discharges for Q2, Q5, and Q10. CFIM hydraulic property tables are used to interpolate reach stage at each return-period discharge, and those stages are compared with cell-level HAND summaries to create binary inundation labels. Formally, for threshold $x \in \{2, 5, 10\}$ and cell i associated with reach r, the label is defined as

$$Y_{i,x} = \mathbb{I}\big(\mathrm{HAND}_{i,p10} \leq S_r(Q_x)\big),$$

where $S_r(Q_x)$ denotes modeled stage at reach r for return period Q_x, and $\mathbb{I}(\cdot)$ is the indicator function.

Three LightGBM binary classifiers are trained, one per threshold [5]. HAND variables are excluded from the predictor set because they are algebraically embedded in the label-construction step; this prevents the model from trivially reproducing the label formula. Instead, the model is required to learn adjacent terrain, drainage, and network context that generalizes beyond the explicit thresholding rule. The resulting probabilities are combined into a composite Flood Susceptibility Index:

$$\mathrm{FSI}_i = 0.2\, P_i(Q2) + 0.3\, P_i(Q5) + 0.5\, P_i(Q10),$$

where the Q10 component receives the largest weight because it most closely approximates a planning-relevant flood-frequency threshold.

1.4 Use Cases and User Groups

TerrainGrade is intended for decision settings that require rapid, spatially consistent screening of flood susceptibility. For infrastructure and municipal planning,

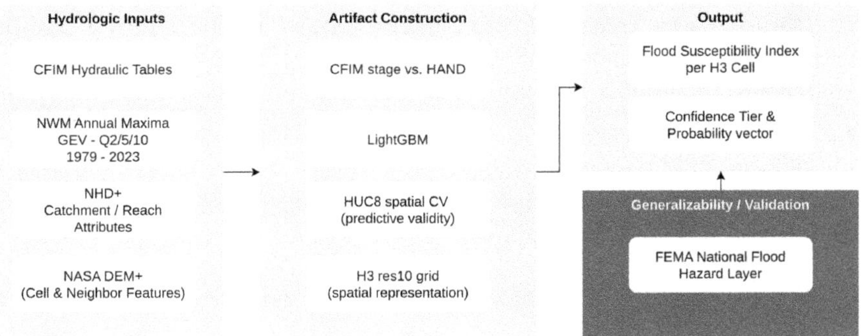

Fig. 1. TerrainGrade artifact overview. FEMA NFHL is used as an external validation benchmark and not as a training target.

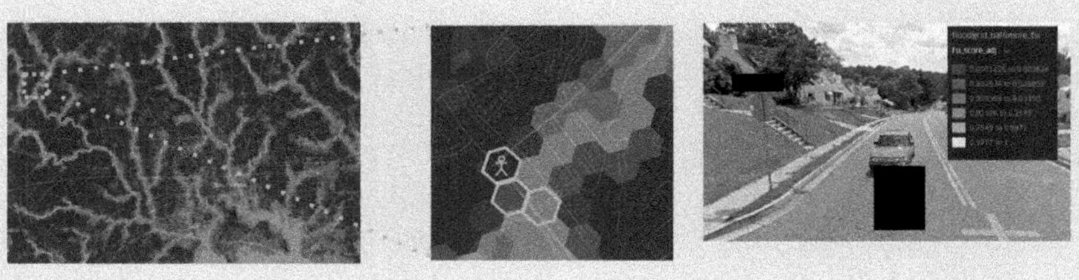

Fig. 2. TerrainGrade artifact in operation. Left: Flood Susceptibility Index surface for the Baltimore region. Middle: individual H3 grid cells representing the spatial prediction units used by the model. Right: street-level context for selected cells, illustrating how TerrainGrade predictions correspond to real-world locations. Note the downward slope, matching an increasing FSI across cells.

the artifact provides a continuous susceptibility surface that can intersect with roads, utilities, facilities, and planned investments. For emergency management, the artifact offers a precomputed, cell-based hazard signal that can support preparedness analysis, prioritization, and scenario planning, especially outside formally mapped FEMA zones. For insurance and risk analytics, the artifact supplies a graded probability vector across multiple return periods rather than a single binary hazard boundary. For research and AI engineering, TerrainGrade provides an ML-ready spatial representation that can be reused for downstream resilience, exposure, or causal modeling tasks (Figs. 1 and 2).

2   Significance to Research

Following the pathways framework for design research on AI [1], TerrainGrade occupies the predictive artifact position in the artifact typology. Its primary abstraction contribution is a new design problem formulation: how to generate continuous, ML-ready flood susceptibility surfaces from open federal hydrologic infrastructure without depending on regulatory map products. This positions the artifact toward the "new design problems" region of the abstraction spectrum [3], with emergent design insights about spatial representation, label construction, and structure-preserving evaluation that generalize beyond the flood domain to geospatial risk modeling more broadly. The artifact's connection to the IS cumulative tradition on disaster resilience is anchored by prior work establishing the conceptual distinction between binary regulatory classifications and continuous vulnerability gradients in disaster-affected communities [9].

TerrainGrade contributes to design science and geospatial informatics in three ways. First, it operationalizes H3 as a machine-learning representation for flood susceptibility analysis. Existing flood datasets are typically organized as irregular polygons, reaches, or raster tiles. TerrainGrade instead treats the discrete grid cell as the computational unit of analysis, which simplifies neighborhood feature construction, hierarchical aggregation, and model deployment across administrative and hydrologic boundaries.

Second, the artifact demonstrates a hydrologically grounded method for label construction. Return-period discharge estimates from NWM are translated into stage (stream/water height) using CFIM hydraulic relationships, and stage is then compared with HAND-derived terrain position to produce cell-level inundation labels. This creates training supervision that is physically interpretable and decoupled from FEMA regulatory products. Because HAND is excluded from the predictor set after being used in label construction, the model is pushed to learn a broader spatial structure rather than simply restating the threshold rule.

Third, the artifact contributes to an evaluation design appropriate for spatial machine learning. Leave-one-HUC8-out cross-validation respects watershed structure, reducing leakage that would arise under random folds. The artifact therefore is not only a predictive model instance, but also a replicable methodological template for building and testing grid-based flood susceptibility systems.

These contributions crystallize into three prescriptive design principles for geospatial risk artifact development [1]: (1) *represent predictions on a uniform hierarchical spatial grid*—discrete, addressable cells unify feature construction, storage, and deployment across administrative boundaries; (2) *derive supervision from physically grounded simulation rather than regulatory products*—decoupling labels from the intended benchmark enables genuinely independent external validation; and (3) *evaluate spatial predictive models using hydrologically coherent holdouts*—watershed-based folds respect spatial autocorrelation and yield defensible out-of-sample estimates.

3 Significance to Practice

The principal practical contribution of TerrainGrade is that it can be instantiated from an open national data infrastructure, satisfying DR3. The Maryland pilot draws on NOAA NWM retrospective hydrology, CFIM hydraulic property tables, NHDPlus HR network and catchment attributes, NASADEM-derived terrain features, and FEMA NFHL for external benchmarking [6,8]. The artifact therefore avoids proprietary data dependencies and is suitable for reproducible deployment on standard cloud infrastructure.

Table 1. Out-of-fold AUC under leave-one-HUC8-out spatial cross-validation, Maryland pilot (2,195,973 H3 cells; 21 HUC8 folds).

Threshold	OOF AUC (LightGBM)	OOF AUC (Baseline)
Q2—50% annual exceedance	0.984	0.624
Q5—20% annual exceedance	0.978	0.630
Q10—10% annual exceedance	0.969	0.630

The three-threshold probability design also addresses a practical weakness in binary floodplain products. Regulatory boundaries are useful for compliance decisions, but operational planning often requires a graded notion of hazard. Two locations outside a mapped special flood hazard area may still have materially different susceptibility profiles. By returning $P(Q2)$, $P(Q5)$, and $P(Q10)$ for every cell, TerrainGrade provides a structured probability vector that can support screening, prioritization, and portfolio-level comparison.

Finally, the external comparison to FEMA is practically important. FEMA Special Flood Hazard Areas exhibit substantially higher Flood Susceptibility Index values than non-FEMA areas (0.198 mean increase, Welch t = 131.9; Cohen's d = 0.48), indicating strong alignment between the artifact's probabilistic outputs and existing regulatory floodplain designations despite FEMA data not being used for model training.

4   Evaluation

4.1   Spatial Cross-Validation Results

A Maryland pilot demonstrates the operation of TerrainGrade on a state scale using 2,195,973 H3 cells and 21 HUC8 folds. Table 1 reports out-of-fold (OOF) AUC under leave-one-HUC8-out cross-validation for all three return-period thresholds, satisfying DR4. As a baseline, a logistic regression model that uses only reach hydraulic attributes (log drainage area and stream order) achieved AUC values of 0.624, 0.630, and 0.630 at Q2, Q5, and Q10, respectively. One fold (HUC8 02060001; 478 cells) returned an undefined AUC because all cells were positive at Q2 and was therefore excluded from the aggregate OOF summary.

Feature importance analysis indicates that terrain-derived variables, particularly flow accumulation, elevation, and topographic wetness, dominate model predictions, consistent with established hydrologic understanding.

4.2   Limitations

The Maryland pilot demonstrates the artifact but does not constitute a cross-state generalization test. HUC8-based spatial cross-validation provides a defensible estimate of within-state predictive validity, yet broader transfer will require a multi-state training corpus spanning different physiographic regions. Flat coastal terrain, particularly on the Eastern Shore, also presents reduced stability, which is consistent with known HAND limitations in low-relief environments. In addition, raw elevation features that are useful within Maryland may require additional normalization for cross-state deployment. Future artifact extensions should therefore incorporate geographically diverse training data and additional urban runoff information such as impervious surface fraction.

5   Artifact Availability

The TerrainGrade pipeline is documented at https://aifornaturaldisasters. github.io/terraingrade-md-demo. The Maryland pilot training tables, scored H3 parquet outputs, and model artifacts are archived. Pipeline notebooks are available from the author upon request.

Disclosure of Interests. The authors have no competing interests to declare that are relevant to the content of this article.

References

1. Abbasi, A., Parsons, J., Pant, G., Sheng, O.R.L., Sarker, S.: Pathways for design research on artificial intelligence. Inf. Syst. Res. **35**(2), 441–459 (2024). https://doi.org/10.1287/isre.2024.editorial.v35.n2
2. Brodsky, I.: H3: a hexagonal hierarchical geospatial indexing system. In: Proceedings of the 16th ACM SIGSPATIAL International Conference on Advances in Geographic Information Systems. ACM (2018). https://doi.org/10.1145/3274895.3274919
3. Gregor, S., Hevner, A.R.: Positioning and presenting design science research for maximum impact. MIS Q. **37**(1), 337–355 (2013). https://doi.org/10.25300/MISQ/2013/37.2.01
4. Hevner, A.R., March, S.T., Park, J., Ram, S.: Design science in information systems research. MIS Q. **28**(1), 75–106 (2004). https://doi.org/10.2307/25148625
5. Ke, G., et al.: LightGBM: a highly efficient gradient boosting decision tree. In: Garnett, R. (ed.) Advances in Neural Information Processing Systems, vol. 30, Curran Associates, Inc. (2017). https://doi.org/10.2307/25148625
6. Liu, Y., Tarboton, D.G., Maidment, D.R.: Height above nearest drainage (HAND) and hydraulic property table for CONUS – version 0.21. Technical report, Oak Ridge National Laboratory (2020)
7. Liu, Y.Y., Maidment, D.R., Tarboton, D.G., Zheng, X., Wang, S.: A CyberGIS integration and computation framework for high-resolution continental-scale flood inundation mapping. JAWRA J. Am. Water Resour. Assoc. **54**(4), 770–784 (2018). https://doi.org/10.1111/1752-1688.12660
8. Moore, R.B., et al.: User's guide for the national hydrography dataset plus high resolution (NHDPlus HR). Technical report, U.S. Geological Survey (2025)
9. Roderick, T., Tremblay, M.C., Kohli, R., Castellanos, A., Pengetnze, Y.: When vulnerability drives action: designing forward-looking frameworks for disaster preparedness. Inf. Syst. Res. (2026). https://doi.org/10.1287/isre.2024.1683

Towards Agentic Lecture Production with Human–AI Workflows

Johannes Sahlin[(✉)], Stefan Cronholm, Björn Dahlstrand, and Håkan Sundell

University of Borås, Borås, Sweden
`{johannes.sahlin,stefan.cronholm,bjorn.dahlstrand,`
`hakan.sundell}@hb.se`

Abstract. Higher education teachers need to produce lecture material in multiple formats (slides, notes, audio, and video), but workflows are fragmented across tools and roles. We present a prototype artifact for agentic lecture production, developed and evaluated through a design science process. The core design contribution is to conceptualize each lecture as a computational boundary object that centralizes the transformation chain, preserves process state, supports reproducibility, and makes human–Artificial Intelligence (AI) transitions explicit and traceable. The artifact integrates markdown-based authoring of slide headers, bullet points, and speaker manuscripts, template-aware slide generation, lecture management, Text-To-Speech (TTS), avatar/video pipeline orchestration, and export management in an orchestrated production pipeline. We describe the artifact design, its research and practice significance, and a formative evaluation focused on feasibility, usability, and operational value. Results indicate that the prototype improves workflow coherence and traceability, supports faster iteration from content drafting to multimedia output, and contributes preliminary design knowledge for human-in-the-loop, AI-supported educational production systems.

Keywords: Agentic Workflows · Lecture Production · Human-AI Collaboration · Educational Technology

1 Design of the Artefact

Problem Statement. Lecture production in higher education increasingly relies on multimedia materials that combine written content, slides, audio narration, and video [5]. However, these items are typically produced across disconnected tools. Educators repeatedly shift platforms for writing environments, presentation software, audio-generation services, and video-production systems [5]. This fragmented diversity of tools leads to version drift, duplicated effort, weak traceability between source content and multimedia outputs, and coordination overhead [1,3]. The problem intensifies when lectures must be produced at scale. While Artificial Intelligence (AI)-enabled services increasingly support isolated tasks such as script generation or audio synthesis, workflows remain largely non-integrated. Educators therefore spend considerable effort managing technical coordination rather than refining pedagogical content.

A possible solution to this problem can be that recent research on reasoningaction paradigms in Large Language Models (LLMs) shows how language models can coordinate multi-step tool execution [8]. At the same time, Human-Centered AI principles emphasize maintaining meaningful human oversight and control [4]. Existing research on AI-supported lecture production has largely focused on generating artifacts such as slides, lecture scripts, or instructional videos. While these approaches demonstrate the potential of generative AI for producing educational content, they typically treat generation as an isolated task rather than as part of a coordinated lecture production workflow. Consequently, limited attention has been given to the design of lecture production workflows themselves as humanAI collaborative systems that orchestrate multiple tools, agents, and human interventions.

To address this gap, this study asks: How can an agentic lecture-centered workflow architecture be designed to integrate human authorship with generative AI services while preserving traceability and reproducibility across the lecture production process? This paper presents a prototype artifact that implements such a workflow architecture and evaluates its feasibility in an authentic higher-education context. In this study, agentic refers to human–AI coordinated multi-step tool orchestration in an explicit workflow boundary where AI services perform delegated transformations under human supervision.

Intended User Group. The intended user groups are university teachers, instructional designers, and educational technologists who need to produce lecture material at scale. Secondary users include program coordinators and media support staff who require visibility into lecture status and exports.

Use Case Summary. Table 1 sums the use case and intended practice value.

Table 1. Use case overview

User group	University teachers, instructional designers, and educational technologists
Problem	Fragmented lecture production workflow
Data	Lecture folders containing markdown slides, metadata, institutional presentation templates, source literature, generated audio, avatar profiles, and export artifacts
Objective	- An AI-supported multimedia lecture workflow - Unify content transformation, authoring, generation, and export in one workflow while maintaining lecture structure, alignment - Support human-in-the-loop AI assistance for quality and speed
Benefits	- Reduced production friction and fewer handoff errors - Faster iteration from draft to publishable lecture assets - Better transparency for monitoring and managing exports

Design Process. The artifact was developed iteratively using a design science approach [2] with formative naturalistic evaluation [7]. The process included: (1) problem framing based on observed lecture production pain points; (2) architecture and workflow design; (3) implementation of core services and web interface; (4) formative evaluation through scenario-based use and stakeholder feedback; and (5) refinement of artifact capabilities, including lecture-scoped recording/export management.

Description of the Solution. The core design contribution is to conceptualize lectures as computational boundary objects—an adaptable yet structured coordination artifact enabling collaboration across heterogeneous tools and roles (cf. [6]). In this study, the lecture specification used in the workflow functions as a computational boundary object. Boundary objects are artifacts that enable coordination between different social or technical actors while allowing each actor to interpret the artifact according to its own practices [6]. In the proposed workflow, structured lecture files and associated metadata serve as shared computational representations that coordinate interactions between human authors, generative AI services, and production tools. These artifacts provide a stable reference point that supports traceability and reproducible transformation of lecture content across the workflow. The artifact instantiates this concept in a modular lecture engineering platform. Rather than centering individual tools, the architecture centers a lecture-scoped orchestration boundary coordinating transformations from source material to multimedia outputs.

Figure 1 illustrates the lecture-centered workflow instantiated within the system, showing the transition from material preparation to lecture object generation, with human supervision across stages and AIservices executing the underlying transformations.

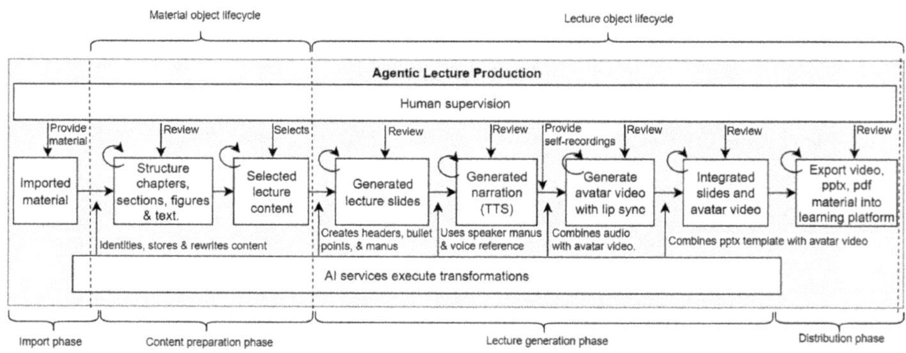

Fig. 1. The lecture artifact acts as a computational boundary object coordinating a multi-stage lecture production workflow with human supervision and AI-driven transformations.

In this boundary, the artifact: (1) centralizes the transformation chain (drafting, structuring, generation, rendering and export) in a lecture-scoped workflow;

(2) retains lecture-related metadata, file references, and job status across stages to support coordination of the production process; (3) supports consistent lecture generation through structural constraints and validation (e.g., slide naming and sequential numbering) prior to media generation and export; and (4) makes human review opportunities explicit by exposing where AI outputs are produced and where lecturers can review, edit, and approve them.

The artifact integrates: (1) web-based lecture authoring and management with LLM-supported transformation of course literature into structured slides and speaker manuscripts; (2) template-aware slide export using institutional presentation templates; (3) media generation services including Text-To-Speech (TTS), avatar lip synchronization, and automated video rendering, where users can record short personal video samples that are used to generate personalized avatar-based lecture videos; (4) background job orchestration and lecture-level export management; and (5) role-based access and import of existing presentations for reuse and refinement.

2 Significance to Research

Artefactual Contributions. The prototype provides a concrete instantiation of an agentic educational production system where content, process state, and outputs are organized around lecture-level boundaries. More specifically, it advances the design concept of *lecture as a computational boundary object*, making cross-stage orchestration traceable and governable. The artifact bridges authoring, generation, and delivery while keeping human decision authority in the loop. It instantiates a broader class of lecture-centered agentic workflow systems characterized by bounded orchestration, persistent process state, and explicit human approval transitions. While evaluated in higher education, the design logic may also inform similar educational production contexts where traceability and human oversight are required.

Theoretical Contributions. The study suggests that multimedia lecture production can be understood not only as a content authoring task but also as a workflow integration challenge. The artifact motivates a view of educational AI support as orchestrated human–AI collaboration across stages rather than isolated model interactions. It further highlights the role of artifact-level traceability for trust and maintainability in AI-supported educational systems, especially when transitions between automated and human-mediated actions are made explicit at lecture scope.

Methodological Contributions. The study shows a prototype-driven approach to advancing educational workflow systems: structuring lecture-centered information models, instrumenting cross-stage transitions, and evaluating not only output quality but also process coherence and recoverability. This approach is particularly relevant in domains where multiple media pipelines evolve rapidly and strict end-to-end automation is neither feasible nor desirable.

3   Significance to Practice

Educator control is supported through opportunities for manual review and editing throughout the workflow. Lecturers can edit slide headers, bullet points, images, and speaker manuscripts before export; preview the generated PowerPoint; review and revise LLM-generated text; listen to generated narration; preview avatar videos; and manually trigger video rendering. Role-based permissions further regulate who can create or modify lecture outputs. As indicated by course deployment and participant feedback, these mechanisms reduce coordination overhead without removing authorial control over final content and publication decisions.

4   Evaluation of the Artefact

Evaluation Design. The evaluation was conducted in four stages. First, the prototype was iteratively tested by the primary researcher together with a small group of colleagues during early development. Second, the system was deployed in an authentic teaching context where the primary researcher used the prototype to produce six video lectures based on course literature. These lectures were used as instructional material in a doctoral-level research course, enabling end-to-end validation of the workflow under realistic conditions. Third, a qualitative study was conducted with six university teachers representing variation in discipline, pedagogical experience, gender, and course level. Each teacher attended an individual two-hour session where they created a lecture using the system. Observations were documented through field notes focusing on interaction patterns, friction points, and workflow strategies. These observations were complemented by ongoing, informal discussions during the sessions while participants interacted with the system, which were also captured in the field notes, where participants reflected on perceived pain points, benefits, and suggested future functionality or changes to the system. The researcher acted as facilitator during the sessions, guiding the discussions, and iterative refinements to the system were made between sessions when feasible.

Findings. Across stages, the system demonstrated stable end-to-end execution and supported coherent transitions between content authoring and multimedia generation. During course deployment, five video lectures based on distinct textbook chapters were produced in a single working day, indicating operational feasibility and production efficiency. Teacher sessions provided formative feedback on system interaction, including friction points, workflow strategies, perceived benefits, and proposed improvements. For example, one participant described the system as a "really good tool for distance learning". At the same time, participants expressed a desire for greater control over AI-supported functionality, such as being able to "decide how many slides it generates".

Limitations. The evaluation is formative and context-bound. The participant group was limited in size, and long-term adoption effects remain to be studied.

Future work will include longitudinal studies and comparative analyses with traditional production workflows.

5 Implementation and Access

The prototype is implemented as a web-based system with a Python/FastAPI backend and a Svelte frontend. Lecture data is stored in structured folders in a content repository, while background jobs are persisted in a database. The system integrates LLM-based services through external Application Programming Interfaces (APIs) and locally executed models, enabling flexible deployment. An embedded LLM chat interface supports editing lecture markdown fields (headers, bullet points, and speaker manuscripts), with tool coordination handled via structured API calls and Model Content Protocol (MCP)-based integration.

The implementation includes role-based authentication, lecture management APIs, template and media integration points, and export/job administration views. The current implementation is suitable for local and small-team deployment and can serve as a research platform for iterative artifact evolution. A demonstration video is available here: <<link>>.

6 Conclusion

This paper presented a prototype for agentic lecture production in higher education. The artifact shows how a lecture-centered workflow coordinates content transformation and multimedia generation while maintaining human oversight. Treating each lecture as a computational boundary object centralizes transformations, preserves process state, and makes human–AI transitions traceable. The formative evaluation indicates that the architecture improves workflow coherence, traceability, and production efficiency while preserving educator control. More broadly, the study contributes design knowledge on structuring human-centered, AI-supported production systems around coordinated multistage workflows. Future work will focus on longitudinal validation and refinement of design principles for agentic, human-in-the-loop educational workflows.

References

1. Azad, A.K., Nahar, S.: Challenges faced by teachers to use multimedia in classroom and students' perception from it: a case study on a selected college in bangladesh. J. Manage. Bus. Educ. **7**(1), 54–69 (2024)
2. Hevner, A.R., March, S.T., Park, J., Ram, S.: Design science in information systems research. MIS Q. 75–105 (2004)
3. Klein, C.: Understanding the relevance of digital media in higher education. Int. J. Technol. Educ. Sci. **7**(1), 71–82 (2023)
4. Shneiderman, B.: Human-Centered AI. Oxford University Press (2022)
5. Staneviciene, E., Žekienė, G.: The use of multimedia in the teaching and learning process of higher education: a systematic review. Sustainability **17**(19) (2025)

6. Star, S.L., Griesemer, J.R.: Institutional ecology, 'translations' and boundary objects: Amateurs and professionals in Berkeley's museum of vertebrate zoology, 1907-39. Soc. Stud. Sci. **19**(3), 387–420 (1989)
7. Venable, J., Pries-Heje, J., Baskerville, R.: FEDS: a framework for evaluation in design science research. Eur. J. Inf. Syst. **25**(1) (2016)
8. Wu, Q., et al.: AutoGen: enabling next-gen LLM applications via multi-agent conversations. In: First Conference on Language Modeling (2024)

Designing a Human-In-The-Loop Clustering Information System for Automotive Field Observations

Lukas-Orlando Ulmer[1,2]([envelope]) [iD], Nicole Schempp[1,2] [iD], and Miriam Gräf[1] [iD]

[1] Technical University of Darmstadt, 64289 Darmstadt, Germany
ulmer@is.tu-darmstadt.de
[2] Dr. Ing. H.C. F. Porsche AG, Porscheplatz 1, 70435 Stuttgart, Germany

Abstract. Detecting emerging failure patterns in automotive aftersales requires analyzing large volumes of heterogeneous repair data at very low initial occurrence rates. Machine learning can cluster similar failures, but domain expertise is crucial for early novelty detection in context-dependent environments. We present a Human-in-the-Loop Information System that integrates expert feedback into model-driven clustering. Using Design Science Research, we derived four design principles based on Cognitive Fit Theory and practitioner insights, instantiated in a web-based prototype. In empirical evaluation, field analysts indicated that aligning cluster information with analytical tasks reduced cognitive load and enhanced reasoning. This study contributes design knowledge for Human-in-the-Loop Information Systems, demonstrating how human expertise and model-driven approaches can collaborate effectively to support failure detection.

Keywords: Human-in-the-Loop · Interactive Clustering · Design Science Research · Human-AI Collaboration · Cognitive Fit Theory

1 Introduction and Motivation

Field analysts in the automotive industry face increasing pressure to identify emerging technical failures, as rising product complexity and the increasing volume, heterogeneity, and ambiguity of repair data make the task more challenging [e.g., 2, 5, 6]. Analysts must classify incoming repair cases, detect recurring patterns, and determine if symptoms reflect known issues or indicate novel failures, a process which is highly context dependent, cognitively demanding, and reliant on technical experience [e.g., 1, 9].

While machine learning (ML) methods offer substantial benefits for pattern detection and similarity-based clustering, decision authority and quality control remain with human experts. Analytical tools must therefore support, not replace, expert judgment. These developments highlight the need for Human-in-the-Loop Information Systems (HITL IS) that support collaboration between ML models and domain experts. Such systems must provide cognitively aligned representations of repair case clusters, enabling more efficient analytical reasoning and earlier identification of relevant issues. Yet design knowledge for HITL IS in automotive aftersales remains limited.

© The Author(s), under exclusive license to Springer Nature Switzerland AG 2026
S. Chatterjee et al. (Eds.): DESRIST 2026, LNCS 16607, pp. 389–394, 2026.
https://doi.org/10.1007/978-3-032-28570-6_35

This raises the central research question of this study: *How can HITL IS be designed to enable field analysts to integrate model-driven cluster suggestions with expert judgment to improve the identification of novel failure patterns?* To address this question, we develop, instantiate, and evaluate design principles (DPs) for HITL IS that support the interpretive clustering tasks of field analysts. Grounded in Cognitive Fit Theory (CFT) [13], and informed by extensive practitioner insights, we derive theory-driven and practically validated DPs and instantiate them in a web-based prototype that aims to support ML-assisted clustering processes and product quality decision-making.

2 Design of the Artifact

The artifact builds on CFT [13], which emphasizes the importance of aligning task characteristics with information representation, while preserving practical prerequisites and expert authority. Following the Design Science Research (DSR) approach by Peffers (2007), five MRs were identified, from which twelve design requirements (DRs) were derived and subsequently generalized into four DPs (Fig. 1). These were instantiated in a prototype and evaluated in a practitioner-oriented study [12]. The resulting design knowledge contributes guidance for designing HITL IS that integrates ML capabilities with human expertise in product quality decision processes.

The research was initiated through seven exploratory workshops involving nine practitioners from field analysis and quality management. Applying a Design Thinking perspective [e.g., 4, 10], the workshops produced 144 user stories related to current challenges and opportunities in the field observation process. The user stories were analyzed using open coding based on grounded theory principles [7]. The codes were subsequently consolidated into thematic categories following Braun & Clarke's (2006) thematic analysis approach [3].

Content related to non-functional aspects or organizational conditions was excluded from scope. The remaining categories were complemented by a literature review on HITL IS and formed the basis for deriving meta requirements (MRs) grounded in CFT, reflecting the relationships between task demands, data representation, and cognitive processing [13]. Mapping these MRs with practitioner insights resulted in twelve DRs, which were generalized into DPs (Fig. 1).

All DPs were instantiated in a web-based prototype, simulating the workflow of field analysis. The prototype represents the first iteration of the DSR cycle and serves to demonstrate the operationalization of the DPs rather than to optimize clustering algorithm performance.

To evaluate the artifact, a video-based demonstration of a realistic usage scenario was provided to workshop participants and field analysts. Participants completed a structured questionnaire based on the NASA Task Load Index framework (NASA-TLX) [8], assessing perceived usefulness, transparency, and cognitive workload. This evaluation provided an initial assessment of user-perceived cognitive support for the proposed DPs as instantiated in the prototype.

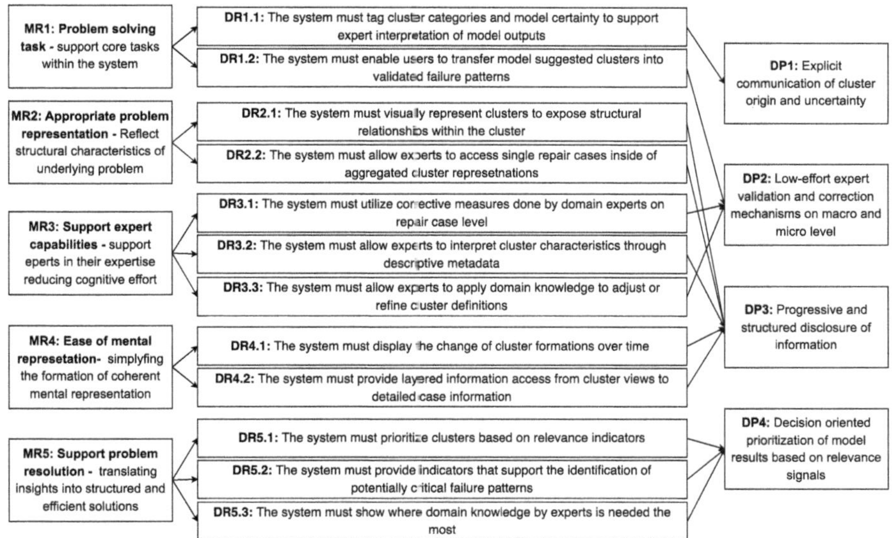

Fig. 1. Meta requirements, design requirements and -principles grounded in CFT [13]

2.1 Problem Statement and Intended User Group

Automotive aftersales organizations continuously monitor vehicles in the field to detect quality issues at an early stage [e.g., 9, 1_]. Increasing product diversity, more complex system architectures, and heterogeneous data sources have made the classification of repair cases more challenging [e.g., 2, 5, 6]. Moreover, the interpretive classification still depends heavily on expert judgment due to ambiguous documentation, contextual nuances, and the lack of standardized workflows [e.g., 2].

Prior research consistently highlights that automotive failure classification requires substantial technical reasoning and cannot be fully automated [e.g., 5]. Consequently, organizations face a widening gap: the dimensionality and workload of classification tasks continue to increase, while the available expert capacity remains static. At the same time, current toolchains emphasize monitoring functions rather than supporting interactive analytical tasks. Analysts frequently rely on spreadsheets and fragmented system views, leading to high manual effort and inconsistent detection of emerging failure patterns [e.g., [11].

Research on field failure analytics largely focuses on forecasting techniques [e.g., [6], using survival models, time-series models, ML approaches, and knowledge-based systems [e.g., [1]. However, early stage detection of novel failure clusters requires interpretive assessment of present repair cases rather than prediction of future failures. This results in a research gap concerning HITL IS designed to support clustering, interpretation, and expert-guided case assignment.

The study addresses this gap by developing a HITL IS artifact that combines model-driven cluster suggestions with expert authority and interpretive reasoning. The objective is to reduce cognitive workload and manual effort while enabling earlier and more consistent detection of emerging failure topics.

2.2   Use Cases: Human-In-The-Loop Field Observations

The prototype supports field analysts' tasks related to reviewing repair cases. Field analysts determine whether each case corresponds to an existing failure pattern or constitutes a new issue. This classification process is non-routine, as each case includes heterogeneous information like textual customer complaint descriptions, repair actions, replaced components, fault codes, multimedia attachments, contextual metadata, and optional diagnostic or historical data. The workflow therefore requires interpretive reasoning rather than predefined labeling. Analysts must evaluate whether the constellation of symptoms matches known patterns or indicates a new issue, which is a decision that is inherently experience-driven.

2.3   System Features

The artifact was deployed as a web-based prototype on a client machine. The objective was to evaluate HITL IS DPs rather than the performance of clustering algorithms. To balance realistic practical evaluation with experimental control, cluster structures and underlying data were artificially generated to replicate the structure and heterogeneity of real repair data. This approach aligns with DSR objectives of demonstrating DPs and interaction mechanisms over algorithm optimization. The prototype features two interface views (Fig. 2).

The cluster overview (**A**) lists identified clusters by size and relevance, indicating potentially critical failure patterns (**DP4**), labels each cluster with its model origin and model confidence, supporting the expert interpretation of the uncertainty of the proposed clusters (**DP1**) and shows a validation marker indicating which clusters have not been analyzed yet, with additional aggregated details available via mouseover tooltips. Selecting a cluster opens the cluster view (**B**) in a new browser tab, displaying cluster metadata, the centroid, a modular scatterplot, and a layered line diagram showing time progression. In a single view, users can explore cluster and repair case details from a macro to a micro level (**DP3**).

At the macro level, cluster definitions can be edited by changing, adding, or removing features that describe the cluster, and at the micro level, single cases can be removed from the cluster. Validated clusters can be dragged into a classification heatmap to monitor changes in failure patterns over time (**DP2**). Overall, the prototype operationalizes the derived DPs by aligning problem representation, expert experience, and field analysis tasks to reduce the cognitive load. A prototype video is available at https://drive.google.com/file/d/19_lO1rvguXistd86kUSra1ub81n6PF0T/view?usp=sharing.

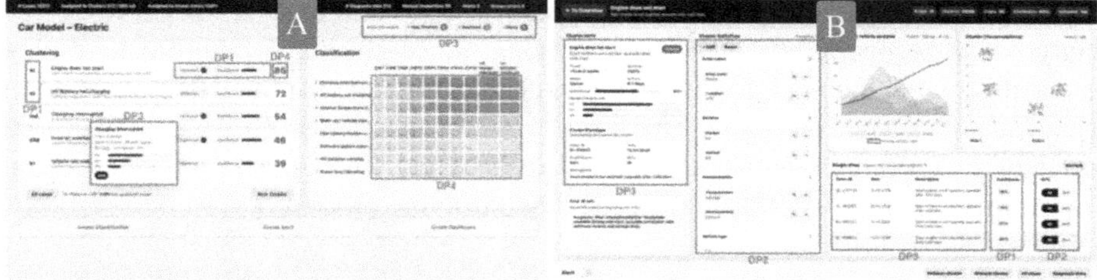

Fig. 2. Overview (A) & cluster (B) view of HITL IS prototype with applied design principles.

3   Evaluation

A key requirement of this study was that the HITL IS enables users to effectively interact with and refine model-generated clusters. To assess this, a survey-based evaluation was conducted with $n = 20$ practitioners (female: 4, male: 16), including those involved in the prior workshops. Participants watched an eight-minute video demonstrating the prototype and its core interaction features.

Survey items, adapted from the NASA-TLX [8], measured perceived mental demand, time pressure, effort, frustration and success using seven-point Likert scales, where lower values indicate more positive perceptions. Responses were tested against the neutral midpoint (4) using a one-sample Wilcoxon signed-rank test [14] (Fig. 3).

Results indicated significantly lower mental demand ($p = 0.009$), time pressure ($p = 0.004$), and frustration ($p < 0.001$), while perceived effort ($p = 0.132$) and success ($p = 0.336$) did not differ significantly from the neutral midpoint value. Overall, the HITL IS prototype implementing the proposed DPs imposed a low cognitive burden on users.

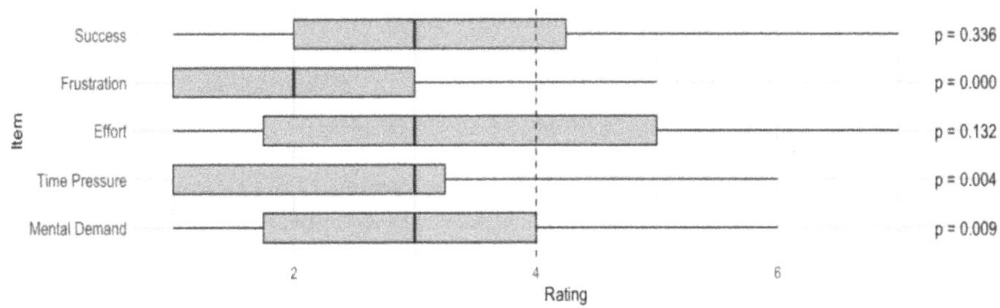

Fig. 3. Boxplot diagram of the perceived properties of the HITL IS prototype.

4   Significance to Research and Practice

This paper contributes to IS research by proposing DPs for HITL IS in analytical clustering tasks. While prior research on HITL IS has predominantly focused on algorithmic performance, less attention has been given to the design of interactive IS that effectively integrates expert feedback. Grounded in the CFT, this study shows how aligning human feedback mechanisms with appropriately represented clustering information can reduce the cognitive load in heterogeneous data environments. The resulting generalized DPs extend HITL IS research beyond the automotive aftersales domain.

For practitioners, the proposed artifact demonstrates how a novel workflow for field analysis can be operationalized. By combining model-generated failure pattern clusters with structured human feedback, the IS enables efficient identification of emerging technical issues while leveraging analysts' long-term experience. This approach lays the groundwork for further innovations in field analysis and other domains in which human feedback must be incorporated into analytical clustering processes.

Disclosure of Interests. The authors have no competing interests to declare that are relevant to the content of this article.

References

1. Babakmehr, M., .: Data-driven framework for warranty claims forecasting with an application for automotive components. Engineering Reports **6**(5) (2024). https://doi.org/10.1002/eng2.12764
2. Blischke, W.R., Karim, M.R., Murthy, D.P.: Warranty Data Collection and Analysis (2011). https://doi.org/10.1007/978-0-85729-647-4
3. Braun, V., Clarke, V.: Using thematic analysis in psychology. Qual. Res. Psychol. **3**(2), 77–101 (2006). https://doi.org/10.1007/978-0-85729-647-410.1191/1478088706qp063oa
4. Brown, T.: Design thinking. Harv. Bus. Rev. **86**(6), 84–92 (2008)
5. Buyvol, P., Makarova, I., Voroshilov, A., Krivonogova, A.: The Process of Identifying Automobile Joint Failures during the Operation Phase: Data Analytics Based on Association Rules. Information **14**(5), 257 (2023). https://doi.org/10.3390/info14050257
6. Carvalho, T.P., et al.: A systematic literature review of machine learning methods applied to predictive maintenance. Comp. Indus. Eng. **137**, 106024 (2019). https://doi.org/10.1016/j.cie.2019.106024
7. Corbin, J., Strauss, A.: Basics of Qualitative Research, 3rd ed., Techniques and Procedures for Developing Grounded Theory (2014). https://doi.org/10.4135/9781452230153
8. Hart, S.G., Staveland, L.E.: Development of NASA-TLX (Task Load Index): results of empirical and theoretical research. In Advances in Psychology **52**, 139–183 (1988). https://doi.org/10.1016/S0166-4115(08)62386-9
9. Jardine, A.K., Lin, D., Banjevic, D.: A review on machinery diagnostics and prognostics implementing condition-based maintenance. Mech. Syst. Signal Process. **20**(7), 1483–1510 (2006). https://doi.org/10.1016/j.ymssp.2005.09.012
10. Johansson-Sköldberg, U., Woodilla, J., Çetinkaya, M.: Design Thinking: Past, Present and Possible Futures. Creat Innov Manage **22**(2), 121–146 (2013). https://doi.org/10.1111/caim.12023
11. Khoshkangini, R., et al.: Early Prediction of Quality Issues in Automotive Modern Industry. Information **11**(7), 354 (2020). https://doi.org/10.3390/info11070354
12. Peffers, K., Tuunanen, T., Rothenberger, M.A., Chatterjee, S.: A Design Science Research Methodology for Information Systems Research. Journal of Mgmt. Inf. Sys. **24**(3), 45–77 (2007). https://doi.org/10.2753/MIS0742-1222240302
13. Vessey, I., Galletta, D.: Cognitive Fit: An Empirical Study of Information Acquisition. Inf. Syst. Res. **2**(1), 63–84 (1991). https://doi.org/10.1287/isre.2.1.63
14. Wilcoxon, F.: Individual Comparisons by Ranking Methods. Biometrics Bulletin **1**(6), 80 (1945). https://doi.org/10.2307/3001968

Bridging the Gap: A Hybrid Intelligence Decision Support System for B2B Pricing

Tobias Hornbogen[1], Josef Valentin[1]([✉]), Thomas Haskamp[2], and Jan vom Brocke[2]

[1] Hasso-Plattner-Institut, Prof.-Dr.-Helmert-Str. 2-3, 14482 Potsdam, Germany
{tobias.hornbogen,josef.valentin}@student.hpi.uni-potsdam.de
[2] Universität Münster, Schlossplatz 2, 48149 Münster, Germany
{thomas.haskamp,jan.vom.brocke}@uni-muenster.de
https://hpi.de/en/ , https://www.uni-muenster.de/en/

Abstract. B2B pricing in high-velocity wholesale environments is typically delegated to frontline sales agents, yet time pressure and information asymmetry lead to systematic over-discounting that erodes margins. While data-driven automation promises a remedy, the absence of rejected quotes from historical transaction data creates a fundamental censoring problem: the margin-maximizing price is likely unrecoverable, and black-box optimization cannot be validated against the true business objective. Static floor-and-target rules, the dominant alternative, ignore transaction-level heterogeneity. We present a hybrid intelligence Decision Support System developed with a large German finishing trades wholesaler processing over 3 million annual transactions. The artifact uses K-Nearest Neighbors as a Case-Based Reasoning mechanism to retrieve historical transactions with comparable elasticity profiles, defined by customer characteristics, product attributes, order size, and market timing, and constructs transaction-specific price corridors from the empirical discount distribution of the matched set. Glass-box retrieval enables domain experts to inspect neighbors, assess comparability, and iteratively recalibrate similarity weights, treating model output as a refinable heuristic rather than an authoritative optimum. An offline simulation on 160,000 recent transactions estimates revenue uplifts of 8 to 12% and profit uplifts of 27 to 39% across conservative to optimistic negotiation scenarios, and field validation with experienced sales agents confirmed corridor plausibility. From the design we extract two generalizable principles for decision support under target misalignment: prefer transparent architectures that enable iterative calibration when the optimization target is a biased proxy, and derive adaptive decision boundaries from empirical distributions of comparable cases to balance delegation with margin discipline.

Keywords: Dynamic Pricing · Decision Support System · Censored Data

© The Author(s), under exclusive license to Springer Nature Switzerland AG 2026
S. Chatterjee et al. (Eds.): DESRIST 2026, LNCS 16607, pp. 395–403, 2026.
https://doi.org/10.1007/978-3-032-28570-6_36

1 Design of the Artifact

While B2C markets have widely adopted algorithmic pricing, B2B pricing remains a human-driven negotiation shaped by customer relationships, product complexity, and local market knowledge. This study addresses the design problem of decision support for delegated B2B pricing under censored transaction data. In collaboration with a large-scale German finishing trades wholesaler (anonymized as WholesaleCo), we designed a hybrid intelligence pricing artifact for high-velocity sales settings. With over 3 million historical transactions processed by counter and telephone sales agents who set prices within defined floor-to-list-price ranges, the organization faces the challenge of reconciling centralized margin discipline with decentralized sales autonomy. Its primary users are frontline sales agents: inside sales staff handling high-velocity phone and counter transactions, field sales representatives requiring mobile access and alignment with inside quotes, and junior staff who lack the market intuition of experienced colleagues. The resulting artifact instantiates this design objective as a web-based Decision Support System (DSS) that leverages Case-Based Reasoning to construct interpretable, transaction-specific price corridors and is designed to augment human judgment rather than replace it.

1.1 Problem Statement

WholesaleCo delegates pricing authority to frontline sales agents to capitalize on local market knowledge and customer-specific price elasticity. Delegation is theoretically optimal when agents hold private elasticity information [11]. However, interviews with branch managers and sales agents suggested that instead of capitalizing on market knowledge, sales agents regularly over-discount. This happens because WholesaleCo's high-speed counter and telephone sales afford no opportunity to acquire the necessary information. Important factors that actually determine price elasticity, such as specific customer history, are unavailable during the negotiation, and time pressure leads agents to default to price concessions as a substitute for the cognitively demanding task of selling on value [7]. Analysis of WholesaleCo's transaction data confirms the effect: transactions that are comparable on the factors that should determine price elasticity consistently exhibit discount spreads exceeding 20% points (interquartile range), indicating that realized prices depend more on individual agent behavior than on market conditions. One possible design response is data-driven automation (predicting an "optimal" discount), but this path faces structural barriers rooted in the data itself.

WholesaleCo's historical transaction data contain only accepted deals; rejected quotes go entirely unrecorded. This severe censoring means the optimal price may not even be identifiable from the observed data [2]. Without a recoverable ground truth, no model output can be validated against the actual business objective (the margin-maximizing price) regardless of the modeling approach employed. Transparency therefore becomes a core requirement for the artifact: any recommendation must expose its reasoning so that domain experts can assess whether it reflects genuine market signal or artifacts of the data it was trained on.

Taken together, these constraints rule out both ends of the automation spectrum. Black-box optimization cannot derive transaction-specific optimal prices because the optimization target is likely unrecoverable from censored, agent-biased data. Static safeguards such as uniform floor and target prices - a common tool to address over-discounting - are either too broad to have an impact (when using large ranges) or re-centralize pricing through one-size-fits-all constraints that ignore transaction-level heterogeneity (when using small ranges). For example, a high volume private label sale for a regular customer may have an optimal discount much higher than a new customer buying a non-private label for the first time. The core design objective therefore shifts from price optimization to decision support. Any viable artifact must satisfy two requirements that follow from the failures identified above. First, it must adapt its guidance to the specific elasticity profile of each transaction rather than imposing uniform constraints. Second, because its recommendations cannot be validated against a known ground truth, it must make the basis of its recommendations transparent so that domain experts can assess, challenge, and iteratively recalibrate the model's assumptions.

1.2   Description of Features

The artifact is guided by a simple design premise: while we cannot estimate the acceptance probability for a given price, we can identify historical transactions that should exhibit similar price elasticity based on shared customer characteristics, product attributes, order size, and market timing. The matched set then provides an empirical distribution of realized discounts for that elasticity profile. Because unobserved conditions, such as competitive pressure or customer urgency, introduce variance beyond what the matching captures, the design pursues two objectives: to capture as many elasticity-relevant factors as possible and to sample from the resulting distribution conservatively enough to exclude likely noise while still counteracting systematic over-discounting.

To instantiate these requirements, a central design decision is to use K-Nearest Neighbors (KNN) as a Case-Based Reasoning (CBR) mechanism [1]. Rather than training a model that outputs a point prediction, KNN retrieves the concrete historical transactions most similar to the current quote request in terms of factors relevant to price elasticity. Agents can inspect the retrieved neighbors and assess whether the comparison is appropriate. The algorithm computes a weighted Euclidean distance between the current request Q and each historical transaction H_i: $\mathrm{Dist}(Q, H_i) = \sqrt{\sum w_j (q_j - h_{ij})^2}$. Feature weights w_j were both derived from academic literature and calibrated iteratively with domain experts to reflect which factors most strongly determine price elasticity in this market. Transactions are first filtered for having the same product category [13]. The factors considered for the weighting are, in order of importance, log order gross value [13], log order quantity [13], log customer product frequency [12], log customer potential [16], industry order size ratio [12], log customer order number [16] and log customer portfolio breadth [10]. Because each weight directly corresponds to a business-interpretable factor, sales managers could evaluate whether the similarity metric aligned with their understanding of what"comparable deal" means, leading to an iterative refinement of the weights across three design cycles. For instance, the initial feature set grouped products by category (e.g., paint with paint), causing the system to retrieve transactions for premium brand products as neighbors for private-label quotes. The resulting corridors were systematically too aggressive, because private-label customers expect, and historically receive, substantially larger discounts than brand-name buyers. Inside sales agents identified this mismatch by inspecting the retrieved neighbors, and the similarity metric was adjusted accordingly.

The matched set of neighbors provides a distribution of historically realized discounts for transactions with comparable elasticity profiles. From this distribution, the artifact constructs a pricing corridor rather than a single recommended price in order to preserve agent autonomy while bounding it with empirical evidence. This directly addresses the agent's core need during a phone or counter interaction: a defensible starting price and a clear limit for concessions if the customer pushes back. The target price is set at the 20th percentile, excluding the most favorable 20% of outcomes, which we assume disproportionately reflect unobserved favorable conditions rather than replicable pricing. The floor is set at the 50th percentile (median): given that the upper half of the distribution demonstrates that customers with similar elasticity profiles accepted lower discounts, is assumed to largely reflect the over-discounting the system is designed to counteract. Agents operate within this corridor based on situational judgement and the retrieved neighbors are inspectable in the UI to allow plausibility assessment. We arrived at the specific numbers through iterative refinement with senior sales agents.

The final design element addresses the censored data problem directly. Sales agents log the outcome of each quote (accepted, rejected, or modified final price). In the current prototype, rejection data is collected but not yet integrated into the retrieval engine; future iterations will use rejection logs to recalibrate corridor boundaries by incorporating evidence on where prices exceed actual willingness to pay. This transforms the system from a static retrieval engine into a learning system that progressively reduces the gap between the modeled elasticity factors and the true drivers of customer behavior.

2   Significance to Research

Decision support systems in negotiation settings face a structural problem that standard modeling improvements cannot resolve. The only available supervised learning target, the set of accepted transaction prices, confounds genuine market conditions with systematic agent bias, and the two cannot be separated without observing the counterfactual: the prices at which customers would have walked away. This is not merely a noisy-label problem. Standard econometric remedies each fail because they make assumptions that cannot be guaranteed or are not reliable enough to be useful in practice: Heckman selection models require an exclusion restriction that is unverifiable without rejection data [8], and Double ML estimates population-level treatment effects rather than the transaction-specific recommendations agents need in real time [3]. The optimization target in such settings is therefore fundamentally ill-defined [2]. No offline accuracy metric can confirm whether a recommendation reproduces historical bias or captures genuine market signal. In design science research terms, this constitutes a wicked problem in the sense of Hevner et al. [9]: the problem requirements are inherently unstable because the ground truth against which any solution would be evaluated is itself unrecoverable from the available data.

We argue that for this class of problem, where the business goal cannot be expressed as a loss function, ML approaches can still generate value, but their output must be treated as a refinable heuristic rather than an authoritative optimum. This makes glass-box modeling essential, not primarily for user trust or adoption as in standard algorithm aversion accounts [5], but as a calibration mechanism that enables iterative convergence toward a goal that resists formal specification. Rudin [14] argues that inherently interpretable models should replace post-hoc explanations of black boxes in high-stakes settings; our artifact instantiates this principle in a context where interpretability serves a more specific function than trust alone: it is the mechanism through which domain knowledge enters the model. The CBR architecture [1] makes this calibration concrete: stakeholders can examine which historical transactions the system treats as comparable, evaluate whether the similarity factors capture the right elasticity drivers, and identify where the model's assumptions diverge from market reality. This reflects the iterative build-and-evaluate cycle central to design science research [9], in which artifact construction is grounded in the academic knowledge base (here, pricing delegation theory [11] and elasticity driver research [12,13]) while evaluation within the application environment drives refinement that neither source of knowledge could achieve alone. In our case, the weight recalibration prompted by sales agents identifying private-label mismatches (described in Sect. 1.2) exemplifies exactly this interplay between designed artifact and situated evaluation. The resulting system aligns with the hybrid intelligence paradigm [4], which defines superior outcomes as those achievable only through the combination of human and artificial intelligence, with each component continuously improving through interaction with the other.

A second design challenge concerns not how the model reasons but what form its guidance takes. As introduced in the problem statement, static floor and target prices are the dominant governance mechanism for controlling agent over-discounting [15], but they impose uniform constraints that ignore transaction-level heterogeneity. The artifact addresses this by deriving decision boundaries from the empirical distribution of comparable deals rather than from centrally imposed rules. This means corridors adapt automatically to local conditions: they are tight where comparable transactions show pricing consensus, indicating well-understood elasticity, and wide where legitimate price variation exists, indicating unobserved factors the model cannot capture. This property preserves agent discretion precisely where it is most valuable, in ambiguous situations where situational knowledge matters, while constraining it where the evidence suggests over-discounting rather than informed judgment. The corridors thereby offer a design-level approach to resolving the tension between delegation and centralization that motivates the artifact's design [11,15]. Rather than choosing one or the other, the system constructs a middle ground in which the degree of agent autonomy is calibrated empirically for each transaction.

Following Gregor and Hevner's [6] knowledge contribution framework, we position our artifact as an improvement: applying known solution components (CBR, percentile-based corridors) to a known problem class (pricing DSS under censored data), but combining them in a novel configuration that yields two generalizable design principles. Both respond to the same underlying condition, an optimization target that is unrecoverable from the available data, but address distinct layers of the design problem: DP1 concerns model architecture, while DP2 concerns the structure of the system's output.

DP1 (Calibration Through Transparency): When the ML optimization target is a systematically biased proxy for the business objective, prefer glass-box approaches that expose the model's reasoning to domain experts, enabling iterative calibration toward a goal that cannot be formally specified as a loss function.

DP2 (Adaptive Decision Boundaries): When contextual heterogeneity renders both full automation and static rules inadequate, construct decision boundaries from empirical distributions of comparable cases. This allows the system to tighten guidance where historical evidence is consistent and preserve agent discretion where legitimate variation signals unobserved factors.

3   Significance to Practice

While the artifact was developed with WholesaleCo, the underlying challenge is widely generalizable across B2B firms in fast-paced markets that delegate pricing to frontline sales. Since the data censoring constraint is the usual case in practice [2], it makes profit-optimal pricing targets difficult to identify and black-box automation hard to validate. The practical contribution is twofold. First, the artifact demonstrates transaction-specific pricing support under accepted-only data. Second, by logging quote outcomes, it builds a basis for future refinements and more advanced pricing models. This is achieved by integrating a feedback system into the currently recommended price range, which logs customer acceptance and rejection of a given discount.

For WholesaleCo the artifact translates key user pain points into an actionable workflow that fits high-velocity counter and telephone sales. The practical impact is an expected revenue and profit uplift through three mechanisms. First, margin leakage by systematic over-discounting is adressed by the price corridor which shifts the discount torward better than median outcomes observed for comparable transactions. This can increase realized margin on a large volume of transactions without requiring rigid, centrally imposed rules. Second, by reducing

15. Stephenson, R.P., Cron, W.L., Frazier, G.L.: Delegating pricing authority to the sales force: the effects on sales and profit performance. J. Mark. **43**(2), 21–28 (1979). https://doi.org/10.2307/1250736
16. Zhang, Y., Netzer, O., Ansari, A.: Dynamic targeted pricing in B2B relationships. Mark. Sci. **33**(3), 317–337 (2014). https://doi.org/10.1287/mksc.2013.0842

LLM Buddy: An AI-Augmented Research Environment for Auditable Design Science

Anthony T. Vigil[✉] [iD] and Matthew T. Mullarkey [iD]

Muma College of Business, University of South Florida, Tampa, FL 33620, USA
`{anthonyvigil,mmullarkey}@usf.edu`

Abstract. As Large Language Models (LLMs) become integral to design science research, a new software paradigm known as 'promptware' has emerged. In this paradigm, the prompts that drive artifact development are themselves critical, first-class software artifacts requiring systematic documentation and engineering rigor. However, traditional version control tools capture only code changes, leaving the rationale behind AI-assisted decisions invisible and irreproducible. LLM Buddy is a desktop-based research-instrumentation environment for eADR that captures prompts and LLM responses across interfaces, links them to the files they shaped, and preserves the resulting design rationale as an auditable, rollbackable research trace. It provides multimodal prompt capture, prompt-to-file association, automated rollback, and structured session records for eADR reporting. Developed and evaluated through six Elaborated Action Design Research (eADR) iterations, LLM Buddy captured 1,555 prompts during a longitudinal field deployment at the University of South Florida, supporting the identification of recurring prompt interaction patterns, including what the authors term Conversational Forking, and aiding recovery from a critical file corruption incident through its automated versioning system.

Keywords: Design Science Research · Promptware Engineering · Large Language Models · Prompt Management · Research Transparency · Traceability · eADR

1 Design of the Artifact

1.1 Problem Statement

Large Language Models are becoming crucial for creating artifacts in Design Science Research, fundamentally transforming traditional software engineering [1], but a significant methodological issue remains: conventional version control systems, such as Git, can record code modifications but not the underlying rationale, including the prompts, context, and reasoning behind AI-driven development choices. Chen et al. [2] identify prompt versioning and traceability as a key open challenge, noting the need for specialized tools that go beyond traditional version control to track prompt iterations and document modifications. This chasm poses a threat to the transparency, reproducibility,

S. Chatterjee et al. (Eds.): DESRIST 2026, LNCS 16607, pp. 404–410, 2026.
https://doi.org/10.1007/978-3-032-28570-6_37

and auditability of AI-augmented research [3], and exemplifies the broader 'prompt-ware crisis' [2] in which prompt development remains largely ad hoc and unsystematic. This concern is amplified within iterative approaches such as Elaborated Action Design Research (eADR) [4], where subsequent design cycles are founded upon the documented reflections of prior stages.

The problem compounds across several dimensions: researchers interact with LLMs through multiple channels, making comprehensive prompt capture difficult; prompts remain ephemeral conversational turns with no inherent connection to the files they influence; and rapid AI-assisted development can outpace manual documentation, risking both data loss and the loss of methodological insights.

Addressing these multidimensional challenges requires transitioning from conventional software development tools to dedicated AI-Augmented Research Environments. Such environments must move beyond simple code tracking to treat human-AI interactions as first-class methodological artifacts, seamlessly integrating prompt provenance with version control to ensure rigorous, auditable design science.

1.2 Intended User Groups and Use Cases

LLM Buddy targets three primary user groups: (1) DSR researchers conducting iterative design cycles [5] who need comprehensive audit trails of AI-assisted artifact development; (2) academics using LLMs as research instruments who must demonstrate methodological rigor and transparency; and (3) software development teams employing AI pair-programming who require traceability between prompts and code changes. The tool addresses use cases ranging from single-researcher dissertation projects to collaborative, multi-person design efforts where prompt provenance is essential for knowledge transfer and reproducibility.

1.3 Description of Features

LLM Buddy is a Python desktop application with a PySide6/Qt 6 interface and a shared data layer that consolidates prompt and response records from four capture modes: Chrome extension, HTTPS proxy, Claude Desktop MCP integration, and manual entry. Together, these modes route human inputs and AI outputs into a unified repository for later analysis and traceability.

At the heart of the software's methodological value is its capacity to bind specific project files directly to the conversational inputs that shaped their creation or modification. Researchers can create these links in real time while prompting the LLM or add them retroactively, establishing a transparent chain of evidence between AI interactions and resulting artifacts.

To protect against data loss, the environment continuously observes the active project directory for modifications. Whenever the volume of changes surpasses a user-defined token limit, the software autonomously creates a time-stamped snapshot of the entire project. If an AI-generated code change causes issues, researchers can use the recovery feature to inspect these historical snapshots, visualize the exact alterations through color-coded differences, and selectively revert specific files to their earlier, stable states.

Preparing context for an AI model is streamlined through an aggregation tool that allows users to compile entire directories or specific files into a cohesive text block, using extension filters to exclude irrelevant data and customizable headers and footers to structure the output. As this context is built, a live token estimation engine powered by tiktoken provides instant feedback, ensuring researchers do not exceed the specific context window constraints of their chosen language model.

To maintain rigorous project organization, interactions and modifications are encapsulated within distinct, named research sessions. When a researcher concludes a session, the system autonomously drafts a comprehensive summary detailing the statistical breakdown of prompts used, API consumption metrics, and a ledger of all file alterations. Complementing this is an integrated logging system specifically tailored for Elaborated Action Design Research, which automatically timestamps and records critical actions like file aggregations or system rollbacks, creating a living audit trail alongside the researcher's manual annotations. An integrated analytics dashboard visualizes prompt frequency over time, LLM platform distributions, and token usage trends, enabling researchers to identify interaction patterns and resource allocation across design cycles.

2   Significance to Research

Following established guidelines for positioning DSR contributions [6], the primary contribution of LLM Buddy is not another interface for using LLMs, but a prototype research-instrumentation environment for eADR. It turns otherwise ephemeral AI interactions into auditable research trace by combining multimodal prompt capture, prompt-to-file linkage, rollbackable project snapshots, and eADR-aligned session summaries in one integrated environment. In their work, Chen et al. outline a conceptual roadmap highlighting 27 open research areas for promptware engineering, including versioning and traceability, as well as prompt-centric IDEs [2]. LLM Buddy offers an early, field-evaluated response to several of these opportunities, grounding the theoretical framework in a working prototype deployed across a longitudinal eADR project. Methodologically, LLM Buddy was developed as instrumentation for documenting prompt-driven design work when conventional development methods proved insufficient for preserving rationale, interaction history, and reflective notes in LLM-augmented eADR projects.

While functioning primarily as an AI-augmented environment for DSR, the empirical trace data captured by LLM Buddy also acts as an instrument for Empirical Method Engineering [7], answering calls to account for how non-human agents shape software development trace data [8]. The tool reframes prompts as first-class research artifacts rather than ephemeral conversation turns, addressing the emerging reproducibility crisis in AI-assisted research where the rationale for design decisions is routinely lost. The artifact is also released as open source with an LLM-readable code snapshot.

The tool contributes to the DSR methodology in three ways. First, it extends Method Engineering principles [9] to the domain of AI-augmented research by evolving traditional computer-aided tools into dynamic AI-Augmented Research Environments. This provides automated instrumentation for a process that previously relied on researcher discipline alone. Second, systematic prompt capture makes non-linear LLM problem-solving patterns visible, including the Conversational Forking pattern observed in the field deployment [10].

Third, LLM Buddy addresses the tension between speed and rigor in AI-augmented DSR. The eADR methodology requires documented reflection at each iteration boundary [4], yet the pace of LLM-driven development can outstrip manual documentation. By automating capture, versioning, and session summarization within an integrated environment, the tool is intended to reduce the documentation burden and, in this field deployment, appeared to improve the completeness and usability of the resulting audit trail. The research session feature directly maps to eADR cycles, producing structured summaries that function as ready-made methods appendices.

3 Significance to Practice

Regarding practical impact [6], LLM Buddy addresses the growing need for accountability in AI-augmented professional and research workflows. Organizations adopting these workflows face critical questions of intellectual property attribution, data privacy, and regulatory compliance that require knowing exactly which AI interactions produced which outputs within a secure, local-only environment. By functioning as a comprehensive AI-Augmented Research Environment, the tool's file-to-prompt association feature supports traceability between AI interactions and resulting artifacts without forcing disruptive changes to existing development practices.

The tool's multimodal capture architecture offers practical value. Instead of constraining researchers to standardize on a single LLM interface, LLM Buddy functions as an unobtrusive layer, intercepting user interactions across their established platforms: web-based chat through a Chrome extension, desktop applications via MCP, and programmatic APIs using a proxy. This design philosophy is intended to reduce adoption friction by allowing researchers to work across their existing LLM interfaces.

The automated backup and rollback system proved its practical value during the research that produced LLM Buddy. A critical incident during development resulted in multiple file corruptions from an errant LLM-generated code change. The rollback system enabled complete restoration to a stable version, saving approximately two weeks of development work. This incident illustrates the potential utility of the rollback feature as a safety net in AI-assisted development, where a single poorly constructed prompt can cascade into widespread file modifications.

4 Evaluation of the Artifact

LLM Buddy was evaluated through longitudinal field deployment during a six-iteration eADR project at the University of South Florida [10]. Across this deployment, the artifact captured 1,555 prompts spanning Claude, Gemini, and ChatGPT and evolved through 14 versions from an initial code-compilation utility to the present multimodal environment. The evaluation focused on four prototype-oriented criteria: (1) capture feasibility across interfaces, (2) traceability between prompts and modified files, (3) recovery utility during AI-assisted failure events, and (4) support for eADR reporting and reflection.

Evidence included sustained authentic use across six eADR iterations, successful rollback-based recovery from a multi-file corruption incident, incorporation of session summaries into research deliverables, and formative expert appraisal through live demonstrations. Together, these results provide in-situ evidence of LLM Buddy's prototype maturity, practical utility, and methodological relevance for prompt-centric auditable development in eADR practice. The evaluation also generated formative feedback that informed the artifact's iterative evolution while yielding summative evidence from sustained field use. Although broader cross-team validation remains future work, the present study demonstrates that the artifact is viable, usable, and valuable in an authentic research setting.

4.1   Field Deployment Results

Throughout the longitudinal assessment phase, the recording framework successfully archived 1,555 distinct AI prompts across prominent language models, including Claude, Gemini, and ChatGPT [10]. The system maintained a continuous log of these exchanges across six comprehensive Elaborated Action Design Research phases, beginning with method engineering and concluding with the integration of security protocols. This extensive repository of interaction data yielded three primary observations from field deployment.

First, analysis of the historical prompt data revealed a recurring interaction pattern that the authors formalize as Conversational Forking. This strategy represents a departure from traditional linear prompting, instead encouraging users to purposefully splinter their dialogue with the AI to test various hypotheses simultaneously before merging the best results into a final solution. Based on this observation, the tool now operationalizes the pattern through a dedicated Prompt Explorer panel that provides visual tree-based conversation management with branch creation, checkout, merging, and fork-point metadata tracking.

Second, the environment's integrated safety protocols supported recovery from a significant file corruption event. During a complex code restructuring task facilitated by artificial intelligence, multiple essential files sustained damage. The environment's automated snapshot infrastructure permitted an immediate restoration to a previously functioning state, suggesting the practical value of integrating rollback and versioning capabilities into AI-assisted workflows.

Finally, the tool supported project reporting by generating summaries that were incorporated into research deliverables. The automatically compiled synopses were incorporated directly into formal research deliverables as methodological appendices.

4.2   Iterative Design Refinement

Consistent with the eADR methodology, LLM Buddy itself underwent iterative refinement based on the researcher's own use. The tool began as a simple code compiler for LLM uploading (v1) and evolved through 14 versions to its current multimodal architecture. Key design decisions driven by field experience included adding the Chrome extension when manual capture proved unreliable and too timely for rapid updates, the rollback feature after a corrupted file lost hours of work, and the research session feature after realizing that prompts could be better organized and mapped to eADR cycles. This co-evolution of the tool and methodology exemplifies the eADR principle of building artifacts to solve immediate research challenges [4].

4.3 Limitations and Future Work

The evaluation was conducted as a longitudinal field deployment within a single eADR project led by the primary researcher. The findings should therefore be interpreted as in-situ evidence of prototype viability, utility, and methodological relevance in an authentic DSR setting, rather than as evidence of broad cross-context generalizability. Within that scope, the study shows that prompt-centric auditable development can be operationalized through multimodal capture, prompt-to-file traceability, rollback support, and research-oriented session summarization.

To support reuse and independent evaluation, LLM Buddy has been released as open-source software together with an LLM-readable markdown snapshot of the codebase. Future work should evaluate the artifact across multiple researchers, teams, and DSR projects, including comparative studies of documentation completeness, traceability, and recovery support relative to conventional workflows. Additional extensions include tighter Git integration, collaborative multi-researcher support, IDE integration, and richer document-format support, including PDF and Word files.

5 System Architecture

Figure 1 illustrates LLM Buddy's modular architecture. Four independent capture recorders (Chrome Extension via Flask API, HTTPS Proxy via mitmproxy, Claude MCP Server, and Manual Entry) feed into a unified Prompt Database backed by SQLite storage.

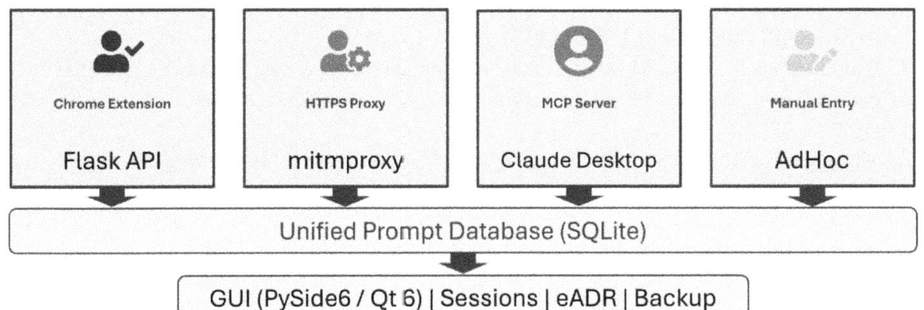

Fig. 1. LLM Buddy system architecture. Four independent capture recorders feed a unified database consumed by the GUI application.

6 Conclusion

LLM Buddy addresses a central methodological gap in AI-augmented design science: preserving a verifiable chain from prompt, to artifact change, to research reflection. By capturing prompts and responses across interfaces, linking them to modified files, and packaging them into rollbackable histories and eADR-ready session records, the artifact makes AI-assisted design work inspectable after the fact. The evaluation provides early field evidence that the tool improves traceability and preserves methodological insights in AI-assisted design work. By providing field-evaluated tooling for challenges identified as open research opportunities in the promptware engineering roadmap [2], LLM Buddy bridges conceptual frameworks and practical implementation in AI-augmented design science.

Implementation and Screencast.   An open-source implementation of LLM Buddy, including installation materials, a video demonstration, and an LLM-readable codebase snapshot to enable rapid AI-assisted review of the artifact, is available at: https://github.com/avigi25/LLM-Buddy.

Disclosure of Interests.   The authors have no competing interests to declare that are relevant to the content of this article.

References

1. Banh, L., Holldack, F., Strobel, G.: Copiloting the future: How generative AI transforms Software Engineering. Inf. Softw. Technol. **183**, 107751 (2025)
2. Chen, Z., et al.: Promptware Engineering: Software Engineering for Prompt-Enabled Systems. ACM Transactions on Software Engineering and Methodology (2026)
3. Brundage, M., et al.: Toward trustworthy AI development: mechanisms for supporting verifiable claims. arXiv preprint arXiv:2004.07213 (2020)
4. Mullarkey, M.T., Hevner, A.R.: An elaborated action design research process model. Eur. J. Inf. Syst. **28**, 6–20 (2019)
5. Bichler, M.: Design science in information systems research. Wirtschaftsinformatik **48**(2), 133–135 (2006). https://doi.org/10.1007/s11576-006-0028-8
6. Gregor, S., Hevner, A.R.: Positioning and presenting design science research for maximum impact. MIS Quarterly 337–355 (2013)
7. Brinkkemper, S., Saeki, M., Harmsen, F.: Assembly techniques for method engineering. International conference on advanced information systems engineering, pp. 381–400. Springer (1998)
8. Maruping, L.M., Matook, S.: The evolution of software development orchestration: current state and an agenda for future research. Eur. J. Inf. Syst. **29**, 443–457 (2020)
9. Brinkkemper, S.: Method engineering: engineering of information systems development methods and tools. Inf. Softw. Technol. **38**, 275–280 (1996)
10. Vigil, A.T.: Adaptive Multi-Agent Intelligence: A Dynamic Data Management System for Enhanced Data Quality and Reconciliation. Muma College of Business, vol. Doctorate, p. 156. University of South Florida, ProQuest (2026)

Author Index

S. Chatterjee et al. (Eds.): DESRIST 2026, LNCS 16607, pp. 411–412, 2026.
https://doi.org/10.1007/978-3-032-28570-6

GPSR Compliance
The European Union's (EU) General Product Safety Regulation (GPSR) is a set
of rules that requires consumer products to be safe and our obligations to
ensure this.

If you have any concerns about our products, you can contact us on

ProductSafety@springernature.com

In case Publisher is established outside the EU, the EU authorized
representative is:

Springer Nature Customer Service Center GmbH
Europaplatz 3
69115 Heidelberg, Germany